New Perspectives on Early Korean Art:
From Silla to Koryŏ

Early Korea Project Occasional Series

Mark E. Byington, Series Editor

New Perspectives on Early Korean Art: From Silla to Koryŏ

Edited by Youn-mi Kim

Early Korea Project
Korea Institute
Harvard University
2013

New Perspectives on Early Korean Art: From Silla to Koryŏ

Mark E. Byington, Editor

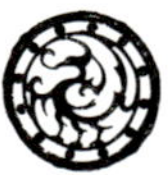

Early Korea Project
Occasional Series

Mark E. Byington, Series Editor

2013

Publisher: Korea Institute, Harvard University
Editorial Board: Martin Bale, Jonathan Best,
Mark Byington, Richard D. McBride II
Copy Editor: Nita Sembrowich
Cover: Kelly Maccioli
Design: Wayne de Fremery, Byungwook Ryu
Proofreader: Beyond Words Proofreading

The Early Korea Project Occasional Series
is a peer-reviewed edited serial published by the Early Korea Project at the
Korea Institute, Harvard University, with the generous
support of the Northeast Asian History Foundation in Seoul, Korea.
Operational funding for the Early Korea Project is provided by the Korea
Foundation in Seoul, Korea.

ISSN 2159-0540
ISBN 978-0-9886928-1-7

Inquiries to: Early Korea, Korea Institute, Harvard University,
Center for Government and International Studies, South Building Room
S228, 1730 Cambridge Street, Cambridge, MA 02138.

Phone: (617) 496-3403. Fax: (617) 495-9976.
Website: http://www.fas.harvard.edu/~ekp/
Email: ekp@fas.harvard.edu.

Acknowledgments

This edited volume could not have been completed without the generous help, significant efforts, and collegial collaboration from many senior scholars, colleagues, and friends. I would like to extend my deepest gratitude to the contributors to this volume, Chung Woothak, Jang Namwon, Rhi Juhyung, and Joo Kyeongmi, who kindly travelled the great distance from Korea to Cambridge, Massachusetts, to present at the art history lecture series organized by the Early Korea Project of the Korea Institute, Harvard University in 2010, who shared with us their cherished research papers, and who have patiently provided constant and tireless help in publishing this volume.

Very special thanks go to Rhi Juhyung, whose expertise and vision have greatly advanced the development of this volume from the first steps in organizing the lecture series to the final steps of the publishing stage. Among his many contributions, I would particularly like to express my gratitude for his guidance in structuring the introduction of this edited volume and introducing a new citation style for the *Samguk yusa* and the *Samguk sagi*, which I explain in the Conventions section of this volume. Professor Rhi's knowledge of Buddhism has also proven beneficial in editing chapters of this volume.

I would also like to express my sincere gratitude to the many other experts and senior colleagues in art history and Korean Studies, who have made this publication more meaningful. Eugene E. Wang, Nancy S. Steinhardt, and Robert D. Mowry kindly served as discussants during the art history lecture series in 2010. Their participation ensured that this project involved a productive communication between experts in art history currently active in Korea and in the United States. I am also grateful to Jane Portal, Robert D. Mowry, Melissa Moy, and Anne Rose Kitagawa for kindly showing art objects in the collection of the Museum of Fine Arts, Boston, and the Arthur M. Sackler Museum, in response to requests from Joo Kyeongmi and Chung Woothak, who needed to examine artworks in the museum collections, including the famous reliquary of the Koryŏ monk Naong 懶翁 (1320-1376) and many pieces of Koryŏ and early Chosŏn Buddhist paintings. Having the opportunity to examine those artworks with true field experts inside the quiet storage area and the object study room of these two museums remains a precious memory for me.

The vision and experience of Mark E. Byington, our series editor, have provided tremendous help from the initiation of the lecture series to the careful editing of this volume. Without his support, advice, and leadership, this volume could not have been completed. Often he took on many more responsibilities and devoted more time than were required of a series editor. By working with him, I have learned much about the responsibilities of an editor. I also would like to extend my sincere thanks to the anonymous reviewer of this volume, who kindly provided a careful review and insightful comments, which greatly improved the quality of this volume.

Editing the five chapters in this volume has been assisted and significantly facilitated by many senior scholars and friends. In the final editing stage, Yukio Lippit and Eugene E. Wang shared their expertise whenever I needed their advice, for which I am truly grateful. I would like to thank Seunghee Jeon for translating portions of the original Korean material (Chapters One and Four of this volume were originally submitted in Korean). Copy editor Nita Sembrowich patiently edited the five chapters of this volume multiple times. Julia Deems and Naoki Yamamoto provided final touches to further improve the writing style of some chapters, while Yun-hee Lee proofed the manuscript for Romanization of Korean terms. Martin Bale has provided advice throughout the process, from the lecture series to this publication.

Many friends devoted their invaluable time to produce this volume. At Harvard, Scott Walker, of the Harvard Map Collection, designed the maps appearing near the beginning of this volume. Jina Kim, at the Korea Institute, helped to coordinate parts of the preparatory processes; Kelly Maccioli designed the cover; and Lea J. Park helped to redraw some of the illustrations and label the maps. At Yale, Yong Cho, a student research assistant, devoted significant time to making this volume more polished and complete.

I also would like to thank the National Museum of Korea, the Gyeongju National Museum, the Gyeongju Research Institute of Cultural Heritage, and other institutions that provided us with images of objects in their collections. Kim Dong-yeol and Jeong Ji-eun gave much help in securing copyrights for the photographs from the Gyeongju Research Institute of Cultural Heritage and the National Museum of Korea. I am also grateful to Chung Woothak for sharing many of his rare photographs of Koryŏ Buddhist paintings for use in this volume. I also appreciate that photographers Ahn Jangheon and Ha Jigwon allowed us to use their photographs in Chapter Three of this volume.

Funding for the lecture series and the publication of this volume was generously provided by the Northeast Asian History Foundation in Seoul, Korea. Operational support for the Early Korea Project, which produced this volume, was provided by the Korea Foundation in Seoul, Korea. The publication of this book was also supported, in part, with Publications Funds of Yale's History of Art Department and the East Asian Studies Faculty Research Fund from the Council on East Asian Studies at Yale University.

Abbreviations and Conventions

Ch.   Chinese

Jp.   Japanese

Kr.   Korean

Sk.   Sanskrit

T   *Taishō shinshū Daizōkyō* 大正新脩大蔵経 [Taishō edition of the Buddhist canon]. Edited by Takakusu Junjirō 高楠順次郎 and Watanabe Kaigyoku 渡辺海旭. 100 vols. Tokyo: Taishō Issaikyō Kankōkai, 1924-1934.

Transliterations of Asian languages follow the romanization systems commonly used in academic publications: McCune-Reischauer for Korean, pinyin for Chinese, and revised Hepburn for Japanese.

Citations from the *Taishō shinshū Daizōkyō* are listed in the following manner: Taishō serial number; Taishō volume number; page number, register (a, b, or c), and, if applicable, line number(s)—for example, T2145, 55:39a21-23. The title of the cited sutra is marked in the footnote only when the sutra title is not clearly identified in the main text.

Citations from the *Samguk yusa* 三國遺事 (Memorabilia of the Three Kingdoms) and the *Samguk sagi* 三國史記 (History of the Three Kingdoms) are based on the 2003 and 2011 editions by the Academy of Korean Studies. Citations from the *Samguk yusa* are listed in the following manner: title of the work; volume number of the original manuscript; title of the article in romanization; reference information about the edition of the Academy of Korean Studies; the Academy of Korean Studies volume number; the Academy of Korean Studies page number(s), for example:

Samguk yusa 三國遺事 5: "Taesŏng hyo ise pumo Sinmunwangdae," Han'guk Chŏngsin Munhwa Yŏn'guwŏn 韓國精神文化研究院
[Academy of Korean Studies], ed., *Yŏkchu Samguk yusa* 譯註 三國
遺事 [Annotation and translation of the *Samguk yusa*] (Seoul: Ihoe
Munhwasa, 2003), 4:376-377.

When the *Samguk yusa* or the *Samguk sagi* appears again within the
same chapter, it uses an abbreviated form—for example, *Samguk yusa* 5:
"Myŏngnang Sinin," *Yŏkchu Samguk yusa*, 4:225-226.

For the "Pon'gi" 本紀 (Annals) sections of the *Samguk sagi*, the reign
year is used in place of the article title, for example:

Samguk sagi 三國史記 7: King Munmu, nineteenth year, Han'gukhak
Chungang Yŏn'guwŏn 韓國學中央研究院 [Academy of Korean
Studies], ed., *Yŏkchu Samguk sagi* 譯註 三國史記 [Annotation and
translation of the *Samguk sagi*] (Sŏngnam: Han'gukhak Chungang
Yŏn'guwŏn Ch'ulp'anbu, 2011), 1:183.

Citations from other primary texts, including the *Tongguk Yi Sangguk chip*
東國李相國集, the *Koryŏsa* 高麗史, the *Chosŏn wangjo sillok* 朝鮮王朝實錄,
the *Sinjŭng Tongguk yŏji sŭngnam* 新增東國輿地勝覽, the *Nihon shoki* 日本書
紀, and the *Hou Hanshu* 後漢書, follow a similar footnote style, which identifies the volume numbers of both the original manuscript and modern reprint.

All other editorial styles found in this volume follow the standards
employed by the Early Korea Project, including the romanization of author
names in footnotes. In footnotes, therefore, this volume uses McCune-Reischauer for the author's name and, when applicable, identifies the author's
chosen spelling of his or her own name in parentheses—for example: Chŏng
Ut'aek (Chung Woothak) 鄭于澤. Also following the Early Korea Project's
editing style, this volume uses a hyphen in the name of Korean Buddhist
monasteries or temples—for example: Kamsan-sa 甘山寺. Traditional Chinese characters are used for primary texts, publications written in traditional
Chinese characters, and historic names of places and kingdoms. Simplified
Chinese characters are used for publications written in simplified Chinese
characters as well as modern names of places and people. Accordingly Chinese characters unique to Korea and Japan are used for Korean and Japanese
terms as well as book titles.

Maps, Figures, and Tables

New Perspectives on Early Korean Art: From Silla to Koryŏ

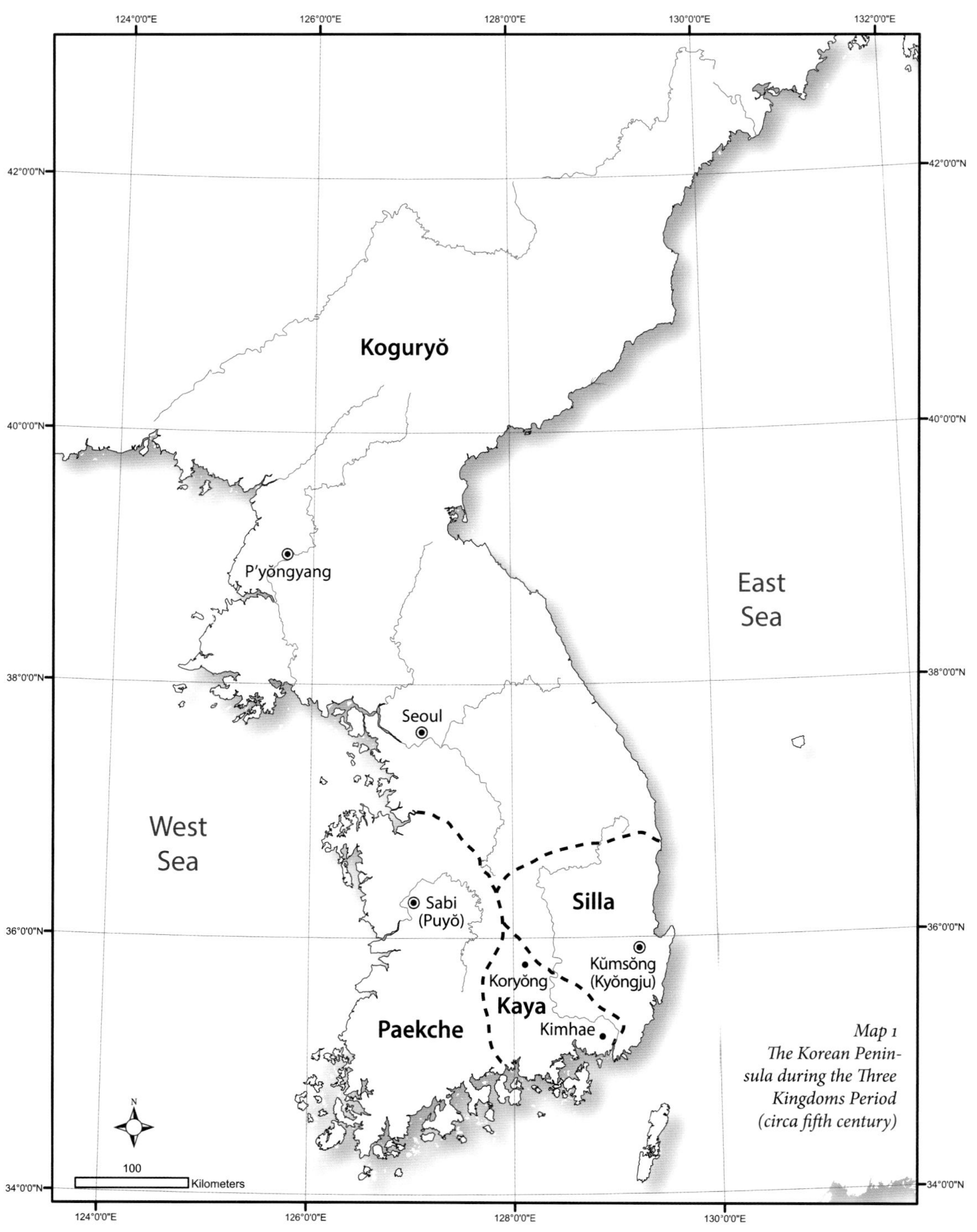

Map 1
The Korean Peninsula during the Three Kingdoms Period (circa fifth century)

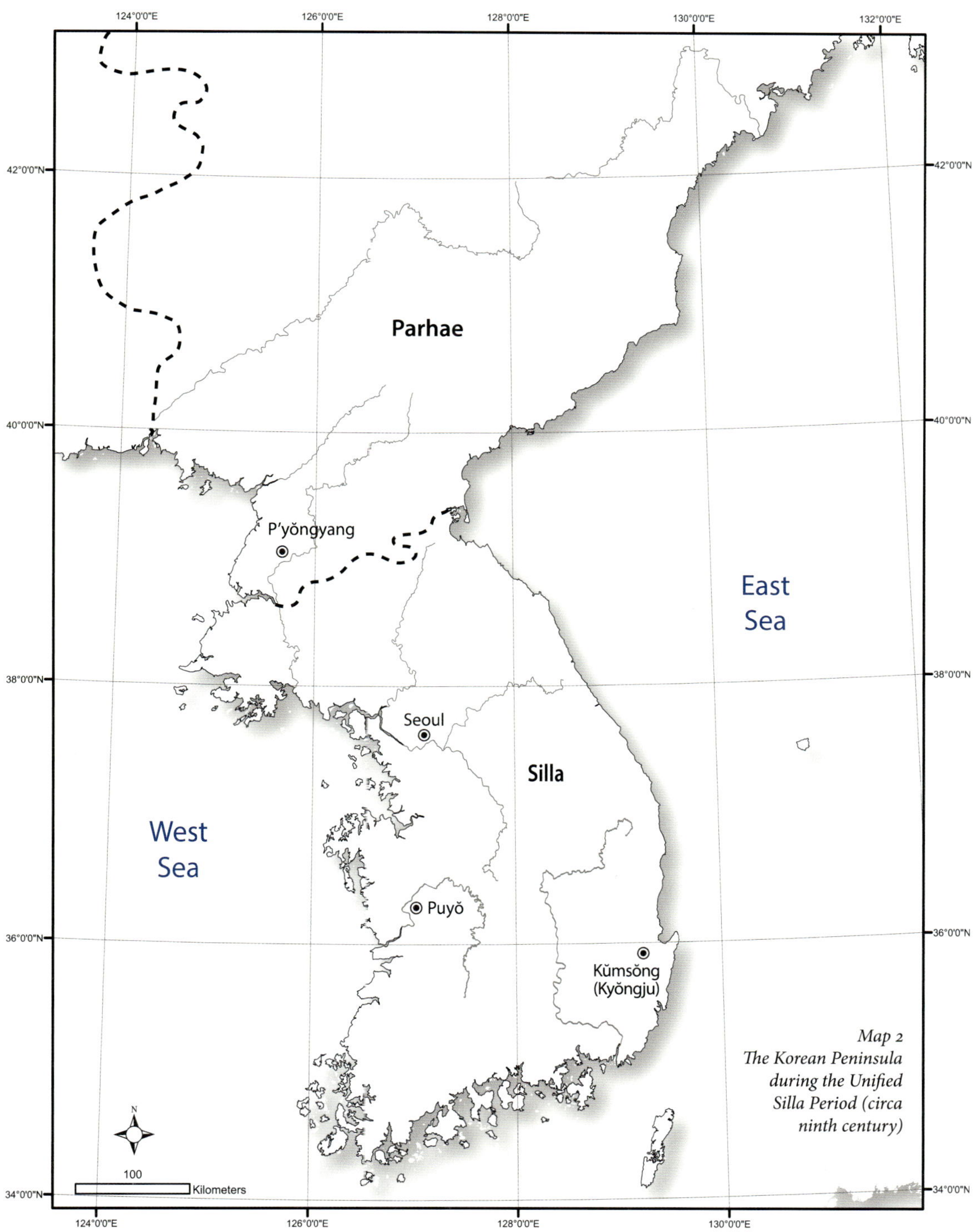

124°0'0"E
126°0'0"E
128°0'0"E
130°0'0"E
132°0'0"E
42°0'0"N
40°0'0"N
38°0'0"N
36°0'0"N
34°0'0"N
Parhae
P'yŏngyang
East
Sea
West
Sea
Seoul
Silla
Puyŏ
Kŭmsŏng
(Kyŏngju)
N
100
Kilometers
Map 2
The Korean Peninsula
during the Unified
Silla Period (circa
ninth century)

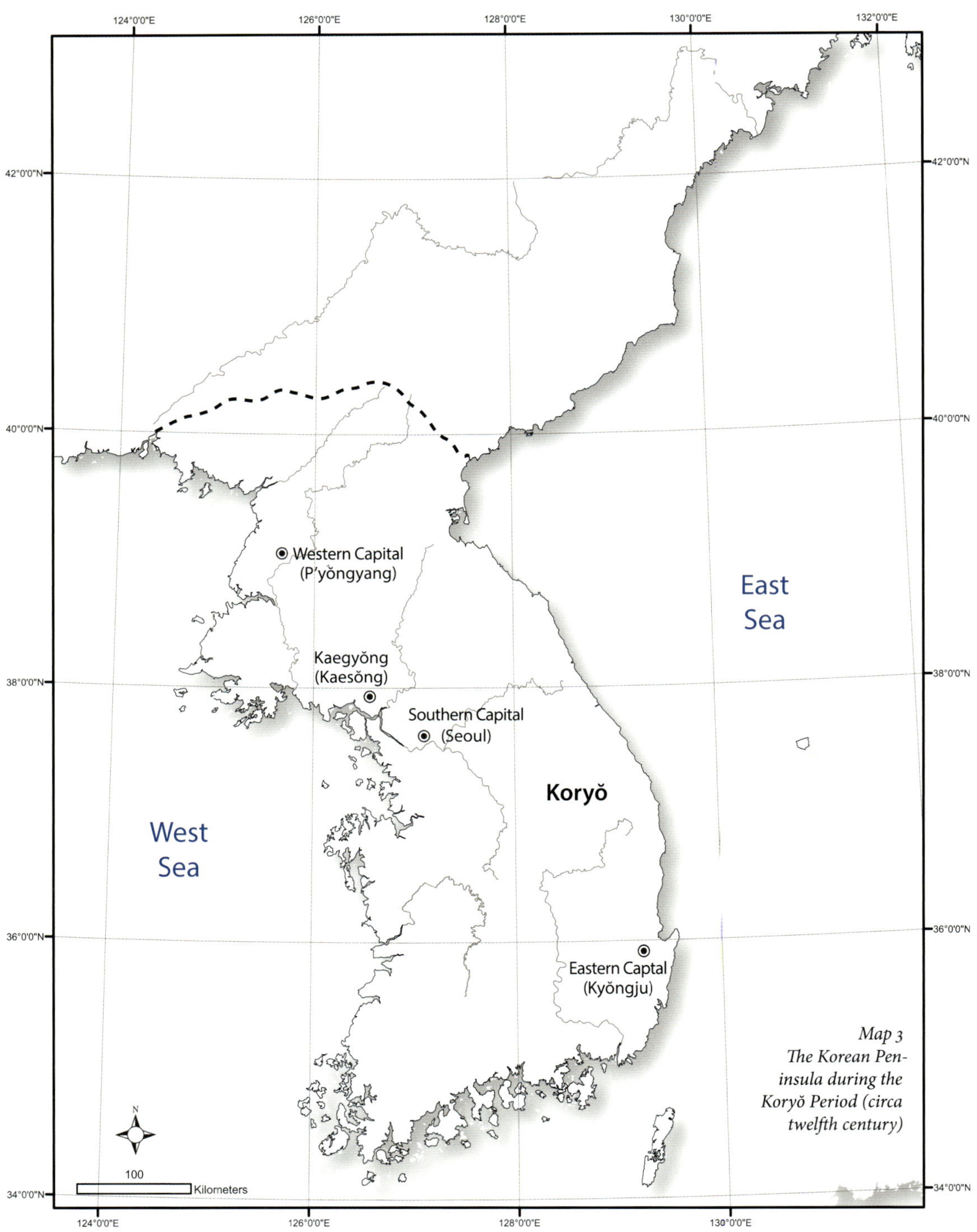

Map 3
The Korean Peninsula during the Koryŏ Period (circa twelfth century)

Introduction

Youn-mi Kim

In understanding the history and culture of early Korea, visual art plays an indispensable role, one with immense importance. Diverse visual artifacts with varying degrees of artistic value not only show the creative achievements of the early periods of Korean history, but also provide invaluable evidence about multiple aspects of the lives of the people of that time. This is particularly important given the fact that contemporaneous literary evidence is extremely limited for early Korean history. Discussions of the artworks in the present edited volume, from gold adornments recovered from tombs to Buddhist paintings scattered in modern museums and private collections, provide understanding of the religious practice, aesthetics, cross-cultural exchange, and everyday life of the people who made, used, appreciated, and circulated them that could not be gleaned in other ways. At the same time, a better understanding of Korean art and its stylistic features shared with arts of neighboring countries can also help us render a more vivid historical account of East Asia, illuminating the complicated interregional cultural exchanges in this area. Consequently, the scope of the following chapters in this volume often goes beyond the conventional realm of "national" art history, in effect offering thorough investigations of cross-cultural dialogues among Korea, China, Japan, and even South and Southeast Asian countries.

Because of the inherent importance and broad ramifications of visual art of Korea, the Early Korea Project at Harvard University called together a panel of specialists in Korean art in 2010. Whereas the previous conferences and publications sponsored by the Early Korea Project illuminated early Korean history primarily from the perspective of archaeology, the 2010 lecture series focused on visual culture and art history. The present volume consists of five chapters developed from the papers presented at this lecture series.

Like the previous volume of the Early Korea Project Occasional Series, titled *State and Society in Middle and Late Silla* (2010), the current volume maintains a focus on Silla 新羅 (traditional dates 57 B.C.E.-935 C.E.) while extending the time range to include Koryŏ 高麗 (918-1392). This inclusion allows us to consider a number of important issues and subfields of Korean art history, such as the origin of porcelain in the Korean peninsula and the study of Koryŏ Buddhist paintings.

The field of art historical scholarship in Korea has experienced rapid growth during the last several decades, as institutes of higher education began to adopt art history as an academic discipline in their regular curricula. From the initial establishment in Korea of both graduate and undergraduate programs in art history from the mid-1970s to the early 1980s, the field has rapidly developed into a dynamic and expansive presence within Korean academia. In addition to a number of academic journals devoted to art history, hundreds of monographs, edited volumes, and exhibition catalogues published in Korea are now available. It would not be an exaggeration to say that it has now become difficult for young Korean scholars in Korea to find an unexplored topic for a master's thesis or doctoral dissertation if they simply follow traditional methodologies. Naturally, the field of art history in Korea is gradually embracing more diverse approaches introduced from the West, from social history of art to semiotics, and producing more creative thematic studies on various types of visual art. It is, however, unfortunate that these works remain inaccessible to those scholars who do not have access to materials written in the Korean language. In keeping with the main objective of the Early Korea Project—providing Western readers with up-to-date scholarship on Korean history, as presented by scholars active in the field, to help close the gap that remains in English language scholarship—the present volume introduces recent scholarship in representative art media.

In 2010 the Early Korea Project at Harvard University invited four specialists—Joo Kyeongmi, Rhi Juhyung, Chung Woothak, and Jang Namwon—to present their research on various aspects of early Korean art history. They delivered lectures on Silla gold crafts, Silla Buddhist sculpture, Koryŏ porcelain, and Koryŏ Buddhist painting, respectively. Lastly, Youn-mi Kim, then a Ph.D. candidate at Harvard University, joined the series to give a talk on Silla Buddhist architecture.

The first three chapters of this volume examine representative media of Korean Buddhist art. Religious art, especially Buddhist art, constitutes one of the most important groups of extant artworks from Silla and Koryŏ. Buddhism became the major driving force in creating new types of visual art in Silla after it was officially recognized and accepted in the sixth century.[1] After the transmission of Buddhism, sculpture rose as a mainstream art form, and Buddhist temples began to reshape the urban environment of the capital area. The surviving visual artifacts and textual records related to Buddhism, however, are relatively limited. In Korean art history, only a very few paintings produced before Koryŏ have survived. The exception is the well-preserved murals inside the Koguryŏ 高句麗 (trad. 37 B.C.E.-668 C.E.) tombs, which are concentrated around present-day Pyongyang in North Korea and Ji'an 集安 in the northeastern part of China. As for Silla, the majority of the remaining examples are paintings that adorn various crafts including lacquerware, with the exception of a small fragment of an illustration from the *Flower Ornament Sutra* (Ch. *Huayan jing* 華嚴經) scroll (ca. 754). The earliest and most important category of Korean painting is Koryŏ Buddhist painting. It was only in the 1970s that art historians began to rediscover Koryŏ Buddhist paintings, which were scattered in various collections throughout the world, especially in Japan, where they had been misidentified as Chinese or Japanese works. Chung Woothak is one of the pioneers whose work led to the rediscovery of Koryŏ Buddhist paintings, and he has a superb knowledge of the techniques used in their production, through which Koryŏ Buddhist paintings can be uniquely identified. In Chapter One, "Iconography, Technique, and Context in Koryŏ Buddhist Painting," Chung explores the production process as well as the subject matter and socio-religious contexts of Koryŏ Buddhist painting. Chung's research is based on analyses of the rich data he collected over decades through firsthand examination and fine-grained observations—which sometimes even utilized microscopic analysis—of rare Koryŏ Buddhist paintings scattered throughout many countries. Chung's chapter also demonstrates his new academic approach, further revealing the unique qualities of Koryŏ Buddhist paintings through comparison with Chinese Buddhist paintings from the Song 宋 (960-1127) and Xixia 西夏 (1038-1227) periods.

Study of Korean Buddhist art of earlier periods is a challenging task due to the insufficiency of surviving historical texts. The *Samguk sagi* 三國史記

---

[1] While Koguryŏ and Paekche respectively adopted Buddhism in 372 and 384, it took much longer for Silla aristocrats to do so. Only after Ich'adon 異次頓 (506-527) voluntarily martyred himself in 527 during King Pŏphŭng's 法興 (r. 514-540) reign did Silla aristocrats begin to accept this foreign religion that originated in India.

(History of the Three Kingdoms) and the *Samguk yusa* 三國遺事 (Memorabilia of the Three Kingdoms), the two earliest surviving texts on early Korean history, were respectively compiled in the twelfth and the thirteenth centuries, several centuries after Silla disappeared from the Korean peninsula. To overcome the problem of limited data, Chapters Two and Three take an interdisciplinary approach to throw more light on early Korean Buddhist art and practice, and in doing so, they explore the boundaries between art history, archaeology, and epigraphy. In Chapter Two, "Seeing Maitreya: Aspiration and Vision in an Image from Early Eighth-Century Silla," Rhi Juhyung draws our attention to two images from Kamsan-sa. These images carry unusually long inscriptions on the back of their mandorlas and are thus exceptionally well documented in terms of information about the circumstances of their creation. Focusing on the image of the Maitreya bodhisattva, which is identifiable as such through inscriptions, Rhi explores why this bodhisattva takes an idiosyncratic iconographic form virtually unparalleled in Buddhist iconography. He seeks to answer this question from the patron's experience of visualizing Maitreya as descending from the Tuṣita heaven for an encounter with a devotee. In Chapter Three, "(Dis)assembling the National Canon: Seventh-Century "Esoteric" Buddhist Ritual, the *Samguk yusa*, and Sach'ŏnwang-sa," Youn-mi Kim examines a controversial passage from the *Samguk yusa* about the Munduru 文豆婁 Ritual performed in seventh-century Silla—the earliest extant record of "esoteric" Buddhist ritual in Korea. Through interdisciplinary analyses of the passage that examine external texts as well as surviving archaeological remains at Sach'ŏnwang-sa 四天王寺 and reliquaries from the Kamŭn-sa 感恩寺 twin pagodas, Kim suggests that, contrary to previous scholarly skepticism about the reliability of this passage in Western academia, it is highly likely that the Munduru Ritual was indeed performed at Sach'ŏnwang-sa in the seventh century. Together, these two chapters not only address the limitations of textual research for studying early Korean Buddhism, but also demonstrate that considering archaeological remains and art historical data can enhance our understanding of Buddhist practices in early Korea.

The last two chapters of the present volume explore representative genres of craft from Korea. Ceramics are an especially important genre of Korean art. Excavations of Silla tombs have yielded diverse ceramics that probably had ritual functions. But these ceramics were primarily earthenware and stoneware, fired at relatively lower temperatures, and thus were not yet porcelain. The origin of porcelain in the Korean peninsula is a much-debated issue. Until the 1990s specialists in Korean ceramics erroneously thought that porcelain production in Korea began in late Unified Silla, mostly in the ninth century. As more kiln sites have been excavated and more information about Chinese kilns has become available, however, the previous theory has been revised, and now it is clear that Koryŏ artisans were the first to produce porcelain in the Korean peninsula. In order to bring to light recent scholarship on the early production of porcelain in Korea, we have decided to include some of the ongoing debates on Koryŏ works in this volume. Unlike previous scholarship that primarily focused solely on the influence of southern Chinese kilns, Chapter Four, "The Development of Koryŏ Porcelain and the Chinese Ceramic Industry in the Tenth Century," by Jang Namwon, demonstrates Koryŏ's selective adoption from various regions in China in the tenth century. Jang's research is groundbreaking in that she illuminates the Koryŏ porcelain industry's connection to northern Chinese dynasties, especially Liao 遼 (907-1125). Her new approach solves several important problems left unanswered by previous scholarship—most significantly, the problem of the reversed chronology of the *bi*-shaped foot (Kr. *okhwanjŏ* 玉璧底) and the jade-ring-shaped foot (Kr. *okhwanjŏ* 玉環底) of Koryŏ, which deviates from the chronological development of ceramics in China.

Another important group of crafts in Korean art history is gold metalwork excavated from royal tombs of Silla. Approximately 1,700 to 1,800 Silla tombs survive, and roughly two hundred of these are believed to belong to the royal family. Of the various objects excavated from Silla's royal tombs, the most spectacular and important are gold crafts. Members of the royal family buried in excavated Silla tombs were often found with sumptuous gold earrings, gold belts with many pendants, gold crowns, and even gilded bronze shoes. Many scholars have tried to elucidate the origin of the gold adornments from Silla tombs because these gold crafts are unique both in style and quantity: no other region in East Asia has tombs that boast such high proportions of gold ornaments among the tomb objects. In Chapter Five, "The Gold Jewelry of Ancient Silla: Syncretism of Northern and Southern Asian Cultures," Joo Kyeongmi traces the origin of the gold crowns and gold earrings excavated from Silla's royal tombs. While previous scholarship primarily focused on their relationship to northern Eurasia and northeast China, Joo proposes to revise this view, suggesting that such an approach reflects Japanese colonial period (1910-1945) scholars' rather propagandistic argument that Silla had an isolated and lineal culture influenced by invaders and immigrants from the north. Joo's claim finds support in her demonstration that Silla's thick gold earrings with pendants were created as a synthesis of the thin earrings with pendants worn by northern Eurasian nomadic people and the thick earring style transmitted from South and Southeast Asia.

It is my hope that this present volume will be a foundation for the study of early Korean art by making its latest academic achievements available to a wide range of readers in various fields, especially those without access to Korean language scholarship. In addition, I consider a variety of new findings and arguments disclosed in the following pages timely and sincere responses from Korean scholars to an increasing interest in Korean art and culture in the West during the last few decades. With its shared interest in the socio-religious and cross-cultural aspects of the arts of Silla and Koryŏ, *New Perspectives on Early Korean Art* ultimately opens up a new forum for studies of early Korea in the global context.

1

Iconography, Technique, and Context in Koryŏ Buddhist Painting

Chung Woothak

Koryŏ Buddhist painting began to draw attention in the autumn of 1978, with the opening of the "Special Exhibition of Koryŏ Buddhist Paintings" (Jp. Tokubetsuten Kōrai Butsuga 特別展高麗仏画) at the Museum Yamato Bunkakan, in Nara 奈良, Japan.[1] Thereafter, as a result of significant research and increased interest, the number of Buddhist paintings identified as works from the Koryŏ period (918-1392) has increased every year, and now exceeds 150 pieces.[2] The significance of Koryŏ Buddhist paintings is unmistakable: with virtually no secular paintings from the same period remaining, they are the only extant materials through which we may observe the trends of Koryŏ paintings.

Although the Koryŏ Buddhist paintings that survive were mostly produced during a period spanning roughly 150 years in late Koryŏ, they

---

[1] For the catalogue of this exhibition, see Yamato Bunkakan 大和文華館, *Tokubetsuten Kōrai butsuga: Waga kuni ni shōraisareta ringoku no konjiki no hotoketachi* 特別展高麗仏画: わが国に請来された隣国の金色の仏たち [Special exhibition of Koryŏ Buddhist painting: The golden Buddhas brought from Korea to our country] (Nara: Yamato Bunkakan, 1978).

[2] Kikutake Jun'ichi 菊竹淳一 and Chŏng Ut'aek (Chung Woothak) 鄭于澤, eds., *Koryŏ sidae ŭi purhwa* 高麗時代의 佛畵 [Buddhist paintings of the Koryŏ period], 2 vols. (Seoul: Sigongsa, 1997). This book presents 133 examples of Buddhist paintings. Since its publication, however, more Koryŏ Buddhist paintings have been newly discovered in Japan, the United States, and Europe. The same book was also published in Japanese by the same publisher in 2000. Kikutake Jun'ichi and Chŏng Ut'aek, eds., *Kōrai jidai no butsuga* 高麗時代の仏画 [Buddhist paintings of the Koryŏ period] (Seoul: Sigongsa, 2000).

differ from Buddhist paintings of the subsequent Chosŏn period (1392-1910) as well as those of China, Japan, and other areas in East Asia. Thanks to invigorated research activities in recent years, Koryŏ Buddhist painting has been firmly established as one of the major areas of research in East Asian art history.[3] Employing the research results accumulated thus far, this chapter aims to offer a brief account of the distinctive characteristics of Koryŏ Buddhist painting, including its iconography, techniques, and production purposes.

Rediscovery and Academic Research

There are no references to Koryŏ Buddhist painting in the major contributions to the history of Korean art published under the period of Japanese colonial rule (1910-1945), including *Chōsen koseki zufu* 朝鮮古蹟圖譜 (Illustrated book of Korean historical remains),[4] O Sech'ang's *Kŭnyŏk sŏhwa ching* 槿域書畫徵 (Biographical compendium of Korean painters and calligraphers) published in 1928,[5] or the art historian Ko Yusŏp's writings of the 1940s. This means that no Koryŏ Buddhist paintings in color were known to exist in Korea before the late 1970s, with the exception of four heavily damaged ink paintings of the Five Hundred Arhats in the collection of the National Museum of Korea.

On display at the aforementioned exhibition at the Museum Yamato Bunkakan were forty-nine Buddhist paintings from the Koryŏ period, many of which had previously been misclassified either as works of Chinese origin or under erroneous titles (fig. 1.1).[6] For example, *Amitābha and the Eight Great Bodhisattvas* (Kr. *Amit'a p'altae posalto* 阿彌陀八大菩薩圖) displayed in this exhibition had long been misidentified as *Śākyamuni and the Eight Great Bodhisattvas* (Kr. *Sŏkka p'altae posalto* 釋迦八大菩薩圖).[7] Not surpris-

----

[3] Regarding the results of research on Koryŏ Buddhist paintings, see the bibliography of Koryŏ Buddhist painting in Kikutake Jun'ichi and Chŏng Ut'aek, eds., *Koryŏ sidae ŭi purhwa*, 2: 136-137.

[4] Chōsen Sōtokufu 朝鮮總督府 [Governor-General of Korea], ed., *Chōsen koseki zufu* 朝鮮古蹟圖譜 [Illustrated book of Korean historical remains], 15 vols. (Tokyo: Chōsen Sōtokufu, 1915-1935).

[5] O Sech'ang 吳世昌, *Kŭnyŏk sŏhwa ching* 槿域書畫徵 [Biographical compendium of Korean painters and calligraphers] (Kyŏngsŏng [Seoul]: Kyemyŏng Kurakpu, 1928).

[6] The exhibition at the Museum Yamato Bunkakan was held from October 18 through November 19 in 1978. It was curated by Yoshida Hiroshi 吉田宏志.

[7] Editor's Note: Following academic convention, the word "painting" (Kr. *to* 圖) is omitted in the English translations of painting titles. The literal translation

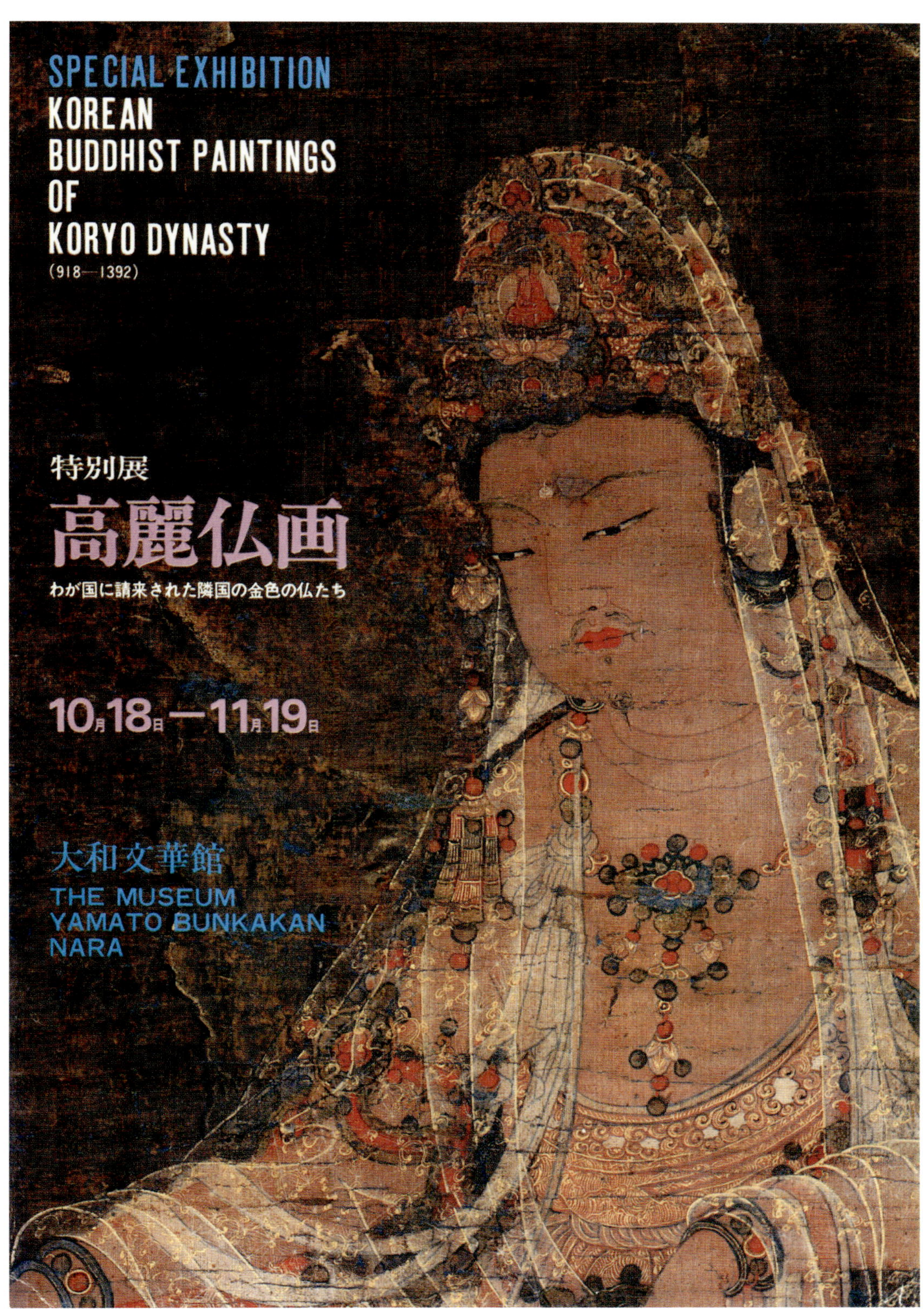

Figure 1.1 Cover image of the catalogue of "Special Exhibition of Koryŏ Buddhist Paintings" at the Museum Yamato Bunkakan, in Nara, Japan. Courtesy of Museum Yamato Bunkakan.

ingly, Yoshida Hiroshi, the curator of this exhibition, had to face serious objections and criticisms for his decision to reclassify the majority of Buddhist paintings on display as Koryŏ paintings. At the time, they were still believed to be Chinese. In the end, however, the exhibition revealed the existence of a superb Buddhist art—Koryŏ Buddhist paintings surviving in and outside of Korea—and eventually proved to be the pivotal moment in establishing Koryŏ Buddhist painting as an independent field of academic study.

Following this exhibition, Koryŏ Buddhist paintings were presented to the public on a large scale in the special exhibition "Koryŏ, Eternal Beauty" (Kr. Koryŏ, Yŏngwŏn han Mi 高麗, 영원한 美) held in 1993 at the Ho-Am Art Museum.[8] The exhibition was intended to quench the thirst of the many people who wanted to see the paintings in person. This exhibition has great significance because it served as the first exhibition of Koryŏ Buddhist paintings held in Korea, introducing the existence and importance of these forgotten treasures to many Koreans. Subsequently, a number of Koryŏ Buddhist paintings were displayed in the "Great National Treasures of Koryŏ Exhibition" (Kr. Tae Koryŏ Kukpojŏn 大高麗國寶展) in 1995.[9] These events provided an opportunity for scholars to recognize Koryŏ Buddhist painting as an important research theme and for the general public to appreciate it as one of the beautiful arts of Korea.

In autumn 1997, a multitude of Koryŏ Buddhist paintings, including those shown to the public for the first time, were put on display in the exhibition "Buddhist Art of Koryŏ and the Yi Dynasty" (Jp. Kōrai, Richō no Bukkyō Bijutsuten 高麗・李朝の仏教美術展) held at the Yamaguchi Prefectural Museum of Art in Japan.[10] In May 2006, several previously unknown

---

of *Amit'a p'aldae posalto*, for example, would be *Amitābha and the Eight Great Bodhisattvas Painting*.

[8] For more about this exhibition, see Hoam Misulgwan 湖巖美術館 [Ho-Am Art Museum], *Koryŏ yŏngwŏn han mi: Koryŏ purhwa t'ŭkpyŏlchŏn* 高麗, 영원한 美: 高麗佛畫特別展 [Koryŏ, eternal beauty: Special exhibition of Koryŏ Buddhist painting] (Seoul: Samsŏng Misul Munhwa Chaedan, 1993).

[9] For this exhibition's catalogue, see Hoam Misulgwan 湖巖美術館 [Ho-Am Art Museum] et al., eds., *Tae Koryŏ kukpojŏn* 大高麗國寶展 [Great national treasures of Koryŏ exhibition] (Seoul: Samsŏng Munhwa Chaedan and Hoam Gaellŏri; Yongin: Hoam Misulgwan, 1995).

[10] For more on this exhibition, see Iwai Tomoji 岩井共二 and Fukushima Tsunenori 福島恒德, eds., *Kōrai, Richō no Bukkyō bijutsuten* 高麗・李朝の仏教美術展 [Buddhist Art of Koryŏ and the Yi Dynasty] (Yamaguchi: Yamaguchi Kenritsu Bijutsukan, 1997).

Koryŏ Buddhist paintings drew attention when the exhibition titled "National Treasures at Dongguk University" (Kr. Tongguktae Kukpojŏn 東國大國寶展) was held in commemoration of the one-hundred-year anniversary of the founding of Dongguk University. Most recently, the National Museum of Korea held the largest exhibition of Koryŏ Buddhist paintings to date, titled "Masterpieces of Koryŏ Buddhist Painting" (Kr. Koryŏ Purhwa Taejŏn 高麗佛畫大展), from October to November in 2010, winning wide acclaim from both critics and the general public.

Kumagai Nobuo's article, "Chōsen butsugachō" 朝鮮仏画徵 (Compendium of Korean Buddhist paintings) published in *Chōsen gakuhō* 朝鮮学報 in 1967, was the first academic writing that acknowledged the existence of Koryŏ Buddhist painting.[11] Focusing on the Buddhist paintings of the Chosŏn period, this article introduced a total of seventy-five Buddhist paintings—twenty-four of which were identified as Koryŏ works—providing an opportunity to understand some aspects of Koryŏ Buddhist painting.

The first monograph that dealt with Koryŏ Buddhist painting as its main theme was *Kōrai butsuga* 高麗仏画 (Koryŏ Buddhist painting), published in 1981 by the Japanese newspaper company Asahi Shinbun.[12] Consolidating the results of the exhibition at the Yamato Bunkakan, the book primarily offered black-and-white reproductions of the paintings. In the same year, another book titled *Koryŏ purhwa* 高麗佛畫 (Koryŏ Buddhist painting) was published in Korea as part of the *Han'guk ŭi mi* 韓國의 美 (Beauty of Korea) series.[13] Published in 1997, *Koryŏ sidae ŭi purhwa* 高麗時代의 佛畫 (Buddhist paintings of the Koryŏ period), which featured a total of 133 paintings known at the time of publication, received praise as the most comprehensively compiled body of Koryŏ Buddhist painting.[14] This book provided the results of on-site research and hundreds of high-definition photos showing the details of the paintings, covering nearly as much information as one can obtain from actually seeing objects and thereby contributing to the vitalization of research in related fields.[15]

---

[11] Kumagai Nobuo 熊谷宣夫, "Chōsen butsugachō" 朝鮮仏画徵 [Compendium of Korean Buddhist paintings], *Chōsen gakuhō* 朝鮮学報 44 (1967): 1-114.

[12] Kikutake Jun'ichi 菊竹淳一 and Yoshida Hiroshi 吉田宏志, eds., *Kōrai butsuga* 高麗仏画 [Koryŏ Buddhist painting] (Tokyo: Asahi Shinbunsha, 1981).

[13] Yi Tongju 李東洲 ed., *Koryŏ purhwa* 高麗佛畫 [Koryŏ Buddhist painting] (Seoul: Chungang Ilbosa, 1981).

[14] Kikutake Jun'ichi and Chŏng Ut'aek, eds., *Koryŏ sidae ŭi purhwa*.

[15] For a discussion of how Koryŏ Buddhist paintings became known to scholars

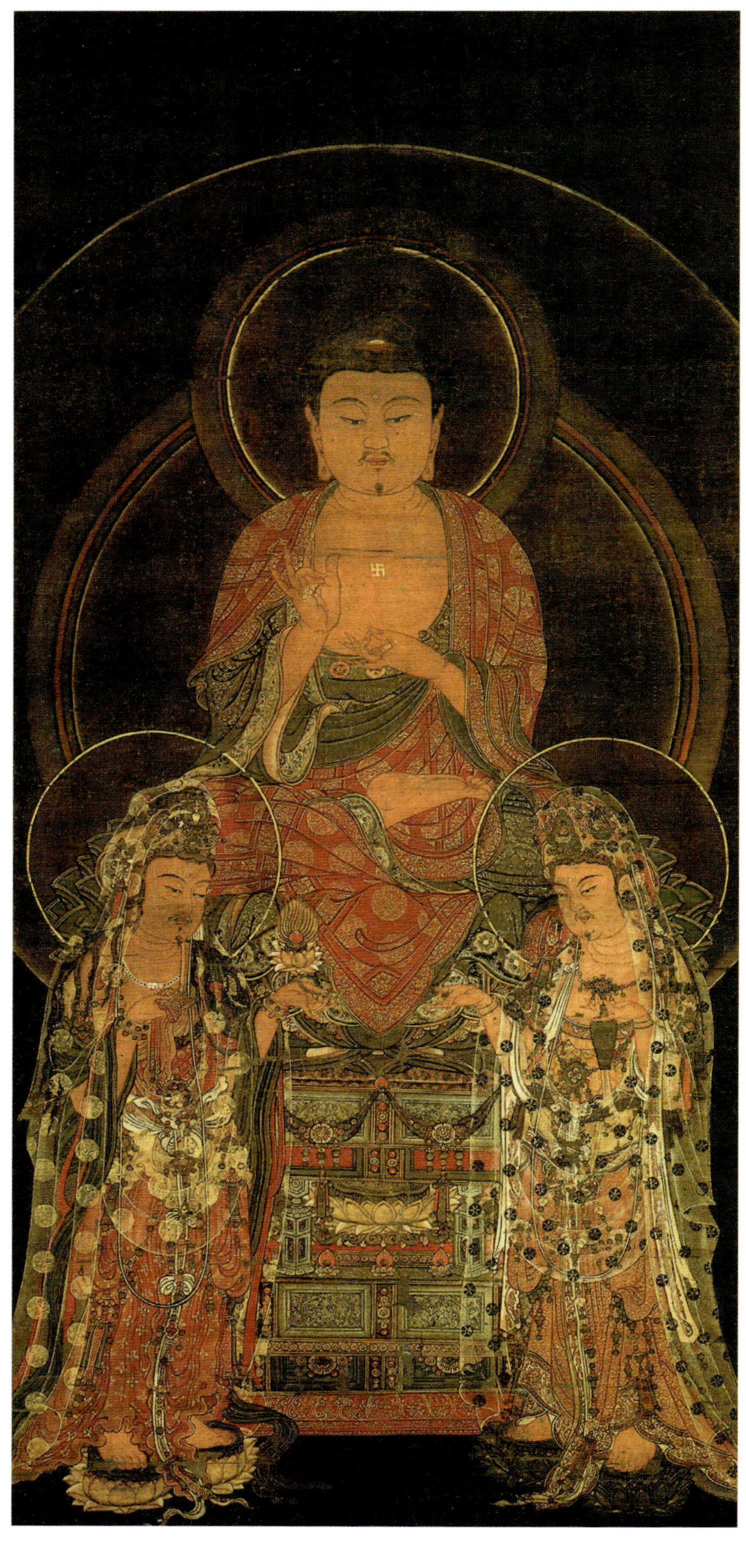

Figure 1.2 Amitābha Triad. *Koryŏ, fourteenth century. Hanging scroll, ink and color on silk. 139.0×87.9cm. Nezu Museum, Japan. Courtesy of the author.*

Iconography and Imitativeness[16]

Iconography and Iconology

More than 150 Buddhist paintings of the Koryŏ period have been identified thus far, with 120-odd pieces found in Japan and others in collections in Korea, the United States, and other countries. While it is hard to say that Koryŏ Buddhist painting is diverse in its iconographic content, it still comprises a range of iconographies that came from exoteric Buddhism, including Buddhas and bodhisattvas. Among them, works associated with Amitābha Buddha were preferred as objects of worship across all Buddhist schools, periods, and states due to the common belief that Amitābha Buddha presides over the Western Pure Land. In most cases, these paintings are divided into two iconographic features: Amitābha preaching the Buddhist law in the Western Pure Land (fig. 1.2), and Amitābha welcoming the soul who has attained rebirth into the Western Pure Land (fig. 1.3).

Buddhist paintings related to Amitābha also include various examples of *Illustration of the Introductory Chapter of the Visualization Sutra* (Kr. *Kwan'gyŏng sŏbun pyŏnsangdo* 觀經序分變相圖) and *Illustration of the Sixteen Contemplations in the Visualization Sutra* (Kr. *Kwan'gyŏng simnyukkwan pyŏnsangdo* 觀經十六觀變相圖). The scriptural basis for their iconography is the *Sutra of the Contemplation on the Buddha of Immeasurable Life* (Ch. *Guan wuliangshou jing* 觀無量壽經), also known as the *Visualization Sutra* (Ch. *Guan jing* 觀經).[17] This sutra is one of the principal scriptures of the Pure Land belief that describes methods of visualizing the Western Pure Land as well as the reasons, means, and processes enabling a believer to be reborn in the Western Pure Land with the guidance of Amitābha.

Bhaiṣajyaguru Buddha, also known as Medicine Buddha (Ch. Yaoshi rulai 藥師如來), is the Buddha of the Eastern Pure Land of Crystal Radiance, believed to fulfill the devotees' wishes to be delivered from illness and bring good fortune to them by granting benefits in the present world.

---

and a list of relevant publications, see Chŏng Ut'aek 鄭于澤, "Koryŏ purhwa ui yŏngyŏk" 高麗佛畫의 領域 [The field of Koryŏ Buddhist painting], *Pulgyo misul sahak* 佛教美術史學 5 (November 1997): 212-214.

[16] Editor's Note: "Imitativeness" is a translation of the Korean word *mosasŏng* 模寫性. The author of this chapter uses this word to describe the tendency to copy previous iconography and composition, which is widely observed in Koryŏ Buddhist paintings.

[17] T365, 12:340b-346b.

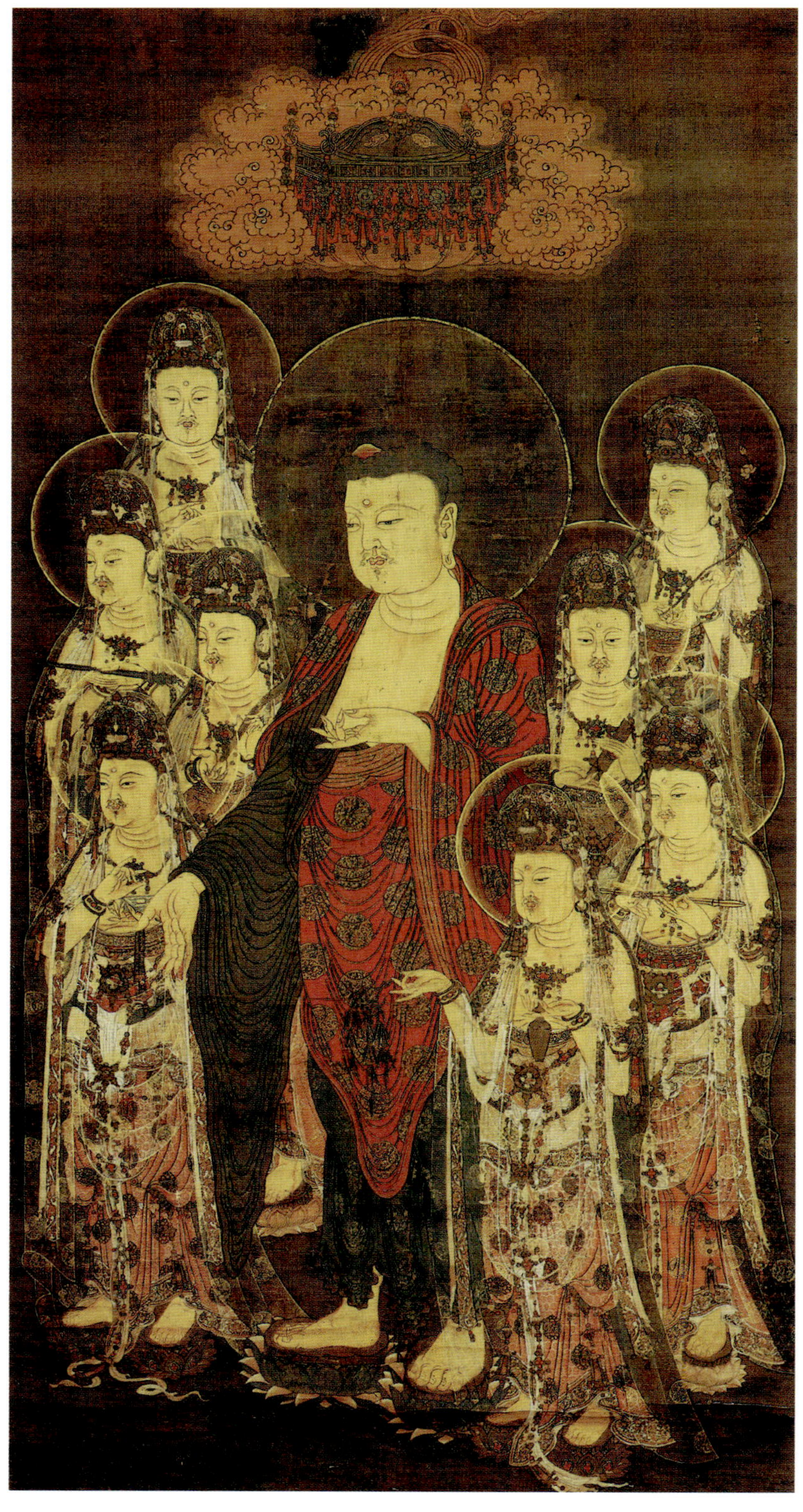

Figure 1.3 Descent of Amitābha and the Eight Great Bodhisattvas. *Koryŏ, fourteenth century. Hanging scroll, ink and color on silk. 173.1×91.1cm. Jōkyōji, Japan. Courtesy of the author.*

Currently, three Koryŏ paintings are identified as depicting this figure, including *Bhaiṣajyaguru Buddha* (Kr. *Yaksa yŏrae tokchondo* 藥師如來獨存圖), which portrays the Buddha alone, and *Bhaiṣajyaguru Preaching the Law* (Kr. *Yaksa sŏlpŏpto* 藥師說法圖), which portrays Bhaiṣajyaguru Buddha attended by Sūryaprabha bodhisattva (Kr. Ilgwang posal 日光菩薩) and Candraprabha bodhisattva (Kr. Wŏlgwang posal 月光菩薩) as well as by eight other bodhisattvas and the twelve guardian generals.

It is plausible to assume that a considerable number of Buddhist paintings associated with Vairocana Buddha or the *Flower Ornament Sutra* (Ch. *Huayan jing* 華嚴經)—the main Buddha and the principal sutra of the Avataṃsaka School—were produced as well, because the Avataṃsaka School was very popular in Koryŏ at the time. There are, however, only a few known examples extant today. A painting titled *Fifteen Thousand Buddhas* (Kr. *Man-ochŏn pulto* 萬五千佛圖) from Fudōin 不動院 is filled with tiny images of numerous Buddhas and bodhisattvas (fig. 1.4). Some scholars have suggested that this is the pictorial representation of the following passage from the *Flower Ornament Sutra*: "The moment Vairocana Buddha gains awakening, rays of great light emanate from his body to illuminate the world in ten directions, and a cloud of transformation bodies of the Buddha emerges from every pore," or "The transformation Buddhas emerge from every pore of the body like a cloud and fully infuse all the worlds in ten directions."[18]

Maitreya is known as the future Buddha who resides in the Tuṣita heaven as a bodhisattva. It is believed that Maitreya will descend to earth as Buddha at the time of the Latter Days of the Dharma (Ch. *mofa* 末法)—the era of darkness that emerges many years after the *parinirvāṇa* of the historical Buddha Śākyamuni—and deliver teachings three times to bring all sentient beings to salvation. There are four extant Koryŏ paintings related to Maitreya: three examples of *Illustration of the Sutra on Maitreya's Rebirth Below* (Kr. *Mirŭk hasaenggyŏng pyŏnsangdo* 彌勒下生經變相圖), and one example of *Maitreya Buddha Triad* (Kr. *Mirŭk samjondo* 彌勒三尊圖).

Tejaprabhā, the Buddha who is regarded as the personification of the North Star in Buddhism, is believed to have the power to control natural disasters and ward off misfortunes. The paintings of Tejaprabhā depict Tejaprabhā Buddha and a diverse attendant group of Daoist origin. Only

---

[18] Kikutake Jun'ichi 菊竹淳一, "Koryŏ purhwa ui t'ŭksŏng" 高麗佛畫의 特性 [Features of Koryŏ Buddhist paintings], in *Koryŏ sidae ŭi purhwa* 高麗時代의佛畫 [Buddhist paintings of the Koryŏ period], ed. Kikutake Jun'ichi and Chŏng Ut'aek, vol. 2 (Seoul: Sigongsa, 1997): 12-13.

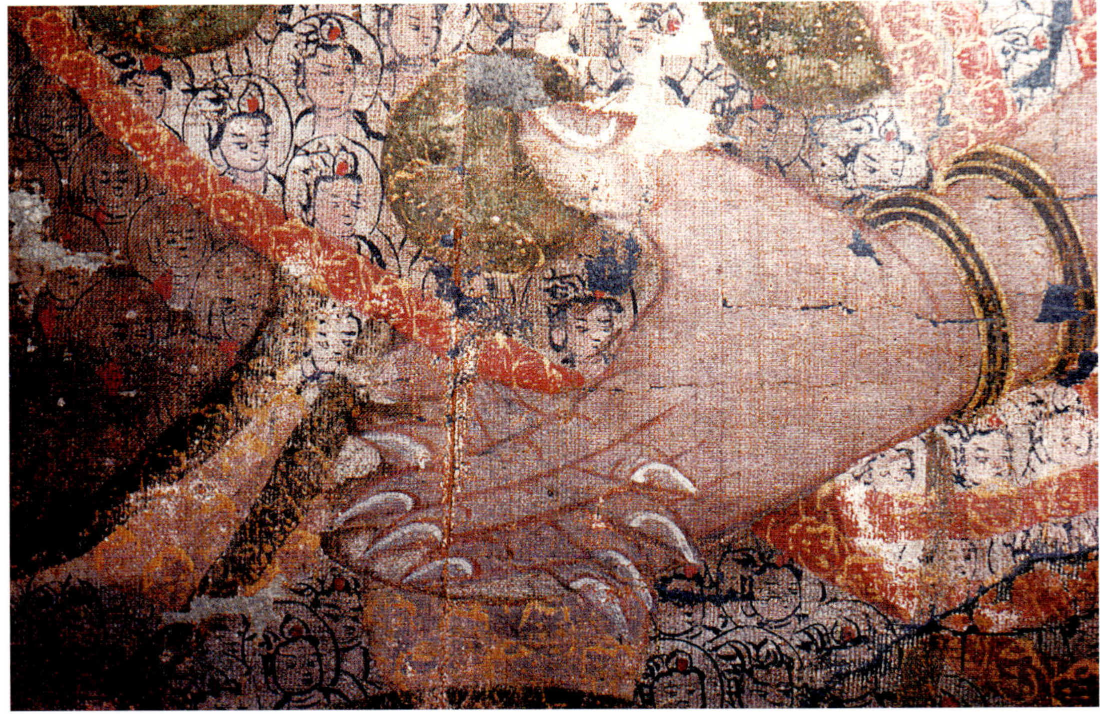

Figure 1.4 Fifteen Thousand Buddhas *(detail). Koryŏ, thirteenth century.
Hanging scroll, ink and color on silk. Fudōin, Japan. Courtesy of the author.*

one such painting has been identified from Koryŏ, which is now in the collection of the Museum of Fine Arts, Boston. This iconography came into being by merging Buddhist and Daoist elements.

Best known among Koryŏ Buddhist paintings are the representations of Avalokiteśvara, the bodhisattva who symbolizes compassion and is believed to deliver sentient beings from calamities and lead them to paradise. In other words, he grants both benefits in the present world and salvation in the next life. The chapter of "Universal Gate of Avalokiteśvara Bodhisattva" (Ch. *Guanshiyin pusa pumen pin* 觀世音菩薩普門品) in the *Miaofa lianhua jing* 妙法蓮華經 (Lotus Sutra)[19] is commonly referred to as the

---

[19] T262, 9:56c–62b.

20

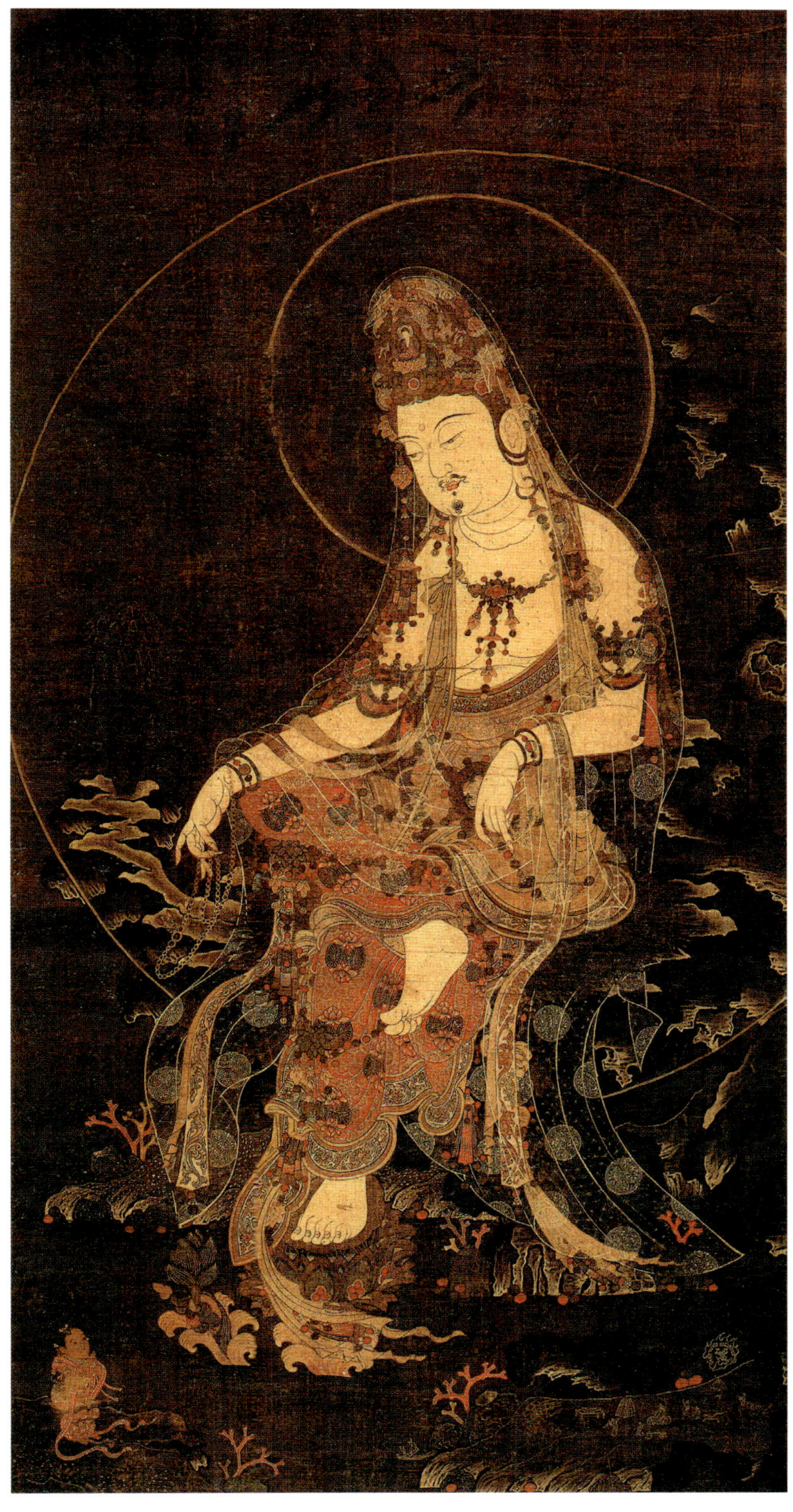

Figure 1.5 Water-Moon Avalokiteśvara. *Koryŏ, fourteenth century. Hanging scroll, ink and color on silk. 109.5×57.8cm. Tanzan Jinja, Japan. Courtesy of the author.*

Kwanŭmgyŏng 觀音經 (Sutra of Avalokiteśvara) and functions as the most representative scripture that describes Avalokiteśvara bodhisattva's benevolent nature and merits, as well as the benefits that devotees will receive.

In most Koryŏ Buddhist paintings depicting Avalokiteśvara (fig. 1.5), the bodhisattva is seated on a rocky outcrop in a half-lotus position (having one leg crossed and the other hanging); in the background are bamboo stalks and in the foreground is a willow branch placed in a *kundika* bottle (Kr. *chŏngbyŏng* 淨瓶). At the left bottom corner, where Avalokiteśvara gazes down, the boy Sudhana can be seen. This iconography is based on the "Chapter on Entry into the Realm of Reality" (Sk. *Gaṇḍa-vyūha*, Ch. *Ru fajie pin* 入法界品) of the *Flower Ornament Sutra*, illustrating the content detailed in this chapter: the abode of Avalokiteśvara is Mount Potalaka by the sea, and Avalokiteśvara welcomes the boy Sudhana, who had journeyed to find good teachers (Ch. *shan zhishi* 善知識) in his quest for awakening.

In Koryŏ Buddhist paintings, Kṣitigarbha, the bodhisattva who oversees the netherworld, is represented singly or in the form of either *Kṣitigarbha Triad* (Kr. *Chijang samjondo* 地藏三尊圖), *Kṣitigarbha and the Ten Kings* (Kr. *Chijang siwangdo* 地藏十王圖), or other forms. The iconography of Kṣitigarbha can be classified into two types: the *śrāvaka* (Kr. *sŏngmun* 聲聞) type, showing Kṣitigarbha with the shaven head of a monk, or the kerchief type, showing Kṣitigarbha wearing a monk's scarf on his head. The scriptural sources for the iconography of the former are the *Dizang shilun jing* 地藏十輪經 (Sutra of ten cakras of Kṣitigarbha) and the *Dizang pusa yigui* 地藏菩薩儀軌 (Ritual manual of Kṣitigarbha bodhisattva),[20] but no scriptural association is found for the latter among Buddhist sutras. Nevertheless, the image of Kṣitigarbha wearing the monk's kerchief appears in a number of paintings from Dunhuang and in the records of miraculous stories, including the *Huanhun ji* 還魂記 (Record of a returned soul) and the *Dizang pusa lingyan ji* 地藏菩薩靈驗記 (Record of the miracles of Kṣitigarbha bodhisattva). These records suggest that this iconographical feature was established by the ninth century at the latest.[21]

Paintings like *Standing Avalokiteśvara and Kṣitigarbha* (Kr. *Kwanŭm chijangbosal pyŏngnipto* 觀音地藏菩薩竝立圖) and *Standing Amitābha Buddha and Kṣitigarbha Bodhisattva* (Kr. *Amit'a yŏrae chijangbosal pyŏngnipto*

---

[20] *Dizang shilun jing* T 411, 13:721a-777c; *Dizang pusa yigui* T 1158, 20:652a-c.

[21] Chŏng U-t'aek, "Chikuzen Zendōji no Jizō bosatsu-zu" 筑前善導寺の地藏菩薩図 [A Kṣitigarbha painting at Chikuzen Zendōji], *Bijutsushi* 美術史 36, no. 2 (1987): 110-125.

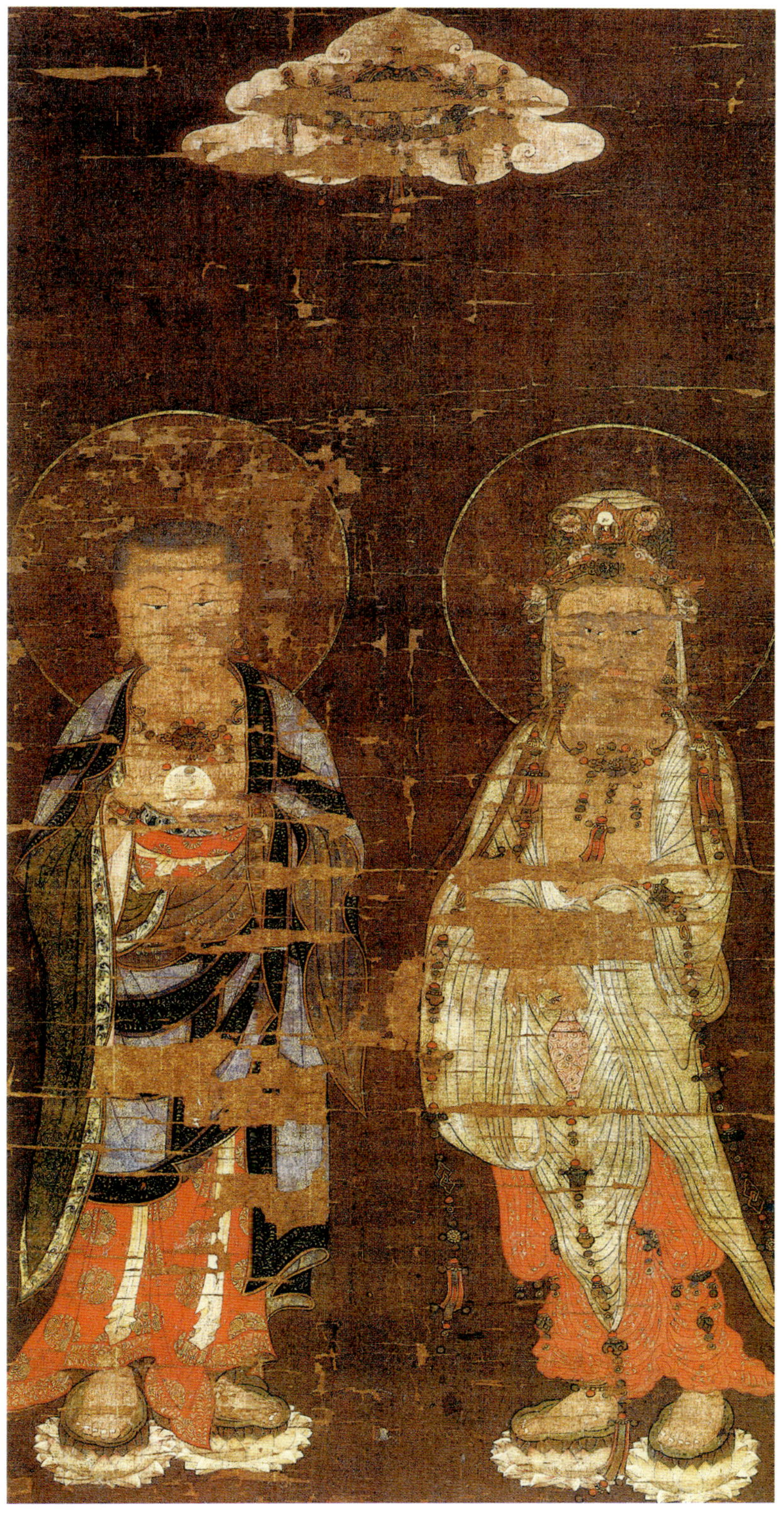

Figure 1.6 Standing Avalokiteśvara and Kṣitigarbha. *Koryŏ, fourteenth century. Hanging scroll, ink and color on silk. 99.0×52.5cm. Saifukuji, Tsuruga, Japan. Courtesy of the author.*

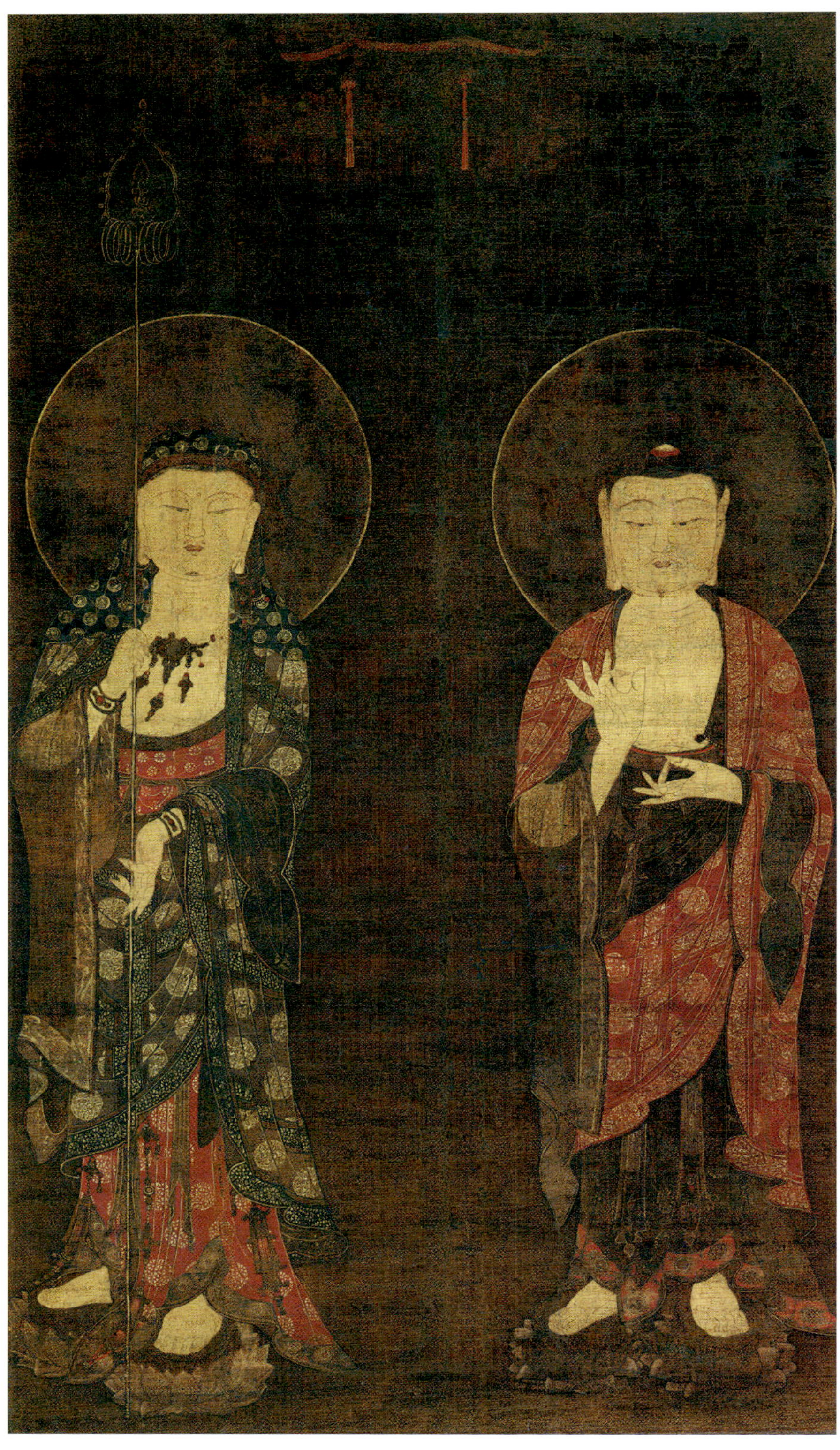

Figure 1.7 Standing Amitābha Buddha and Kṣitigarbha Bodhisattva. *Koryŏ, fourteenth century. Hanging scroll, ink and color on silk. 94.6× 55.6cm. The Metropolitan Museum of Art, Rogers Fund, 1913 (13.5) Image © The Metropolitan Museum of Art.*

阿彌陀如來地藏菩薩竝立圖) include only the deities associated with the Pure Land and the Buddhist netherworld in their composition (figs. 1.6, 1.7). These paintings seem to have been produced in parallel with the development of the Pure Land belief. Representing these two standing deities in color in a single composition is unique to Koryŏ and has not yet been observed in other East Asian countries.

There are also paintings of arhats, highly advanced spiritual practitioners. The remaining painting types are *Śākyamuni and Sixteen Arhats* (Kr. *Sŏkka simnyuk nahando* 釋迦十六羅漢圖), *Five Hundred Arhats* (Kr. *Obaek nahando* 五百羅漢圖) painted in a single scroll, and parts of a set of *Five Hundred Arhats* paintings, in which each arhat is portrayed on an independent scroll.[22] Additionally, there also remain, albeit in rather limited quantity, paintings of Indra (Kr. Chesŏk 帝釋), who, as a resident of the City of Śakra (Ch. Shanjian cheng 善見城) in Mount Sumeru, is believed to protect Buddhist teaching. There are also a few surviving paintings of Marīcī (Kr. Marijich'ŏn 摩利支天), which may have been related to the Marīcī Ritual that was held on countless occasions in Koryŏ for the purpose of protecting Buddhist law and the state.[23]

Among the roughly 150 surviving Koryŏ Buddhist paintings, some 55 are associated with Amitābha Buddha, 42 with Avalokiteśvara bodhisattva, and 24 with Kṣitigarbha, all of them adding up to approximately 120 paintings. It is then possible to say that iconographies related to these three deities constitute most of the surviving Buddhist paintings in Koryŏ. Of course, textual records attest that the actual production of Koryŏ Buddhist paintings had been more diverse in its iconographic content. Still, there is no written record about paintings of the Buddha preaching the *Lotus Sutra* or the *Flower Ornament Sutra*, which are most representative of the teachings of exoteric Buddhism. I would argue that such preponderance of a few iconographies observed in surviving Koryŏ Buddhist paintings reflects the personal devotion of aristocrats, rather than particular Buddhist schools

---

[22] Regarding the time period and purpose of production for this *Five Hundred Arhats*, see Chŏng Ut'aek 鄭于澤, "Kōrai jidai no Rakan gazō" 高麗時代の羅漢画像 [Arhat images of the Koryŏ period], *Yamato bunka* 大和文華 92 (September 1994): 35-49; Sin Kyŏnghŭi 辛廣姬, "Han'guk ŭi nahando yŏn'gu" 韓國의 羅漢圖研究 [A study of the arhat paintings of Korea] (Tongguk Taehakkyo paksa hagwi nonmun 東國大學校博士學位論文 [Dongguk University Ph.D. Dissertation], 2010): 92-124.

[23] For the photographs of the Koryŏ Buddhist paintings not provided in this paper, see illustrations in Kikutake Jun'ichi and Chŏng Ut'aek, *Koryŏ sidae ŭi purhwa*.

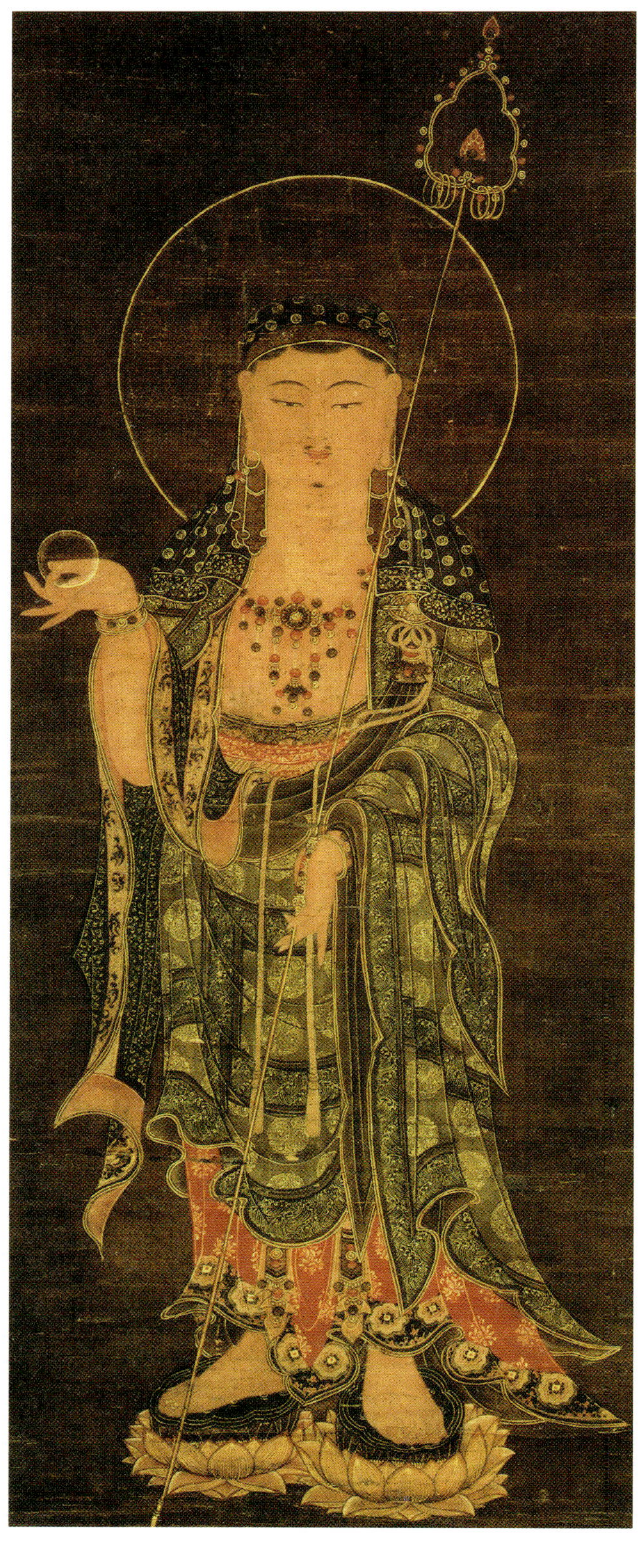

Figure 1.8 Kṣitigarbha. *Koryŏ, fourteenth century. Hanging scroll, ink and color on silk. 107.6×43.5cm. Nezu Museum, Japan. Courtesy of the author.*

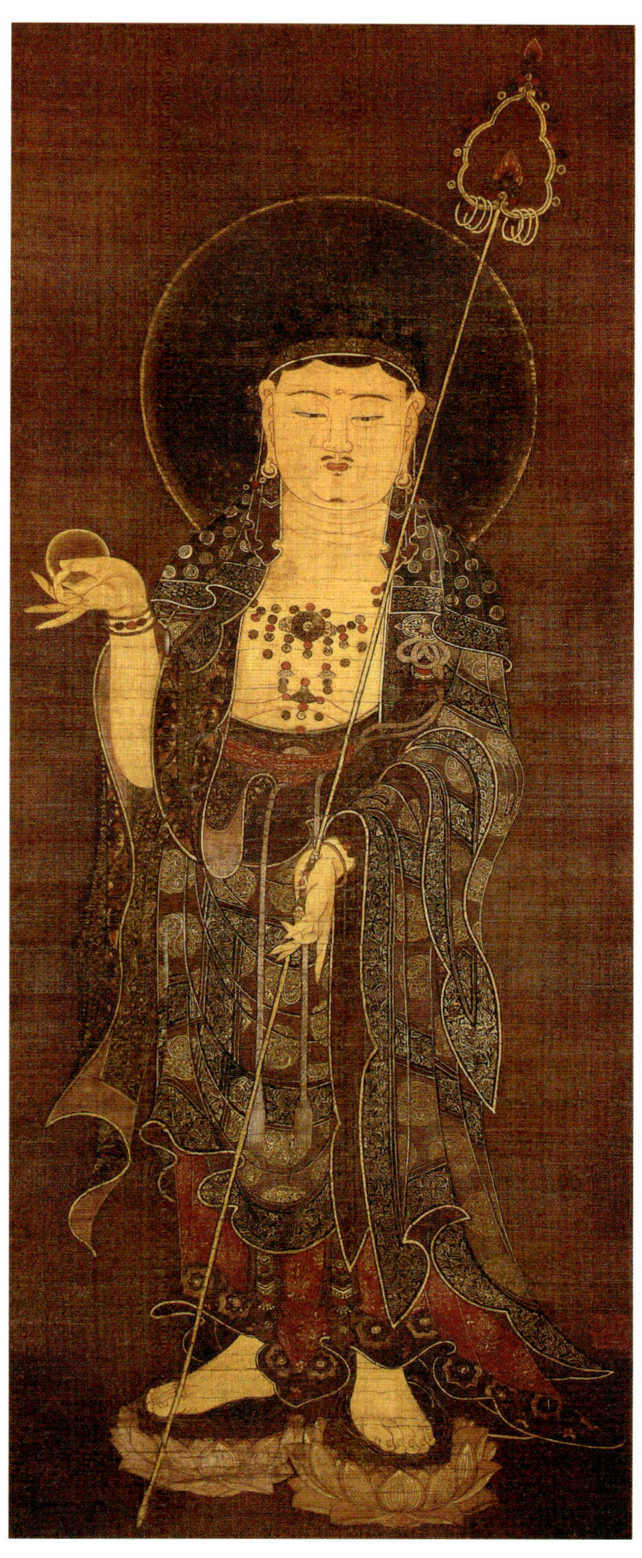

Figure 1.9 Kṣitigarbha. *Koryŏ, fourteenth century. Hanging scroll, ink and color on silk. 105.1×43.9cm. Tokugawa Art Museum, Japan. Courtesy of the author.*

and doctrinal persuasion of the time. At the same time, extant Koryŏ Buddhist paintings are painted on silk, and except for a few examples, most of them are too small in size to be fit for enshrinement in a Buddhist monastery. It is hard to conjecture how knowledgeable these aristocrats were with regard to Buddhism (even though they owned these paintings), but they seem to have held at least some belief in gaining benefits in the present world and salvation in the next life. If we take into consideration the instances in Japan, where a person contemplated a painting of the *Descent of Amitābha* (Jp. *Amida raigō-zu*, Kr. *Amit'a naeyŏngdo* 阿彌陀來迎圖) or other paintings related to the Pure Land at his or her deathbed, this conjecture should appear not too far from what was actually the case in Koryŏ. Later in this chapter, I will expand more on the background of the production of Koryŏ Buddhist paintings.

Copying of Iconographies—Imitativeness

Some Koryŏ Buddhist paintings resemble one another so closely, having nearly identical iconographies and similar application of colors, that it is difficult to tell them apart. This feature deserves attention in that it represents one of the characteristics of Koryŏ Buddhist painting—imitativeness, or the re-creation of iconographies through imitation.[24]

For example, the two paintings of Kṣitigarbha (one in the Nezu Museum and the other in the Tokugawa Art Museum) resemble each other so closely that it is hard to distinguish one from the other when comparing them using black and white photographs (figs. 1.8, 1.9). A comparison of full-color reproductions of the two paintings reveals some measure of difference. Still, it is not possible to fully grasp their differences by studying the reproductions alone. To begin with, the face of Kṣitigarbha in the Tokugawa Art Museum appears to be larger than that of Kṣitigarbha in the Nezu Museum, and yet this is an optical illusion created by the reproduction. In fact, their actual sizes are nearly the same.

While the outlines of the garment of Kṣitigarbha in the Tokugawa Art Museum are doubly delineated, flowing with a sense of flexibility, those of the garment of Kṣitigarbha in the Nezu Museum are drawn in relatively thick, single lines that are stiffened and exaggerated. In other words, Kṣi-

---

[24] On the imitativeness of Koryŏ Buddhist paintings, see Chŏng Ut'aek 鄭于澤, "Koryŏ purhwa e issŏsŏ tosang ŭi chŏnsŭng" 高麗佛畵에 있어서 圖像의 傳承 [Transmission of iconographies in Koryŏ Buddhist painting], *Misulsahak yŏn'gu* 美術史學研究 192 (1991): 2-25.

tigarbha in the Nezu Museum clearly displays both the artist's intention to depict the outlines more distinctly as well as the limitations of exaggeration and reduction found in any copy. Through this, the two paintings' relationship of original and copy can be discerned as well as their temporal sequence.

Two examples of the *Illustration of the Sutra on Maitreya's Rebirth Below* at Chion'in 知恩院 and Shinnōin 親王院 demonstrate the imitativeness of Koryŏ Buddhist painting as well as changes in painting style during their production period (figs. 1.10, 1.11).[25] The painting at Shinnōin was produced in 1350, as can be ascertained from its inscription, but there is no inscription or external record that indicates the production date of the painting at Chion'in. As was true in the previous example, discerning the exact relationship between these two works from photographs alone is nearly impossible, whether we want to understand which is derived from which or the temporal sequence. But when examining the actual paintings, one can find significant differences. As if faithfully reflecting the description in the scripture "The central floor of the City of Ketumati (Ch. *Chitoumo dacheng* 翅頭末大城) is made of diamonds . . . ,"[26] the painting at Chion'in portrays the floor in the foreground of the Buddha decorated with a pattern consisting of diamond shapes, creating an illusion of spatial depth. On the other hand, the painting at Shinnōin simply depicts the floor with intersecting horizontal and diagonal lines, a choice that obscures any sense of depth or materiality. In addition, their temporal sequence—the relationship of original to copy— is readily recognizable in the narrative scene in which King Rangqu 穰佉王 has his hair shaved so as to renounce secular life. In the painting at Chion'in the monk shaving the king has a solemn and profound countenance that expresses both joy and sadness. On the other hand, the painting at Shinnōin depicts the monk with much exaggeration and a lack of serenity—to the point of revealing his teeth—which hardly befits the solemn occasion of the king's entering the priesthood (figs. 1.12, 1.13).

Three paintings depicting a *Descent of Amitābha Triad* (Kr. *Amit'a samjon naeyŏngdo* 阿彌陀三尊來迎圖) at Hōdōji 法道寺, Sen'oku Hakukokan 泉屋博古館, and the Brooklyn Museum exemplify the Koryŏ Buddhist paintings' imitativeness and modification in the process of copying prior

---

[25] Regarding the two paintings, see Donohashi Akio 百橋明穂, "Kōrai no Miroku-geshō-kyō-hensō-zu ni tsuite" 高麗の弥勒下生経変相図について [Regarding Koryŏ's *Illustration of the Sutra on Maitreya's Rebirth Below*], *Yamato bunka* 大和文華 66 (March 1979): 1–12.

[26] *Foshuo Mile dachengfo jing* 佛說彌勒大成佛經. T456, 14:431b17.

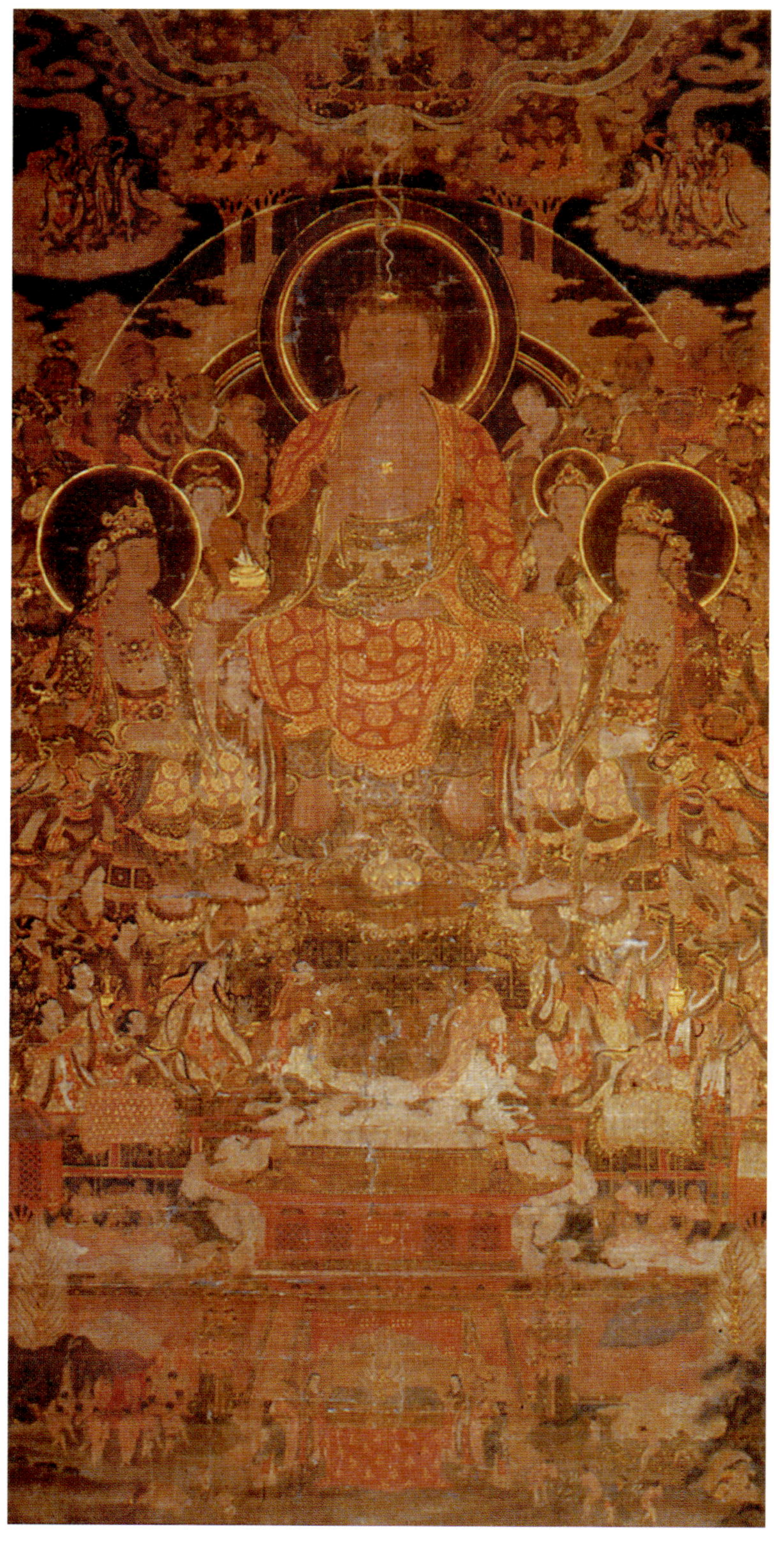

Figure 1.10 Illustration of the Sutra on Maitreya's Rebirth Below. *Koryŏ, ca. 1300. Hanging scroll, ink and color on silk. 171.8×92.1cm. Chion'in, Japan. Courtesy of the author.*

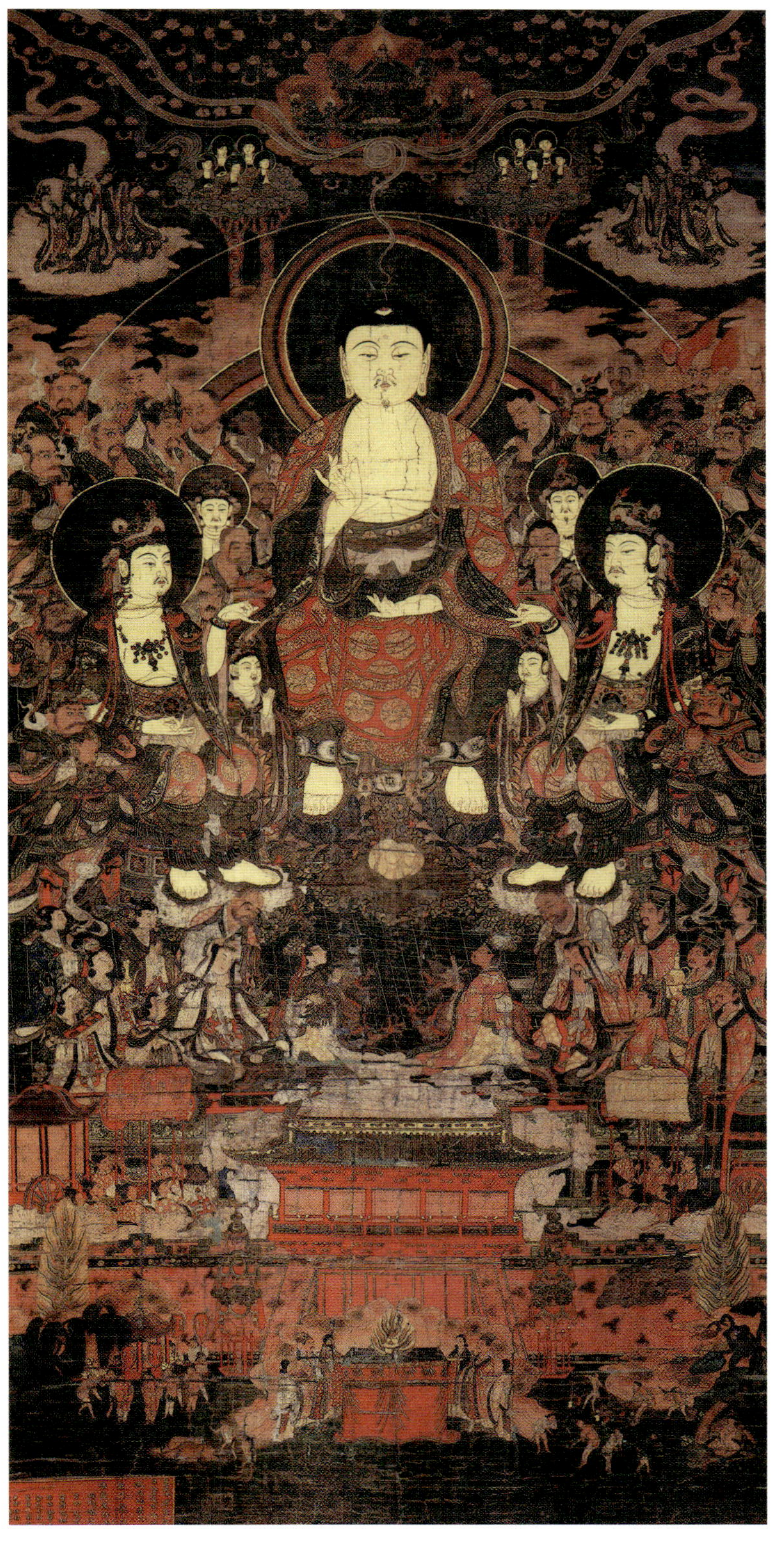

Figure 1.11 Illustration of the Sutra on Maitreya's Rebirth Below. *Koryŏ, 1350. Hanging scroll, ink and color on silk. 178.0×90.3cm. Shinnōin, Japan. Courtesy of the author.*

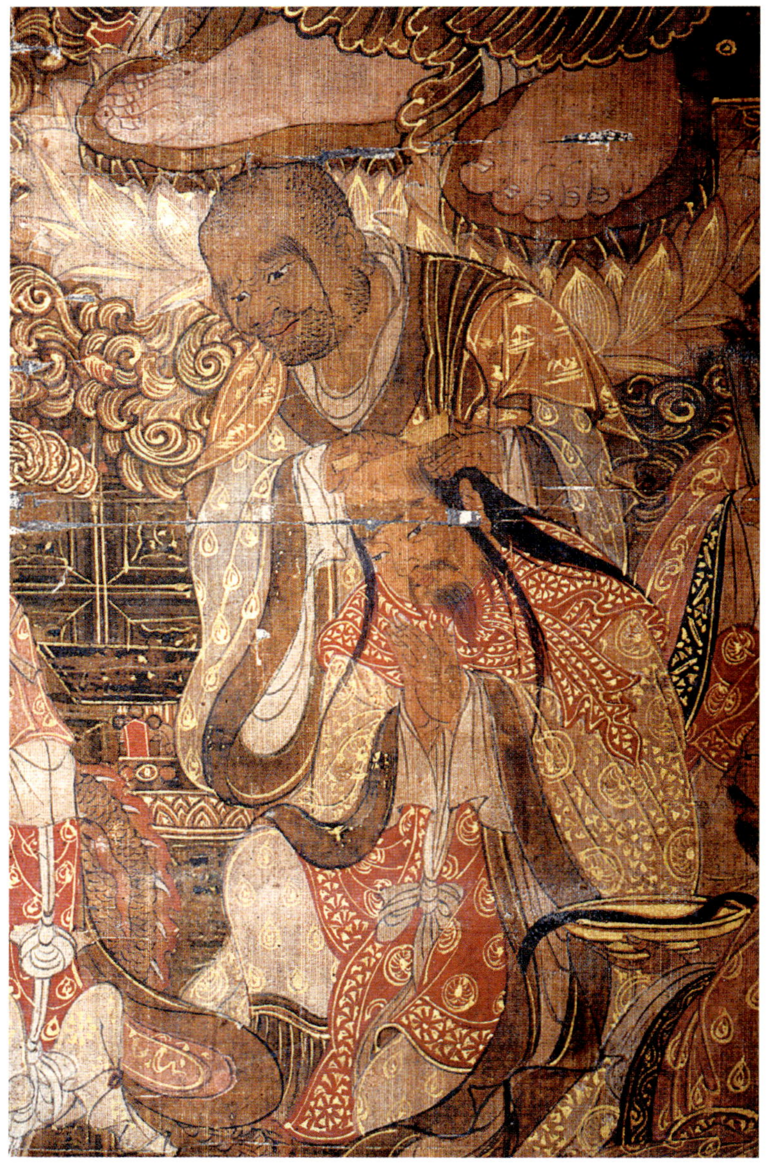

Figure 1.12 Detail of figure 1.10. Courtesy of the author.

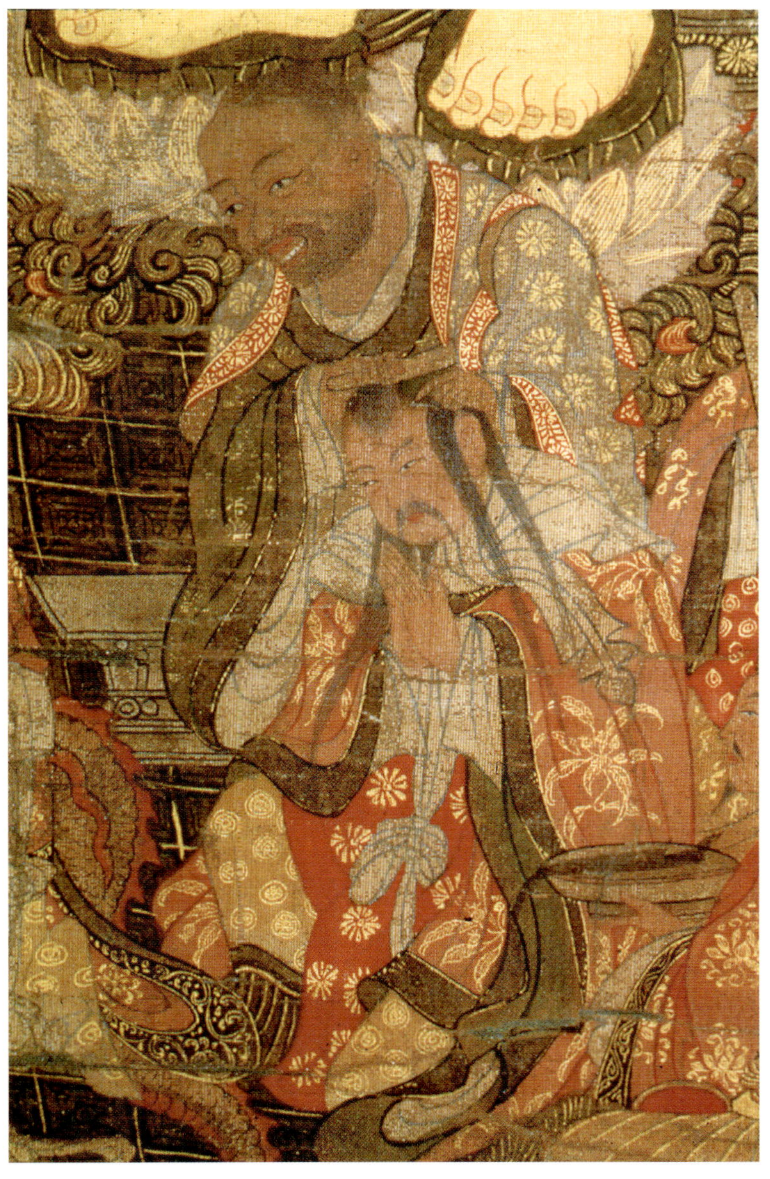

Figure 1.13 Detail of figure 1.11. Courtesy of the author.

models.[27] Unlike the conventional *Descent of Amitābha Triad*, shown in the painting in the MOA Museum of Art in Atami, Japan, in these paintings, departing from convention, Avalokiteśvara bodhisattva holds a willow branch raised to shoulder height in the left hand, and Mahāsthāmaprāpta bodhisattva holds a lotus branch in both hands. Stylistic analysis of these paintings suggests that the painting at Hōdōji was the first to be produced; the other two seem to be copies of the former, although these later paintings seem to have been produced during different periods.[28] Meanwhile, both the *Descent of Amitābha* formerly in the collection of the Shimazu family 島津家 and the one in Hagiwaradera 萩原寺 portray Amitābha in a very unusual pose, with the Buddha turning his torso toward the right as if looking backward, while moving his body to the left (figs. 1.14, 1.15). Lotus flowers on the picture plane seem to symbolize the deceased soul going to the Western Pure Land, and it appears that Amitābha is checking to see whether the soul is duly following.

These two paintings show some differences in the depiction of the Buddha's robe, but the iconographies are almost the same, because both works share nearly identical posture, composition, and patterns. My previous study has shown that the painting at Hagiwaradera was produced by imitating the painting of the Shimazu family while faithfully reflecting contemporaneous trends in painting style.[29]

The tendency to copy iconographies from prior models often observed in Koryŏ Buddhist paintings is also prominent in paintings of *Water-Moon Avalokiteśvara* (Kr. *Suwŏlgwanŭmdo* 水月觀音圖). Although some variants

----

[27] For further discussion of these works, see Chŏng Ut'aek 鄭于澤, "Kōrai jidai no Amida sanzon" 高麗時代の阿弥陀三尊 [Amitābha triad of the Koryŏ period], *Sen'oku Hakukokan kiyō* 泉屋博古館紀要 5 (1988): 50-70.

[28] A different opinion is presented in Pak Young-sook, "Amitabha Triad: A Koryŏ Painting in the Brooklyn Museum," in *Sambul Kim Wŏllyong kyosu chŏngnyŏn t'oeim kinyŏm nonch'ong* 三佛金元龍教授停年退任記念論叢 [Festschrift for the retirement of Sambul, Professor Kim Wŏllyong], ed. Sambul Kim Wŏllyong Kyosu Chŏngnyŏng T'oeim Kinyŏm Nonch'ong Kanhaeng Wiwŏnhoe 三佛金元龍教授停年退任記念論叢刊行委員會 [Committee for the Publication of Festschrift for the Retirement of Sambul, Professor Kim Wŏllyong], vol. 2 (Seoul: Ilchisa, 1987): 513-536.

[29] For more discussion of this work, see Kikutake Jun'ichi 菊竹淳一, "Kōrai jidai raigō bijutsu no ichi irei: Kagawa Hagiwaradera no Amida Nyōrai ritsuzō" 高麗時代来迎美術の一遺例—香川・萩原寺の阿弥陀如来立像 [One extant example of Amitābha Descent art from the Koryŏ period: *Standing Amitābha Buddha* in Hagiwaradera in Kagawa Prefecture], *Yamato bunka* 大和文華 72 (February 1984): 15-24.

34

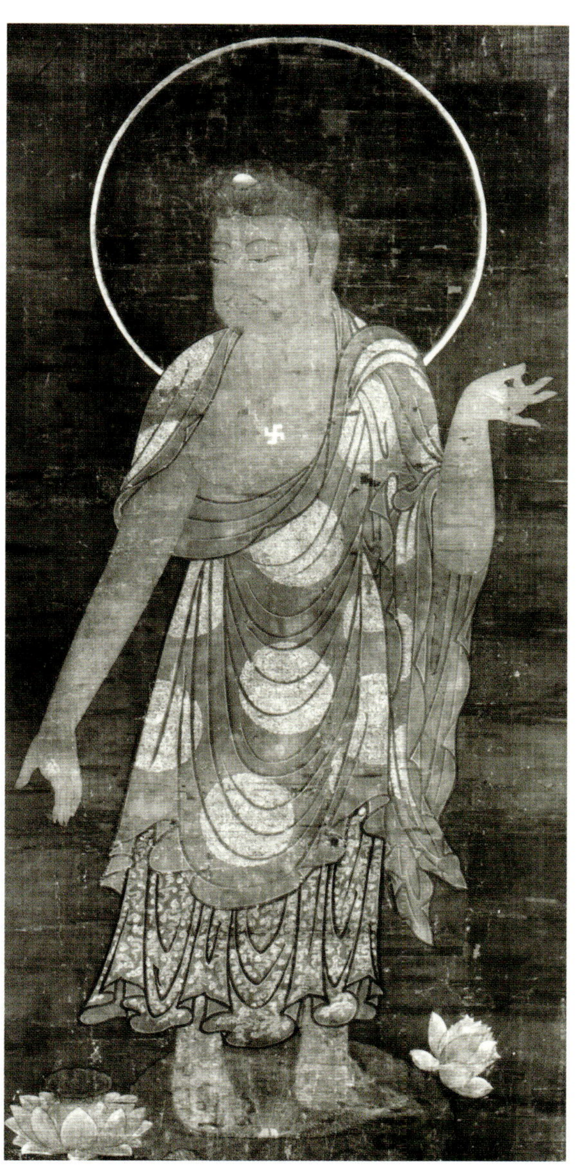

Figure 1.14 Descent of Amitābha *(infrared photograph). Koryŏ, 1286.*
Hanging scroll, ink and color on silk. 203.5×105.1cm. Formerly in the
collection of the Shimazu Family, Japan. Courtesy of the author.

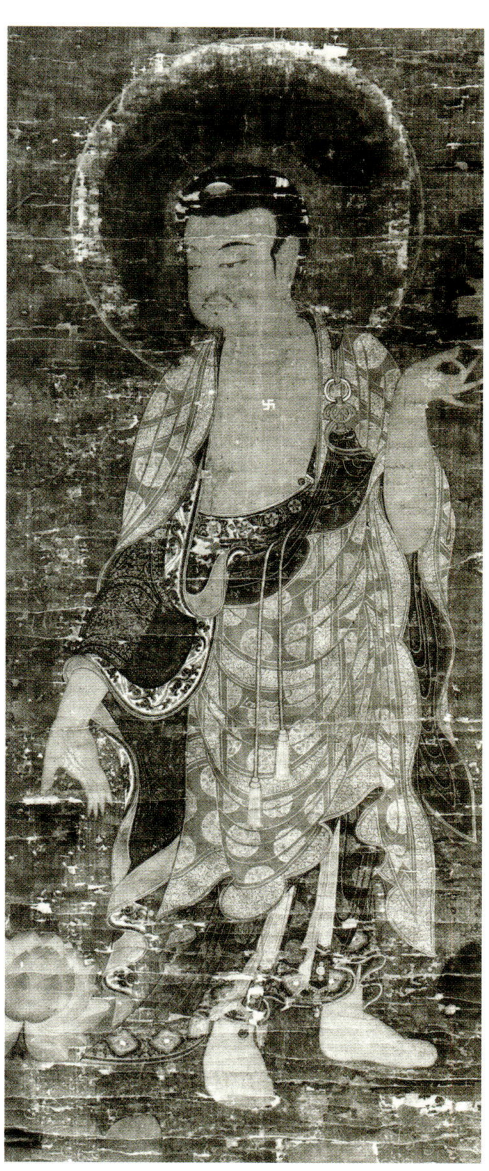

Figure 1.15 Descent of Amitābha. *Koryŏ, fourteenth*
century. Hanging scroll, ink and color on silk. 110.8×50.4cm.
Hagiwaradera, Japan. Courtesy of the author.

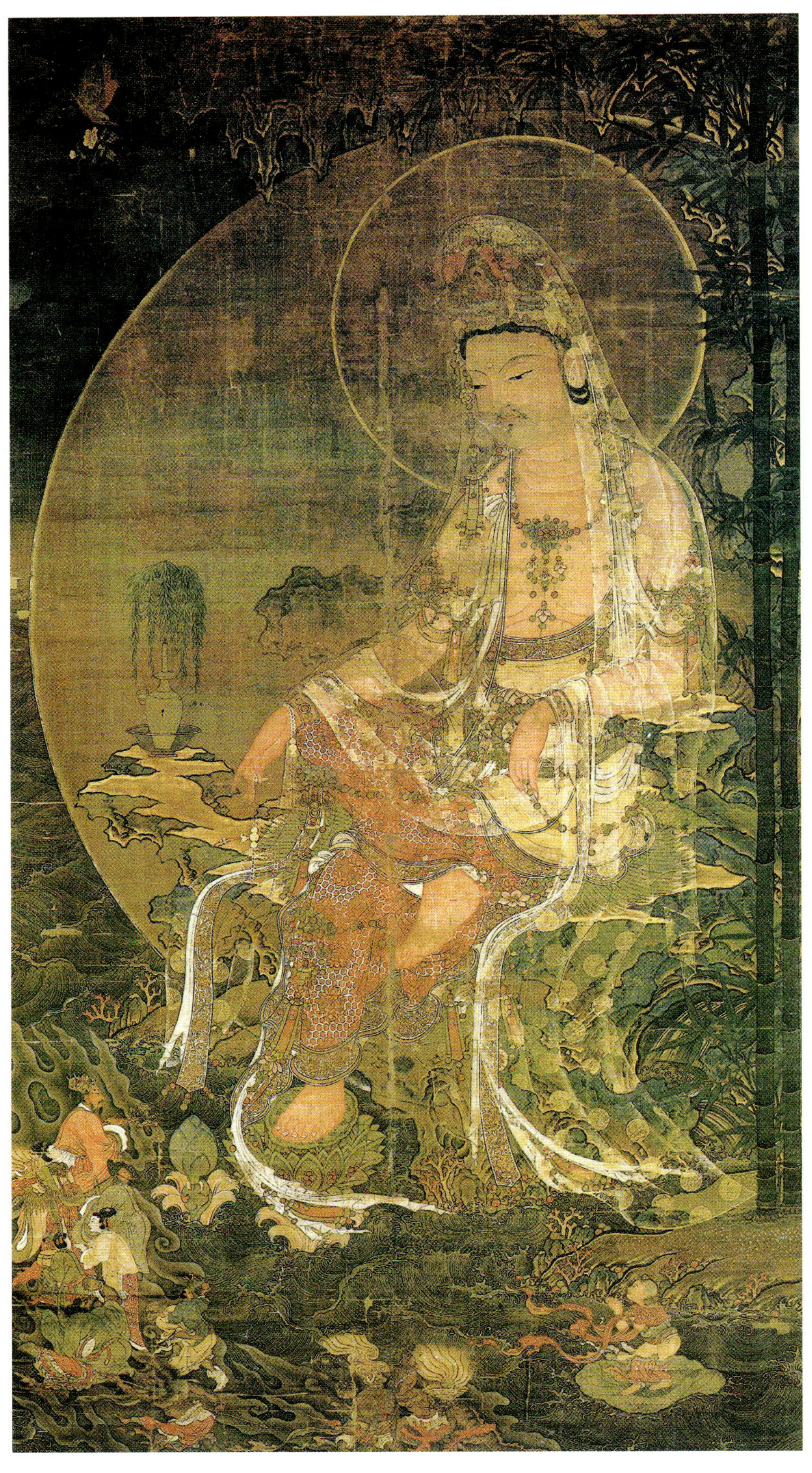

Figure 1.16 Water-Moon Avalokiteśvara. *Koryŏ, fourteenth century. Hanging scroll, ink and color on silk. 227.9×125.8cm. Daitokuji, Japan. Courtesy of the author.*

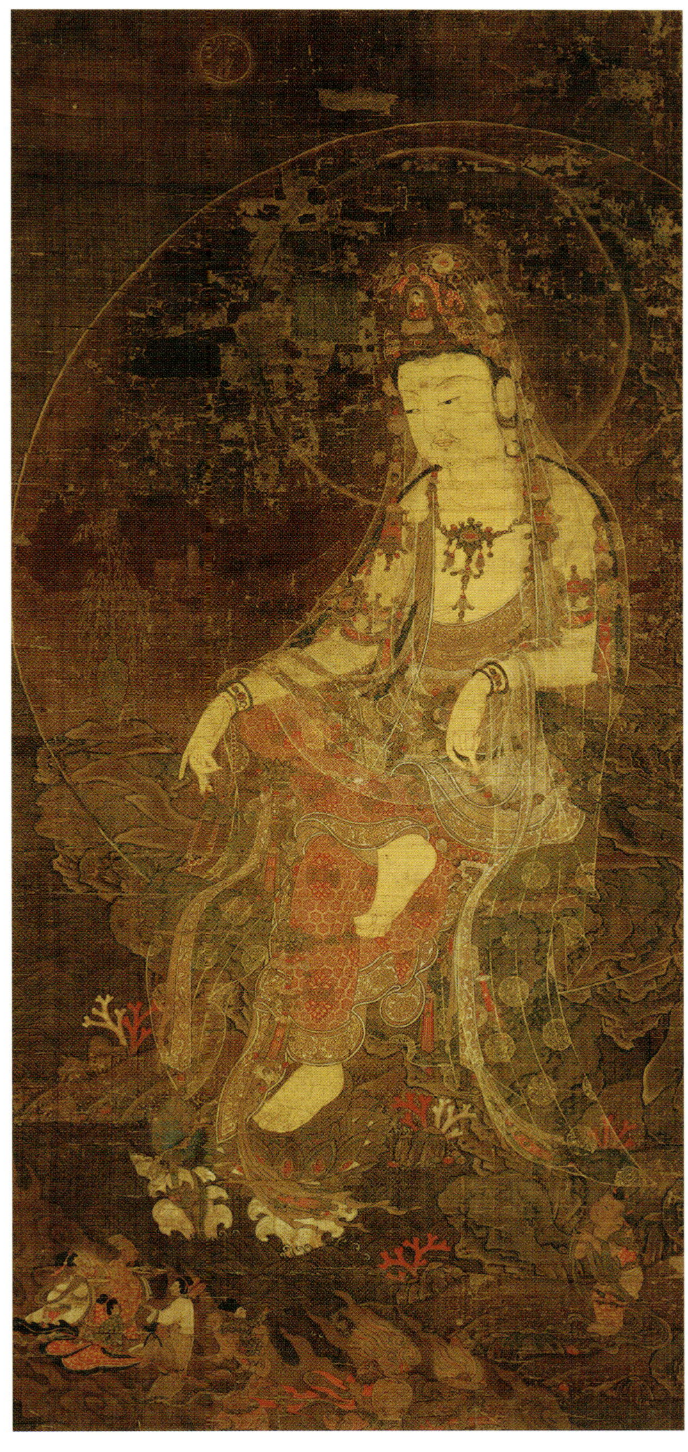

Figure 1.17 Water-Moon Avalokiteśvara. *Koryŏ, fourteenth century. Hanging scroll, ink and color on silk. 113.7×55.3cm. The Metropolitan Museum of Art, Charles Stewart Smith Collection, Gift of Mrs. Charles Stewart Smith, Charles Stewart Smith Jr., and Howard Caswell Smith, in memory of Charles Stewart Smith, 1914 (14.76.6) Image © The Metropolitan Museum of Art.*

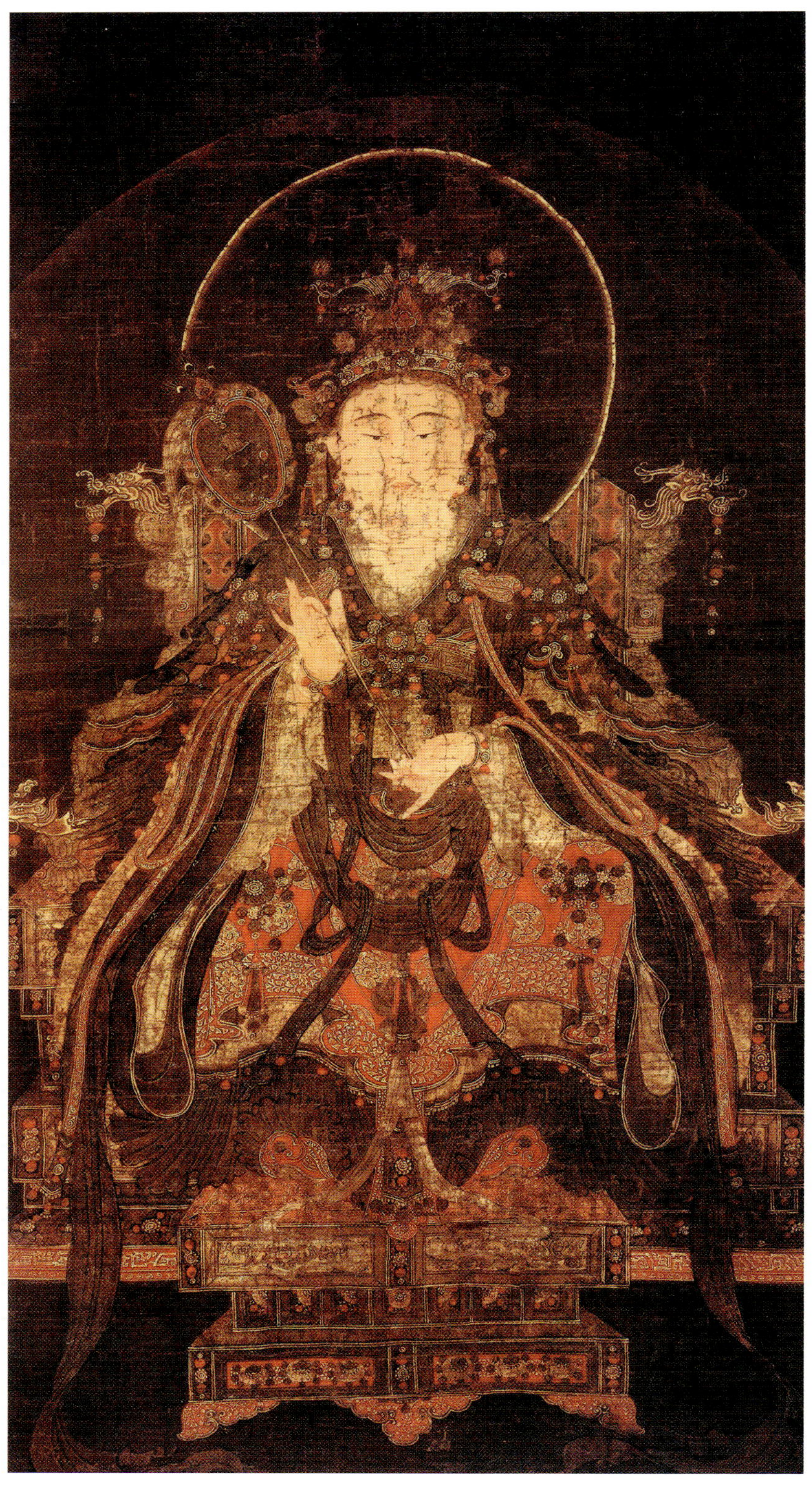

Figure 1.18 Indra. *Koryŏ, fourteenth century. Hanging scroll, ink and color on silk. 97.9×54.5cm. Shōtakuin, Japan. Courtesy of the author.*

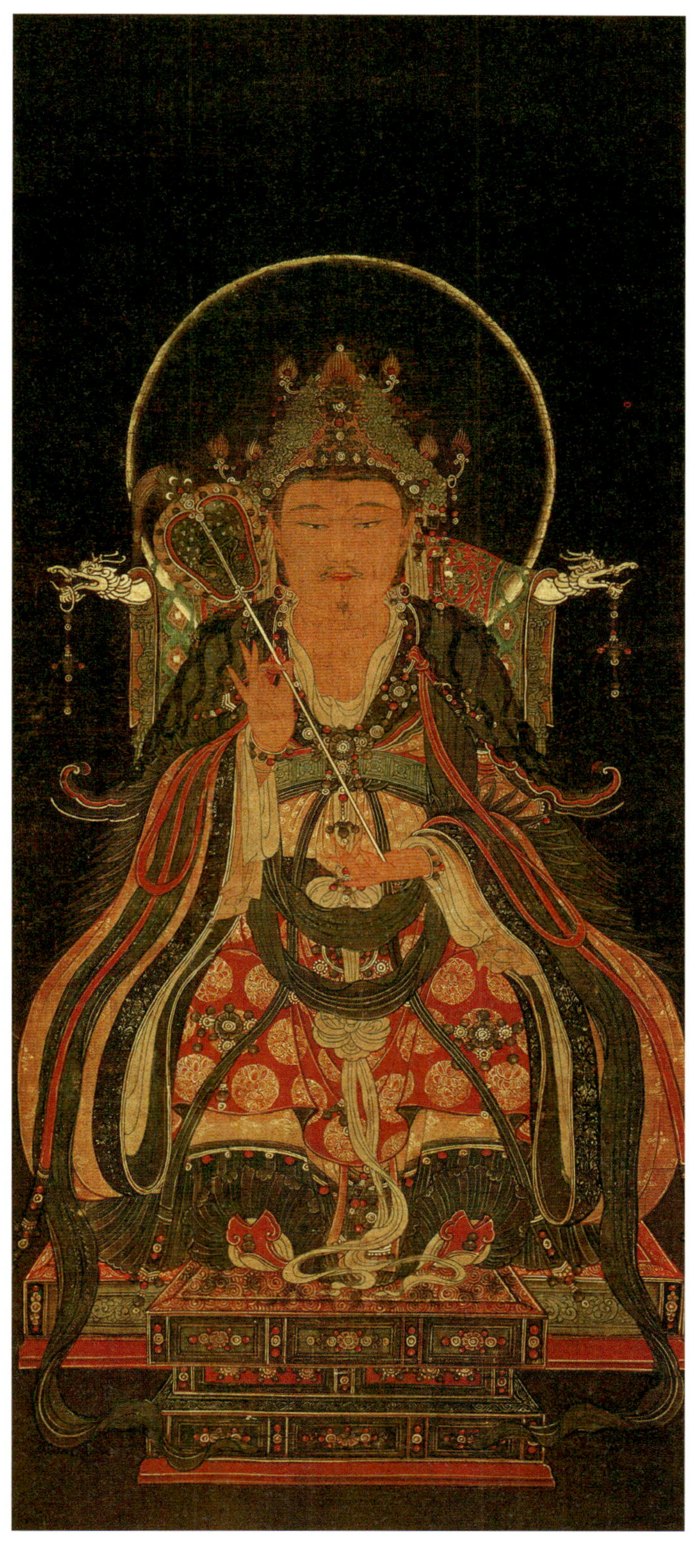

Figure 1.19 Indra. *Koryŏ, fourteenth century. Hanging scroll, ink and color on silk. 116.6×52.8cm. Seikadō Bunkō Art Museum, Japan. Courtesy of the author.*

exist, these paintings exhibit a striking resemblance to one another. They consist of Avalokiteśvara, slightly turning to the right, seated on a rocky outcrop in the half-lotus posture, the *kundika* bottle holding a willow branch, the boy Sudhana, two bamboo stalks, and so on. The basic color tones of the works are also more or less the same. Thus, it can be said that *Water-Moon Avalokiteśvara* of Koryŏ is faithful to the tradition and shows a marked imitativeness. There do exist, however, works like the *Water-Moon Avalokiteśvara* in Daitokuji 大德寺 and another in the Metropolitan Museum of Art that attempted differentiation, whether intentionally or not. To be specific, the bottom of the painting at Daitokuji depicts figures bringing offerings and the upper left side of the picture includes a blue bird (fig. 1.16). The bottom of the painting at the Metropolitan Museum of Art also portrays figures bringing offerings, sharing the same iconographical implications (fig. 1.17). Nonetheless, the composition of these figures in the Metropolitan Museum of Art painting is less organic than the work at Daitokuji. This may be the result of the artist's attempt to differentiate the painting from the one at Daitokuji or simply the result of the artist's lack of expressive skills. Considering the fact, however, that the painting at the Metropolitan Museum of Art omits the blue bird shown in Daitokuji and instead depicts the moon, it is clear that the artist attempted to differentiate the iconography, be the results positive or negative.

Further, the paintings of Indra at Shōtakuin 聖澤院 and at the Seikadō Bunkō Art Museum are also good examples of the creation of new iconographies through imitation (figs. 1.18, 1.19). Partly due to their stylistic differences, the two works appear to show different iconographies, but they actually show nearly identical postures and compositions, with the latter a simpler version than the former. Therefore, it is evident that the artist of the Seikadō Bunkō Art Museum piece was aware of the work at Shōtakuin at the time of its production; this is another instance in which one can detect the artist's will both to faithfully reflect the stylistic trends of the time and to stake a claim for originality.

Iconographic Succession from Koryŏ to Chosŏn
In the Chosŏn kingdom, which followed Koryŏ, a policy of "revering Confucianism and suppressing Buddhism" (Kr. *sungyu ŏkpul* 崇儒抑佛) was adopted. As a result, Chosŏn Buddhist painting, when compared to that of the Koryŏ period, is of lesser quality. During the early Chosŏn period, however, figures associated with the royal family still supported the production of Buddhist paintings. In the mid-sixteenth century, in

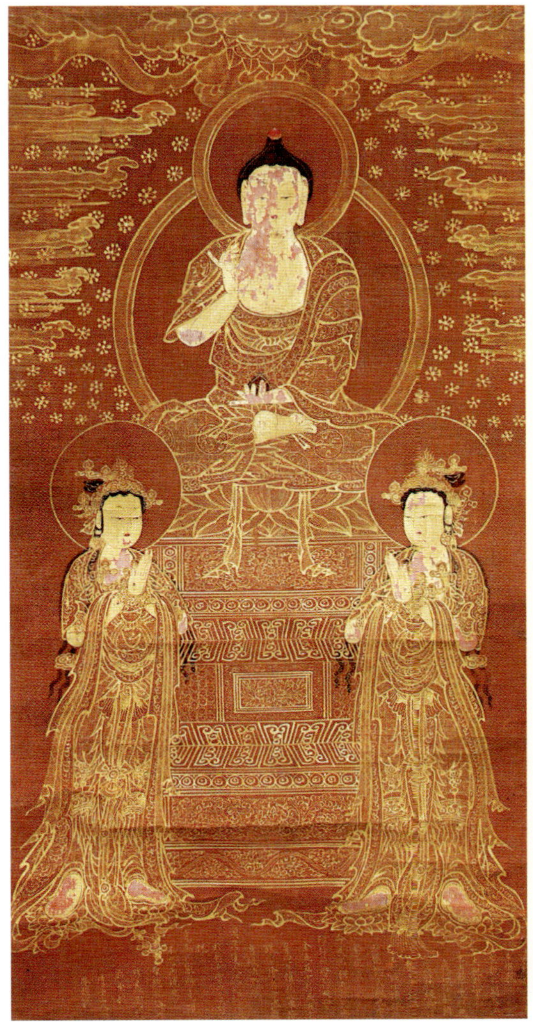

Figure 1.20 Bhaiṣajyaguru Triad. *Chosŏn, 1565.*
Hanging scroll, gold on red silk. 58.7×30.8cm.
Tokugawa Art Museum, Japan. Courtesy of the author.

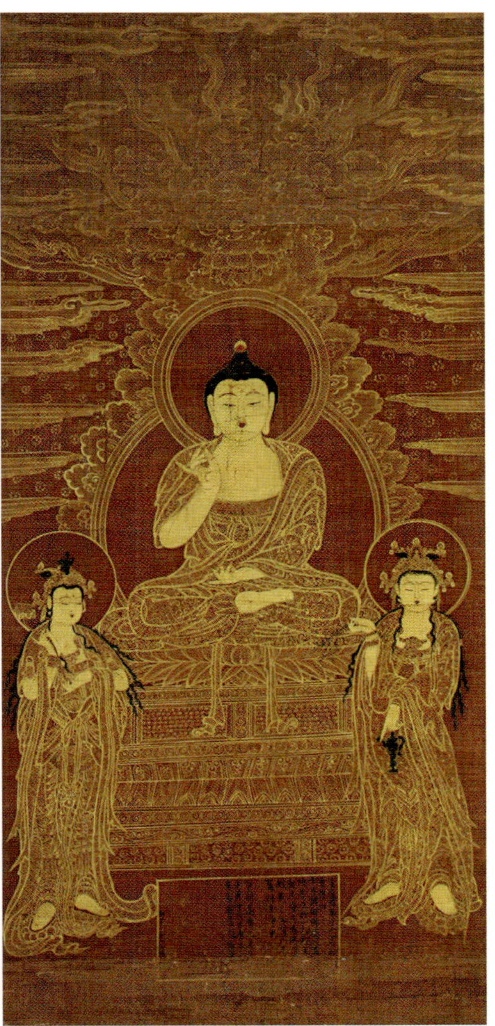

Figure 1.21 Amitābha Triad. *Chosŏn, 1581.*
49.5×33.3cm. Hanging scroll. Private Collection,
Korea. Courtesy of the author.

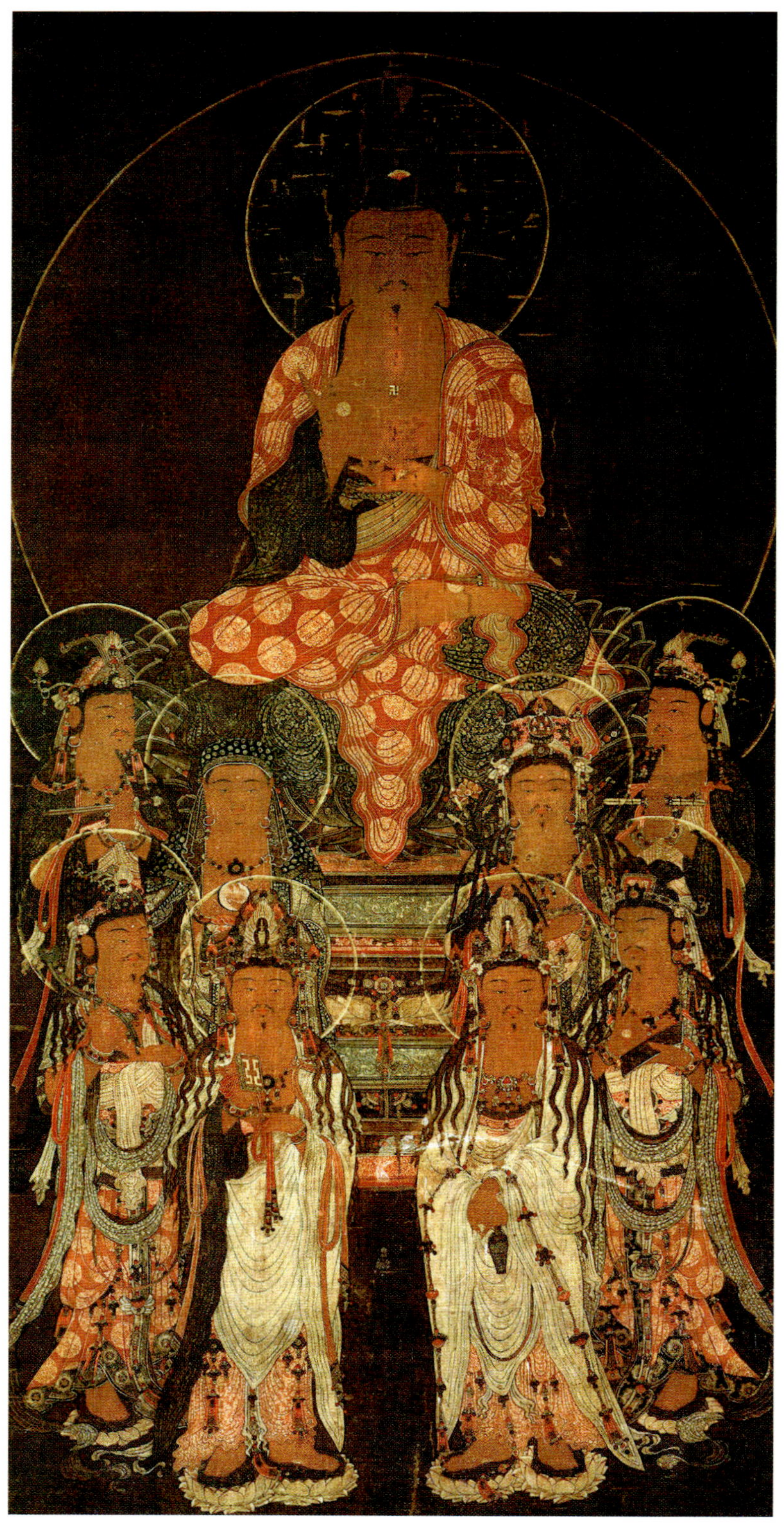

Figure 1.22 Amitābha with the Eight Great Bodhisattvas. *Koryŏ, 1320. Hanging scroll, ink and color on silk. 177.3×91.2cm. Matsuodera, Japan. Courtesy of the author.*

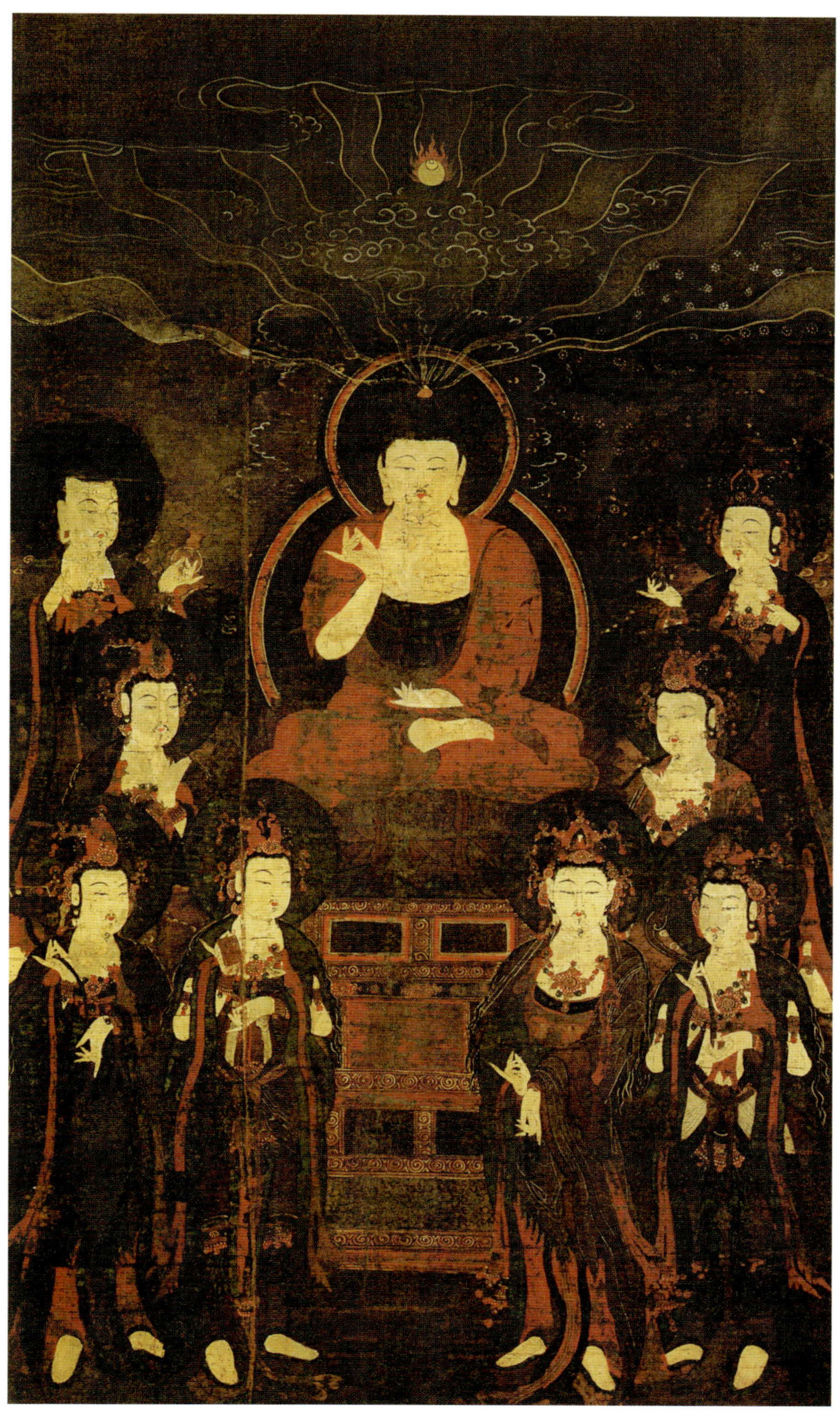

Figure 1.23 Amitābha with the Eight Great Bodhisattvas. *Chosŏn, fifteenth century. Hanging scroll, ink and colcr on silk. 128.3×78.5cm. Private Collection, Korea. Courtesy of the author.*

particular, as part of the enthusiastic pro-Buddhist policy pursued under Queen Regent Munjŏng 文定王后 (1501-1565), the mother of the juvenile King Myŏngjong 明宗 (1534-1567, r. 1545-1567), a number of Buddhist paintings were produced. These Buddhist paintings of the early Chosŏn period attempted to create new styles that befit the trends of the new era and differ from those of Koryŏ paintings, and yet at the same time they actively embrace the Koryŏ Buddhist painting style.

The *Amitābha Triad* at the Nezu Museum is a Buddhist painting in the typical Buddha triad form from the Koryŏ period: the Buddha is seated in a lotus position on the lotus throne, which is located on top of a raised pedestal at the center of the image, flanked by a standing bodhisattva on either side (fig. 1.2). This type of composition continued to be used in early Chosŏn Buddhist paintings of the fifteenth and sixteenth centuries, such as paintings of *Bhaiṣajyaguru Triad* commissioned in 1565 by Queen Regent Munjŏng and now dispersed to many collections, including the Tokugawa Art Museum (fig. 1.20) and the National Museum of Korea; and the *Amitābha Triad* of 1581, currently held in a private collection in Korea (fig. 1.21).[30]

The *Amitābha with the Eight Great Bodhisattvas* of 1320 in the collection of Matsuodera 松尾寺, representing the main Buddha flanked by eight bodhisattvas, is one of the most important Buddhist paintings of the Koryŏ period in that it is a very rare color example of *Amitābha with the Eight Great Bodhisattvas* in East Asia (fig. 1.22). The Chosŏn-period *Amitābha with the Eight Great Bodhisattvas* in a private collection in Korea (fig. 1.23), presumably from the early fifteenth century, faithfully incorporates the iconography of Koryŏ Buddhist painting reflected in the Matsuodera piece. The *Illustration of the Sixteen Contemplations in the Visualization Sutra* of 1465 at Chion'in is another example demonstrating the strong continuity from Koryŏ Buddhist painting to Chosŏn Buddhist painting. According to its inscription, this work, painted by Yi Maenggŭn 李孟根, was commissioned by two princes, Prince Hyoryŏng 孝寧大君 (1396-1486), the second son of King T'aejong 太宗 (r. 1400-1418), and Prince Wŏlsan 月山大君 (1454-1488), the older brother of King Sŏngjong 成宗 (r. 1470-1494). Even at first glance, this painting is very similar to the *Illustration of the Visualization Sutra* (1323) of the Koryŏ period, which is in the same Buddhist monastery, Chion'in. They are so similar that they might be regarded

---

30 Chŏng Ut'aek 鄭于澤, "Chosŏn chŏn'gi kŭmsŏnmyo *Amit'a samjondo* illye" 朝鮮前期金線描阿彌陀三尊圖一例 [A case of early Chosŏn Amitābha triad with gold line-drawing], *Misulsa yŏn'gu* 美術史研究 22 (2008): 151-168.

as nearly identical, in spite of the fact that some differences exist in composition, forms, and coloring.[31]

The *Standing Avalokiteśvara and Kṣitigarbha* from the early fifteenth century at Amyōin 阿名院 portrays the two bodhisattvas in a single hanging scroll (fig. 1.24), and it is no exaggeration to say that this painting is one of the most representative examples of faithful adherence to the iconographies of Koryŏ Buddhist painting. No other example of an independent painting depicting Avalokiteśvara and Kṣitigarbha together in a single composition has been found in China or Japan, and this iconography was unique to Korea during the late Koryŏ to the early Chosŏn period. Only three examples of *Standing Avalokiteśvara and Kṣitigarbha* are known from the Koryŏ period: the paintings at Saifukuji 西福寺 (fig. 1.6) and at Minamihokkeji 南法華寺 in Japan, and a work in a private collection in Korea (fig. 1.25). The painting at Amyōin is especially similar to the work in the private collection in Korea. While the two works differ in that the former was drawn only using gold lines and the latter was painted using colors, they are identical in the positioning and posture of the two bodhisattvas and the attributes in their hands. Even the depictions of the three Buddhas—probably transformation Buddhas (Kr. *hwabul* 化佛) and Buddhas of Other Lands (Kr. *t'abangbul* 他方佛)—appearing above the two bodhisattvas are identical. Therefore, it is highly plausible that the early-fifteenth-century Amyōin painting was based on the Koryŏ painting in the private collection in Korea.[32]

---

[31] Chŏng Ut'aek 鄭于澤, "Chosŏn wangjo shidae chŏn'gi kungjŏng hwap'ung purhwa ŭi yŏn'gu" 朝鮮王朝時代 前期 宮廷畫風 佛畫의 研究 [Research on Buddhist paintings in court painting style from the early Chosŏn kingdom], *Misul sahak* 美術史學 13 (1999): 131-133.

[32] Chŏng Ut'aek 鄭于澤, "Ilbon Aich'i-hyŏn chiyŏk Chosŏn shidae chŏn'gi purhwa ŭi chosa yŏn'gu" 日本 아이치현 (愛知縣) 지역 조선시대 전기 불화의 조사 연구 [An examination of early Chosŏn Buddhist paintings in Aichi Prefecture, Japan], *Misulsa nondan* 美術史論壇 33 (2011): 39-40. As mentioned earlier, the Metropolitan Museum of Art has a Koryŏ-period painting representing Amitābha Buddha and Kṣitigarbha bodhisattva standing next to each other from the late fourteenth century. It is a unique iconography not seen elsewhere in East Asia, and it presumably developed under the influence of the preceding paintings of *Standing Avalokiteśvara and Kṣitigarbha* (fig. 1.7). I propose that the contemporaneous religious belief regarding salvation underlies this iconography that portrays only the presiding deities of the Western Pure Land and the netherworld, and that the iconography of *Standing Avalokiteśvara and Kṣitigarbha* was also adopted in this context.

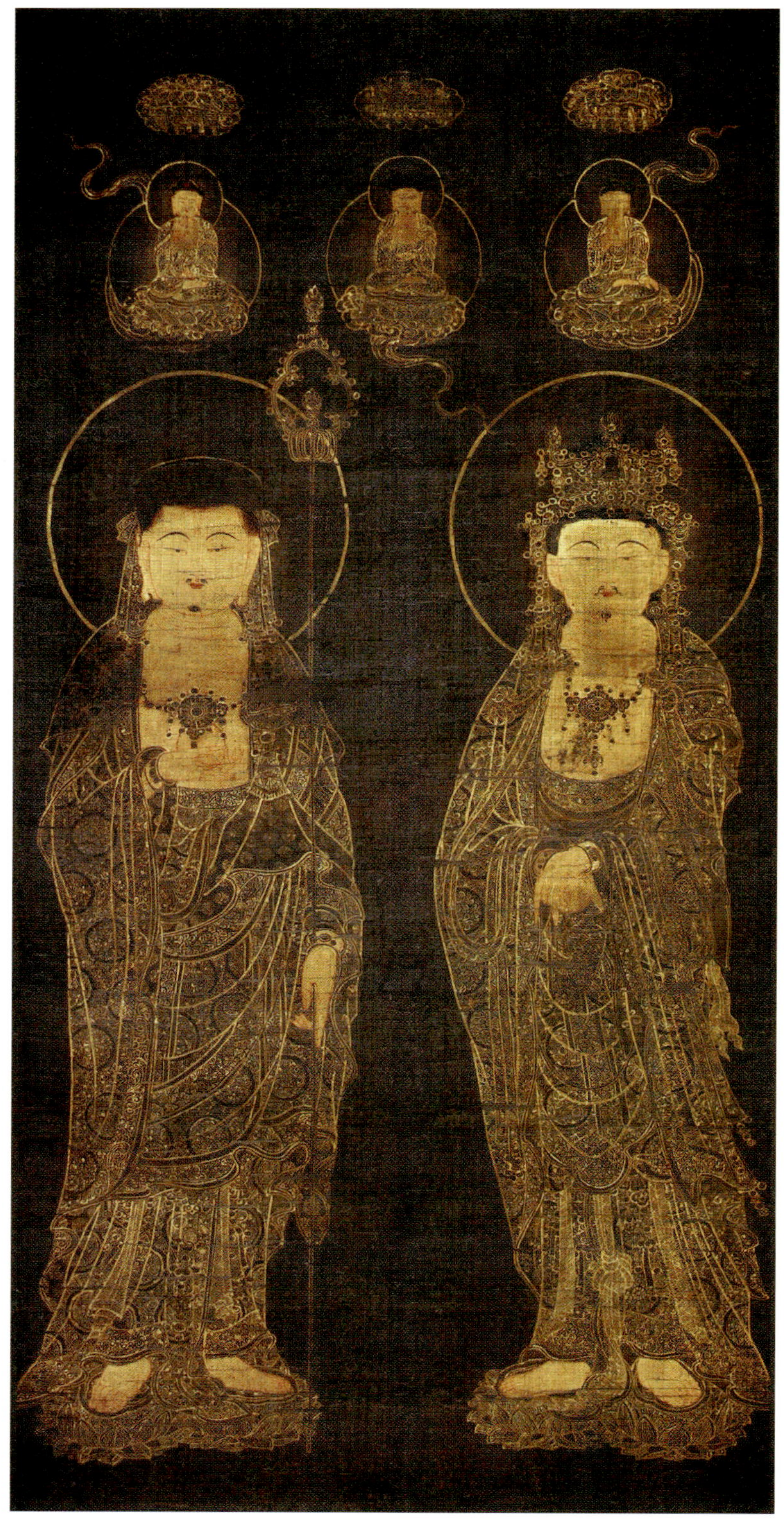

Figure 1.24 Standing Avalokiteśvara and Kṣitigarbha. *Chosŏn, early fifteenth century. Hanging scroll, gold on indigo blue silk. 90.0×45.2cm. Amyōin, Japan. Courtesy of the author.*

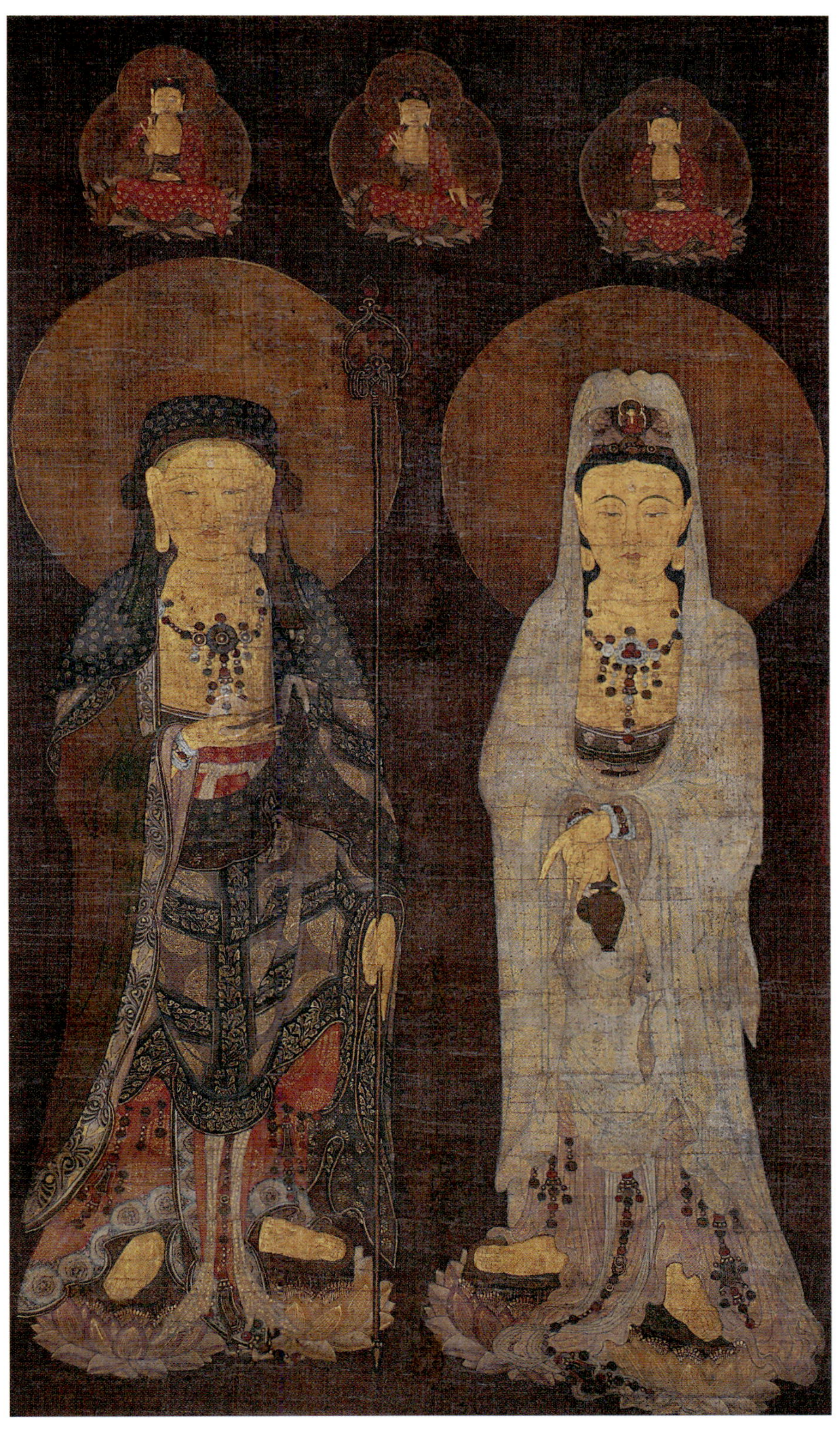

Figure 1.25 Standing Avalokiteśvara and Kṣitigarbha. *Koryŏ, fourteenth century. Hanging scroll, ink and color on silk. 75.4×44.7cm. Private Collection, Korea. Courtesy of the author.*

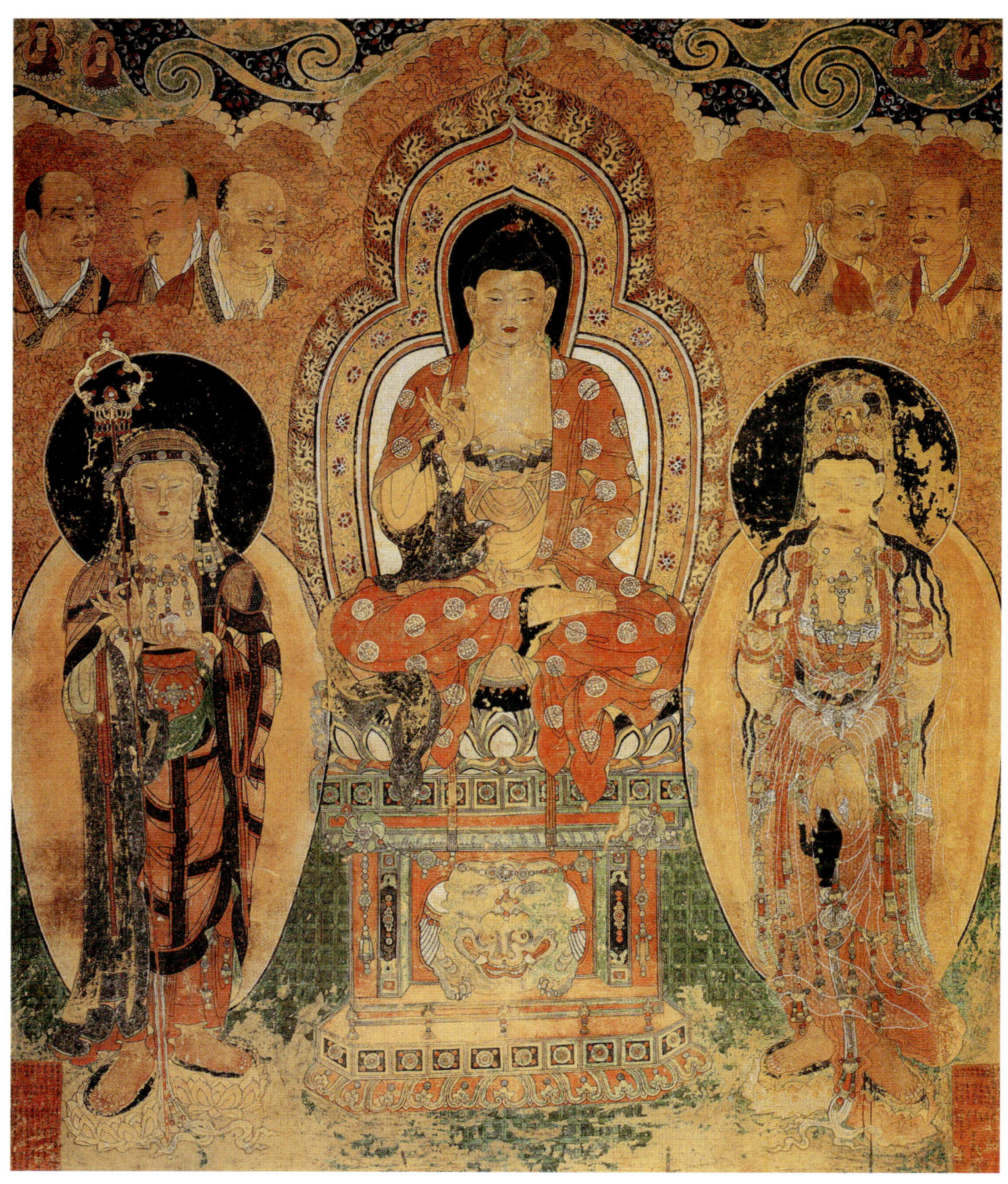

Figure 1.26 Amitābha Triad. *Chosŏn, 1476. Mural. Muwi-sa, Korea. Courtesy of the author.*

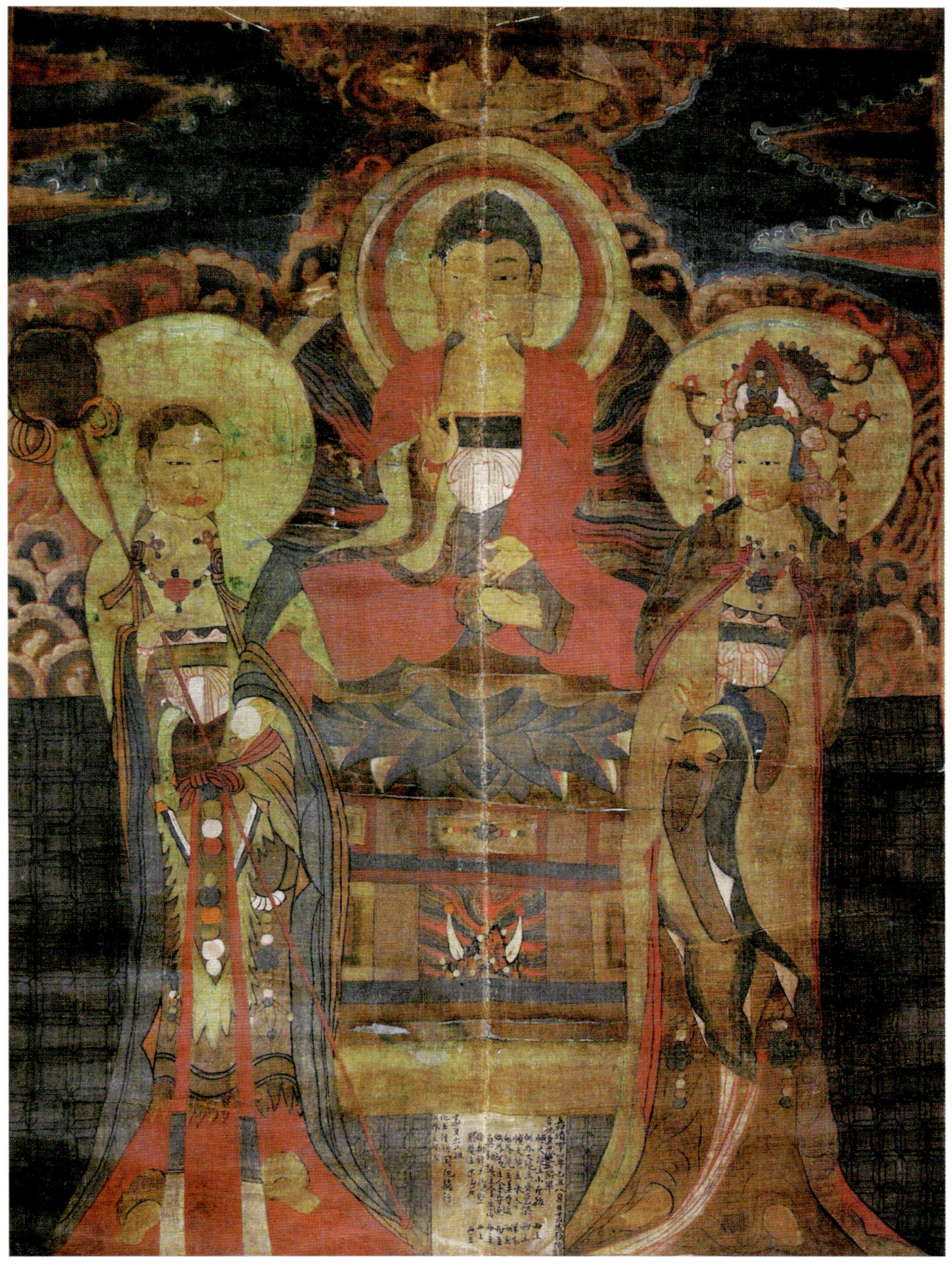

Figure 1.27 A̱mitābha Triad. *Chosŏn, 1565. Hanging scroll, ink and color on hemp cloth. 89.5×66.9cm. Shōgakuji, Japan. Courtesy of the author.*

Meanwhile, the mural of *Amitābha Triad* of 1476 at the Hall of Amitābha's Pure Land (Kr. Kŭngnakchŏn 極樂殿) of Muwi-sa 無爲寺 (fig. 1.26) of the Chosŏn period appears to have adopted some aspect of iconographic traditions from Koryŏ Buddhist painting. This mural portrays Kṣitigarbha in place of Mahāsthāmaprāpta as the attendant to the right of the Amitābha Buddha. This iconography, widespread from the late fourteenth century in Koryŏ, has been regarded as a unique feature of Koryŏ Buddhist painting. As the *Amitābha Triad* at Shōgakuji 正覚寺 painted in 1565 shows, the iconography in which Kṣitigarbha appears in place of Mahāsthāmaprāpta continued until sixteenth-century Chosŏn (fig. 1.27).[33]

Representation Techniques of Koryŏ Buddhist Painting

Since representation techniques faithfully reflect the contemporaneous sensitivities to form and aesthetics, as in all types of art genres, careful examination of techniques offers important evidence regarding a Buddhist painting's characteristics, uniqueness, and country of origin. While iconographies in Buddhist art can be shared across time periods as well as among diverse countries and regions, representation techniques are clearly differentiated.[34]

Koryŏ Buddhist painting used three colors—red, green, and blue—as principal color choices, and pigment types are also few in number. Despite this rather limited variation in colors, Koryŏ Buddhist paintings produced hundreds of years ago have remained vivid and beautiful, thanks to their artists' special method of using pigments: almost all pigments, as well as the three principal colors of red, green, and blue, were applied in their original form without other pigments being mixed in. This was probably due to the artists' understanding of the most fundamental nature of pigments: that color saturation (Kr. *ch'aedo* 彩度) decreases as more pigments are mixed together.

---

[33] Chŏng Ut'aek, "Ilbon Aich'i-hyŏn chiyŏk Chosŏn shidae chŏn'gi purhwa ŭi chosa yŏn'gu," 41.

[34] For the representation and technique of Koryŏ Buddhist painting, see Chŏng Ut'aek 鄭于澤, "Koryŏ purhwa ŭi tosang kwa arŭmdaum: kŭ p'yohyŏn kwa kipŏp" 高麗佛畵의 圖像과 아름다움: 그 表現과 技法 [The iconography and beauty of Koryŏ Buddhist painting: Its representation and technique], in *Koryŏ sidae ŭi purhwa* 高麗時代의 佛畵 [Buddhist paintings of the Koryŏ period], ed. Kikutake Jun'ichi and Chŏng Ut'aek, vol. 2 (Seoul: Sigongsa, 1997): 27-30; Chŏng Ut'aek, "Koryŏ purhwa ui yŏngnyŏk," 211-233; Chung Woothak, "Identity of Goryeo Buddhist Painting," *Korean Art and Archaeology* 4 (2010): 21-23.

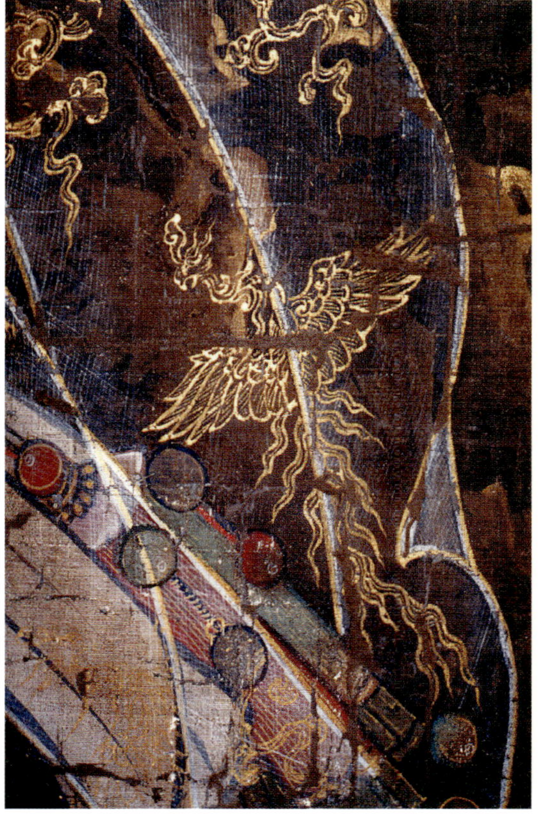

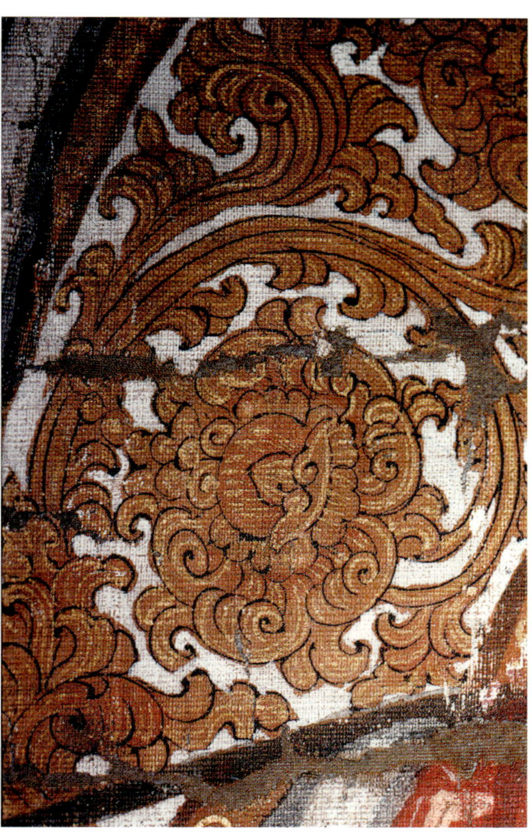

Figure 1.28 Water-Moon Avalokiteśvara *(detail).*
Koryŏ, 1310. Hanging scroll, ink and color on silk.
Kagami Jinja, Japan. Courtesy of the author.

Figure 1.29 Water-Moon Avalokiteśvara *(detail).*
Koryŏ, 1310. Hanging scroll, ink and color on silk.
Kagami Jinja, Japan. Courtesy of the author.

The most excellent example of the coloring techniques typical of
Koryŏ Buddhist painting is the *Water-Moon Avalokiteśvara* of 1310 at
Kagami Jinja 鏡神社. Here the texture of a thin veil is created using minute lines of white pigment, over which clouds and a phoenix are painted
in sequence to create a sense of compactness (fig. 1.28). Moreover, the strips
forming the hem of the heavenly robe, although only a very small part,
are depicted by first coating the entire surface of the strips with ocher and

then painting the tiny white part that actually forms the background of the ocher-colored pattern (fig. 1.29). This application of colors in reverse order is an extremely calculated technique intended to avoid any decrease in color saturation, which would have occurred if white had been painted under the ocher-colored pattern and subsequently mixed in. In addition, in a Koryŏ Buddhist painting, one type of pigment is rarely, if ever, applied with varied saturation or luminosity (Kr. *myŏngdo* 明度). In other words, in a single picture, one hue has the same value and intensity even when applied in different parts of the painting.

I think that the use of primary colors and the simplicity of color values also have a close relationship to the rich application of the gold pigment known as *kŭmni* 金泥.[35] The gold color in Koryŏ Buddhist paintings comes from pure gold, and it was used to depict nearly all contours, with the exception of the deity's body parts, as well as various types and shapes of decorative patterns (fig. 1.30). Koryŏ Buddhist paintings are painted with primary colors because the effect of the gold pigment is amplified when primary colors, rather than neutral colors or non-primary colors, are used for background and also when the colors' saturation and luminosity remain high. In other words, the artists of Koryŏ Buddhist paintings were well aware of how to use gold effectively, and for them gold ultimately served as a tool to give vitality to the picture. The gold lines of Koryŏ Buddhist paintings are all drawn using a brush, and the *kirikane* 切金/截金 technique typical of Japanese Buddhist paintings—the technique of applying thinly cut pieces of gold leaf—is not used.

Various types of decorative patterns are employed in Koryŏ Buddhist paintings. They seem to maintain some measure of consistency although their types vary according to their location in the painting. This is probably either because there were basic rules for the use of decorative patterns or because the artists tried to uphold tradition. For example, in terms of decorative patterns used for the Buddha's robe, the arabesque-medallion pattern (Kr. *tangch'o wŏnmun* 唐草圓文) is most frequently used, while the lotus-medallion pattern (Kr. *yŏnhwa wŏnmun* 蓮華圓文) and the floral-arabesque-medallion (Kr. *posang tangch'o wŏnmun* 寶相唐草圓文) are also used occasionally. For the Buddha's great robe, nearly all paintings use the cloud-phoenix pattern (Kr. *unbongmun* 雲鳳文). The Buddha's skirt is decorated with an oval-shaped lotus pattern and the lotus-arabesque-medallion

---

[35] Editor's Note: *Kŭmni*, gold pigment used for calligraphy or painting, is made by mixing powder of crushed gold with glue or starch.

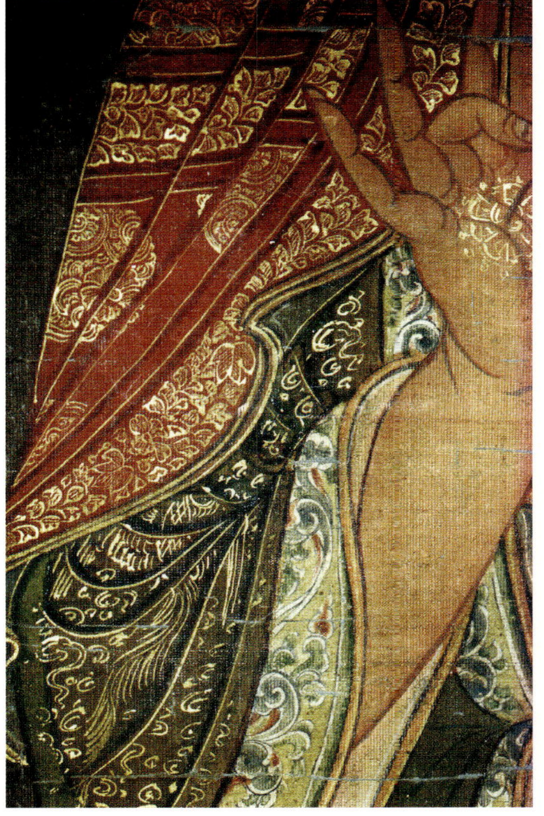

Figure 1.30 Detail of figure 1.2. Courtesy of the author.

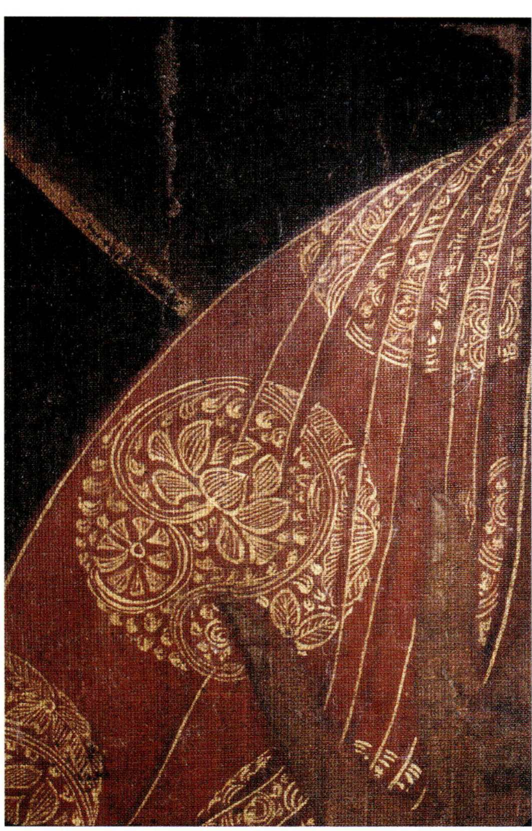

Figure 1.31 Detail of figure 1.22. Courtesy of the author.

pattern (Kr. *yŏnhwa tangch'o wŏnmun* 蓮華唐草圓文), or, less frequently, the cloud pattern (Kr. *unmun* 雲文).[36]

The patterns used for the images of Avalokiteśvara are more diverse than those for Buddha. For the skirt, the turtle-shell pattern (Kr. *kwigammun* 龜甲文) is mostly used as the base pattern, on top of which are added oval-shaped patterns, each containing symmetrical lotuses at the top and

---

[36] Regarding various decorative patterns, see Chŏng Uťaek, "Koryŏ purhwa ŭi tosang kwa arŭmdaum," 29-30.

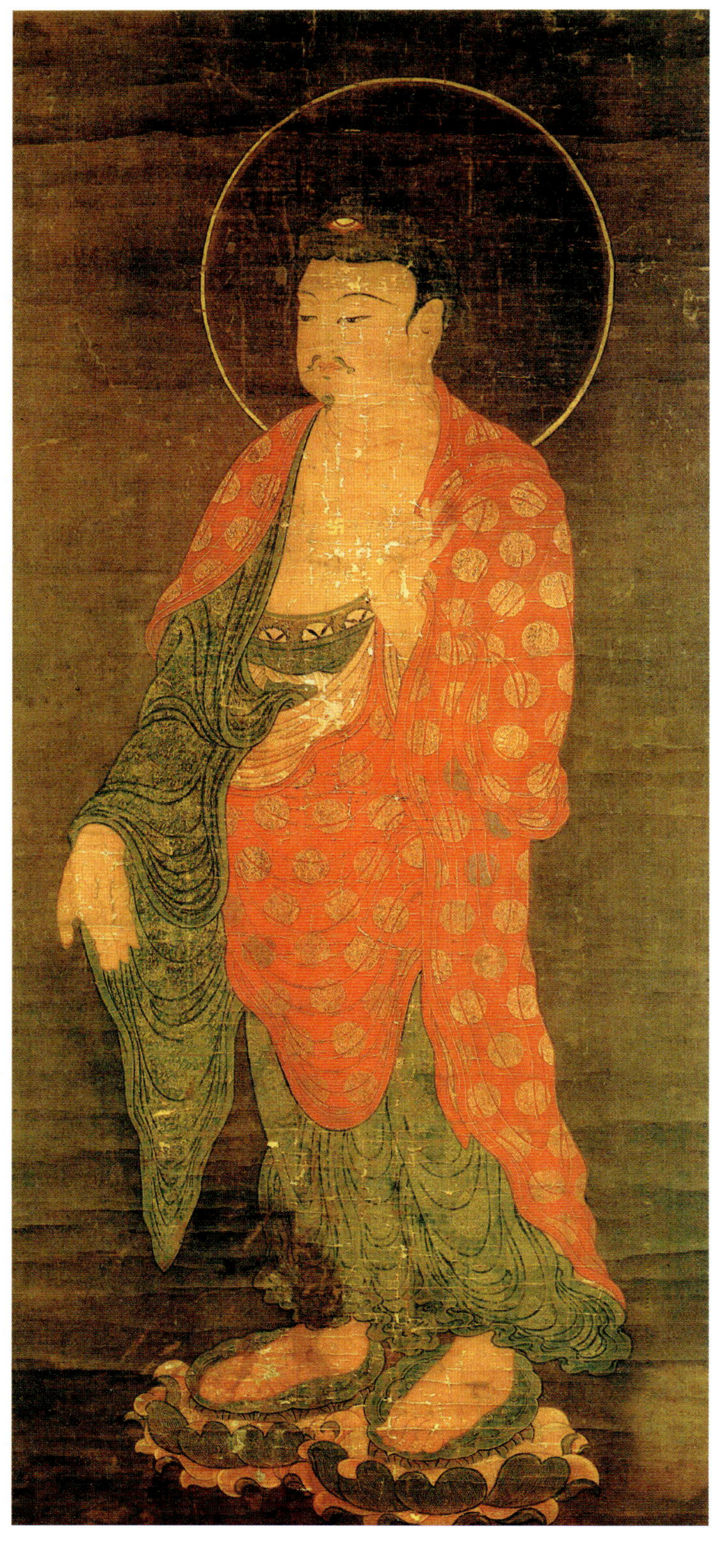

Figure 1.32 Descent of Amitābha. *Koryŏ, fourteenth century. Hanging scroll, ink and color on silk. 184.0×86.5cm. Shōbōji, Japan. Courtesy of the author.*

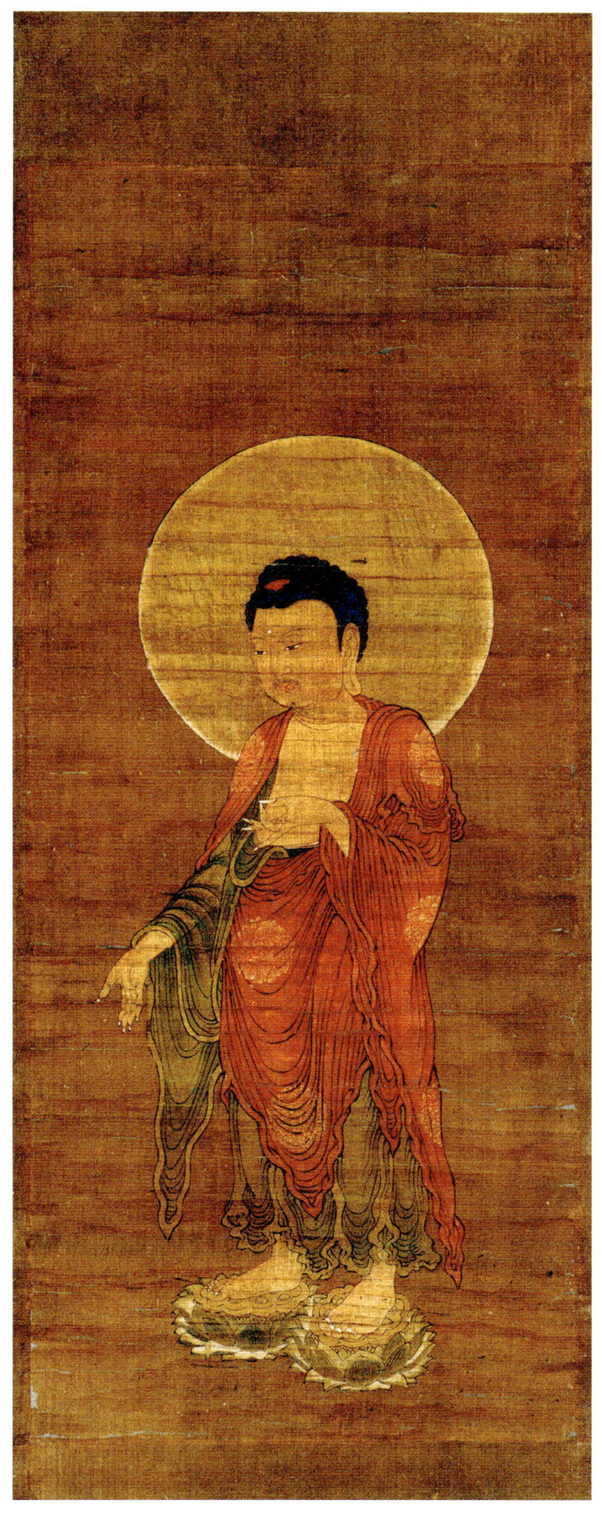

Figure 1.33 Descent of Amitābha. *Southern Song (1127-1279). Hanging scroll, ink and color on silk. Private Collection, Korea. Courtesy of the author.*

bottom. Sometimes a seven-treasure pattern (Kr. *ch'ilbomun* 七寶文) is used in place of the turtle-shell pattern. The hem of the skirt is invariably decorated with a peony-arabesque pattern (Kr. *moktan tangch'omun* 牧丹唐草文). For the veil, the hemp-leaf pattern (Kr. *mayŏmmun* 麻葉文) is depicted over the entire surface as the base pattern, on top of which the arabesque-medallion pattern, the lotus-medallion pattern, the floral-medallion pattern (Kr. *hwawŏnmun* 花圓文), or, in a few instances, the cloud-phoenix pattern is arranged in appropriate size to decorate it.

Among the patterns used for Koryŏ Buddhist paintings, the arabesque-medallion pattern is notable because it is the pattern used most frequently and the one that has the most diverse shapes (fig. 1.31). This is the decorative pattern quintessential to Koryŏ Buddhist paintings of the thirteenth and fourteenth centuries. Because it is used with such consistency, it offers valuable clues for dating Koryŏ Buddhist paintings: the time of the painting's production can be inferred based on the development of this particular pattern. Moreover, the arabesque-medallion pattern is unique to Koryŏ Buddhist painting and is not found in Chinese or Japanese Buddhist paintings, regardless of their time period or subject matter. Hence, presently it is an important detail by which to ascertain the painting's country of origin. If a painting has this pattern, it would certainly be a Koryŏ Buddhist painting from the thirteenth to fourteenth centuries. On the other hand, Buddhist paintings using the lotus-arabesque-medallion pattern that survive in Japan or other countries are largely copies that date to later periods.[37]

Unlike the case of Koryŏ Buddhist painting, it is nearly impossible to offer a simple definition of representation techniques in Chinese Buddhist painting, which include many factors that vary by period, region, function, material, and painter. Moreover, the Chinese Buddhist paintings I have examined may not be representative of their respective time periods and regions, so saying anything about their representational techniques is risky. In comparing the representation techniques of the Buddhist paintings of Koryŏ and China, I risk making an error based on a superficial and impressionistic judgment. Nevertheless, even if we do not consider the particular circumstances under which the Buddhist paintings were produced, these two groups of paintings retain invariably different elements. Hence, although the examples are rather limited and have been chosen for

---

[37] Regarding the lotus-arabesque pattern of Koryŏ Buddhist paintings, see Chŏng U-t'aek, "Chikuzen Zendōji no Jizō bosatsu-zu," 112-114.

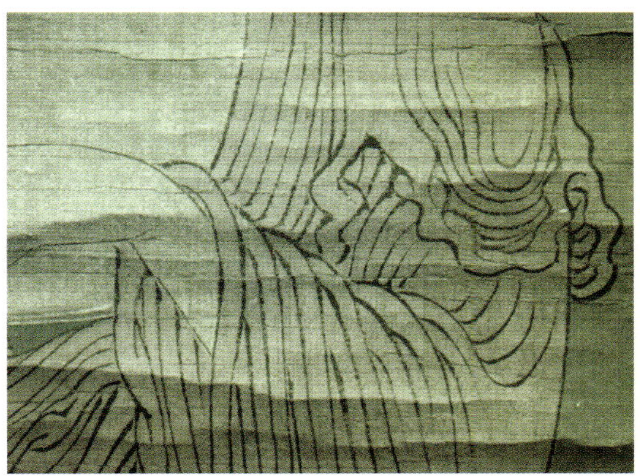

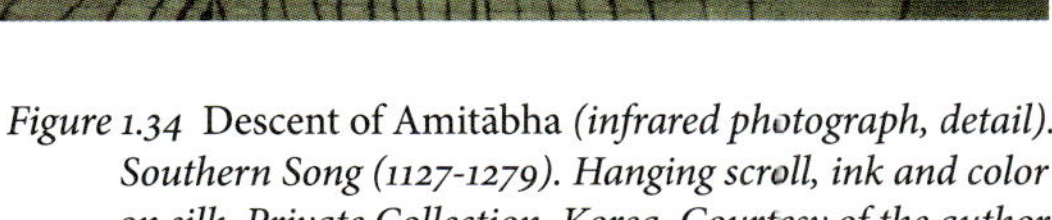

Figure 1.34 Descent of Amitābha *(infrared photograph, detail).*
Southern Song (1127-1279). Hanging scroll, ink and color
on silk. Private Collection, Korea. Courtesy of the author.

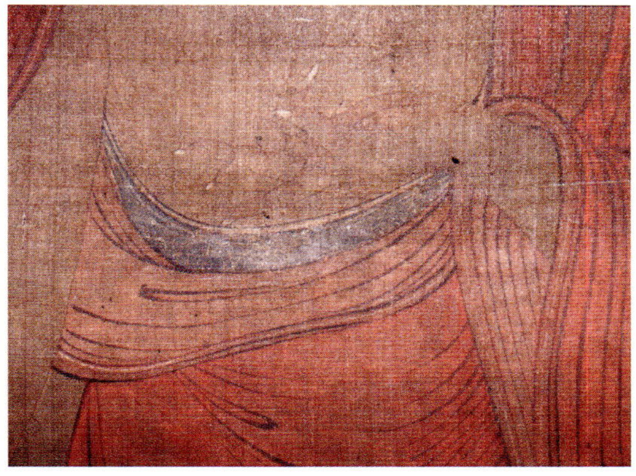

Figure 1.35 Puyue *(date unknown),* Amitābha Triad *(detail).*
Southern Song (1127-1279). Hanging scroll, ink and color on silk.
249.7×60.9cm. Shōjōkein, Japan. Courtesy of the author.

the sake of convenience, here I attempt to point out some obvious differences between the two.[38]

For instance, when comparing the *Descent of Amitābha* of Koryŏ at
Shōbōji 正法寺 (fig. 1.32) to the *Descent of Amitābha* from Song (960-1279)
China in a private collection (fig. 1.33), a close examination reveals quite a
significant difference even though the two paintings use nearly identical
basic coloring, posture, and costume for the Buddha. Above all, compared
to the Shōbōji work, the Chinese painting exhibits a restrained use of decorative patterns but a pronounced use of line drawing (fig. 1.34). Additionally, it depicts the Buddha's right arm delicately observed through the great
robe as if the robe were translucent.[39] This examination of the paintings
of *Descent of Amitābha* suggests that the Buddhist painting from China

---

[38] For the connection between Buddhist paintings of Koryŏ and China, see
Chŏng Ut'aek 鄭于澤, "Koryŏ ŭi Chungguk purhwa sŏnt'aek kwa pyŏnyong" 고려
의 중국불화 선택과 변용 [Adoption and adaptation of Chinese Buddhist painting
in Koryŏ], *Misulsa yŏn'gu* 美術史研究 25 (2011): 109-136.

[39] Although this difference is especially prominent between these two paintings,
the technique of representing the transparent great robe of a Buddha was applied
in quite a few Koryŏ Buddhist paintings as well. See Chŏng U-t'aek, "Chikuzen
Zendōji no Jizō bosatsu-zu," 112.

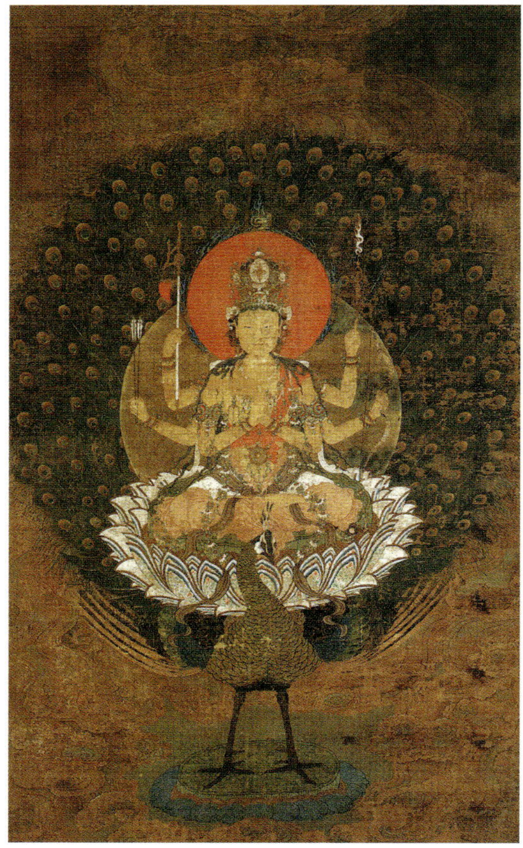

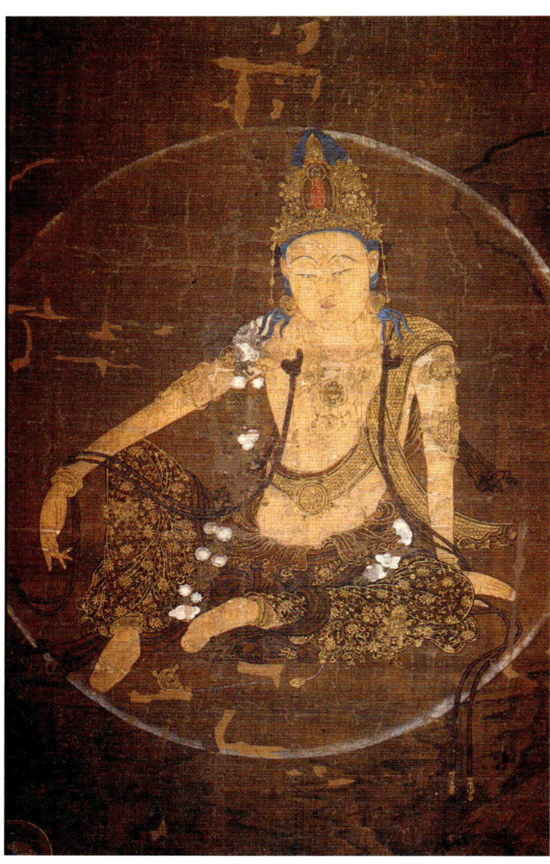

Figure 1.36 Mahāmayūrī. *Northern Song (960-1126).
Hanging scroll, ink and color on silk. 167.1×102.6cm.
Courtesy of Ninnaji, Kyoto, Japan.*

Figure 1.37 Cintāmaṇi-cakra Avalokiteśvara *(detail). Southern Song (1127-1279). Hanging scroll, ink and color on silk.
101.5×50.8cm. Nezu Museum, Japan. Courtesy of the author.*

conveys a stronger sense of the material reality of the depicted figure, rather
than the decorative feeling observed in the Koryŏ Buddhist painting. Such
representational techniques from Chinese Buddhist painting that feature
line drawing can be seen not only in Buddhist paintings that emphasize
the presence of the deity but also in paintings aimed basically at creating a
dreamlike atmosphere, as in the case of the *Amitābha Triad* painted by the
Chinese painter Puyue 普悦 (fig. 1.35).

58

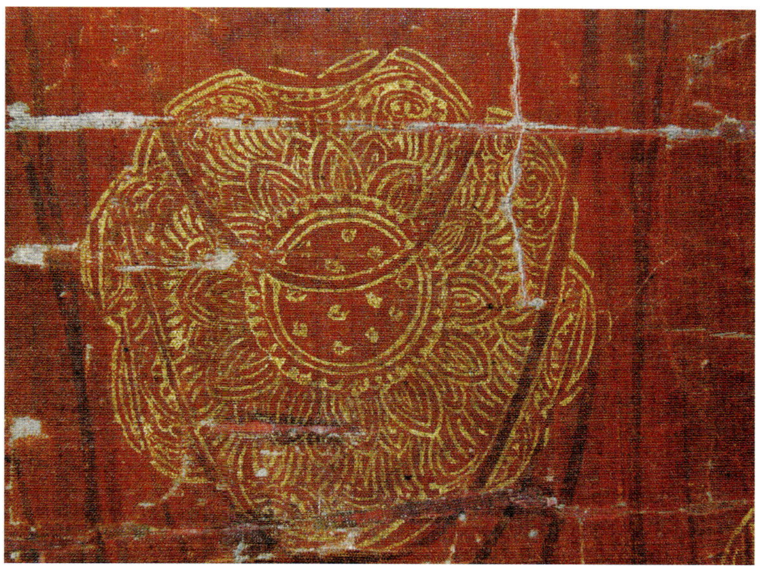

Figure 1.38 Amitābha Buddha *(detail). Southern Song (1127-1279). Hanging scroll,
ink and color on silk. Konrenji, Japan. Courtesy of the author.*

As can be easily observed in the paintings of *Mahāmayūrī* (Ch. *Kong-qiao mingwang xiang* 孔雀明王像) at Ninnaji 仁和寺, Kyoto (fig. 1.36), which is widely referred to as the greatest Buddhist painting of Northern Song, and *Cintāmaṇi-cakra Avalokiteśvara* (Ch. *Ruyilun guanyin tu* 如意輪觀音圖) at the Nezu Museum, Tokyo (fig. 1.37), which preserves the style of Southern Song painting, Chinese Buddhist paintings are more sensuous as well as very diverse in color and decorative pattern than are Koryŏ Buddhist paintings. Contemporaneous Chinese Buddhist paintings have a stronger tendency to create volume and a sense of reality through color gradation than do Koryŏ Buddhist paintings. But it should also be noted that while the decorative patterns of the Chinese Buddhist paintings of Song and Yuan 元 (1271-1368) are as varied as their colors, the arabesque-medallion pattern (fig. 1.31)—the pattern most frequently used in Koryŏ Buddhist paintings—is not used as the central pattern for the Buddha's robe (fig. 1.38) and is not used anywhere in Chinese Buddhist paintings.

Koryŏ Buddhist paintings divide the surface of the background, painted in a primary color, into tiny pieces through the use of layers of very

59

thin lines; typically, no space is left unadorned. In other words, by forming a "micro world" through layered depiction, the artists of Koryŏ Buddhist paintings strove to create a world of mysterious beauty, in which
a sense of depth can be felt. This technique of layered depiction seems to
have been one means of escaping from conventional iconographies, and this
technique can be regarded as one characteristic of Koryŏ Buddhist painting. In other words, within the extremely limited confines of predefined
iconographies and compositions, artists were left with little room fully to
demonstrate their abilities and thus likely sought to differentiate their work
through intricate details. The tendency toward the decorativeness observed
in Koryŏ Buddhist paintings is presumably due to this meticulous attention
to intricate details.

Production Context and Purpose

As explained above, most iconographic groups of Koryŏ Buddhist
paintings—including *Kṣitigarbha Bodhisattva*, *Illustration of the Sutra on
Maitreya's Rebirth Below*, and *Water-Moon Avalokiteśvara*—include works
that resemble one another down to minute details. Regardless of the date
of production, Koryŏ Buddhist paintings have a strong tendency to strive
persistently for homogeneity not only in technique but also in iconography. Moreover, the extant Koryŏ Buddhist paintings, with a few exceptions, are uniformly only about one meter high, and thus not appropriate for enshrinement in monasteries as an apparatus for devotion. During
Koryŏ, the majority of paintings enshrined in monasteries for devotion
were murals, as attested by the number of written records and the surviving
examples from Koryŏ and early Chosŏn, including the murals at Pusŏk-sa
浮石寺, Pongjŏng-sa 鳳停寺, and Muwi-sa.

One may attribute the homogeneity of iconography, composition, and
size observed in Koryŏ Buddhist paintings to certain Buddhist doctrines or
to the conservatism of Korean art; however, I argue that the reason is more
intimately related to the purpose of the commission, the place of enshrinement, and the paintings' function, all of which reflect contemporaneous
Buddhist belief. In light of this, trends in Buddhism and Buddhist belief
practices in Koryŏ are worth attention.

Since its foundation, the Koryŏ kingdom adopted Buddhism as the
state religion, and this prompted the establishment of various Buddhist
schools. The Buddhist doctrines of these schools are so complex and mutu-
ally interconnected that it is not easy to comprehend or investigate their
actual condition and true nature. From the twelfth century, however, Koryŏ

Buddhism, having formed close connections with the central governing elite, gradually lost its true character and moved away from its traditional role in society. In response, the renowned monks Chinul 知訥 (1158-1210) and Yose 了世 (1163-1245) attempted to reform Koryŏ Buddhism's doctrinal structure and belief system by launching a movement to set up religious organizations known as *kyŏlsa* 結社, including Chŏnghye kyŏlsa 定慧結社 and Paengnyŏn kyŏlsa 白蓮結社. After the mid-thirteenth century, however, Koryŏ Buddhism again colluded with a particular group within the ruling class, became conservative, and lost its social foundation. Especially starting with the Yuan dynasty's political interference in Koryŏ in the late thirteenth century, practicing Buddhism to gain worldly benefits by accumulating religious merit became the prevalent motivation, regardless of specific schools or doctrines. This resulted in the faith's individualization, leading members of the royal family and other influential families to compete in constructing personal monasteries (Kr. *wŏnch'al* 願剎, or *wŏndang* 願堂) and in commissioning illustrated scriptures using gold and silver for accumulation of religious merit. The reason that the vast majority of surviving Koryŏ Buddhist paintings portray Amitābha, Avalokiteśvara, or Kṣitigarbha—the paintings commissioned in order to wish for good fortune in this world and salvation in the afterlife—is probably because Koryŏ Buddhist paintings reflect these contemporaneous religious trends.

A passage in the *Tongguk Yi Sangguk chip* 東國李相國集 (Collected works of State Councilor Yi of the Eastern Kingdom) testifies to the existence of personal monasteries: "One bay of the building was arranged as a Buddhist shrine to cultivate one's mind. The place was even equipped to hold all kinds of Buddhist rituals . . ."[40] Meanwhile, the story detailed in *Wangnang panhon chŏn* 王郎反魂傳 (The story of the returned soul of Wangnang) provides important clues that should be considered when speculating on the purpose behind the relatively small size of Amitābha paintings from Koryŏ. In this Buddhist novel, the main character's late wife, then in hell, appears in a dream and instructs her husband to hang a

---

[40] *Tongguk Yi Sangguk hu chip* 東國李相國後集 11:7-9 "朴樞府有嘉堂記", original manuscript reprinted in Minjok Munhwa Ch'ujinhoe 民族文化推進會 [Korean Classics Research Institute], ed., *Kugyŏk Tongguk Yi Sangguk chip* 국역동국이상국집 [Translation of Collected Works of State Councilor Yi of the Eastern Kingdom] (Seoul: Minjok Munhwa Ch'ujinhoe, 1979): 6:62-63. The reproduction of the original manuscript is included in the back part of this book, which has pagination marked in Chinese characters.

painting of Amitābha on the western wall for worship and contemplation. Because he follows her instructions, he not only escapes being taken to the underworld but also prolongs his life. Japanese paintings depicting a person contemplating hanging scrolls such as the *Descent of Amitābha* or the *Illustration of the Sixteen Contemplations in the Visualization Sutra* at his or her deathbed also provide clues to infer how Koryŏ Buddhist paintings were used in similar contexts.

I think that the similarities in technique and iconography of Koryŏ Buddhist paintings resulted from the patrons' limited range of social class as well as the homogeneity of the paintings' production purposes and enshrinement locations. The composition of Koryŏ Buddhist paintings tends to amplify only the central subject such as the main deity. The paintings did not need to be expository, probably because the devotees who commissioned and appreciated them were members of the royal family or aristocrats who already had good knowledge of Buddhism and Buddhist literature. This is also the reason that Koryŏ Buddhist paintings are imbued with a strong conceptual quality.[41]

**Comparison with Iconography from
Chinese Buddhist Painting and Composition**
The Chinese influence on Korean art, although it varies in degree according to genre, cannot be denied, and seems to have taken diverse forms. Hence, the level of originality of Korean art is often determined by analyzing the extent of its differentiation from Chinese art. As expected, since Buddhism is a foreign religion transmitted through China, the earlier the time period, the stronger the Chinese influence.

Koryŏ and China not only were geographically adjacent but also maintained a long relationship, sometimes close and sometimes rather distant. Although the two countries are supposed to have had considerable influence on each other through their shared belief in Buddhism, unfortunately there is such a dearth of written records about Buddhist paintings that it is difficult even to speculate about the historical circumstances of such influence when relying solely on the written documents.

The most frequently cited record regarding the exchange of Buddhist art between Koryŏ and China is the documentation about the painting of *Five Hundred Arhats*. Fascicle One, "Sega" 世家, in the *Koryŏsa* 高麗史 (History

---

[41] The circumstances and purpose of production of Koryŏ Buddhist paintings are discussed in detail in Chung Woothak, "Identity of Goryeo Buddhist Painting," 21-23.

of Koryŏ) includes a passage, "[In 923] Yun Chil 尹質 went to the Liang state as emissary, returned, and presented the painting of *Five Hundred Arhats*. [The King] had it enshrined at Sungsan-sa 嵩山寺 in Haeju 海州."[42]

The "Gaoliguo" 高麗國 section in Fascicle Six of the *Tuhua jianwen zhi* 圖畫見聞志 (Record of paintings seen and heard) records that in 1076 a Koryŏ envoy brought a number of painters to China and had them study the murals of Xiangguosi 相國寺, then paint copies in Hŭngwang-sa 興王寺 in Kaegyŏng 開京, the capital of Koryŏ.[43] This is another indispensable reference when discussing the exchange of paintings between the two countries.

Considering the close geographical and historical relationship between the two countries, records on the exchange of Buddhist paintings between Koryŏ and China are inexplicably scanty. Records of evaluations of Koryŏ Buddhist paintings in China do exist, albeit in bits and pieces. For instance, the *Huajian* 畫鑒 (Examination of painting) written by Tang Hou 湯垕 (fl. 1322) records, "Tang Zai 湯載 of the Song dynasty said that the paintings of Avalokiteśvara of Koryŏ are very exquisite, and this style originated from Yuchi Yiseng 尉遲乙僧. Yuchi Yiseng was a foreigner who was very skilled at making Buddhist paintings whose color was so intense that it looked as if the figure might spring out from the silk."[44] Although limited to the paint-

---

[42] *Koryŏsa* 1:17, T'aejo 太祖 6.6.10, Yŏnhŭi Taehakkyo Tongbanghak Yŏn'guso 延禧大學校東方學研究所 [The Institute of Far Eastern Studies Chosun Christian University], ed., *Koryŏsa* 高麗史 [History of Koryŏ], 3 vols. (Seoul: Yŏnhŭi Taehakkyo Ch'ulp'anbu, 1955): 1:42. Editor's Note: The Liang dynasty in this record is Later Liang 後梁 (907-923), one of the short-lived dynasties during the Five Dynasties and Ten Kingdoms period in China.

[43] Guo Ruoxu 郭若虛 (fl. 1070-1075), *Tuhua jianwen zhi* (Beijing: Renmin Meishu Chubanshe, 1963): 6:156-157.

[44] For the original texts and translations of respective materials, see Kikutake Jun'ichi 菊竹淳一 and Chŏng Ut'aek (Chung Woothak) 鄭于澤, "Koryŏ purhwa munhŏn charyo" 高麗佛畫文獻資料 [Historical documentation data of Koryŏ Buddhist painting], in *Koryŏ sidae ŭi purhwa* 高麗時代의 佛畫 [Buddhist paintings of the Koryŏ period], ed. Kikutake Jun'ichi and Chŏng Ut'aek, vol. 2 (Seoul: Sigongsa, 1997): 118-129. For a detailed discussion about the exchange of Buddhist paintings between the two countries, see Kikutake Jun'ichi 菊竹淳一, "Kōrai butsuga ni miru Chūgoku to Nihon" 高麗仏画にみる中国と日本, in *Kōrai butsuga* 高麗仏画 [Koryŏ Buddhist painting], ed. Kikutake Jun'ichi 菊竹淳一 and Yoshida Hiroshi 吉田宏志 (Tokyo: Asahi Shinbunsha, 1981): 9-14. Regarding exchange of secular paintings between Koryŏ and China, see An Hwijun (Ahn, Hwi-Joon) 안휘준, "Koryŏ mit Chosŏn ch'ogi ŭi tae Chung hoehwa kyosŏp" 고려 및 조선초기의 對

ings of Avalokiteśvara, this passage provides evidence that Koryŏ Buddhist paintings were highly regarded in China.

Nearly all iconographies of the Koryŏ Buddhist paintings are based on the scriptures of exoteric Buddhism, and as pointed out earlier, the majority of paintings depict three iconographies—Amitābha, Avalokiteśvara, and Kṣitigarbha. Hence, the Koryŏ Buddhist paintings cannot be said to have an abundant variety of iconographies. This is probably because most of the surviving Koryŏ Buddhist paintings are hanging scrolls commissioned for individual worship while the majority of Buddhist paintings of the time were monastery murals that were undoubtedly painted with diverse subjects. Unfortunately, only a few Koryŏ monasteries remain that preserve the original setting inside their halls.[45] Given that the extant Koryŏ Buddhist paintings show the holistic characteristics of Interpenetrated Buddhism (T'ong Pulgyo 通佛教) and were commissioned for personal religious practice by aristocrats, it is natural that their iconographies are limited. In any event, even when all recorded iconographies are considered, Koryŏ Buddhist paintings are still relatively lacking in variety, in comparison to Chinese Buddhist paintings, which encompass various iconographies drawn from both exoteric and esoteric Buddhism and even from Daoism and folk beliefs.

Differences between the Buddhist iconographies of Koryŏ and China perhaps seem more dramatic than they were in fact; this may be due to comparative analyses that do not include consideration of religious practices, enshrinement sites, painting functions, and commission purpose. Because only a few Buddhist paintings enshrined in Koryŏ monasteries remain—particularly murals—such simplistic comparative analyses can lead to misleading results. At any rate, Koryŏ presumably selectively adopted elements of Chinese Buddhist painting. For instance, it seems that it was

---

中 회화교섭 [Koryŏ and early Chosŏn's exchange of paintings with China], in *Han'guk hoehwasa yŏn'gu* 한국회화사연구 [Research on Korean painting history] (Seoul: Sigongsa, 2000): 285-297.

[45] Written records testify that the mural was the main format for paintings adorning Koryŏ monasteries. This is also proved by the surviving examples, such as the mural at the Hall of the Founder (Kr. Chosadang 祖師堂) at Pusŏk-sa from Koryŏ and the mural behind the main altar of the Main Buddha Hall (Kr. Taeungjŏn 大雄殿) at Pongjŏng-sa from early Chosŏn. In particular, the Buddhist paintings, presumably dated to 1476, found inside the Hall of Amitābha's Pure Land at Muwi-sa are all murals. They are representative early Chosŏn works continuing the earlier tradition from Koryŏ and suggest that most Buddhist paintings enshrined inside Buddhist halls during the earlier period were also murals.

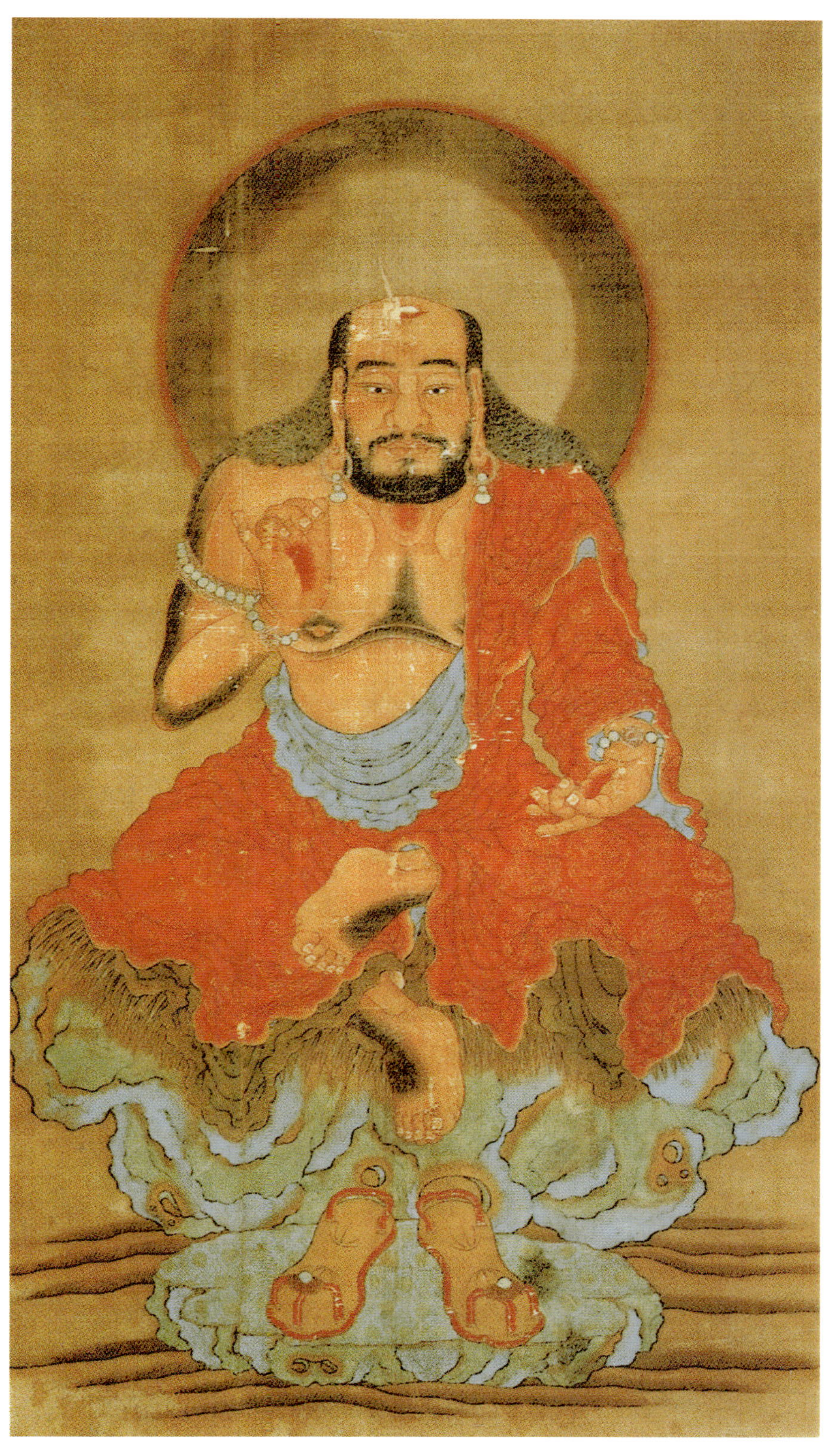

Figure 1.39 Attributed to Yan Hui (date unknown), Śākyamuni Triad (detail). Yuan (1271-1368). Hanging scroll triptych, ink and color on silk. 135.7×77.2cm, each hanging scroll. Courtesy of Rokuōin, Japan.

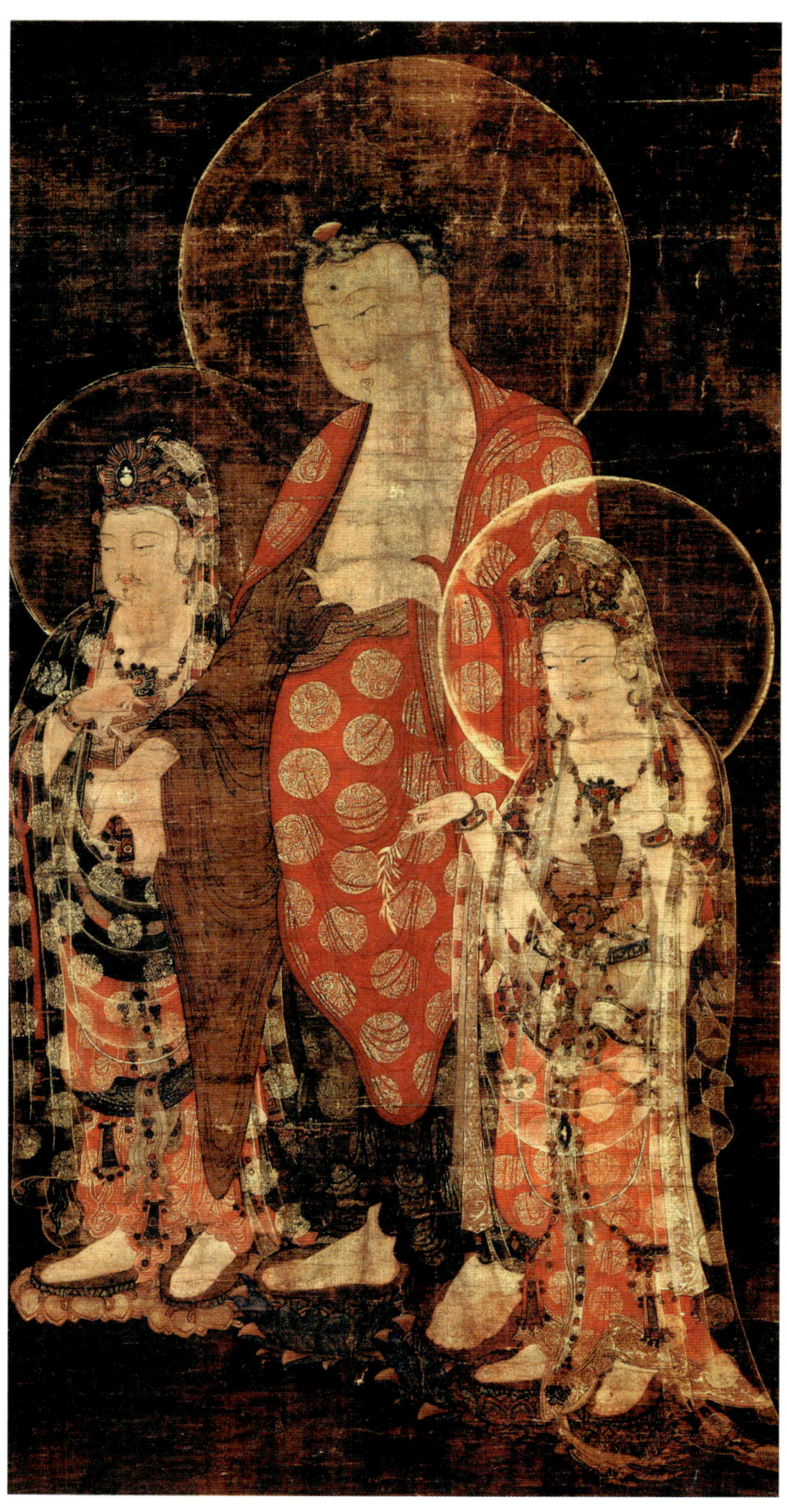

Figure 1.40 Descent of Amitābha Triad. *Koryŏ (918-1392). Hanging scroll, ink and color on silk. 100.9×54.2cm. MOA Museum of Art, Atami, Shizuoka Prefecture, Japan. Courtesy of the author.*

hardly acceptable for the Koryŏ people to adopt iconographies derived from esoteric Buddhism, such as *Mahāmayūrī* (fig. 1.36) and *Cintāmaṇi-cakra Avalokiteśvara* (fig. 1.37); paintings of nirvana; or iconographies that drastically deviate from the typical Buddha and bodhisattva images, such as the *Śākyamuni Triad* of Rokuōin 鹿王院 in Kyoto (fig. 1.39). It seems that Koryŏ selected only those iconographies acceptable for adoption even when copying the Xiangguoxi's murals in China.[46]

In terms of composition, Koryŏ Buddhist paintings depicting deities show a strong tendency to emphasize only the main subject, such as the principal deity. For instance, Koryŏ's examples of *Descent of Amitābha*, contrary to those of China and Japan, do not depict clouds, and Koryŏ paintings of *Amitābha Preaching the Law* often represent only the Amitābha Buddha or the Amitābha triad. These tendencies contrast with those of the Buddhist paintings of China, which strove to connect the compositional elements in an organic relationship and to convey the narrative through the composition. This difference in composition between Koryŏ and Chinese Buddhist paintings may originate from different production dates and the artistic sensitivity unique to each country; however, the decisive difference is rather more closely associated with the patron's social status, purpose of production, and painting function. For example, Koryŏ's *Descent of Amitābha Triad* in the MOA Museum of Art depicts only the Buddha and bodhisattvas (fig. 1.40), just like most other Koryŏ paintings of the same subject, even omitting the cloud that symbolizes the "descent," as if the deities were frozen in the air. Hence, people without prior knowledge would not understand the meaning of the painting. In contrast to Koryŏ paintings, the Chinese paintings of the descent of Amitābha—as one can see in Eikandō Zenrinji's 永観堂禅林寺 *Descent of Amitābha Triad*, a Kamakura period 鎌倉時代 (1185-1333) painting heavily influenced by the Song dynasty painting style—portray the cloud as if it were flowing from the foreground of the picture toward the background so that the triad seems to be approaching the viewer, giving a virtual experience of witnessing the Amitābha Buddha's "descent" from the Western Pure Land (fig. 1.41).

---

[46] Regarding the subjects and the painters of the murals at Xiangguoxi, including Wang Renshou 王仁壽 (?-959), Gao Yi 高益 (fl. tenth century), Gao Wenjin 高文進 (fl. tenth century), and Wang Daozhen 王道眞 (fl. tenth century), see Guo Ruoxu 郭若虛 (fl. 1070-1075), *Tuhua jianwen zhi*, 2:53; 3:69; 3:75; 6:19-150. For more about the murals of Xiangguoxi, see Kikutake Jun'ichi, "Kōrai butsuga ni miru Chūgoku to Nihon," 9-14.

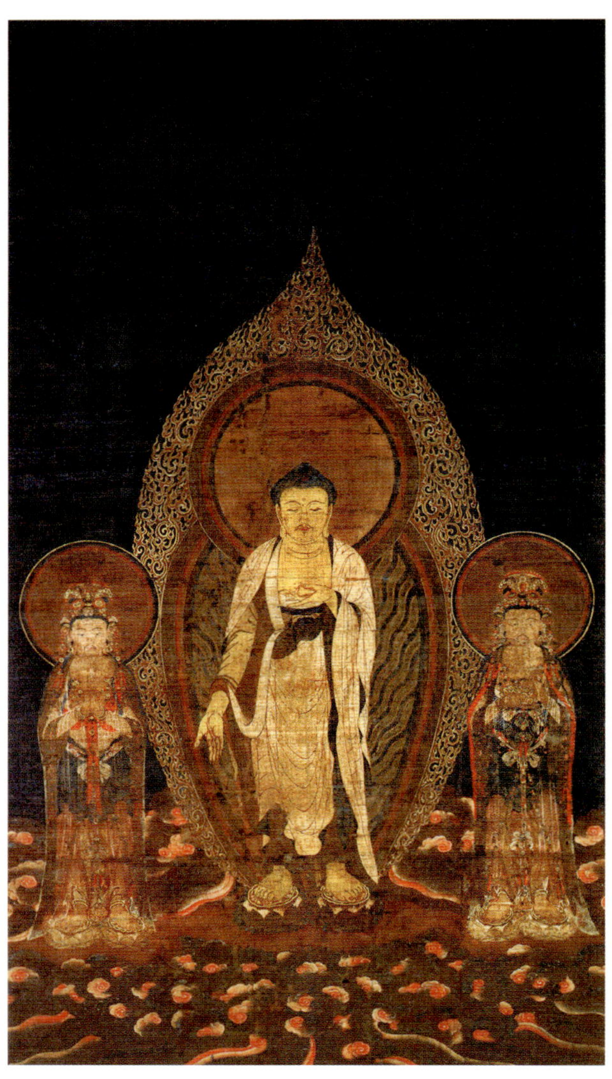

Figure 1.41 Descent of Amitābha Triad. *Kamakura (1185-1333). Hanging scroll, ink and color on silk. 102.8×57.4cm. Courtesy of Eikandō Zenrinji, Kyoto, Japan.*

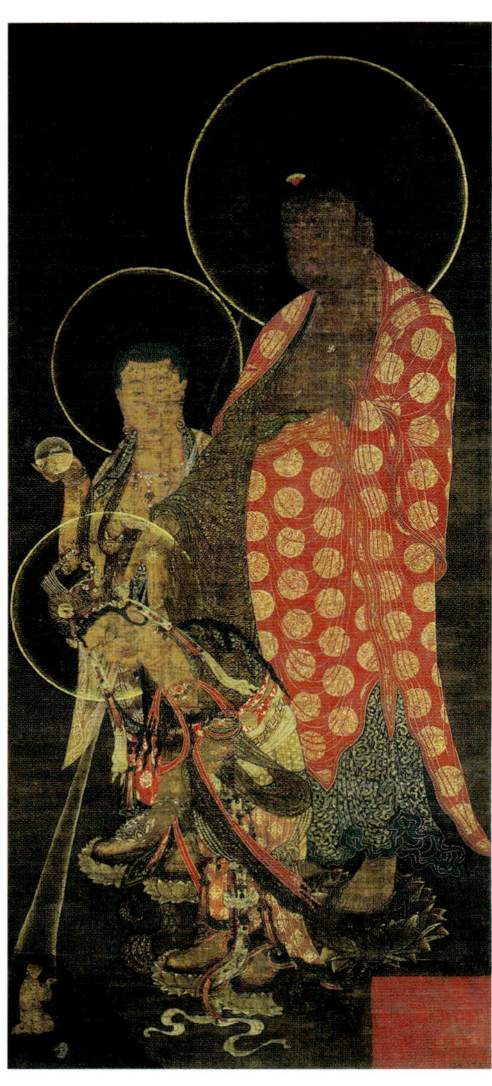

Figure 1.42 Descent of Amitābha Triad. *Koryŏ (918-1392). Hanging scroll, ink and color on silk. 110.0×51.0cm. Courtesy of the Leeum, Samsung Museum of Art, Korea.*

The same tendency can also be clearly understood through the *Descent of Amitābha* in the collection of the Leeum, Samsung Museum of Art in Korea (fig. 1.42). This painting faithfully represents the Amitābha's "descent" as explicated in scripture so that the viewer can easily understand the painting; in other words, this painting deviates from the typical iconography of Koryŏ Buddhist paintings. Still, in comparison with the Xixia 西夏 state's (1038-1227) *Descent of Amitābha* (fig. 1.43), which is presumed to be its iconographical origin, even this Koryŏ painting tends to emphasize the subject, which is one of the characteristics of Koryŏ Buddhist paintings in general. The Xixia painting depicts the "soul" of the deceased,[47] not to mention the cloud, and its compositional elements are connected so organically and with such expository clarity that it visually convinces the viewer that attaining rebirth in the Western Pure Land is both realistic and possible.[48]

In a broad sense, most Koryŏ Buddhist paintings do not widely diverge from the iconographic categories of Chinese Buddhist painting, but they have a number of differences in representational technique and their artists consistently strove to differentiate their work from Chinese Buddhist paintings. A good example is the *Avalokiteśvara Bodhisattva* (fig. 1.44) held in a private collection in Korea. When compared with the renowned *White-Robed Avalokiteśvara* of Daitokuji in Kyoto, painted by the Southern Song Chan monk-painter Muqi Fachang 牧谿法常 (ca.1210-1269) in the thirteenth century, this painting has no essential difference in iconography;

---

[47] Editor's Note: The "soul" appears at the end of the small trail of cloud rising from the head of the deceased standing in the lower left corner of the painting. Unlike the deceased, who is wearing an ordinary long brown robe, the "soul" is dressed in a heavenly robe and elegant scarves. The "soul" depicted in this painting is about to take a seat on the lotus pedestal held in the hands of two bodhisattvas, and is simultaneously illuminated by the white light emanating from the head of the Buddha.

[48] For the relationship between this Koryŏ painting and the iconography of Xixia's Buddhist painting, see Chŏng Ut'aek (Chung Woothak) 鄭于澤, "Koryŏ purhwa ŭi tokchasŏng" 高麗佛畫의 獨自性 [The originality of Koryŏ Buddhist painting], in *Han'guk misul ŭi chasaengsŏng* 韓國美術의 自生性 [Indigenous nature of Korean art], ed. Han'guk Misul ŭi Chasaengsŏng Kanhaeng Wiwŏnhoe 한국미술의 자생성 간행위원회 [Committee for the Publication of *Han'guk misul ŭi chasaengsŏng*] (Seoul: Han'gil Art, 1999): 154-158; Chŏng Ut'aek (Chung Woothak) 鄭于澤, "Shirukurōdo to Kōrai butsuga" シルクロードと高麗仏画 [The Silk Road and Koryŏ Buddhist painting], in *Kodai Tōhoku Ajia no bunka kōryu* 古代東北アジアの文化交流 [Cultural exchange in ancient Northeast Asia] (Matsue: Hōkōsha, 1995): 91-98.

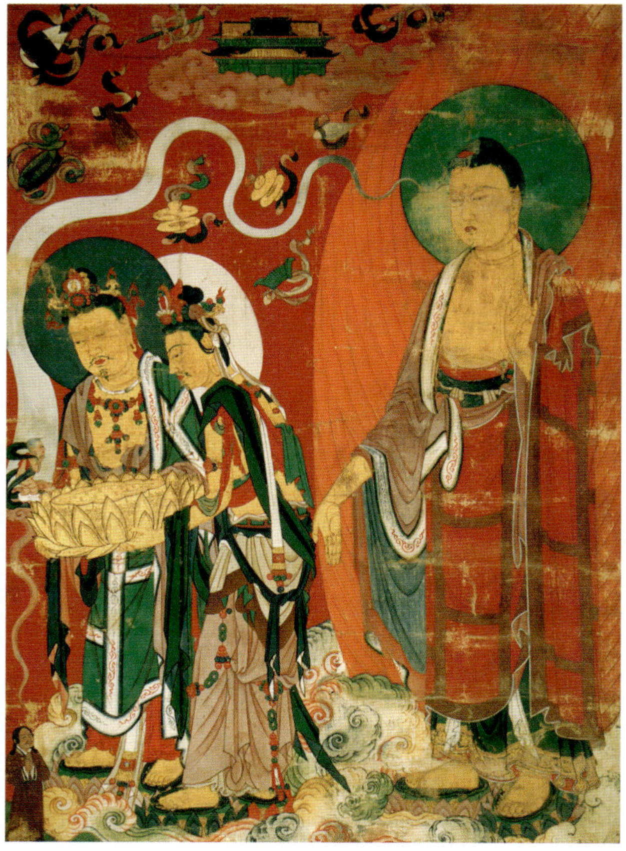

Figure 1.43 Descent of Amitābha Triad. *Xixia (1038-1227).
Hanging scroll, ink and color on silk. 84.8×63.8cm.
Photograph © The State Hermitage Museum / photo by
Vladimir Terebenin, Leonard Kheifets, Yuri Molodkovets.*

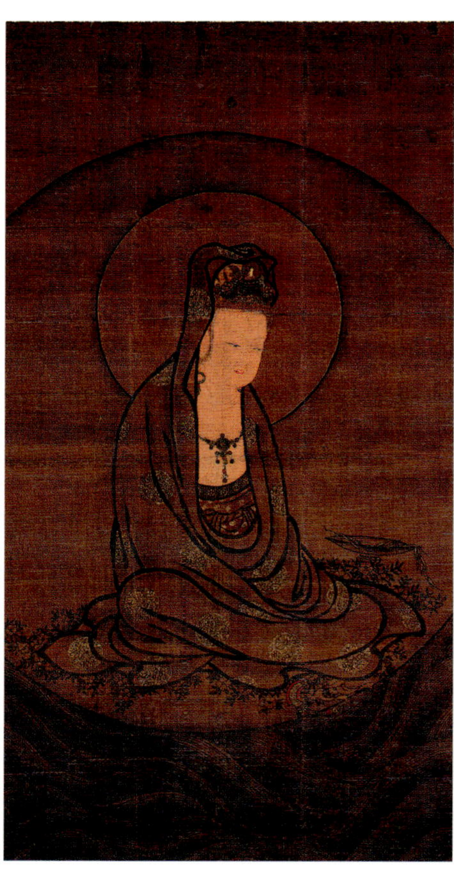

Figure 1.44 Avalokiteśvara Bodhisattva.
*Koryŏ (918-1392). Hanging scroll, ink and color
on silk. 91.5×42.3cm. Private Collection, Korea.
Courtesy of the author.*

this can be seen through Avalokiteśvara's nearly identical way of dressing as well as the posture of the deity and the folds of the robe, notwithstanding some difference in the background, the *kundika* bottle, and the seat. Nevertheless, by fully understanding the essence of the Chinese iconography and faithfully reflecting traditional Koryŏ Buddhist painting techniques, this

70

Avalokiteśvara Bodhisattva from Koryŏ did not stop at merely adopting the iconography but also succeeded in recreating it through modification.[49]

The original meaning and function of Buddhist iconography tends to undergo frequent modification in the course of transmission, reception, comprehension, and acculturation. At a time when travel was difficult for geographical and environmental reasons, it was primarily the iconography, namely an image, that was transmitted, and it was often not easy to adopt the fundamental concepts surrounding its production or the doctrinal interpretations behind it. Therefore, one needs to consider the following questions: Does Koryŏ Buddhist painting display clear understanding of the original meaning of the iconographical prototype during the process of reception? Does the process of transmission involve changes in the essential nature of the prototype iconography?

Korean Buddhism strongly shared Interpenetrated Buddhism's characteristic embrace of various teachings of exoteric Buddhism. As a result, when examined through extant records and surviving material data, Koryŏ Buddhist paintings show little difference in iconography or style that reflects teachings of dissimilar Buddhist schools. Hence, I have suggested that Koryŏ did not have "sectarian art" (Jp. *shūha bijutsu* 宗派美術), which did exist in China and Japan. The iconographies of Koryŏ Buddhist painting may look similar to those of China, but it is difficult to assume that the sectarian beliefs or doctrines behind the iconographies were also adopted.

Conclusion

Korean Buddhist painting has persistently upheld past tradition from its early development to the present. The extant Koryŏ Buddhist paintings represent only those of the late Koryŏ period, which spans from the late thirteenth to the late fourteenth centuries, but they have immense importance in Korean art history, opening a window through which we can observe the artistic trends of the entire Koryŏ period as well as the dynamics of the overall history of Korean painting. Although Koryŏ Buddhist paintings are somewhat lacking in iconographical variation and in the sense of rhythmical movement, their beauty resides in the harmony between

---

[49] For a detailed discussion of this *Avalokiteśvara Bodhisattva* in a private collection in Korea, including its date and relationship with Chinese Buddhist painting, see Chŏng Ut'aek (Chung Woothak) 鄭于澤, "Sinch'ul Koryŏ sidae *Suwŏl kwanŭmdo*" 新出 高麗時代 水月觀音圖 [A newly discovered Koryŏ-period painting of Water-Moon Avalokiteśvara], *Tongak misul sahak* 東岳美術史學 2 (2001): 103-119.

constituent visual elements and in their exquisite and sophisticated details. In addition, Koryŏ Buddhist painting excels in its effective amplification of the subject as well as in visual effects intended for the viewer at close proximity, thus befitting their role as objects of personal worship. As is the case for Buddhist painting of any other period or country, Koryŏ Buddhist painting retains its uniqueness and originality. These are undoubtedly the canonical masterworks of Korean Buddhist painting.

Seeing Maitreya: Aspiration and Vision in an Image from Early Eighth-Century Silla

2

Rhi Juhyung

Extraordinary Images

In writing a narrative on early Korean Buddhist art, one faces perennial difficulties that stem from the inherent nature of materials in the field. In contrast to the fields of Chinese or Japanese Buddhist art, only a meager number of images that would have had high cultic importance to contemporaneous Buddhists remain. Literary evidence from both epigraphical and historical sources, which would have greatly helped in contextualizing images, is also extremely limited. This has not only restricted the methodological prospects of researchers, but has also led to the academic discourse on Korean Buddhist art being dominated by a small number of images, of which the most notable are probably two renowned pensive bodhisattvas (fig. 2.1) and the Buddha in Sŏkkuram 石窟庵.[1] Nonetheless, even with these three images, which feature prominently in modern accounts of early Korean Buddhist art, absolutely nothing is known from the epigraphical or historical sources about the pensive bodhisattvas, and we only have a brief account in the *Samguk yusa* 三國遺事 regarding the patronage of the Sŏkkuram Buddha by Kim Taesŏng 金大城.[2]

---

[1] For illustrations of the other famous pensive bodhisattva and the Sŏkkuram Buddha, see Lena Kim, *Buddhist Sculpture of Korea* (Elizabeth, NJ, and Seoul: Hollym, 2007): Plates I-44, 45, II-26.

[2] *Samguk yusa* 三國遺事 5: "Taesŏng hyo ise pumo Sinmunwangdae," Han'guk Chŏngsin Munhwa Yŏn'guwŏn 韓國精神文化研究院 [Academy of Korean Studies], ed., *Yŏkchu Samguk yusa* 譯註 三國遺事 [Annotation and translation of the *Samguk yusa*] (Seoul: Ihoe Munhwasa, 2003), 4:376-382.

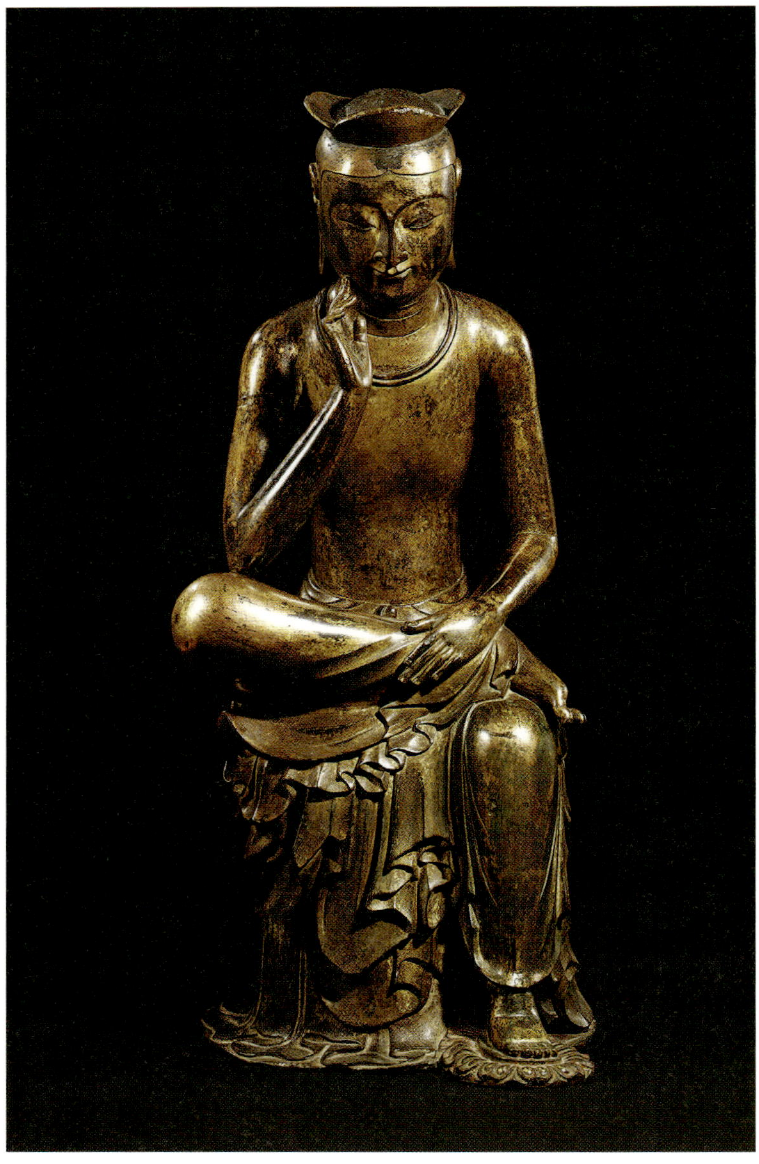

Figure 2.1 *Maitreya Bodhisattva. Silla, early seventh century.*
National Museum in Seoul. Courtesy of the National Museum of Korea.

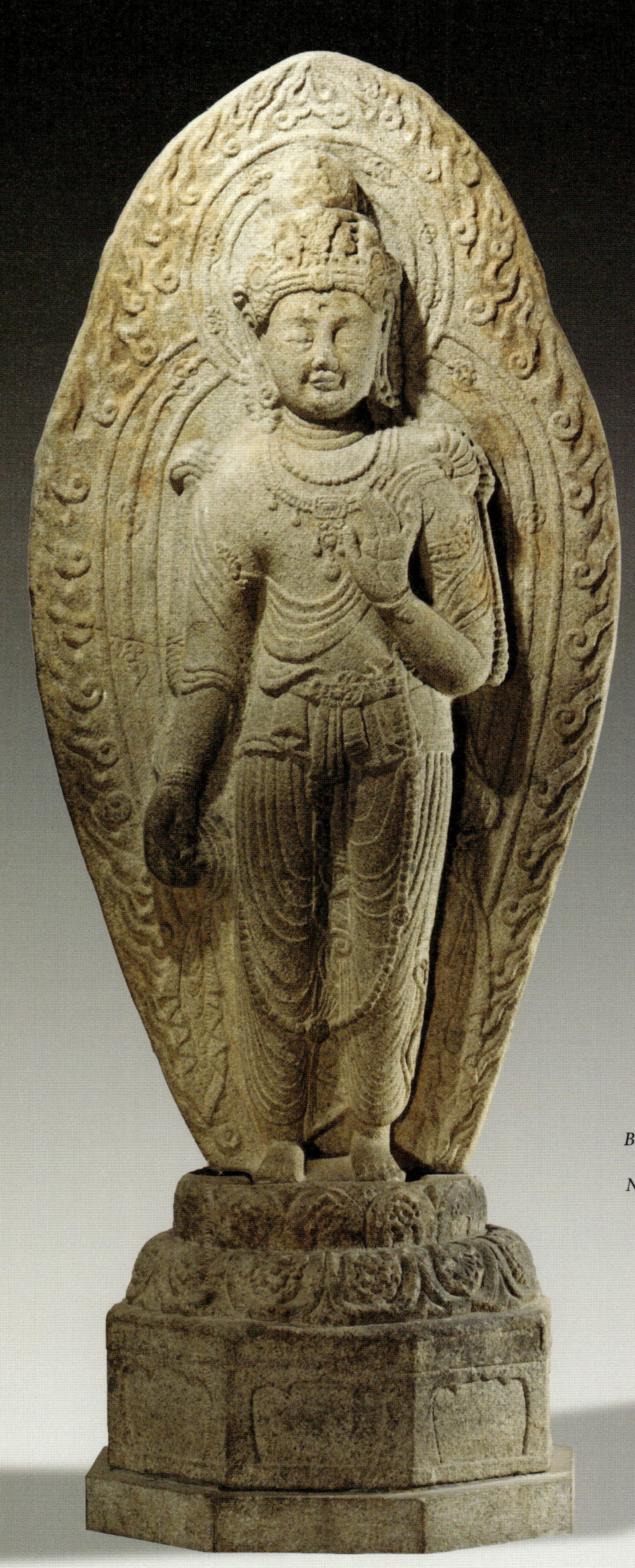

Figure 2.2 Maitreya Bodhisattva, from Kamsan-sa, Kyŏngju. Silla, 719. National Museum in Seoul. Courtesy of the National Museum of Korea.

Two stone images, a Buddha and a bodhisattva from Kamsan-sa 甘山
寺, a Buddhist temple in Kyŏngju 慶州, are probably the most conspicuous exceptions in this regard (figs. 2.2, 2.3). Datable to around 719, they are
large, visually gripping images, and were obviously installed as main cult
statues in the temple. More importantly, they carry unusually long inscriptions carved on the back of their mandorlas, which provide rich information about the subjects of the images, the donor, his career and personal
aspirations, and the reasons for the statues' creation (for translations of the
inscriptions, see the appendix at the end of this chapter).[3] As a result, we
are exceptionally well informed about these images in terms of the circumstances of their dedication.[4] This chapter explores these two images with a

---

[3] The inscriptions have been published in a number of works, beginning with
Chōsen kinseki sōran 朝鮮金石總覽 [Comprehensive collection of Korean epigra-
phy] (Keijō [Seoul]: Chōsen Sōtokufu, 1919): 1.34-36. The most frequently cited
source (with a Korean translation) today is in *Han'guk kodae kŭmsŏngmun* 韓國古
代金石文 [Ancient inscriptions of Korea], ed. Han'guk Kodae Sahoe Yŏn'guso 韓
國古代社會研究所 [Research Institute of Ancient Korean Society] (Seoul: Karak-
kuk Sajŏk Kaebal Yŏn'guwŏn, 1992): 3.293-302 (trans. Kim Namyun 金南允), which
is available on the website of the National Research Institute of Cultural Heritage
(http://gsm.nricp.go.kr). Some mistakes found in this translation have been cor-
rected in my translation in the appendix. See n. 74.

[4] A number of studies have been written on these two images and their inscriptions: Suematsu Yasukazu 末松保和, "Kanzanji Miroku sonzō oyobi Amidabutsu no
kakō kōki" 甘山寺彌勒尊像及び阿彌陀佛の火光後記 [Inscriptions on the back of
the flame mandorla of the Maitreya and Amitābha images from Kamsan-sa], *Chōsen*
朝鮮 (Dec. 1932): 63-72, later compiled in Suematsu's *Shiragi shi no shomondai* 新
羅史の諸問題 [Various problems in Silla history] (Tokyo: Tōyō Bunkō, 1954): 450-
460 (citations in this chapter will refer to the 1954 edition); Ayukai Fusanoshin 鮎貝
房之進, *Zakkō* 雑攷 [Miscellaneous observations] 6-1 (Keijō: Chikazawa Shuppan-
sha, 1934): 13-24; Katsuragi Sueji 葛城末治, *Chōsen kinseki kō* 朝鮮金石考 [Study
of Korean epigraphy] (Keijō: Ōsakayagō Shoten, 1935): 200-210; Nakagiri Isao 中
吉功, "Shiragi Kanzanji sekizō Miroku Amidazō ni tsuite" 新羅甘山寺石造弥勒阿弥
陀像について [On stone images of Maitreya and Amitābha of Silla from Kamsan-
sa], *Chōsen gakuhō* 朝鮮學報 9 (1956): 275-288; Chin Hongsŏp 秦弘燮, "Kyŏngju
Kamsansaji Sungboksaji ŭi chosa: Silla oak chosagi kisa" 慶州 甘山寺址 崇福寺址의
調査: 新羅五惡調査記 其四 [A survey of the sites of Kamsan-sa and Sungbok-sa in
Kyŏngju: The records of surveys on the Five Mountains of Silla, no. 4], *Kogo misul*
考古美術 6, no. 5 (1965): 73-74; Mun Myŏngdae 文明大, "Silla Pŏpsangjong (Yugajong) ŭi sŏngnip munje wa kŭ misul: Kamsan-sa Mirŭk posalsang mit Amit'a pulsang kwa kŭ myŏngmun ŭl chungsim ŭro" 新羅 法相宗(瑜伽宗)의 成立 問題와 그 美

76

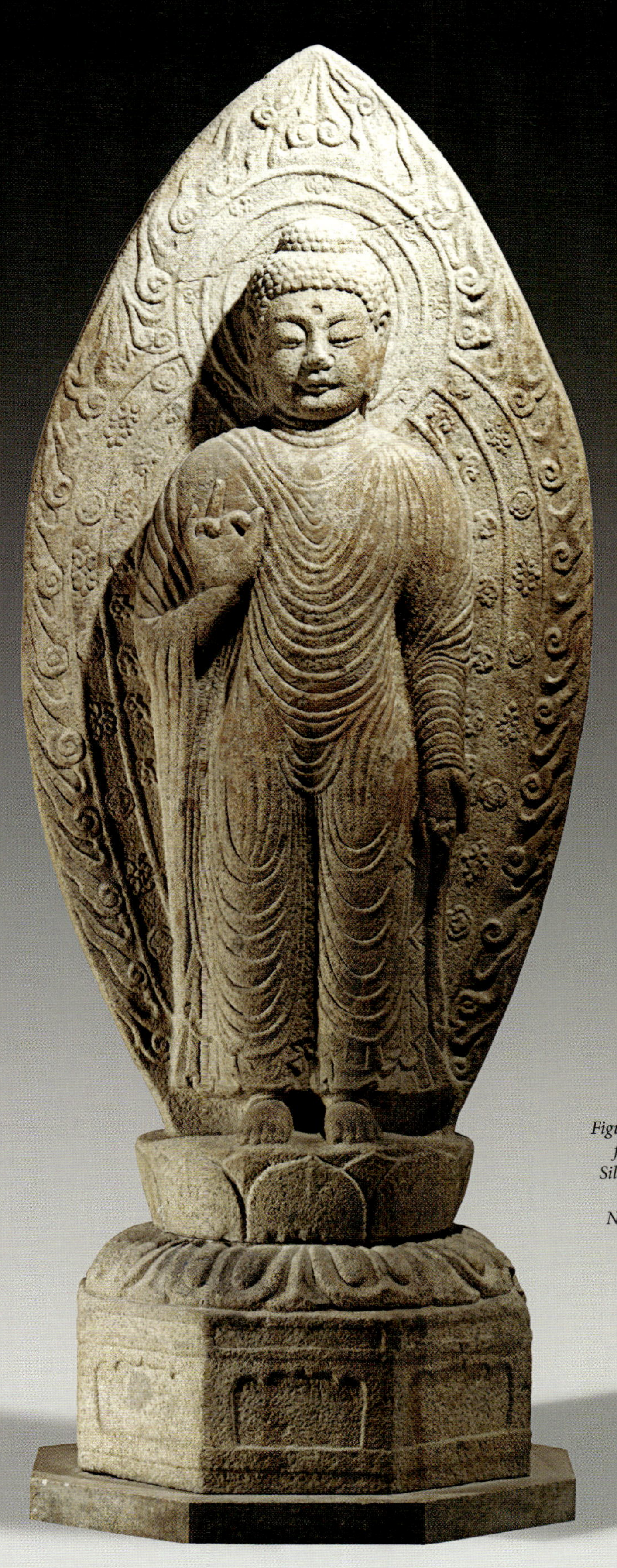

Figure 2.3 *Amitābha Buddha, from Kamsan-sa, Kyŏngju. Silla, 719. National Museum in Seoul. Courtesy of the National Museum of Korea.*

special focus on the bodhisattva and addresses diverse aspects of Buddhist image-making in early eighth-century Silla.

Images and Inscriptions

These two images were first brought to the attention of modern scholars in 1915, when Japanese colonial officers found them lying in rice paddies near a mountain slope to the south of Kyŏngju. The same year they were transported to Seoul and displayed in an exhibition organized by the Japanese colonial government to promote industrial production in Korea. After the exhibition they entered the Colonial Government Museum, whose collections were

---

術: 甘山寺 彌勒菩薩像 및 阿彌陀佛像과 그 銘文을 中心으로 [The formation of the *Dharmalakṣaṇa* school of Silla and its art: With a focus on the Maitreya bodhisattva image and the Amitābha Buddha image from Kamsan-sa and their inscriptions], *Yŏksa hakpo* 歷史學報 62 (1974): 75-105, and 63 (1974): 133-162, later compiled with slight revision under the title "Silla Pŏpsangjong (Yugajong) ŭi sŏngnip munje wa Kamsan-sa Mirŭk Amit'a pulsang" 新羅 法相宗(瑜伽宗)의 成立 問題와 甘山寺 彌勒 阿彌陀佛像 in his *T'ongil Silla Pulgyo chogaksa yŏn'gu (sang): wŏnŭm kwa kojŏnmi* 統一新羅 佛教彫刻史 研究(上): 圓音과 古典美 [Study of the Buddhist sculpture of the Unified Silla, vol. 1: Perfect sound and classical beauty] (Seoul: Yegyŏng, 2003): 72-110 (citations in this paper refer to the 2003 edition); Kim Lina (Lena Kim) 金理那, "Shiragi Kanzanji nyoraishiki butsuzō no imon to Nihon butsuzō no kankei" 新羅甘山寺如来式仏像の衣文と日本仏像の関係 [Relationship between the drapery pattern of the Kamsan-sa Buddha type of Silla and that of Japanese Buddha images], *Bukkyō geijutsu* 佛教藝術 110 (1976): 3-24; Saitō Tadashi 齋藤忠, "Shiragi no sōsei kara mita Kanzanjiseki sekizō Amida nyōraizō Miroku bosatsuzō meibun no ichi kaishaku" 新羅の葬制から見た甘山寺跡石造阿弥陀如来像弥勒菩薩像銘文の一解釈 [An interpretation of the inscriptions of the stone Amitābha Buddha and Maitreya bodhisattva images from Kamsan-sa in light of Silla funerary practice], *Chōsen gakuhō* 99/100 (1981): 131-141; Kim Yŏngmi 金英美, "Sŏngdŏk wangdae chŏnje wangkwŏn e taehan il koch'al: Kamsan-sa Mirŭksang Amit'asang myŏngmun kwa kwallyŏn hayŏ" 聖德王代 專制王權에 대한 一考察: 甘山寺 彌勒像·阿彌陀像 銘文과 관련하여 [A reflection on the authoritarian kingship in the reign of King Sŏngdŏk: In relation to the inscriptions of a Maitreya image and an Amitābha image from Kamsan-sa], *Idae sawŏn* 梨大史苑 22/23 (1988): 369-392; So Hyŏnsuk 蘇鉉淑, "Kamsan-sa Mirŭk posal ipsang kwa Amit'a yŏrae ipsang yŏn'gu" 甘山寺 彌勒菩薩立像과 阿彌陀如來立像 研究 [Study of the Maitreya bodhisattva image and the Amitābha Buddha image from Kamsan-sa] (Ihwa Yŏja Taehakkyo sŏksa hagwi nonmun 梨花女子大學校碩士學位論文 [Ewha Womans University M.A. Thesis], 1999). Of these, the works by Mun Myŏngdae and So Hyŏnsuk present the most in-depth discussions regarding the religious significance of the images.

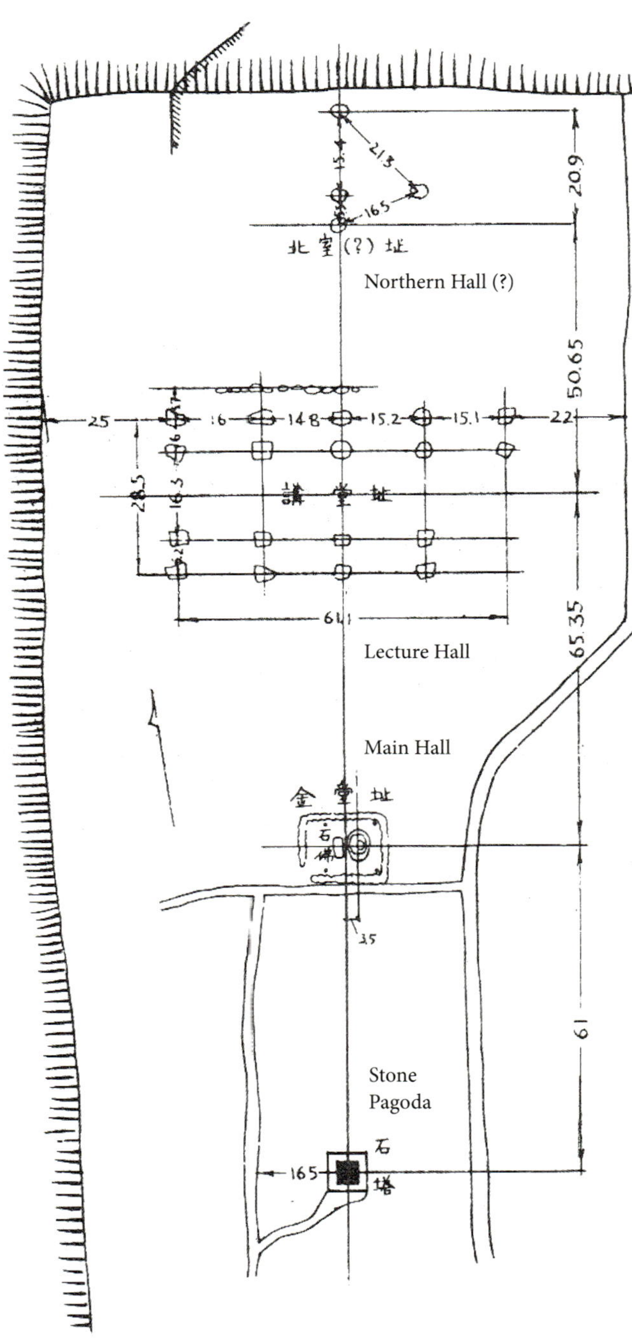

Figure 2.4 Plan of Kamsan-sa, from a survey in 1929. From Fujishima Gaijirō 藤島亥治郎, *Chōsen kenchiku shiron* 朝鮮建築史論 *(Keijō [Seoul], 1935): fig. 131.*

eventually absorbed into the collection of the National Museum of Korea in Seoul. Remains of a temple were also located at the site in a survey conducted in 1929.[5] The temple was of a modest size, its compound measuring sixty meters by thirty meters (fig. 2.4). Most of its buildings had disappeared long before its discovery, except for the remains of a three-story stone pagoda, which was partially reconstructed in 1965 (fig. 2.5).[6] The site of a lecture hall on the northernmost side was indicated by the stone bases for wooden pillars, though the site of the main hall at the center of the temple was barely recognizable. Even the former is now no longer there, and a new modern temple has been built on the western side of the old temple site (fig. 2.6).[7]

The Buddha and the bodhisattva from Kamsan-sa, which are currently on display in the Buddhist sculpture gallery at the National Museum of Korea in Seoul, measure 174 and 183 centimeters high, respectively, not including the mandorla and pedestal of each. These measurements are approximately six *ch'ŏk* 尺, or *chi*, regardless of which *chi*, from Eastern Wei or from Tang, was used during this period.[8] They correspond roughly to the

---

[5] The information above about the discovery of the images and the site is from Fujishima Gaijirō 藤島亥治郎, *Chōsen kenchiku shiron* 朝鮮建築史論 [On the history of Korean architecture] (Keijō [Seoul], 1935): 196, and Nakagiri Isao, "Shiragi Kanzanji sekizō Miroku Amidazō ni tsuite," 275. The 1929 survey was conducted by Fujishima, who was then working as a surveyor for the Japanese colonial government.

[6] Chin Hongsŏp, "Kyŏngju Kamsansaji Sungboksaji ŭi chosa: Silla oak chosagi kisa," 73-74.

[7] The most recent excavation was made in 2001 on the area around the stone pagoda and the assumed location of the main hall. The excavation revealed the remains of two buildings, perhaps the main halls from two different periods. However, the work, conducted on a small scale for less than a month, did not clarify the relationship of the two buildings to the plan made during the 1929 survey, and the report is rather clumsily written. See Chungang Munhwajae Yŏn'guwŏn 中央文化財研究院, *Kyŏngju Kamsansa pŏptangji* 慶州 甘山寺 法堂址 [Remains of shrines at Kamsan-sa of Kyŏngju] (Kyŏngju: Chungang Munhwajae Yŏn'guwŏn and Kamsan-sa, 2001).

[8] The determination of measures used in the design of ancient Korean architecture or sculpture is a complex and controversial problem. It is generally believed that the *ch'ŏk* adopted from the Tang *chi* (c. 29.7 centimeters) was employed in Silla from the late seventh century. However, with Kamsan-sa, Fujishima Gaijirō, who conducted the 1929 survey, suggests that the *chi* of Eastern Wei (c. 29.97 centimeters) was in use. Arai Hiroshi points out that a deviation from the above measures, a unit of approximately 30.8 centimeters, was applied. Fujishima Gaijirō, *Chōsen kenchiku shiron*, 196-198; Arai Hiroshi 新井宏, *Maboroshi no kodai shaku* まぼろしの古代尺 [Phantasmal ancient

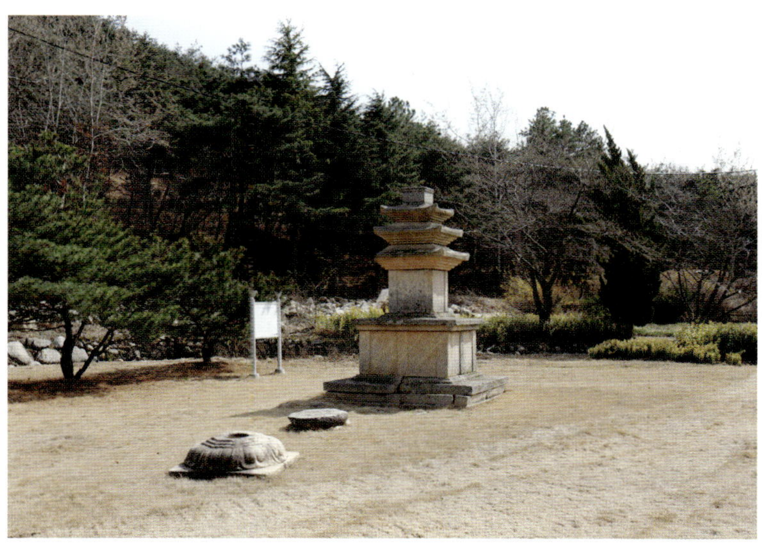

*Figure 2.5 The site of Kamsan-sa with a pagoda (currently incomplete),
facing south. Photograph by Rhi Juhyung.*

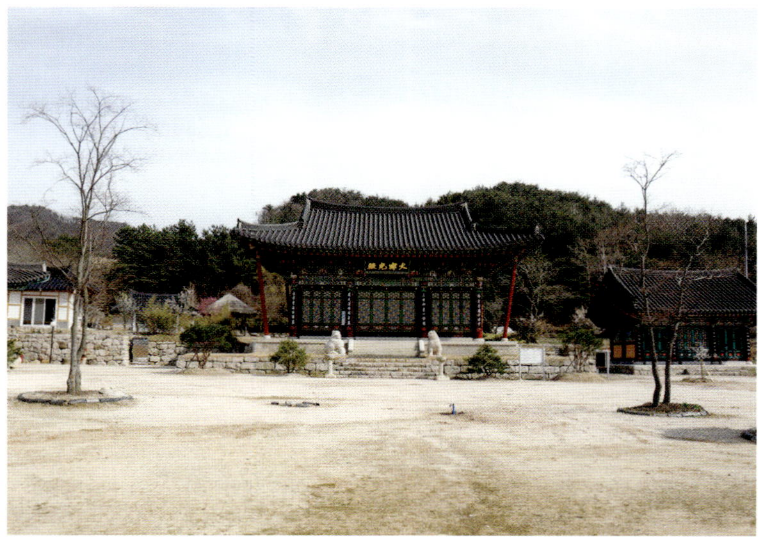

Figure 2.6 Modern temple at the Kamsan-sa site. Photograph by Rhi Juhyung.

average size of extant cult statues that were most likely installed indoors in Silla Buddhist temples. For instance, a sandstone Buddha at the Kyŏngju National Museum is 174 centimeters high, and a gilded-bronze Buddha from Paengnyul-sa 栢栗寺 is 177 centimeters high, as are many other images from the Unified Silla period.[9] Although sculptors probably did not measure dimensions as meticulously as architects did, they must have had a sense of what size—usually a little taller than an average-sized human—would fit an ordinary building. With their mandorlas and pedestals, the Kamsan-sa Buddha and bodhisattva are as tall as 275 and 252 centimeters, as other images of similar size would have been. We know at least that the bodhisattva image was enshrined in the main hall, whose exact dimensions are not clearly known.[10] According to a survey conducted by Fujishima Gaijirō in 1929, the lecture hall facing south measured 18.51 meters wide and 8.63 meters long,[11] and we can assume that, as was usual, the main hall was smaller than the lecture hall. The dedication was thus an ambitious venture for the commissioner of the images.

The patron's name is known through the inscriptions on the images (for the following discussions concerning the inscriptions, also see the translations in the appendix). He was named Kim Chisŏng 金志誠 in the inscription of the bodhisattva and Kim Chijŏn 金志全 in that of the Buddha. It is clear that the two are different names for the same person, as all of the other details about his family relations recorded in the inscriptions are identical.[12] A Korean scholar,

---

shaku] (Tokyo: Yoshikawa Kōbunkan, 1992): 21-53. Regarding the measures used in ancient Korea, also see Yi Chongbong 李宗峯, *Han'guk chungse toryanghyŏngje yŏn'gu* 韓國中世度量衡制研究 [Study of the weight and measure system in medieval Korea] (Seoul: Hyean, 2001): 65-76; Pak Hŭngsu 朴興秀, *Han-Chung toryanghyŏng chedosa* 韓中度量衡制度史 [History of the weight and measure systems in Korea and China] (Seoul: Sŏnggyun'gwan Taehakkyo Ch'ulp'anbu, 1999): 518-555.

[9] For the sandstone Buddha, see Hwang Suyŏng 黃壽永, *Kukpo* 國寶 [National treasures], vol. 4 (Seoul: Yegyŏng sanŏpsa, 1985): pl. 74; for the Paengnyul-sa Buddha, see Lena Kim, *Buddhist Sculpture of Korea*, pl. II-31.

[10] See p. 86.

[11] Fujishima Gaijirō, *Chōsen kenchiku shiron*, 198. The measurements originally given by Fujishima are in the Japanese *shaku* (Kr. *chŏk*, Ch. *chi*): 61.1 *shaku* by 28.5 *shaku*, which equal 18.51 by 8.63 meters.

[12] Suematsu Yasukazu, "Kanzanji Miroku sonzō oyobi Amidabutsu no kakō kōki," 454-455; Ayukai Fusanoshin, *Zakkō*, 14-16; Katsuragi Sueji, *Chōsen kinseki kō*, 204-208; Mun Myŏngdae, "Silla Pŏpsangjong (Yugajong) ŭi sŏngnip munje wa Kamsan-sa Mirŭk Amit'a pulsang," 78.

82

Ch'oe Wansu, has suggested that Kim Chisŏng of the bodhisattva inscription changed his name to Kim Chijŏn a year later, when the Buddha image was dedicated; according to Ch'oe, changing *sŏng* 誠 meaning "sincerity" to *jŏn* (*chŏn*) 全 meaning "wholeness" may have accorded with the orders of the king, who lauded Kim's propitious conduct.[13] This is simply speculation, but it is a possible explanation for the change, unless the two names were simply used alternatively. The inscription informs us that Kim Chisŏng (or Kim Chijŏn; I will use the former throughout this paper to avoid confusion) built a temple called Kamsan-sa with a stone Amitābha image and a stone Maitreya image on the fifteenth day of the second month, seventh year of the Kaiyuan 開元 reign, the cyclical year *kimi* (or *jiwei*) 己未. Although the term Buddha or bodhisattva is not mentioned specifically, we can easily see that the Maitreya was meant for a bodhisattva image, as there is only one Buddha, not two Buddhas: though Maitreya can be either Buddha or bodhisattva, Amitābha cannot be a bodhisattva's name. The bodhisattva was thus Maitreya, and the Buddha was Amitābha. The seventh year of the Tang Kaiyuan reign, the cyclical year *kimi*, corresponds to the eighteenth year of King Sŏngdŏk 聖德 (r. 702-737) of Silla and approximately to 719 of the Common Era. Interestingly, the last two lines of the Amitābha inscription indicate that after accomplishing this meritorious deed, Kim Chisŏng died the following year, on the twenty-second day of the fourth month of the year *kyŏngsin*, or *gengshen* 庚申, or 720 C.E., at the age of sixty-nine. This information was most likely added posthumously to the Amitābha image after the completion of the image and its inscription.[14]

---

[13] Ch'oe Wansu 崔完秀, *Han'guk pulsang ŭi wŏllyu rŭl ch'ajasŏ 2: Mirŭk hasaeng kwa Amit'a ch'urhyŏn* 韓國 佛像의 源流를 찾아서 2: 彌勒下生과 阿彌陀 出現 [Searching for the origin of ancient Korean Buddhist images 2: The descent of Maitreya and the emergence of Amitābha] (Seoul: Taewŏnsa, 2007): 236-241. Ayukai Fusanoshin suggests the change was an attempt to avoid a name identical to that of the king (Sŏngdŏk), who, he presumes, changed the name from Ch'ŏnjung 天中 to Hŭnggwang 興光 and to Chisŏng between the king's seventeenth year (when the Maitreya inscription was written) and two to three years later (when the Amitabha inscription was actually carved). Ayukai Fusanoshin, *Zakkō*, 15-16. However, if that is the reason, he would have changed the entire given name, not just the character *sŏng*. Furthermore, the account that the king was also named Chisŏng, which is, according to the *Samguk sagi* 三國史記, found in the *Tangshu* 唐書 but actually appears in another source, *Cefu yuangui* 冊府元龜 (dated 1005), is probably a mistake for reporting the name of the envoy Kim Chisŏng, who was sent by the king to the Tang court in 705. See n. 15 in this chapter.

[14] Katsuragi Sueji, *Chōsen kinseki kō*, 207-208. Mun Myŏngdae disagrees with

Though Kim Chisŏng is hardly known in literary sources, the inscriptions contain abundant information about him.[15] They indicate that he had acquired the rank of *chungach'an* 重阿湌 or double *ach'an*, an advanced rank within that of *ach'an*, the sixth rank in the seventeen office ranks of Silla.[16] Because he was awarded the rank of *chungach'an* rather than the higher fifth rank, *taeach'an* 大阿湌 (greater *ach'an*), scholars have suspected that he was of *yuktup'um* 六頭品 status, head-rank six in the bone-rank grades of Silla, members of which could not be promoted beyond the sixth rank.[17]

Katsuragi, suggesting that the Amitābha image was completed together with the inscription after the death of Kim Chisŏng. Mun Myŏngdae, "Silla Pŏpsangjong (Yugajong) ŭi sŏngnip munje wa Kamsan-sa Mirŭk Amit'a pulsang." 97. Kim Yŏngmi raises the possibility that the remarks on the death of Kim Chisŏng's mother and father, which appear separately in the two inscriptions, are also later carvings. Kim Yŏngmi, "Sŏngdŏk wangdae chŏnje wangkwŏn e taehan il koch'al," 373-374.

[15] The only other instances in which Kim Chisŏng appears in literary sources are in the Chinese *Cefu yuangui* and the Korean *Samguk sagi*. The *Samguk sagi* says in a note, "The *Tangshu* 唐書 refers to [King Sŏngdŏk] as Kim Chisŏng." *Samguk sagi* 8: King Sŏngdŏk, first year, Han'gukhak Chungang Yŏn'guwŏn, ed., *Yŏkchu Samguk sagi* 譯註 三國史記 [Annotation and translation of the *Samguk sagi*] (Sŏngnam: Han'gukhak Chungang Yŏn'guwŏn Ch'ulp'anbu, 2011): 1:190. However, neither the *Tangshu* nor the *Xin Tangshu* 新唐書 has such an account, and this anomaly is apparently due to the confusion of Kim Pusik 金富軾, the author of the *Samguk sagi* (dated 1145). Kim Pusik's source must have been the *Cefu yuangui* (scroll 970), which says, "In the third month of the first year of Shenlong 神龍 [705; the fourth year of King Sŏngdŏk], the king of Silla, Kim Chisŏng, sent an envoy to the [Tang] court." Based on the account in the *Samguk sagi* that King Sŏngdŏk's name was Yunggi 隆基 and later Ch'ŏnjung 天中, not Chisŏng, Suematsu Yasukazu has argued that the *Cefu yuangui* most likely put the character *qian* 遣 (meaning "send") mistakenly not after "the king of Silla," but after "Kim Chisŏng" and that the correct sentence should have been ". . . the king of Silla sent Kim Chisŏng as an envoy to the [Tang] court." Thus, this record actually refers to Kim Chisŏng's trip to China as a Silla envoy in 705. Suematsu Yasukazu, "Kanzanji Miroku sonzō oyobi Amidabutsu no kakō kōki," 459-460. Suematsu's interpretation is accepted by most scholars. The record for the same year in the *Samguk sagi* simply says, "In the third month, an envoy was sent to Tang and paid a tribute."

[16] As to the seventeen official ranks of Silla, see Ki-baik Lee, *A New History of Korea*, trans. Edward Wagner and Edward Shultz (Seoul: Ilchogak, 1984): 50-51.

[17] Pyŏn T'aesŏp 邊太燮, "Silla kwandŭng ŭi sŏngkyŏk" 新羅官等의 性格 [The nature of the official ranks of Silla], *Yŏksa kyoyuk* 歷史教育 1 (1956): 62-82; Mun

In the office he rose as high as *sirang* 侍郎 (deputy minster) of the *Chipsabu* 執事部, the chancellery, and seems to have been a close aide to Prince Kaewŏn 愷元, the sixth son of King Muyŏl 武烈 (r. 654-661), who served as *sangdaedŭng* 上大等, the head of the Silla aristocrats, between 695 and 704 (during the reigns of King Hyoso 孝昭 [692-702] and King Sŏngdŏk [702-737]).[18] In the Maitreya inscription Kim Chisŏng prays especially for Prince Kaewon "to get away from bustling worldly matters full of defilements and to attain the exquisite reward of no rebirth."

Kim Chisŏng was a cultivated man. The inscriptions say that he was an avid reader of Chinese classics, such as the *Laozi Daodejing* 老子道德經 and the *Zhuangzi* 莊子, and the Buddhist philosophical treatise *Yujia shidilun* 瑜伽師地論, a Chinese translation of the *Yogācārabhūmi-śāstra* by Asaṅga. This account of Kim Chisŏng is specific enough not to be a mere embellishment, although we do not know how common such erudition was among contemporary Silla intellectuals.

Kim Chisŏng made the two images principally for his deceased parents, but he also prayed for the king, Prince Kaewŏn, and his own brothers, sisters, deceased wife, and current wife. The Maitreya image was possibly meant for his mother, while the Amitābha image was intended for his father, as each of them is mentioned separately in the inscriptions on the two images. His father died at forty-seven, and his mother at sixty-six. Because Kim Chisŏng was sixty-eight when he had the images made, the dedication was made at least twenty to forty years after the deaths of his parents. This suggests that the dedication was not simply planned to memorialize his deceased parents. Rather, and more importantly, it was intended to transfer merit to those from whom he benefited or with whom he had family ties while looking ahead to the end of his life, which was only a year away.

The donation of Kim Chisŏng's estate at Kamsan 甘山 funded the building of the temple and the production of the two images. The carving of the images must have been a costly enterprise. Although Kim Chisŏng was not of the highest aristocratic class in Silla, he apparently had enough resources to finance the project. The Amitābha inscription shows that the

---

Myŏngdae, "Silla Pŏpsangjong (Yugajong) ŭi sŏngnip munje wa Kamsan-sa Mirŭk Amit'a pulsang," 87-88.

[18] *Samguk sagi* 8: King Hyoso, fourth year, King Sŏngdŏk, fifth year, *Yŏkchu Samguk sagi*, 12:189, 190; Mun Myŏngdae, "Silla Pŏpsangjong (Yugajong) ŭi sŏngnip munje wa Kamsan-sa Mirŭk Amit'a pulsang," 88-89; Ch'oe Wansu, *Han'guk pulsang ŭi wŏllyu rŭl ch'ajasŏ 2*, 239-241.

inscription, or both inscriptions,[19] were composed by Ch'ong 聰, a *nama* 奈
麻 in the eleventh office rank, who is sometimes identified as Sŏl Ch'ong 薛
聰, the son of the great monk Wŏnhyo 元曉,[20] and that the calligraphy was
done by the monk Sŏk Kyŏngyung 釋京融 and the layman Kim Ch'wiwŏn
金驟源. In many ways, the inscriptions are invaluable documents for the
social and intellectual history of contemporary Silla.

Maitreya and a Devotee

The two Kamsan-sa images demonstrate advanced three-dimensionality,
bodily form, and dress and drapery types in comparison with earlier Korean
images, such as the Buddha triads from Samhwaryŏng 三花嶺 and Pae-ri
拜里 (fig. 2.7) in Kyŏngju (both datable to the early seventh century), and
one in the Kunwi 軍威 cave (late seventh century).[21] The Kamsan-sa images
follow generally the so-called Tang style in their predilection for naturalism

---

[19] Remarks on Ch'ong as well as the two calligraphers appear near the end of the
Amitābha inscription, and, as most scholars agree, it is not clear whether they also
apply to the Maitreya inscription. Kim Yŏngmi suggests that only the Amitābha
inscription was composed by Ch'ong, while the Maitreya inscription must have
been written by Kim Chisŏng himself. Kim Yŏngmi, "Sŏngdŏk wangdae chŏnje
wangkwŏn e taehan il koch'al," 374. Although the deliveries are in the third person
in both inscriptions, the tone is somewhat different, especially in the description
of the donor. Laudatory remarks about the donor, which are more conspicuous in
the Amitābha inscription, are not clearly visible in the Maitreya inscription; rather,
we find in the latter humbling characterizations such as "While trying to amend
wrongs without cleverness, he barely escaped judicial punishment." Closely reading
the two inscriptions, I find myself more than sympathetic with Kim Yŏngmi's suggestion. Still, the prose styles are quite similar between the two inscriptions. It is,
then, perhaps the case that the Maitreya inscription was written by Kim Chisŏng
and polished by Ch'ong, who wrote the Amitābha inscription by rephrasing Kim's
words in the Maitreya inscription in a more coherent order. The Amitābha inscription specifies that Ch'ong wrote it by royal order. Although the two images were
dedicated together, as indicated in the Maitreya inscription, the two inscriptions
were possibly written under different circumstances.

[20] Katsuragi Sueji, *Chōsen kinseki kō*, 209-210. Mun Myŏngdae has expressed
skepticism about Katsuragi's suggestion without specifying a reason, while Ch'oe
Wansu has agreed with Katsuragi. Mun Myŏngdae, "Silla Pŏpsangjong (Yugajong)
ŭi sŏngnip munje wa Kamsan-sa Mirŭk Amit'a pulsang," 89. Ch'oe Wansu, *Han'guk
kodae pulsang ŭi wŏllyu rŭl ch'ajasŏ 2*, 241.

[21] For the triad from Samhwaryŏng and the Buddha in the Kunwi cave, see Lena
Kim, *Buddhist Sculpture of Korea*, pls. I-33, II-2.

and corporeality, but they are somewhat stiffer and more restrained than contemporary or slightly earlier Tang images (fig. 2.8). As a result, Korean scholars have sought their parallels in Chinese images produced during the early part of the seventh century.[22] Though this conservatism may be the product of idiosyncratic Chinese prototypes, which may have influenced them, images from Silla tend to exhibit a similar restraint in adopting naturalistic configurations transmitted from Tang. In any case, this is not seemingly the result of a delay or regression in the transmission of a visual style. Silla and Tang had close diplomatic ties during this period, and Silla sent envoys to the Tang court once or twice a year. Through such official as well as private contacts, such as frequent travels of Buddhist monks, the latest achievements in Chinese literary and material culture were promptly conveyed to Silla. For example, a Buddhist sutra called the *Wugou jingguang datuoluoni jing* 無垢淨光大陀羅尼經, or the *Great Dhāraṇī Sutra of Immaculate and Pure Light*, translated into Chinese by Mituoshan 彌陀山 in 704, was found in a reliquary datable to 706 from a Buddhist pagoda at the site of Hwangbok-sa 皇福寺 in Kyŏngju; this means that the sutra was transmitted to Silla within only two years of its Chinese translation.[23] Kim Chisŏng himself was also an envoy sent to the Tang court in the third month of 705,[24] and some have suggested that he brought the sutra to Silla.[25] Kim Chisŏng was in a position to be best informed about the most up-to-date developments in Chinese Buddhism. He could have been able to employ the latest visual style from China.

Though a virtual pair, the two images differ slightly, especially in their mandorlas and pedestals. Due to these differences, as well as anomalies found in the Amitābha inscription, some scholars have questioned the contemporaneity of these two images. In addition to the remark on Kim Chisŏng's death in 720 in the Amitābha inscription, which was discussed above, as most likely a later carving, the inscription records the post he held

---

[22] Mun Myŏngdae, "Silla Pŏpsangjong (Yugajong) ŭi sŏngnip munje wa Kamsan-sa Miruk Amit'a pulsang," 92-99; Ch'oe Wansu, *Han'guk kodae pulsang ŭi wŏllyu rŭl ch'ajasŏ 2*, 242-253.

[23] Also for two golden Buddhas discovered inside a reliquary from the Hwangbok-sa pagoda datable to around 692 and 706 respectively, see Lena Kim, *Buddhist Sculpture of Korea*, pls. II-12, 13.

[24] See n. 15 above.

[25] So Hyŏnsuk, "Kamsan-sa Miruk posal ipsang kwa Amit'a yŏrae ipsang yŏn'gu," 41; Ch'oe Wansu, *Han'guk kodae pulsang ŭi wŏllyu rŭl ch'ajasŏ 2*, 239.

in the *Chipsabu* as *sirang*. However, the *Samguk sagi* 三國史記, a major historical source about ancient Korea, tells us that *sirang* was created to replace *chŏndaedŭng* 典大等 as late as 747.[26] Based on this apparent anachronism, the Korean scholar Mun Myŏngdae has argued that the Amitābha image, as well as the temple itself, was completed as late as thirty or more years after the creation of the Maitreya image.[27] However, it seems absurd that the carving of a stone statue of this size would have taken as many as three decades, even if we allow for an impressive amount of labor. Furthermore, if the Amitābha image had been created thirty years later, it would not have displayed the same visual homogeneity as the Maitreya image. As to the title *sirang*, the Japanese scholar Suematsu Yasukazu attributes the anomaly to a mistake in the *Samguk sagi*, an argument that makes more sense.[28] Perhaps an advanced technological examination of the inscription's calligraphy will solve this mystery, but this has not yet been attempted. I believe that the two images must have been made in the same workshop within a year of each other, while the minor differences in the mandorlas and pedestals are most likely the result of different hands.

The Maitreya inscription begins by mentioning the creation of a stone Amitābha image and a stone Maitreya image. Although the Amitābha image is named first, preceding the Maitreya image in the inscription, it was actually the Maitreya that was made first. Furthermore, the Maitreya was possibly the principal image in the main hall of the temple. The *Samguk yusa*, another important source for ancient Korean history, particularly on Buddhism, quotes part of the inscriptions on both the Maitreya and the Amitābha and calls the Maitreya "the primary [image] of the golden hall" (*kŭmdangju* 金堂主).[29] The Amitābha inscription recorded in the same text right after the Maitreya inscription lacks the phrase at the beginning. It is not impossible that the phrase was omitted to avoid repetition. Even if this were the case, it is worth noting that this source places the Maitreya image before the Amitābha, and the relative importance of the Maitreya image is evident. Whether the two images were housed together in the main hall is not at all clear, but obviously, Iryŏn 一然 (1206-1289), the author of the

---

[26] *Samguk sagi* 38: "Chikkwan sang," *Yŏkchu Samguk sagi*, 1:518.

[27] Mun Myŏngdae, "Silla Pŏpsangjong (Yugajong) ŭi sŏngnip munje wa Kamsan-sa Mirŭk Amit'a pulsang," 97-99.

[28] Suematsu Yasukazu, "Kanzanji Miroku sonzō oyobi Amidabutsu no kakō kōki," 454-455.

[29] *Samguk yusa* 3: "Namwŏlsan," *Yŏkchu Samguk yusa*, 3:306-308.

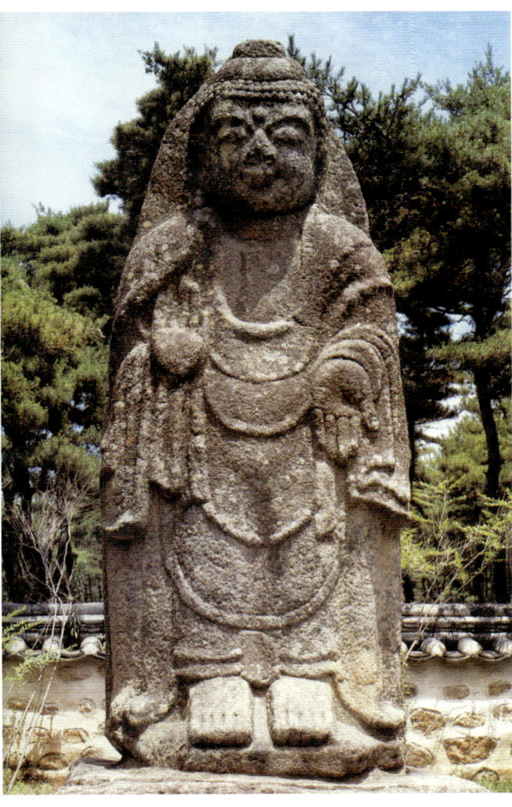

Figure 2.7 *Buddha, Pae-ri, Kyŏngju. Silla, early seventh
century. From Hwang Suyŏng 黃壽永, Sŏkpul 石佛 (Seoul:
Yegyŏng Sanŏpsa, 1935): Plate 12.*

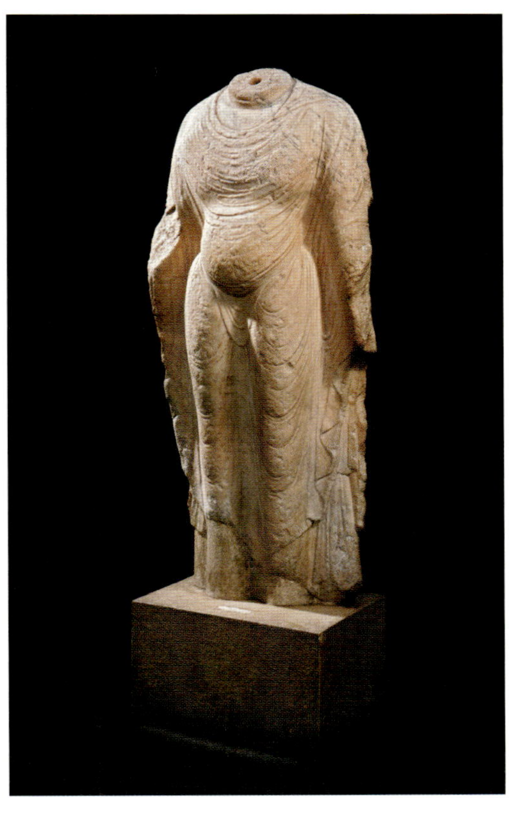

Figure 2.8 *Buddha. Tang, early eighth century.
© Victoria and Albert Museum, London.*

Samguk yusa, saw the Maitreya image standing at the center of the main
hall during the thirteenth century.

In the Buddhist pantheon, a Buddha is obviously superior to a bodhisattva in its hierarchy. But why then was the bodhisattva Maitreya
treated as more important than the Buddha Amitābha at Kamsan-sa? This
was obviously due to the special meaning attached to Maitreya bodhisattva
by Kim Chisŏng. The inscriptions repeatedly state that Kim Chisŏng was
an ardent admirer of the *Yogācārabhūmi*: "He aspired to the profundity
and serenity of Asaṅga['s treatise]"; "He thoroughly studied the teachings

89

of the seventeen stages [of the *Yogācārabhūmi*]"; "Revering and yearning
after the true creed presented by Asaṅga, he often read the *Yogācārabhūmi*."
Asaṅga (or Much'ak 無著 in the inscriptions) was an eminent Indian
master of the Yogācāra school active in the fourth century, to whom the
Yogācārabhūmi was conveyed by Maitreya bodhisattva from the Tuṣita
heaven. The *Datang xiyuji* 大唐西域記 by Xuanzang 玄奘, who brought the
Indian text to China in 645 and produced the first complete translation in
Chinese several years later, writes:

> To the southwest of the city [the capital of Ayodhyā] five or six
> *li*, in an extensive grove of mango trees, is an old monastery; this
> is where Asaṅga bodhisattva pursued his studies and directed the
> men of the age. Asaṅga bodhisattva went up by night to the palace
> of Maitreya bodhisattva, and there received the *Yogācārabhūmi-
> śāstra*, the *Mahāyānasūtrālaṅkāra*, the *Madhyāntavibhāga-śāstra*,
> etc., and by day declared these to the great congregations, in their
> deep principles.[30]

Thus, the repeated reference to Asaṅga in the Kamsan-sa inscriptions
does not merely indicate Kim Chisŏng's admiration for Asaṅga but suggests, more significantly, his devout reverence for the text's ultimate exponent, Maitreya. The identity of Maitreya, who taught Asaṅga, is debated
in modern scholarship—as to whether he was a celestial bodhisattva at the
stage of *ekajātipratibaddha* (on the candidacy of one more birth) or a historical person—but the second possibility seems to be taken less seriously
at present.[31] The attribution of the *Yogācārabhūmi* to Maitreya in Chinese
Buddhism can be understood as the miraculous transmission of the text
from Maitreya bodhisattva to Asaṅga. Along with the *Yogācārabhūmi*, this

---

[30] Samuel Beal, trans., *Si-yu-ki, Buddhist Records of the Western World*, vol. 1
(London: Trübner, 1884): 226 (with modification); cf. T2085, 51:896b.

[31] For various ideas regarding the identity of Maitreya in relation to the
Yogācārabhūmi, see Ui Hakuju 宇井伯壽, *Indo tetsugakushi* 印度哲學史 [History of
Indian philosophy] (Tokyo: Iwanami Shoten, 1932): 335-386; Hakamaya Noriaki
袴谷憲昭, "Yugakōha no bunken" 瑜伽行派の文献 [Literature of Yogācāra], *Kōza
daijō Bukkyō* 講座大乗仏教, vol. 8: *Yuishiki shisō* 唯識思想 (Tokyo: Shujūsha, 1982):
84-85; Florin Deleanu, *The Chapter on the Mundane Path (Laukikamārga) in the
Śrāvakabhūmi: A Trilingual Edition (Sanskrit, Tibetan, Chinese), Annotated Translation and Introductory Study* (Tokyo: The International Institute for Buddhist
Studies, 2006): 1:154-156, 194-196.

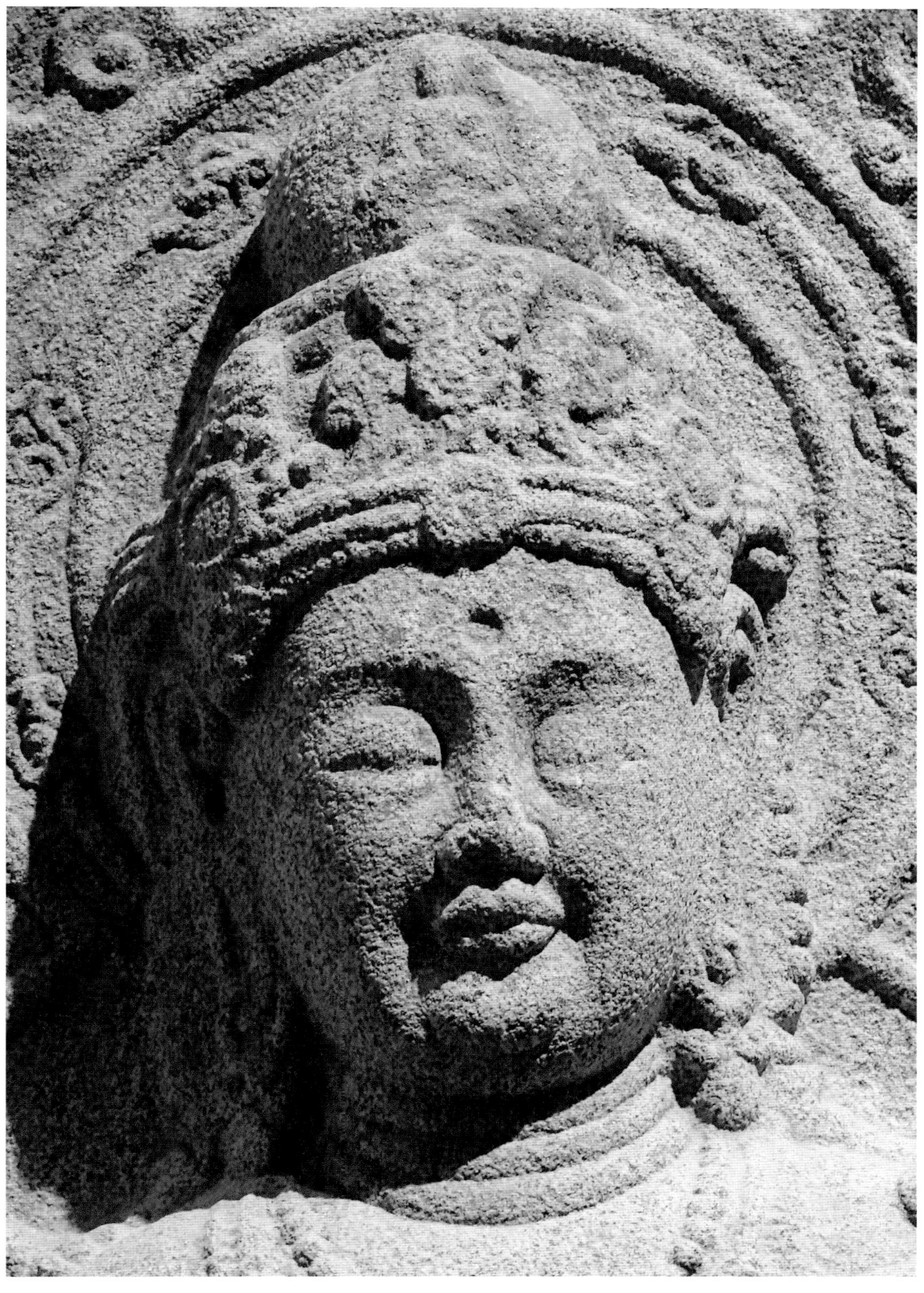

*Figure 2.9 Detail of Figure 2.2.
Photograph by Rhi Juyung.*

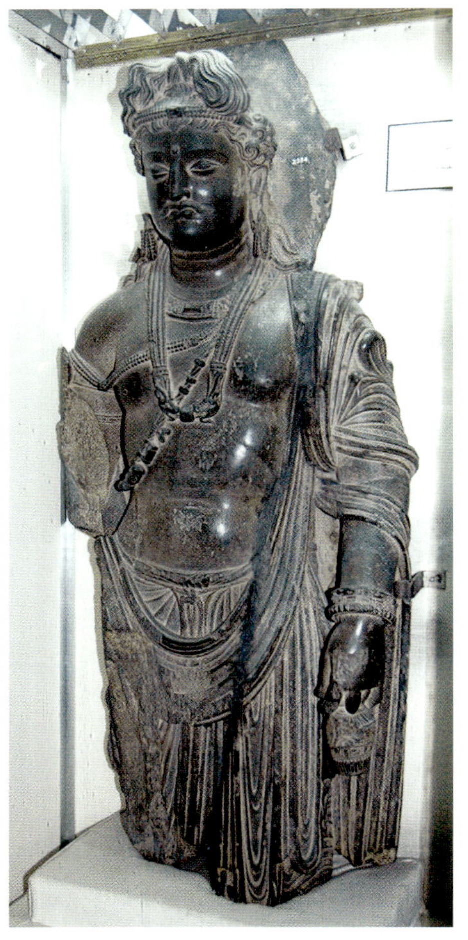
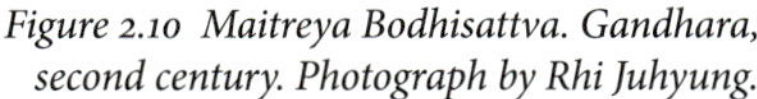

Figure 2.10 *Maitreya Bodhisattva. Gandhara,
second century. Photograph by Rhi Juhyung.*

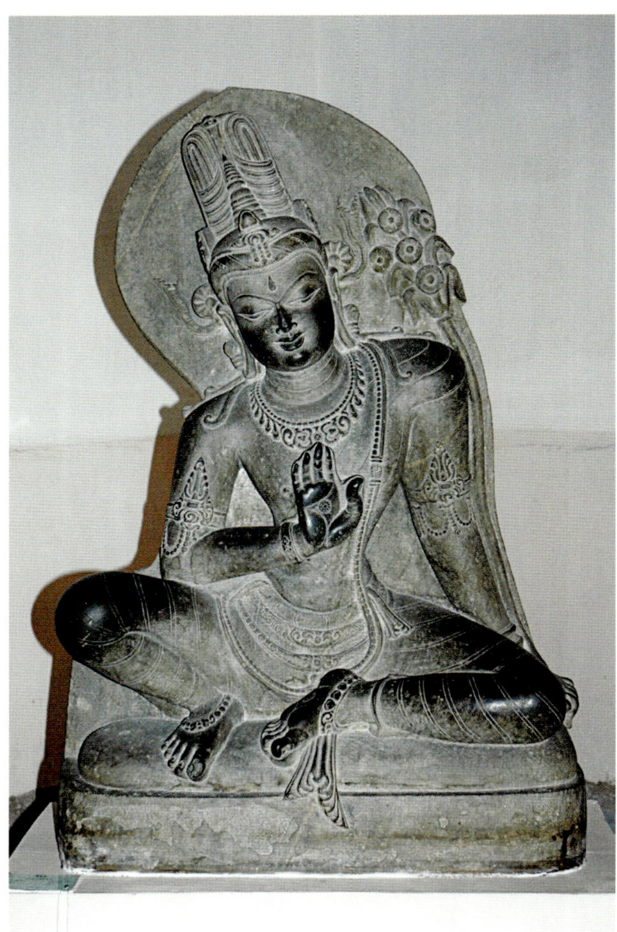

Figure 2.11 *Maitreya Bodhisattva, from Hasra Kol,
tenth century. Patna Museum. Photograph by EPIBM.*

tradition must have been well known in Silla. It was thus Maitreya bodhisattva who lay behind Kim Chisŏng's admiration for the *Yogācārabhūmi*,
and Maitreya represented in the Kamsan-sa image is none other than the
bodhisattva as the legendary exponent of the text.

Maitreya Descending

Here we face a more difficult question: Why does the Kamsan-sa Maitreya take such a singularly idiosyncratic form? The Kamsan-sa Maitreya is a standing image wearing a headdress decorated with a small Buddha in the center (fig. 2.9). This is iconographically almost unparalleled in the bodhisattva Maitreya in East Asia, including Korea. On the Indian subcontinent, standing images of Maitreya bodhisattva are found throughout history in the regions from Gandhara to eastern India. They usually hold a water bottle in the earlier periods (fig. 2.10) and later often a sprig of *nāgapuṣpa* flowers (fig. 2.11).[32] A small Buddha in a headdress is not seen in any bodhisattvas that can be securely confirmed as Maitreya; instead, an Indian-style stupa is commonly carved on the headdress in later periods (fig. 2.11).[33] In China, images of Maitreya bodhisattva were commonly made during the fifth and sixth centuries, usually in the crossed-ankle pose (fig. 2.12), identified as the bodhisattva in the Tuṣita heaven, and occasionally in the pensive pose, perhaps identifiable as the bodhisattva in his last human incarnation (fig. 2.13).[34] However, the standing type is seldom found among images

---

[32] Miyaji Akira 宮治昭, "Indo ni okeru Miroku zuzō no hensen" インドにおける弥勒図像の変遷 [Transformation of the iconography of Maitreya in India], in his *Nehan to Miroku no zuzōgaku* 涅槃と弥勒の図像学 [Iconology of the *mahāparinirvāṇa* and Maitreya] (Tokyo: Yoshikawa Kōbunkan, 1992): 355-386; Inchang Kim, *The Future Buddha Maitreya: An Iconological Study* (New Delhi: D.K. Printworld, 1997). For Maitreya images holding a *nāgapuṣpa* flower in Korea, see Son Yŏngmun 孫永文, "Koryŏ sidae yonghwa suin Mirŭk tosang yŏn'gu" 高麗時代 龍華手印 彌勒圖像 研究 [Study of the iconography of Maitreya holding *nāgapuṣpa* in the Koryŏ period], *Misulsahak yŏn'gu* 美術史學研究 252 (2006): 122-129.

[33] Miyaji Akira presents two Indian examples from Kushan Mathura and Gupta Sarnath, but neither of them is clearly Maitreya. Miyaji Akira, "Indo ni okeru Miroku zuzō no hensen," figs. 204, 211. Also see Inchang Kim, *The Future Buddha Maitreya*, 66-69, 128-129, figs. 35, 36, 104. I believe that the example that Miyaji cites from Kushan Mathura represents Siddhārtha bodhisattva. See Yi Chuhyŏng (Rhi Juhyung) 李柱亨, "K'usyan sidae Mat'ura posalhyŏng ilkki" 쿠샨시대 마투라 菩薩型 읽기 [Reading bodhisattva types from Kushan Mathura], *Kogo yŏksahak chi* 考古歷史學誌 16 (2000): 405-406.

[34] For the identification of Maitreya in these two types as one in the Tuṣita heaven and one in the last human incarnation, see *Chūgoku sekkutsu Tonkō Bakkōkutsu* 中國石窟 敦煌莫高窟, vol. 1 (Tokyo: Heibonsha, 1981): explanations of plates 18, 19. Since the relevant remarks appear only in the Japanese edition, not in the Chinese edition, they are most likely the ideas of Tō Kengō 鄧健吾 (Higashiyama Kengō 東山健吾), who wrote supplements to the plate explanations originally written by Chinese

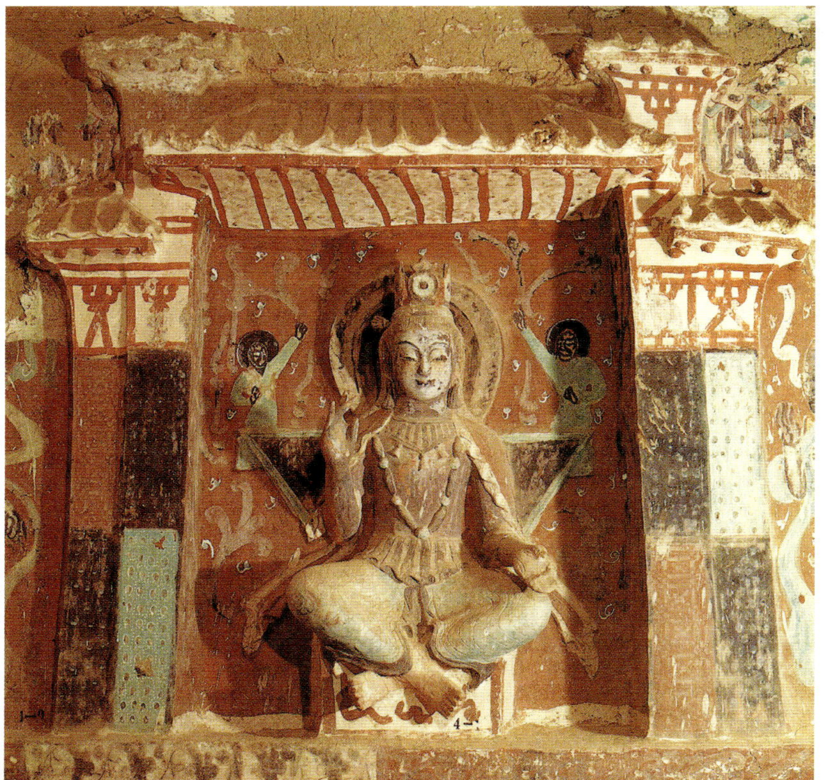

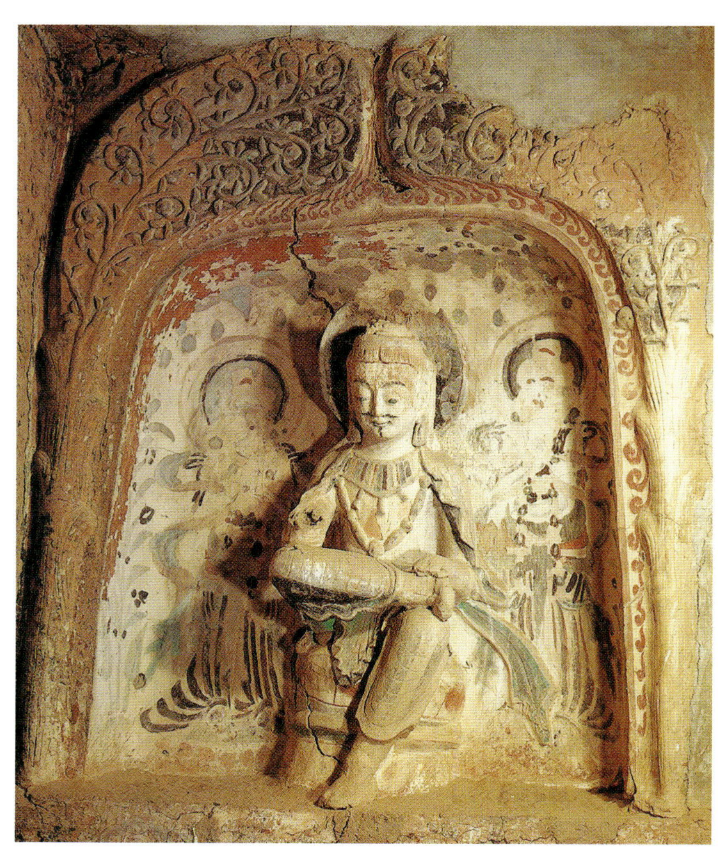

Figure 2.13 Pensive Bodhisattva, Dunhuang Cave 275, China. Early fifth century, China. From 敦煌文物研究所 [Dunhuang Research Institute], ed., Dunhuang Mogao ku 敦煌 莫高窟, vol. 1. (Beijing: Wenwu Chubanshe, 1982): Plate 19.

identified as Maitreya by their inscriptions.[35] On the contrary, standing bodhisattvas are frequently identified as Avalokiteśvara, and often hold a lotus in the early period and a water bottle and/or a willow twig later on (fig. 2.14).[36] From the late sixth century on, a standing Avalokiteśvara frequently bears a small Buddha in the headdress (fig. 2.15). This pattern was generally followed in Korea, except that a crossed-ankle pose Maitreya was apparently never adopted. According to these iconographic conventions, the Kamsan-sa Maitreya is apparently much closer to bodhisattva images known as Avalokiteśvara. Without the inscriptions, modern scholars would have readily identified it as Avalokiteśvara.

How did this deviation from the conventional iconographic pattern come about? It is hard to imagine that this was a decision made by the sculptor. During the previous two centuries in Silla, Maitreya, both as a Buddha and a bodhisattva, enjoyed great popularity in the Buddhist cultic practice. The pensive type was well established in visual representations of

scholars. The identification of bodhisattva images in the pensive pose in China in general, often called *siwei* 思惟 figures in Chinese, is a much more complex issue. Although some scholars prefer to identify the majority of them as Siddhārtha (Jung-hee Lee, "The Origins and Development of the Pensive Bodhisattva Images of Asia," *Artibus Asiae* 53.3/4 [1993]: 317-344), the presence of Maitreya among them is generally acknowledged despite differences in interpreting their significance (Yu-min Lee, "The Maitreya Cult and Its Art in Early China" [Ph.D. dissertation, Ohio State University, 1983]: 301-315; Denise Leidy, "The Ssu-wei Figure in Sixth-Century A.D. Chinese Buddhist Sculpture," *Archives of Asian Art* 43 [1990]: 21-37). For Maitreya images in the crossed-ankle pose in China, see Ishimatsu Hinako 石松日奈子, "Chūgoku kōkyaku bosatsuzō kō" 中国交脚菩薩像考 [Study of Chinese crossed-ankle bodhisattva images], in her *Hokugi Bukkyō zōzōshi no kenkyū* 北魏仏教造像史の研究 [Study on the history of Northern Wei Buddhist images] (Tokyo: Buryukke, 2005): 219-240.

[35] Maitreya bodhisattva in the standing type is found among only a handful of examples from the third and fourth centuries, which exhibit conspicuous influence from India. One of these rare examples is a gilded bronze image in the Fujii Yurinkan. Marylin Rhie, *Early Buddhist Art of China and Central Asia*, vol. 1 (Leiden: Brill, 1999): Plate. III and fig. 2.32. Also see Yu-min Lee, "The Maitreya Cult and Its Art in Early China," 264-269; Lee Yumin 李玉珉, "Sui Tang zhi Mile xinyang yu tuxiang" 隋唐之彌勒信仰與圖像 [Maitreya cult and iconography during Sui and Tang], *Yishuxue* 藝術學 1 (1987): 91-117.

[36] For Chinese Avalokiteśvara images that hold a lotus, a jewel, or a willow twig as well as their significance, see Kang Hŭijŏng 姜熺靜, *Chungguk Kwanŭm posalsang yŏn'gu* 中國觀音菩薩像研究 [Study of Chinese Avalokiteśvara images] (Seoul: Ilchisa, 2004): 71-204.

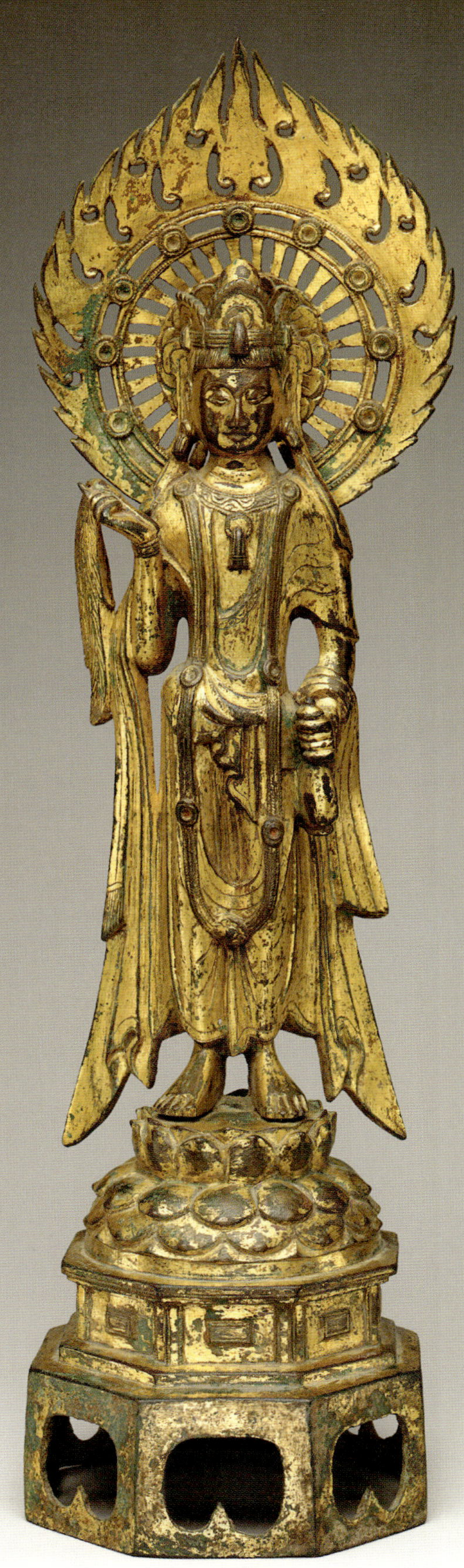

Figure 2.14 *Avalokiteśvara Bodhisattva. Sui, late sixth century. The Metropolitan Museum of Art, Rogers Fund, 1912 (12.161) Image © The Metropolitan Museum of Art.*

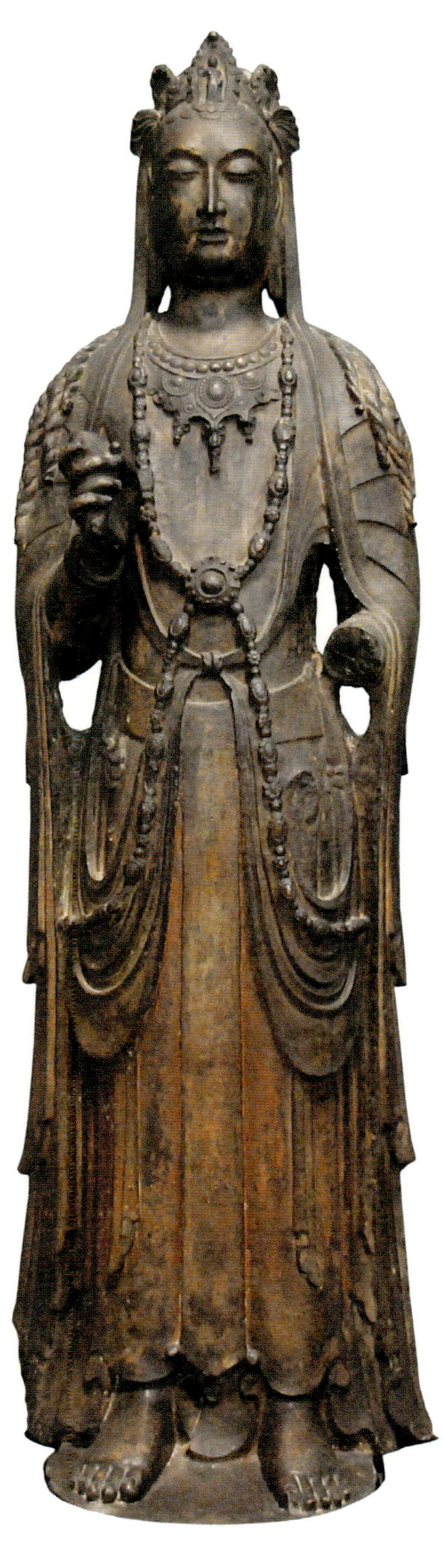

Figure 2.15 Avalokiteśvara Bodhisattva, from Xiangdangshan, China. Late sixth century. Penn Museum. Photograph by Rhi Juhyung.

Maitreya as a bodhisattva (fig. 2.1). Although in China the type was apparently used both for the prince Siddhārtha and the bodhisattva Maitreya, it seems to have been exclusively used for Maitreya in Silla.[37] Despite disagreement among specialists, I believe that the two famous gilded-bronze pensive images at the National Museum in Seoul were both in Buddhist temples in Kyŏngju.[38] From the late seventh century on, Maitreya bodhisattva ceased to enjoy the same popularity in image-making, but there is no doubt that the two pensive images were worshiped in Kyŏnjgu. If one were commissioned to make a Maitreya image, it would have been natural to turn to this eminent type. However, a different decision was made for the Kamsan-sa Maitreya.

Most likely, Kim Chisŏng himself deliberately selected the unique iconography that we see in the Kamsan-sa image. What might have brought about this choice? One cannot rule out the possibility that a fresh impetus was provided by the transmission of a new prototype from outside Korea. Since such a type would have been hardly known in China, it might have been an Indian type, if not itself directly transmitted from India. During the sixth and seventh centuries in India, Maitreya bodhisattva was commonly portrayed as a standing attendant figure in a Buddha triad, along with Avalokiteśvara, as we see in Buddhist caves from this period in Aurangabad and Ellora.[39] A metal figurine representing Maitreya in such a form could have been brought to Silla. However, a weakness of this hypothesis is that Maitreya images from India usually have a stupa on the headdress, not a Buddha, and there is little evidence to support it substantially. This theory of Indian inspiration is thus far short of being a satisfactory answer to our question. The Kamsan-sa Maitreya is a puzzling figure that cannot be explained by a transmission model familiar to art historians.

---

[37] For pensive bodhisattvas in China and Korea, see Denise Leidy, "The Ssu-wei Figure in Sixth-Century A.D. Chinese Buddhist Sculpture," 21-37; Junghee Lee, "The Origins and Development of the Pensive Bodhisattva Images of Asia," 317-349.

[38] Yi Chuhyŏng (Rhi Juhyung), "Han'guk Pulgyo chogak ŭi chasaengsŏngnon ŭl wihan sogo" 韓國 佛教彫刻의 自生性論을 위한 小考 [Reflections for a discourse on the autonomous character of Korean Buddhist sculpture], in *Han'guk misul ŭi chasaengsŏng* 韓國美術의 自生性 [The autonomous character of Korean art] (Seoul: Han'gilsa, 1999): 118-119. For the controversy regarding the origins of the two pensive bodhisattvas among the three kingdoms, see a brief survey by Kim Lina (Kim Lena), "Kukpo pan'ga sayusang chejakkuk ŭl al su ŏptta" 國寶 半跏思惟像 製作國을 알 수 없다 [National-treasure pensive bodhisattvas: The countries of origin are unknown], *Gana Art* (July & August 1994): 40-43.

[39] Miyaji Akira, "Indo ni okeru Miroku zuzō no hensen," 365-376.

98

The most plausible source for the imagery of the Kamsan-sa Maitreya is perhaps Kim Chisŏng's own visionary experience of the bodhisattva. Accounts concerning Maitreya's miraculous transmission of the *Yogācārabhūmi* to Asaṅga in Buddhist sources are full of elements that could have easily prompted visualization. An account in the *Posoupandou fashi zhuan* 婆藪槃豆法師傳 or the *Biography of Vasubandhu*, translated into Chinese by Paramārtha in the sixth century, is the most elaborate.

> Thinking that it would not be right to drop it [the doctrine of nothingness peculiar to Hīnayāna] altogether, he [Asaṅga, called also Vasubandhu[40]] went up to the Tuṣita heaven . . . and inquired of Maitreya, the bodhisattva, who expounded for him the doctrine of nothingness belonging to Mahāyāna. When he returned to Jambudvīpa he investigated by the methods explained to him, and soon became enlightened. . . . He afterwards often went up to the Tuṣita heaven in order to ask Maitreya the doctrine of the Mahāyāna sutras. The bodhisattva expounded it extensively for him. Whenever he acquired anything, he used to come back to Jambudvīpa to teach it to others. Most of those hearing him did not believe him. Asaṅga, teacher of the dharma, then prayed, saying: "I now intend to make all beings fully believe in the doctrine of Mahāyāna. I only pray thee, O Great Master, to come down to Jambudvīpa and propound Mahāyāna in order that all beings may be fully convinced of it." Maitreya, thereupon, in accordance with his prayer, came down to Jambudvīpa at night, flooding it with great rays of light, had a large assembly of those connected with (the dharma) called in a lecture hall, and began to recite the *Sutra of the Seventeen Stages (Saptadaśabhūmi).* After having recited a passage he would explain its purport. The *Seventeen Stages* was finished during the nights of four months. Although all were together in one and the same hall listening to the discourse, it was, nevertheless, only Asaṅga, teacher of the dharma, who had access to the bodhisattva Maitreya, while the others could merely hear him from afar. At night, all together heard the religious discourse by Maitreya, while in the daytime Asaṅga, teacher of the dharma, commented once again, for the sake of the others, upon

---

[40] Although Vasubandhu is known as a younger brother of Asaṅga, the *Biography of Vasubandhu* says that all three brothers of Asaṅga went initially by the same name, Vasubandhu.

what was taught by the bodhisattva. In this way all the people could
hear and believe in the doctrine of Mahayana.[41]

This text is by far the most detailed source for the miraculous encounter between Maitreya and Asaṅga. While the *Datang xiyuji* by Xuanzang
speaks only of Asaṅga ascending to the Tuṣita heaven to hear lectures from
Maitreya (see p. 88), the *Biography of Vasubandhu* tells of Maitreya descending to our world in a sumptuous vision.

The account in the *Biography of Vasubandhu* must have been well
known to Buddhists in China and Korea during the seventh and eighth
centuries. For example, the Chinese master Huizhao 慧沼, who succeeded
Kuiji 窺基 as a patriarch of the Faxiang 法相 or *Dharmalakṣaṇa* school
established with Xuanzang's translation of the *Yogācārabhūmi*, describes the
incident in his *Chengweishilun liaoyideng* 成唯識論了義燈, a commentary
on the *Chengweishilun*, and his narrative is obviously based on the *Biography of Vasubandhu*.

[Although Asaṅga heard the theory of emptiness pertaining to
Hīnayāna from the *arhat* Piṇḍola] the meaning was not secure,
and the logic was not proper. Therefore, with supernatural power
he went up to the Tuṣita heaven and asked Maitreya bodhisattva. The bodhisattva explained the theory of emptiness pertaining
to Mahāyāna. He came back and meditated, immediately attaining enlightenment. Thus, he was named Asaṅga, which means
"No attachment." Later many times he went to the Tuṣita heaven
and questioned Maitreya on the meaning of Mahāyāna sutras. He
explained to other people what he had heard, but many of them
did not trust it. He suddenly made a wish that he would ask the
Maitreya bodhisattva to descend and preach on Mahāyāna, having
the sentient beings see the bodhisattva and all gain belief. Then, at
night when the bodhisattva descended as Asaṅga had wished, he
emitted great light and assembled those who had good conditions.
Maitreya preached on the *Seventeen Stages* in Ayodhyā. Although
they were in the same hall, only Asaṅga was able to have access to
the bodhisattva, and the others only heard the preaching or saw
mysterious occurrences. At the time, Master Asaṅga preached for

---

[41] Takakusu Junjiro, trans., "The Life of Vasu-bandhu by Paramārtha," *T'oung
Pao*, 2nd ser., 5-3 (1904): 273-274 (with modification), cf. T2049, 50:188c.

the others, and thus they first developed belief in the meaning of
the dharma of Mahāyāna.[42]

A description in the *Yujialunji* 瑜伽論記, a vast commentary on the
Yogācārabhūmi, by the Silla monk Tullyun 遁輪, who was active in China
possibly during the late seventh century, is also similar.

Asaṅga attained the first stage (*bhūmi*) and achieved the great
light *samādhi* and the great miraculous power. He paid homage to
the Great Mercy [i.e., Maitreya] and asked to preach this treatise
[*Yogācārabhūmi*], etc. Maitreya bodhisattva agreed to Asaṅga's wish.
Every night, the bodhisattva descended from the Tuṣita heaven to
Asaṅga's meditation cell[43] and preached on the verses of five trea-
tises: the *Yujialun* 瑜伽論 (*Yogācārabhūmi*), the *Fenbieguansuo
mingfenbie yujialun* 分別觀所名分別瑜伽論,[44] the *Dazhuangyan-
lun* 大莊嚴論 (*Mahāyānasūtrālaṅkāra*), the *Bianzhongbianlun* 辨
中邊論 (*Madhyāntavibhāga*), and the *Jingangboruolun* 金剛般若論
(*Vajracchedikaprajñāpāramitāsūtra-śāstra*).[45] At the time, among his
disciples, some saw light without seeing the countenance of the bodhisattva or hearing the teaching; some saw the countenance without hearing the teaching; some saw the countenance and heard the
teaching. However, as the succession of time is far away, their names

---

[42] T1832, 43:659c-660a.

[43] *Chanxing* 禪省. This term seems to be found nowhere except for this text.
Karashima Seishi, whom I consulted for its meaning, suggests that it was probably
derived from the Sanskrit word *prahāṇa-śālā* and was an equivalent for *chanfang* 禪
坊 or 禪房. I thank Prof. Karashima for providing this information.

[44] A text by the name of the *Fenbieguansuo mingfenbie yujialun* does not seem
to be found elsewhere in the Buddhist textual tradition, and what its title exactly
means is not clear. In the Jinling 金陵 edition used for collation with the Shūkyō
daigaku 宗教大學 edition in the creation of the Taishō edition, one of the characters
in the title, *suo* 所, is written differently as *xing* 行, and my colleague Ahn Sungdoo
(An Sŏngdu 安性斗) suspects that the *Fenbieguanxing mingfenbie yujialun* 分別觀
行名分別瑜伽論 perhaps makes better sense.

[45] It is interesting that Tullyun includes the *Vajracchedikaprajñāpāramitāsūtra-
śāstra* as well as the text of an otherwise unknown title, *Fenbieguansuo mingfenbie yujialun*, as writings transmitted by Maitreya, while Xuanzang specifies
only three texts, the *Yogācārabhūmi-śāstra*, the *Mahāyānasūtrālaṅkāra*, and the
Madhyāntavibhāga-śāstra.

are lost. Only Asaṅga and the celestial beings were edified by Maitreya and received all the teaching.[46]

During the period when cultural contact between Tang and Silla was almost instantaneous, as we saw in the transmission of the *Wugou jingguang datuoluoni jing*,[47] these texts must also have quickly reached the Buddhists of Silla. The accounts of the miraculous encounter described in these texts would have left a deep impression on anyone who was interested in the *Yogācārabhūmi*, such as Kim Chisŏng. Reading the *Yogācārabhūmi*, Kim Chisŏng could have easily visualized Maitreya in the manner in which the bodhisattva is described in these texts. Kim Chisŏng's vision of Maitreya was apparently the bodhisattva descending from the Tuṣita heaven. If it had been the vision of Maitreya residing in Tuṣita, he would have chosen a seated image instead of the standing one.[48]

Seeing Maitreya
Visualization was a popular practice in early Chinese Buddhism; so was visualization directed to Maitreya, as attested by literary sources.[49] Chinese monastic experience in the Maitreya visualization usually speaks of monks in the middle of a *samādhi* ascending to the Tuṣita heaven and meeting

---

[46] T1828, 42:311b.

[47] It is also notable that the *Jinguangming zuishengwang jing* 金光明最勝王經 translated by Yijing 義淨 in 703 was brought to Silla in the next year by an envoy, Kim Sayang 金思讓, who reached China in 703. So Hyŏnsuk, "Kamsan-sa Mirŭk posal ipsang kwa Amit'a yŏrae ipsang yŏn'gu," 40-41, cf. *Samguk sagi* 8: King Sŏngdŏk, third year, *Yŏkchu Samguk sagi*, 1:190.

[48] When I presented this paper for the second time, at a meeting of the Association of Art History and Visual Culture in Seoul in June 2010, the discussant Nam Dongsin, a Buddhist history specialist, suggested that Sŏl Ch'ong, the son of Wŏnhyo, who has been identified as the composer of the Kamsan-sa inscriptions by some scholars, could have influenced Kim Chisŏng's choice of the iconographic type for Maitreya. Ch'ong in the inscriptions was possibly none other than Sŏl Ch'ong, and thus Nam Dongsin's imaginative suggestion is quite stimulating. However, it would be difficult to pursue this possibility without any supporting evidence.

[49] Liu Huida 刘慧达, "Beiwei shiku yu chan" 北魏石窟与禅 [Northern Wei caves and meditation], *Kaogu xuebao* 考古学报, no. 3 (1978): 337-352, especially, 346-349, cf. Alexander Soper, *Literary Evidence for Early Buddhist Art in China* (Ascona: Artibus Asiae, 1959): 214-216.

Maitreya.[50] Its principal scriptural source, the *Guan Milepusa shangsheng
Doushuaitian jing* 觀彌勒菩薩上生兜率天經 or the *Sutra of the Visualization of Maitreya's Rebirth Above in the Tuṣita Heaven* translated by Juqu
Jingsheng 沮渠京聲 in the fifth century, recounts in detail the way Maitreya
in Tuṣita should be visualized, and describes Maitreya reborn in the Tuṣita
heaven in the following words:

> At the time, in the Maṇi hall on the Seven Treasures terrace in
> the Tuṣita heaven a lion pedestal will suddenly appear. [Maitreya will be] seated cross-legged on a lotus. His body will be
> in the golden *jambūnada* color. He will be sixteen *yojana* tall.
> All thirty-two *lakṣaṇas* and eighty *anuvyañjanas* will be present in beautiful form. The hair on the *uṣṇīṣa* will be of the color
> of purple *vaiḍūrya*. The celestial crown will be decorated with
> *śakrābhilagna maṇi* and thousands of billions of *kiṃśuka* jewels.
> The crown will have ten billion colors, and in each color innumerable hundreds of thousands of incarnate (*nirmāṇa*) Buddhas
> will be present with attendant incarnate bodhisattvas.[51]

The sutra also explains the merit to be obtained by making Maitreya
images.

> If a sentient being in the future, having heard the compassion of
> the bodhisattva, makes an image, decorates it with incense, flowers, clothes, banners and umbrellas, worships it, and meditates on
> it, then when that person is about to die, Maitreya bodhisattva will
> emit light from the *ūrṇa* on his eyebrows and arrive with heavenly
> beings to greet the person. Then, the person will immediately attain
> rebirth [in the Tuṣita heaven].[52]

Numerous Maitreya images created in early Chinese Buddhist art—
especially in the Dunhuang, Yungang, and Longmen caves during the fifth
and sixth centuries—accord with these textual descriptions (fig. 2.12). It is

---

[50] *Gaosengzhuan* 高僧傳, T2059, 50:339c (Zhiyan 智嚴), 399b (Daofa 道法);
Mingsengzhuan chao 名僧傳抄, in *Xuzangjing* 續藏經, no. 1523: 358b; cf. Soper, 32
(no. 33, Daofa).

[51] T452, 14:419c.

[52] T452, 14:420b.

believed that they represent the bodhisattva in the Tuṣita heaven, and that
a number of them are linked to the practice of visualization.[53] This early perception of and practice about Maitreya that parallels the *Sutra of the Visualization of Maitreya's Rebirth Above* must have affected the Buddhists of Silla
when they imagined Maitreya, although the visual imagery of Maitreya in
Korea took a somewhat different course, as Maitreya images in the crossed-
ankle pose, the most prevalent type in China, were never employed in Korea.

In any case, that such visualization was taken seriously by the Buddhists
of Silla is reflected in Wŏnhyo's commentary on the *Sutra of the Visualization of Maitreya's Rebirth Above*, the *Mirŭk sangsaenggyŏng chongyo* 彌勒上
生經宗要. In this commentary Wŏnhyo discusses what visualization in the
sutra means and what constitutes this practice.

> Visualization here is of two kinds. The first is to visualize the majes-
> tic adornments of the [Tuṣita] heaven as the setting for rebirth, and
> the second is to visualize the superiority of receiving rebirth [there]
> as a bodhisattva. One concentrates one's thoughts in a detailed
> visual examination and so this [technique] is called *samādhi*.[54]

While elucidating the concordances and discrepancies between three
major sutras on Maitreya—the *Sutra of the Visualization of Maitreya's
Rebirth Above*, the *Sutra on Maitreya's Rebirth Below* (*Mile xiasheng jing*
彌勒下生經),[55] and the *Sutra on Maitreya's Achieving Buddhahood* (*Mile*

---

[53] Ishimatsu Hinako, "Chūgoku kōkyaku bosatsuzō kō," 219-240; Stanley K.
Abe, "Art and Practice in a Fifth-Century Chinese Buddhist Cave Temple," *Art Ori-
entalis* 20 (1990): 8-9. Eileen Hisang-ling Hsu argues that a large number of pensive
figures in sixth-century China, affixed with the word *siwei*, developed into representations of pious Maitreya devotees "in seated meditational posture visualizing (*siwei*
or *guan* 觀) themselves in the company of Maitreya in Tuṣita." Eileen Hsiang-ling
Hsu, "Visualization Meditation and the Siwei Icon in Chinese Buddhist Sculpture,"
Artibus Asiae 62.1 (2002): 5-32, especially, 8, 27. Her suggestion is interesting, but
whether the term *siyu* can be interpreted in conjunction with visualization, as she
argues, seems to need further corroboration.

[54] Alan Sponberg's translation in "Wŏnhyo on Maitreya Visualization," in *Maitreya, the Future Buddha*, ed. A. Sponberg and H. Hardacre (Cambridge: Cambridge
University Press, 1988): 98, cited here with slight modification; cf. T1773, 38:299c.

[55] Besides the *Mile xiasheng jing* translated by Dharmarakṣa (T453), two other
Chinese versions are extant with an identical title, *Mile xiasheng chengfo jing* (T454,
T455), each translated by Kumārajīva and Yijing.

dachengfo jing 彌勒大成佛經)[56]—Wŏnhyo returns to the problem of visualization, and distinguishes three different kinds of visualization according to the three different grades of people.

> The highest grade of people are those who either cultivate the *samādhi* of Buddha visualization or who take repentance as their method of practice. In their present body they will succeed in seeing Maitreya. According to the quality of their mind, the image they see will be either great or small. This is taught in the *Sutra of the Sea of the Samādhi of Buddha Visualization* (*Guanfo sanmei hai jing* 觀佛三昧海經) and the *Expanded Dhāraṇī* (*Dafangdeng tuoluoni jing* 大方等陀羅尼經).
>
> The middle grade of people are those who either cultivate the *samādhi* of Buddha visualization or who [practice] by performing pure deeds. After having given up this [present] body, they will be reborn in the Tuṣita heaven, there to see Maitreya and attain the stage of non-retrogression (*butuizhuan* 不退轉, *avinivartanīya*). This is as is taught in the *Sutra [of the Visualization] of Maitreya's Rebirth Above.*
>
> The lowest grade of people cultivate the various good deeds—generosity (*dāna*), morality (*śīla*), etc.—and, upon that base, produce a vow wishing to see Maitreya. After giving up their [present] body, they incur rebirth in accord with their past deeds until the time when Maitreya completes the path [and is reborn on earth]. They will see Maitreya then and attain deliverance as part of the three assemblies. This is as taught in the *Sutra on Rebirth Below* and the *Sutra on Achieving Buddhahood.*
>
> Thus those for whom the *Sutra [of the Visualization] of Maitreya's Rebirth Above* was [taught] are people of the middle grade, where the other two sutras are for the benefit of the people of the lowest grade.[57]

According to Wŏnhyo, only those in the highest grade can visualize Maitreya in the present life, while for those in the lower grades visualization is possible in the Tuṣita heaven only after the current life or after numerous lives when Maitreya attains buddhahood. Because Kim Chisŏng's vision of Maitreya embodied in the Kamsan-sa image is apparently not a vision of

---

[56] Translated by Kumārajīva (T456).

[57] Based on Sponberg's translation with slight modification: "Wŏnhyo on Maitreya Visualization," 99-100; cf. T1773, 38:300b.

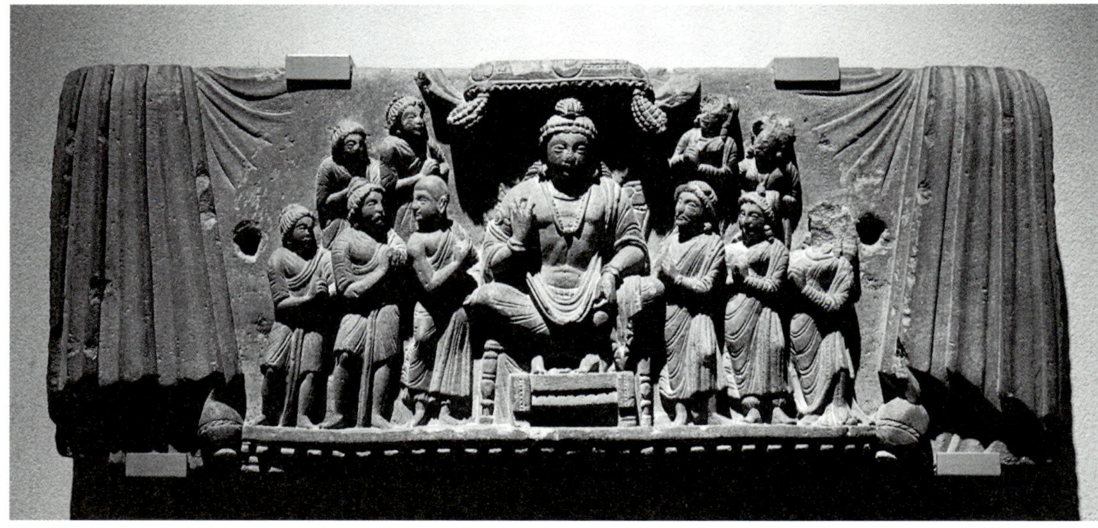

Figure 2.16 *Maitreya Bodhisattva. Gandhara, second-third century. Musuem für Asiatische Kunst, Berlin. Photograph by Rhi Juhyung.*

him in the Tuṣita heaven, but most likely an encounter with him in the present life, it is unique, unlike that of the *Sutra of the Visualization of Maitreya's Rebirth Above* or those of the other two major sutras on Maitreya. His visualization of Maitreya would thus correspond to that of the highest grade in Wŏnhyo's classification. Wŏnhyo does not mention the *Yogācārabhūmi* for visualization of this kind because the text does not specifically concern the practice of visualization.[58] The learned layman Kim Chisŏng quite possibly

---

[58] It is interesting to note that he speaks of the *Sutra of the Sea of the Samādhi of Buddha Visualization*, one of the primary scriptures that elucidate visualization. The sutra, which has been cited by some scholars to explain the distinctive significance embodied in Sŏkkuram, was evidently well known in Silla. See Yi Kiyŏng (Rhi Ki-yong) 李箕永, "Sŏkkuram kwa tongnyong: Sŏkkuram choyŏng ŭi sasangjŏk paegyŏng" 石窟庵과 毒龍: 石窟庵 造營의 思想的 背景 [Sŏkkuram and a poisonous dragon: Ideas behind the creation of Sŏkkuram], in his *Chonggyo sahwa* 宗教史話 [Stories in the history of religion] (Seoul: Han'guk Pulgyo Yŏn'guwon, 1978): 89-94; Mun Myŏngdae, *T'ohamsan sŏkkul* 吐含山石窟 [Mount T'oham cave] (Seoul: Hanŏn, 2000): 211-224.

106

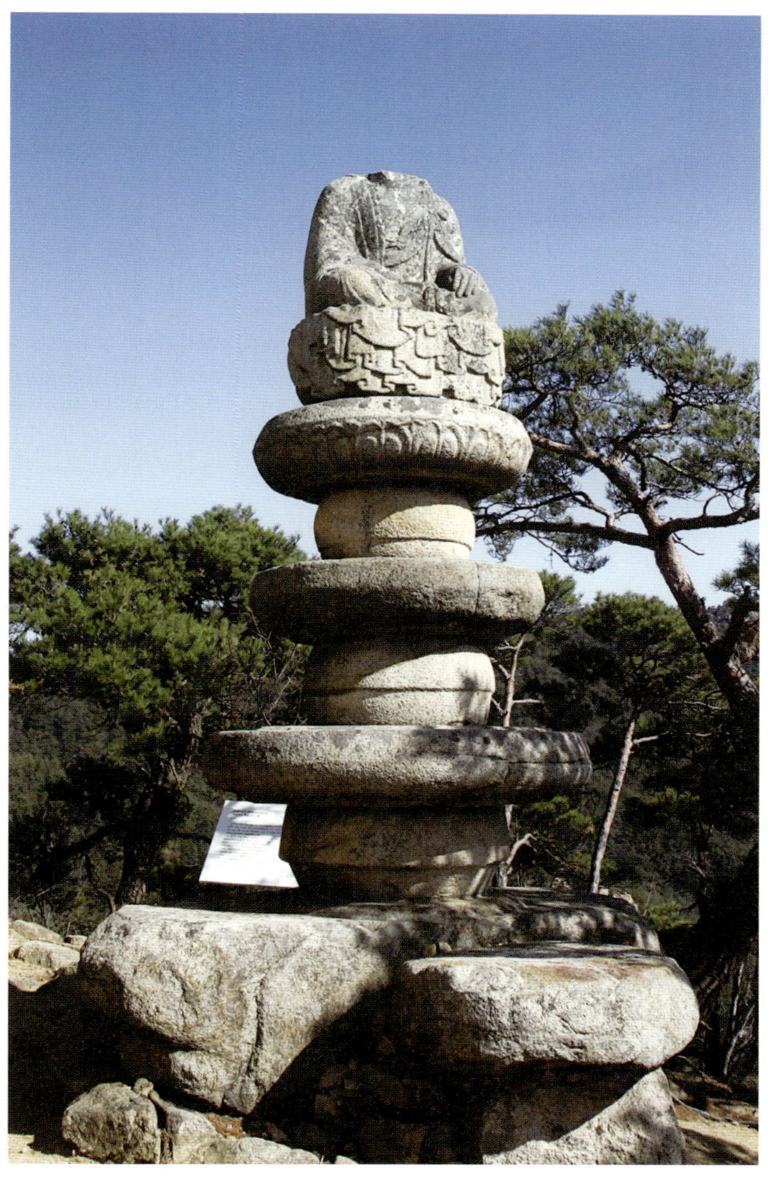

Figure 2.17 *Maitreya Bodhisattva, Yongjanggye, Namsan, Kyŏngju.
Silla, eighth century. Photograph by Rhi Juhyung.*

read Wŏnhyo's works including this commentary, though we do not know whether he was conscious of the sophisticated distinctions of visualization in his aspiration for Maitreya. Also, we cannot tell whether Kim Chisŏng envisaged Maitreya through a systematic *samādhi* practice or simply in a casual dream. In terms of images thus created in the mind of Kim Chisŏng, the difference between the two methods would not have been significant.[59] In any case, Kim Chisŏng could have devised an iconographic type, unprecedented in earlier Buddhist visual imagery of Maitreya, based on his own visualization experience of Maitreya descending before him.

Maitreya in the crossed-ankle pose, an iconographic type probably created in the Northwest of the Indian subcontinent,[60] could also have originated in visualization experiences (fig. 2.16). The type was immensely popular and was thus replicated in large numbers in early Chinese Buddhism, but the moment of its origin was probably forgotten entirely among the Chinese. By contrast, parallels for Kim Chisŏng's Maitreya are rare in later Silla Buddhist art, and the image apparently did not leave a meaningful imprint on later developments in Silla Buddhist art. Instead, it seems to have been an incidental aberration, although one supposes that many people saw the image in Kamsan-sa.[61] Perhaps his fellow Silla Buddhists

---

[59] In the *Pratyutpannasamādhi-sūtra*, one of the principal texts on visualization in early Indian Buddhism, envisioning in a dream is an important method of visualization. "If they concentrate their thoughts with undistracted minds on the *Tathāgata* Amitāyus for seven days and nights, then, when a full seven days and nights have elapsed, they see the Lord and *Tathāgata* Amitāyus. Should they not see that Lord during the daytime, then the Lord and *Tathāgata* Amitāyus will show his face to them in a dream while they are sleeping." Paul Harrison, *The Samādhi of Direct Encounter with the Buddhas of the Present: An Annotated English Translation of the Tibetan Version of the Pratyutpanna-Buddha-Sammukhavathita-Samādhi-Sūtra* (Tokyo: The International Institute for Buddhist Studies, 1990): 32.

[60] Ishimatsu Hinako, "Chūgoku kōkyakubosatsuzō kō," 220-221.

[61] A stone Buddha quite close to the Kamsan-sa Amitābha is inside a cave at Mit'aam 彌陀庵, Yangsan 梁山. Ch'oe Sŏng-ŭn 崔聖銀, *Sŏkpul maaebul* 石佛 磨崖佛 [Stone Buddhas and rock-cut Buddhas] (Seoul: Yegyŏng, 2004): 110-111, Plate 33. It is slightly smaller in size, somewhat different in clothing, and stiffer in details, but otherwise very close to the Kamsan-sa Amitābha. Also identified as Amitābha, the Yangsan Buddha is most likely a copy of the Kamsan-sa Amitābha, which suggests that the latter was considered a valuable model for replication. The Kamsan-sa Maitreya may also have been copied, but a Maitreya in the identical form is seldom found among later images.

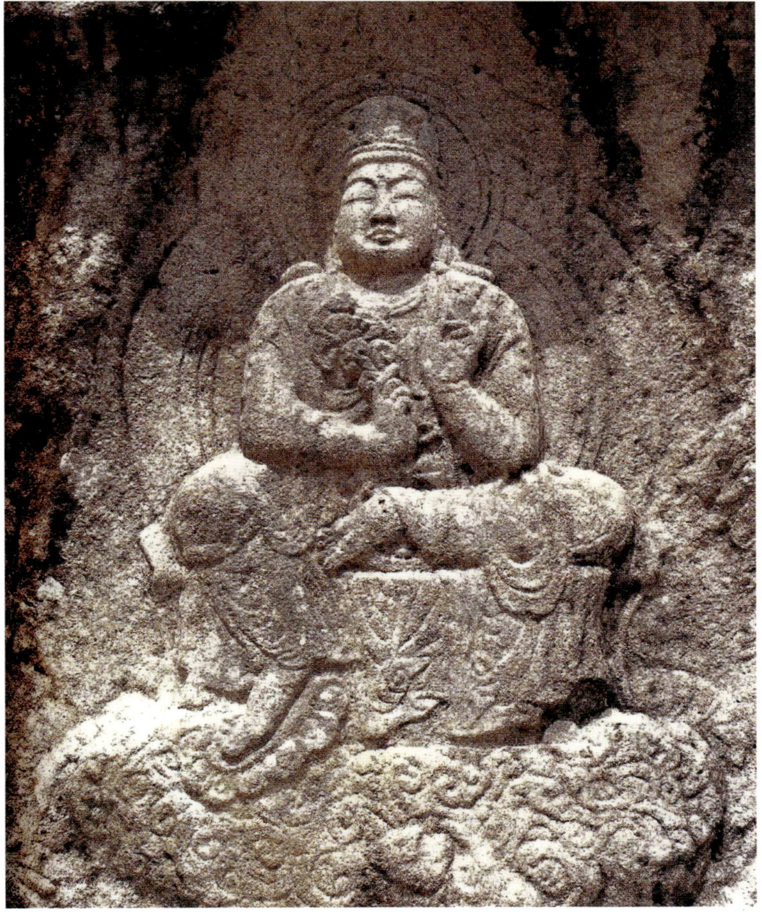

Figure 2.18 *Maitreya Bodhisattva, Sinsŏnam, Namsan, Kyŏngju.
Silla, eighth century. Photograph by Rhi Juhyung.*

thought the type too similar to the better-established standing bodhisattva type of Avalokiteśvara to be useful as a distinctive type for Maitreya, since *differentiation* is an important key to the success of an iconographic type. The *Samguk yusa* records a Maitreya image in the temple Yongjang-sa 茸長 寺 adored by T'aehyŏr 太賢, a master of the Korean *Dharmalakṣaṇa* school

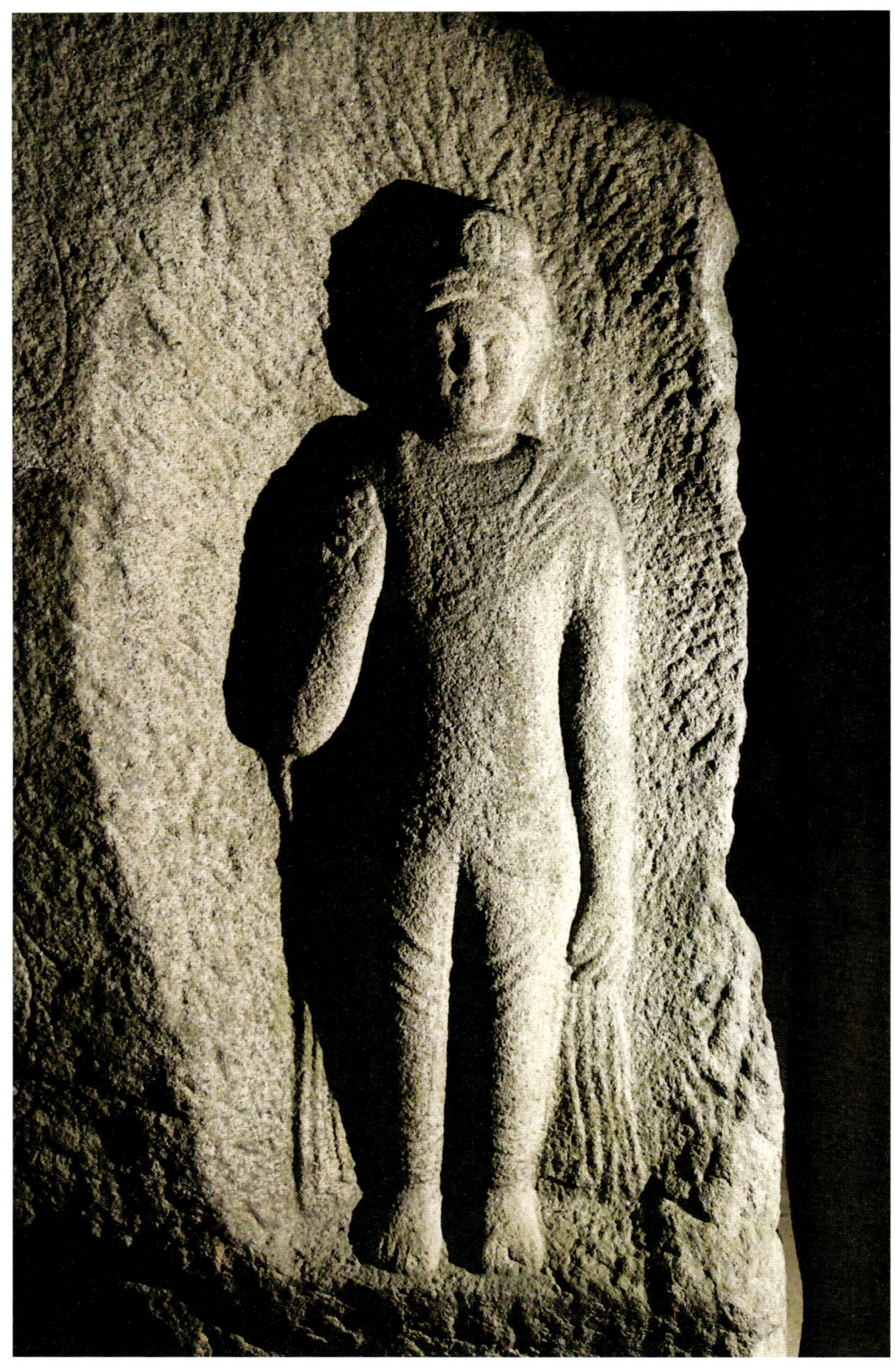

Figure 2.19 Maitreya Bodhisattva, the Kulbul-sa site, Kyŏngju. Silla, mid-eighth century. Photograph by Song Jinhyup.

and active during King Kyŏngdŏk's reign (742-765) (fig. 2.17).⁶² This Maitreya was a seated image signifying the bodhisattvas's presence in the Tuṣita heaven.⁶³ Another bodhisattva carved on a rock face at Sinsŏnam 神仙庵 near Ch'ilburam 七佛庵 in Kyŏngju, which we can identify as Maitreya by the *nāgapuṣpa* twig held in his right hand, is seated on a cloud with his right leg hanging down, in a position somewhat similar to the pensive type (fig. 2.18).⁶⁴ The only example in the standing pose comparable to the Kamsan-sa Maitreya and also identifiable as Maitreya bodhisattva is an image carved on the north face of a square boulder at Kulbul-sa 掘佛寺 datable to the mid-eighth century (fig. 2.19).⁶⁵ This may have been a rare attempt to replicate the Kamsan-sa Maitreya type.

Two Destinations

In addressing the Maitreya image from Kamsan-sa, we also need to make sense of its relationship to the Amitābha image from the same temple. Where was the Buddha installed in the temple? What significance did it have in relation to the Maitreya?

As for the placement of the Amitābha, some scholars have suggested that it was installed in the lecture hall separately from the Maitreya in the main hall. A parallel has been drawn from another account from the *Samguk yusa*, in which a Maitreya Buddha and an Amitābha Buddha were placed separately in the main hall and the lecture hall of a temple on Mount Paegwŏl 白月 founded where the two practitioners Nohil Pudŭk 努詰夫得 and Taldal Pakpak 怛怛朴朴 supposedly attained buddhahood as Maitreya and Amitābha respectively.⁶⁶ It has also been noted that in Kōfukuji

---

⁶² *Samguk yusa* 4: "Hyŏn Yuga Hae Hwaŏm," *Yŏkchu Samguk yusa*, 4:197-203.

⁶³ Although many scholars usually regard this image as a Maitreya Buddha, Mun Myŏngdae thought it a Maitreya bodhisattva. Mun Myŏngdae, "T'aehyŏn kwa Yongjang-sa ŭi pulsang chogak" 太賢과 茸長寺의 佛像彫刻 [T'aehyŏn and a Buddha image at Yongjang-sa], in his *T'ongil Silla Pulgyo chogaksa yŏn'gu sang: wŏnŭm kwa kojŏnmi* (2003): 123-127 (originally published in *Paeksan hakpo* 白山學報 17 [1974]).

⁶⁴ Son Yŏngmun, "Koryŏ sidae yonghwa suin Mirŭk tosang yŏn'gu," 139-140.

⁶⁵ Kim Lina (Kim Lena), "Kyŏngju Kulbulsaji ŭi samyŏn sŏkpul e taehayŏ" 慶州掘佛寺址의 四面石佛에 대하여 [On the four-sided Buddha images of the Kulbul-sa site in Kyŏngju], in her *Han'guk kodae Pulgyo chogaksa yŏn'gu* 韓國古代佛教彫刻史研究 [Study in the history of ancient Korean Buddhist sculpture] (Seoul: Ilchogak, 1989): 259 (originally published in *Chindan hakpo* 震檀學報 39 [1975]: 43-68).

⁶⁶ *Samguk yusa* 3: "Namwŏlsan isŏng Nohil Pudŭk Taldal Pakpak," *Yŏkchu Samguk yusa*, 3:216-232.

興福寺 in Japan, a Maitreya and an Amitābha were placed separately in the main hall and the lecture hall during the Nara period (710-794).[67] However, in Kōfukuji the Maitreya is not the only image in the main hall, which also housed an image of Śākyamuni Buddha. Furthermore, the Maitreya of Kōfukuji was most likely a Buddha, not a bodhisattva. The Maitreya on Mount Paegwŏl was also a Buddha. Despite the fact that the legend speaks of Maitreya and Amitābha installed simultaneously on Mount Paegwŏl, we cannot be certain of the relevance of two images on Mount Paegwŏl and the Kamsan-sa images to each other. Alternately, considering the symmetrical configurations of the two images, especially in hand gestures, it has been suggested that they stood side by side in the main hall.[68] This is supported by a question: If the two images had been intended to be installed in separate halls, would they necessarily have been created in identical dimensions and formats? Although the current evidence does not allow us fully to answer these questions, it may be more reasonable to suppose that the two images were in the same building, which is the main hall of the temple.

Mun Myŏngdae, who proposed the separate installation of Maitreya and Amitābha in the main hall and the lecture hall, has suggested that the simultaneous devotion to Maitreya and Amitābha was a distinctive phenomenon of the *Dharmalakṣaṇa* school in Silla, as in Kōfukuji, which was also a temple of the *Dharmalakṣaṇa* school in Japan.[69] However, even though Kim Chisŏng was an avid reader of the *Yogācārabhūmi* and an ardent devotee of Maitreya, it is not at all clear whether he and his temple were affiliated with the *Dharmalakṣaṇa* school. Mun Myŏngdae tends to stress prominent sectarianism in the visual imagery of Silla Buddhism, but this view has been questioned by a number of Buddhist history specialists.[70]

---

[67] *Kōfukuji ryūki* 興福寺流記 [Records of Kōfukuji], in *Dainihon Bukkyō zensho* 大日本佛教全書 [Compendium of Japanese Buddhist literature], vol. 123: 6-7, 16-17.

[68] Ch'oe Wansu suggests that, for the reason above, the two images were originally made to be housed in the same hall, but in another place in the same book he writes that they were installed separately in the golden hall and the lecture hall. Ch'oe Wansu, *Han'guk kodae pulsang ŭi wŏllyu rŭl ch'ajasŏ 2*, 240, 246. So Hyŏnsuk thinks that the two images were together in the main hall. So Hyŏnsuk, "Kamsan-sa Mirŭk posal ipsang kwa Amit'a yŏrae ipsang yŏn'gu," 60-63.

[69] Mun Myŏngdae, "Silla Pŏpsangjong (Yugajong) ŭi sŏngnip munje wa Kamsan-sa Mirŭk Amit'a pulsang," 106-109.

[70] The nature of Buddhist sects or sectarianism is one of the pivotal issues in the study of early and medieval Korean Buddhism. According to the assessment of Hŏ Hŭngsik, a specialist in medieval Korean Buddhism, sectarianism in the proper sense

Others point out, as negative evidence for Mun Myŏngdae's theory, examples from China outside the context of the *Dharmalakṣaṇa* school in which Maitreya and Amitābha were simultaneously dedicated. For instance, in the sixth century Master Nanyue Huisi 南嶽惠思, despite being a devout follower of the *Lotus Sutra*, created and worshipped images of Maitreya and Amitābha together after hearing lectures from the two deities in a dream.[71] Placing Maitreya and Amitābha together on a single monument or inside a single space, not for doctrinal reasons but to appropriate popular devotions, was not uncommon in Chinese Buddhist art.[72]

Likewise, it is possible that Kim Chisŏng, while creating a Maitreya based on his own experience of visualization, may have simply added an Amitābha, the Buddha of the Western Pure Land (Sukhāvatī) where many contemporary Buddhists in Silla aspired to be reborn. In doing so, he may have provided two potential destinations for rebirth for those on whose behalf he prayed. He perhaps hoped that his parents and many other deceased relatives would find a new abode in one of these two places—Maitreya's Tuṣita or Amitābha's Sukhāvatī. Kim Chisŏng himself did not live long after the initiation of this project. No doubt he longed for a rebirth in the Tuṣita heaven, and perhaps considered Amitābha's Sukhāvatī as expedient means (*upāya*) for those not fully initiated.[73] However, when two differ-

---

appears in Korean Buddhism only in the ninth century during the late Unified Silla period. Hŏ Hŭngsik 許興植, "Kyojong ojongp'asŏl ŭi pip'an" 敎宗 五宗派說의 批判 [Criticism on the theory of five scriptural schools], in his *Koryŏ Pulgyosa yŏn'gu* 高麗佛教史研究 [Studies in the history of Koryŏ Buddhism] (Seoul: Ilchogak, 1986): 127-144; also see Kim Yŏngt'ae 金煐泰, *Han'guk Pulgyosa kaesŏl* 韓國佛教史概說 [A comprehensive history of Korean Buddhism] (Seoul: Kyŏngsŏwŏn, 1986): 18; Ch'ae Sangsik 蔡尚植, "Han'guk chungse Pulgyo ŭi ihae panghyang" 韓國 中世佛教의 理解 方向 [Toward understanding medieval Korean Buddhism], *Kogo yŏksa hakchi* 9 (1993): 321.

[71] T2060, 50:562c, cf. Li Yumin, "Sui Tang zhi Mile xinyang yu tuxiang," 92-94; So Hyŏnsuk, "Kamsan-sa Mirŭk posal ipsang kwa Amit'a yŏrae ipsang yŏn'gu," 43-44.

[72] So Hyŏnsuk, "Kamsan-sa Mirŭk posal ipsang kwa Amit'a yŏrae ipsang yŏn'gu," 53-55.

[73] It is well known that Silla Buddhists debated the superiority of the two paradisiacal realms of Amitābha and Maitreya. For example, Wŏnhyo thought Amitābha's Sukhāvatī superior to Maitreya's Tuṣita, while Kyŏnghŭng asserted otherwise. An Kyehyŏn suggests that Wŏnhyo's view was expressed as an expedient means to recommend devotion to Amitābha from the standpoint emphasizing Amitābha, and not intended to support the absolute superiority of Amitābha's

ent paradisiacal realms of rebirth are present, would one perceive either one of them to be more real? Fundamentally speaking, Maitreya's Tuṣita might have been as hollow as Amitābha's Sukhāvatī. In Kim Chisŏng's case, however, even if the two images were placed side by side in the main hall of Kamsan-sa, he was not forced to face such disturbing questions, for he passed away before the Amitābha image was completed for dedication. We do not know whether he ever met Maitreya in the Tuṣita heaven afterward.

 * The part of this chapter on the interpretation of the iconograpic singularity of the Kamsan-sa Maitreya image was published in Korean with slight adaptation: "Mirŭk ŭl mannada: Kamsansa mirŭk posalsang ŭi hyŏngsik kwa ŭimi e taehan haemyŏng" 미륵을 만나다: 감산사 미륵보살상의 형식과 의미에 대한 해명 [The vision of Maitreya in an image from Kamsan-sa], *Misulsa wa sigak munhwa* 미술사와 시각문화 9 (2010): 8-26.

**Appendix: Translations of
the Inscriptions of the Two Kamsan-sa Images**[74]

1. Maitreya inscription

開元七年己未二月十五日重阿飡金志誠奉
爲亡考仁章一吉飡亡妣觀肖里敬造甘
山寺一所石阿彌陀像一軀石彌勒像一軀
盖聞至道玄微不生不滅能仁眞寂無去無來
所以顯法應之三身隨機拯濟表天師之十號
有願咸成弟子志誠生於聖世歷任榮班
無智略以匡時僅免罹於刑憲性諧山水慕莊
老之逍遙志重眞宗希無著之玄寂年六十有
七致王事於清朝遂歸田於閒野披閱五

Sukhāvatī. An Kyehyŏn 安啓賢, *Silla chŏngt'o sasangsa yŏn'gu* 新羅淨土思想史研究 [Study of the history of thoughts in Pure Land Buddhism in Silla] (Seoul: Hyŏnŭmsa, 1987): 57-60, 92-98, 156-157.

[74] In making these translations, I have consulted translations by Kim Namyun, Mun Myŏngdae, and Ch'oe Wansu along with comments by Suematsu Yasukazu, Ayukai Fushanoshin, Katsuragi Sueji, and Nakagiri Isao. For these works, see n. 3, 4, and 13 above. Attempts have been made to correct mistakes in both translations by Mun Myŏngdae and Kim Namyun. I would like to thank Nam Dongsin for offering much help in this regard.

千言之道德弃名位而入玄窮研十七地之法
門壤色空而俱滅尋復降旌命於草廬典
遍都之劇務雖在官而染俗塵外之心無捨罄
志誠之資業建甘山之伽藍伏願以此微誠上
資國主大王履千年之遐壽延萬福之鴻
休愷元伊湌公出有漏之羇埃證无生之妙果
弟良誠小舍玄度師姊古巴里前妻古老里後
妻阿好里兼庶兄及漢一吉湌一憧薩湌聰敬
大舍妹首盻買里及无邊法界一切衆生同出
六塵咸登十號縱使誠☑有盡此願无窮劫石
已消尊容不☑无求不果有願咸成如有順此
心願者庶同營其善因也亡姚官肖里夫人
年六十六古人成之東海欣支邊散之

Kaiyuan 開元 seventh year (719),[75] the cyclical year *kimi* 己未, second month, fifteenth day,[76] Kim Chisŏng in the rank of *chungach'an* 重阿湌[77] reverently built a temple, Kamsan-sa, and made a stone image of Amitābha and a stone image of Maitreya sincerely for his deceased father, Injang 仁章, who reached the rank of *ilgilch'an* 一吉湌,[78] and his deceased mother, Kwanch'ori 觀肖里.[79] One hears that the ultimate truth, which is profound and abstruse, is neither born nor destroyed, and that the Capable of Being Benevolent (*nŭngin*, Ch. *nengren* 能仁, Buddha), who is truly serene, neither goes nor comes. Therefore, by revealing the three bodies [of Buddha] such as the dharma body (*pŏp*, Ch. *fa* 法, *dharmakāya*) and the respondent body (*ŭng*, Ch. *ying* 應, *saṃbhogakāya*), [the Buddha] delivers [sentient

---

[75] The eighteenth year of King Sŏngdŏk of Silla.

[76] The fifteenth day of the second month is the nirvana day of Śākyamuni Buddha. The date for the dedication of the two images or at least one of them may have been especially chosen for this occasion.

[77] Double *ach'an*. It is located between the sixth rank *ach'an* 阿湌 and the fifth rank *taeach'an* 大阿湌 in the office rank system of Silla. *Chungach'an* along with *samjungach'an* (triple *ach'an*) and *sajungach'an* (quadruple *ach'an*) is commonly understood to signify promotions from *ach'an* within the sixth rank for those belonging to the grade of head-rank six, who were not allowed to ascend beyond the sixth rank.

[78] The seventh rank in the office rank system of Silla.

[79] *Kwan* 觀 in Kwanch'ori is written with a different Chinese character, *kwan* 官, at the end of this inscription. The use of alternative Chinese characters for proper names was a common practice in Silla.

beings] according to their capabilities,[80] and by manifesting his ten epithets (*sipho*, Ch. *shihao* 十號)[81] such as the Teacher of Gods and Humans (*śāstā*

---

[80] The clause 所以顯法應之三身隨機拯濟, especially its first part, has not been properly translated in earlier works. Mun Myŏngdae translates it into Korean, which could be rendered in English: "Therefore, the exoteric teaching follows this, and the Buddhas of the three bodies of the dharma, the reward (*saṃbhoga*) and the transformation (*nirmāṇa*) deliver sentient beings according to their capabilities." He reads *hyŏnbŏp* (Ch. *xuanfa*) 顯法 as "exoteric teaching." Mun Myŏngdae, "Silla Pŏpsangjong (Yugajong) ŭi sŏngnip munje wa Kamsan-sa Mirŭk Amit'a pulsang," 83. Ch'oe Wansu translates this in a similar way. With regard to reading *hyŏnbŏp* as the exoteric teaching, one should point out that the clause 顯法應之三身隨機拯濟 obviously parallels the following clause 表天師之十號有願成成 structurally, and *hyŏn* was apparently used as a verb corresponding to *p'yo* (Ch. *piao*) 表, therefore Mun and Ch'oe's readings cannot be upheld. Ch'oe Wansu, *Han'guk kodae pulsang ŭi wŏllyu rŭl ch'ajasŏ 2*, 234. On the other hand, Kim Namyun thinks that *hyŏn* signifies the "body of manifestation" in the sense of *nirmāṇakāya* and thus translates into Korean as: "Therefore, the Buddhas of the three bodies—the body of manifestation, the body of dharma, and the body of respondent—deliver according to [their] capabilities. . . ." See her translation in *Han'guk kodae kŭmsŏngmun*, 3:300. However, the *nirmāṇakāya*, usually *yingshen* 應身 or *huashen* 化身 in Chinese translations, was never translated as *xuanshen* (Kr. *hyŏnsin*) 顯身 in the textual tradition, and the three bodies of the Buddha were never counted in any traditions in the order of *xuan* 顯, *fa* (Kr. *pŏp*) 法, and *ying* (Kr. *ŭng*) 應, i.e., *nirmāṇakāya, dharmakāya*, and *saṃbhogakāya*. Part of the reason for this confusion stems from the fact that in the phrase 法應之三身 the character *po* (Ch. *bao*) 報 (respondent) for *saṃbhogakāya* is omitted. But one should note that in the phrase 天師之十號 the character *in* (Ch. *ren*) 人, which should have been in *ch'ŏninsa* (Ch. *tianrenshi*) 天人師 (*śāstā devamanuṣyānām*), is also missing. In the phrase 法應之三身, *ŭng* (Ch. *ying*) 應 can be understood as either *saṃbhogakāya* or *nirmāṇakāya*, since it was used differently depending on whether the three bodies of the Buddha are counted as *fa-bao-ying* 法報應 or *fa-ying-hua* 法應化. I translated *ŭng* in the sense of *saṃbhogakāya* because the preceding verb *hyŏn* could imply the manifestation of *dharmakāya* and *saṃbhogakāya*.

[81] Ch'oe understands *ch'ŏnsa* (Ch. *tianshi*) 天師 as the heavenly lord in Daoism and *sipho* (Ch. *shihao*) 十號 as the ten epithets of the Daoist deity. Ch'oe Wansu, *Han'guk kodae pulsang ŭi wŏllyu rŭl ch'ajasŏ 2*, 234. However, even if Kim Chisŏng was fond of reading the Daoist writings of Laozi and Zhuangzi, the overall religious penchant in his inscriptions is prominently Buddhist, and the *ch'ŏnsa sipho* must also be read in the Buddhist context. For the *sipho* that appears later in this inscription, Ch'oe also translates it as being those of the Buddha. It seems unlikely that the same term was used with meanings derived from the two different contexts.

devamanuṣyānām), [the Buddha] makes whatever wishes fulfilled. The disciple Chisŏng was born in a sacred time and took up honorable posts.[82] While trying to amend wrongs without cleverness, he barely escaped judicial punishment.[83] By nature he harmonized with the mountains and rivers, admired the "Wandering Beyond" (*xiaoyao* 逍遙) of Zhuangzi and Laozi, cherished the true creed (Buddhism), and aspired to the profundity and serenity of Asaṅga['s treatise].[84] At sixty-seven, having accomplished the royal affairs in the clean court, he retired to his land in a peaceful wilderness.[85] Reading through the *Daodejing* 道德經 in five thousand characters, he abandoned [desire for] fame and offices and entered the realm of the profound. Thoroughly studying teachings of the seventeen stages [of the *Yogācārabhūmi*], he [realized] the breaking down of form and emptiness and their total destruction. As the royal banner was hung over his thatched dwelling, he assumed [again] a bustling duty. Despite being in office and

---

[82] Most parts of this inscription seem to have been originally composed on the basis of Kim Chisŏng's own words (see n. 19 above). However, it is written principally in the third person, although there are parts where the distinction between the first and third persons is not clear. In order to avoid confusion, especially in its relation to the Amitābha inscription, which was obviously written by a person other than Chisŏng, I used the third person in my translation.

[83] Mun Myŏngdae suggests that Kim Chisŏng was perhaps expelled from the office with the *chungsi* Sunwŏn 順元 on a charge of treason by the *ich'an* Kyŏngyŏng in the ninth year of King Hyoso (700). Mun Myŏngdae, "Silla Pŏpsangjong (Yugajong) ŭi sŏngnip munje wa Kamsan-sa Mirŭk Amit'a pulsang," 79. This may be a simple conjecture based on his presumption that Sunwŏn had a close tie to Kaewŏn. Ch'oe Wansu suspects, on the other hand, that Kim Chisŏng was implicated along with Prince Kaewŏn in the expulsion of Queen Sŏngjŏng 成貞 and the murder of the crown prince Chunggyŏng 重慶, and that this infuriated the king.

[84] Based on this sentence as well as his remark on his reading of the *Daodejing* and the *Yogācārabhūmi*, many scholars have pointed out that Kim Chisŏng's devotion to Buddhism was intricately interwoven with his sympathy for Daoism. Suematsu Yasukazu, "Kanzanji Miroku sonzō oyobi Amidabutsu no kakō kōki," 457-458; Katsuragi Sueji, *Chōsen kinseki kō*, 210; Nakagiri Isao, "Shiragi Kanzanji sekizō Miroku Amidazō ni tsuite," 284-288. However, Mun Myŏngdae disagrees, considering that Kim Chisŏng's attraction to Daoism was limited to its philosophical aspects only. Mun Myŏngdae, "Silla Pŏpsangjong (Yugajong) ŭi sŏngnip munje wa Kamsan-sa Mirŭk Amit'a pulsang," 80-81.

[85] If Kim Chisŏng died at sixty-nine in 720 (see the last two lines in the Amitābha inscription), his retirement would have been in 718, a year before the founding of Kamsan-sa.

[exposed to] corrupt mundanity, he never gave up his mind to outworldliness. Spending all of his possessions, he founded a temple at Kamsan. Prostrating himself, he prays that the lord of the kingdom, the great king, will enjoy the longevity of a thousand years and ten thousand great fortunes will be bestowed widely; that Prince Kaewŏn 愷元,[86] *ich'an* 伊飡,[87] will get away from bustling worldly matters full of defilements and attain the exquisite reward of no rebirth; that his younger brothers, Yangsŏng 良誠,[88] *sosa* 小舍,[89] the monk Hyŏndo 玄度, his elder sister Kop'ari 古巴里, his former wife Korori 古老里,[90] his second wife Ahori 阿好里, his stepbrothers, Kŭphan 及漢, *ilgilch'an*, Ildong 一憧, *salch'an* 薩飡,[91] and Ch'onggyŏng 聰敬, *taesa* 大舍,[92] his younger sister Suhilmaeri 首肹買里, and all sentient beings in the endless realm of dharma will get out of the world of the six kinds of defilements and ascend to the realm of the ten epithets (Buddha). Even if the sincerity may have a limit, may the wish have no bound. Even if the stones may be worn down in endless eons, may the honorable countenances [of the Buddha and the bodhisattva] not [disappear]. If one seeks after, may there be a reward, and may whatever wishes be fulfilled. May those who vow for these wishes strive for this virtuous cause. His deceased mother, Lady Kwanch'ori 官肖里, passed at sixty-six, and [her remains] were scattered on the shore of the East Sea at Hŭnji 欣支.[93]

---

[86] See p. 83 above.

[87] The first rank in the office rank system of Silla.

[88] Yangsŏng 梁誠 in the Amitābha inscription.

[89] The thirteenth rank in the office rank system of Silla.

[90] Korori 古路里 in the Amitābha inscription.

[91] The eighth rank in the office rank system of Silla.

[92] The twelfth rank in the office rank system of Silla.

[93] Kim Yŏngmi thinks that this sentence is not part of the original written by Kim Chisŏng. See also n. 14 above. With regard to Hŭnji 欣支, Ayukai identifies it with Kŭnoji 斤烏支 in the Geography section of the *Samguk sagi*: "Imjŏng District 臨汀縣 was originally changed from Kŭnoji District by King Kyŏngdŏk. It is the present Yŏngil District 迎日縣." *Samguk sagi* 34: "Chiri il," *Yŏkchu Samguk sagi*, 1:479. Ayukai suggests that Hŭnji is derived from Kŭnoji with *o* 烏 dropped, while *kŭn* and *hŭn* were interchangeable. Ayukai Fusanoshin, *Zakkō*, 17; Suematsu Yasukazu, "Kanzanji Miroku sonzō oyobi Amidabutsu no kakō kōki," 455. Kim Namyun translates, ". . . were scattered by the rocks on the East Sea" (*Han'guk kodae kŭmsŏngmun*, 3:301, 302). Also, the remark on scattering bone ashes (*sankol* or *san'gu* 散骨) has been noted as evidence for the practice in ancient Korea. See Ayukai Fusanoshin, *Zakkō*, 18-19; Saitō Tadashi, "Shiragi no sōsei kara

2. Amitābha inscription

若夫至道者不生不滅猶表跡於周宵能仁者若去若
來尚流形於漢夢濫觴肇自西域傳燈及至東土遂乃
佛日之影奄日域以照臨貝葉之文越洱川而啓發龍
宮錯峙鴈塔駢羅舍衛之境在斯極樂之邦密爾有重
阿湌金志全誕靈河岳降德星辰性叶雲霞情友山水
蘊賢材而命代懷智略以佐時朝鳳闕而銜綸則授尚
舍奉御逡雞林而曳綬則任執事侍郎年六十七懸車
致仕避世閑居侔四皓之高尚辭榮養性同兩疎之見
機仰慕無著眞宗時時讀瑜伽之論兼愛莊周玄道日
日覽逍遙之篇以爲報德慈親莫如十號之力酬恩
聖主無過三寶之因故奉爲國主大王伊湌愷
元公亡考亡姚亡弟小舍梁誠沙門玄度亡妻古路
里亡妹古寶里又爲妻阿好里等捨其甘山莊田建此
伽藍仍造石阿彌陀像一軀伏願託此微因超昇
彼岸四生六道並證菩提
開元七年歲在己未二月十五日奈麻聰
撰奉教沙門釋京融大舍金驟源▨▨▨
亡考仁章一吉湌年卌七古人成之東海
欣支邊散也後代追愛人者此善助在哉
金志全重阿湌敬生已前此善業造歲▨
十九庚申年四月廿二日長逝爲▨之

With regard to the ultimate truth, it is neither born nor destroyed, but its trace was [first] shown on a night in Zhou.[94] With regard to the Capable

---

mita Kanzanjiseki sekizō Amida nyōraizō Miroku bosatsuzō meibun no ichi kaishaku," 134-140.

[94] This reflects one of the Chinese traditions about the birth of the Buddha. The *Zhoushu yiji* 周書異記, attributed to Wang Fu 王浮 of Western Jin, states that the Buddha was born on the night of the eighth day of the fourth month in the twenty-fourth year of King Zhao 昭王 (r. ca. 995-977 B.C.E.: he is actually thought to have ruled for nineteen years). This became a prevalent tradition in China, and many important later sources, such as the *Fozu tongji* 佛祖統紀 (twenty-sixth year of King Zhao) and the *Fozu lidai tongzai* 佛祖歷代通載 (twenty-fifth year of King Zhao), also adopt similar dates for the birth of the Buddha. This tradition was apparently known to ancient Korean Buddhists, as evidenced, besides the Kamsansa Amitābha inscription, in the correspondence between the Northern Qi monk Fashang 法上 and a Koguryŏ prime minister Wang Kodŏk 王高德 during the late

of Being Benevolent, he neither goes nor comes, but his form was [first] revealed in the dream of a Han [emperor].[95] The origin started in the western regions, and the dharma lantern reached the land in the east. Thus, the shadow of the sun of the Buddha shed light on the land where the sun had been hidden, and the scriptures on palm-leaves crossed the P'ae River 浿水[96] and enlightened [the people in the east]. Dragon palaces soar interlocking with one another,[97] and pagodas spread like wild geese. The region of Śrāvastī is right here, and the land of Sukhāvatī is nearby. Kim Chijŏn 金志全, *chungach'an*, was born with spirit from mountains and rivers and bestowed with virtues by heavenly bodies. His character harmonized with clouds and sunset glows, and his sentiment befriended mountains and rivers. Endowed with wisdom and talent, he received the royal order and served with sagacity. He attended the court and cherished the royal order. Awarded the *pongŏ* 奉御 of *sangsa* 尚舍,[98] he reverently served the king and became prominent in Kyerim 雞林 (Silla), pulling the cord of the seal. Thus, he was appointed to *sirang* 侍郎 of *Chipsabu* 執事部. At sixty-seven, he resigned from officialdom. He shunned worldliness and lived in peace like the Four Graybeards (*sihao* 四皓)[99] with lofty virtues. He avoided

---

sixth century, cited in the *Xu gaosengzhuan* (T2060, 50:485b). See Ren Jiyu 任繼愈 ed., *Zhongguo fojiaoshi* 中國佛教史 [History of Chinese Buddhism], vol. 1 (Beijing: Zhongguo Shehui Kexue Chubanshe, 1981): 49-52.

[95] This refers to the famous tradition concerning the transmission of Buddhism to China, according to which the Buddha first appeared as a golden man in the dream of the emperor Mingdi 明帝 (r. 57-75 C.E.) of the Han dynasty. Ren Jiyu ed., *Zhongguo fojiaoshi*, vol. 1: 96-98.

[96] The present Taedong 大同 River, which became the border between Silla and Tang at the finalization of the unification war during the late seventh century.

[97] The dragon palaces here apparently indicate Buddhist temples. This sentence probably means that Buddhist temples stood majestically, like dragon palaces.

[98] Mun Myŏngdae considers *sangsa* as a post, which manages food and clothing in the palace, and Kim Namyun adopts this interpretation in her translation. Mun Myŏngdae, "Silla Pŏpsangjong (Yugajong) ŭi sŏngnip munje wa Kamsan-sa Mirŭk Amit'a pulsang," 85; *Han'guk kodae kŭmsŏngmun*, 3:298, n. 47. The *sangsa*, which is not found in the *Samguk sagi* or the *Samguk yusa*, is probably an office, like the one with the same name in Tang, that oversaw the installation and management of makeshift ceremonial facilities, and *pongŏ* is its director. Kim Yŏngmi, "Sŏngdŏk wangdae chŏnje wangkwŏn e taehan il koch'al," 387-388.

[99] Or called Shangshan sihao 商山四皓, the Four Graybeards of Shangshan. The four Chinese scholars, Dong Yuangong 東園公, Qi Liji 綺里季, Yongli Xiansheng 用

luxury and cultivated his mind like the Two Shu 疏.[100] who saw the right time. Revering and yearning after the true creed of Asaṅga, he often read the *Yogācārabhūmi*. He also loved the profound path of Zhuangzi and read the chapter "Wandering Beyond" every day. In repaying parents' kindness, nothing is comparable to doing it with the power of the ten epithets (Buddha), and in repaying the grace of the sacred lord, nothing surpasses doing it with the cause of the three jewels. Therefore, he donated his estate at Kamsan and founded this temple for the lord of the kingdom, the great king, Prince Kaewǒn, *ich'an*, his deceased father and mother, his deceased younger brothers, Yangsǒng, *sosa*, and the monk Hyǒndo, his deceased wife Korori, his deceased sister Kobori 古寶里,[101] and his present wife Ahori, and so forth.[102] Also making a stone image of Amitābha, he prays in prostration that this small cause will lead one to ascend to the other shore and that the sentient beings of the four births and of the six paths will attain enlightenment. Kaiyuan seventh year, the cyclical year *kimi*, second month, fifteenth

里先生, and Xia Huanggong 夏黃公, had served as officials, but left the government and became recluses to protest against the despotic rule of Shihuangdi 始皇帝 of the Qin dynasty.

[100] The Two Shu are two Han-dynasty officials, Shu Guang 疏廣 and his nephew Shu Shou 疏受. They are lauded for having retired at the height of their careers.

[101] As suggested by Ayukai, Kobori here is probably the same person as Kop'ari 古巴里 in the Maitreya inscription. A drawback to this supposition may be that Kop'ari is specified as *cha* (Ch. *zi*) 姊, an elder sister, while Kobori is written as *mae* (Ch. *mei*) 妹, a younger sister. However, Ayukai points out that in Korean *mae* is commonly used for a sister regardless of seniority, while *cha* was reserved for an elder sister, as we can see in the use of *chahyŏng* 姊兄 (husband of an elder sister for a male) and *maebu* 妹夫 or *maehyŏng* 妹兄 (husband of a sister for a male), and this was probably the case in ancient Silla. Ayukai Fusanoshin, *Zakkō*, 16.

[102] Unlike the Maitreya inscription, many beneficiaries of the merit transferred with the making of the images in the Amitābha inscription are said to be dead, such as in Yangsǒng and the monk Hyǒndo (the deceased younger brothers), Korori (the deceased wife), and Kobori (or Kop'ari, the deceased sister). It seems quite unlikely that all of them died suddenly within the short interval that might have existed between the writing of the two inscriptions, unless a disastrous epidemic had broken out, which then would have been noted somewhere in the Amitābha inscription. Probably they were already dead by the time of the writing of the Maitreya inscription, but were not specifically mentioned. There are slight differences in style between the two inscriptions, and one has to acknowledge that they were not written simultaneously.

day, Ch'ong 聰,[103] *nama* 奈麻,[104] following the [royal] order, composed this,
and the monk Sŏk Kyŏngyung 釋京融 and Kim Ch'wiwŏn 金驟源, *taesa*
大舍,[105] [following the order, did the calligraphy].[106] His deceased father
Injang, *ilgilch'an*, passed at forty-seven, and [his remains] were scattered on
the shore of the East Sea at Hŭnji. For the posterity who misses him, may
there be help from this virtuous deed.[107] Kim Chijŏn, *chunga'chan*, reverently accomplished this deed, and passed at [sixty-]nine,[108] the cyclical year
kyŏngsin, fourth month, twenty-second day.

---

[103] Ch'ong is quite possibly Sŏl Ch'ong, the son of Wŏnhyo. Although the classical Chinese employed in the two inscriptions occasionally shows domesticated
Korean literary elements, they are beautifully written by one who seems quite
knowledgeable scholastically, and Nam Dongsin suspects that there would have
been very few who would have been capable of composing such prose in contemporary Silla. For a discussion of the Silla vernacular style visible in the inscriptions, see
Ayukai Fusanoshin, *Zakkō*.

[104] The eleventh rank in the office rank system of Silla.

[105] The twelfth rank in the office rank system of Silla.

[106] Kim Yŏngmi thinks that the inscription originally ended with this sentence.
Kim Yŏngmi, "Sŏngdŏk wangdae chŏnje wangkwŏn e taehan il koch'al," 373.

[107] The inscription would have been complete here, and the following last sentence, which refers to the death of Kim Chijŏn, must be an insertion made right
after the incident. Katsuragi Sueji, *Chōsen kinseki kō*, 208.

[108] 歲☒十九. Most scholars agree that this probably indicates the age of Kim
Chisŏng at the time of death and that the illegible character must be *-yuk* (Ch. *liu*)
六, six. A small anomaly is that the character *se* (Ch. *Sui*) 歲 is used here, while *nyŏn*
(Ch. *nian*) 年 is found in other parts referring to the ages. Mun Myŏngdae proposes
an alternative: that the missing character may be *chae* (Ch. *zai*) 在 and the phrase
could be read "in the year nineteen" of King Sŏngdŏk, which happened to be the year
kyŏngsin (720) when Kim Chisŏng died. See Mun Myŏngdae, "Silla Pŏpsangjong
(Yugajong) ŭi sŏngnip munje wa Kamsan-sa Mirŭk Amit'a pulsang," 91–92.

ic # chapter header number displayed as decorative "3"

3

(Dis)assembling the National Canon: Seventh-Century "Esoteric" Buddhist Ritual, the *Samguk yusa*, and Sach'ŏnwang-sa

Youn-mi Kim

S tudying a time period or a region that has left few textual records is a daunting task. The time when the Korean peninsula was ruled by the Three Kingdoms—Koguryŏ (trad. 37 B.C.E.-668 C.E.), Paekche (trad. 18 B.C.E.-660 C.E.), and Silla (trad. 57 B.C.E.-935 C.E.)[1]—is one of those time periods that has challenged scholars because of its significant lack of contemporaneous records. Fragmentary records from this period—epigraphs from the three kingdoms, records regarding these kingdoms scattered in contemporaneous Chinese and Japanese texts, and some Buddhist commentaries written by monks of this period—are insufficient to offer a complete picture of Korean history before the tenth century. Despite the lack of historical records written during the Three Kingdoms period, studies of the Three Kingdoms and Unified Silla constitute a significant portion of scholarly literature on Korean history and art, especially in Korean academia.

How then have researchers attempted to study the Three Kingdoms of Korea? Two texts have served as primary sources of information about the

---

[1] Silla unified the Korean peninsula in 668. Modern scholars often use the term "Unified Silla" (Kr. T'ongil Silla 統一新羅) for the period between 668 and 935. For the modern coinage of this term, see Richard D. McBride II, "Introduction," in *State and Society in Middle and Late Silla*, ed. Richard D. McBride II (Cambridge, MA: Korea Institute, Harvard University, 2010): 3.

history of the Three Kingdoms: the *Samguk sagi* 三國史記 (History of the Three Kingdoms), compiled around 1145 by a group of scholars led by Kim Pusik 金富軾 (1075-1151) following an order of King Injong 仁宗 (r. 1122-1146), and the *Samguk yusa* 三國遺事 (Memorabilia of the Three Kingdoms), compiled around 1281 by the monk Iryŏn 一然 (1206-1289).[2] In particular, the latter has served as the foundation for the study of early Korean Buddhist history because it offers records of many events related to the history of Buddhism.[3] Unfortunately both texts were compiled several centuries after the demise of these kingdoms. The late compilation dates as well as the inclusion of myths and miracle stories, especially in the *Samguk yusa*, have led to debates over the reliability of these texts. Since such debates tend to evolve around issues that can easily arouse nationalistic sentiments, there has always been discord among scholars, with some scholars viewing the texts as precious historical data, and others viewing the same texts as spurious fabrications.

I hope to offer an escape from this predicament. In this chapter, through a case study of an important passage from the *Samguk yusa* about an early "esoteric" ritual exhibiting Buddho-Daoist characteristics,[4] I aim to provide,

---

[2] Since the 1980s, however, a number of Korean scholars have argued that more than one compiler created the *Samguk yusa*, suggesting different figures or a group of people around Iryŏn as possible participants in the compilation. The philological study of the *Samguk yusa*—research into its different editions and publication dates—also constitutes an important part of the academic literature concerning the *Samguk yusa* produced by Korean scholars in recent years.

[3] For a brief history of the *Samguk yusa*'s rise as an important historical source in the twentieth century, see Park Daejae, "Doubts about the Edition of the *Samguk yusa*," *International Journal of Korean History* 13 (2009): 17-19.

[4] These types of ritual were often categorized as practices of "miscellaneous esotericism," which is a translation of the term *zōmitsu* 雜密. In modern scholarship, *zōmitsu* forms a binary system with "pure esotericism" (Jp. *junmitsu* 純密), the systemized "esoteric" Buddhism introduced to East Asia in the eighth century. In this binary system, as implied by the names of the two categories, *junmitsu* is regarded as superior to *zōmitsu*. As scholars have recently pointed out, however, the binary division between *zōmitsu* and *junmitsu* is a modern creation. A number of scholars have observed that such a distinction between *zōmitsu* and *junmitsu* did not exist in China, and even in Japan usage of these two terms as binary concepts first appeared only in Ekō's 慧光 (1666-1734) writing. Ryūichi Abe, *The Weaving of Mantra: Kūkai and the Construction of Esoteric Buddhist Discourse* (New York: Columbia University Press, 1999): 152-154; Robert Sharf, *Coming to Terms with Chinese Buddhism: A Reading of the Treasure Store Treatise* (Honolulu: University of Hawaiʻi Press, 2002): 267. To avoid the simplistic binary notion and hierarchical bias implied in

if not a perfect solution, then at least useful suggestions on how to productively use the *Samguk yusa*. This chapter shows that it is possible to read the *Samguk yusa* contents in the context of relevant visual and material evidence as well as other external texts. By taking such an interdisciplinary approach, I believe, one can make more productive use of this rich but problematic document. Although it still remains unknown to many Western scholars, there exist quite abundant archaeological and art historical data from the Three Kingdoms period and Unified Silla that retain traces of early Korean Buddhism. Through my careful reading of these precious data sources, this chapter explores the diverse and interesting intersection between Buddhology and art history in the context of seventh-century Korea.

Another goal of this chapter is to throw some light on the early history of Korean "esoteric" Buddhism, which is also a topic of heated debate. The passage of the *Samguk yusa* that will be investigated below is a short record about a ritual known as Munduru 文豆婁,[5] meaning Mudrā (religious hand gesture or seal), purportedly performed in the early 670s at about the time when Silla unified the peninsula, bringing an end to the Three Kingdoms period. This passage about the Munduru Ritual has been critical in shaping modern scholars' understanding of early Korean

---

the term *zōmitsu*, in this chapter I simply use the term "early" esoteric Buddhism. Koichi Shinohara is currently writing a book on the development of early "esoteric" Buddhist *dhāraṇī* rituals to elaborate systemized "esoteric" Buddhist rituals of the eighth century. The term "esotericism/esoteric Buddhism" (Ch. *mijiao* 密教) itself has become contentious in contemporary Buddhist studies as well, since Buddhist "esotericism," as pointed out by Robert Sharf, did not form an independent form of teaching or school in China. The term *mijiao* was used to designate "esoteric" teachings and practices only in the tenth century in China. Robert Sharf, *Coming to Terms with Chinese Buddhism*, 263-278, especially 269. In Korea, there were two distinctive esoteric Buddhist schools, Sinin 神印 and Ch'ongji 摠持, at least from the time of the Koryŏ kingdom. So I do not use quotation marks when referring to esoteric Buddhism of Koryŏ. For more on this subject, see Henrik H. Sørensen, "On the Sinin and Ch'ongji Schools and the Nature of Esoteric Buddhist Practice under the Koryŏ," *International Journal of Buddhist Thought and Culture* 5 (2005): 49-84. Following the recent remarkable study of esoteric Buddhism in *Esoteric Buddhism and the Tantras in East Asia*, this chapter uses the term "esoteric" Buddhism as one that comprehensively includes diverse esoteric practices before and after the introduction of the systemized tantric Buddhist tradition to East Asia in the eighth century. See Charles D. Orzech, Henrik H. Sørensen, and Richard K. Payne, eds., *Esoteric Buddhism and the Tantras in East Asia* (Leiden and Boston: Brill, 2011).

[5] For the meaning of "Munduru," see page 142.

"esoteric" Buddhism because it is one of the few records mentioning "esoteric" Buddhist practices in Korea before the Koryŏ period (918-1392). Depending on their different interpretations of this passage—from the record about the starting point of the Korean esoteric Buddhist school known as Sinin 神印 to a fabricated origin story about a much later ritual practice—scholars have offered quite different views on early Korean "esoteric" Buddhism.

Neither indiscriminately trusting this record nor simply dismissing it as untrustworthy, this chapter aims to provide a more sophisticated and refined understanding of this earliest record about an "esoteric" Buddhist ritual in Korea. I begin with comparing the passage in the *Samguk yusa* with earlier and later texts in an attempt to discern what textual comparison will reveal with regard to the subject of analysis. Next, through a further examination of the nature of this ritual in a larger context of the history of "esoteric" Buddhism in East Asia, I explore the question of when this ritual began to be practiced in the Korean peninsula. Lastly, by exploring archaeological and art historical data from the seventh century, I examine whether material data can enhance our understanding of this important passage. Simply proving the validity of this passage is not my goal; instead, in this chapter I hope to demonstrate the extent to which an intertextual reading and interdisciplinary methodology can deepen our understanding of early Korean Buddhism and Buddhist art.

The Earliest Record of "Esoteric" Buddhist Ritual in Korea

The *Samguk yusa* reference to the Munduru Ritual is important because our current understanding of the early history of "esoteric" Buddhism in the Korean peninsula drastically changes depending on the interpretation of this passage. The passage appears in the section of the *Samguk yusa* titled "King Munmu whose posthumous title was Pŏmmin" (*Munho Wang Pŏmmin* 文虎王法敏). It would not be an exaggeration to state that King Munmu's 文武 (r. 661-681) reign was the most eventful time in the history of the Silla kingdom. Through a series of wars, Silla finally conquered Paekche (trad. 18 B.C.E.-660 C.E.) and Koguryŏ (trad. 37 B.C.E.-668 C.E.), the other two kingdoms of the peninsula. Silla, initially the weakest among the Three Kingdoms, managed to turn the tables through its military alliance with China's Tang empire (618-907). By the end of this extended unification process, however, Silla's relationship with Tang suddenly went sour, as a serious territorial dispute emerged over the newly conquered lands, eventually leading to the Silla-Tang War (670-676).

126

According to a passage included in the "Munho Wang whose posthumous title was Pŏmmin" article of the *Samguk yusa*, the Munduru Ritual was practiced to protect Silla as the Silla-Tang War was about to begin. The passage explains that King Munmu, discovering that Tang was planning to launch a military attack against Silla, summoned a monk named Myŏngnang 明朗 (fl. seventh century) and asked for providential help. The monk advised the king to build Sach'ŏnwang-sa 四天王寺, or Four Heavenly Kings Monastery, as a site at which to perform a ritual. Because time was lacking, a monastery was instead created using silk textiles as a temporary measure, and the monk performed the Munduru Ritual at the temporarily built monastery immediately before the two countries began to battle. The *Samguk yusa* ascribes Silla's victory in battles in 670 and 671 to the ritual's efficacy. The relevant passage reads:

> [Myŏng]nang told [King Munmu], "There is Sinyu Forest 神遊林 on the southern side of Mount Nang 狼山. Build Sach'ŏnwang-sa in that place, and install a ritual place. Then all should be fine." At that time, a messenger from Chŏngju reported, "Countless Tang soldiers approached our border, and [their warships] are patrolling on the sea." The king summoned Myŏngnang and said, "The issues have become extremely urgent. What should we do?" [Myŏng]nang said, "[We] should temporarily build [a monastery] with colorful silk." Thereupon [they] built a monastery using colorful silk, made images of *obangsin* 五方神 (the Deities of the Five Directions) with grass, and twelve Yoga (Kr. Yuga 瑜伽) monks, the leader of whom was Myŏngnang, performed the secret Munduru Ritual. Furious wind and waves sank all the Tang warships, even before Tang and Silla had a battle. Later rebuilt and officially launched, the monastery was named Sach'ŏnwang-sa. The ritual platform [at the monastery] has not been damaged until today. <The *Kuksa* 國史 says that the renovation and formal opening of the monastery took place in the first year of the Tiaolu 調露 reign, which was the year of *kimyo* 己卯 [679].>[6] Later in the year of *sinmi* 辛未 (671), Tang once more dispatched Zhao Xian 趙憲 as general of the army, and fifty thousand soldiers again came to

---

[6] The sentence in angled brackets is an interlinear note. In the original passage from the *Samguk yusa*, the interlinear note appears in smaller characters than the characters of the main text.

defeat [Silla]. They performed the [Munduru] Ritual again, and the
warships sank as before.[7]

朗奏曰, 狼山之南有神遊林, 創四天王寺於其地 開設道場則可矣. 時
有貞州使走報曰, 唐兵無數至我境, 迴槧海上. 王召明朗曰, 事已逼
至如何. 朗曰, 以彩帛假搆宜矣. 乃以彩帛營寺, 草搆五方神像, 以瑜
伽明僧十二員, 明朗爲上首, 作文豆婁秘密之法. 時唐羅兵未交接, 風
濤怒起, 唐船皆沒於水. 後改刱寺, 名四天王寺, 至今不墜壇席 <國
史云改刱在調露元年己卯> 後年辛未, 唐更遣趙憲爲帥, 亦以五萬兵
來征, 又作其法, 船沒如前.[8]

Korean Buddhologists generally regard this ritual as one of the major
events in the early history of Korean esoteric Buddhism, and many think
that the monk Myŏngnang who performed this ritual later founded the
Sinin School, one of two Korean esoteric Buddhist schools.[9] On the other
hand, Henrik H. Sørensen, a specialist in Korean esoteric Buddhism, does
not view this passage as a trustworthy historical record, and has suggested
that the practice of the Munduru Ritual probably began only in the eleventh century under Koryŏ, the polity that succeeded Silla.[10] This opinion
conforms with his view that the majority of records about "esoteric" Bud-

---

[7] All English translations in this chapter are by the author.

[8] *Samguk yusa* 2: "Munho Wang Pŏmmin," Han'guk Chŏngsin Munhwa
Yŏn'guwŏn 韓國精神文化研究院 [Academy of Korean Studies], ed., *Yŏkchu
Samguk yusa* 譯註 三國遺事 [Annotation and translation of the *Samguk yusa*]
(Seoul: Ihoe Munhwasa, 2003), 2:22-23. The sentence appearing in angled brack-
ets is an interlinear note.

[9] See publications of Kwŏn Sangno, Yi Chongik, Pak T'aehwa, and Mun Myŏngdae
for the account that the Sinin School was founded during the time of Myŏngnang. For
a list of their publications discussing this issue, see Sŏ Yun'gil 서윤길, *Han'guk milgyo
sasangsa* 한국밀교사상사 [History of Korean esoteric Buddhist thought] (Seoul:
Unjusa, 2006): 324, footnote 68. Sŏ Yun'gil, however, argues that the Sinin School
became an independent school only in 936 under the Koryŏ kingdom. See Sŏ Yun'gil,
Han'guk milgyo sasangsa, 324-326. It is clear that Myŏngnang has been regarded as the
founder of this esoteric school since the thirteen century, if not earlier, when Iryŏn
compiled the *Samguk yusa*. The *Samguk yusa* records that Myŏngnang had been to
Tang China and describes him as the founder of the Sinin School. See *Samguk yusa* 5:
"Myŏngnang Sinin," *Yŏkchu Samguk yusa*, 4:225-226.

[10] Henrick H. Sørensen, "On the Sinin and Cho'ngji Schools," 49-84, especially 58-59.

dhism from the Three Kingdoms period in Korea, which mostly come from the *Samguk yusa*, are fabrications modeled on stories having similar patterns found in earlier Chinese texts.[11]

Here we find drastically differing views on this *Samguk yusa* passage among scholars. How shall we deal with this quandary? Simply following one of the opinions will not deepen our understanding of early Korean "esoteric" Buddhism; instead, it will only contribute to the ever-widening gap between the two camps. To resolve this issue, I will first identify key information provided in this record and then compare it with external texts as well as archaeological data.

The passage from the *Samguk yusa*, although brief, provides several pieces of key information about the ritual under discussion:

1. The name of the ritual was Munduru 文豆婁,[12] meaning *mudrā*.
2. The ritual was performed in order to protect the state.
3. The ritual was performed under Silla in 670 and 671 during the reign of King Munmu.
4. The ritual was performed at the Sach'ŏnwang-sa site located on Mount Nang 狼.
5. The ritual used statues of the Deities of the Five Directions (Kr. *obangsin* 五方神).
6. After the war, permanent buildings were built at the Sach'ŏnwang-sa site, which were completed in 679.
7. The monk Myŏngnang performed the ritual with twelve eminent Yoga monks.[13]

---

[11] See Henrick H. Sørensen, "Early Esoteric Buddhism in Korea: Three Kingdoms and Unified Silla (ca. 600-918)," in *Esoteric Buddhism and the Tantras in East Asia*, ed. Charles D. Orzech, Henrik H. Sørensen, and Richard K. Payne (Leiden and Boston: Brill, 2011): 575-579.

[12] The meaning of this word will be explained more fully below.

[13] Some scholars have previously suggested that the term "Yoga monks" in this passage refers to Yogācāra monks. Because the record is about an "esoteric" Buddhist ritual, however, I agree with Sŏ Yun'gil, a specialist in Korean esoteric Buddhism, who suggests that "Yoga monks" in this context means monks who practice esoteric Buddhism's three mysteries (瑜伽三密). Sŏ Yun'gil, *Han'guk milgyo sasangsa*, 174-175. About the three mysteries appearing in early Buddhist texts, see Charles D. Orzech and Henrik H. Sørensen, "Mudrā, Mantra, Mandala," in *Esoteric Buddhism and the Tantras in East Asia*, ed. Charles D. Orzech, Henrik H. Sørensen, and Richard K. Payne (Leiden and Boston: Brill, 2011): 83-87.

8. The ritual platform at Sach'ŏnwang-sa was intact when the monk Iryŏn composed the *Samguk yusa* in the thirteenth century during the Koryŏ period.

For the convenience of the reader, this chapter will use the above numbers when referring to these key points in the following sections.

External Texts

In this section, I examine the *Samguk yusa* passage through a traditional method commonly used by historians—comparison with external textual sources. Four external texts from different genres, from an anthology compiled by a scholar-official to the official history composed by royal order, provide some useful records concerning the Munduru Ritual; this information can then be compared with the above key information from the *Samguk yusa* passage. As will be shown below, intertextual reading of these external documents helps understand the nature of the Munduru Ritual during the Koryŏ period, but does not tell us much about its practice during the Silla period. The four texts show that key points 2 and 4 were true at least from early Koryŏ to early Chosŏn (1392-1910), and that key point 6—that the construction of Sach'ŏnwang-sa was completed in 679—was not a simple fabrication by the compiler of the *Samguk yusa* but a quotation from an older text.

The first external text that can be used for comparison is the *Tongguk Yi Sangguk chip* 東國李相國集 (Collected works of State Councilor Yi of the Eastern Kingdom), an anthology of works by the Koryŏ scholar-official Yi Kyubo 李奎報 (1168-1241). A prose work in this anthology, titled "Prose for the Munduru Ritual at Vajra Monastery in the Western Capital" (Sŏgyŏng Kŭmgang-sa Munduru Toryangmun 西京金剛寺文豆婁道場文), shows that the Munduru Ritual was practiced under Koryŏ during Yi Kyubo's lifetime and that the purpose of this ritual at that time was state protection.[14] As the title of this work clearly indicates, Yi Kyubo composed it for the Munduru

---

[14] The "Western Capital" 西京 in the title appears as the "Same Capital" 同京 in the original text. This means that it is the same capital that appears in the title of the previous prose work included in the anthology. The title of the previous prose work begins with the word "Western Capital." *Tongguk Yi Sangguk chip* 39:9, original manuscript reprinted in Minjok Munhwa Ch'ujinhoe 民族文化推進會 [Korean Classics Research Institute], ed., *Kugyŏk Tongguk Yi Sangguk chip* 국역동국이상국집 [Translation of *Collected Works of State Councilor Yi of the Eastern Kingdom*] (Seoul: Minjok Munhwa Ch'ujinhoe, 1979): 5:24. The reproduction of the original manuscript is included in the back part of this book, which has pagination marked in Chinese characters.

Ritual practiced at the monastery named Vajra located in Koryŏ's Western Capital, which is present-day Pyongyang 平壤, North Korea.[15] Yi Kyubo's composition invokes religious protection of the state. It reflects a chaotic time for Koryŏ between the mid-twelfth and mid-thirteenth centuries, a period tainted by wars and rebellions. In the final passage of his prose composition, Yi Kyubo pleads with Buddhist deities to protect his country:

> [I] bend my body to rely on your spiritual power's response, [so that] wars will be loosened and suspended, worries of indignity caused by foreign countries will permanently disappear; the state will be sublime and numinous for a long time; and [we can] effortlessly enjoy the happiness of revived prosperity.[16]

曲借神通之應兵戈韜戢永無外侮之虞社稷靈長坐撫中興之慶.

Yi Kyubo's prose, especially the sentence quoted above, suggests that the purpose of the Munduru Ritual as practiced during Koryŏ was state protection and peace. This text validates key point 2, but only during Koryŏ. It does not confirm that the ritual was practiced for state protection during the Silla period.

The second text that provides more information about this ritual is the *Koryŏsa* 高麗史 (History of Koryŏ), which was compiled between 1449 and 1451. The *Koryŏsa* contains many records of various types of Buddhist rituals performed by the Koryŏ court, including records of nine Munduru Ritual performances.[17] The dates of the Munduru Ritual performances

---

[15] Koryŏ had three capitals (Kr. *samgyŏng* 三京)—the Central Capital (Kaegyŏng 開京, present-day Kaesŏng 開城), the Western Capital (present-day Pyongyang), and the Eastern Capital (present-day Kyŏngju). The usage of the term "Three Capitals" became complicated when Koryŏ installed the Southern Capital in Yangju 楊州 in 1067. The location of the Southern Capital's palace is inferred to be near the site of the Blue House (Ch'ŏngwadae 青瓦臺) in Seoul, South Korea. After the installation of the Southern Capital, the Koryŏ people often used the term "three capitals" to indicate the Central, Western, and Southern Capitals, excluding the declining Eastern Capital. In addition, the same term, "three capitals," was sometimes used to denote only the three local capitals: the Western, Eastern, and Southern Capitals.

[16] The literal translation of the last phrase (坐撫中興之慶) is "touch the joy of restoration while sitting."

[17] The examples of the Munduru Ritual performances recorded in the *Koryŏsa* include the performance at Sach'ŏnwang-sa on the fourth day of the seventh month

recorded in the *Koryŏsa* range from 1074 to 1217, with a concentration
occurring in the early twelfth century.

These records regarding the Munduru Ritual practice from the *Koryŏsa*
verify that Sach'ŏnwang-sa was one of the places this ritual was performed
under the Koryŏ kingdom (key point 4). The *Koryŏsa* record of the fourth
day of the seventh lunar month of 1074 (the twenty-eighth year of King
Munjong's 文宗 reign) reads,

On the day *kyŏngja*, [they] performed the Munduru Ritual at
Sach'ŏnwang-sa in the Eastern Capital for twenty-seven days, and
thereby subdued a barbarian military attack.

庚子設文豆婁道場於東京四天王寺二十七日以禳蕃兵.[18]

---

of 1074 (*Koryŏsa* 9:12, Munjong 文宗 28.7.4); the one practiced on the eleventh day
of the fourth lunar month in 1101 [the sixth year of Sukchong's reign] (*Koryŏsa* 54:1,
chi 志 8 *ohaeng* 五行 2); the one at Chinjŏng-sa 鎮靜寺 on the twenty-eighth day of
the seventh lunar month in 1108 (*Koryŏsa* 12:37, Yejong 睿宗 3.7.28); those performed
at Hŭngbok-sa 興福寺, Yŏngmyŏng-sa 永明寺, Changgyŏng-sa 長慶寺, Kŭmgang-sa
金剛寺, and other monasteries on the eleventh day of the lunar fourth month in 1109
(*Koryŏsa* 13:3-4, Yejong 4.4.11); and the two performances at Hyŏnsŏng-sa 賢聖寺, one
on the twenty-seventh day of the fourth lunar month in 1217 (*Koryŏsa* 22:11, Kojong 高
宗 4.4.27) and one on the nineteenth day of the twelfth lunar month in the same year
[the fourth year of Kojong's reign] (*Koryŏsa* 22:14, Kojong 4.12.19). I used the Yŏnhŭi
University (Yonsei University) edition of *Koryŏsa*. For the original texts of the above
Koryŏsa passages, see Yŏnhŭi Taehakkyo Tongbanghak Yŏn'guso 延禧大學校東方學研
究所 [The Institute of Far Eastern Studies Chosun Christian University], ed., *Koryŏsa*
高麗史 [History of Koryŏ], 3 vols. (Seoul: Yŏnhŭi Taehakkyo Ch'ulp'anbu, 1955) [here-
after *Yŏnhŭi Taehakkyo Koryŏsa*], 1:186; 2:125; 1:257; 1:260; 1:443; 1:444. The dates
refer to the traditional Korean lunar calendar. Because the ritual of 1109 was performed
in multiple monasteries and the article records the names of four monasteries, I count
them as separate ritual performances. I would like to point out that there were clearly
more occasions of the Munduru Ritual performances not recorded in the *Koryŏsa*. We
can notice, for example, that the Munduru Ritual for which Yi Kyubo wrote the prose
piece was not mentioned in the *Koryŏsa*. Sŏ Yun'gil has also suggested that the Buddhist rituals recorded in the *Koryŏsa* are only some of the rituals actually performed
during Koryŏ. He pointed out that records of annual Buddhist rituals were often omitted for the sake of brevity and that the many records of the king's visits to local monasteries also imply unrecorded Buddhist rituals performed during those visits. Sŏ Yun'gil,
Han'guk milgyo sasangsa yŏn'gu (Seoul: Pulgwang Ch'ulp'anbu, 1993): 508-510.

[18] *Koryŏsa* 9:12, Munjong 28.7.4, *Yŏnhŭi Taehakkyo Koryŏsa*, 1:186. A literal

Koryŏ's Eastern Capital was Kyŏngju 慶州, the former site of the capital of Silla. Mount Nang—the mountain identified as the location of Sach'ŏnwang-sa in the *Samguk yusa*—was also located in this place. These details corroborate that Sach'ŏnwang-sa in this *Koryŏsa* record of 1074 is the monastery mentioned in the *Samguk yusa* passage.

Furthermore, the nine performances of the Munduru Ritual recorded in the *Koryŏsa* also affirm that Koryŏ practiced this ritual for state protection (key point 2). With the exception of the two occasions in 1217 when the Munduru Ritual was performed at Hyŏnsŏng-sa 賢聖寺 for unstated purposes, the ritual was clearly recorded to have been performed each time in order to win victory in war or subdue military attack.[19] In particular, this ritual was most frequently performed in the early twelfth century when Koryŏ was waging a series of battles with the Jurchens, who were gradually gaining military power on Koryŏ's northern frontier. The unspecified purposes of the two ritual practices of 1217 may have been related to state protection as well: comprehensive reading of the entire record of the year 1217 in the *Koryŏsa* suggests that the ritual may have been performed in order to repel the Kitans of Later Liao 後遼 (1216-1219), who were invading and plundering Koryŏ that year.[20]

The third external text, *Chosŏn wangjo sillok* 朝鮮王朝實錄 (Annals of the Chosŏn dynasty), records a performance of the Munduru Ritual as late as the year 1400 in the early Chosŏn period.[21] This is the latest docu-

---

translation of the first phrase of this sentence (設文豆婁道場) is "installed a ritual place/altar of the Munduru [Ritual]." In Korea, the phrase *sŏl toryang* 設道場 is often translated as "perform a ritual." As Koichi Shinohara has pointed out to me, however, this phrase suggests that a certain kind of altar was installed to practice "esoteric" Buddhist ritual.

[19] The record of the occasion for each ritual is very short, usually only one or two sentences. In order to understand more about the military attack or the war mentioned in each record of the Munduru Ritual performance, one has to read the records from the same month or year. For more about the original sources from the *Koryŏsa*, see the list in footnote 17 of this chapter.

[20] The Kitan's Liao state fell to the Jin 金 (1115-1234) in 1125. The remaining Kitan people, however, briefly founded the short-lived Later Liao polity, also known as Great Liao (Ch. Da Liaoguo 大遼國), when the Mongols began to conquer the Jin in the early thirteenth century. Driven away by the Mongols from their territory, between 1216 and 1219 the Kitans of the Later Liao invaded Koryŏ. In 1219, Koryŏ subjugated the invading Kitans through a military alliance with the Mongols.

[21] 設祈禳文豆婁道場于賢聖寺七日. *Chŏngjong sillok* 定宗實錄 3:14, Chŏngjong

mented practice of the Munduru Ritual. As Buddhism soon lost favor in the Chosŏn court, it seems that afterward this Buddhist ritual was not practiced by royal patrons.

The last text having a relevant intertextual relationship with the *Samguk yusa* passage is the above-mentioned *Samguk sagi*, the official history of the Three Kingdoms of Korea, which was compiled under Koryŏ. Comparative reading reveals that the completion date of 679 noted in the *Samguk yusa* (key point 6) was derived from this official historical work. According to the *Samguk yusa* passage, Sach'ŏnwang-sa had been temporarily built with silk textiles in preparation for the Munduru Ritual performance in 670 at the beginning of the Silla-Tang war, and permanent wooden buildings were erected at the monastery site in 679, two years after the end of the Silla-Tang war. In the above *Samguk yusa* passage, this completion date appears in an interlinear note.[22] This interlinear note, written in smaller characters than those used for the main text in the original manuscript, explains, "The *Kuksa* says the renovation and formal opening of the monastery took place in the first year of the Tiaolu reign, which was the year of *kimyo* [679]."[23] There are several different opinions regarding the identity of the text *Kuksa* (State history) repeatedly quoted in the *Samguk yusa*. As for the *Kuksa* quoted in this specific interlinear note, however, it is clear that it indicates the *Samguk sagi*,[24] since the same content is found in this text's entry for the eighth month of the nineteenth year of King Munmu's reign, which records that "Sach'ŏnwang-sa has been completed" (*Sach'ŏnwang-sa sŏng* 四天王寺成)

2.3.15 (*kyŏngjin* 庚辰), original manuscript reprinted in Kuksa P'yŏnch'an Wiwŏnhoe 國史編纂委員會 [National Institute of Korean History], ed., *Chosŏn wangjo sillok* 朝鮮王朝實錄 [Annals of the Chosŏn dynasty] (Seoul: Tongguk Munhwasa, 1955): 1:167b. The second year of King Chŏngjong's reign corresponds to the year 1400 in the Western calendar.

[22] I marked the interlinear note with angled brackets in my translation of the *Samguk yusa* passage provided earlier in this chapter.

[23] "Tiaolu" was one of the reign titles of emperor Gaozong (r. 649-683) of China's Tang empire, and its first year corresponds to the year 679. During the Koryŏ period, it was common to use the title of the Chinese reign in official records. Depending on changing international politics, Koryŏ chose to use Song, Liao, or other Chinese dynasties' reign titles. There were, however, several Koryŏ kings, such as T'aejo 太祖 (r. 918-943), Kwangjong 光宗 (r. 949-975), and Kyŏngjong 景宗 (r. 975-981), who used their own Koryŏ titles.

[24] This does not mean that all the records titled *Kuksa* appearing in the *Samguk yusa* citations refer to the *Samguk sagi*.

in this month.[25] The nineteenth reign year of King Munmu corresponds to the year 679, thereby matching the monastery's completion date in the above *Samguk yusa* passage. In writing this passage, the compiler was referencing the earlier text when available. The fact that the monastery's completion date came from the *Samguk sagi*'s quotation of the previous official history attests that this date for the completion of Sach'ŏnwang-sa is at least not a pure fabrication by the compiler of the *Samguk yusa*. The matching document in the *Samguk yusa* and the *Samguk sagi*, however, does not fully verify that the completion date of 679 is a trustworthy record. Although the latter text, an official history of the Three Kingdoms, is widely accepted as a much more reliable text than the former, its credibility is unfortunately still a matter for debate.[26]

Comparison with external texts so far has proved useful, but at the same time reveals an apparent limit in evaluating the *Samguk yusa* passage under examination. Although it provides relatively rich information about the nature and practices of the Munduru Ritual in later dynasties, it does little to illuminate this ritual under the Silla kingdom. This is where archaeological, art historical, and other types of data come in, as will be discussed in a later part of this chapter.

Epigraphs and Internal Signs
As shown above, external texts do not give many clues about whether the Munduru ritual was ever practiced in seventh-century Silla. This rather frustrating limitation of using external texts to evaluate the contents of the *Samguk yusa* is not unique to this passage about the Munduru Ritual. Much of the content of the *Samguk yusa* cannot be authenticated by external texts, since most of the earlier or contemporaneous texts produced on the Korean peninsula did not survive.

As a small suggestion to remedy this predicament to some degree, before further discussing the passage about the Munduru Ritual, I want

---

[25] *Samguk sagi* 7: King Munmu, nineteenth year, Han'gukhak Chungang Yŏn'guwŏn 韓國學中央研究院 [Academy of Korean Studies], ed., *Yŏkchu Samguk sagi* 譯註 三國史記 [Annotation and translation of the *Samguk sagi*] (Sŏngnam: Han'gukhak Chungang Yŏn'guwŏn Ch'ulp'anbu, 2011), 1:183.

[26] The *Samguk sagi* obviously includes some errors. Most scholars would agree that this is the case. The problem arises, however, in that some believe that the text is mostly trustworthy except for small errors, while others argue that a large portion of this text was fabricated.

to draw the reader's attention to quotations included in the *Samguk yusa*, since they can be useful in identifying relatively trustworthy information in this text. The *Samguk yusa* has quite a few long and short quotations, the sources for which are clearly marked. The quotation from the *Kuksa* documenting the completion date of Sach'ŏnwang-sa included in the above passage about the Munduru Ritual is one such example. These quotations come from inscriptions as well as various writings from preceding dynasties in Korea and China. Some are embedded in the main text and are written in the same size characters, and some appear as interlinear notes written in smaller characters.

Some of the epigraphs excavated in modern times show that certain types of quotations in the *Samguk yusa* came from epigraphs collected in the Korean peninsula. One good example is the reliquary inscription (872) found at the pagoda site at Hwangnyong-sa 皇龍寺 (569), meaning Imperial Dragon Monastery, located in present-day Kyŏngju (fig. 3.1).[27] The inscription provides a good opportunity to understand how Iryŏn used epigraphic data (fig. 3.2). Hwangnyong-sa—a palace turned into a Buddhist monastery during its construction[28]—was an unprecedentedly large and ambitious Silla monastery. Following the advice of the famous monk Chajang 慈藏 (590-658), the Silla royal family built a monumental nine-story wooden pagoda at this monastery in 645.[29] This pagoda stood at Hwang-

---

[27] A few historical records spell this monastery's name as Hwangnyong-sa 黃龍寺, meaning Yellow Dragon Monastery. As shown in the reliquary inscription from the monastery and many other records, however, the correct name of this monastery is Hwangnyong-sa 皇龍寺, Imperial Dragon Monastery. The latter name is also widely used by modern scholars.

[28] *Samguk sagi* 4: King Chinhŭng, fourteenth year, *Yŏkchu Samguk sagi*, 1:135.

[29] *Samguk sagi* 5: King Sŏndŏk, fourteenth year, *Yŏkchu Samguk sagi*, 1:147-148. While the *Samguk sagi* records that this pagoda was first created (Kr. *ch'angjo* 創造) in 645, the reliquary inscription from this pagoda, which will be discussed below, records that construction of the pagoda began and its heart pillar erected in 645, while the construction of the pagoda was completed the following year. This suggests that people placed much importance on the erection of the heart pillar, the most symbolically significant part of the pagoda, and the enshrinement of the Buddha relics beneath it; it also demonstrates that this act was regarded as the complement of the pagoda. When the relic is enshrined, the pagoda is consecrated and transformed into a sacred monument. Such a momentous event must have been celebrated with an appropriate Buddhist ceremony. This becomes more evident in that the compiler of the *Samguk yusa*, who referred to this reliquary inscription, also

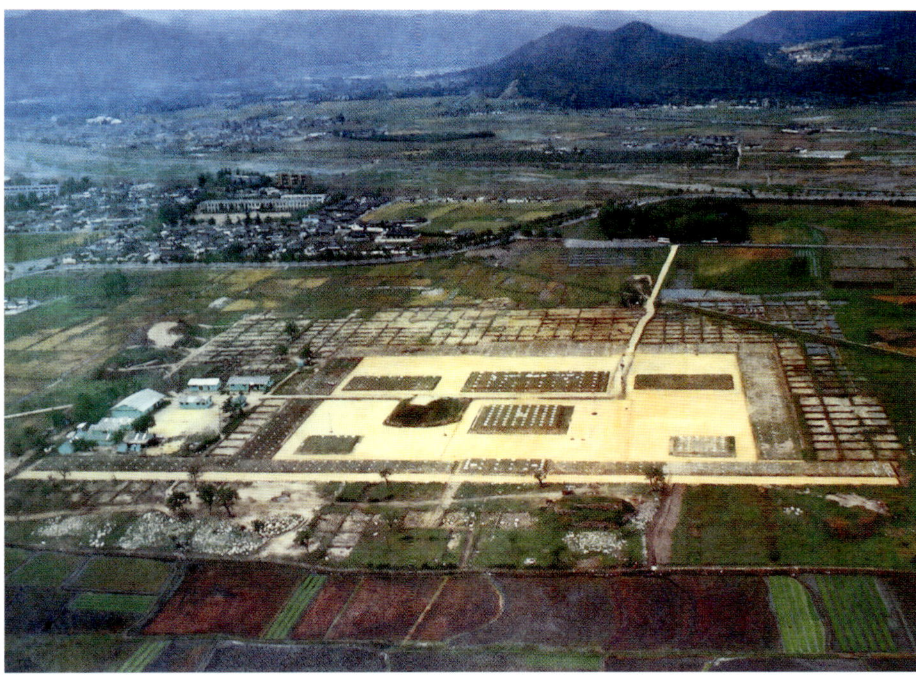

Figure 3.1
Hwangnyong-
sa site, Kyŏngju,
Korea.
Courtesy of
the Gyeongju
Research Insti-
tute of Cultural
Heritage.

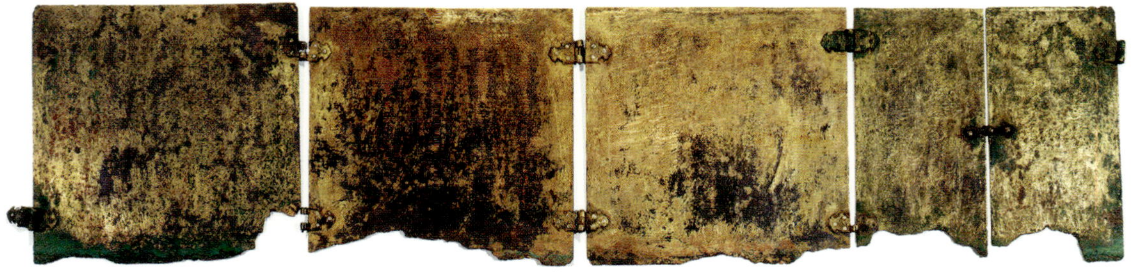

Figure 3.2 Reliquary casket, from the Hwangnyong-sa Pagoda site, Kyŏngju, Korea.
Silla, 872. Gilt-bronze. 22.5×94cm. Courtesy of the National Museum of Korea.

nyong-sa until the Mongols invaded the Korean peninsula and reduced it to ashes in 1238. Although the pagoda was lost many centuries ago, its stone bases, showing that each of the pagoda's four sides had seven bays, remained mostly intact until the twentieth century. In December 1964, however, looters took the pagoda reliquaries and accompanying objects from the relic crypt inside the central stone base, which initially supported the heart pillar (Kr. *ch'alchu* 刹柱) of the pagoda.[30] Fortunately the looters were caught two years after the robbery, and the stolen objects, which had been sold to a private collector, were sent to the National Museum of Korea. Among the objects retrieved were two nested gilt-bronze caskets, forming part of a reliquary set. The smaller gilt-bronze casket had seventy-four lines of inscription titled *Hwangnyong-sa ch'alchu pon'gi* 皇龍寺刹柱本記 (Record of the heart pillar at Hwangnyong-sa) engraved on the recto and verso of its three sides.[31] The casket lost its bottom plate due to natural processes over the many centuries it stayed underground. The illustration in this chapter shows the unfolded sidewalls of this casket, connected with hinges (fig. 3.2). The width and height of each plate, except for the frontal plate divided into two pieces in the center, are 23.5 centimeters and 22.5 centimeters, respectively.

---

recorded the completion date of the pagoda as 645 instead of 646. *Samguk yusa* 3: "Hwangnyong-sa Kuch'ŭngt'ap," *Yŏkchu Samguk yusa*, 3:130.

[30] The "heart pillar" means the central pillar of a wooden Buddhist pagoda. Buddha's relics were often enshrined inside the stone supporting the heart pillar, so that the reliquary could not be taken out without moving the enormous heart pillar.

[31] For a transcription of the entire inscription and annotations on its content, see Hwang Suyŏng 黃壽永, "Silla Hwangnyong-sa Kuch'ŭngt'apchi: Ch'alchu pon'gi e taehayŏ" 新羅 皇龍寺 九層塔誌: 刹柱本記에 대하여 [Record of the Nine-story Pagoda at Hwangnyong-sa from Silla: Regarding the *Record from the Heart Pillar*], *Misul sahak yŏn'gu* 美術史學研究 116 (1972): 275-277; Hwang Suyŏng 黃壽永, "Silla Hwangnyong-sa Kuch'ŭng mokt'ap ch'alchu pon'gi wa kŭ sarigu" 新羅 皇龍寺九層木塔 刹柱本記와 그 舍利具 [*Record from the Heart Pillar of the Nine-story Pagoda* of Hwangnyong-sa from Silla and the pagoda's reliquary], *Tongyanghak* 東洋學 3 (1973): 269-328. For a translation of the inscription into modern Korean with thorough annotations, see Han'guk Kodae Sahoe Yŏn'guso 韓國古代社會研究所 [Research Institute of Korean Ancient Society], ed., *Yŏkchu Han'guk kodae kŭmsŏngmun* 譯註韓國古代金石文 [Annotation and translation of ancient inscriptions of Korea], vol. 3 (Seoul: Karak-kuk Sajŏk Kaebal Yŏn'guwŏn, 1992): 364-375. *Yŏkchu Han'guk kodae kŭmsŏngmun* contains one minor error: the thirtieth reign year of King Chinhŭng 眞興 (r. 540-576), the completion year of Hwangnyong-sa, is not 574, but corresponds to 569.

The content of the inscription, dated to 872, shows that this reliquary was enshrined during the pagoda's restoration under the reign of King Kyŏngmun 景文 (r. 861-875). Discovered at the Hwangnyong-sa site in 1960s, this reliquary inscription reveals that Iryŏn referred to epigraphs from the Korean peninsula when compiling the *Samguk yusa*. This inscription was cited in the *Samguk yusa*'s "Nine-story Pagoda at Hwangnyong-sa" (Hwangnyong-sa Kuch'ŭngt'ap 皇龍寺九層塔).[32] This article includes two very short quotations of epigraphs from Hwangnyong-sa. One is included in the main text and reads, "*Ch'alchugi* 刹柱記 (Record from the [pagoda] heart pillar) says that the pinnacle of the pagoda is 42 *ch'ŏk* tall and the body of the pagoda is 183 *ch'ŏk* tall."[33] The name of the original text, *Ch'alchugi*, implies that this text is the reliquary inscription enshrined under the pagoda's heart pillar. The *Ch'alchugi* indeed includes information regarding this pagoda's height,[34] indicating that the compiler of the *Samguk yusa* undeniably referred to this particular reliquary inscription.[35] Since the pagoda used

---

[32] It was Hwang Suyŏng, one of the first generation of Korean art historians after the colonial period, who first examined this inscription in 1972. Hwang found that the *Samguk yusa*'s "Nine-story Pagoda at Hwangnyong-sa" article quoted this inscription, and that the official historical work *Samguk sagi* also has records conforming to the contents of this inscription. See Hwang Suyŏng, "Silla Hwangnyong-sa kuch'ěng mokt'ap," 278-279. For *Samguk yusa*'s "Nine-story Pagoda at Hwangnyong-sa" article, see *Samguk yusa* 3: "Hwangnyong-sa Kuch'ŭngt'ap," *Yŏkchu Samguk yusa*, 3:128-130. Since its discovery in the 1960s, this inscription from the Hwang-nyong-sa pagoda has been well known among Korean scholars, but it is not widely known in Western academia. When I say that this ancient inscription matches the records in the *Samguk yusa* and the *Samguk sagi*, my colleagues usually show immediate interest and curiosity. It is quite interesting, however, that this discovery did not come as much of a surprise for Hwang Suyŏng, who saw many archaeological remains corresponding to records in the *Samguk yusa*.

[33] 刹柱記云. 鐵盤已上高四十二尺, 已下一百八十三尺. *Samguk yusa* 3: "Hwangnyong-sa Kuch'ŭngt'ap," *Yŏkchu Samguk yusa*, 3:129. The literal translation of this quotation is "*Record from the [Pagoda] Heart Pillar* says that the height of [the pagoda] above the iron plate is 42 *ch'ŏk* and below [the iron plate] is 183 *ch'ŏk*." The "iron plate" refers to the metal component forming the lowest bottom part of the pagoda's metal pinnacle. This part of the pagoda pinnacle is also called "dew plate" (Kr. *noban* 露盤). The *ch'ŏk* is a traditional measurement unit in East Asia.

[34] For the height of the pagoda in the reliquary inscription, see Hwang Suyŏng, "Silla Hwangnyong-sa Kuch'ŭng mokt'ap," 278; Han'guk Kodae Sahoe Yŏn'guso, ed., *Yŏkchu Han'guk kodae kŭmsŏngmun*, 368.

[35] Hwang Suyŏng, "Silla Hwangnyong-sa Kuch'ŭng mokt'ap," 278-279. It is quite

the measurement unit known as the Koryŏ *chŏk* 高麗尺 in which one *chŏk* was 35.63 centimeters,[36] the original height of this pagoda including the pinnacle part was about 80.2 meters. Iryŏn noted the source of this pagoda height probably because the exact pagoda height was not common knowledge that he could draw on from memory and he had to refer to a transcription of the reliquary inscription.

Another quotation in the *Samguk yusa*'s "Nine-story Pagoda at Hwangnyong-sa" reveals that the compiler cited the epigraph to explain that there were two different accounts of why this pagoda was built. This quotation appears as an interlinear note, which reads, "*Sajunggi* 寺中記 (Record from the monastery) says that [the monk Chajang] was given the idea of building the pagoda [at Hwangnyong-sa] at the meditation master Yuanxiang's dwelling on Mount Zhongnan."[37] After reading the entire article, one realizes that the compiler added this short quotation to inform the reader that the *Sajunggi*, an epigraph from the monastery, describes a version of the story that differs slightly from the version provided in the main text. In the story recounted in the main text, the monk Chajang encountered a man with supernatural power (Kr. *sinin* 神人) near Lake Taihe 太和 in China, who told Chajang to return to Silla and build a nine-story pagoda at Hwangnyong-sa in order to make neighboring countries surrender to Silla. In this version of the story, the man with supernatural power later turns out to be the father of the dragon protecting Hwangnyong-sa in Silla.[38] On the other hand, the version of the story recorded in the reliquary inscription from the monastery's pagoda site is more realistic: In this version, a meditation master called Yuanxiang 圓香 (dates unknown), not the father of the

---

surprising that the compiler of the *Samguk yusa* knew the precise information from this inscription that had been written four centuries earlier and then buried under the pagoda. As one of the attendees of my presentation at Harvard in February 2012 has pointed out, it is likely that there was a transcription of this reliquary that was being circulated when the *Samguk yusa* was compiled. I appreciate her comment.

[36] Kungnip Kyŏngju Munhwajae Yŏn'guso 國立慶州文化財研究所 [Gyeongju National Research Institute of Cultural Heritage], *Sach'ŏnwang-sa: Kŭmdangji palgul chosa pogosŏ* 四天王寺 I: 金堂址 발굴조사보고서 [Sach'ŏnwang-sa I: Main Buddha hall site excavation report] (Kyŏngju-si: Kungnip Kyŏngju Munhwajae Yŏn'guso, 2012): 341, chart 12.

[37] 寺中記云. 於終南山圓香禪師處. 受建塔因由. The literal translation of the phrase, "su kŏnt'ap inyu" 受建塔因由 is "received the reason and cause to build the pagoda." *Samguk yusa* 3: "Hwangnyong-sa Kuch'ŭngt'ap," *Yŏkchu Samguk yusa*, 3:128.

[38] *Samguk yusa* 3: "Hwangnyong-sa Kuch'ŭngt'ap," *Yŏkchu Samguk yusa*, 3:128.

dragon, tells Chajang to build the nine-story pagoda to protect Silla.[39] The fact that the meditation master's name is the same reveals that this is the version of the story mentioned in the *Samguk yusa* quotation. Evidently Iryŏn knew both versions of the story. Unfortunately Iryŏn does not clarify the source of the legend of the man with supernatural power at Lake Taihe that he relates in detail in the main text of the *Samguk yusa* article. As a result, ironically, we can only know the source of the story that Iryŏn treated as a secondary version of the story and hence only briefly mentioned in the interlinear note, while the source of the version of the story detailed in the main text remains unknown.

Among the works quoted in the *Samguk yusa*, those works titled *Sajunggi, Sajung kogi* 寺中古記 (Old record from the monastery), and *Ch'alchugi* are epigraphs collected from monastery and pagoda sites in the peninsula. These quotations, although appearing under generic titles, are mostly epigraphic documents from specific monastery and pagoda sites which are discussed in the sections of the *Samguk yusa* that cite those epigraphs. Understanding Iryŏn's usage of Korean epigraphs is very important in that it would help us better to comprehend the way Iryŏn composed the *Samguk yusa* and therefore better to understand the nature of this text. According to my brief research, the *Samguk yusa* includes more than seven quotations from works titled *Sajunggi* or *Sajung kogi*, whose contents and nature deserve more careful study in the future. For this chapter concentrating on the Munduru Ritual at Sach'ŏnwang-sa, however, it suffices to point out that Iryŏn referred both to epigraphs and to received texts and that he from time to time marked his source when quoting them.

Besides this specific type of quotation from epigraphic data, general quotations in the *Samguk yusa* also faithfully preserve information from the original texts. For example, in a 2006 article, Richard McBride examined four lengthy citations in the *Samguk yusa* that were derived from

---

[39] For a translation of the inscription into modern Korean with thorough annotations, see Han'guk Kodae Sahoe Yŏn'guso, ed., *Yŏkchu Han'guk kodae kŭmsŏngmun*, 364-375. It seems that more than one epigraph from Hwangnyong-sa was available to the compiler of the *Samguk yusa* when he composed the "Nine-story Pagoda at Hwangnyong-sa" section. For example, the final part of this section quotes the *Sajung kogi* (Old record from the monastery), and the quotation includes some information not found in the reliquary inscription. *Samguk yusa* 3: "Hwangnyong-sa Kuch'ŭngt'ap," *Yŏkchu Samguk yusa*, 3:130. This means that the *Sajunggi* mentioning the meditation master Yuanxiang, quoted in the *Samguk yusa*, could be another epigraph from Hwangnyong-sa that is not extant today, recording a similar content.

earlier texts from Korea and China, as well as one epigraph from Silla, and
concluded that the compiler of the *Samguk yusa* did not change or distort
the contents of the quoted text, although he often summarized or rephrased
the original sources.[40]

All these observations suggest that although the *Samguk yusa* is
regarded as a less reliable text than other historical documents written
earlier in China and Korea, at least the quotations it includes should be
treated in a similar way that scholars would have treated the original epigraphs or texts cited, had those epigraphs or texts survived. For example,
the renowned Korean monk Anhong's 安弘 (fl. sixth century) proposal
to build a nine-story pagoda at Hwangnyong-sa for state protection, as
described in his *Tongdo Sŏngnipki* 東都成立記, was cited in the "Nine-story
Pagoda at Hwangnyong-sa" article of the *Samguk yusa*.[41] Unfortunately, the
Tongdo Sŏngnipki does not survive today. In this case, it would be proper
for a scholar to treat the specific quotation from this book included in
the *Samguk yusa* as he or she would treat the same information from the
Tongdo Sŏngnipki if that text had survived. Even though quotations are
often short and occupy only a small portion of the *Samguk yusa*, information included in those quotations, however meager, would serve as useful
data about early Korean Buddhism especially because most ancient Korean
texts have been lost.

Ritual from Silla or Koryŏ?

Now we can move on to consider the *Samguk yusa* passage about the
Munduru Ritual. As discussed above, external texts clearly verify that this
ritual was practiced under the Koryŏ kingdom to ensure state protection
from the eleventh century onward, but they do not verify much about the
ritual's practice in seventh-century Silla. Here, one can posit the possibility
that the practice of this ritual began only in Koryŏ times, and that the story
of Silla's practice of the Munduru Ritual was fabricated later. Is it not possible that the monk Iryŏn, who witnessed the Munduru Ritual performed
at Sach'ŏnwang-sa located in the former capital of Silla, gave the ritual an
imagined origin in Silla based on his observation of the contemporaneous

---

[40] Richard D. McBride's article shows that the *Samguk yusa*'s quotations often
abbreviate and rephrase the original texts, but do not add incorrect or fabricated
information. Richard D. McBride II, "Is the *Samguk yusa* Reliable? Case Studies from
Chinese and Korean Sources," *The Journal of Korean Studies* 11, no. 1 (2006): 163-190.

[41] *Samguk yusa* 3: "Hwangnyong-sa Kuch'ŭngt'ap," *Yŏkchu Samguk yusa*, 3:129.

ritual, especially if he had—although one can't prove it—a need to give the ritual more authority?

Further examination of the nature of this ritual in the larger context of East Asian "esoteric" Buddhism, however, suggests that this is less likely to be true. Scholars unanimously agree that the primary textual source of the Munduru Ritual is the seventh fascicle of the *Foshuo guanding jing* 佛說灌頂經, or the *Consecration Sutra Preached by the Buddha* (hereafter *Consecration Sutra*),[42] an opinion first put forward by Pak T'ae-hwa in his 1965 article.[43] Key points 1 (the name of the ritual was Munduru) and 5 (usage of statues of the Deities of the Five Directions) connect this ritual, practiced

------

[42] T1331, 21:495a-536b. This sutra had several different names, such as the *Da guanding shenzhou jing* 大灌頂神呪經, meaning the *Great Consecration Supernatural Incantation Sutra*. Strickmann recognized the importance of "apocryphal" Buddhist sutras, which reflect and adopt Chinese indigenous religious practices, and argued that the *Consecration Sutra* is "a repository of practice and oral tradition." For more about the *Consecration Sutra*, see Michel Strickmann "The *Consecration Sūtra*: A Buddhist Book of Spells," in *Chinese Buddhist Apocrypha*, ed. Robert E. Buswell, Jr. (Honolulu: University of Hawai'i Press, 1990): 75-118; Oka Sumiaki 阿純章, "*Kanjōkyō* ni okeru jujutsu no juyō" 『灌頂経』における呪術の受容 [Embrace of incantation in the *Consecration Sutra*], *Tendai gakuhō* 天台学報 39 (October 1997): 179-185; Oka Sumiaki 阿純章, "*Kanjōkyō* no seiritsu ni tsuite" 『灌頂経』の成立につ いて [On the establishment of the *Consecration Sutra*], *Waseda Daigaku daigakuin bungaku kenkyūka kiyō* 早稲田大学大学院文学研究科紀要 41, no.1 (1996): 97-108; Endō Yusuke 遠藤 祐介, "*Kanjōkyō* no yakusha ni tsuite" 『灌頂経』の訳者につい て [On the translator of the *Consecration Sutra*], *Mikkyōgaku kenkyū* 密教学研究 36 (March 2004): 45-64.

[43] Pak T'ae-hwa 朴泰華, "Silla sidae ŭi milgyo chŏllaego" 新羅時代의 密敎 傳 來考" [Study on the transmission of esoteric Buddhism during the Silla period], in *Hyosŏng Cho Myŏnggi Paksa hwagap kinyŏm Pulgyo sahak nonch'ong* 曉城趙明基博士 華甲記念佛教史學論叢 [Festschrift on Buddhist history in honor of Hyosŏng, Doctor Cho Myŏnggi, for his sixty-first birthday], ed. Hyosŏng Cho Myŏng-gi Paksa Hwagap Kinyŏm Pulgyo Sahak Nonmunjip Kanhaeng Wiwŏnhoe 曉城趙明基博士 華甲記念佛教史學論叢刊行委員會 [Committee for the Publication of Festschrift on Buddhist History in Honor of Hyosŏng, Doctor Cho Myŏnggi, for his Sixty-First Birthday] (Seoul: Tongguk Taehakkyo, 1965): 73-74. For more about this ritual, see Ko Ikchin 高翊晋, "Silla milgyo ŭi sasang naeyong kwa chŏn'gae yangsang" 新羅密 敎의 思想内容과 展開樣相 [Thoughts and evolution of Silla esoteric Buddhism], in *Han'guk milgyo sasang yŏn'gu* 韓國密教思想研究 [Research on Korean esoteric Buddhist thought], ed. Pulgyo Munhwa Yŏn'guwŏn 佛教文化研究院 [Research Institute of Buddhist Culture] (Seoul: Pulgyo Munhwa Yŏn'guwŏn, 1986): 145-161.

on the Korean peninsula, with the *Consecration Sutra*. In the seventh fascicle of this sutra, titled "Sutra of Consecration Seal and Great Spell That Subjugate Māra, as Preached by the Buddha" (*Foshuo guanding fumo fengyin dashenzhou jing* 佛說灌頂伏魔封印大神呪經),[44] the Buddha, responding to Indra's (Ch. Tian dishi 天帝釋) request,[45] expounds on a ritual named "Munduru" 文頭婁 (Ch. Wentoulou).[46] This ritual was performed to help people with various difficulties, especially sick people. The name of this ritual comes from the thaumaturgic power of wooden seals inscribed with the names of deities. The wooden seals are called "Munduru" and used for healing and for other efficacies in the *Consecration Sutra*. The word "Munduru" in this sutra is the same word as "Munduru" 文豆婁, the name of the "esoteric" ritual as recorded in the *Samguk yusa*, the *Koryŏsa*, and other Korean texts. "Munduru" (either spelled 文頭婁 or 文豆婁) is a transliteration of the Sanskrit term *mudrā*.[47] *Mudrā* can be either apotropaic Buddhist seals (Ch. *yin* 印),[48] or religious hand gestures (Ch. *shouyin* 手印) that were used by monks for ritual performances or formed by Buddhist deities as iconographic signs. In East Asian Buddhist texts, however, the Sanskrit term *mudrā* usually appeared as translated Chinese words, *yin* (seal) or *shouyin* (hand gesture or hand seal), and this specific transliteration of the term "Munduru" was very rarely used. To the best of my knowledge, the word "Munduru" does not appear in other Buddhist sutras, which makes the matching names of the two rituals all the more noteworthy. Moreover, just as in the Munduru Ritual described in the *Samguk yusa*, the Deities of the Five Directions (Kr. *obangsin*, Ch. *wufangshen* 五方神) play an important

---

[44] T1331, 21:515a-517b. Michel Strickmann provided a translation of the beginning half of this seventh fascicle from the *Consecration Sutra* in his book, *Chinese Magical Medicine*, ed. Bernard Faure (Stanford: Stanford University Press, 2002): 132-136.

[45] Tian dishi can be also translated as "Heavenly Sovereign Śakra."

[46] To avoid confusion, I use the Korean pronunciation, instead of Chinese pronunciation, of this ritual explained in this *Consecration Sutra* fascicle.

[47] Ōmura Seigai 大村西崖, *Mikkyō hattatsushi* 密教發達志 [Record on the development of esoteric Buddhism] (Tokyo: Bussho Kankōkai Zuzōbu, 1918): 1:132; Sŏ Yun'gil, *Han'guk milgyo sasangsa*, 169; Michel Strickmann, *Chinese Magical Medicine*, 316, no. 21.

[48] Michel Strickmann suggested that Chinese Buddhists adopted the practice of using seals for healing and thaumaturgic efficacy from the Daoist tradition. See Michel Strickmann, *Chinese Magical Medicine*, 123-193.

role in the ritual explained in the *Consecration Sutra*.[49] Probably not coincidentally, the Deities of the Five Directions are also deities that rarely appear in Buddhist sutras. The *Samguk yusa* and the *Consecration Sutra* are the only texts that mention these deities among the texts included in the *Taishō shinshū daizōkyō*, the Buddhist canon compiled in Japan in the early twentieth century. In short, the matching names of the ritual and the principal deities provide a strong connection between the ritual recorded in the *Samguk yusa* and the one explained in the *Consecration Sutra*.[50]

Most significantly, the "Munduru" Ritual explained in the seventh fascicle of the *Consecration Sutra* is categorized as an early "esoteric" ritual of a type popular before the eighth century. More specifically, this ritual is an early "esoteric" Buddhist ritual that exhibits influence from Daoist practices.[51] This type of ritual is distinguished from the highly developed and systemized "esoteric" Buddhism that was introduced to East Asia in the eighth century by a group of Indian monks. The *Taishō shinshū daizōkyō* attributes the translation of the *Consecration Sutra* to Śrīmitra (Ch. Bo

---

[49] T1331, 21:515a-c. In addition to the *Consecration Sutra*, only a few other Buddhist texts mention the Deities of the Five Directions.

[50] One needs to consider, however, that many of the rituals explained in the Buddhist canon do not document actual ritual performances. Ritual practices evolve and become modified as they spread to different regions and as time passes. Therefore, while I agree that a very strong relationship exists between this ritual and the sutra, the "Munduru" Ritual explained in the *Consecration Sutra* is not necessarily exactly the same as the Munduru Ritual *practiced* in Korea. In other words, small deviations between the Munduru Ritual *practice* and the descriptions in the *Consecration Sutra* do not prove that there is no relationship between them. At the same time, as I will discuss more in this chapter, one should not depend too much on this text when reconstructing the Munduru Ritual practiced in Korea. For an example of a *dhāranī* ritual modified from the Tang to Liao and Heian Japan, see Youn-mi Kim, "Eternal Ritual in an Infinite Cosmos: The Chaoyang North Pagoda (1043-1044)," (Ph.D. dissertation, Harvard University, 2010): 216-307; Youn-mi Kim, "The Secret Link: Tracing Liao in Japanese Shingon Ritual," *Journal of Song-Yuan Studies* (forthcoming, 2014).

[51] For more about the Daoist influence on the *Consecration Sutra*, see Michel Strickmann, "The *Consecration Sūtra*," 75-118; Michel Strickmann, *Chinese Magical Medicine*, 113-119, 132-140, 185, 187, 192; Kang Ubang 姜友邦, *Wŏnyung kwa chohwa: Han'guk kodae chogaksa ŭi wŏlli* 圓融과 調和: 韓國古代彫刻史의 原理 [Synthesis and harmony: Principle of the history of ancient Korean sculpture] (Seoul: Yŏrhwadang, 1990): 190-197; Oka Sumiaki, "*Kanjōkyō* ni okeru jujutsu no juyō," 179-185; Oka Sumiaki, "*Kanjōkyō* no seiritsu ni tsuite," 97-108.

Shilimiduoluo 帛尸梨蜜多羅, d. 343 C.E.), a Kuchean monk who was active in the capital city of Eastern Jin 東晉 (317-420 C.E.). Ōmura Seigai, however, pointed out that this attribution is incorrect because its twelfth fascicle was composed by the monk Huijian 慧簡 in 457,[52] as explained in the *Chu sanzang jiji* 出三藏記集 (Compilation of notes on the translation of the Tripiṭaka).[53] More recent scholarship also suggests that this sutra was written in China's Jiangnan 江南 area around 457 by Huijian or by people in Huijian's circle.[54] Oka Sumiaki has pointed out the strong Daoist influence in the *Consecration Sutra*,[55] and Michel Strickmann argued that the "Munduru" Ritual from the seventh fascicle of this sutra is essentially a Daoist ensigillation ritual—a ritual that uses magical seals—in Buddhist guise.[56] This type of "apocryphal" Buddhist sutra written in China with strong Daoist influence became old-fashioned after the eighth century when monks from India, such as Śubhakarasiṃha (637-735), Vajrabodhi (671-741), and Amoghavajra (705-774), introduced to China systemized "esoteric" Buddhism, which, according to Robert Sharf, was regarded as "new technology."[57] After the introduction of the systemized "esoteric" Buddhism to China, its new "ritual technology" gained the favor of the imperial court. The early "esoteric" rituals, although they did not completely disappear, were no longer a leading form of Buddhist ritual.

If the practice of the Munduru Ritual began in the time of Koryŏ rather than Silla, one needs to find plausible reasons why the Koryŏ court in the eleventh century suddenly began to practice this ritual, which by that time was rather old-fashioned. One convincing reason has been suggested by Sørensen. Observing that there is no trace of similar rituals practiced in either Tang or Song 宋 (960-1279) China,[58] Sørensen suggested that Koryŏ

---

[52] Ōmura Seigai, *Mikkyō hattatsushi*, 1:126-133, especially 129-130.

[53] T2145, 55:39a21-23.

[54] Michel Strickmann, "The *Consecration Sūtra*," 79-81, 90-93; Endō Yusuke, "*Kanjōkyō* no yakusha ni tsuite," 45-64; Oka Sumiaki, "*Kanjōkyō* ni okeru jujutsu no juyō," 179-185; Oka Sumiaki, "*Kanjōkyō* no seiritsu ni tsuite," 97-108.

[55] Oka Sumiaki, "*Kanjōkyō* ni okeru jujutsu no juyō," 179-185; Oka Sumiaki, "*Kanjōkyō* no seiritsu ni tsuite," 97-108.

[56] Michel Strickmann, *Chinese Magical Medicine*, 132-140.

[57] As for the systemized "esoteric" rituals as new technology in eighth-century China, see Robert Sharf, *Coming to Terms with Chinese Buddhism*, 263-278, especially 276-278.

[58] Henrik H. Sørensen, "On the Sinin and Ch'ongji Schools," 59. Absence of records of the actual *practice* of the Munduru (Ch. Wentoulou) Ritual suggests

began to practice this ritual because the *Consecration Sutra* drew the attention of Korean monks in the eleventh century when the Koryŏ court had the ambitious project of creating the *Koryŏ Taejanggyŏng* 高麗大藏經 (Koryŏ Tripiṭaka).[59] According to this view, the *Consecration Sutra*'s explanation of how to prevent disaster and adversity probably attracted Koryŏ Buddhist monks, who were looking for sutras that might help protect the state.

This suggestion, however, is not sufficiently convincing to support the idea that this old-fashioned Buddhist ritual suddenly received the patronage of the Koryŏ royal court. First, instruction on how to avoid disasters and gain worldly benefits using ritual or Buddhist incantation (*dhāraṇī*) is a feature commonly found in numerous early esoteric Buddhist sutras included in the *Koryŏ Taejanggyŏng*. The content of the *Consecration Sutra* itself, therefore, offers little explanation of how this specific sutra would have caught the attention of Koryŏ monks. Even within the *Consecration Sutra*, this "Munduru" Ritual is just one of many ritual practices, all of which promise various worldly benefits. Second, the discrepancy between the *Consecration Sutra* and the Koryŏ texts regarding the believed efficacy of the Munduru Ritual suggests that it was not the discovery of this sutra that triggered practice of the ritual in the Korean peninsula. As explained previously, the *Koryŏsa* and *Tongguk Yi Sangguk chip* attest that Koryŏ people performed the Munduru Ritual for state protection when there were wars and rebellions, but the *Consecration Sutra* states that this ritual is especially efficacious in healing disease, among other disasters. This discrepancy suggests that the practice of the Munduru Ritual was not simply triggered by an accidental discovery of the sutra. Lastly, it would have been fairly difficult to create a new ritual based on the terse instruction provided in the *Consecration Sutra*, since this sutra is not a ritual manual. On a related note, we need to further consider what role any text could have played in the formation of a new ritual tradition. Buddhist rituals, especially esoteric rituals, were usually transmitted from teacher to disciples through training and practice, thus forming the source of the ritual's

---

either that it was not practiced at all during the Tang and Song or that this type of ritual was not sponsored by the imperial family or powerful patrons and thereby was left unrecorded. In either case, royal patronage and the high level of importance given to this ritual are unique to the Korean peninsula.

[59] Henrik H. Sørensen, "On the Sinin and Ch'ongji Schools," 58-59. Although I very much respect Sørensen's scholarship, I find this particular suggestion to be less convincing.

authenticity. A randomly discovered old sutra would not create or authenticate a new ritual practice unless a special event occurred that made people believe in the efficacy of the new ritual.

Before moving on, I also want to point out the problem of many Korean scholars' attempts to reconstruct the Munduru Ritual using contents of the *Consecration Sutra*. Even though it might have preserved some oral traditions of fifth-century China as Strickmann has argued, the *Consecration Sutra* is not a descriptive record of what people practiced but essentially a prescriptive text. On the other hand, all the Korean texts cited in this chapter are, regardless of their faithfulness to fact, essentially descriptive records. This means that a gap might exist between what was stated in the sutra composed in fifth-century China and what people actually practiced in the Korean peninsula in later times. Besides the issue of the ritual's intended efficacy, quite a few other discrepancies can be found between the prescriptive texts in the *Consecration Sutra* and the descriptive documents from Korea describing this ritual. A ritual practice often continuously evolves and changes, which naturally creates variations of the same ritual when practiced in different regions and time periods. Therefore one should not expect a one-to-one match between the actual practice of the Munduru Ritual in Korea and the prescriptive explanation of the ritual in the *Consecration Sutra* several centuries earlier in China, even though there are apparent connections between them.[60] In other words, reconstructing the particulars of the Munduru Ritual practice in Korea using this descriptive text entails a methodological error. What is clear from the *Consecration Sutra* is that the Munduru Ritual practiced in the Korean peninsula was an early "esoteric" Buddhist ritual mixed with Daoist practices.

Considering the nature of the Munduru Ritual—a ritual related to the fifth-century early "esoteric" sutra that became old-fashioned before the eighth century—seventh-century Silla is a more plausible starting point for this ritual practice than eleventh-century Koryŏ. If this ritual had been practiced by Silla's royal court due to its efficacy in providing state protection, as recorded in the *Samguk yusa*, this would explain why this particular ritual remained as a popular and unique tradition in the Korean peninsula until the time of Koryŏ. As explained earlier in this chapter, this ostensibly ancient Buddhist ritual was actually practiced until around 1400 under the Chosŏn kingdom. In this context, it is also notable that there is evidence

---

[60] For the same reason, small deviations between the Munduru Ritual practice and *Consecration Sutra* descriptions do not necessarily mean that the two are unrelated.

that the *Consecration Sutra* was already well known in seventh-century Silla; Buddhist texts, including the *Tōiki dentō mokuroku* 東域傳燈目錄 (Record of the transmission of the lamp to the Eastern Regions) compiled in 1094 by Eichō 永超,[61] record that the eminent Silla monk Kyŏnghŭng 憬興/璟興 (fl. seventh century) composed the *Kwanjŏnggyŏng so* 灌頂經疏 (Commentary of the Consecration Sutra) in two fascicles.[62] This seventh-century commentary on the *Consecration Sutra* refutes the assumption that this sutra began to receive attention only in the eleventh century. This shows that the *Consecration Sutra* was a well-known sutra in the Korean peninsula in the seventh century.[63] One more interesting point is that, as

---

[61] T1152, 55:1152b18-20.

[62] For more about this commentary, see Tongguk Taehakkyo Pulgyo Munhwa Yŏn'guso 東國大學校佛教文化研究所 [Dongguk University Research Institute for Buddhist Culture], ed., *Han'guk Pulgyo ch'ansul munhŏn ch'ongnok* 韓國佛教撰述文獻總錄 [Complete list of Korean Buddhist literature and texts] (Seoul: Tongguk Taehakkyo Ch'ulp'anbu, 1976): 43. The monk Kyŏnghŭng composed about forty-seven written works about Buddhist teachings, out of which four works have survived. For a complete list of Kyŏnghŭng's writings, see Han T'aesik 韓泰植, "Kyŏnghŭng ŭi saengae e kwanhan chae koch'al" 憬興의 生涯에 관한 재고찰 [Re-examination of the life of Kyŏnghŭng], *Pulgyo hakpo* 佛教學報 28 (1991): 210-212. Quite a few Japanese scholars, in particular Watanabe Kenshō, studied the monk Kyŏnghŭng, especially from the 1960s to the 1980s. For example, see Watanabe Kenshō 渡辺顯正, *Shiragi Kyōgō shi Jutsumonsan no kenkyū* 新羅・憬興師述文贊の研究 [Research on writings by Silla monk Kyŏnghŭng] (Kyoto: Nagata Bunshōdō, 1978). According to Michel Strickmann, the *Consecration Sutra* has the earliest description of consecration as an actual Buddhist ritual, known as *abhiṣeka*. Michel Strickmann, "The *Consecration Sūtra*," 81-85. The *abhiṣeka* ritual originated from the royal investiture ritual in India. The royal implication of this ritual could have made the *Consecration Sutra* more popular at the royal court of Silla and Koryŏ. I appreciate Mimi Yiengpruksawan's comment on this.

[63] There is an interesting record about the monk Kyŏnghŭng in the *Samguk yusa*. In the section titled "Kyŏnghŭng usŏng" 憬興遇聖, the *Samguk yusa* records that King Munmu left a will at his deathbed and asked his son to appoint Kyŏnghŭng as *kuksa* 國師 (National Teacher), and that King Munmu's son appointed him as *kungno* 國老 (National Elder). If this record is true, it is worth noting that the monks Kyŏnghŭng and Myŏngnang are both related to King Munmu as well as to the *Consecration Sutra*. It seems that the compiler of the *Samguk yusa* also referred to epigraphic data regarding the monk Kyŏnghŭng since the conclusion of this section mentions a stele called the "Samnang-sa Stele" 三郎寺碑, which recorded the virtuous deeds of the monk Kyŏnghŭng. Unfortunately since the compiler does not

Strickmann has pointed out, among all the printed versions of the *Conse-cration Sutra* from premodern times, only the Korean version had its fas-cicles in correct sequential order,[64] a detail that may also suggest the special position this sutra enjoyed in the Korean peninsula.

Considering all these points, Silla seems to be a more plausible starting point for the Munduru Ritual practice than eleventh-century Koryŏ. If this ritual was practiced by Silla's royal court and was known for its efficacy in protecting the state, it would also explain why this particular ritual remained as a popular and unique tradition in the Korean peninsula long after this type of early "esoteric" ritual went out of fashion in China. Bearing in mind all these pieces of circumstantial evidence suggesting the possibility that the initial practice of the Munduru Ritual took place under Silla rather than Koryŏ, let us investigate the archaeological remains related to this ritual.

Archaeological Remains

This chapter has so far analyzed the *Samguk yusa* passage mainly in light of the external texts and historical context. Now this chapter will exam-ine whether our understanding of this passage further changes if we take archaeological data into consideration. Are there any relevant archaeologi-cal remains related to this *Samguk yusa* passage? What deserves our atten-tion in this *Samguk yusa* passage is the venue mentioned for the perfor-mance of the Munduru Ritual—Sach'ŏnwang-sa. According to the *Samguk yusa* passage, the Silla people built this monastery in Sinyu Forest on the southern side of Mount Nang.

As a matter of fact, the ruins of the Sach'ŏnwang-sa site remain at the very southernmost foot of Mount Nang in present-day Paeban-dong 排盤洞 in Kyŏngju, the city which had been the capital of Silla, located in North Kyŏngsang Province 慶尚北道 (fig. 3.3).[65] The monastery site sits

---

include a direct quotation from this stele, it is difficult to know what part of the article about the monk Kyŏnghŭng came from this stele inscription. *Samguk yusa* 5: "Kyŏnghŭng usŏng," *Yŏkchu Samguk yusa*, 4:262-263. A small stele fragment, which is possibly a piece from the Samnang-sa Stele, is currently in the collection of Dankook University Museum, but only a few characters in the inscription on the stele fragment remain legible.

[64] Michel Strickmann, "The *Consecration Sūtra*," 111-112, no. 18.

[65] While a number of academic articles about this monastery site have been written in Korean, the site has not been widely known among Western scholars. Juhyung Rhi's (Yi Chuhyŏng 李柱亨) paper, "Monks, Dragons, and Guardians: Sach'ŏnwangsa, an Esoteric Buddhist Temple in the Unified Silla," presented in 2007

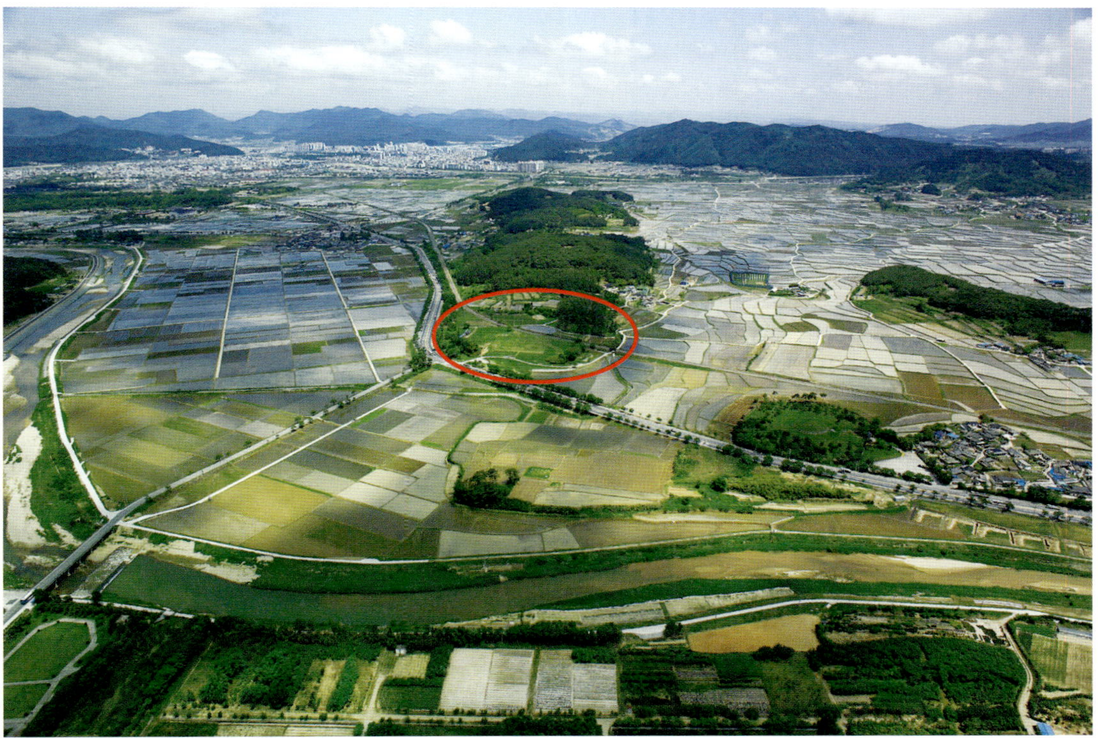

*Figure 3.3 Sachŏnwang-sa site before excavation, Paeban-dong, Kyŏngju.
Courtesy of the Gyeongju Research Institute of Cultural Heritage.*

at a height of 53.3 meters above sea level. Several gazetteers and geography books from the Chosŏn period provide a continuous record of this monastery, including the *Sinjŭng Tongguk yŏji sŭngnam* 新增東國輿地勝覽 (Newly augmented survey of the geography of the Eastern Kingdom) completed in 1530.[66] An interlinear note added to the title of the

<hr>

at *An International Conference on Esoteric Buddhist Tradition in East Asia: Text, Ritual and Image*, is the only paper about this monastery written in English. This conference, organized by Youngsook Pak, was held at Yale University with the support of the Korea Foundation. This paper will be soon published in the conference volume.

[66] *Sinjŭng Tongguk yŏji sŭngnam* 21:30, original manuscript reprinted in *Kugyŏk sinjŭng Tongguk yŏji sŭngnam* 國譯新增東國輿地勝覽新增東國輿地勝覽

poem, "Sach'ŏnwang-sa Site" (Ch'ŏnwang-saji 天王寺址), by Kim Sisŭp 金時習 (1435-1493), in the *Maewŏltang chip* 梅月堂集 (Anthology of Maewŏltang), comments that "Today [the monastery] became a residential dwelling."[67] Since the anthology was published in 1583, this interlinear note, probably added by compilers, suggests that Sach'ŏnwang-sa lost its religious function before the end of the sixteenth century. One short record suggests that the buildings at this monastery site had been destroyed by the mid-eighteenth century; specifically, it was recorded in the *Yŏjidosŏ* 輿地圖書 (Book of geographical information with maps), which was compiled between 1757 and 1765, that "Sach'ŏnwang-sa, located to the south of Mount Nang, is currently in an abandoned state."[68]

The ruins of Sach'ŏnwang-sa began to draw the scholarly interest of archaeologists and art historians in the early twentieth century. Although the monastery's original buildings were destroyed several centuries ago, floor tiles and fragments of glazed terracotta reliefs scattered at the monastery site attracted Japanese scholars' attention during the Japanese colonial period (1910-1945) (fig. 3.4). Ayukai Fusanoshin 鮎貝房之進 (1864-1946), Harada Yoshito 原田淑人(1885-1974), and Fujita Ryōsaku 藤田亮策 (1892-1960), among others, investigated the monastery site, measuring the size of the remaining base stones of lost buildings and collecting roof tiles and terracotta reliefs from the ruins.[69] In 1963, following the colonial

---

[Translation of the *Newly Augmented Survey of the Geography of the Eastern Kingdom*] (Seoul: Minjok Munhwa Ch'ujinhoe, 1970): 3:83 The reproduction of the original manuscript is included in the back part of this edition, which has pagination marked in Chinese characters.

[67] 今爲人家. For the original text of this poem in its entirety, see Kungnip Kyŏngju Munhwajae Yŏn'guso, *Sach'ŏnwang-sa*, 54.

[68] 四天王寺 在浪山南麓今廢. The original text requoted from Han Myŏnghŭi 한명희, "Sach'ŏnwang-sa kŭmdang ŭi pogwŏn e kwanhan yŏn'gu" 사천왕사 금당의 복원에 관한 연구 [Research on the restoration of the main hall of Sach'ŏnwang-sa] (Myŏngji Taehakkyo sŏksa hagwi nonmun 明知大學校碩士學位論文 [Myongji University M.A. Thesis], 2010): 12, no. 11.

[69] For reports on the investigation of the Sach'ŏnwang-sa site from 1918 and 1922, see Chōsen Sōtokufu 朝鮮總督府 [Governor-General of Korea], ed., *Taishō shichi-nendo koseki chōsa hōkoku* 大正七年度古蹟調査報告 [Report of the survey on historical remains in the year 1918] (Keijō [Seoul]: Chōsen Sōtokufu, 1922); Chōsen Sōtokufu 朝鮮總督府 [Governor-General of Korea], ed., *Taishō jūichi-nendo koseki chōsa hōkoku* 大正十一年度古蹟調査報告 [Report of the survey on historical remains in the year 1922] (Keijō: Chōsen Sōtokufu, 1925). For black and

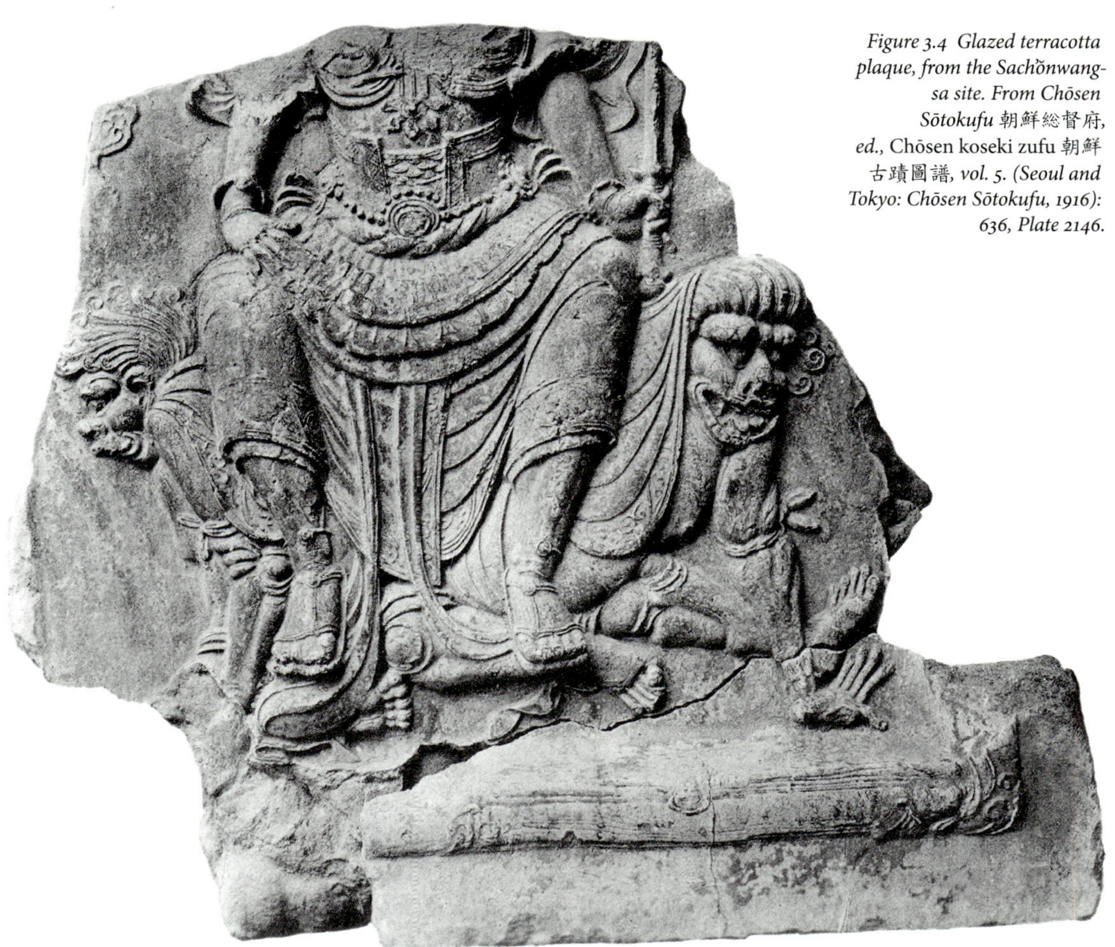

Figure 3.4 Glazed terracotta plaque, from the Sach'ŏnwang-sa site. From Chōsen Sōtokufu 朝鮮総督府, *ed.,* Chōsen koseki zufu 朝鮮古蹟圖譜, *vol. 5. (Seoul and Tokyo: Chōsen Sōtokufu, 1916): 636, Plate 2146.*

white photographs of floor tiles and fragments of terracotta reliefs published during the Japanese colonial period, see Chōsen Sōtokufu 朝鮮總督府 [Governor-General of Korea], ed., *Chōsen koseki zufu* 朝鮮古蹟圖譜 [Illustrated book of Korean historical remains] (Seoul and Tokyo: Chōsen Sōtokufu, 1915-1935): 5:636-638, 644. For a brief history of the investigations conducted at the Sach'ŏnwang-sa site during the Japanese colonial period, see Kungnip Kyŏngju Munhwajae Yŏn'guso, *Sach'ŏnwang-sa*, 58-60. For a list of scholarly publications on Sach'ŏnwang-sa written in Korean, Japanese, Chinese, and English, see Kungnip Kyŏngju Munhwajae

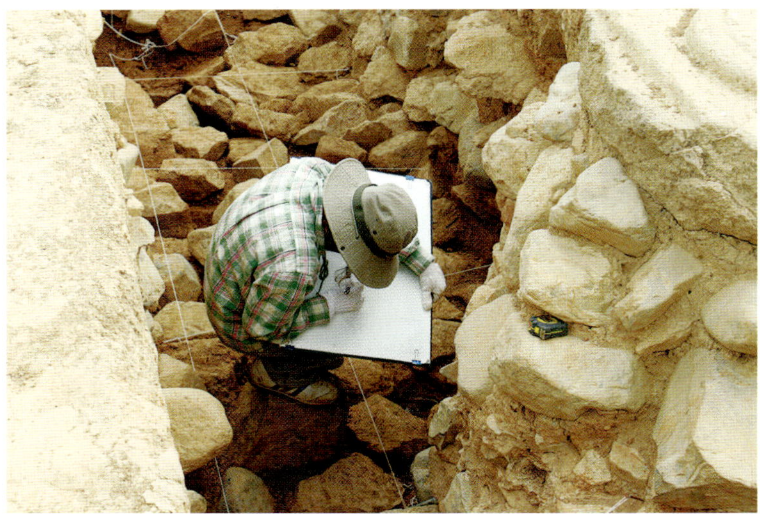

*Figure 3.5 Excavation of the Sachŏnwang-sa site in 2010.
Courtesy of the Gyeongju Research Institute of Cultural Heritage.*

period, the Korean government designated the monastery site as Historic Site (Sajŏk 史蹟) No. 8.

It is the current archaeological excavation, which began in April 2006, however, that provides a more comprehensive understanding of the original ground plan and the construction date of Sach'ŏnwang-sa (fig. 3.5).[70] Conducted by Gyeongju National Research Institute of Cultural Heritage, this excavation-in-progress has revealed the monastery's full ground plan (fig. 3.6). In addition to the main hall and the twin pagodas, whose base stones were briefly examined during the colonial period, the excavation has uncovered remains of corridors that originally surrounded the monastery precinct to form two courtyards, the main monastery gate site to the south of

Yŏn'guso 國立慶州文化財研究所 [Gyeongju National Research Institute of Cultural Heritage], *Silla hoguk ŭi yŏmwŏn: Sach'ŏnwang-sa* 신라 호국의 염원: 四天王寺 [Silla's wish for state protection: Sach'ŏnwang-sa] (Kyŏngju-si: Kungnip Kyŏngju Munhwajae Yŏn'guso, 2008): 149-153.

[70] For a description of the results of the excavation between 2006 and 2011, see Kungnip Kyŏngju Munhwajae Yŏn'guso, *Sach'ŏnwang-sa*, 1-409.

154

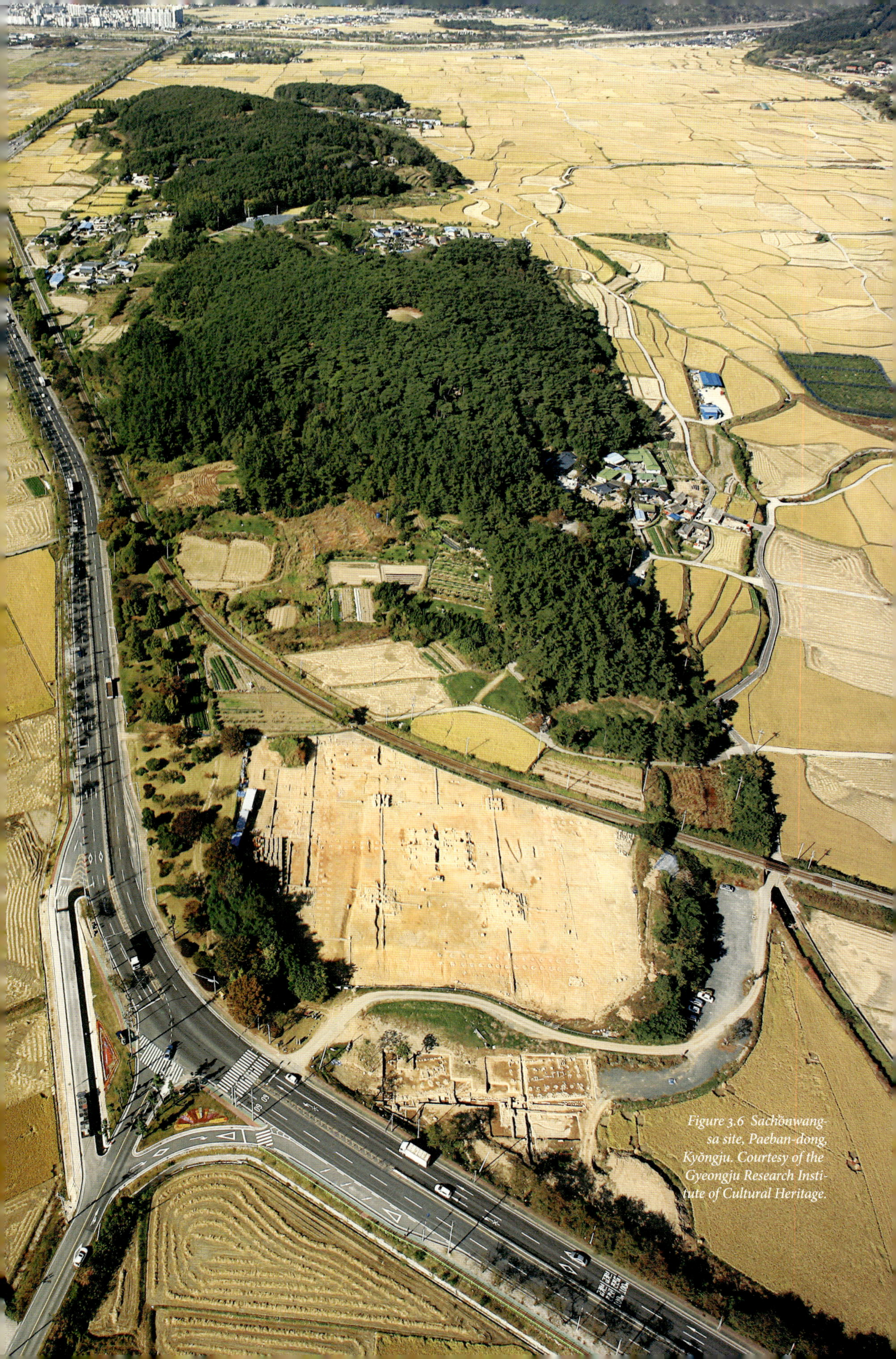

Figure 3.6 Sach'ŏnwang-sa site, Paeban-dong, Kyŏngju. Courtesy of the Gyeongju Research Institute of Cultural Heritage.

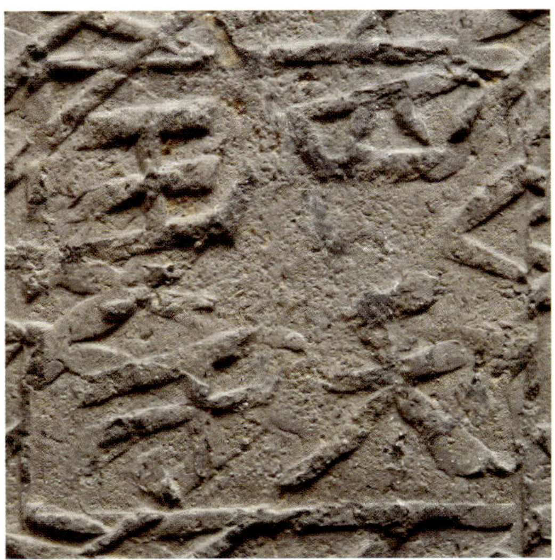

Figure 3.7 *Roof tile with an inscription, "Sach'ŏnwang-sa" (detail), from the Sach'ŏnwang-sa site. Courtesy of the Gyeongju Research Institute of Cultural Heritage.*

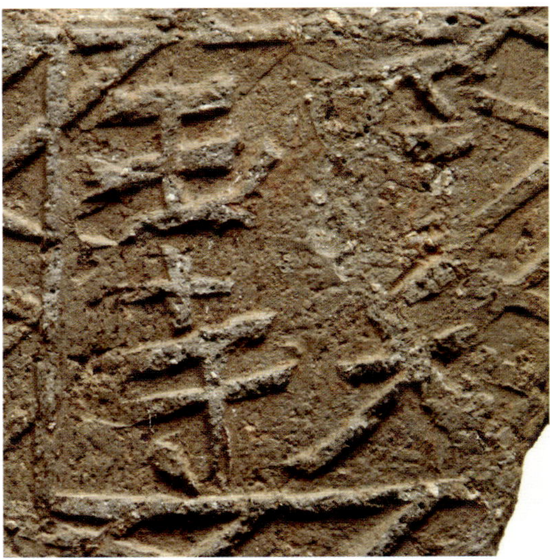

Figure 3.8 *Roof tile with an inscription, "Sach'ŏnwang-sa" (detail), from the Sach'ŏnwang-sa site. Courtesy of the Gyeongju Research Institute of Cultural Heritage.*

the main Buddha hall, evidence of a lecture hall located to the north of the main Buddha hall, and traces of two stone bridges crossing the monastery's small drainage ditch. The excavation has also uncovered quite a few important objects, including thirteen different kinds of roof tiles stamped with the four characters "Sach'ŏnwang-sa" 四天王寺 (figs. 3.7, 3.8),[71] and other objects indicating the approximate date of the monastery.[72] Seven pieces of floor tiles with floral patterns (Kr. *posanghwamunjŏn* 實相華紋塼), for

---

[71] Kungnip Kyŏngju Munhwajae Yŏn'guso, *Sach'ŏnwang-sa*, 238-242, 350-352. For more about various kinds of tiles excavated from this monastery site, see Kungnip Kyŏngju Munhwajae Yŏn'guso 國立慶州文化財研究所 [Gyeongju National Research Institute of Cultural Heritage], *Kyŏngju Sach'ŏnwang-saji wa* 경주 사천왕 사지 瓦 [Tiles from the Sach'ŏnwang-sa site] (Kyŏngju: Kungnip Kyŏngju Munhwajae Yŏn'guso, 2011): 1-182.

[72] Since the excavation reports also refer to the *Samguk yusa* for dating some of the excavated materials, in this chapter I have cautiously selected only materials verified through scientific analysis, dated inscription, and stylistic analysis.

example, have a shape similar to that of a floor tile inscribed with the date 680 (the second year of the Tiaolu 調露) excavated from nearby Anap Pond 雁鴨池, the pond and palace site created during the reign of King Munmu, thereby helping to date the monastery (fig. 3.9).[73] In addition, the monastery site has yielded earthenware pieces from the seventh century.[74] Also conforming to the recorded date of the monastery is the result of the AMS (Accelerator Mass Spectrometry) radiocarbon dating of charred organic material found under the pedestal of the sculpture at the main Buddha hall. The AMS result roughly matches the recorded monastery completion date of 679 (key point 6). It suggests calendrical dates between 660 and 730, which has a probability of 42.9 percent probable at the 68.2 percent confidence level, and the midpoint of this range is 695 C.E.[75]

This scientific as well as stylistic dating of the archaeological remains of Sach'ŏnwang-sa strengthens the possibility that the Munduru Ritual explained in the *Samguk yusa* was actually practiced not under Koryŏ, but under Silla. Given the date of the archaeological remains of Sach'ŏnwang-sa, what deserves our attention is the state-protection function of this monastery during the Silla period. Sach'ŏnwang-sa together with Hwangnyong-sa and Kamŭn-sa 感恩寺 (ca. 682) served as the three major state-protection monasteries (*hoguk sach'al* 護國寺刹) of Silla.[76] Although the Four Heavenly Kings are generally understood as protectors of Buddhist law, in the context of seventh-century Silla, where state-protection Buddhism (*hoguk Pulgyo* 護國佛敎) was the dominant form of religious practice, the Four Heavenly Kings were especially worshipped as divine protectors of the country.[77] Such worship originates from the Four Heavenly Kings chapter in the

---

[73] Kungnip Kyŏngju Munhwajae Yŏn'guso, *Sach'ŏnwang-sa*, 264-269, 356.

[74] Kungnip Kyŏngju Munhwajae Yŏn'guso, *Sach'ŏnwang-sa*, 358. For images of the floor tiles with floral patterns excavated from the Sach'ŏnwang-sa site, see Kungnip Kyŏngju Munhwajae Yŏn'guso, *Sach'ŏnwang-sa*, 264-269. The monastery site also had porcelains of later periods because the monastery continued to be in use until the early Chosŏn period.

[75] Kungnip Kyŏngju Munhwajae Yŏn'guso, *Sach'ŏnwang-sa*, 396-400.

[76] Richard D. McBride, *Domesticating the Dharma: Buddhist Cults and the Hwaŏm Synthesis in Silla Korea* (Honolulu: University of Hawai'i Press, 2008): 28. For more about the state-protection function of Sach'ŏnwang-sa, see Kim Sanghyŏn 金相鉉, "Sach'ŏnwang-sa ŭi ch'anggŏn kwa ŭiŭi" 四天王寺의 創建과 意義 [Establishment of Sach'ŏnwang-sa and its meaning], *Silla wa Nangsan* 신라와 낭산 [Silla and Mount Nang] (Kyŏngju: Silla Munhwa Sŏnyanghoe, 1996): 125-144.

[77] For more about Four Heavenly Kings worship in Silla, see Sim Hyosŏp 沈曉

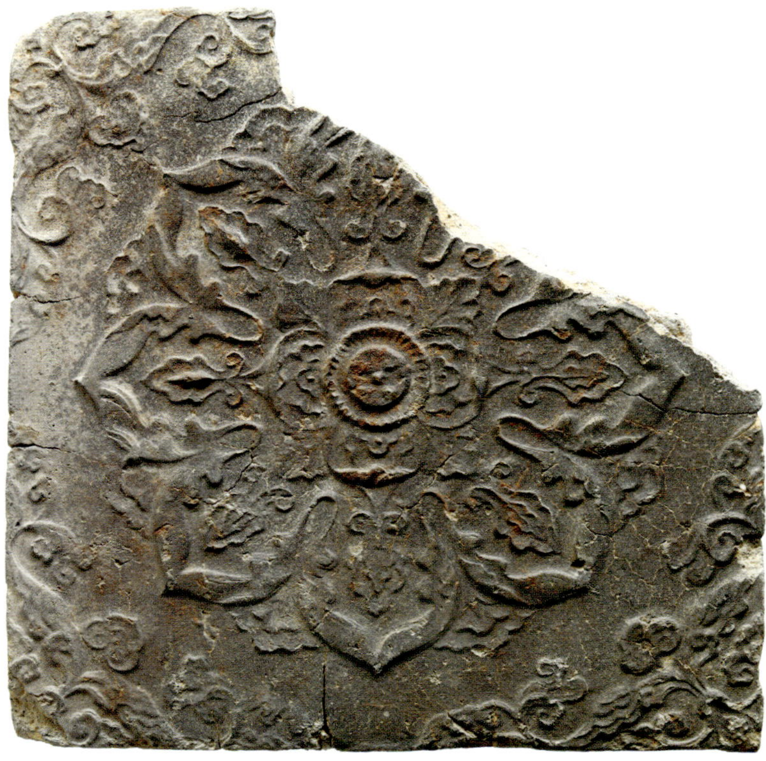

*Figure 3.9 Tile inscribed with the date 680 (the second year of the Tiaolu 調露),
excavated from Anap Pond, Kyŏngju, Korea. Gyeongju National Museum.
Courtesy of the Gyeongju Research Institute of Cultural Heritage.*

Jinguangming jing 金光明經 (hereafter *Golden Light Sutra*), in which these
Heavenly Kings promise the Buddha that they will protect the country
whose king venerates the *Golden Light Sutra*.[78] Much ink has been spilled
about the Four Heavenly Kings images from Silla. According to the most
recent scholarship by Im Yŏngae, Silla's production of the Four Heavenly

---

燮, "Silla Sachŏnwang sinang ŭi suyong kwa chŏn'gae" 新羅 四天王信仰의 受容과 展
開 [Reception and evolution of Four Heavenly Kings worship in Korea], *Tongguk
sahak* 東國史學 30 (1996): 113-146.
    [78] T663, 16:341b.

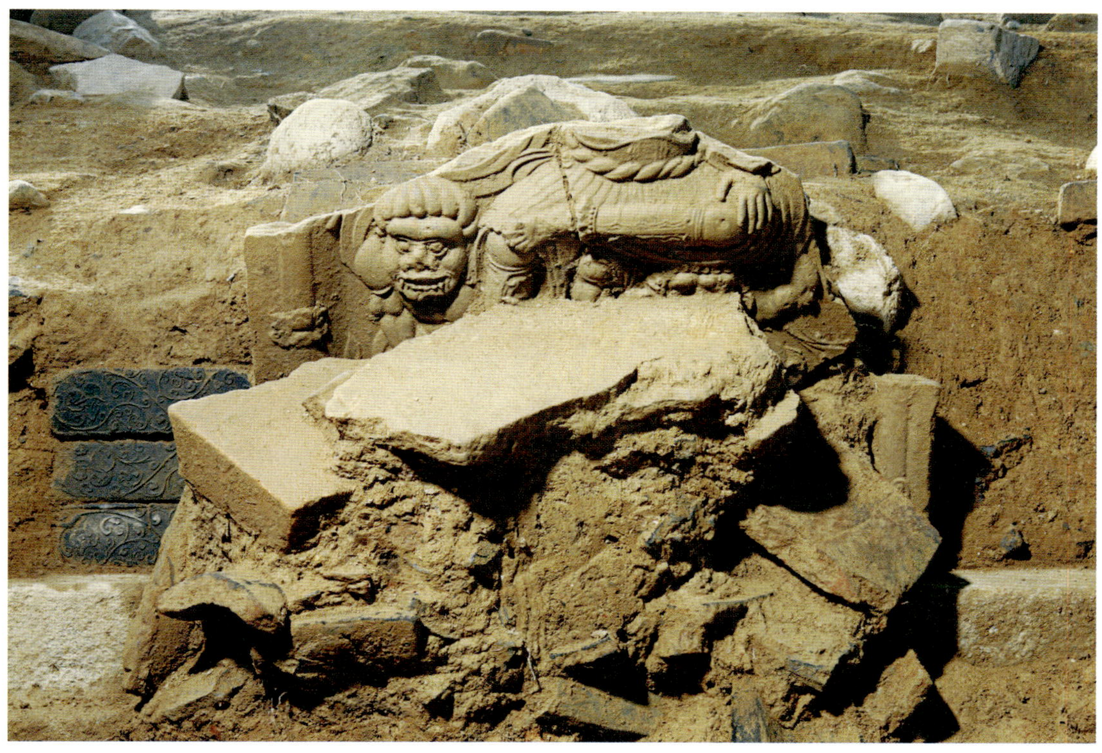

*Figure 3.10 Glazed terracotta plaque at the Sach'ŏnwang-sa excavation site
(Plaque C at the north side pedestal of the east pagoda).
Courtesy of the Gyeongju Research Institute of Cultural Heritage.*

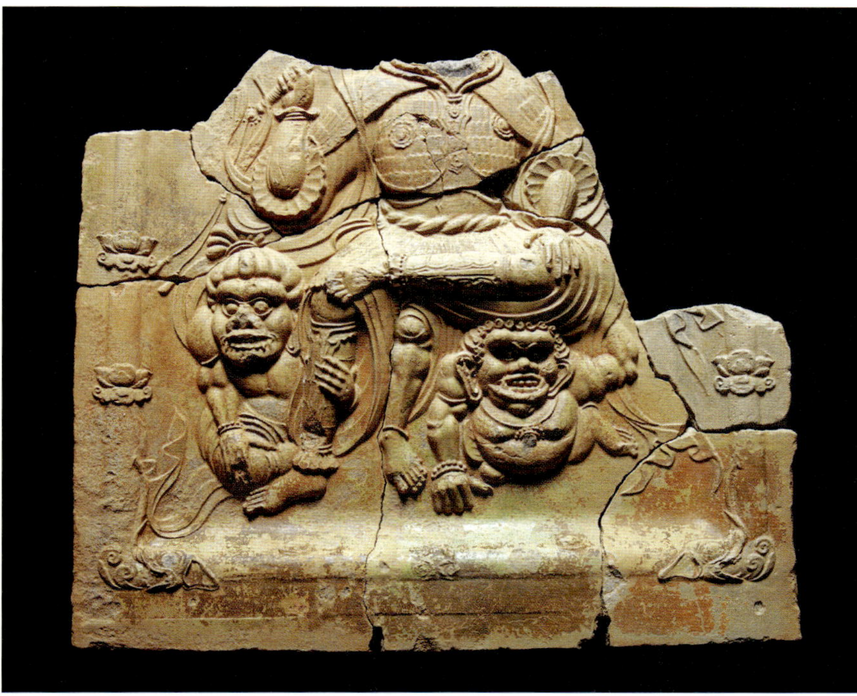

*Figure 3.11 Glazed
terracotta plaque newly
excavated from the
Sach'ŏnwang-sa site
(Plaque C from the
north side pedestal of
the east pagoda).
Courtesy of the
Gyeongju Research
Institute of Cultural
Heritage.*

Kings images began with the construction of Sach'ŏnwang-sa.[79] Im Yŏngae suggests that although Silla already had Hwangnyong-sa, the grandiose state-protecting monastery, the introduction of Four Heavenly Kings worship necessitated the construction of a new state-protection monastery to enshrine these new state-protecting deities, which resulted in the construction of Sach'ŏnwang-sa. The status of Sach'ŏnwang-sa as the state-protection monastery during the Silla period conforms to the nature of the Munduru Ritual as the state-protection ritual.

Glazed terracotta tiles with reliefs of guardian deities excavated from this monastery site provide archaeological data that further reveal the state-protection function of Sach'ŏnwang-sa (figs. 3.10, 3.11). Although only their fragments were found, the elegant shape and naturalistic style of these guardian reliefs are among the reasons this monastery site has attracted scholarly attention since the early twentieth century. Assembled fragments show that each terracotta tile, sixty-nine centimeters wide and eighty-six centimeters tall, bears an image of a deity seated on two demons, wearing armor, and holding a sword or a bow (figs. 3.12, 3.13, 3.14). The fierce face with bulging eyes, big nose, and mustache is believed to have its prototype in figures from Central Asia.[80] The naturalistic style and Central Asian physiognomy reveal that these terracotta images were made in the seventh century in the style of Tang Buddhist art.[81] Identification of these images has been a long-debated issue. Until the recent archaeological excavation, they were widely accepted as images of the Four Heavenly Kings.[82] There

----

[79] Im Yŏngae (Lim Youngae) 林玲愛, "'Sŏkkuram Sach'ŏnwang-sang' ŭi tosang kwa Pulgyo kyŏngjŏn" '석굴암 사천왕상'의 도상과 불교 경전 [The iconography of the "Four Heavenly Kings at Sŏkkuram" and the Buddhist sutra], *Kangjwa misulsa* 講座美術史 37 (2011): 25-26.

[80] This does not mean that these reliefs have a direct connection to Central Asian people or art.

[81] Kang Ubang, *Wŏnyung kwa chohwa*, 182-184.

[82] Kang Ubang's in-depth study published in 1979 was most influential in supporting this identification. Kang Ubang 姜友邦, "Sach'ŏnwang-saji ch'ult'o ch'aeyu ch'ŏnwang pujosang ŭi pogwŏnjŏk koch'al: obangsin kwa Sach'ŏnwang-sang ŭi chohyŏngjŏk sŭphap hyŏnsang" 四天王寺址 出土 彩釉天王浮彫像의 復元的 考察: 五方神과 四天王像의 造形的 習合現象 [Restorational examination of glazed Heavenly Kings relief images excavated from the Sach'ŏnwang-sa site: Formal synthesis of the Deities of the Five Directions and the Four Heavenly Kings], *Misul charyo* 美術資料 25 (1979): 1-46. This article was later included in his book, *Wŏnyung kwa chohwa*, 159-201.

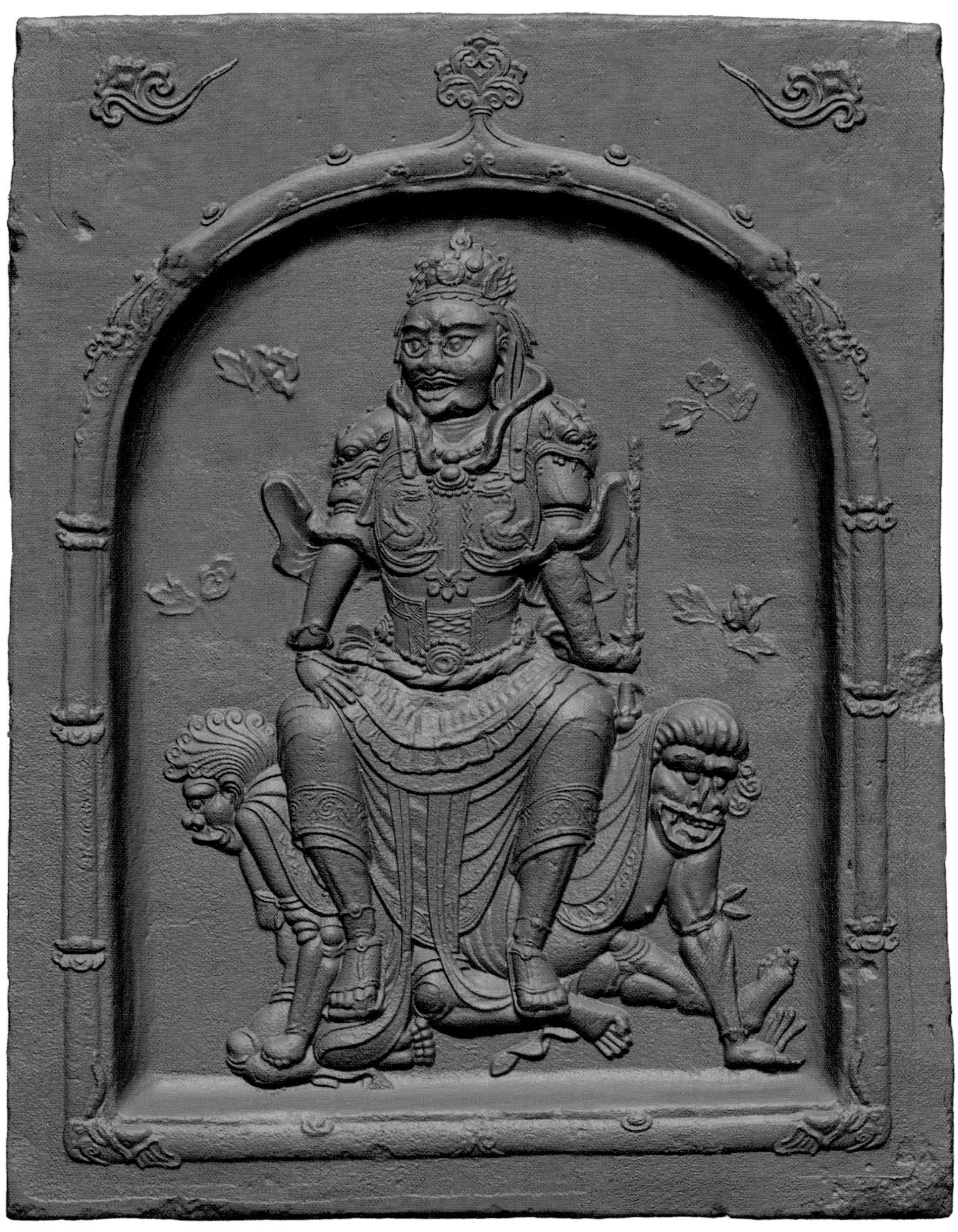

Figure 3.12 Computer software-assisted reconstructed image of Glazed Terracotta Plaque A.
Courtesy of the Gyeongju Research Institute of Cultural Heritage.

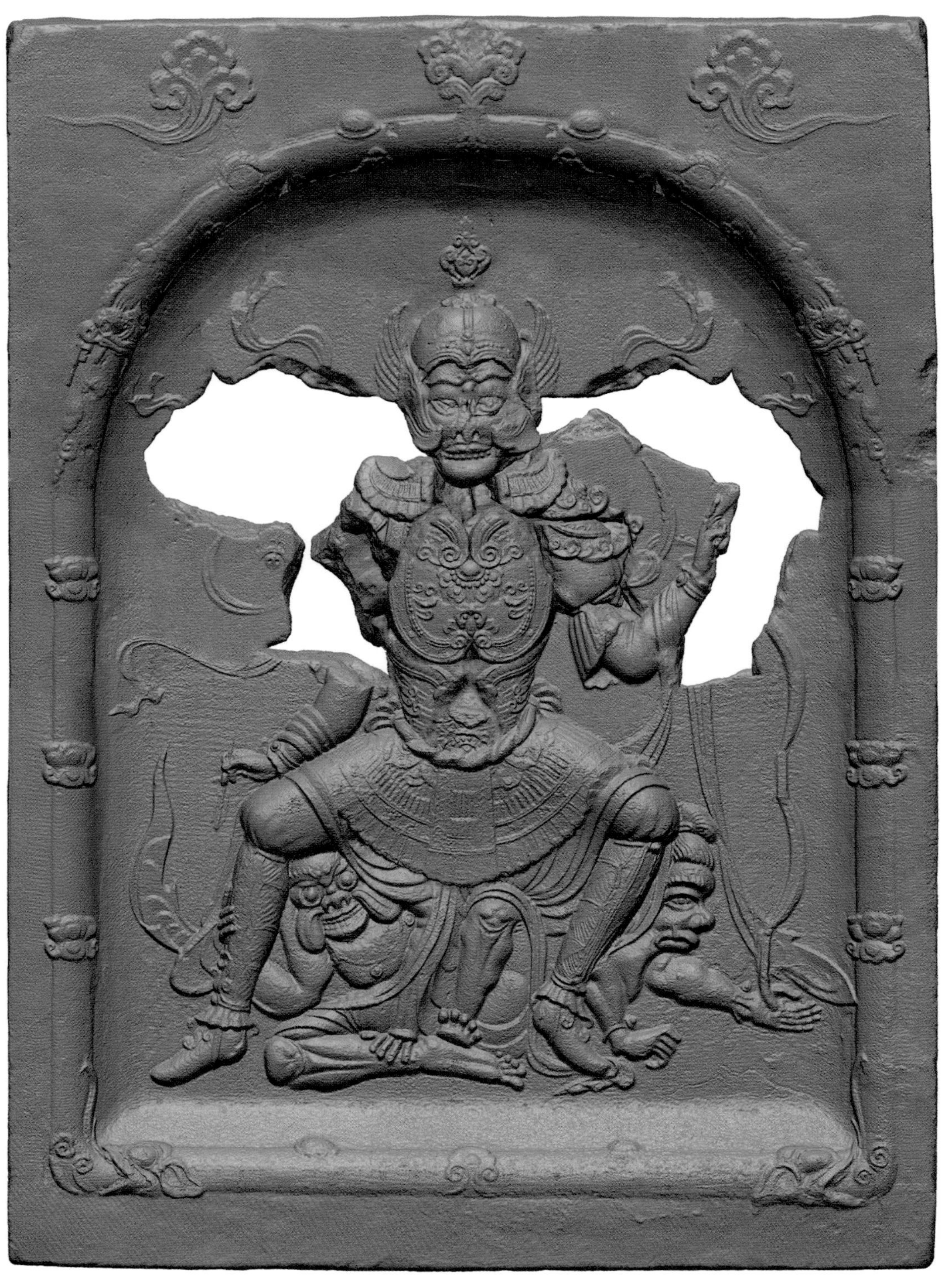

Figure 3.13 Computer software-assisted reconstructed image of Glazed Terracotta Plaque B. Courtesy of the Gyeongju Research Institute of Cultural Heritage.

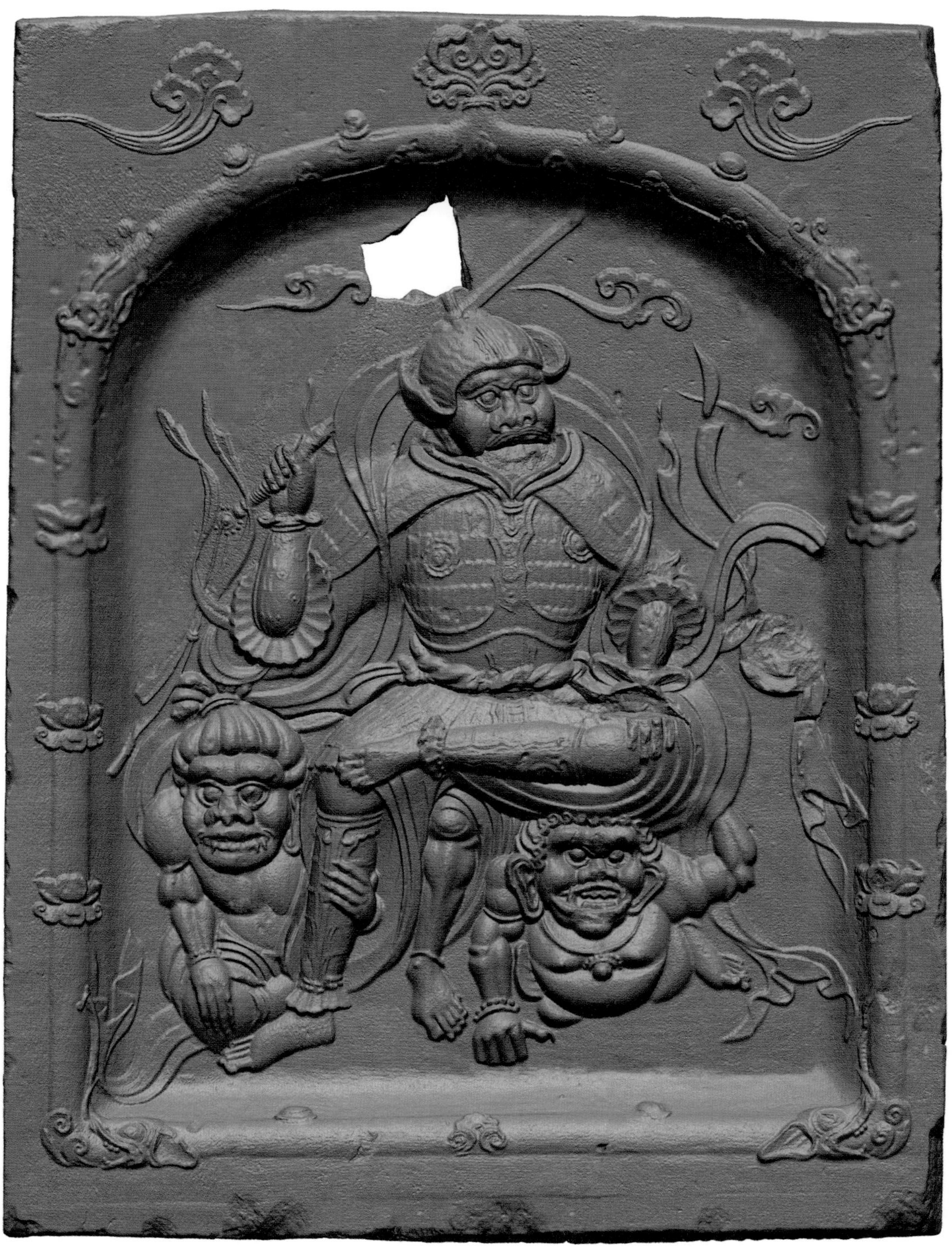

*Figure 3.14 Computer software-assisted reconstructed image of Glazed Terracotta Plaque C.
Courtesy of the Gyeongju Research Institute of Cultural Heritage.*

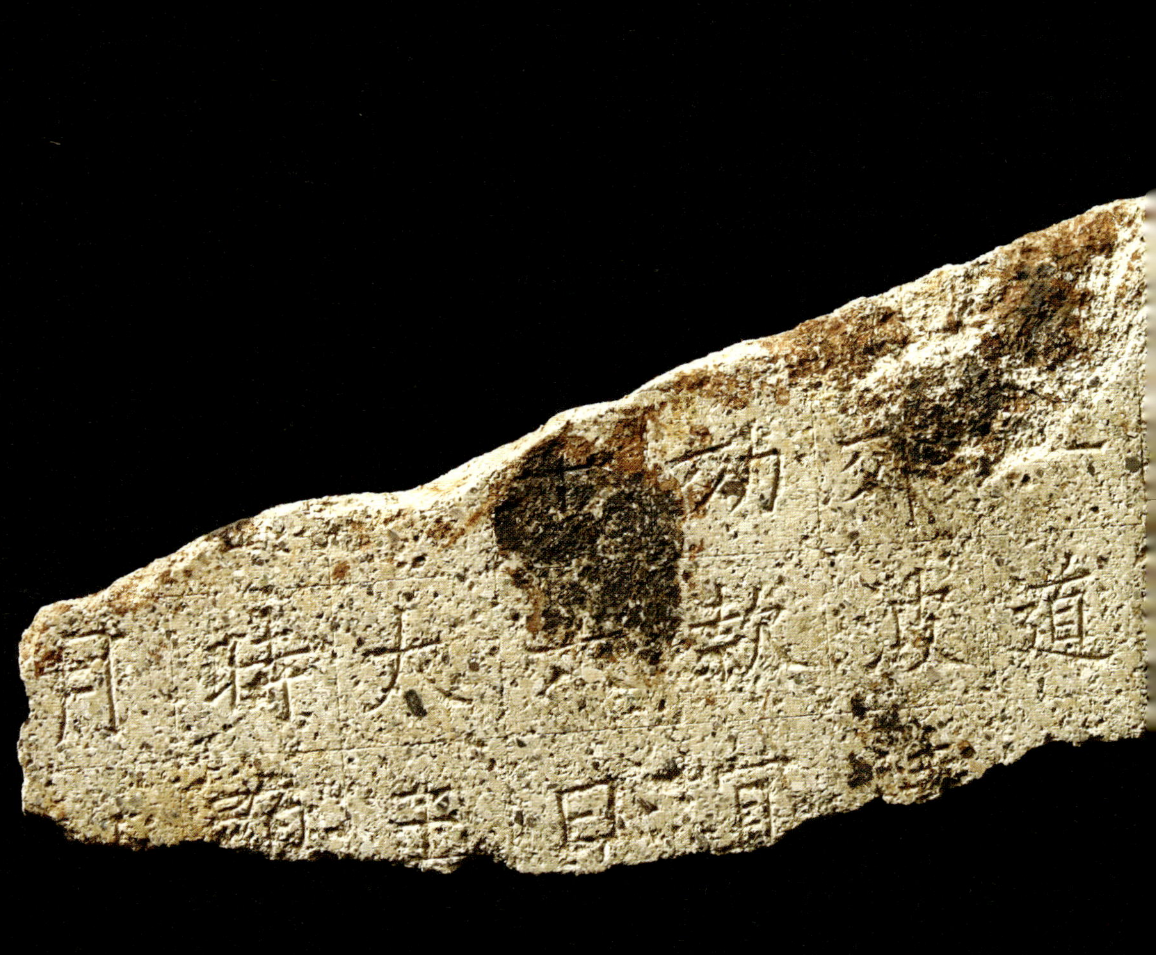

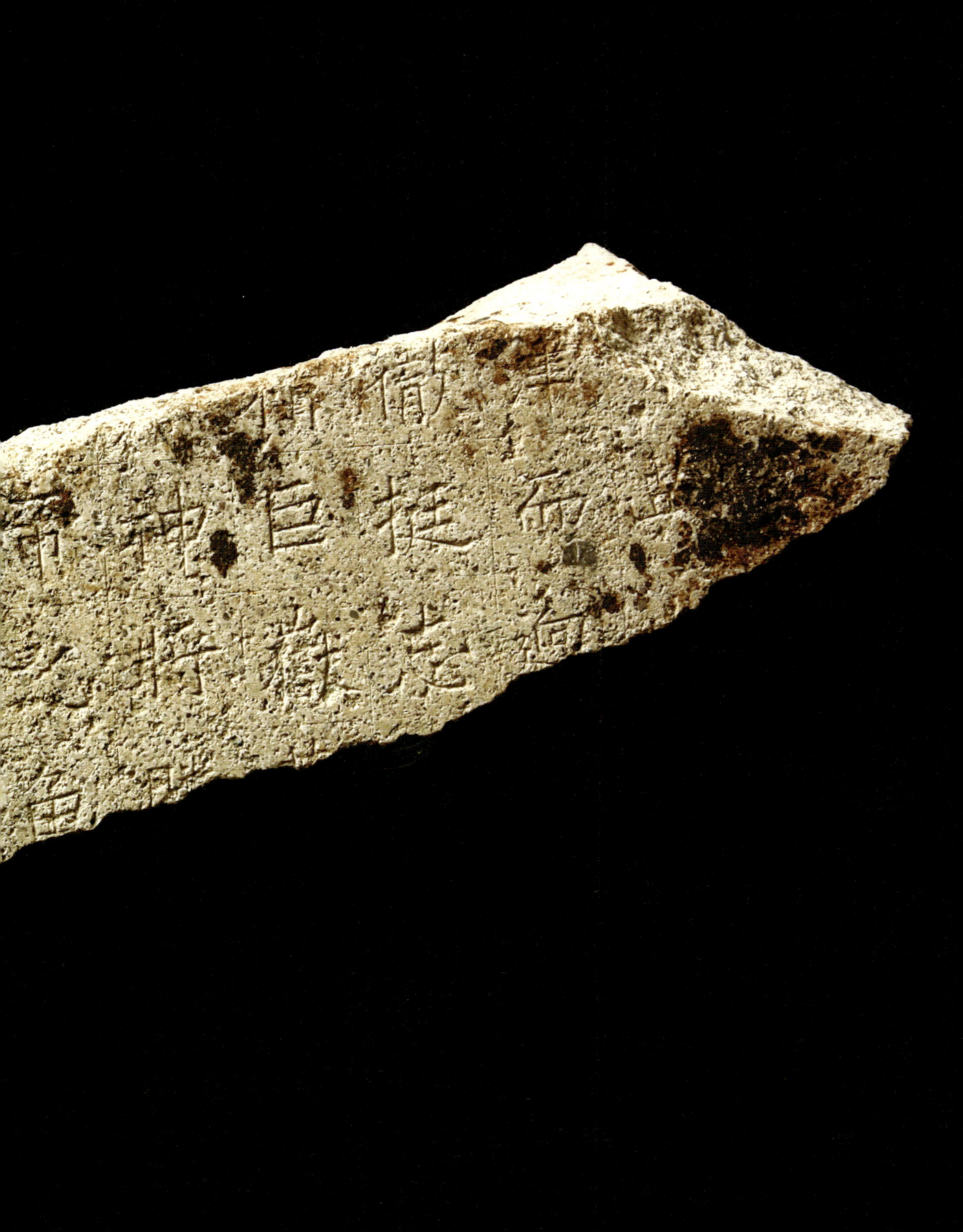

*Figure 3.15 Fragment of a stone stele, from the Sachŏnwang-sa site.
11.0×55.0×14.0cm. Courtesy of the Gyeongju Research Institute of Cultural Heritage.*

was also an opinion, although less widely accepted, that these terracotta images represent the Eight Kinds of Beings (Kr. P'albujung 八部衆).[83] Surprisingly, the result of the recent archaeological excavation supports neither of these opinions. The excavation instead has revealed that there were three kinds of terracotta images. Two sets of the three images were attached to each side of the pagoda's pedestal, and therefore twenty-four images in total surrounded the pagoda. This puzzling number does not fit either the Four Heavenly Kings or the Eight Kinds of Beings. Following the excavation, Im Yŏngae has convincingly argued that these terracotta images are generic guardian deities, which cannot be identified as either Four Heavenly Kings or Eight Kinds of Beings.[84] She further suggested that they should be understood as *shenwang* 神王, the guardian deities often appearing in the *Consecration Sutra*.[85] Im Yŏngae's new argument is very convincing, but at the same time there is a possibility that these guardian images, although their concept came from the *Consecration Sutra*, were known under the more generic name *sinjang* 神將 (guardian general or guardian deity) among the Silla people who made them. The fragment of the stone stele excavated from the Sach'ŏnwang-sa site in 2011 also supports this idea, because among the several legible letters is included the clearly engraved word *sinjang* (fig. 3.15).[86] Although images of *sinjang* became prevalent in

---

[83] Mun Myŏngdae, *Wŏnŭm kwa chŏkchomi: T'ongil Silla Pulgyo chogaksa yŏn'gu, ha* 圓音과寂照美: 統一新羅 佛教彫刻史研究(下) [Beauty of the Buddha's perfect voice and wisdom: Research on the history of Buddhist sculpture of the Unified Silla 2] (Seoul: Yegyŏng, 2003): 28, 242-244. As Kang Ubang pointed out, however, the Eight Kinds of Beings became widespread only after the mid-ninth century in the Korean peninsula.

[84] Im Yŏngae (Lim Youngae) 林玲愛, "Sach'ŏnwang-saji sojosang ŭi chonmyŏng" 四天王寺址 塑造像의 尊名 [Name of the images modeled with clay from the Sach'ŏnwang-sa site], *Misulsa nondan* 美術史論壇 27 (2008): 7-37. Im Yŏngae thinks that the images of the Four Heavenly Kings, which did not survive, were probably enshrined inside the pagoda or main Buddha Hall of this monastery.

[85] In the *Consecration Sutra*, the Deities of the Five Directions of the Munduru Ritual are one of these *shenwangs*. Several passages of the seventh fascicle of this sutra call them *wufang shenwang* 五方神王, *Shenwang* of Five Directions. T1331, 21:515b14, b16, c14.

[86] For more about this stele fragment, see Choe Changmi 최장미, "Sach'ŏnwang-saji palgul chosa sŏngkwa wa ch'ujŏng sajŏkpi p'yŏn" 사천왕사지 발굴조사 성과와 추정 사적비편 [The achievement of the excavation of the Sach'ŏnwang-sa site and the stele fragment inferred to be from the stele of the monastery history], *Mokkan*

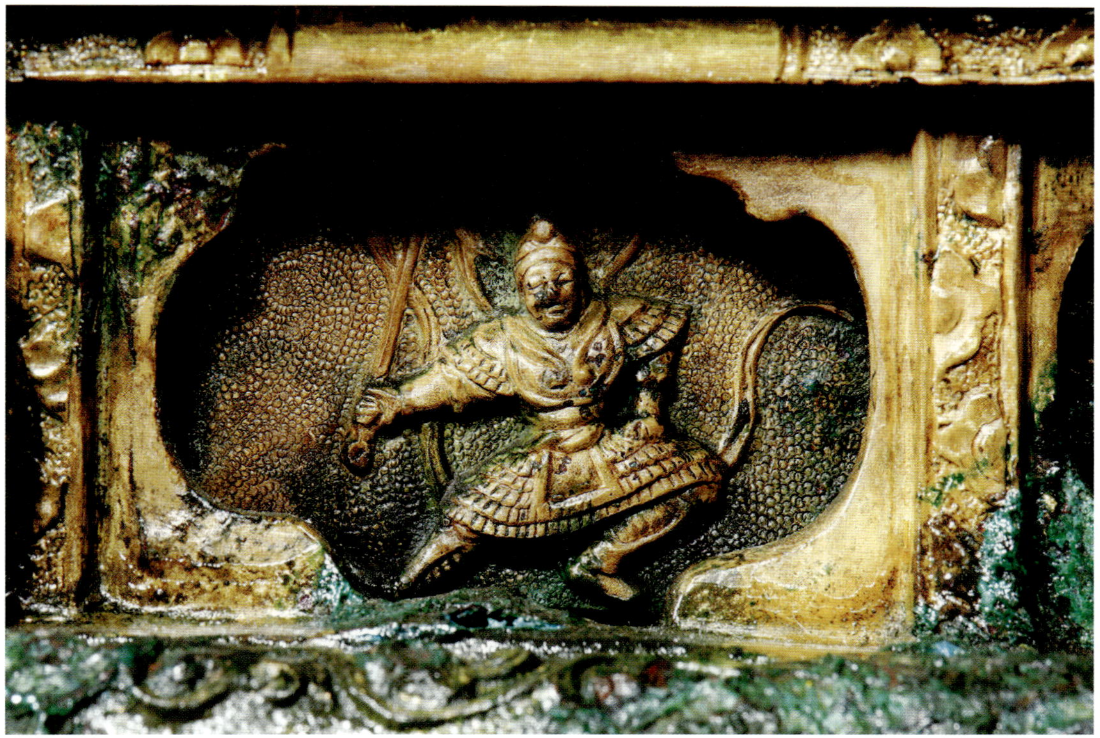

*Figure 3.16 Inner reliquary, from the east pagoda of Kamŭn-sa (detail).
Courtesy of the National Museum of Korea.*

later periods, these terracotta images constitute one of the earliest examples of *sinjang* images remaining in Korea. In fact, they are one of three such surviving examples from the seventh century: the other two examples are the set of eight *sinjang* images engraved on the bronze reliquary casket (ca. 645) from the nine-story pagoda of Hwangnyong-sa and the two sets of four *sinjang* figurines inside the niches on the pedestal of the inner reliquaries from the Kamŭn-sa twin pagodas (fig. 3.16).[87] It is significant that these earliest three extant examples of *sinjang* images are from the three

---

kwa muncha 목간과 문자 8 (December 2011): 171-184.

[87] Im Yŏngae, "Sach'ŏnwang-saji sojosang ŭi chonmyŏng," 21-22.

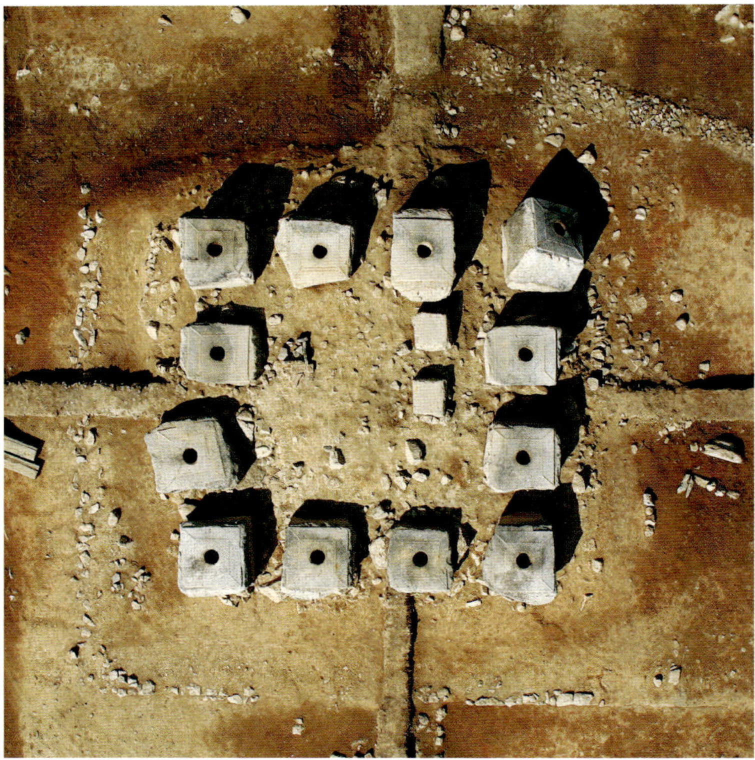

*Figure 3.17 West stone remains behind the main Buddha hall site at the Sachŏnwang-sa site.
Courtesy of the Gyeongju Research Institute of Cultural Heritage.*

major state-protection monasteries of Silla. This strongly suggests that under the specific context of the seventh century these images of *sinjang*, which did not have specific iconographic features but looked similar to the Four Heavenly Kings, were also generally related to state protection. This was probably because the iconographic difference between *sinjang* and the Four Heavenly Kings was not fully understood in the seventh century when the iconography of the Four Heavenly Kings as divine state protectors was newly introduced to Silla.

The most notable archaeological remains at this monastery site that may have a direct connection with the Munduru Ritual, however, are unique stone installations placed behind the main Buddha hall site. There

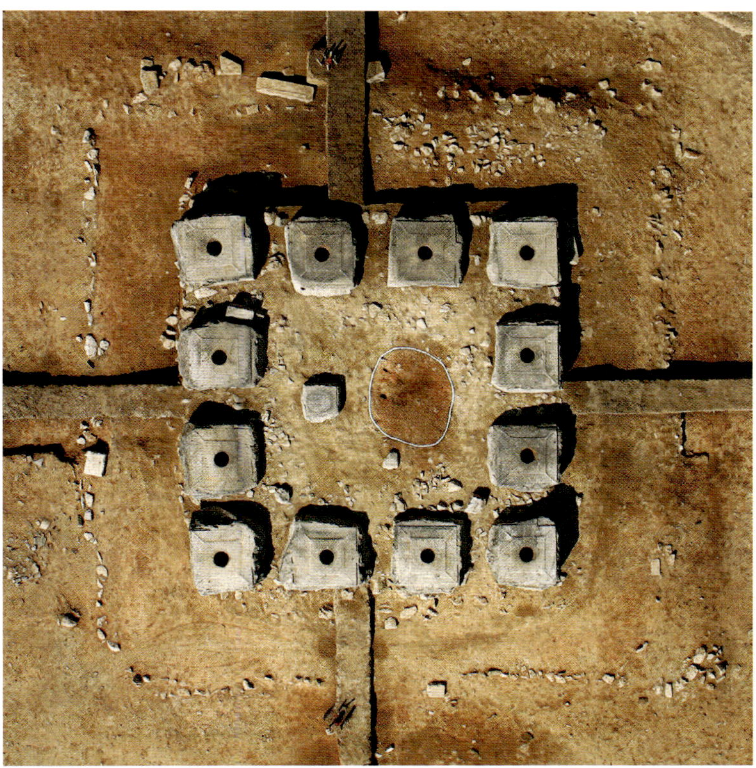

Figure 3.18 East stone remains behind the main Buddha hall site at the Sachŏnwang-sa site. Courtesy of the Gyeongju Research Institute of Cultural Heritage.

are two sets of mysterious stone remains, facing each other in the east and the west, placed in this monastery's courtyard between the main Buddha hall and the lecture hall sites (figs. 3.17, 3.18). Together with the main Buddha hall and paired pagodas to the south of the main hall, these two sets of stone remains create an almost mandalic monastery ground plan, one unprecedented in the Korean peninsula (fig. 3.19).[88] Each stone installation

---

[88] Some scholars have argued that this monastery plan is related to a Buddhist mandala. For example, see Kim Sangt'ae (Kim Sang-Tae) 김상태 and Pak Ŏngon (Park Eon-Kon) 박언곤, "Sach'ŏnwang-sa ŭi milgyojŏk tŭksŏng e kwanhan yŏn'gu" 四天王寺의 密教的 特性에 關한 硏究 [Research about the esoteric Buddhist features

consists of twelve pieces of square stone, whose width and length are about ninety centimeters long. The twelve stones are neatly arranged to form a square ground plan. In the center of each stone is a round hole, twenty-two centimeters wide and twenty-three centimeters deep. Surrounding the hole is a raised square form. Diagonal lines connect each corner of this square with the corresponding corner of the stone (fig. 3.20). As architectural historians Fujishima Gaijirō and Ko Yusŏp pointed out during the Japanese colonial period, the shape of these stones differs from that of ordinary base stones for pagodas found in Korea, which typically show few decorations.[89] For example, they are markedly different from the contemporaneous stone bases of the twin pagodas at Sach'ŏnwang-sa (fig. 3.21) and those of the above-mentioned nine-story wooden pagoda at Hwangnyong-sa. The twelve holes in these stone installations are not relic crypts not only because they are too small but also because a relic crypt usually appears only in the central stone supporting the heart pillar.

In his articles published in 1996 and 2002, Chang Ch'ungsik argued that these trimmed stones were not bases for wooden architecture, but the *tansŏk* 壇席 or remains of the ritual platform for the Munduru Ritual mentioned in the *Samguk yusa* (key point 8).[90] Chang Ch'ungsik suggested,

---

of Sach'ŏnwang-sa], *Taehan kŏnch'uk hakhoe nonmunjip* 大韓建築學會論文集 24, no. 2 (2004): 151-158.

[89] Fujishima Gaijirō 藤島亥治郎, "Chōsen kenchiku shiron, sono ichi" 朝鮮建築史論(其一) [Historical essay on Korean architecture 1], *Kenchiku zasshi* 建築雜誌 530 (1930): 255-329; reprinted in *Chosŏn kŏch'uk saron* (Seoul: Kyŏngin Munhwasa, 1982): 59-60; Ko Yusŏp 高裕燮, *Chosŏn t'app'a ŭi yŏn'gu* 韓國塔婆의 研究 [Research on Korean pagodas] (Seoul: Ŭryu Munhwasa, 1954): 11-12. Chang Ch'ungsik also agrees that these stones were not base stones for wooden pagodas. See his "Silla Nangsan yujŏk ŭi che munje (I): Sach'ŏnwang-saji rŭl chungsimŭro" 新羅 狼山遺蹟의 諸問題 (I): 四天王寺址를 中心으로 [Various problems of Silla's cultural remains at Mount Nang 1: Focusing on the Sach'ŏnwang-sa site], *Silla munhwaje haksul palp'yohoe nonmunjip* 新羅文化祭學術發表會論文集 17 (1996): 15-36. Before Chang Ch'ungsik's 1996 article, following colonial-period scholars' suggestions, many people believed that these stones were ruins of twin sutra pavilions (Kr. *kyŏngnu* 經樓), or a paired sutra pavilion and bell pavilion (Kr. *chongnu* 鐘樓). But there is no concrete evidence supporting such beliefs. In his 1930 article, Fujishima Gaijirō wrote that he was the first person to argue that these stones were sutra pavilion sites, but at the same time he admitted that there is no single convincing explanation for the function of these stones.

[90] Chang Ch'ungsik, "Silla Nangsan yujŏk ŭi chemunje (I)," 15-36; Chang Ch'ungsik, "Silla Sach'ŏnwang-saji tansŏk ŭi koch'al" 新羅 四天王寺址 壇席의 考察

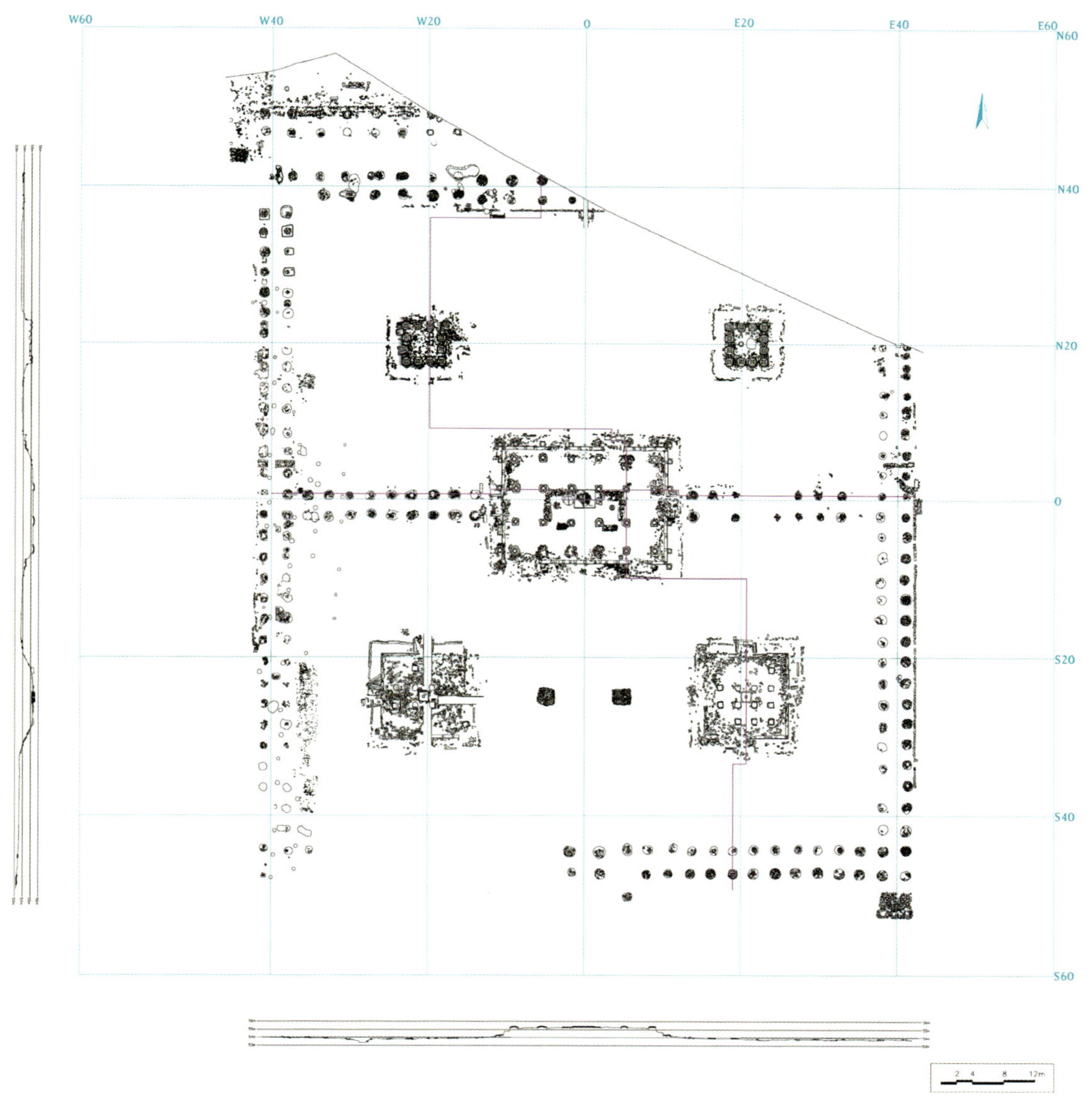

Figure 3.19 *Ground plan of Sachŏnwang-sa revealed after excavation.*
Courtesy of the Gyeongju Research Institute of Cultural Heritage.

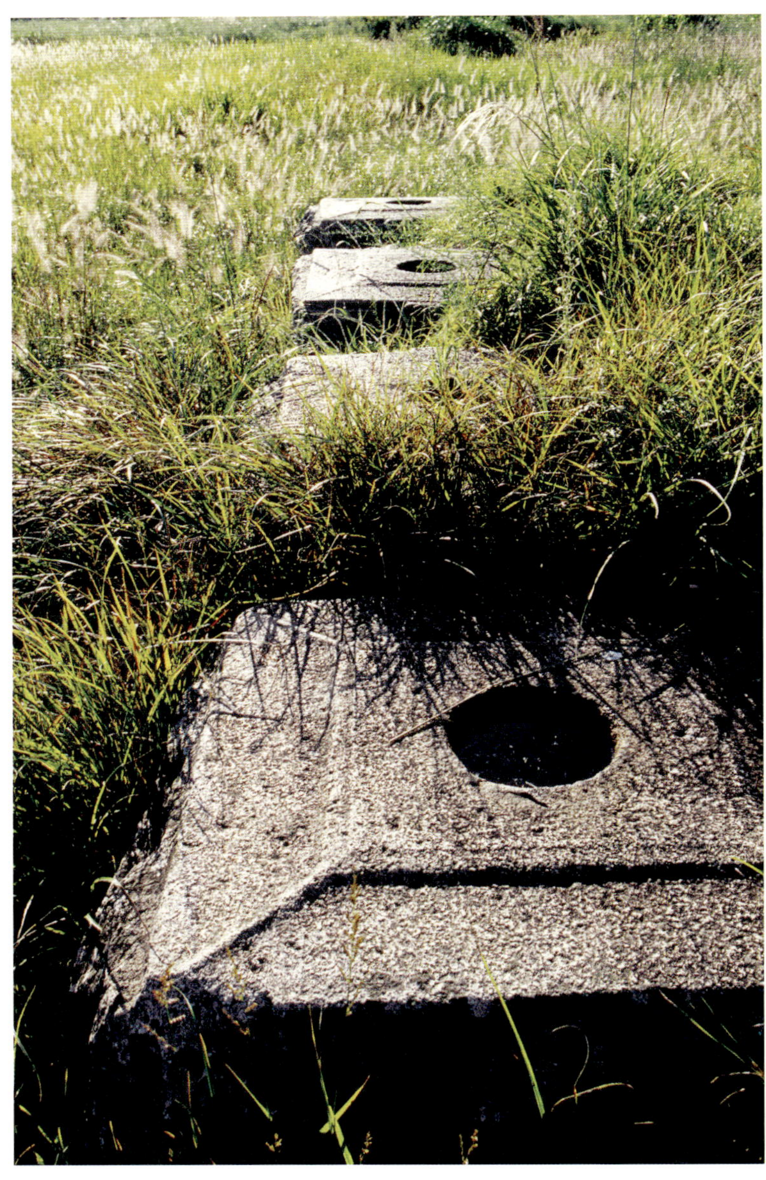

Figure 3.20 *Stone remains at the Sachŏnwang-sa site (detail).*
Courtesy of Ahn Jangheon.

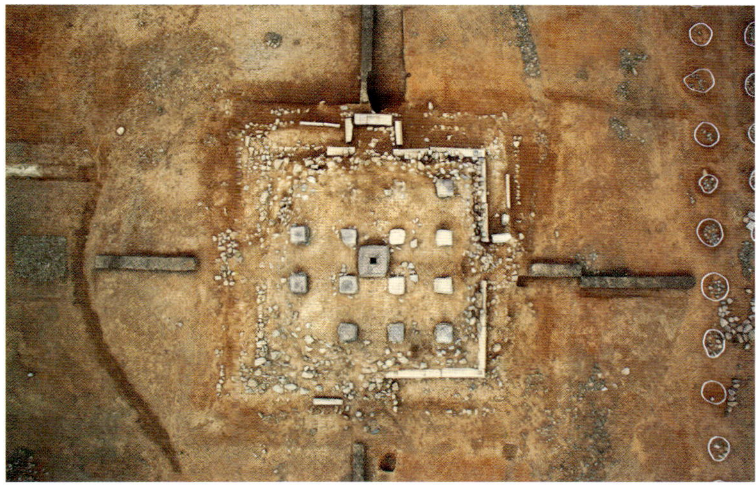

*Figure 3.21 Stone bases of the east pagoda at the Sachŏnwang-sa site.
Courtesy of the Gyeongju Research Institute of Cultural Heritage.*

based on the seventh fascicle of the *Consecration Sutra*, that the holes in
these stones were used to insert round pieces of wood (Kr. *wŏnmok* 圓木),
or logs, inscribed with the names of the Deities of the Five Directions and
their retinues. As explained above, these inscribed logs serving as thaumaturgic seals are called "Munduru" in this ritual, and the name of this ritual comes from these wooden seals. Chang Ch'ungsik also suggested that
the number of the stones in each stone installation symbolized the twelve
Yoga monks who performed the Munduru Ritual under the direction of
the monk Myŏngnang. This new suggestion has been positively accepted
among many scholars. The interim excavation report of 2012, while await-
ing complete excavation of the stone installations, identifies these two stone
remains as "sites inferred to be ritual platforms."[91]

  While waiting for the complete excavation result to be published by the
Gyeongju National Research Institute of Cultural Heritage, I want to add

---

[Examination of the ritual platform at Sachŏnwang-sa from Silla], *Pulgyo hakpo*
佛教學報 39 (2002): 7-23.
  [91] 推定壇席址. See Kungnip Kyŏngju Munhwajae Yŏn'guso, *Sachŏnwang-sa*,
82-86.

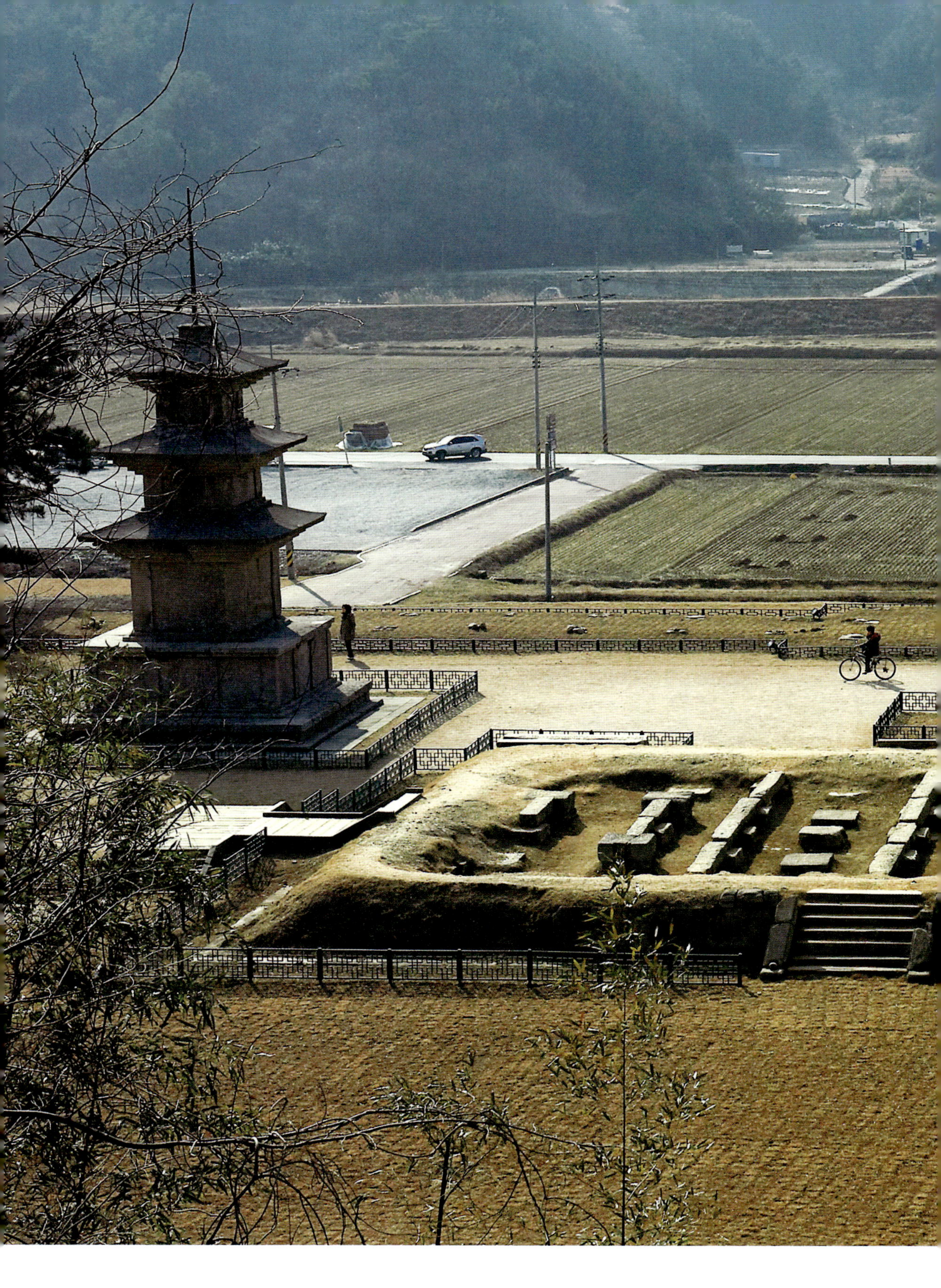

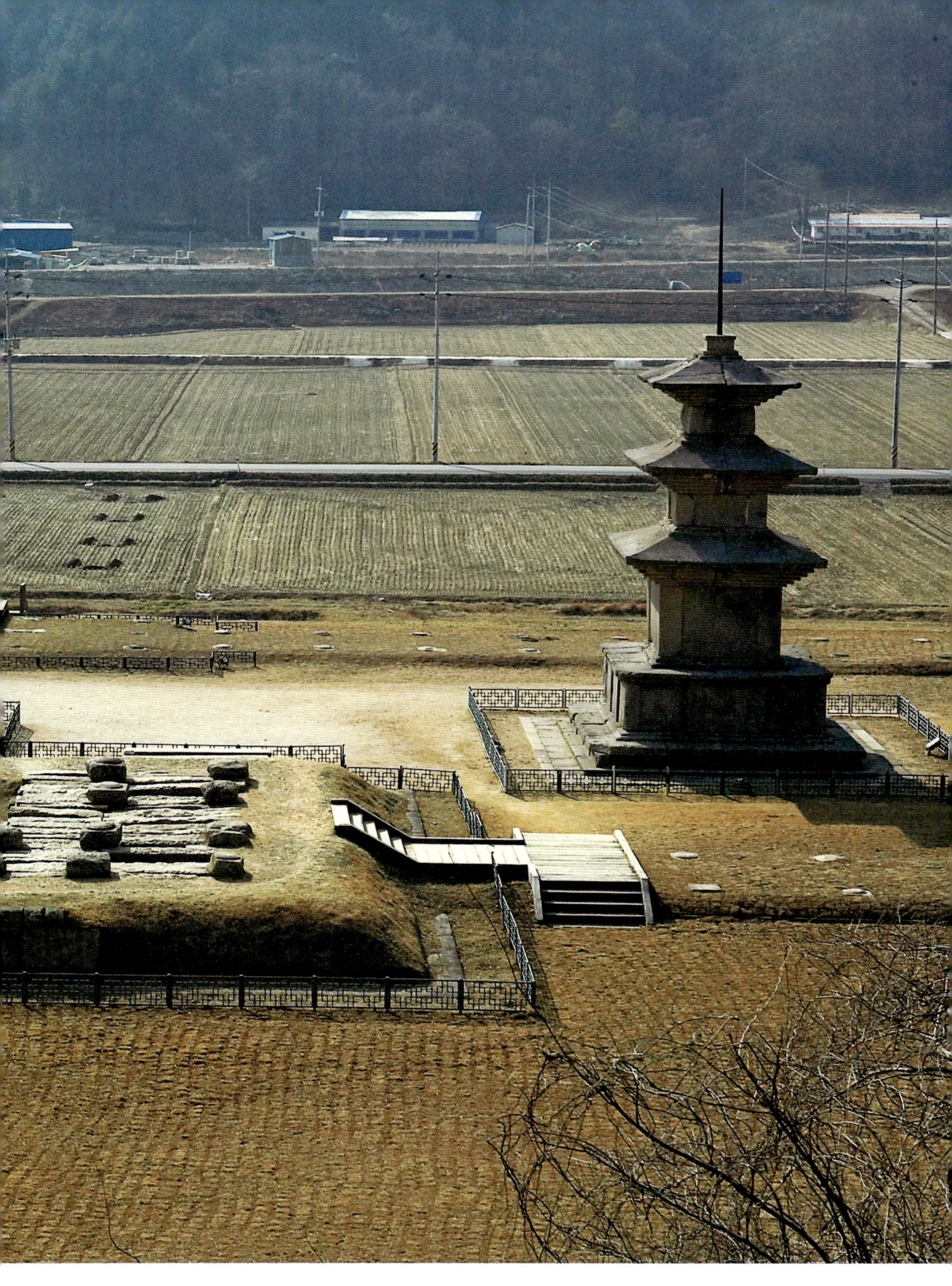

Figure 3.22 Twin pagodas of Kamŭn-sa (view from the north side of the monastery site), Yangbung-myŏn, Kyŏngju. Silla, ca. 682. Courtesy of Ha Jigwon.

a few observations that reinforce Chang Ch'ungsik's suggestion. In addition
to the unusual decorations on these stones, their arrangement also indicates
that they were not base stones for a typical wooden structure. In traditional
East Asian timber architecture, the basic spatial unit is the bay defined by
two pillars. If the twelve stones served as bases for wooden architecture, the
structure would have been a three-by-three-bay building. The space between
two stones in these installations, however, is about sixty-four centimeters,
too narrow to form one bay for a normal wooden building. The sixty-four-
centimeter distance between stones is even shorter than the length of each
stone that forms these stone remains. Also strange is that, unlike in a normal pagoda or building site, only a few base stones were found inside the
square ground plan (compare figs. 3.17 and 3.18 and fig. 3.21). It is difficult to
find similarly arranged stones at monastery sites elsewhere. This means that
either a special wooden structure having an unusual form was built above
these stones, or there was no wooden building at all. Additionally, the size
of the small wooden log on which the names of the deities were written,
explained in the *Consecration Sutra*, is noteworthy. In the sutra, Indra asks
the Buddha, "What should be the length and breadth of the Munduru
(*mudrā*) made of round pieces of wood?" and the Buddha answers, "The
length and breadth [should be] seven *fen* by seven *fen*."[92] In modern units
of measurement, one *fen* 分 is about 3.03 centimeters, and seven *fen* is about
21.21 centimeters. Interestingly, a small log about twenty-one centimeters
tall and twenty-one centimeters wide would exactly fit into the holes on the
stones forming the two stone remains at the Sach'ŏnwang-sa site (fig. 3.20).
Were wooden logs inscribed with deities' names inserted into the stones?
Were superstructures of some kind enshrining the inscribed wooded pieces
built over the stone? Although details regarding the usage of these mysterious stones remain as yet unclear, these unprecedented stone installations
from the Silla period at least suggest that this monastery was designed to

---

92 員木文頭婁縱廣幾許 佛言縱廣七七分. T1331, 21:515b18. Strickmann trans-
lated the phrase "*qiqifen*" 七七分 in the Buddha's answer to "7 inches by 0.7 inch,"
but I see no reason to interpret the second *qi* 七, which simply means seven, as 0.7.
Michel Strickmann, *Chinese Magical Medicine*, 134. Chang Ch'ungsik suggested
that *qiqifen* means seven multiplied by seven, hence 49 *fen*, which is about 148
centimeters. Chang Ch'ungsik, "Silla Sach'ŏnwang-saji tansŏk ŭi koch'al," 15. From
reading the entire fascicle, however, one can understand that this round wooden
object is a seal (*mudrā*) placed on the chest of a sick person during the ritual (持
此神印致病者身 當胸上而安之). A forty-nine-inch long log would be too heavy to
place on a sick person's chest.

have a special function that other contemporaneous Korean monasteries did not have. As Koichi Shinohara pointed out to me, the word *toryang* 道場/道場 in the phrase "install a ritual space 開設道場" implies that the ritual space had a certain kind of esoteric ritual altar. In the seventh century, painted mandalas to be hung over ritual altars had yet to appear, but mandalas painted on the ground for ritual practice or mandalas as ritual altars already existed.[93] It is plausible that these stone installations arranged in mandalic format were the ritual altar/platform mentioned in the *Samguk yusa* passage,[94] and that, as Chang Ch'ungsik suggested, the "ritual platform" Iryŏn saw at this monastery in the thirteenth century consisted of these stone installations (key point 8).

Reliquary Reminiscence of the Ritual

Now we will briefly examine the inner reliquary excavated from the east pagoda of Kamŭn-sa, since it can serve as visual evidence to connect this ritual with King Munmu (key point 3). Kamŭn-sa, one of the three major state-protection monasteries of Silla, as mentioned above, is also a fortunate case in which archaeological data as well as relatively reliable textual records have survived. The archaeological remains of Kamŭn-sa, which still retains its three-story twin pagodas made of stone (fig. 3.22), are located in present-day Yongdang-ni 龍堂里, Yangbung-myŏn 陽北面 in Kyŏngju. The first excavation of the Kamŭn-sa site was conducted in 1959 by the National Museum of Korea with the financial support of the Harvard-Yenching Institute (figs. 3.23, 3.24).[95] This was the first modern archaeological excavation conducted by Korean archaeologists.

Fortunately, the *Samguk yusa* includes a quotation from an epigraph from Kamŭn-sa. It explains that King Munmu initiated the construction of this monastery but passed away in 681 before its completion, and his son King Sinmun (r. 681-692) completed the construction for his father

---

[93] I appreciate Koichi Shinohara's comments on this. For more about early "esoteric" Buddhism in East Asia, see his "The All-gathering Maṇḍala Initiation Ceremony in Atikūa's Collected *Dhāraṇī* Scriptures: Reconstructing the Evolution of Esoteric Buddhist Ritual," *Journal Asiatique* 298, no. 2 (2010): 389-420.

[94] In East Asian languages, the plural form and the singular form are often undifferentiated. So the *tansŏk* in the *Samguk yusa* can be either singular or plural.

[95] For the excavation report, see Yun Mubyŏng (Youn Moo-byong) 尹武柄 and Kim Chaewŏn 金載元, *Kamŭn-saji palgul chosa pogosŏ* 感恩寺址 發堀調査報告書 [Excavation report of Kamŭn-sa site] (Seoul: Ŭryu Munhwasa, 1961): 1-202.

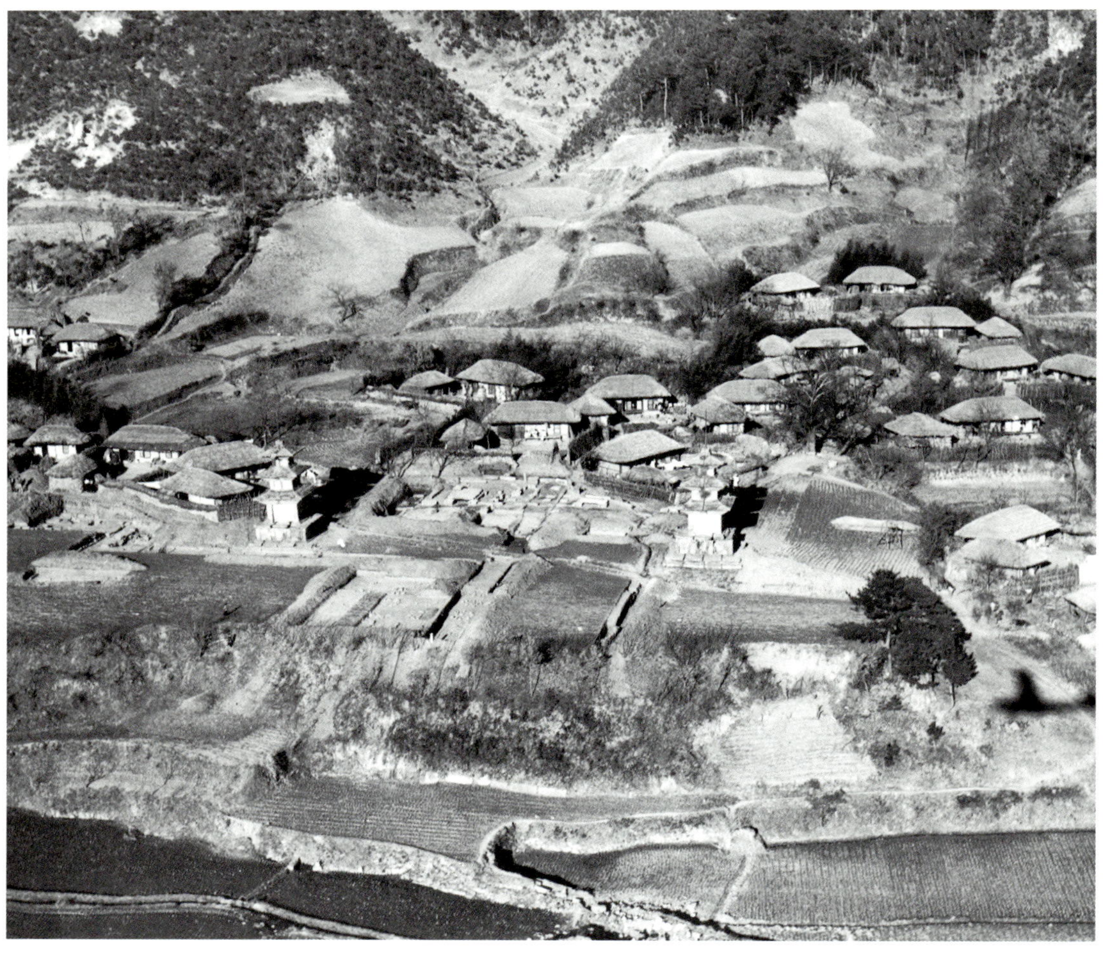

Figure 3.23 Kamŭn-sa site before excavation. Courtesy of Youn Moo-byong.

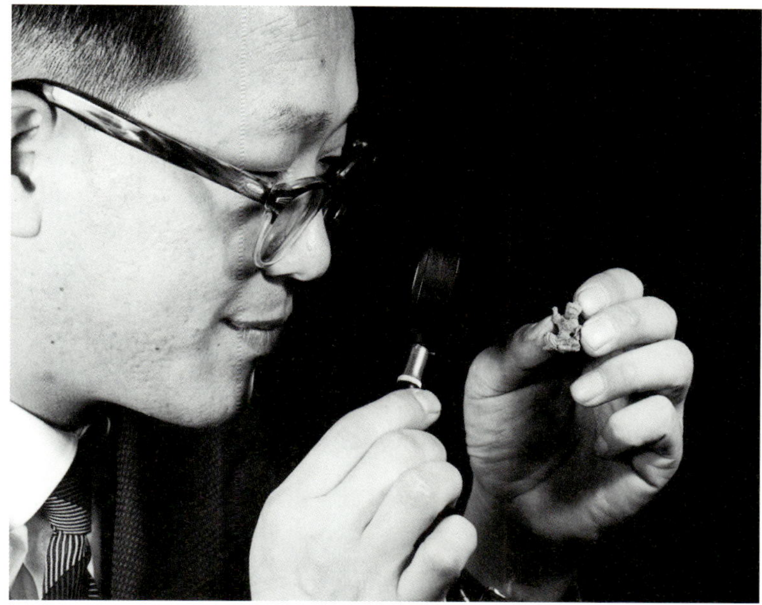

Figure 3.24 Archaeologist Youn Moo-byong (Yun Mubyŏng 尹武炳) examining a figurine excavated from the west pagoda of Kamŭn-sa. Courtesy of Youn Moo-byong.

one year after King Munmu's death. As a result, King Munmu became the patron as well as dedicatee of this monastery.[96] The beginning half of the quotation reads:

> *Sajunggi*[97] says that King Munmu wanted to quell the Japanese military. Therefore he began to construct this monastery. He passed away

---

[96] Based on the location of the monastery and the records in the *Samguk sagi*, the official history of the Three Kingdoms, some scholars have suggested that Kamŭn-sa served as *wŏndang* 願堂, or a commemorative monastery, of King Munmu. Yi Yŏngho 李永鎬, Kim Ch'angho 金昌鎬, and Kim Wŏnju 金源周, "Silla sŏngjŏn sawŏn ŭi sŏngnip" 新羅 成典寺院의 成立 [Establishment of Silla's *sŏngjŏn* monastery], *Silla munhwajae haksul palp'yo taehoe nonmunjip* 新羅文化際 學術發表 大會論文輯 14 (1993): 247-288.

[97] As discussed earlier in this chapter, records of this type are epigraphic data collected from monasteries.

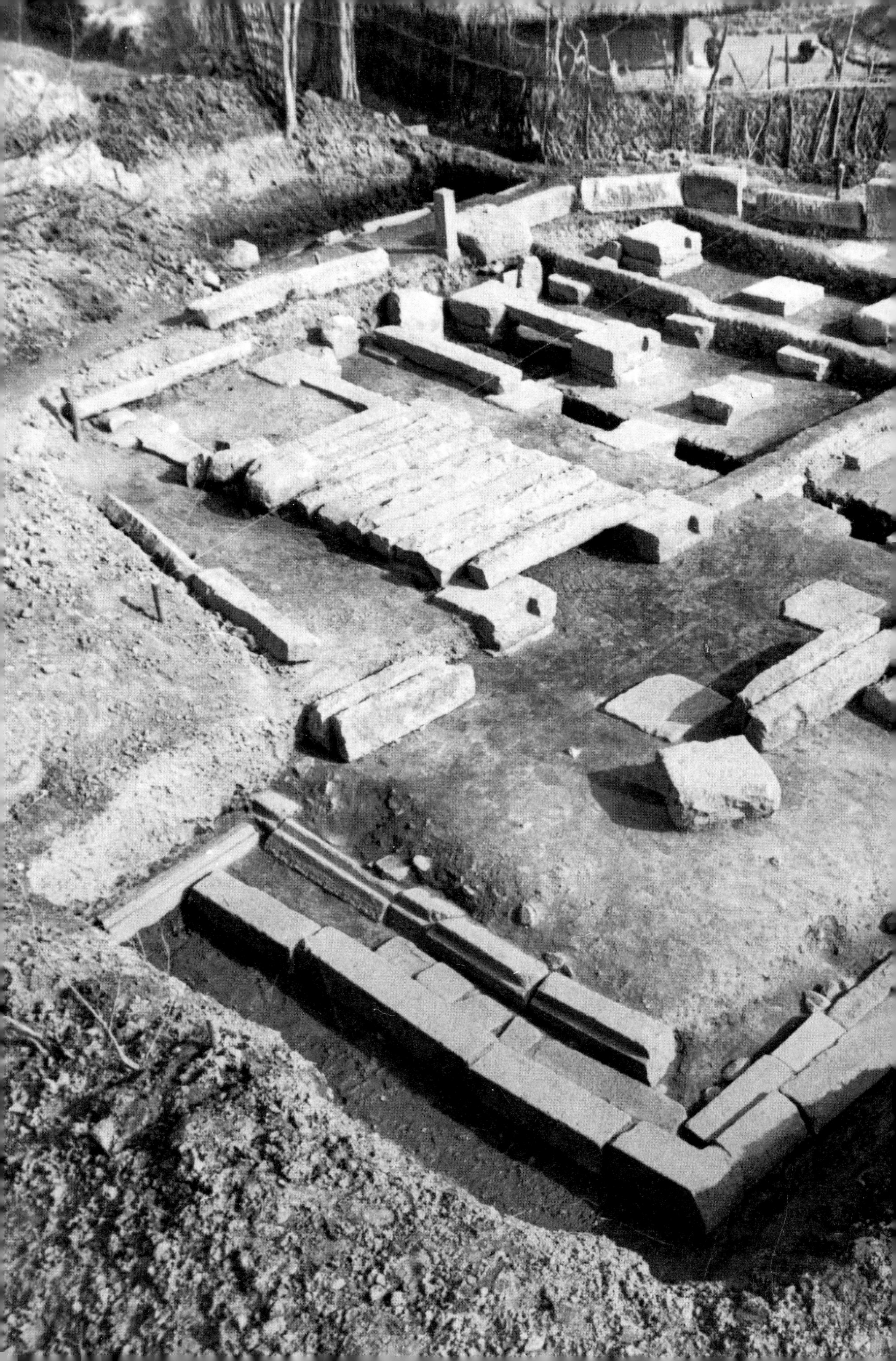

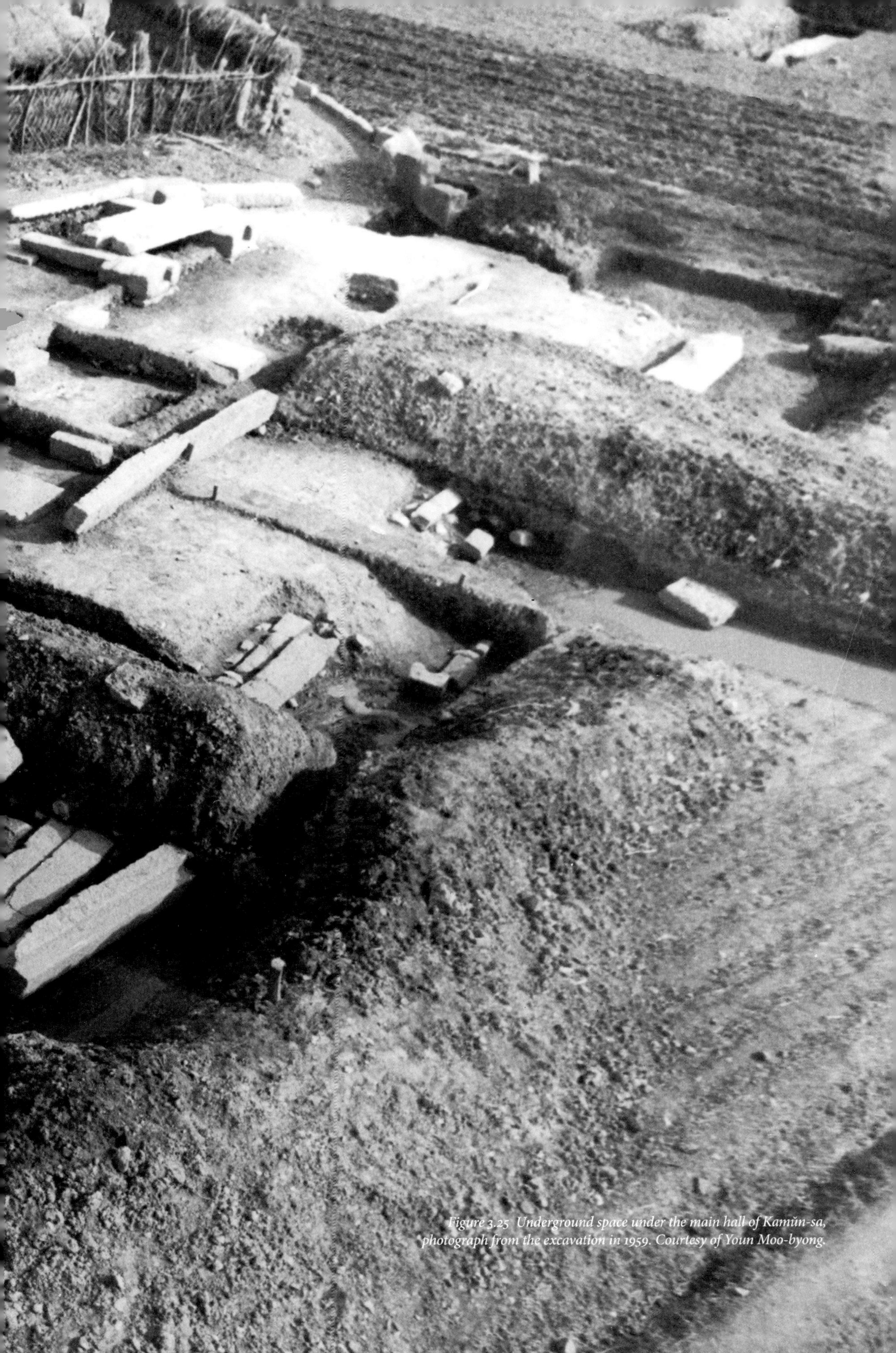

Figure 3.25 Underground space under the main hall of Kamŭn-sa,
photograph from the excavation in 1959. Courtesy of Youn Moo-byong.

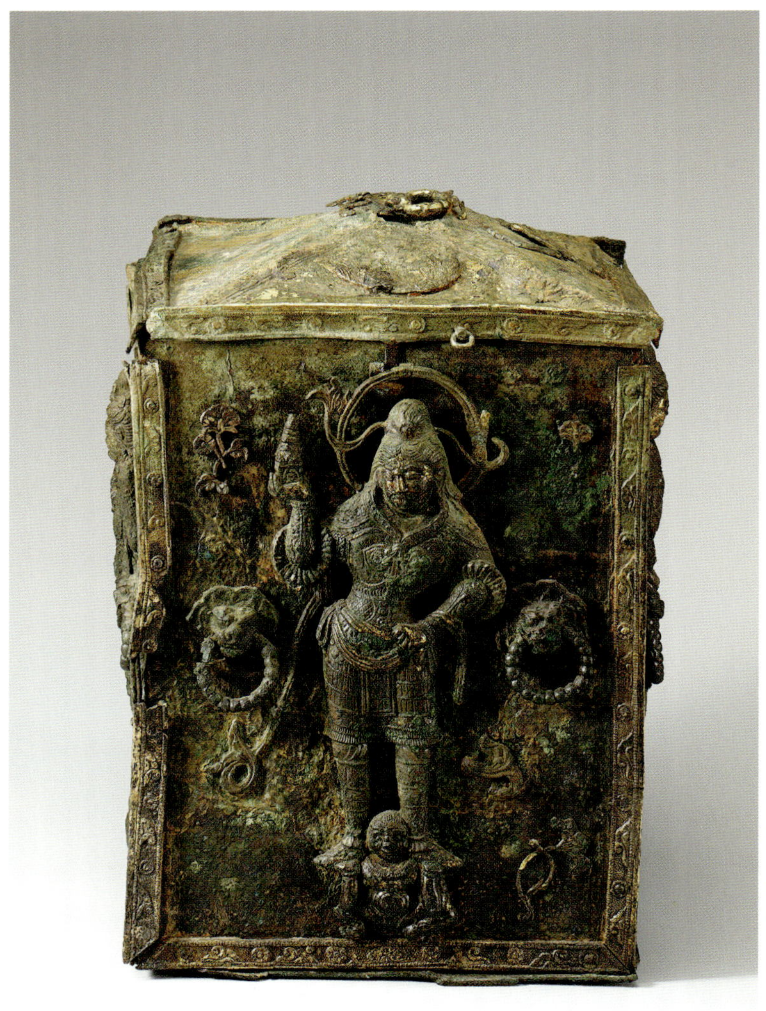

*Figure 3.26 Outer reliquary, from the west pagoda of Kamŭn-sa. Silla, ca. 682.
31.0×18.8×18.8cm. Courtesy of the National Museum of Korea.*

182

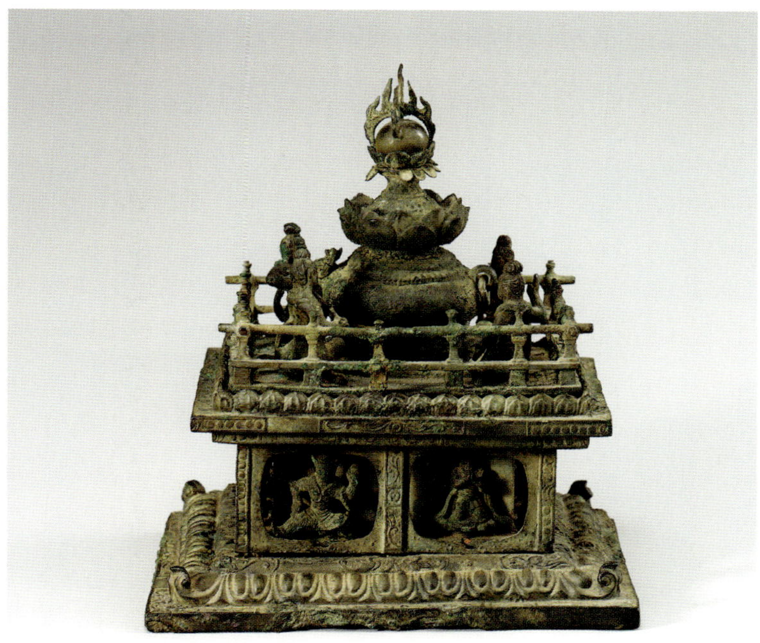

*Figure 3.27 Inner reliquary, from the west pagoda of Kamŭn-sa (without the canopy part).
Silla, ca. 682. Courtesy of the National Museum of Korea.*

before completing [the monastery], and became a dragon in the sea.
His son [King] Sinmun ascended to the throne and completed [the
construction of Kamŭn-sa] in the second year of the reign of Kaiyao
開耀 (682). [King Sinmun] had a hole opened toward the east under
the stone steps of the main Buddha hall. It was a preparation for the
dragon to enter the monastery and coil itself up . . .[98]

寺中記云, 文武王欲鎮倭兵, 故始創此寺, 未畢而崩, 爲海龍. 其子神
文立, 開耀二年畢.排金堂砌下, 東向開一穴, 乃龍之入寺旋繞之備.

---

[98] *Samguk yusa* 2: "Manp'asikchŏk," *Yŏkchu Samguk yusa*, 2:45.

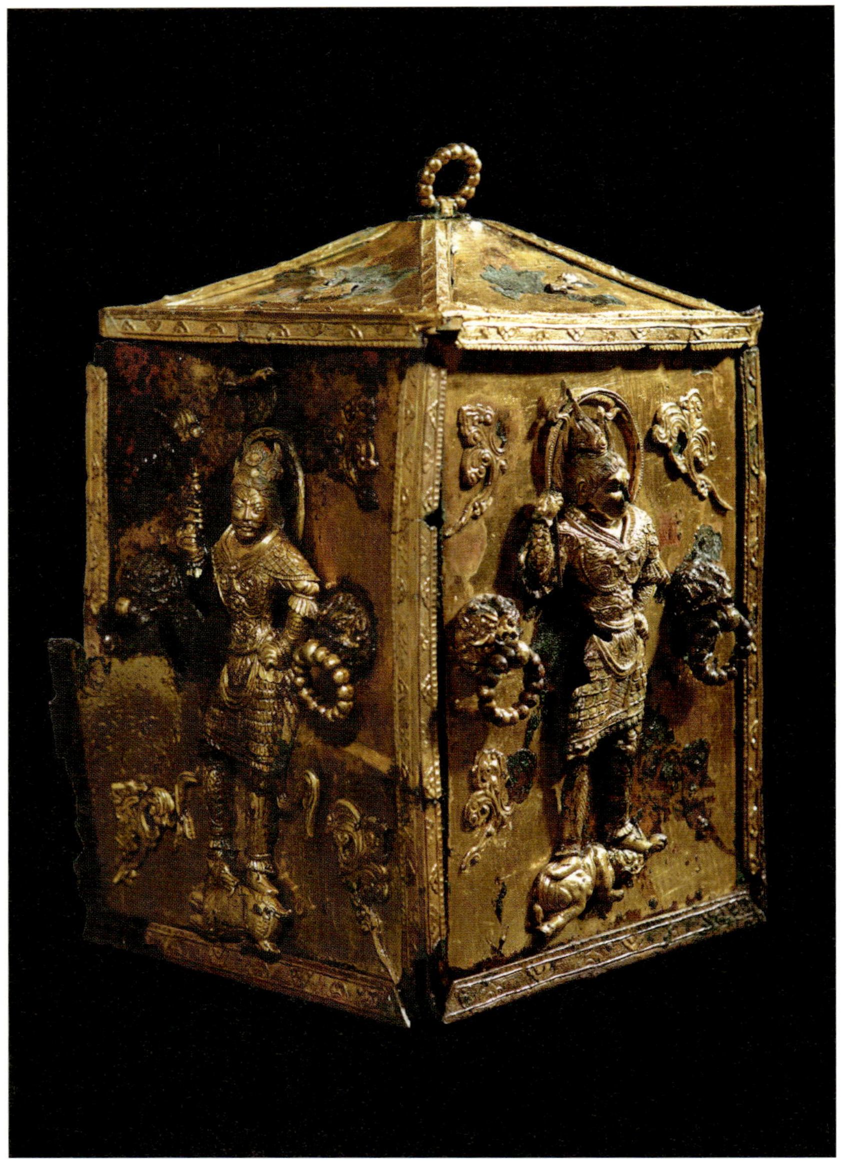

Figure 3.28 *Outer reliquary, from the east pagoda of Kamŭn-sa. Silla, ca. 682.
30.2×18.9×18.9cm. Courtesy of the National Museum of Korea.*

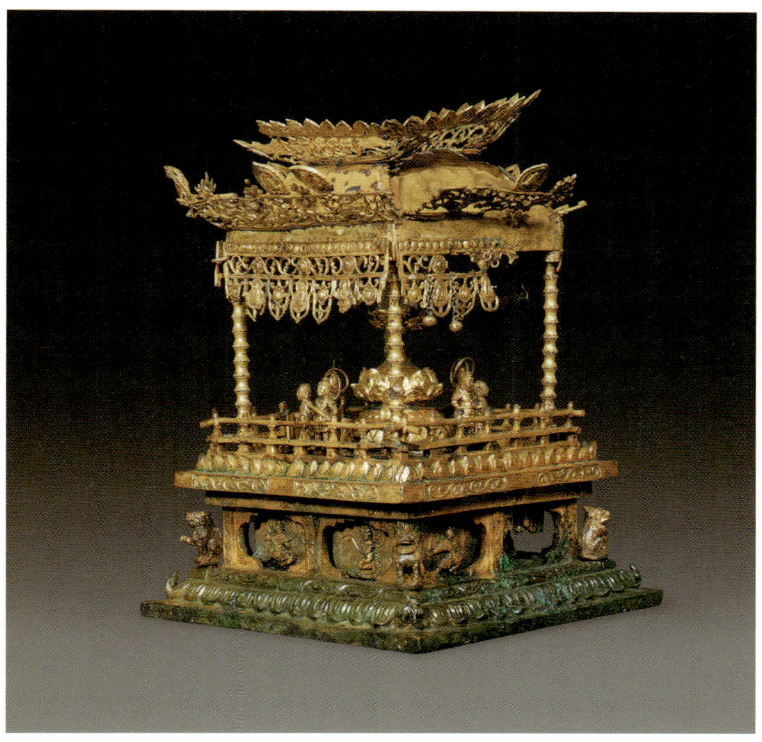

Figure 3.29 Inner reliquary, from the east pagoda of Kamŭn-sa. Silla, ca. 682.
18.8×14.6×14.6cm. Courtesy of the National Museum of Korea.

Although parts of this record are closer to myth than history, especially the story about the dragon, surprisingly the 1959 excavation of the
Kamŭn-sa site discovered a mysterious underground space under the main
hall (fig. 3.25), which conforms to the space that was prepared to invite the
dragon reincarnation of King Munmu to the monastery recorded in the
above quotation.[99] The excavation of 1959 also found an unprecedentedly

99 Yun Mubyŏng and Kim Chaewŏn, *Kamŭn-saji palgul chosa pogosŏ*, 3-4,
19-28; Kungnip Kyŏngju Munhwajae Yŏn'guso 國立慶州文化財研究所 [Gyeongju
National Research Institute of Cultural Heritage], *Kamŭn-sa palgul chosa pogosŏ*
感恩寺 發堀調査報告書 [Excavation report of Kamŭn-sa], (Kyŏngju: Kungnip

sophisticated reliquary set from the west pagoda (figs 3.26, 3.27). A matching reliquary set was discovered from the east pagoda in 1996 during the pagoda restoration (figs. 3.28, 3.29).[100]

The complete reliquary sets, which have unique and complicated design, will be the subject of a separate publication. What is relevant for the discussion in this chapter is the inner reliquary from the east pagoda of Kamŭn-sa. The design of this exquisite inner reliquary, especially that of the eight figurines on its pedestal, is unique and is not seen anywhere else in East Asia. The reliquary has an architectural form in which four pillars on a high platform support a canopy. On the platform, eight figurines surround the relic container placed in the center (fig. 3.30). Among the eight figurines, the four standing in each of the four corners of the platform are figures of monks. Despite their tiny size, ranging from 2.8 to 3.2 centimeters tall, these monk figurines have fascinating details, including especially their hand gestures and the objects in their hands. The one in the southeast corner holds an object similar to the ritual apparatus *vajra*.[101] The monk in the southwest corner also holds an unidentifiable object. The one in the northwest forms a *varada mudrā* with his left hand, but the object that was initially inserted in the hole of his right hand is now lost. The northeastern monk is secretly hiding his left hand in his robe under his right hand. These intentionally differentiated hand gestures and ritual objects show that the artisan put special emphasis on these details to imply that the monks are performing a certain kind of ritual action. One more detail to note is that these four monk figurines do not fit any known Buddhist iconography. In Buddhist art, the most frequently appearing monk images are those of young Ānanda and old Kāśyapa, the two disciples of the Śākyamuni Buddha; the ten disciples of the Buddha; and *arhat* images often made in sets of sixteen, eighteen, or five hundred.

Kyŏngju Munhwajae Yŏn'guso, 2009): 221-222.

[100] For the excavation report of the reliquary sets from the east pagoda of Kamŭn-sa, see Kungnip Munhwajae Yŏn'guso Misul Kongye Yŏn'gusil 국립문화재 연구소 미술공예연구실 [Research Team on Art and Craft at the National Cultural Properties Research Institute], *Kamŭnsaji tong samch'ŭng sŏkt'ap sari changŏm* 감은 사지 동 삼층석탑 사리장엄 [Reliquaries from the east pagoda of the Kamŭn-sa site] (Seoul: Kungnip Munhwajae Yŏn'guso, 2010): 1-235.

[101] For the drawing showing details of these four monk figurines, see Kungnip Munhwajae Yŏn'guso Misul Kongye Yŏn'gusil, *Kamŭnsaji tong samch'ŭng sŏkt'ap sari changŏm*, 103, Drawing 2.

What is even more unique is that these four monks are grouped together in this reliquary with four guardian figurines. Standing between the monks, the four guardian figurines, wearing scale armor and holding weapons, are positioned in the four cardinal directions of the reliquary's platform.[102] Taking a closer look, we see halos behind the guardians' heads, indicating that they are not ordinary human beings but some sort of deities. The small pagoda in the hand of the northern guardian indeed indicates that these four figurines are the Four Heavenly Kings. A small pagoda is the most distinctive attribute of Vaiśravaṇa, the Northern Heavenly King. In fact, images of the Four Heavenly Kings from Kamŭn-sa are the earliest surviving example of these deities in the Korean peninsula.[103] In short, both the images of four monks and the Four Heavenly Kings are unprecedented in previous reliquaries of the Korean peninsula, and the iconography grouping them together into a set is seen only in this Kamŭn-sa reliquary.

This unique design reveals that the reliquary figurines were not made by simply following a previous visual tradition or known iconography. What would have triggered creation of this unique design, if it did not come from preexisting visual models? Considering that this reliquary is from Kamŭn-sa, built by and dedicated to King Munmu, the strong resonance between the Munduru Ritual and reliquary design is all the more significant. As the readers of this chapter may already have noticed, this reliquary design has an uncanny resonance with the Munduru Ritual as examined above. As explained in the *Samguk yusa*, a group of Yoga monks led by Myŏngnang performed the Munduru Ritual using the statue of the Deity of Five Directions. The term "Yoga monks" in this context means monks who practice *mantra* (Buddhist incantation), *mudrā*, and mandala (visualization).[104] The monk figurines in the reliquary are forming *mudrā*, and some even seem to have slightly open mouths as if they are reciting incantations. The Deities of the Five Directions, as explained in the *Consecration Sutra*, take the form of guardian deities wearing armor and carrying

---

[102] For images showing details of these four figurines, see Kungnip Munhwajae Yŏn'guso Misul Kongye Yŏn'gusil, *Kamŭn-saji tong samch'ŭng sŏkt'ap sari changŏm*, 99, Plate 1.

[103] Im Yŏngae, "Sŏkkuram Sach'ŏnwang-sang ŭi tosang kwa Pulgyo kyŏngjŏn," 25-26. Im Yŏngae thinks that Sach'ŏnwang-sa had images of the Four Heavenly Kings but that they did not survive.

[104] See footnote 13 of this chapter. *Mantra, mudrā*, and visualization are also important in the Munduru Ritual explained in the seventh chapter of the *Consecration Sutra*.

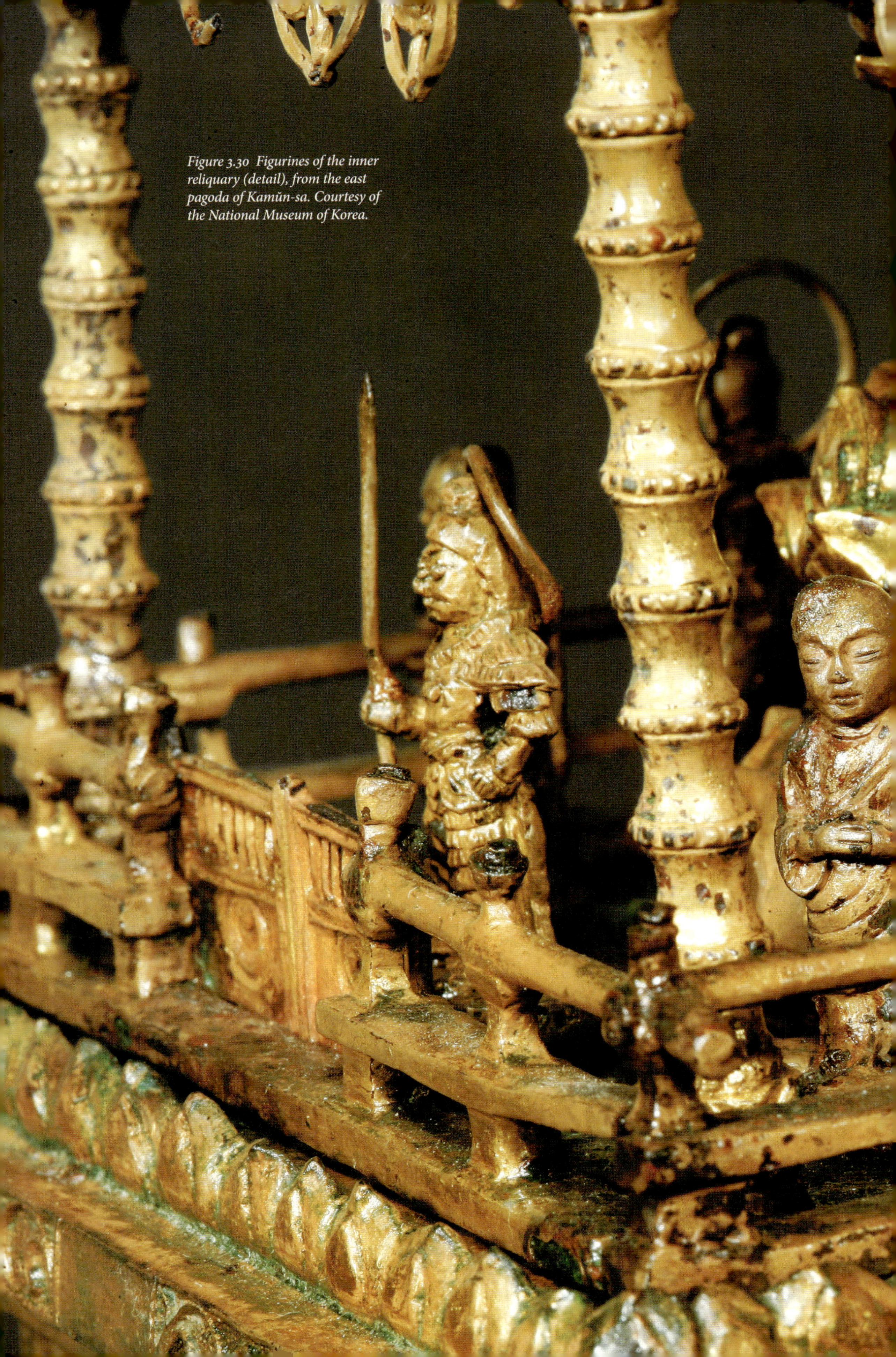

Figure 3.30 Figurines of the inner reliquary (detail), from the east pagoda of Kamŭn-sa. Courtesy of the National Museum of Korea.

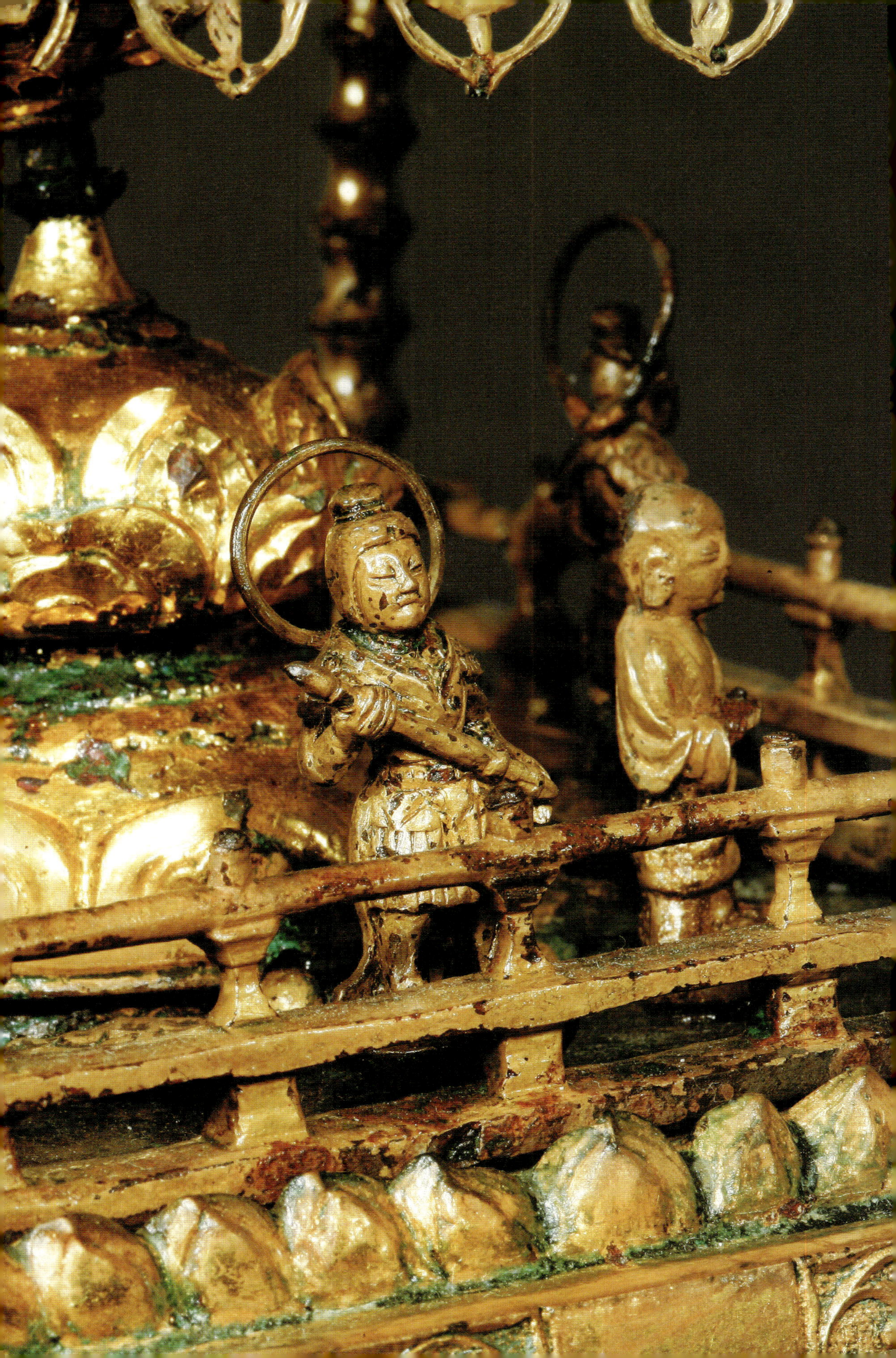

weapons.[105] What is particularly relevant here is Kang Ubang's argument that the shape of the Deities of the Five Directions was probably modeled after that of the Four Heavenly Kings at Sach'ŏnwang-sa.[106] According to him, the Munduru Ritual in the *Consecration Sutra*, which assimilated indigenous East Asian religious practices into Buddhism, promoted the synthesis of Silla's indigenous religion with Buddhism. In the process, religious arts also reflected such synthesis, and the Deities of the Five Directions, which retained the nature of the indigenous religion, were visualized in the form of the Four Heavenly Kings. In the *Consecration Sutra*, Indra indeed promises that the Four Heavenly Kings will protect this Munduru Ritual of the Deities of the Five Directions.[107]

I would not want to argue that these figurines faithfully represent the Munduru Ritual. Rather, the design of the reliquary responded to contemporaneous religio-political events and was inspired by the Munduru Ritual. Although it is not a faithful representation of the Munduru Ritual, the reliquary clearly borrowed motifs from the Munduru Ritual, a ritual performed during the reign of King Munmu for the sake of the state, in order to symbolize state protection.

Conclusion

In this postmodern era, many historians acknowledge that complete and objective reconstruction of the past is an impossible task. Study of ancient history and art in any culture involves a certain level of speculation and interpretation. While keeping in mind the limits of modern knowledge of the past, in this chapter I attempted to open up the possibility of productively using the *Samguk yusa* through an interdisciplinary approach to the text, using archaeological data as well as intertextual readings. Careful "understanding" of ancient Korean Buddhist history obtained through an interdisciplinary approach that neither simply ignores nor naively trusts the value of the *Samguk yusa* as a meaningful historical source, I believe, can add more depth to our prior conceptions of Korean Buddhist history.[108]

As a stepping-stone to new approaches to the *Samguk yusa*, this chapter takes an interdisciplinary approach to its passage about the Munduru

---

[105] T1331, 21:515c.

[106] Kang Ubang, *Wŏnyung kwa chohwa*, 190-197.

[107] T1331, 21:516a.

[108] In Korean history, the time before Koryŏ is often categorized as ancient history (Kr. *kodaesa* 古代史).

Ritual to provide a case study. Inspection of external texts and relevant archaeological materials suggests that it is highly probable that this early "esoteric" ritual was actually performed during the Silla period under King Munmu's reign, and that this ritual practice also served to shape one characteristic of later Korean esoteric Buddhism, in which early "esoteric" ritual mixed with Daoist tradition was patronized by the royal court as late as the fifteenth century. This chapter has also shown that the religious art of Unified Silla sensitively responded to its socio-religious environment.

This chapter represents an endeavor to connect not just the present and the past but also Western Buddhologists and Korean art historians. Communication between modern scholars and premodern materials flows only in one direction—scholars can only make educated inferences using fragmentary or mute data; this relationship will necessarily remain one-sided, but the relationship among scholars from differing disciplines and regions is something we can work to develop further. Prominent scholars of Korean Buddhism, such as Henrik H. Sørensen, have already discussed Buddhist art and architecture in their own scholarship, but I hope that a growing number of scholars of Korean Buddhism will more actively engage archaeological and art-historical materials in their future studies. Through the cross-disciplinary and interregional approach I have conducted in this chapter, we can collaborate in drawing a more vivid and accurate picture of socio-religious activities in early Korea.[109]

---

[109] Using visuals can also produce interesting and new types of studies of Korean Buddhist history for later periods, including modern times, as recent works by young scholars with mixed disciplinary backgrounds have demonstrated. Today more young scholars have official training in both Korean art history and Korean Buddhism, such as Dr. Se-Woong Koo and Dr. Maya Kerstin Stiller. I look forward to the new generation of scholars' contributions to the fields of both art history and Buddhology.

4

The Development of Koryŏ Porcelain and the Chinese Ceramic Industry in the Tenth Century[1]

Jang Namwon

Introduction

It is well known that the Koryŏ (918-1392) ceramic industry was greatly influenced during its early stages and establishment by Yuezhou kilns 越州窯 in southern China. The structure of and construction method for kilns during this period as well as the style of porcelain ware confirm this fact.[2] Koryŏ's porcelain production first became active in the

---

[1] Editor's Note: In order to prevent confusion, I provide a brief explanation of the terminology used in this chapter. The term "porcelain" here is a translation of *chagi* 磁器/瓷器. In East Asia, ceramics (Kr. *tojagi* 陶磁器, Ch. *taociqi* 陶瓷器, Jp. *tōjiki* 陶磁器) were traditionally divided into two groups, *togi* 陶器 and *chagi*. The former is often translated as "earthenware" or "pottery" and the latter as "porcelain." *Chagi* includes both celadon ware fired with a 1200-1350°C reducing flame and white ceramic fired with a 1300-1350°C reducing flame, while ceramics fired at a lower temperature are usually categorized as *togi*. In different cultural regions, however, the definition of porcelain varies. In the West, which has a different way of categorizing ceramics, the term "porcelain" designates only ceramics that were completely vitrified by high-temperature fire inside the kiln, and in this categorization, celadon would not be considered to be porcelain.

[2] For detailed discussions of the relationship between the early Koryŏ ceramic industry and the southern Chinese ceramic industry, see Yi Chongmin 李鍾玟, "Sihŭng Pangsan-dong ch'ogi ch'ŏngja yoji ch'ult'op'um ŭl t'onghae pon chungbu chiyŏk chŏnch'ugyo ŭi unyŏng sigi" 시흥 방산동 초기청자 요지 출토품을 통해 본 중부지역 전축요의 운영시기 [The period of brick kiln operation in the central

tenth century, and porcelains first appeared in Hwanghae Province 黃海道 and Kyŏnggi Province 京畿道 near the capital Kaegyŏng 開京. The influence of Yuezhou kilns in Zhejiang Province 浙江省, China, on these early Koryŏ kiln sites has been widely observed in vessel styles, shaping methods, the size (over forty meters long) and construction materials (brick) of kilns, kiln tools, and methods of stacking and arranging vessels inside the kiln. The brick kiln excavated at Pangsan-dong 芳山洞 in Sihŭng 始興, Kyŏnggi Province, in 1997 and 1998 is a representative example showing such influence. The Pangsan-dong kiln is very similar to the typical southern Chinese kilns, which developed along the Yangtze River from the Tang (618-907), Five Dynasties (907-960), and Song (960-1279) periods in China. Similarities include brick kiln construction methods, firing techniques, types and shapes of porcelain ware, and inscriptions. Therefore, it can be inferred that early Koryŏ owes its Chinese-style kilns and much of its porcelain production technology to migrant artisans from Zhejiang Province in China. This hypothesis is based on research results that have accumulated over the last decade, and it has become the most widely accepted theory on the early development of the Koryŏ porcelain industry.

However, from the second half of the tenth century, it appears that the Koryŏ porcelain industry also began incorporating new elements from northern China into its firing techniques, choice of types and shapes of vessels, as well as ornamentation techniques and decorative patterns. For example, soon after Koryŏ kilns began to produce Yuezhou kiln-style celadon, they simultaneously produced white porcelains that required work methods and processes very different from those used in the production of celadon. Also, some porcelain items of the period have a style that differs from the traditions of southern China. In particular, we should closely observe when the tea bowl with the *haemurigup* 해무리굽 type foot was

---

peninsula examined through items excavated from the Sihŭng Pangsan-dong early celadon kiln sites], *Misul sahak yŏn'gu* 美術史學研究 228/229 (2001): 65-97; Yi Hŭigwan 이희관, "Han'guk ch'ogi ch'ŏngja e issŏsŏ haemurigup wan munje ŭi chaegŏmt'o: Han'guk ch'ŏngja chejak ŭi kaesi sigi munje ŭi haegyŏl ŭl wihayŏ" 한국 초기청자에 있어서 해무리굽 완 문제의 재검토 - 한국청자 제작의 개시시기 문제의 해결을 위하여 [Re-examination of the *bi*-shaped foot in early Korean celadon: To solve the problem of dating the beginning of Korean celadon production], *Misul sahak yŏn'gu* 237 (2003): 5-48; Kang Kyŏngsuk 강경숙, "Koryŏ chŏn'gi toja ŭi taejung kyosŏp" 고려전기 도자의 대중교섭 [Early Koryŏ ceramics' cultural exchange with Chinese ceramics], in *Koryŏ misul ŭi taeoe kyosŏp* 高麗 美術의 對外交涉 [Foreign relations in Koryŏ art] (Seoul: Yegyŏng, 2004): 193-248.

produced and how its production changed over time. This type of foot was introduced to Koryŏ much later than it appeared in southern China, and in Koryŏ it was initially produced in white porcelain instead of celadon.[3] This suggests that we should re-examine the early history of Koryŏ celadon and white porcelain as well as its relationship with the Chinese ceramic industry. In addition, it is worth noting that inlay and underglaze-iron painting (Kr. *ch'ŏrhwa* 鐵畫) techniques developed in northern Chinese kilns appeared in Koryŏ during the second half of the tenth century.[4] Accordingly, we can presume that the Koryŏ ceramic industry, although initiated as a result of close contact with the southern Chinese ceramic industry, soon began to incorporate various ceramic technologies and styles from regions other than southern China as the industry further developed. Therefore, this study aims to re-examine the relationship between Koryŏ and China with respect to Koryŏ's reception of new ceramic technologies and styles from diverse regions of China and to discuss its significance.

Early Koryŏ's Porcelain Industry and the Northern and Southern Chinese Kilns

Debates concerning the Date of the Commencement of Celadon Production in Koryŏ

In 1989, a kiln site was excavated at Wŏnsan-ni 圓山里 in Paekch'ŏn 白川, Hwanghae Province in North Korea. This site yielded celadon with the inscriptions "the third year of the Chunhua 淳化 reign period (992)" and "the fourth year of the Chunhua reign period (993)."[5] In the early 1990s,

---

[3] Editor's Note: *Haemurigup*, meaning a foot in the shape of a solar halo, is a Korean term for the Chinese word *yubidi* 玉璧底, "*bi*-shaped foot." The Chinese name originates from its shape, which looks similar to the jade *bi* disk found in ancient China. Here, the author is pointing out that the *haemurigup* of Koryŏ has characteristics somewhat different from those of southern China: unlike in Koryŏ, in China this type of foot was most frequently used for celadon bowls during the Tang and Five Dynasties periods that preceded Koryŏ. This discrepancy between the Koryŏ and Chinese *haemurigup* has puzzled many scholars of Korean ceramics.

[4] Chang Namwŏn (Jang Namwon) 장남원, *Koryŏ chunggi ch'ŏngja yŏn'gu* 고려중기 청자 연구 [Research on mid-Koryŏ celadon] (Seoul: Hyean, 2006): 58.

[5] Kim Yŏngjin 김영진, "Hwanghae-namdo Pongch'ŏn-gun Wŏnsan-ni ch'ŏngjagi kamat'ŏ palgul kallyak pogo" 황해남도 봉천군 원산리 청자기 가마터 발굴 간략보고 [A brief report on the excavation of the celadon kiln site in Wŏnsan-ni, Pongch'ŏn County, South Hwanghae Province], *Chosŏn kogo yŏn'gu* 조선고고연구, no. 2 (serial

the archaeological surface survey of celadon kiln sites around Kangjin 康津, South Chŏlla Province 全羅南道 in South Korea, propelled studies about the beginning and technological genealogy of early celadon production.[6] Through genealogical studies of kiln sites in the midwestern and southern regions of the Korean peninsula, scholars confirmed that early celadon kiln sites in the midwestern region largely adopted Chinese-style brick kilns and technology, whereas celadon kiln sites in the southwestern region chiefly used the traditional Korean earthen kiln (Kr. *t' och'ugyo* 土築窯).

In the 1990s, due to lack of knowledge about the chronology of kilns in the central region of the Korean peninsula as well as lack of access to Chinese scholarship on Chinese kilns, Korean scholars incorrectly speculated that celadon production began in the Korean peninsula during the ninth century. In particular, they maintained that, because usage of the *haemurigup* (*bi*-shaped foot) tea bowl was at its height during the Tang dynasty in China,[7] production of the *haemurigup* tea bowl almost simultaneously began in the peninsula during the late Unified Silla period.[8] Noticing that

---

number 79) (1991): 2-9; Chosŏn Yujŏk Yumul Togam P'yŏnch'an Wiwŏnhoe 조선유적유물도감편찬위원회 [Committee for the Publication of Illustrated Book of Korean Archaeological Sites and Relics], ed., *Chosŏn yujŏk yumul togam* 朝鮮遺跡遺物圖鑑 [Illustrated book of Korean archaeological sites and relics], vol. 12 (Pyongyang: Chosŏn Yujŏk Yumul Togam P'yŏnch'an Wiwŏnhoe, 1992); Minami Hideo 南秀雄, "Ensanri kamaato to Kaijō shūhen no seiji shiryō" 円山里窯跡と開城周辺の青磁資料 [Celadon excavated at the Wŏnsan-ni kiln site and around Kaesŏng], *Tōyō tōji* 東洋陶磁 22 (1992-1994): 105-120.

 [6] Haegang Toja Misulgwan 海剛陶磁美術館 [Haegang Ceramics Museum], *Kangjin ch'ŏngja yoji chip'yo chosa posogo* 康津青磁窯址 地表調査報告書 [Report of the surface survey of the Kangjin celadon kiln sites], vol. 1: *Kangjin ŭi ch'ŏngja yoji* 康津의 青磁窯址 [The celadon kiln sites in Kangjin] (Kangjin-gun: Haegang Toja Misulgwan, 1992).

 [7] In his 1963 article, Feng Xianming explained that bowls with a *bi*-shaped foot were produced in Yue kilns 越窯 at Shanglin Lake 上林湖, Xishan kilns 西山窯 in Wenzhou 溫州, Changsha kilns 長沙窯, Xing kilns 刑窯, Gongxian kilns 鞏縣窯, Quyang kilns 曲陽窯, Chaozhou 潮州, and Tong'an 同安, stating that they are the best tea vessels. Feng Xianming 冯先铭, "Cong wenxian kan Tang Song yilai yincha fengshang ji taoci chaju de yanbian" 从文献看唐宋以来饮茶风尚及陶瓷茶具的演变 [The evolution of tea drinking customs and ceramic teaware since Tang and Song examined through written documents], *Wenwu* 文物, no. 1 (1963): 10.

 [8] Ch'oe Kŏn 崔健, "Kankoku shoki seiji no bunrui to hensen" 韓国初期青磁の分類と変遷 [Classification and evolution of early Korean celadon], trans. Kira Fumio 吉良文男, *Tōyō tōji* 東洋陶磁 22 (1992-1994): 41-64; Ch'oe Kŏn 崔健, "Koryŏ

the kiln construction technology, the kiln tools, and the *haemurigup* style
from these early Korean kilns showed similarities to those found in use in
Tang China, scholars argued that kilns and related artifacts found in Korea
originated from the same period as the Tang dynasty in China. This argument was mainly based on the belief that the *haemurigup* tea bowls produced in the Korean peninsula were identical in terms of date, shape, and
technology to those produced in the Tang dynasty.[9] Accordingly, until the
mid-1990s scholars could not clearly explain specifically when and how

ch'ŏngja ŭi palsaeng munje: Koryŏ ch'ŏngja ŏnje ŏttŏk'e mandŭrŏjyŏnna" 高麗青
磁의 發生問題—고려청자 언제 어떻게 만들어졌나 [Problem of the origin of Koryŏ
celadon: When and how was Koryŏ celadon made?], *Misulsa nondan* 美術史論壇
1 (1994): 269-294; Ch'oe Kŏn 崔健, "Ch'ŏngja yoji ŭi kyebo wa chŏn'gae" 青磁窯
址의 系譜와 展開 [Genealogy of celadon kiln sites and their development], *Misulsa
yŏn'gu* 美術史研究 12 (1998): 3-20; Yi Hŭigwan 이희관 and Ch'oe Kŏn 崔健, "Koryŏ
ch'ogi ch'ŏngja saengsan ch'eje ŭi pyŏndong kwa kŭ paegyŏng" 高麗初期 青磁生産
體制의 變動과 그 背景 [Changes in the celadon production system in early Koryŏ
and their backgrounds], *Misul sahak yŏn'gu* 美術史學研究 232 (2001): 21-55; Ch'oe
Kŏn 崔健, "Namal Yŏch'o Han'guk chagi ŭi kyeyŏl kwa pyŏnch'ŏn: T'ŭkhi 9-10—
segi chagi ŭi hŭngmang sŏngsoe rŭl chungsim ŭro" 라말여초 한국자기의 계열과
변천—특히 9-10세기 자기의 흥망성쇠를 중심으로 [Genealogy and evolution of
Korean porcelain during the end of Silla and the beginning of Koryŏ: Focusing on
the rise and decline of porcelains in the ninth and tenth centuries], *Che 2-hoe Yongin Sisa Haksul Taehoe Yongin Sŏ-ri Koryŏ paekcha yoji ŭi chaejomyŏng palp'yŏ nonmun yuinmul* 제2회 용인시사학술대회 용인서리 고려백자요지의 재조명 발표논문
유인믈 [Papers presented at the second conference on the city history of Yongin,
a review of the Koryŏ white porcelain kiln sites at Sŏ-ri, Yongin] (Yongin: Yongin
Munhwawŏn, 2000): 47-56.

[9] For Chinese bowls with a *bi*-shaped foot, refer to Feng Xianming 冯先铭, "Xin
Zhongguo taoci kaogu de zhuyao shouhuo" 新中国陶瓷考古的主要收获 [Primary
achievements of the new Chinese ceramic achaeology], *Wenwu* 文物, no. 9 (1965):
6-9, 26-56; Li Zhiyan 李知宴, "Tang dai ciyao gaikuang yu Tangci de fenqi" 唐代瓷
窯概况与唐瓷的分期 [Summary of the Tang dynasty porcelain kilns and temporal
classification of Tang porcelains], *Wenwu* 文物, no. 3 (1972): 34-48; Feng Xianming
冯先铭, "Kinnen ni okeru tōji kōko no shinseika" 近年における陶磁考古の新成果
[New outcomes of ceramic archaeology in recent years], *Kinnen hakken no yōshi
shutsudo Chūgoku tōji ten* 近年発見の窯址出土中国陶磁展 [Exhibition of Chinese
ceramics excavated from recently discovered kiln sites] (Tokyo: Idemitsu Bijutsukan, 1982); Kamei Akinori 亀井明徳, "Tōdai gyokuheki takadai no shutsugen to
shōmetsu jiki no kōsatsu" 唐代玉璧高台の出現と消滅時期の考察 [A study of the
emergence and decline of the vessel with a *bi*-shaped foot and a high pedestal during
the Tang dynasty], *Bōeki tōjiki kenkyū* 貿易陶磁研究 13 (1993): 86-126.

porcelain production emerged in the Korean peninsula, although they could confirm that its birth was closely related to cultural and technological exchanges with China.[10]

Koryŏ Pottery's Relation to the Chinese Ceramic Industry

Early Koryŏ Porcelain and Southern Chinese Kilns
Scholars have presented new theories as Chinese excavation reports on Yuezhou kilns have accumulated and as excavation data from Korean kiln sites have been reinterpreted. Archaeological examinations of site stratigraphy directed scholarly attention to the temporal sequence of the excavated objects, resulting in the discovery that *haemurigup* tea bowls excavated from kiln sites at Pangsan-dong in Sihŭng and at Sŏ-ri 西里 in Yongin 龍仁 are unlike those made in China during the Tang period but similar to those made in China during the Five Dynasties. In particular, with regard to early Korean celadon ware, it was found that the jade-ring-shaped foot (Ch. *yuhuandi*, Kr. *okhwanjŏ* 玉環底), which has a thinner foot ring that was popular during the Five Dynasties, preceded the *bi*-shaped foot (or *haemurigup* in Korean), which has a thicker foot ring that was popular during the Tang dynasty. In other words, the temporal sequence of the two foot types, characteristic of the two sequential periods in China, was reversed in Korea.

Yi Hŭigwan, who determined artisan names by deciphering the inscriptions on ceramics excavated from the kiln site at Pangsan-dong in Sihŭng (the inscriptions include the names Mu 木, Fan 范, and characters inferred to be Wuda 吳達 and Wu 吳), believes that these artisans were related to the group of potters who migrated to Koryŏ from China's Yuezhou area. Noting that they had surnames when the surname system was not yet fully established during the late Silla and early Koryŏ periods, Yi argues that the artisans were naturalized Koreans from China or belonged to the class of Koryŏ officials.[11] Based on the fact that ceramics with inscriptions "the

---

[10] Ch'oe Kŏn, "Kankoku shoki seiji no bunrui to hensen," 41–64.

[11] Yi Hŭigwan 李喜寬, "Sihŭng Pangsan taeyo ŭi saengsan chiptan kwa kaesi sigi munje: Pangsan taeyo ch'ult'o myŏngmun charyo ŭi kŏmt'o" 始興 芳山大窯의 生産 集團과 開始時期 問題 —芳山大窯 出土 銘文資料의 檢討 [The artisan group and the beginning period of Great Pangsan Kiln: Examination of inscriptions excavated from Great Pangsan Kiln], in *Silla munhwaje haksul palp'yohoe nonmunjip* 新羅文 化祭學術發表會論文集 [Papers of the Silla cultural heritage academic conference], vol. 23: *Silla kumsŏngmun ŭi hyŏnhwang kwa kwaje* 新羅 金石文의 현황과 과제 [The present condition and future tasks regarding Silla epigraphs], ed. Silla Munhwa

third year of the Chunhua reign period (992)" and "the fourth year of the Chunhua reign period (993)" as well as inscriptions of surnames of artisans, such as Ch'oe 崔, Wang 王, Yi 李, and Sim 沈, were excavated from the kiln site in Wŏnsan-ni, Paech'ŏn, Hwanghae Province—a site similar to that in Pangsan-dong in terms of its brick kiln structure and excavated ceramics—Yi Hŭigwan suggested that it is highly likely that potters from the Yuezhou kilns in China had also immigrated to this Wŏnsan-ni region.[12]

Further, Yi Chongmin argues that the inscription "Fenghua" 奉化 on ceramic sherds excavated from Pangsan-dong could refer to the Fenghua area near Dongqian Lake 东钱湖 in Zhejiang Province. This hypothesis has yet to be verified by the excavation of kiln sites in the Fenghua area in China. This is, however, a plausible hypothesis, since kiln sites near Shang-lin Lake 上林湖 and Dongqian Lake in Zhejiang Province were major sites of Yuezhou kilns.[13] On a related note, it is significant that compositional analyses of ceramic sherds excavated from the Yuezhou kilns and the Pang-san-dong kiln show similar results.

Consequently, many scholars began to argue that a group of potters trained at the Yuezhou kilns migrated to Pangsan-dong and made bowls with a jade-ring-shaped foot, the major product during the Five Dynasties period in China. This hypothesis on the close connection between south-ern China's Yuezhou kilns and Koryŏ's Pangsan-dong kiln is also supported by the similarity of tools used in both kilns. Considering that scholars from the Five Dynasties, Qiu Yangui 酉彦规 and Piao Yan 朴巖, visited Koryŏ, the former in the second reign year (919) of King T'aejo 太祖 (r. 918-943) and the latter in the sixth reign year (923) of the same king, and consid-ering that the Five Dynasties and Koryŏ maintained an active diplomatic relationship at least until the first half of the tenth century, it is highly likely that artisans from Yuezhou kilns and their skills were introduced to Koryŏ during the first half of the tenth century.[14]

Sŏnyanghoe 신라문화선양회 [Council for Promotion of Silla Culture] (Kyŏngju: Tongguktae Silla Munhwa Yŏn'guso, 2002): 233-277.

[12] Yi Hŭigwan, "Sihŭng Pangsan taeyo ŭi saengsan chiptan kwa kaesi sigi munje: Pangsan taeyo ch'ult'o myŏngmun charyo ŭi kŏmt'o," 254-255.

[13] For more about the kiln sites near Dongqian Lake, see Lin Shimin 林士民, "Zhejiang Ningbo Dongqianhu yaochang diaocha yu yanjiu" 浙江宁波东钱湖窑场调查与研究 [Investigation and research of the Dongqian Lake kiln site in Ningbo, Zhejiang Province], Zhongguo gu taoci yanjiu 中国古陶瓷研究 3 (1990): 47-54.

[14] Yi Hŭigwan, "Sihŭng Pangsan taeyo ŭi saengsan chiptan kwa kaesi sigi munje: Pangsan taeyo ch'ult'o myŏngmun charyo ŭi kŏmt'o," 260-263.

These opinions are the result of intense research. They revise the previous theory that argued that the porcelain industry in the Korean peninsula began in the ninth century simply based on the observation that Chang Pogo 張保皐 (?-846), a powerful figure of the late Silla period, controlled and promoted trade between Silla and Tang China during the time Tang actively produced *haemurigup* tea bowls.

In addition, Yun Yongi suggested that during the time when the ruling power was being centralized by Kings Kwangjong 光宗 (r. 949-975) and Sŏngjong 成宗 (r. 981-997) in the second half of the tenth century, the new ruling authority wanted domestically to produce and supply celadon similar to Chinese celadon. Hence, porcelain potters from the Wuyue Kingdom 吳越 (907-978), famous for the *mise* 秘色 (secret color) of its celadon, may have come to Koryŏ because of the desire of the new ruling authority to produce Koryŏ celadon through interchanges with the Wuyue Kingdom. In particular, Yun argued that Koryŏ pottery (*togi* 陶器) artisans started a porcelain industry in Koryŏ after they learned celadon production technology from Wuyue celadon artisans.[15]

Scholars have also expanded their comparative studies on the characteristics of Koryŏ porcelains based on Chinese excavation reports and analyses. They have conducted in-depth studies on the style of ceramic vessels, the chemical composition of clay and glaze, kiln tools, and firing techniques using the ceramic sherds from bowls, plates, cup stands, kettles, and lids excavated from Wŏnsan-ni in Paech'ŏn, Sŏ-ri in Yongin, Pangsan-dong in Sihŭng, and Yonggye-ri 龍溪里 in Koch'ang 高敞, and compared them with the chronological study of Yue ware from the Yuezhou kilns. As a result, scholars discovered that the ceramics excavated from these Koryŏ kilns and the Yuezhou kilns show similarity in terms of foot styles such as the *bi*-shaped foot (*haemurigup*) and the jade-ring-shaped foot as well as the constitution of ceramic object types, such as plates, cup stands, kettles, and lids. This was also true of the geographical conditions of the kiln site, the size of the kiln—about forty meters long—saggars (Kr. *kappal*, Ch. *xiabo* 匣鉢), and kiln tools.[16] In particular, the chemical composition of the clay as well

---

[15] Yun Yongi 尹龍二, "Koryŏ ch'ŏngja ŭi kiwŏn kwa palchŏn" 고려청자의 기원과 발전 [The origin and development of Koryŏ celadon], *Han'guk tojasa yŏn'gu* 韓國陶瓷史研究 [Research on Korean ceramic history] (Seoul: Munye Ch'ulp'ansa, 1993): 151-152.

[16] Kim Yŏngmi 金英美, "Yue yao yanjiu" 越窯研究 [Research on Yuezhou kilns] (Beijing Daxue boshi yanjiusheng xuewei lunwen 北京大学博士研究生学位论文 [Peking University Ph.D. Dissertation], 2002).

as of the glaze of early Koryŏ celadon was discovered to be similar to those of the celadon from the late Tang and early Northern Song periods found at the kiln sites near Shanglin Lake in Zhejiang Province.[17]

Early Koryŏ Porcelain and the Northern Chinese Kilns

Scholars have by now thoroughly researched the role that the relationship between Koryŏ and southern China played in the development of the ceramic industry in early Koryŏ. In particular, the chemical composition and the types of ceramic products as well as their kiln tools and kilns—the most essential constituents of the ceramic industry—were remarkably similar. Starting from the second half of the tenth century, however, features quite different from those that characterize products of the southern Chinese kilns began to appear in Koryŏ porcelains. During the tenth century new political, diplomatic, and cultural relations began developing in Northeast Asia, as the Liao 遼 (907-1125), Koryŏ, and Song polities were successively established. With this new historical development as a backdrop, Koryŏ kilns of the tenth century exhibit characteristics that seem to have come from the northern Chinese kilns.

Under the rule of the Liao dynasty founded by the Kitans, the ceramic industry prospered in Hebei Province 河北省, Shanxi Province 山西省, and Inner Mongolia, where the Kitans were active. The quantity of production and the types of vessels increased in proportion to the increase in demand for ceramic vessels. At the same time, the quantity of ceramics produced by Liao potters in particular increased. Such trends are observed in the Nanshan kiln 南山窯, which was originally located in the Liao dynasty's Linhuang Administration 臨潢府 surrounding the Supreme Capital (Ch. Shangjing 上京),[18] the Shangjing kiln 上京窯, which was Liao's official kiln (Ch. *Guanyao* 官窯),

---

[17] Haegang Toja Misulgwan 海剛陶磁美術館 [Haegang Ceramics Museum], *Pangsan taeyo: Sihŭng-si Pangsandoing ch'ogi ch'ŏngja paekcha yoji palgul pogosŏ* 芳山大窯—始興市 芳山洞 初期青磁·白磁 窯址 發掘調査報告書 [Great Pangsan Kiln: Excavation report of early celadon and white porcelain kiln site] (Sihŭng-si: Haegang Toja Misulgwan, 2001): 345-358; Lu Jiaxi 卢嘉锡 and Li Jiazhi 李家治, eds., *Zhongguo kexue jishushi: Taoci juan* 中国科学技术史—陶瓷卷 [History of Chinese science and technology: Ceramics] (Beijing: Kexue Chubanshe, 1998): 117-122.

[18] Editor's Note: Linhuang Administration (Ch. Linhuangfu 臨潢府) was the metropolitan area surrounding the Supreme Capital. I followed Wittfogel's translation of *fu* 府. See Karl A. Wittfogel and Fêng Chia-shêng, *History of Chinese Society: Liao, 907-1125* (Philadelphia: American Philosophical Society, 1949): 59, no. 2. The Supreme Capital, which was located in present Balin Left Banner, is one of the five capitals of Liao.

Baiyin kiln 白音窯, and the Gaoluo kiln 高洛窯, all located in Balin Left Banner 巴林左旗 in Chifeng 赤峰, Inner Mongolia, as well as the Gangwa kiln 缸瓦窯 and the Qianwa kiln 乾瓦窯 located in Chifeng, Inner Mongolia. Liao kilns in broader regions, including the Gangguantun kiln 江官屯窯 in Liaoyang City 辽阳市, Liaoning Province 辽宁省, and the Longquanwu kiln 龍泉務窯 in Beijing, show similar trends. The major products of these kilns were white porcelains, black-glazed ware (Ch. *heiyou* 黑釉), and tri-color ware (Ch. *sancai* 三彩).[19]

The relationship between Liao and Koryŏ ceramics has only been partially studied in previous Korean scholarship.[20] Recently, however, primary data have become available from the Liao and Jin 金 (1115-1234) dynasties' kilns in Shanxi Province, Inner Mongolia, and Hebei Province. I have attempted to make thorough and concrete inferences on the relationship between Liao and Koryŏ porcelains in my recent articles, drawing upon Chinese textual and visual data, including excavated tomb murals, that contain information on ceramic vessels and crafts and their usage.[21]

---

[19] Mikami Tsugio 三上次男, "Bokkai, Ryō, Kin, Gen tōjiki seisan no rekishiteki haikei" 渤海·遼·金·元陶磁器生產の歷史的背景 [Historical background of ceramic production in Parhae, Liao, Jin, and Yuan], in *Sekai tōji zenshū* 世界陶磁全集 [Complete works of world ceramics], vol. 13: *Ryō, Kin, Gen* 遼·金·元 [Liao, Jin, and Yuan dynasties], ed. Mikami Tsugio (Tokyo: Shōgakkan, 1981): 131-142; Mikami Tsugio 三上次男, "Bokkai to Ryō no tōji" 渤海と遼の陶磁 [Ceramics of Parhae and Liao], in *Sekai tōji zenshū* 世界陶磁全集 [Complete works of world ceramics], vol. 13: *Ryō, Kin, Gen* 遼·金·元 [Liao, Jin, and Yuan dynasties], ed. Mikami Tsugio (Tokyo: Shōgakkan, 1981): 143-169.

[20] Chŏng Sinok 정신옥, "11-segi mal-12—segi chŏnban Koryŏ ch'ŏngja e poinŭn Chungguk toja ŭi yŏnghyang" 11세기말-12세기전반 高麗青瓷에 보이는 中國陶瓷의 영향 [The influence of Chinese ceramics on Koryŏ celadon from the late eleventh century to the early twelfth century], *Misul sahak* 美術史學 21 (2007): 41-85; Im China 任眞娥, "Koryŏ ch'ŏngja e poinŭn Puksong, Yodae chagi ŭi yŏnghyang" 高麗青磁에 보이는 北宋·遼代 磁器의 影響 [The influence of Northern Song and Liao porcelains on Koryŏ celadon] (Hongik Taehakkyo sŏksa hagwi nonmun 弘益大學校碩士學位論文 [Hongik University M.A. Thesis], 2005): 1-221.

[21] Chang Namwŏn (Jang Namwon) 장남원, "Koryŏ chŏngi haemurigup (okpyŏkchŏ kye) wan ŭi chisok hyŏnsang e taehan ch'uron" 고려전기 해무리굽[옥벽저계] 완의 지속현상에 대한 추론 [Inferences on the continuance of the bowl with a *bi*-shaped foot in early Koryŏ], *Hosŏ sahak* 湖西史學 50 (September 2008): 321-353; Chang Namwŏn (Jang Namwon) 장남원, "Koryŏ ch'o, chunggi chagi sanggam kipŏp ŭi yŏnwŏn kwa palchŏn" 고려 初·中期 瓷器 象嵌技法의 연원과 발전 [The origin and development of the early and mid-Koryŏ period porcelain inlay techniques], *Misulsa hakpo* 美術史學報 30 (June 2008): 159-192.

During this period, Koryŏ had diplomatic relations with both Liao and Song, but Koryŏ had more frequent emissary exchanges with Liao than Song at least until the first half of the twelfth century.[22] Whereas the envoy visits between Song and Koryŏ were under the charge of the authorities in Mingzhou 明州 (present-day Ningbo 宁波 in Zhejiang Province) and focused more on exchanges of goods, the diplomatic relationship between Liao and Koryŏ focused more on direct interchanges between the central governments.

Article Four of the *Hunyo Sipcho* 訓要十條, the Ten Injunctions King T'aejo handed to his trusted military official Pak Surhŭi 朴述熙 (?-945) in the fourth lunar month of the twenty-sixth reign year of King T'aejo (943) for the instruction of his royal descendants, states that Koryŏ need not follow Chinese customs or the Chinese system because the characteristics of the Koryŏ people and of their land are different from those of Chinese people and their land. It further instructs against indiscriminately imitating the Kitan attire and customs because Liao is a barbaric country and its customs and language are different from those of Koryŏ.[23] This passage from the injunction is often regarded as a reflection of Koryŏ's low evaluation of the Kitans. I suggest, however, that it can also imply that the Kitan attire and customs had been introduced to a considerable extent and had become so widespread in Koryŏ around the mid-tenth century that the Koryŏ royal court had to be wary of them. This reading of the passage is supported by the royal edict published in the seventh reign year (1129) of King Injong 仁宗 (1122-1146). This royal edict deplored the gaudy trends and customs of the Kitan people which were indiscriminately introduced to everyone in Koryŏ "from the royal court to ordinary people." Therefore, it is likely that Kitan culture began to spread in Koryŏ in the first half of the tenth century

---

[22] See footnote 20.

[23] *Koryŏsa* 2:14-17, T aejo 太祖 26.4; Yŏnhŭi Taehakkyo Tongbanghak Yŏn'guso 延禧大學校東方學研究所 [The Institute of Far Eastern Studies Chosun Christian University], ed., *Koryŏsa* 高麗史 [History of Koryŏ], 3 vols. (Seoul: Yŏnhŭi Taehakkyo Ch'ulp'anbu, 1955) [hereafter *Yŏnhŭi Taehakkyo Koryŏsa*], 1:54-56. Editor's Note: The original text of Article Four reads 惟我東方, 舊慕唐風, 文物禮樂, 悉遵其制, 殊方異土, 人性各異, 不必苟同. 契丹, 是禽獸之國, 風俗不同, 言語亦異, 衣冠制度, 慎勿效焉. The words "Tang customs" 唐風 in this article designate not only the culture of Tang, but the customs of Han Chinese people in general, which were differentiated from the culture of nomadic peoples in the north. The Tang dynasty no longer existed when King Taejo composed the Ten Injunctions in 943. In Japan, the same character, *kara* 唐, also had a broad connotation and was used as a designation for foreign countries in the Korean peninsula as well as China.

and that cultural interchange between Koryŏ and the Kitan Liao dynasty flourished in the second half of the tenth century.

The Kitan Liao state traded with Koryŏ through Liao's Eastern Capital (Ch. Dongjing 東京), present-day Liaoyang. Liao also used the most direct route from Liaoyang to Koryŏ's Sŏgyŏng 西京 (present-day Pyong-yang) and Kaegyŏng (present-day Kaesŏng) during the wars with Koryŏ.[24] Therefore, it is reasonable to assume that the Kitan culture would have been introduced to Koryŏ by this route that passes through the Liaoyang region if they used land routes. After the Kitans established the Liao state, both the official and unofficial interchange between the Koryŏ and the Kitans increased and the influx of Liao culture and technology increased through the naturalization of Kitan artisans into Koryŏ.

The following passage is from *Xuanhe fengshi Gaoli tujing* 宣和奉使高麗 圖經 (Illustrated account of the Xuanhe reign envoy to Koryŏ) written by Xu Jing 徐兢 (1091-1153) in the first half of the twelfth century:

> I also heard that, among tens of thousands of Kitan prisoners of war surrendered [to Koryŏ], one out of ten was an artisan. [Artisans] with exquisite skills were selected and made to stay in Wangbu 王 府.[25] These days, ritual vessels and clothing have become too elabo-rate, frivolous, and artificial to recover the simplicity and modesty of old days.[26]

This passage suggests that Kitan artisans participated in making the Koryŏ royal crafts and influenced their style. The following passage from the record of the twelfth reign year (1117) of King Yejong 睿宗 (r. 1105-1122) in the *Koryŏsa* 高麗史 (History of Koryŏ) also suggests that there was an ethnic Kitan neighborhood in Koryŏ in the early twelfth century:

---

[24] An Chusŏp 안주섭, *Koryŏ Kŏran chŏnjaeng: Amnokkang yŏnan esŏ chŏn'gae toen yŏngt'o hwakchang chŏnjaeng* 고려 거란전쟁: 압록강 연안에서 전개된 영토 확장 전쟁 [The Koryŏ-Kitan War: War for territorial expansion along the coast of the Amnok River] (Seoul: Kyŏngin Munhwasa, 2003).

[25] Wangbu in this context means Kaegyŏng, the capital city of Koryŏ.

[26] 亦聞契丹降虜數萬人, 其工技十有一擇其精巧者, 留於王府. 比年器服益工弟 浮偽頗多, 不復全日 純質耳. *Xuanhe fengshi Gaoli tujing* 95: "Minshu" 民庶, origi-nal text from Li Shutian 李澍田, ed., *Qing shilu Chaoxian guanxi shiliao zhaibian* 清实录中朝鲜关系史料摘编 [Selected edition of Qing dynasty annals and histori-cal documents about China-Korea relations] (Changchun: Jilin Wenshi Chuban-she, 1991): 19:40.

When [the King] visited Namgyŏng 南京 [Southern Capital], the surrendered Kitans, living in the neighborhood, greeted His Majesty's visit with Kitan songs, dances, and various performances. The King stopped his palanquin and enjoyed it.[27]

Selective Adoption of Kiln Technology and Ceramic Style

Kiln Structure: Brick Kiln

The excavation of the porcelain kiln site at Pangsan-dong in Sihŭng, Kyŏnggi Province, in 1997-1998 revealed new features of Korean kilns that had not been discovered until then, triggering new interest in Koryŏ kilns' relationship with Chinese kilns. Above all, the structure of the kiln suggested its close relationship with Yuezhou kilns in China. If we compare the kiln at Pangsan-dong (fig. 4.1), and the kiln in Silongkou 寺龍口, Cixi 慈溪 City, Zhejiang Province in China (fig. 4.2), we find that their sizes are very similar although the former is slightly shorter: their lengths are thirty-nine meters and forty-nine and a half meters respectively, and both kilns are about two meters in width. They also share a similar structure: the Pangsan-dong rising kiln (Kr. *tŭngyo* 登窯) built with bricks is similar to the Yuezhou dragon kilns (Ch. *longyao* 龍窯); both have entrances on the side; and both have furnaces with a similar shape.

The Pangsan-dong brick kiln had undergone major repairs twice, resulting in a reduction in size from 39 to 36 meters in length and from 2.2 to 0.9 meters in width. The changes in style of ceramics found in the various strata show that this kiln was used for about one hundred years. Analysis of the strata containing abandoned ceramic sherds shows that high-quality celadon and white porcelain are found in the lower, earlier strata. But the higher the stratum, the lower the quality of the porcelain, and the upper strata contain mainly celadon. The kiln is almost the same in shape and size as the Tang and Song dynasties' dragon kilns made with firebricks found in southern China. The types of items produced at the Pangsan-dong kiln—tea bowl with *haemurigup* (*bi*-shaped foot), petal-shaped plate, ewer, and cup stand—also match those of the Yuezhou ware. In addition, the olive

---

[27] 丁卯, 王至南京, 契丹投化人, 散居南京圻内者, 奏契丹歌舞雜戲以迎駕, 王駐蹕觀之. *Koryŏsa* 14:23-2⌐, Yejong 睿宗 12.8.12, *Yŏnhŭi Taehakkyo Koryŏsa*, 1:288. For more about this passage, see Ch'oe Hyesuk 최혜숙, *Koryŏ sidae Namgyŏng yŏn'gu* 高麗時代 南京研究 [Research on the Southern Capital during the Koryŏ dynasty] (Seoul: Kyŏngin Munhwasa, 2004): 107.

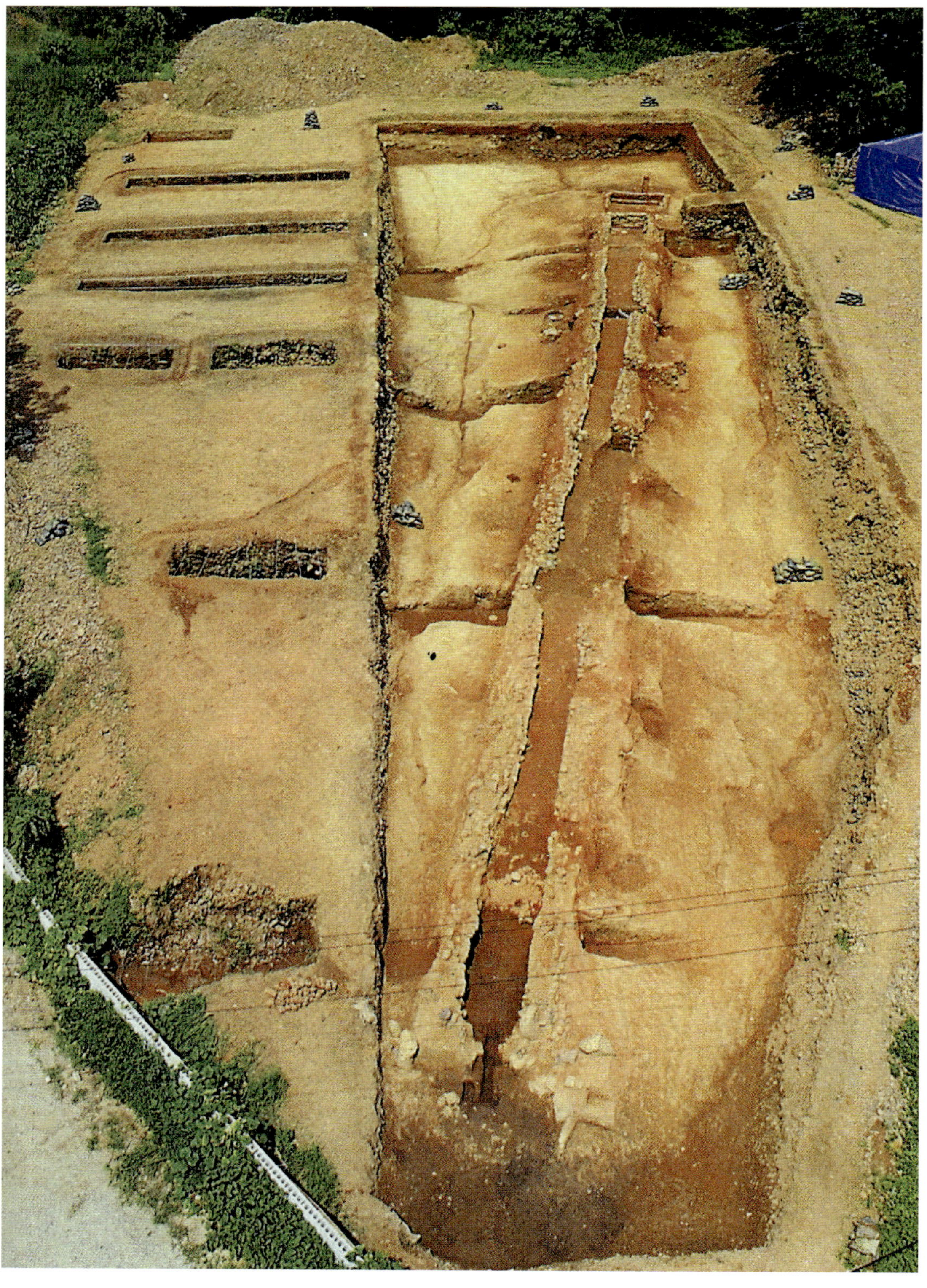

Figure 4.1 Kiln site in Pangsan-dong in Sihŭng, Kyŏnggi Province, Korea. Excavated by Haegang Toja Misulgwan. From Haegang Toja Misulgwan 海剛陶磁美術館, *Pangsan taeyo: Sihŭng-si Pangsandoing ch'ŏgi ch'ŏngja paekcha yoji palgul pogosŏ* 芳山大窯— 始興市 芳山洞 初期青磁 · 白磁 窯址 發掘調查報告書 *(Sihŭng-si: Haegang Toja Misulgwan, 2001): 229.*

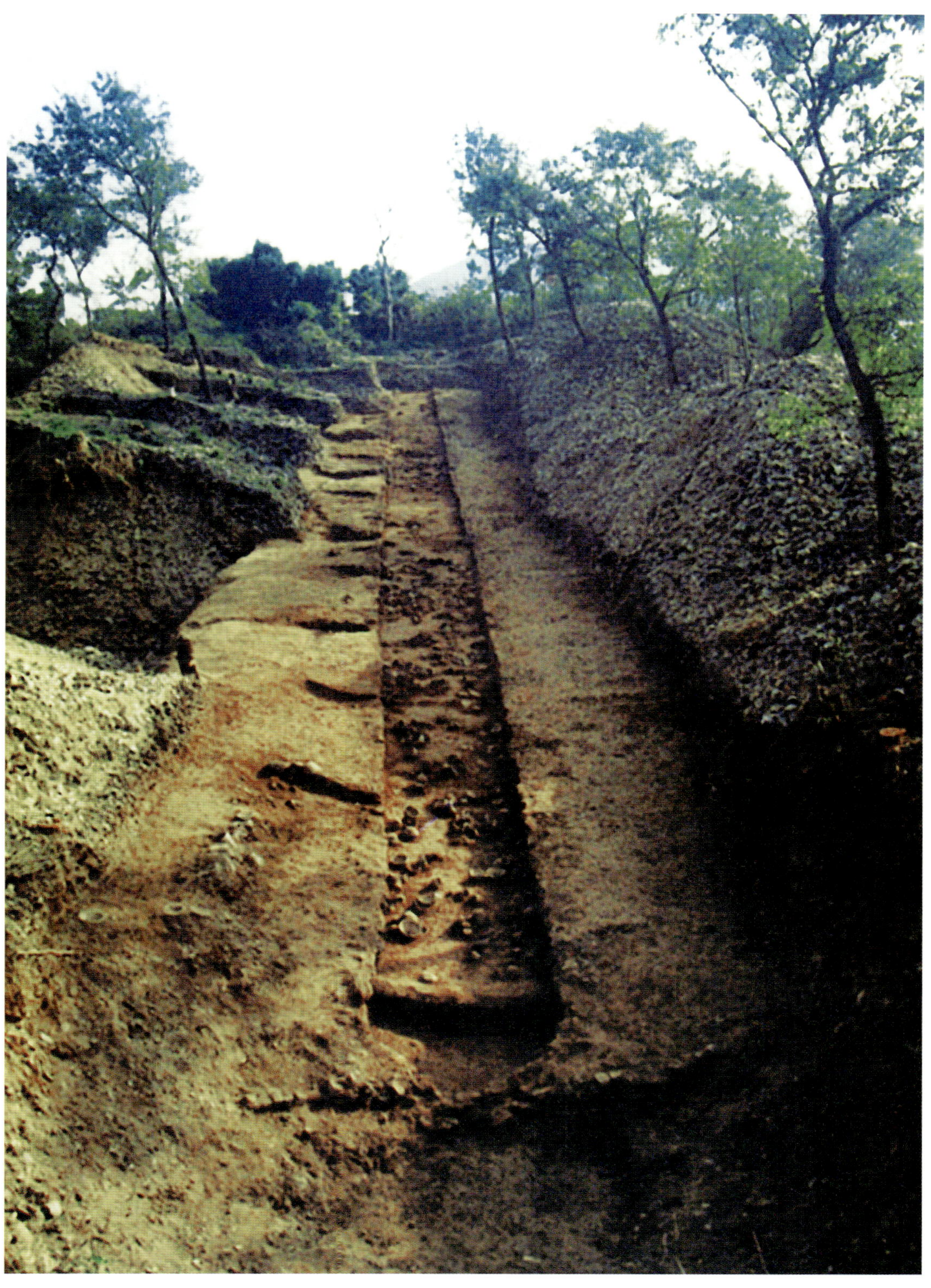

*Figure 4.2 Kiln site in Silongkou in Cixi, Zhejiang Province, China.
Courtesy of the Zhejiang Provincial Institute of Cultural Relics.*

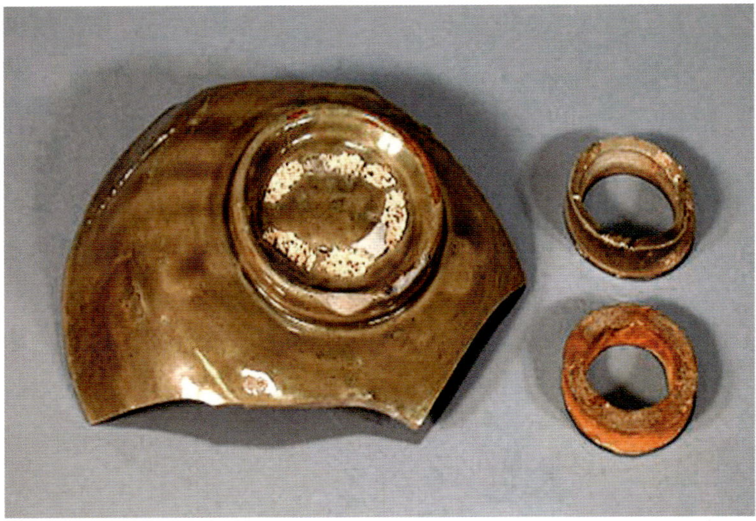

Figure 4.3 Chŏmkwŏn 墊圈 *(ring-shaped support) and a trace of* chŏmkwŏn
*remaining on a ceramic sherd, from the Pangsan-dong kiln site, Sihŭng, Kyŏnggi
Province, Korea. Courtesy of Yi Chongmin.*

green color of the glaze is also similar to that of the Yuezhou celadon from
the late Tang to the Five Dynasties. Furthermore, quite a few ring-shaped
supports (Kr. *chŏmkwŏn* 墊圈) used for firing high-quality ceramic ware
were found at the Pangsan-dong kiln site (fig. 4.3).[28] This indicates the
Pangsan-dong kiln's contemporaneity with other Chinese porcelains that
also used ring-shaped supports and have the inscription "Taiping Wuyin"
太平 戊寅 [the year of Wuyin in the sexagenarian cycle during the Taiping
reign (978)] of the Wuyue Kingdom.[29] Therefore, we can assume that the
kilns in southern China of the same period heavily influenced the Pangsan-
dong kiln in terms of kiln construction technology and operation. In particular, when we compare the kiln tools excavated from the Silongkou kiln

---

[28] Haegang Toja Misulgwan, *Pangsan taeyo*, 159-173.

[29] Editor's Note: These inscribed Wuyue Kingdom porcelains are Yuezhou ware
from the Silongkou kiln site. During the Five Dynasties period, the Wuyue Kingdom ruled the present-day Zhejiang Province, where the Yuezhou kilns, including
the kiln at Silongkou, were located.

site in China (fig. 4.4) with those from the Pangsan-dong and Wŏnsan-ni kilns in Korea (fig. 4.5), we find very similar types of cylindrical saggars, conical saggars, and saggar supports. Accordingly, we can assume the existence of a general connection in kilns between the two regions, including facilities for firing, products, and production and firing methods.

Single Firing and Double Firing

Most Koryŏ potteries in the tenth century finished the ceramic burning process with single firing. In other words, they formed, glazed, and then fired clay only once to finish a ceramic vessel. This contrasts with the double-firing technique, which flourished in the mid-Koryŏ. Double firing has two steps: bisque firing and glaze firing. Bisque firing means firing at a low temperature after shaping the ceramic vessel, and glaze firing is the second firing of the bisque-fired vessel after glazing it at a high temperature, above 1,200° Celsius. The porcelain production process in the Koryŏ during the tenth century shows little trace of double firing. The single-firing technique was generally used at the early Koryŏ kiln sites that were influenced by ceramic technologies of Yuezhou kilns that had been developed beginning in the Five Dynasties period in China—for example, the Koryŏ kilns at Sŏ-ri in Yongin; at Pangsan-dong in Sihŭng; and at Wŏnsan-ni in Paech'on.

Single firing was the primary ceramic firing method in China as well. Exceptions were some official kilns or kilns that were government suppliers, where artisans tried multiple glazing and firing. By repeating the process of glazing and firing at a low temperature two or three times, they could make deeper colors as the layer of glaze thickened. Scholarly investigation of the introduction and establishment of the double-firing technique in Korea is currently in its early stages.[30]

In Koryŏ, double firing became widespread from the late tenth century to the early eleventh century (fig. 4.6).[31] The original technique of double

---

[30] For recent studies on bisque firing of Korean celadon, see Yi Hŭigwan 李喜寬, "Koryŏ pisaek chŏngja ŭi ch'urhyŏn kwa ch'obŏl kui (soso)" 高麗 翡色青磁의 出現과 초벌구이(素燒) [The emergence of Koryŏ jade-green celadon and bisque firing], in *Han, Chung, Il Kukche Haksul Taehoe: Taeoe kyosŏp ŭro pon Koryŏ chŏngja* 한·중·일 국제학술대회—對外交涉으로 본 高麗青磁 [Korea-China-Japan international symposium: Koryŏ celadon seen from the perspective of Koryŏ's foreign relations] (Kangjin-gun: Kangjin Chŏngja Charyo Pangmulgwan, 2003): 16-42.

[31] Yi Chongmin 李鍾玟, "Nambu chiyŏk ch'ogi chŏngja ŭi kyet'ong kwa t'ŭkching" 南部地域 初期 青磁의 系統과 特徵 [The genealogy and characteristics of early celadon in the southern region], *Misulsa yŏn'gu* 16 美術史研究 (2002): 199-228.

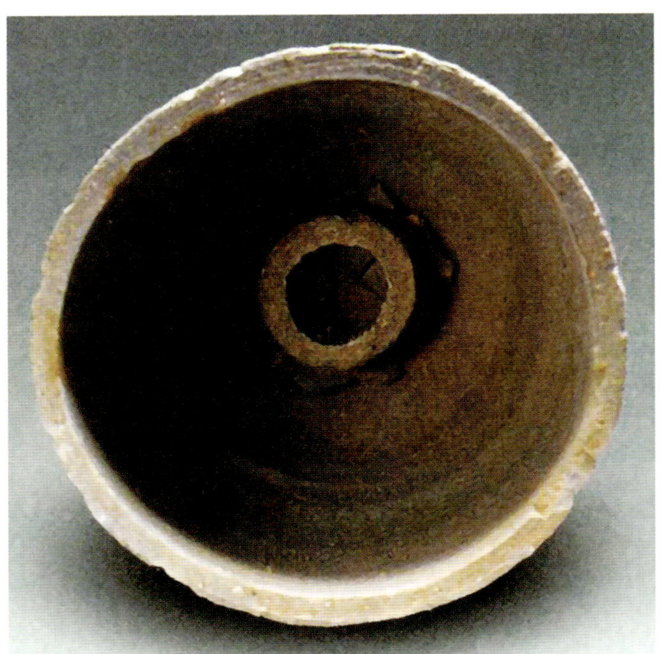
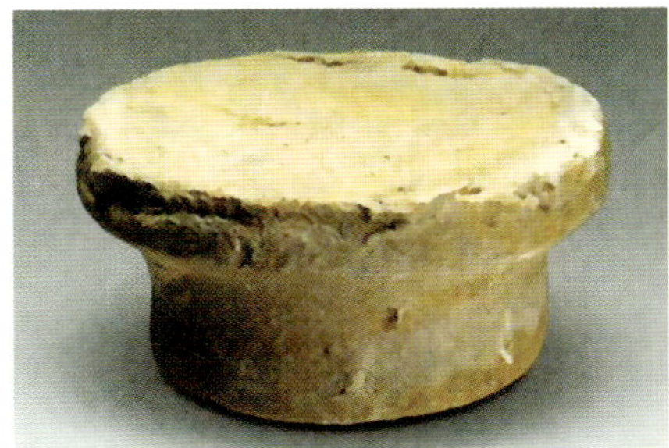
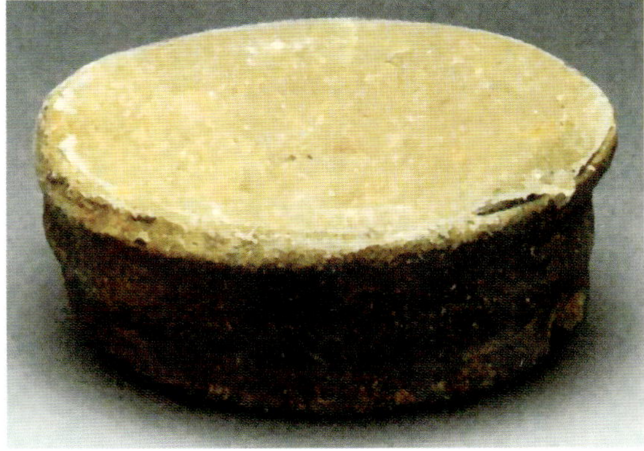

Figure 4.4 Kiln tools excavated from
the Silongkou kiln site in Cixi, Zhejiang
Province, China. Courtesy of the Zhejiang
Provincial Institute of Cultural Relics.

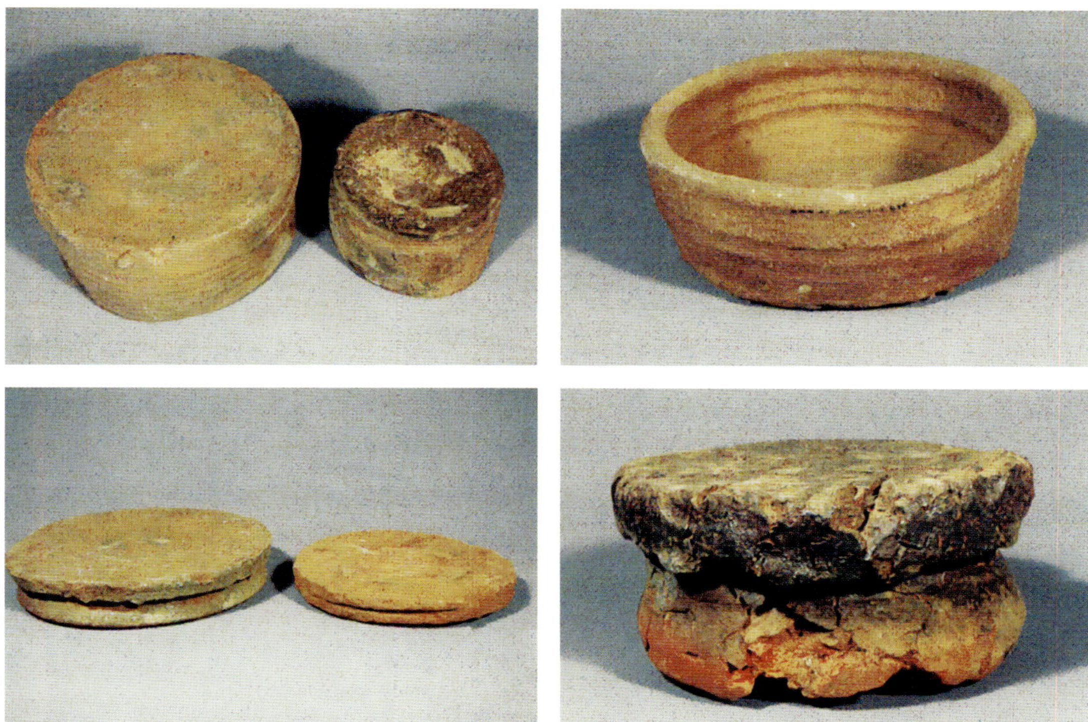

*Figure 4.5 Kiln tools excavated from the Pangsan-dong kiln site, Sihŭng, Kyŏnggi Province, Korea.
Excavated by Haegang Toja Misulgwan. Courtesy of Yi Chongmin.*

firing has not been reported from the southern Chinese kilns of this time
period. A similar firing technique is found in the process of making tri-
color ware (Ch. *sancai* 三彩) in Shaanxi Province and Henan Province 河南
省 during the Tang dynasty. After shaping vessels with white clay, they first
fired them at a high temperature of over 1,000° Celsius before adding glaze,
and then fired them again after glazing them with lead glaze at a lower temperature in order to add colors (fig. 4.7).[32] This technique spread to Parhae

---

[32] Henan Sheng Wenwu Kaogu Yanjiusuo 河南省文物考古研究所 [Henan Provincial Institute of Cultural Relics and Archaeology], Zhongguo Wenwu Yanjiusuo
中国文物研究所 [China National Institute of Cultural Property], and Nihon Nara

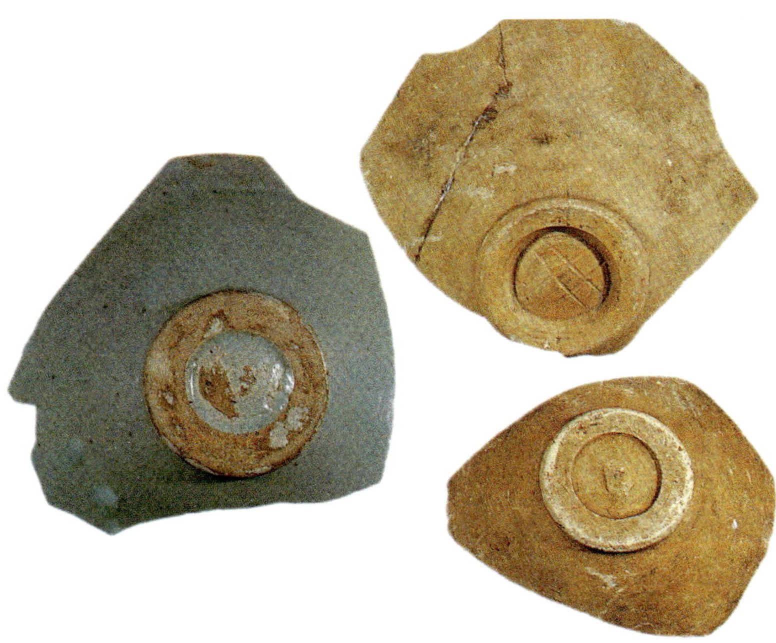

*Figure 4.6 Bisque-fired celadon sherds (right) and a glaze-fired celadon sherd (left),
excavated from Kiln 10 at Yongun-ri, Kangjin, South Chŏlla Province, Korea.
Courtesy of the National Museum of Korea.*

Bunkazai Kenkyūjo 日本奈良文化財研究所 [Japan Nara National Research Institute for Cultural Properties], eds., *Huangye yao kaogu xin faxian* 黄冶窑考古新发现 [New archaeological discovery at the Huangye kiln site] (Zhengzhou Shi: Daxiang Chubanshe, 2005); Henan Sheng Gongyi Shi Wenwu Baohu Guanlisuo 河南省巩义市文物保护管理所 [Cultural Relics Protection and Management Office in Gongyi, Henan Province], ed., *Huangye Tang sancai yao* 黄冶唐三彩窑 [The Tang dynasty tri-color ware kiln at Huangye] (Beijing: Kexue chubanshe, 2000). In particular, researchers discovered that the temperature at the bisque firing stage before glazing was almost 1,100-1,200° C. Asuka Shiryōkan 飛鳥資料館 [Asuka Historical Museum] and Nara Bunkazai Kenkyūjo 奈良文化財研究所 [Nara National Research Institute for Cultural Properties], ed., *Maboroshi no Tōdai seika: Kōya Tō sansaiyō no kōko shinhakken ten* まぼろしの唐代精華―黄冶唐三彩窑の考古新発見展 [Rare treasures of the Tang dynasty: Exhibition on the archaeological new

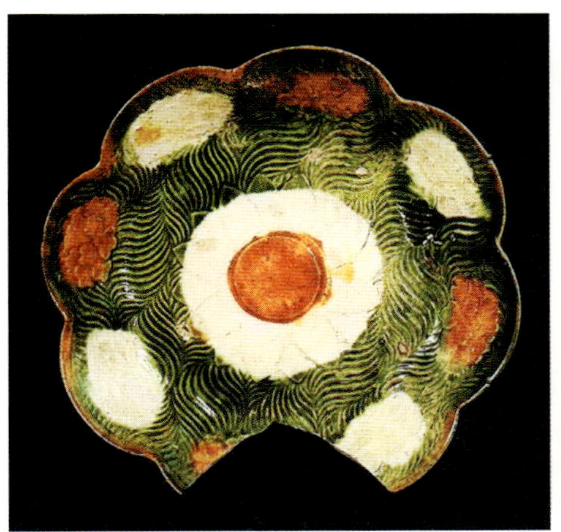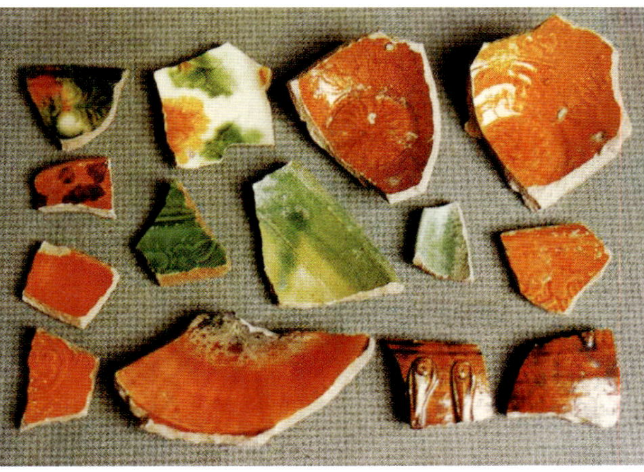

Figure 4.7 *Tri-colored sherds, from the Gangwa kiln in Chifeng, Inner Mongolia. From Lu Jing* 菁路, *Liao dai tao ci* 辽代陶瓷 *(Shenyang: Liaoning Huabao Chubanshe, 2003): 20, Plates 2-41, 2-42.*

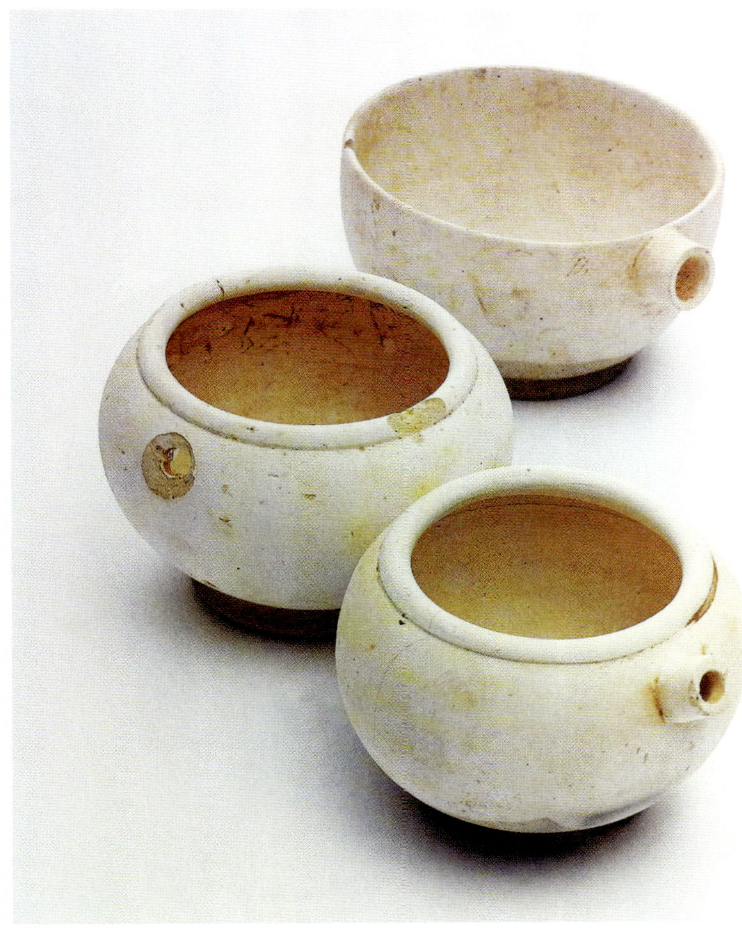

Figure 4.8 Bisque-fired ceramics produced for tri-color glazing, from the Huangye kiln site in Henan Province, China. Henan Sheng Wenwu Yanjiusuo 河南省文物考古研究所, *ed.,* Huangye yao kaogu xin faxian 黄冶窑考古新发现 *(Zhengzhou: Daxiang Chubanshe, 2005): 160, Plate 125.*

渤海 (698-926) and Liao, and as a result continued to be used until after
the tenth century. The tri-color ware technique spread through Shaanxi,
Henan, and Hebei Provinces to Inner Mongolia. After the eleventh century, the tri-color ware technique became very popular in the territories
of Liao and Jin, and we have examples of bisque-fired ceramics produced
for tri-color or white-color glazing (fig. 4.8).[33] Therefore, examination of
the change in Koryŏ's firing method reveals that Koryŏ artisans used the
southern Chinese-style single-firing technique when Yuezhou kiln-style
ceramic technology was introduced in the tenth century, and later gradually advanced to the double-firing technique. Considering the flourishing
of the double-firing technique in Koryŏ, we can infer that the origin of
Koryŏ porcelain technology was not limited to southern China.[34]

Simultaneous Production of Celadon and White Porcelains
As explained earlier, the early Koryŏ porcelain industry was primarily
based on the technology from the Yuezhou kilns of southern China. The
major Yuezhou kiln products are celadon. Interestingly, however, Koryŏ
kilns produced both celadon and white porcelains in the same kiln in the
tenth century, indicating the possibility that the Koryŏ ceramic industry
did not depend solely on technology from southern China. This simultaneous production of celadon and white porcelain was first observed in early
kiln sites in the central region of the Korean peninsula around Kaegyŏng,
the capital of Koryŏ.[35] It is noteworthy that the percentage of white porce-

---

discoveries of the Tang tri-color ceramic kiln at Huangye] (Nara: Kokuritsu Bunkazai Kikō Nara Bunkazai Kenkyūjo Asuka Shiryōkan, 2008): 51.

[33] Beijing Shi Wenwu Yanjiusuo 北京市文物研究所 [Beijing Cultural Relics
Research Institute], ed., *Beijing Longquanwu yao fajue baogao* 北京龙泉务窑发掘
报告 [Excavation report on the Longquanwu kiln] (Beijing: Wenwu Chubanshe,
2002): 82-332.

[34] Shanxi Sheng Kaogu Yanjiusuo 陕西省考古研究所 [Shaanxi Provincial Institute of Archaeology], *Wudai Huangpu yaozhi* 五代黄堡窑址 [The Huangpu kiln
site of the Five Dynasties period] (Beijing: Wenwu Chubanshe, 1997): 196-211;
Shanxi Sheng Kaogu Yanjiusuo and Yaozhou Bowuguan 耀州窑博物馆 [Yaozhou
Kiln Museum], *Song dai Yaozhou yaozhi* 宋代耀州窑址 [The Yaozhou kiln site during the Song dynasty] (Beijing, Wenwu Chubanshe, 1998): 466-471.

[35] In early Koryŏ, white porcelains were mainly produced in Kyŏnggi Province,
including Pangsan-dong in Sihŭng; Sŏ-ri in Yongin; and Chungam-ni in Yŏju.
From the mid-Koryŏ period on, as porcelain production increased, the number
of kilns increased as well, spreading to other regions such as Chech'ŏn, Ch'ilgok,

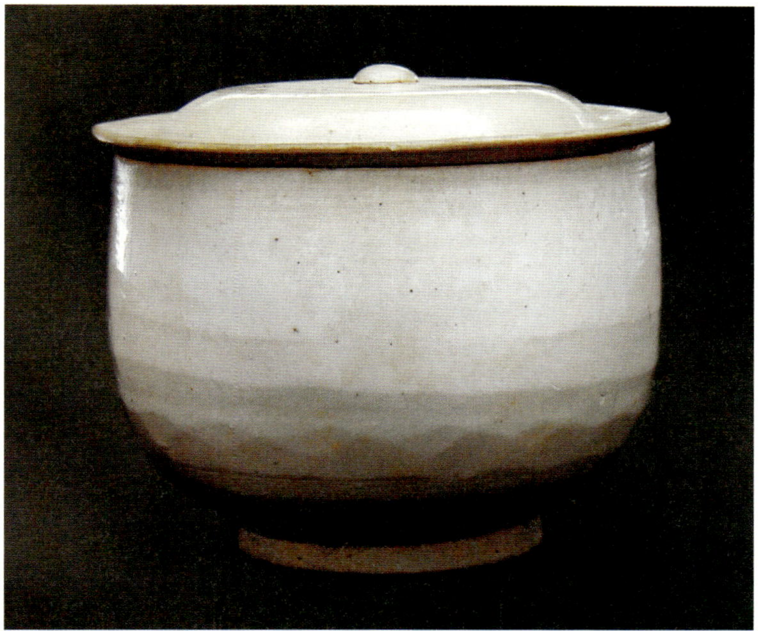

*Figure 4.9 White porcelain bowl with a lid. Jin (1115-1234). Lincheng Prefecture
Cultural Relics Preservation Office, Hebei Province, China. From Beijing Yishu
Bowuguan* 北京艺术博物馆, *ed.,* Zhongguo Xing yao 中国邢窑 *(Beijing: Zhongguo
Huaqiao Chubanshe, 2010): 120, Plate 126.*

lain manufactured together with celadon in the same kiln from these kilns
was fairly high.[36]

---

and Yanggu, where coarser white porcelains were produced due to the coarse soil
native to these areas.

[36] Although white porcelain made up only about seven percent, a very small
proportion, of the total quantity of ceramics produced at Pangsan-dong in Sihŭng,
the ratio of celadon to white porcelain shows a progressive increase in the production of white porcelain: first period (1:0.055), second period (1:0.146), and third
period (1:0.108). See Haegang Toja Misulgwan, *Pangsan taeyo.* The ratio of white
porcelain to celadon progressively increased at Sŏ-ri in Yongin as well: first layer
(26.82:72.35), second layer (87.89:11.15), third layer (98.66:1.06), and fourth layer
(99.80:0.2). See Hoam Misulgwan 湖巖美術館 [Ho-am Art Gallery], *Yongin Sŏ-ri*

215

What was the factor that enabled the sudden production of white porcelain in Koryŏ? To answer this question, we have to recognize the possibility that the Koryŏ kilns were related to the kilns in the northern regions of China. In other words, white porcelain production technology and style, or actual white porcelain, which were widespread in contemporary Hebei, Henan, Shanxi Provinces, and Inner Mongolia, were introduced to Koryŏ, or artisans skilled in white porcelain production technology immigrated to Koryŏ, triggering production of white porcelain in Koryŏ.[37] White porcelain was widely produced in the above-mentioned regions from the Tang dynasty. Scholars had thought that, among the kilns from these regions, the Ding kilns 定窯 in Hebei became the center of the ceramic industry that continued the tradition of northern Chinese white porcelain after the Xing kilns 邢窯 in Hebei closed down around the time of the Five Dynasties. However, the recent discovery of hard white porcelains (Ch. *yingzhi baici* 硬質白瓷) from Song dynasty graves and Jin dynasty strata in the Xingtai 邢台 region, the center of the Xing kilns, has compelled scholars to reconsider the period of activity and the character of the Xing kilns (fig. 4.9). In other words, it has been revealed that the Xing kilns transmitted the ceramic technology and style to many nearby kilns until the time of the Liao and Jin dynasties from the tenth to twelfth centuries.[38] In particular,

---

Koryŏ paekchayo: Palgul chosa pogosŏ 龍仁 西里 高麗白磁窯—發掘調查報告書 [The white porcelain kilns at Sŏ-ri in Yongin: Excavation report], vol. 2 (Seoul: Samsŏng Misul Munhwa Chaedan, 2003).

[37] Chinese white porcelains found at archaeological sites from Koryŏ are mostly Ding ware from the Ding kilns in northern China or Jingdezhen 景德鎮 porcelain in Jiangxi Province, produced from the Five Dynasties to the Jin dynasty. Since the ceramic technologies and artisans from the Ding kilns influenced white porcelains of Jingdezhen produced during the Five Dynasties and early Song, Jingdezhen white porcelains also had strong features from northern China.

[38] Yang Wenshan 杨文山, "Lun Song Jin shiqi Xing yao baici de chixu shengchan" 论宋金时期邢窑白瓷的持续生产 [Discussing the continuing production of white porcelains at the Xing kilns during the Song and Jin periods], in *Xing yao yizhi yanjiu* 邢窑遗址研究 [Research on Xing kiln sites], ed. Xingtai Shi Wenwu Guanlichu 刑台市文物管理处 [Xingtai City Cultural Relics Management Office] and Lincheng Xian Wenwu Baoguansuo 临成县文物保管所 [Lincheng Prefecture Cultural Relics Preservation Office] (Beijing: Kexue Chubanshe, 2007): 330-40; Sheng Wenwu Yanjiusuo 河北省文物研究所 [Cultural Relics Research Institute Hebei Province] and Lincheng Xian Wenwu Baoguansuo 临成县文物保管所 [Lincheng Prefecture Cultural Relics Preservation Office], "Lincheng shanxia Jin dai ciyao yizhi shijue

the proportion of white porcelain is very high among ceramic grave goods in Liao tombs from the mid- to late tenth century to the early eleventh century, as white porcelain began to comprise a greater proportion of ceramic products.[39] Therefore, when Liao kilns began to focus on the production of white porcelain after the tenth century, although essential technology was transmitted through the Ding kilns, the technological tradition of the Xing kilns that mainly produced white porcelain seems to have been widespread in northern China as well. The white porcelain production technology from these northern Chinese kilns could also have been transmitted to Koryŏ through Liao and the Northern Song, the two polities that maintained close relationships with Koryŏ.

Relationship with China Seen through
the Characteristics of Koryŏ Porcelain Products
Among the ceramic vessels produced at early Koryŏ porcelain kilns, the following examples and characteristics suggest a relationship between Koryŏ porcelain and Chinese ceramics.[40]

A. A Ewer with a Trumpet-Shaped Rim Excavated from Pangsan-dong: This ewer looks remarkably similar to the ewer with a trumpet-shaped rim excavated from Ningbo, Zhejiang Province, which was made in the second year (848) of the Dazhong 大中 reign period. The same type of ewer can also be found in the Shanghai Museum collection, which is inscribed: "The seventh year of the Huichang reign period that has been changed to the first year of the Dazhong reign period" 會昌七年改爲大中元年 (847).[41] Another ewer with a lid, also excavated from Pangsan-dong, is quite similar to the white porcelain ewer excavated from the Liao dynasty tomb in Chifeng,

jianbao" 临城山下金代瓷窑遗址试掘简报 [Brief report on the trial trenching at the Jin-dynasty porcelain kiln sites under the Lincheng mountain], in *Xing yao yanjiu* 邢窑研究 [Research on the Xing kilns] (Beijing: Wenwu Chubanshe, 2007): 55-63.

[39] Lu Jing 路菁, *Liao dai taoci* 辽代陶瓷 [Ceramics of the Liao dynasty] (Shenyang Shi: Liaoning Huabao Chubanshe, 2003): 337.

[40] Yi Chongmin, "Sihŭng Pangsan-dong ch'ogi ch'ŏngja yoji ch'ult'op'um ŭl t'onghae pon chungbu chiyŏk chŏnch'ugyo ŭi unyŏng sigi," 65-97.

[41] Editor's Note: This inscription can also be read as "[They] changed the seventh year of the Huichang reign period to the first year of the Dazhong reign period." Since this is an inscription for dating purposes, however, it is more appropriate to read it as a nominal phrase rather than as a sentence with an implied subject and a verb.

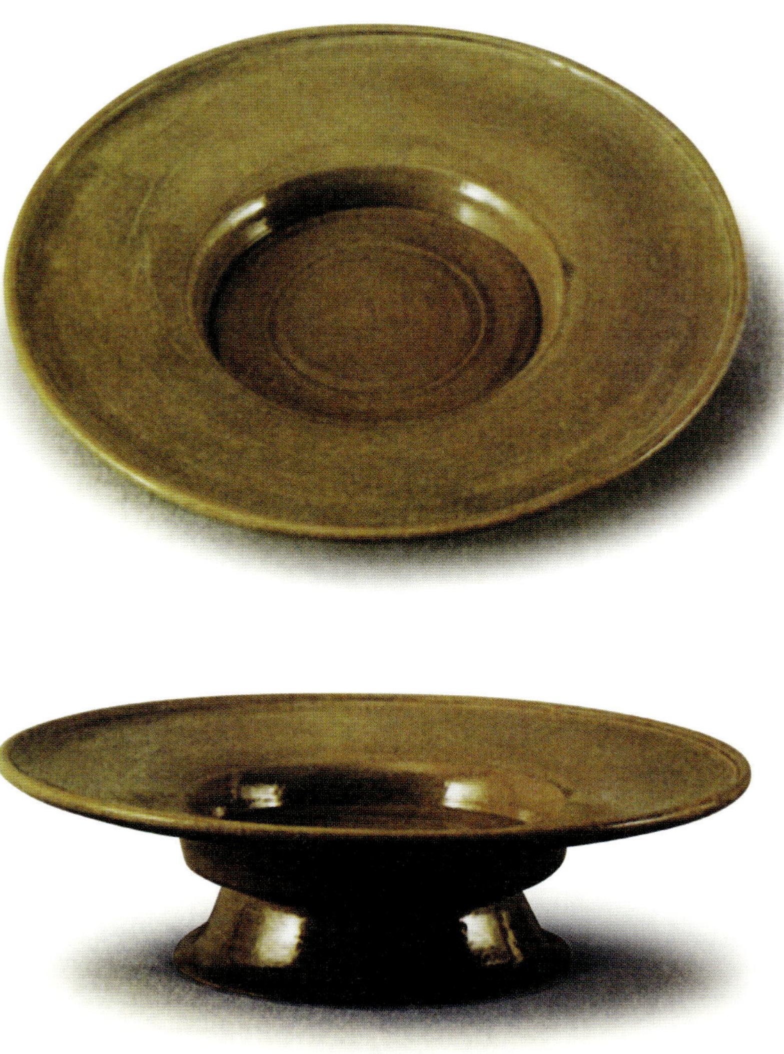

*Figure 4.10 Cup stand, from Allŭng at Konam-ni, Kaesŏng. Excavated by
Sahoe Kwahagwŏn* 社會科學院 *in North Korea. From Chosŏn Yujŏk Yumul
Togam P'yŏnch'an Wiwŏnhoe* 조선유적유물도감편찬위원회, *ed.,* Pukhan ŭi
munhwajae wa munhwa yujŏk 북한의 문화재와 문화유적, *vol. 3 (Seoul:
Sŏul Taehakkyo Ch'ulp'anbu, 2000): 13, Plates 39, 40.*

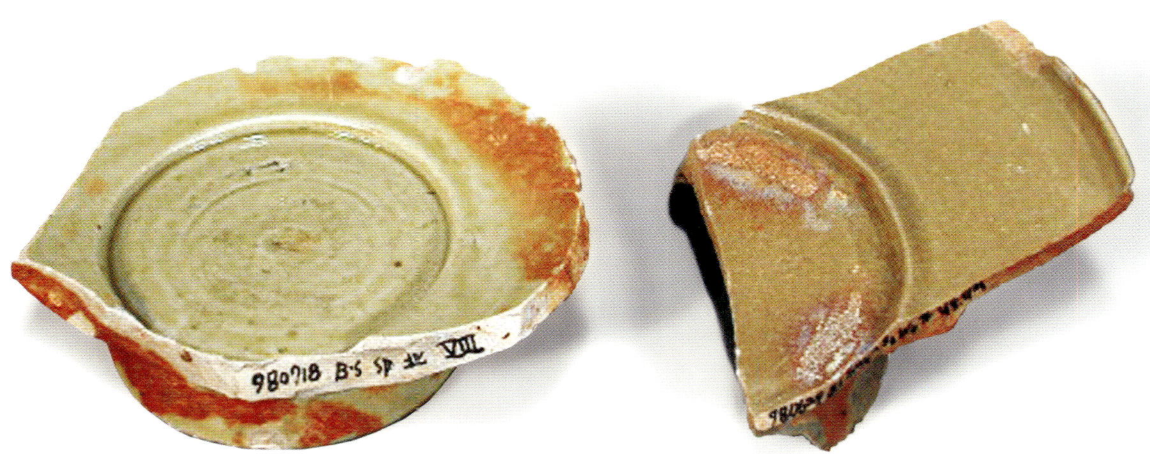

Figure 4.11 Sherds from cup stands, from the Pangsan-dong kiln site, Sihŭng, Kyŏnggi Province, Korea. Excavated by Haegang Toja Misulgwan. Courtesy of Yi Chongmin.

Liaoning Province, that dates to 959 and entombs a Liao emperor's son-in-law who had the title of "King of the Wei Kingdom" 衛國王 (fig. 4.15).[42] Since the celadon ewer with a trumpet-shaped rim excavated from Pangsan-dong has a more narrowly angled rim but more voluminous body and a wider spout than the Liao ewer, it probably postdates the latter.

B. A Celadon Cup Stand Excavated from the Tomb Allŭng 安陵 **at Konam-ni in Kaesŏng City:** Given the date of Allŭng, this cup stand predates 949 (fig. 4.10). It resembles a cup stand made around 940 currently in the collection of the Zhejiang Provincial Museum. Sherds from cup stands similar to Allŭng's cup stand were also found in Pangsan-dong. Therefore, the date of this royal tomb can help identify the duration of the kiln at Pangsan-dong (fig. 4.11).

---

[42] Editor's Note: Based on the inscription from the tomb, Chinese scholars have suggested that the tomb owner is Xiao Shilu 蕭室魯, the husband of the daughter of Emperor Taizu 太祖 (r. 907-926) of Liao. See Jin Yufu 金毓黻, "Liaoguo fuma zeng Weiguo wang muzhiming kaozheng" 辽国驸马赠卫国王墓志铭考证 [Historical investigation of the tomb epitaph of the king of Wei Kingdom, the son-in-law from the Liao dynasty], *Kaogu xuebao* 考古学报, no. 3 (1956): 27-31.

219

C. A Foliate-Rim Bowl Excavated from Allŭng: Although some suggest that this may have been made in China, it is just as likely to have been made in Koryŏ since similar bowls have been excavated from the kilns at Pangsan-dong and Wŏnsan-ni (fig. 4.12).

D. Ring-Shaped Support: This is a kiln tool that was laid under the foot of a ceramic vessel while the vessel was being fired. Bowls excavated from Cixi City, Zhejiang Province, have traces of ring-shaped supports. Some of these bowls have engraved inscriptions, such as "Taiping Wuyin" mentioned above. Ring-shaped supports and ceramic vessel sherds with traces of the use of this support have been found in tenth-century brick kilns located in the central region of the Korean peninsula, including the Pangsan-dong kiln site in Sihŭng. This also suggests that the ceramic industry in early Koryŏ actively adopted firing methods used in southern China's Zhejiang Province.[43]

E. *Haemurigup* Tea Bowl: This is the main item produced in tenth-century Koryŏ. Considered for a long time as a marker of the starting point of early Korean celadon, the *haemurigup* tea bowl produced in Koryŏ was once regarded as a product of the ninth century because it was very popular during the Tang period in China. The development process of the *haemurigup* tea bowl in Koryŏ—from pre-*haemurigup* tea bowl (tea bowl with a jade-ring-shaped foot) through *haemurigup* tea bowl to degenerated *haemurigup* tea bowl—has been confirmed, especially through the investigation of the stratigraphic sequence at the kiln sites at Sŏ-ri in Yongin. Ironically, the thick *haemurigup*—the *bi*-shaped foot—had disappeared almost entirely from the Yuezhou kilns in China and instead the production of the thin jade-ring-shaped foot was booming in the second half of the tenth century. Whereas the bowl with a *bi*-shaped foot predated the bowl with a jade-ring-shaped foot in China, in Koryŏ the sequence is reversed—the bowl with a *bi*-shaped foot postdates the bowl with a jade-ring-shaped foot. Is it because groups of artisans who produced old-fashioned ceramics at the peripheries of Shanglin Lake or Dongqian Lake in Zhejiang Province immigrated to the Korean peninsula and built brick kilns in Pangsan-dong, Wŏnsan-ni, and Sŏ-ri, where they produced bowls with the *bi*-shaped foot, which were already out of fashion in Southern China? Some have argued that this history of

---

[43] Yi Chongmin, "Sihŭng Pangsan-dong ch'ogi ch'ŏngja yoji ch'ult'op'um ŭl t'onghae pon chungbu chiyŏk chŏnch'ugyo ŭi unyŏng sigi," 95.

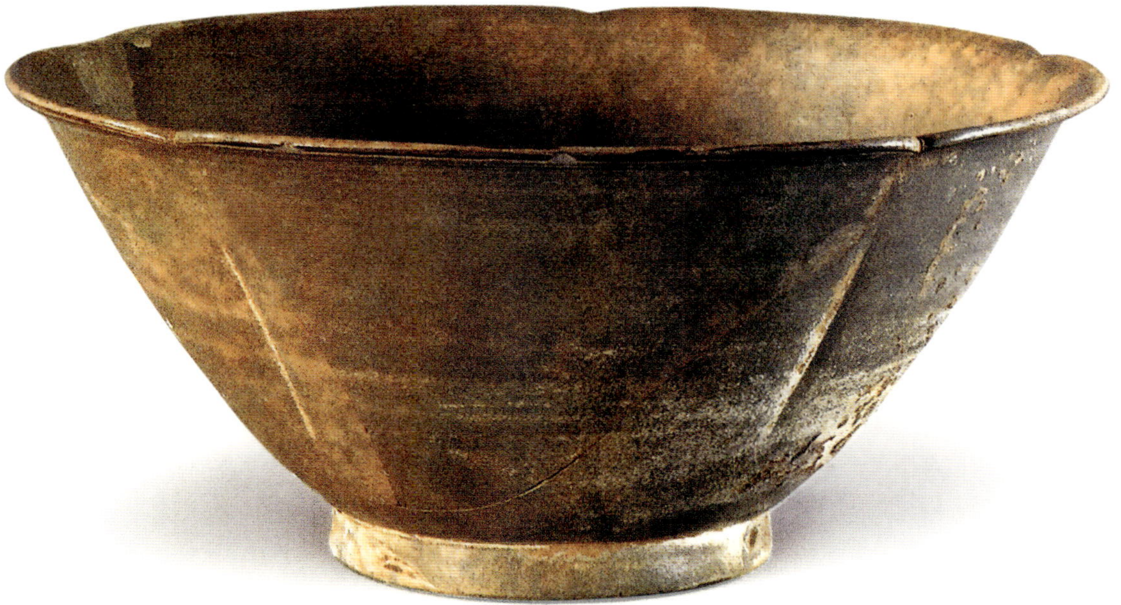

Figure 4.12 Foliate-rim bowl, from Allŭng at Konam-ni, Kaesŏng. Excavated by Sahoe Kwahagwŏn 社會科學院 *in North Korea. From Chosŏn Yujŏk Yumul Togam P'yŏnch'an Wiwŏnhoe* 조선유적유물도감편찬위원회, *ed., Pukhan ŭi munhwa-jae wa munhwa yujŏk* 북한의 문화재와 문화유적, *vol. 3 (Seoul: Sŏul Taehakkyo Ch'ulp'anbu, 2000): 17, Plate 10.*

ceramics in Koryŏ has nothing to do with that of China, and others have argued that Koryŏ artisans introduced the *haemurigup* tea bowl fashionable during the Tang as tea culture thrived in Koryŏ.[44] What were the real reasons for the belated boom of the *haemurigup* tea bowl in Koryŏ?[45] As mentioned above, many ceramic kilns began to appear in the midwestern region of the Korean peninsula from the mid-tenth century, especially near the Koryŏ capital, Kaegyŏng. These include the kiln sites at Pangsan-dong in Sihŭng;[46]

---

[44] Kim Yŏngmi, "Yue yao yanjiu," 113.

[45] For a detailed discussion of this matter, see Chang Namwŏn, "Koryŏ chŏn'gi haemurigup (okpyŏkchŏ kye) wan ŭi chisok hyŏnsang e taehan ch'uron," 321-353.

[46] Haegang Toja Misulgwan, *Pangsan taeyo.*

Chungdŏk 中德 in Sŏ-ri, Yongin;[47] Sangban 上盤 in Sŏ-ri, Yongin;[48] Chun-
gam-ni 中岩里 in Yŏju 驪州;[49] Wŏnhŭng-dong 元興洞 in Koyang 高陽;[50] and
Pugong-ni 釜谷里 in Yangju 楊州,[51] all in Kyŏnggi Province, as well as the
Wŏnsan-ni kiln site in Paech'ŏn, Hwanghae Province,[52] and the T'aesŏng
Kiln Site No. 1 in Namp'o 南浦, South P'yŏngan Province 平安南道.[53]

[47] Hoam Misulgwan, *Yongin Sŏ-ri Koryŏ paekchayo*.

[48] Kijŏn Munhwajae Yŏn'guwŏn 畿甸文化財研究院 [Kyŏnggi Province Research
Institute for Cultural Properties] "Yongin Yidong Sŏ-ri Sangban Koryŏ Paekcha yoji
palgul chosa chido wiwŏnhoe charyo" 용인 이동 서리 상반 고려 백자요지 발굴조사
지도위원회 자료 [Data from the committee directing the excavation of the Koryŏ
white porcelain kiln sites in Sŏ-ri Sangban, Yidong in Yongin] (unpublished data,
November 6, 2001); Kijŏn Munhwajae Yŏn'guwŏn, "Yongin Sŏ-ri Sangban Koryŏ
paekcha yoji 2-ch'a palgul chosa chido wiwŏnhoe charyo" 용인 서리상반 고려백자
요지 2차발굴조사 지도위원회 자료 [Data from the committee directing the second
excavation of the Koryŏ white porcelain kiln sites in Sŏ-ri Sangban, Yongin] (unpublished data, February 2003); Kijŏn Munhwajae Yŏn'guwŏn, "Yongin Sŏ-ri Sangban
Koryŏ Paekchayoji 3-ch'a palgul chosa chido wiwŏnhoe charyo" 용인서리상반 고려
백자요지 3차발굴조사 지도위원회 자료 [Data from the committee directing the third
excavation of the Koryŏ white porcelain kiln site at Sŏ-ri Sangban, Yongin] (unpublished data, January 27, 2004).

[49] Kyŏnggi-do Pangmulgwan 京畿道博物館 [Gyeonggi Provincial Museum and
Yŏju County] et al., *Yŏju Chungam-ni Koryŏ paekcha yoji* 驪州 中岩里 高麗白瓷窯址
[The Koryŏ white porcelain kiln site in Chungam-ni, Yŏju] (Yŏju: Kyŏnggi-do Pang-
mulgwan, 2004).

[50] Han'guk Chŏngsin Munhwa Yŏn'guwŏn 韓國精神文化研究院 [Academy of
Korean Studies], *Han'guk ŭi ch'ŏngja yoji* 한국의 청자요지 [Korean celadon kiln sites]
(Sŏngnam-si: Han'guk Chŏngsin Munhwa Yŏn'guwŏn, 1992).

[51] Chŏn Yŏnggyŏng 全榮京, "Yangju Pugong-ni ch'ongjawan yŏn'gu" 楊州 釜谷
里青磁碗 研究 [Research on celadon bowls from Pugong-ni, Yangju] (Hongik Taehakkyo sŏksa hagwi nonmun 弘益大學校碩士學位論文 [Hongik University M.A.
Thesis], 1993).

[52] Kim Yŏngjin 김영진, "Hwanghae-namdo Pongch'ŏn-gun Wŏnsan-ni ch'ŏngjagi
kamat'ŏ palgul kallyak pogo," 2-9; Chosŏn Yujŏk Yumul Togam P'yŏnch'an
Wiwŏnhoe 조선유적유물도감편찬위원회 [Committee for the Publication of Illus-
trated Book of Korean Archaeological Sites and Relics], ed., "Pongch'ŏn-gun
Wŏnsan-ni chagi kamat'ŏ" 봉천군 원산리 자기가마터 [The porcelain kiln site at
Wŏnsan-ni, Pongch'ŏn County], in *Chosŏn yujŏk yumul togam* 朝鮮遺跡遺物圖
鑑 [Illustrated book of Korean archaeological sites and relics], vol. 12 (Pyongyang:
Chosŏn Yujŏk Yumul Togam P'yŏnch'an Wiwŏnhoe, 1992): 306-321.

[53] Kim Yŏngjin 김영진, *Tojagi kamat'ŏ palgul pogo* 도자기가마터발굴보고 [Exca-
vation report on ceramic kiln sites] (Pyongyang: Sahoe Kwahak Ch'ulpansa, 2002).

Haemurigup tea bowls composed a significant proportion of the product from these kilns. Judging from the stratigraphic sequence, the jade-ring-shaped foot predates the *haemurigup* (*bi*-shaped foot) at these kiln sites of Koryŏ. This sequence is the reverse of that observed in China since the Tang period, which progressed from the *bi*-shaped foot (*haemurigup*) to the jade-ring-shaped foot. Comparative studies of objects excavated from the kiln sites suggest that the transition to the *haemurigup* in Koryŏ took place around the mid- to late tenth century.[54]

It is notable that, in Koryŏ's case, the *haemurigup* tea bowl—the bowl with a foot that has a long diameter and broader foot ring, following the Chinese *bi*-shaped foot—was found mostly at kiln sites where white porcelain was initially the major product, or where celadon and white porcelain were produced together. For example, the kiln sites at Pangsan-dong in Sihŭng, Sŏ-ri in Yongin, and Chungam-ni in Yŏju produced celadon and white porcelain together even when they first began producing ceramics. On the other hand, at kilns where white porcelain was not produced—which includes the kilns at Wŏnsan-ni in Paech'ŏn, Pugong-ni in Yangju, and Wŏnhŭng-dong in Wŏndang—a majority of the bowls had a jade-ring-shaped foot with a narrower foot ring, and the proportion of *haemurigup* tea bowls was low.[55] Why did the production of the *haemurigup* tea bowl begin in the kilns where white porcelain was manufactured together with celadon, such as the kiln sites of Pangsan-dong, Sŏ-ri, and Chungam-ni, or where the main item of production transitioned from celadon to white porcelain?

Considering its function, the popularity of the *haemurigup* tea bowl in Koryŏ could be related to the spread of tea-drinking culture, but this does not explain why Koryŏ artisans specifically chose to copy the Tang tea bowl with a *bi*-shaped foot (*haemurigup*) which had been in vogue almost a century earlier. Moreover, imported Chinese celadon excavated from Koryŏ sites during and after the tenth century consists mostly of bowls with a jade-ring-shaped

---

[54] Yi Chongmin 李鍾玟, *Koryŏ ch'ogi ch'ŏngja yŏn'gu* 고려 초기청자 연구 [Research on early Koryŏ celadon] (Seoul: Paeksan Charyowŏn, 2004).

[55] Together with the Wŏnhung-ni, Wŏnsan-ni, and Sihŭng Pangsan-dong sites, they are kilns where early celadon was produced. But there was no report of a discovery of white porcelain from these kilns, and excavated bowls were mainly those with a jade-ring-shaped foot (Kr. *okhwanjŏ* 玉環底). This type of foot has a larger diameter and narrower surface touching the ground, and there is no engraved circle on the bottom of the vessel's interior. See Chŏn Yŏnggyŏng, "Yangju Pugok-ri ch'ŏngjawan yŏn'gu."

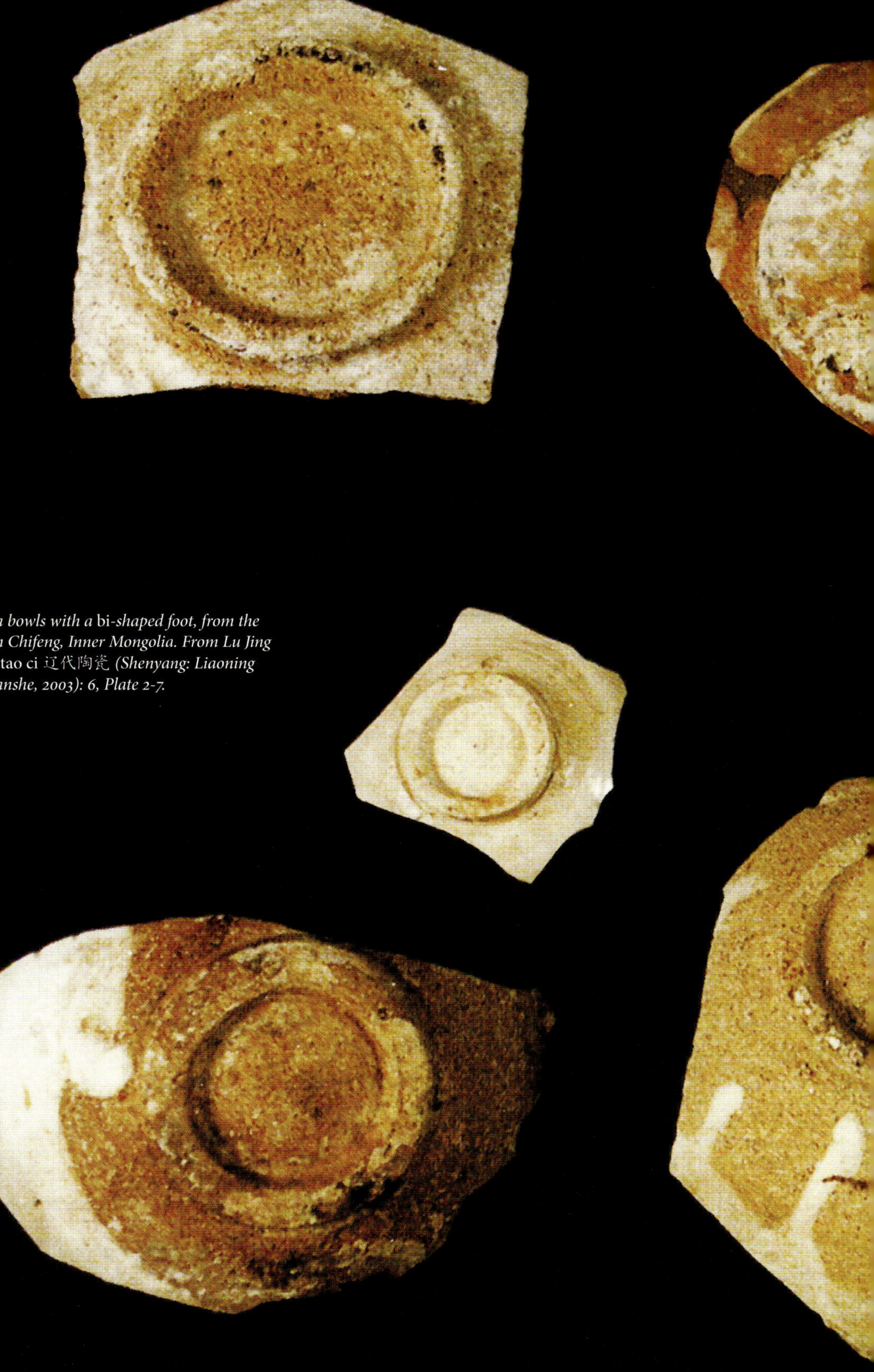

Figure 4.13 *Tea bowls with a bi-shaped foot, from the Gangwa kiln in Chifeng, Inner Mongolia. From Lu Jing* 菁路, *Liao dai tao ci* 辽代陶瓷 *(Shenyang: Liaoning Huabao Chubanshe, 2003): 6, Plate 2-7.*

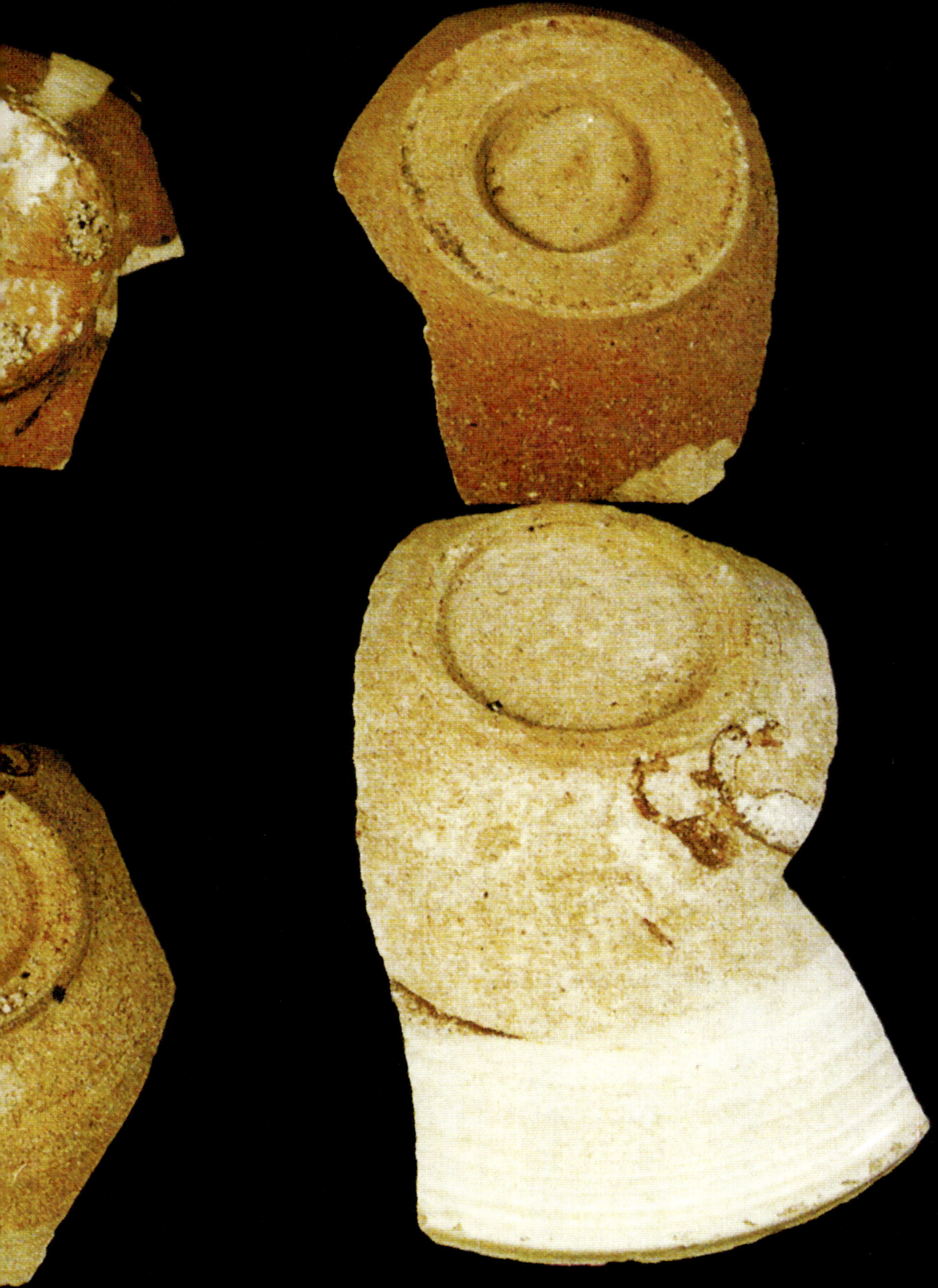

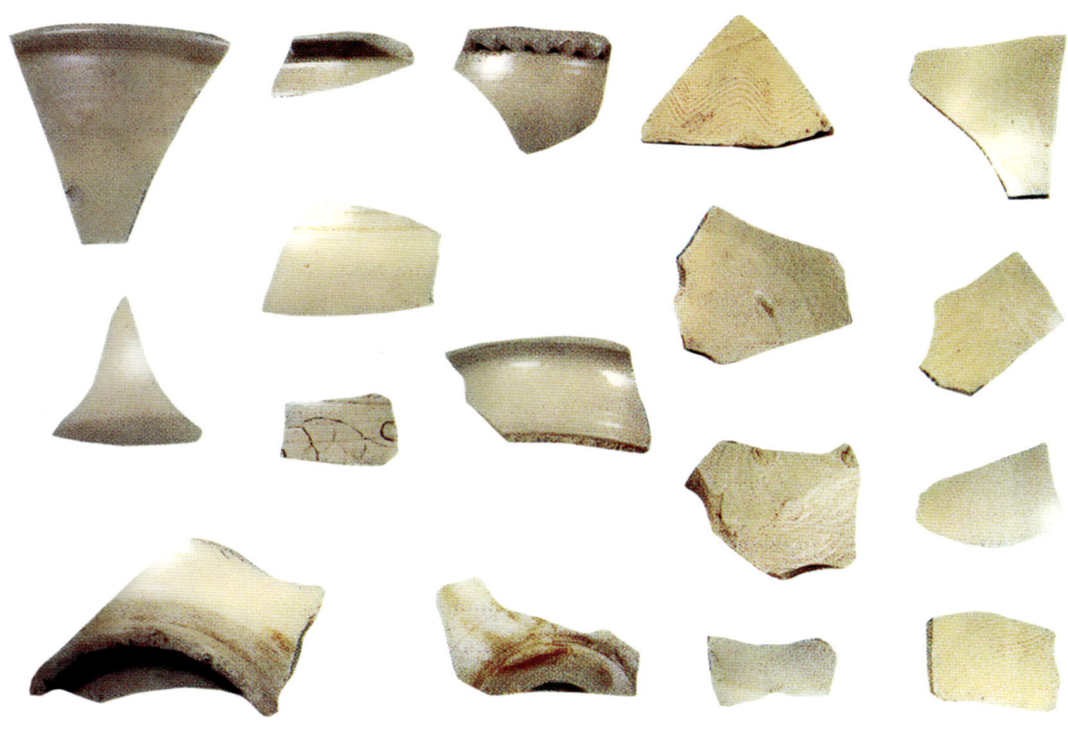

*Figure 4.14 White porcelain sherds, from the Lindong kiln, Shangjing, Inner Mongolia.
Courtesy of the Idemitsu Museum of Arts, Japan.*

foot,[56] and the Song dynasty in China was already transitioning to new
ceramic styles. Above all, tea bowls with a *haemurigup* from Koryŏ differed
from those of Tang China in that they have a clearly engraved circle (Kr.
wŏn'gak 圓刻) on the bottom of the bowl's interior.[57]

---

[56] Yi Chongmin, "Sihŭng Pangsan-dong ch'ogi chŏngja yoji ch'ult'op'um ŭl
t'onghae pon chungbu chiyŏk chŏnch'ugyo ŭi unyŏng sigi," 65-97.

[57] Unlike other cases where patterns were intentionally engraved with a carving
knife by artisans, the circular engraved depression in the Koryŏ dynasty bowl with a

226

Were there kilns in China after the beginning of the tenth century that produced ceramic vessels with a *bi*-shaped foot? Interestingly, during this period in China, bowls with a *bi*-shaped foot were made in areas where Liao and Jin kilns were densely concentrated. Although the sizes and proportions of these Chinese bowls were not exactly the same as those of Koryŏ, tea bowls with a *bi*-shaped foot were produced at the Gangwa kiln in Chifeng (fig. 4.13) and the Lindong kiln 林東窯 in Liao's Supreme Capital (fig. 4.14), both active from the tenth to twelfth centuries. Full excavation reports on these kiln sites have not yet been published. However, through the surface survey conducted by Japanese scholars in the 1940s and investigations by Chinese archaeologists in the 1990s, general information about their production trends, characteristics of the products, and the duration of production have become available.[58] There are also archaeologically datable consumption sites (Kr. *sobi yujŏk* 消費遺蹟) that retain traces of consumption, such as the Liao imperial tombs located in the Inner Mongolia Autonomous Region. Qingling 慶陵 in Balin Left Banner,[59] for example, is inferred to include the tombs of three Liao emperors: Yongqingling 永慶陵 of Shengzong 聖宗 (971-1031), Yongxingling 永興陵 of Xingzong 興宗 (1016-1055), and Yongfuling 永福陵 of Daozong 道宗 (1032-1101). Since it is not clear which tomb belongs to which of the three emperors, the tombs are called Eastern Mausoleum 東陵, Central Mausoleum 中陵, and Western Mausoleum 西陵. White porcelain wares, supposed to have been produced at the Lindong kiln, were excavated at the architectural site accompanying the Eastern Mausoleum,[60] and some of those have a flat and thick foot ring. Also, fragments of white porcelain items with a *bi*-shaped

---

bi-shaped foot was accidentally created when trimming the inside of the vessel with wooden knives or frames.

[58] Lu Jing, *Liao dai taoci*, 337; Yuba Tadanori 弓場紀知, "Ryō Jōkyōhu Lintō kamaato saikentō" 遼上京府林東窯址再檢討 [Re-examination of the Lindong kiln sites in the Supreme Capital Circuit from the Liao dynasty], *Idemitsu Bijutsukan kenkyū kiyō* 出光美術館研究紀要 6 (2000): 115-146.

[59] For discussions concerning this tomb and items excavated from it, see Tamura Jitsuzō 田村實造 and Kobayashi Yukio 小林行雄, *Keiryō: Higashi Mongoria ni okeru Ryōdai teiōryō to sono hekiga ni kansuru kōkogakuteki chōsa hōkoku* 慶陵: 東モンゴリアにおける遼代帝王陵とその壁画に関する考古学的調査報告 [Qingling: Report of the archaeological investigation on the Liao dynasty imperial mausoleums and their murals in East Mongolia], 2 vols. (Kyoto: Kyōto Daigaku Bungakubu, 1953).

[60] The Eastern Mausoleum is assumed to be Yongqingling of Emperor Shengzong 聖宗 (r. 971-1031).

foot were found together with Northern Chinese celadon at the architectural site of the Central Mausoleum, which in turn has helped scholars date the period of activities of these Liao kilns.[61]

Opportunities existed for the influx of artisans and ceramic technologies from northern China into Koryŏ as early as the first half of the tenth century, when Koryŏ and Liao established diplomatic relations and negotiated a peace agreement. The stratigraphic sequence at Pangsan-dong and Sŏ-ri, however, shows that the white porcelains that appear in the strata postdate the early and mid-tenth century. The early and mid-tenth century marks the beginning of the time when Koryŏ began to produce porcelain as the celadon technology was transmitted from southern Chinese Yuezhou kilns. Therefore, it is highly likely that northern artisans joined the Koryŏ kilns after the porcelain industry had become established in Koryŏ, and it led to the production of the *haemurigup* tea bowl together with white porcelains.[62] In addition to the *haemurigup* tea bowl, the above-mentioned white porcelain ewer excavated from the Liao tomb of the King of Wei (959) in Chifeng, Liaoning Province (fig. 4.15), and the celadon ewer with a lid excavated from the Pangsan-dong kiln site show the connection between the Liao and the Koryŏ kilns (fig. 4.16). The ceramics from the eleventh-century kiln sites in Kangjin, South Chŏlla Province, exhibit additional characteristics unique to Korea, as their foot ring becomes thinner and foot diameter smaller. Analysis of the ceramic ware concurrently excavated from these kiln sites, such as wide-rimmed large plates, cup stands, small pots, oil vases, vases with a dish-shaped mouth (Kr. *pan'gubyŏng* 盤口瓶), and arc-shaped plates, reveals that their prototypes are the early celadon from the central region of the Korean peninsula. This suggests that the Chinese-style *haemurigup* tea bowl of the tenth century was evolving into a Koryŏ style in the eleventh century.[63]

As the diplomatic relationship between Koryŏ and Song was renewed during the late eleventh century and as elements of Chinese culture were

---

[61] The Central Mausoleum is assumed to be Yongxingling of Emperor Xingzong 興宗 (r. 1016-1055).

[62] In my opinion, porcelains spread and developed sequentially from the midwestern to southern regions of the Korean peninsula in terms of modeling and production techniques, and kilns in the midwestern region included both kilns that were influenced by northern Chinese white porcelain and kilns that were not influenced.

[63] Yi Chongmin, "Sihŭng Pangsan-dong ch'ogi ch'ŏngja yoji ch'ult'op'um ŭl t'onghae pon chungbu chiyŏk chŏnch'ugyo ŭi unyŏng sigi," 65-97.

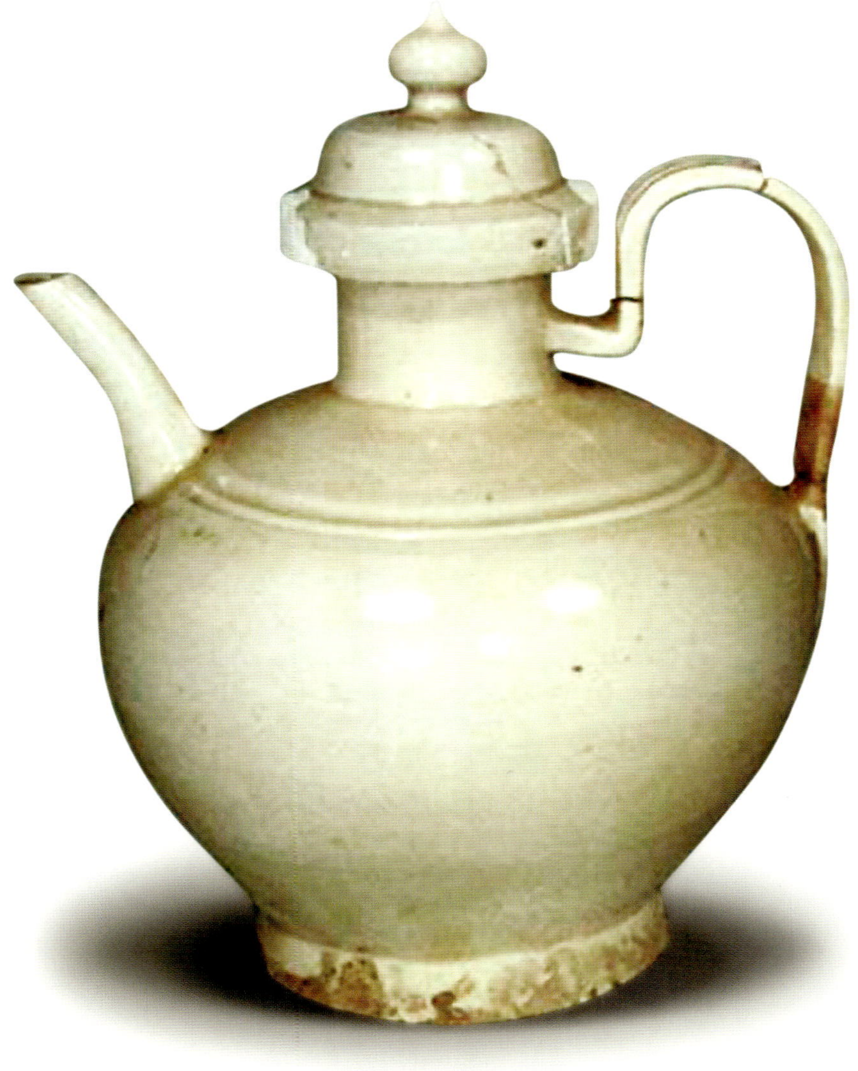

Figure 4.15 *White porcelain ewer, from the Liao tomb of the King of Wei (959) in Chifeng, Laoning Province, China. Courtesy of the Inner Mongolia Museum.*

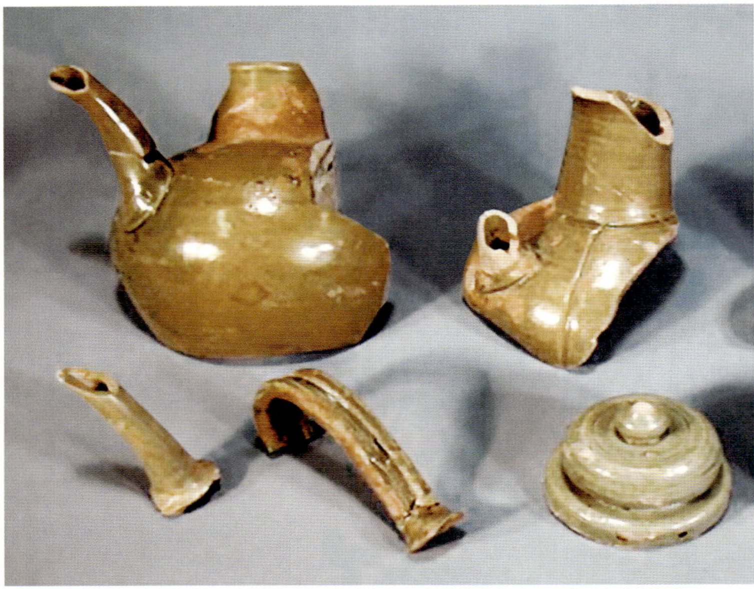

Figure 4.16 Sherds from celadon ewers with a lid, from the Pangsan-dong kiln site, Sihŭng, Kyŏnggi Province, Korea. Excavated by Haegang Toja Misulgwan. Courtesy of Yi Chongmin.

introduced to Koryǒ through formal channels in the first half of the twelfth century, the Koryǒ ceramic industry developed around Kangjin. This period saw changes in shaping methods and technology: new items in the style of the Northern Song (960-1127) emerged and the silica stone support, a firing support for the production of high-quality celadon, was introduced. The *haemurigup* tea bowl, which, I infer, was introduced from northern China after the tenth century, probably continued to be produced until the early twelfth century, although it gradually changed in shape.

F. Introduction of the Inlay Technique:[64] Another characteristic that shows tenth-century Koryǒ ceramic's close relationship with northern China is its inlay technique. This technique had been considered

[64] Chang Namwǒn, "Koryǒ ch'o, chunggi chagi sanggam kipŏp ŭi yŏnwŏn kwa palchŏn," 159-192.

representative of Koryŏ's ceramic production methods in the twelfth and thirteenth centuries, but recent excavations and surveys have revealed that it had also been used in early Koryŏ celadon during the late tenth and early eleventh centuries.[65] It is notable that the inlay technique, which was not used in southern Chinese kilns at that time, was used in Koryŏ during such an early period, when Koryŏ ceramic production was still mostly under the influence of southern China while the influence of northern China was seen only in some white porcelains and a few kinds of ceramic vessels.[66]

Most types of inlay techniques discovered in Koryŏ kilns consist of two types. The first type is a method universally used in Koryŏ celadon and white porcelains. In this method, artisans first engrave or carve out patterns, then fill them with white clay (Kr. *paekt'o* 白土) or iron clay (Kr. *chat'o* 赭土), and finish by smoothing them. The inlay technique used during the Koryŏ period is mostly of this first type. The earliest example of this inlay technique is found on the body of a *changgo* 長鼓, a double-ended, waisted drum, excavated from the Pangsan-dong kiln site in Sihŭng (fig. 4.17). The second type is a method in which artisans first apply a thick coat of iron clay to the surface of the clay that forms the ceramic body, then engrave patterns on this iron-clay-coated surface, and finally fill in the engraved parts with white clay. This type of inlay technique was found in a white porcelain *changgo* excavated from the kiln sites at Sŏ-ri in Yongin (fig. 4.18). A similar technique was used at the Chinsan-ni 珍山里 kiln site in Haenam, South Chŏlla Province, in which artisans applied a thin coat of iron clay, engraved or carved out patterns, and then applied a thin layer of white clay on the patterns with a brush. This is not exactly the same as the second type of inlay technique, but it is based on the same principle.[67]

These two types of inlay techniques were used in slightly different time periods. The first type began to appear at brick kilns in the central region of the Korean peninsula in the late tenth century at the latest. There are

---

[65] Haegang Toja Misulgwan, *Pangsan taeyo*; Hoam Misulgwan, *Yongin Sŏ-ri Koryŏ paekchayo.*

[66] Chŏng Sinok, "11-segi mal-12—segi chŏnban Koryŏ chŏngja e poinŭn Chung-guk toja ŭi yŏnghyang," 42-85; Im China, "Koryŏ chŏngja e poinŭn Puksong, Yodae chagi ŭi yŏnghyang," 1-221.

[67] Mokpo Taehakkyo Pangmulgwan 木浦大學校博物館 [Mokpo National University Museum], *Haenam Chinsan-ni nokch'ŏngja yoji* 海南 珍山里 綠青磁 窯址 [The green celadon kiln site in Chinsan-ni, Haenam] (Haenam-gun: Mokpo Taehakkyo Pangmulgwan, 1992).

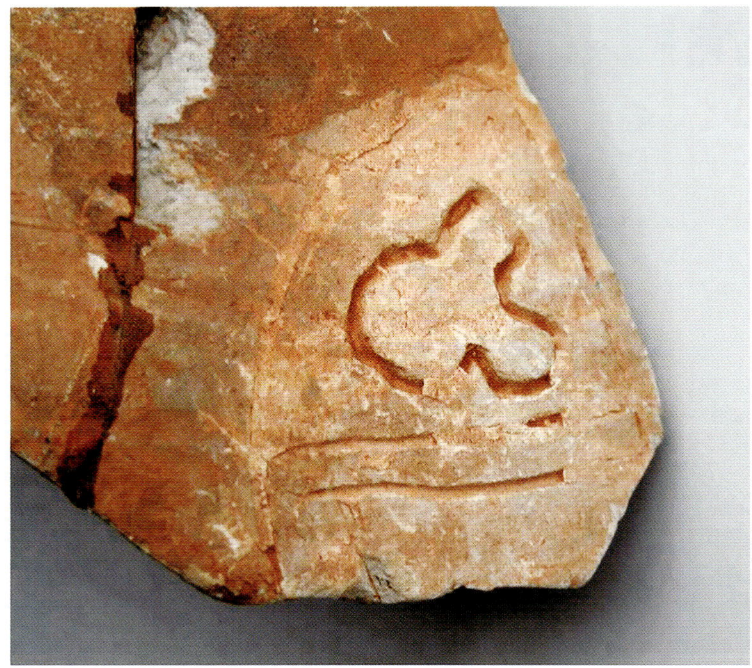

Figure 4.17 Sherd from a changgo 長鼓 with inlay decoration, from the Pangsan-dong kiln site, Sihŭng, Kyŏnggi Province, Korea. Excavated by Haegang Toja Misulgwan. Courtesy of the author.

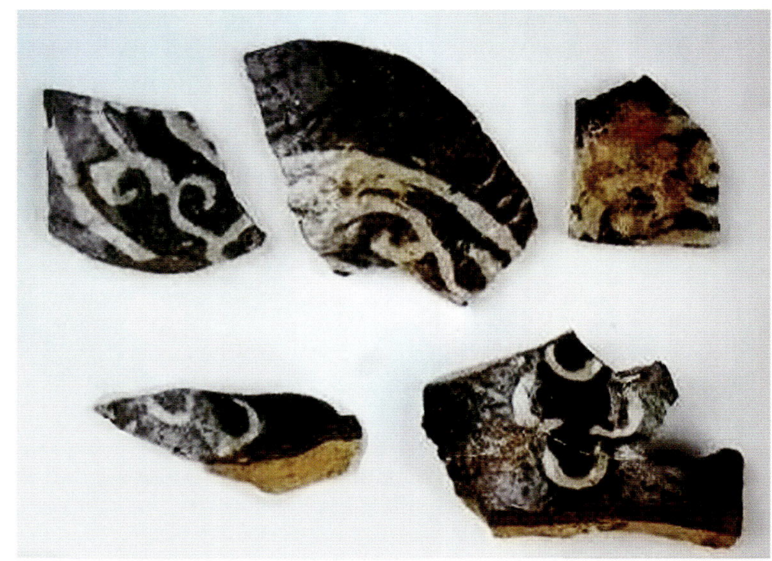

Figure 4.18 Sherds from changgo 長鼓 with inlay decoration, from the Chungdŏk kiln site in Sŏ-ri, Yongin, Kyŏnggi Province, Korea. The Leeum, Samsung Museum of Art. Courtesy of the National Museum of Korea.

no known Chinese examples of inlay technique usage in southern China during this period, whereas similar examples were found at some northern kilns after the Tang period. In other words, the inlay technique of incising or carving out patterns on the clay after forming the ceramic body and filling in the pattern with clay of a different color was mainly found in northern Chinese kilns, suggesting that the development of Koryŏ celadon was not simply related to southern Chinese Yuezhou kilns. In particular, the development of Koryŏ celadon seems to have been related to the kilns of Hebei and Shanxi Provinces, where inlay techniques became popular in the tenth and eleventh centuries.

Cizhou kiln 磁州窯 in Hebei Province in northern China used several different techniques similar to the inlay technique known as *heiyouhuatianbaicai* 黑釉花填白彩 (black-glazed ceramic with engraved pattern filled with white clay), *heitihuaketian* 黑剔花刻填 (ceramic pasted with black clay carved out pattern filled with white clay), *xiangqian* 鑲嵌 (filling incised thin patterns with color clay), and *baiyoutihuatianheicai* 白釉剔花填黑彩 (white-glazed ceramic with engraved pattern filled with black clay).[68] Among these, the "black-glazed ceramic with engraved pattern filled with white clay" technique is similar to the Koryŏ inlay technique. The use of this technique, filling engraved lines with white clay, began in the second half of the tenth century and was at its height in the mid-eleventh century. This technique is similar to the first type of Koryŏ inlay technique in that artisans engrave patterns on the clay that forms the vessel's body and fill the engraved patterns with white clay. When using the *heitihuaketian* technique—a technique highly developed at Cizhou kiln—artisans applied engobe (white or colored clay slip) on the ceramic body, applied iron clay above the engobe, incised patterns, and carved out areas other than the patterns, revealing the engobe. At Jiezhuang kiln 界莊窯 in Hunyuan 渾源 (fig. 4.19), Shanxi Province, artisans first impressed patterns using pattern molds, applied white clay slip on the impressed patterns, and then scratched

---

68 Qin Dashu 秦大樹, "Song, Kŭmdae pukpang chiyŏk chagi ŭi sanggam kongye wa Koryŏ sanggam ch'ŏngja ŭi kwan'gye" 宋·金代 북방지역 瓷器의 象嵌工藝와 高麗 象嵌青瓷의 關係 [The relationship between the inlay technique in northern porcelains during the Song and Jin dynasties and Koryŏ inlay celadon], *Misulsa nondan* 美術史論壇 7 (1998): 45-76; Ren Zhilü 任志录, "Zhongguo zaoqi xiangqianci de kaocha" 中国早期镶嵌瓷的考察 [Study of the early *xiangqian* ceramics of China], *Wenwu* 文物, no. 11 (2007): 74-90; Meng Yaohu 孟耀虎, "Hunyuan yao xiangqian qingci" 渾源窯鑲嵌青瓷 [Inlay celadon of the Hunyaun kiln], *Zhongguo gu taoci yanjiu* 中国古陶瓷研究 12 (2006): 461-471.

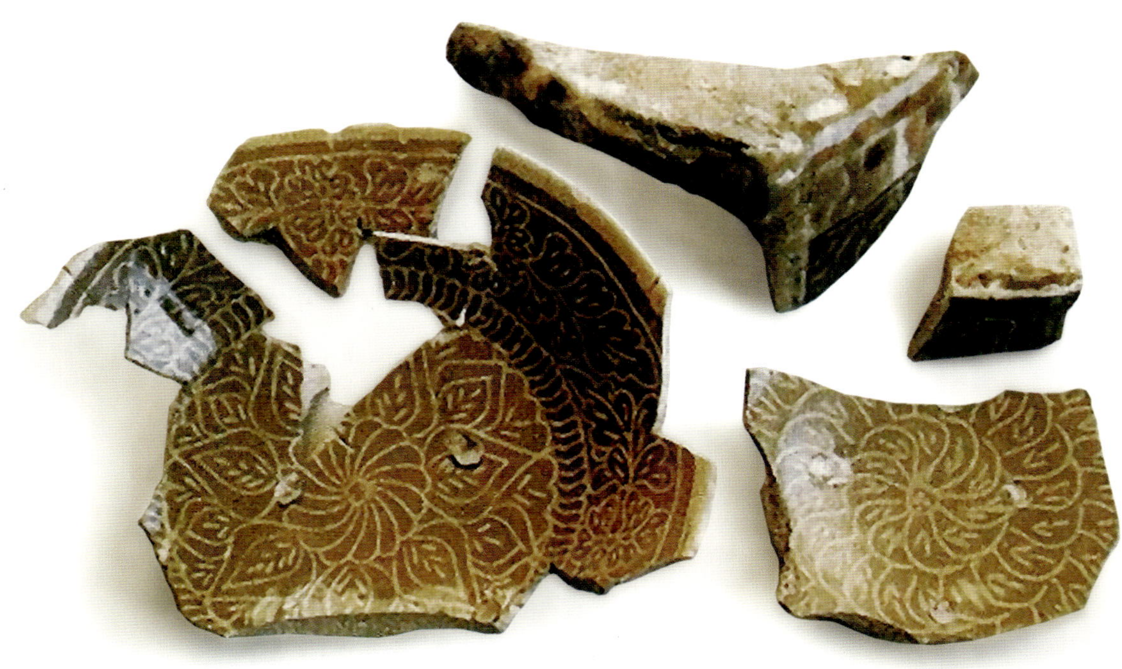

Figure 4.19 Celadon sherds with inlay decoration, from the Jiezhuang kiln in Hunyuan, Shanxi Province, China. From Qin Dashu 秦大樹, *"Song, Kŭmdae pukpang chiyŏk chagi ŭi sanggam kongye wa Koryŏ sanggam chŏngja ŭi kwangye"* 宋·金代 북방지역 瓷器의 象嵌工藝와 高麗 象嵌青瓷의 關係, *Misulsa nondan* 美術史論壇 *7 (1998): 66, Plate 17.*

out the white clay to reveal the pattern. Ceramics using this technique were excavated from Liao dynasty tombs.[69]

---

[69] In addition to the white-glazed ware with flower-pattern carving (白釉刻花) and the white-glazed ware with flower-pattern engraving (白釉剔花) already known to be products of the Hunyuan kiln, the discovery of inlay technique is also reported. See Meng Yaohu 孟耀虎, "Hunyuan yao xiangqian qingci," footnote 63. For the white-glazed ware with flower-pattern carving (白釉刻花) and the white-glazed ware with flower-pattern engraving from this kiln site, see Feng Xianming 冯先铭, "Shanxi Hunyuan gu yaozhi diaocha" 山西渾源古窯址調查 [Examination of the ancient kiln site at Hunyuan, Shanxi], in *Zhongguo gu taoci lunwenji* 中國古陶瓷論文集 [Collected papers on Chinese ancient ceramics] (Hong Kong: Zijincheng Chubanshe and Liangmu Chubanshe, 1987): 177-183.

234

G. Emergence of the Underglaze-Iron Painting Technique:[70] From the late Five Dynasties and early Song, artisans decorated white ceramic vessels with paintings using black pigment made of iron oxide. This decoration method is observed at northern kilns such as the Dangyangyu kiln 當陽峪窯 in Xiuwu 修武, the Hebiji kiln 鶴壁集窯 and Bacun kiln 扒村窯 in Yuxian 禹县, and the Quhe kiln 曲河窯 in Dengfeng 登封, all in Henan Province; the Yaozhou kiln 耀州窯 in Shaanxi Province 陝西省; the Cizhou kiln in Hebei Province; the Jiexiu kiln 介休窯 in Shanxi Province; as well as the Jizhou kiln 吉州窯 in Jiangxi Province 江西省, which was known to have been established by artisans from north Chinese kilns who migrated to southern China.[71] At the Cizhou kiln, in particular, because its local *daqing* clay 大青土 that was used to form the ceramic body was coarse and dark-colored, white clay slip was applied to the ceramic body to hide imperfections as well as to decorate and embellish it. This decoration method influenced kilns in wide areas from the Five Dynasties through the Song, the Liao, and the Jin to the Yuan dynasty (1271-1368), yielding kilns that produced ceramics using this decoration technique, known as *baidiheihua* 白地黑花 (black flower on white background), all over China from north to south.[72] Even underglaze-iron painting was often added on celadon ware without applying white clay slip at the Xicun kiln 西村窯[73] (fig. 4.20) and

---

[70] Chang Namwŏn (Jang Namwon) 장남원, "Koryŏ sidae ch'ŏrhwa chagi ŭi sŏngnip kwa chŏn'gae" 고려시대 철화자기의 성립과 전개 [Establishment and development of Koryŏ porcelains decorated with underglaze-iron painting], *Misulsa nondan* 美術史論壇 18 (June 2004): 41-71.

[71] Yu Jiadong 余家栋 and Ye Wencheng 燁文程, eds., *Jiangxi Jizhou yao* 江西吉州窯 [The Jizhou kiln in Jiangxi Province] (Guangzhou Shi: Lingnan Meishu Chubanshe, 2002).

[72] Beijing Daxue Kaoguxuexi 北京大學考古學系 [Peking University Archaeology Department], Hebei Sheng Wenwu Yanjiusuo 河北省文物研究所 [Cultural Relics Research Institute Hebei Province], and Handan Diqu Wenwu Baoguansuo 邯鄲地區文物保管所 [Handan District Cultural Relics Preservation Office], *Guantai Cizhou yaozhi* 觀台磁州窯址 [The Cizhou kiln sites in Guantai] (Beijing: Wenwu Chubanshe, 1997); Ōsaka Shiritsu Bijutsukan 大阪市立美術館 [Osaka City Museum of Fine Arts], ed., *Shiro to kuro no kyōen: Chūgoku Jishū yōkei tōki no sekai: tokubetsuten* 白と黒の競演: 中国磁州窯系陶器の世界: 特別展 [Contest between white and black: The world of Chinese Cizhou kiln style pottery: Special Exhibition] (Osaka: Ōsaka Shiritsu Bijutsukan, 2002); Hasebe Gakuji 長谷部 樂爾, "Jishūyō" 磁州窯 [Cizhou kiln], *Chūgoku no tōji* 中国の陶磁 7 (Tokyo: Heibonsha, 1996).

[73] Guangzhou Shi Wenwu Guanli Weiyuanhui 廣州市文物管理委員會 [Guangzhou

the Chaozhou kiln 潮州窯[74] in Guangdong Province 广东省, as well as at
the Dehua Qudougong kiln 屈斗宫德化窯 site,[75] and the Cizao kiln 磁竈
窯[76] in Fujian Province 福建省. Furthermore, this same decoration technique was used at kiln sites within Liao and Xixia 西夏 (1038-1227) territories such as the Inner Mongolia Autonomous Region and the Ningxia
Hui Autonomous Region, which were influenced by the Cizhou kiln.[77] A
fragment of a waisted drum with underglaze-iron painting was excavated
even from a late stratum at the Silongkou kiln site in Zhejiang Province, a
kiln representative of Yuezhou kilns of southern China, suggesting that this
technique had widespread use.[78]

Both detailed and simple patterns were used, according to the types of
ceramics. At the same time, ceramics recovered from the sea near Wando

---

City Cultural Relics Management Committee] and Xianggang Zhongwen Daxue
Wenwuguan 香港中文大學文物館 [Art Museum, The Chinese University of Hong
Kong], eds., *Guangzhou Xicun yao* 廣州西村窯 [Xicun kiln in Guangzhou] (Hong
Kong: Xianggang Zhongwen Daxue Zhongguo Kaogu Yishu Yanjiu Zhongxin, 1987).

[74] Guangdong Sheng Bowuguan 廣東省博物館 [Guangdong Provincial Museum]
and Xianggang Daxue Fengpingshan Bowuguan 香港大學馮平山博物館 [Feng-
pingshan Museum, The University of Hong Kong], eds., *Guangdong Tang Song
yaozhi chutu taoci* 廣東唐宋窯址出土陶瓷 [Ceramics excavated from the Tang
and Song kiln sites in Guangdong] (Hong Kong: Xianggang Daxue Fengpingshan Bowuguan, 1985).

[75] Fujian Sheng Bowuguan 福建省博物館 [Fujian Provincial Museum], *Dehua
yao* 德化窑 [Dehua kiln] (Beijing: Wenwu Chubanshe, 1990).

[76] He Zhenliang 何振良 and Lin Demin 林德民, *Cizao yao ci* 磁灶窑瓷 [Cizao
kiln porcelains] (Fuzhou: Fujian Meishu Chubanshe, 2002).

[77] Lu Jing, *Liao dai taoci*, 337.

[78] Zhejiang Sheng Wenwu Kaogu Yanjiusuo 浙江省文物考古研究所 [Zhe-
jiang Provincial Institute of Cultural Relics and Archaeology], Beijing Daxue Kaogu
Wenbo Xueyuan 北京大学考古文博学院 [Peking University School of Archaeology
and Museology], and Cixi Shi Wenwu Guanli Weiyuanhui 慈溪市文物管理委员会
[Cixi City Cultural Relics Management Committee], *Silongkou Yue yaozhi* 寺龙口越
窑址 [The Yue kiln site in Silongkou] (Beijing: Wenwu Chubanshe, 2002): 284. The
use of the underglaze-iron painting technique in southern China cannot be traced
back only to the influence of northern China. There were examples of underglaze-
iron painting during the Wei and Jin periods (220-420), and it is known that underglaze-iron painting was used for celadon from the Yuezhou kilns during the Sui and
Tang periods. However, the underglazed iron found in southern China from the
tenth to twelfth centuries exhibit similarities to those found in northern China in
terms of the patterns and the vessel types on which they appear.

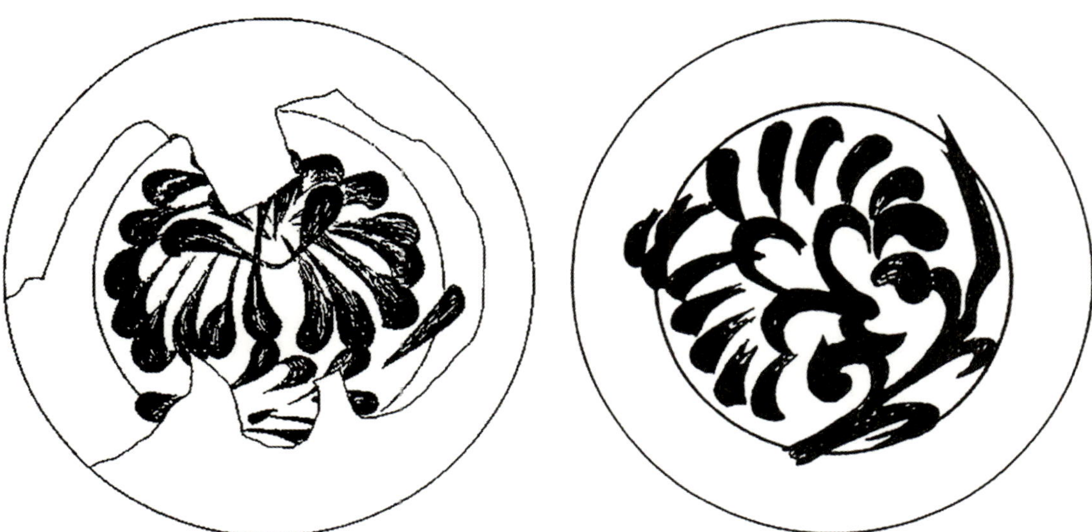

Figure 4.20 *Drawing of underglaze-iron painting on celadon excavated from the Xicun kiln, Guangzhou, Guangdong Province, China. Current whereabouts are unknown. From Guangzhou Shi Wenwu Guanli Weiyuanhui* 廣州市文物管理委員會 *and Xianggang Zhongwen Daxue Wenwuguan* 香港中文大學文物館, eds., Guangzhou Xicun yao 廣州西村窯 (Hong Kong: Xianggang Zhongwen Daxue Zhongguo Kaogu Yishu Yanjiu Zhongxin, 1987): 41, Drawing 30.

were for the most part densely filled with lively paintings executed with underglazed iron (fig. 4.21). On the other hand, examples from other local regions generally showed loosely structured patterns; among these, a simple flower-and-plant-pattern is most common. In general, Koryŏ ceramics painted with underglazed iron display techniques similar to both northern and southern Chinese examples. Similarity to the northern Chinese ceramics, especially to Cizhou ware, is seen in the peony and chrysanthemum patterns, which were created by the sophisticated incision of patterns on the ceramic body covered with black clay including much iron oxide (a technique known as *hŭkchi kakhwa* 黑地刻花), as well as in the overall composition of the painting. The way in which artisans decorated the interior of the ceramic vessel with paintings without applying white slip, however, reveals a similarity to the techniques used in southern Chinese ceramics. Koryŏ porcelains also included vessel types that were similar to those of southern China, such as a washbasin (Ch. *pan* 盤 or *xi* 洗) fashionable in Guangdong and Fujian Provinces in southern China. Therefore, it is hard to assert that

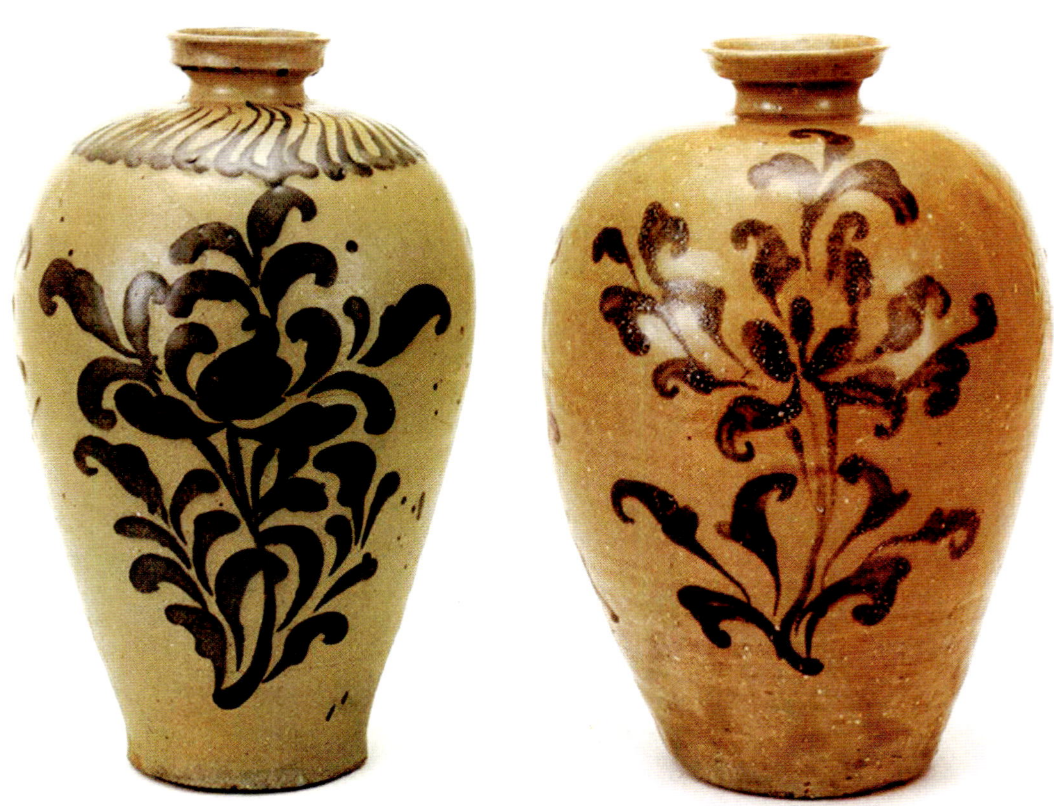

Figure 4.21 *Celadon prunus vase with underglaze-iron painting, excavated from the sea near Wando, Korea. National Research Institute of Maritime Cultural Heritage. Courtesy of the Gwangju National Museum.*

Koryŏ's underglaze-iron painting technique originated entirely from kilns in one specific region in China.

We can infer that the *changgo* with underglaze-iron painting excavated from the uppermost stratum at the Pangsan-dong kiln site in Sihŭng was made between the late tenth and early eleventh centuries through comparative dating and examination of archaeological strata at the Sŏ-ri kiln sites in Yongin. Underglaze-iron painting is also primarily found on *changgo* at the Chungdŏk kiln site at Sŏ-ri in Yongin, suggesting that this technique was booming during the same period. Underglaze-iron painting is also

238

discovered on ceramic pillows at some sites, indicating that this technique was used mostly for special ceramic ware.[79] This was also a period when white porcelain production increased at the brick kilns in the central region of the Korean peninsula and when the kilns at Sŏ-ri in Yongin, which mainly produced bowls with Koryŏ-style *haemurigup*, were the most active. If we compare this site temporally with the Pangsan-dong site in Sihŭng, it falls into the period immediately following the last stage of the Pangsan-dong site. Therefore, we can infer that the introduction and development of the underglaze-iron painting technique occurred during the late tenth century to early eleventh century. In sum, although the underglaze-iron painting techniques of northern and southern Chinese kilns seem to have been introduced to Koryŏ with a slight sequential difference, it is inferred that northern Chinese elements were more influential during the stage when the underglaze-iron painting techniques were first introduced to Koryŏ.

Conclusion

This chapter has examined the relationship between the Koryŏ ceramic industry and the northern and southern Chinese ceramic industry during the tenth century. This study has shown that the launching and the development of the early Koryŏ ceramic industry were closely related to the Chinese ceramic industry, both in terms of production technology and ceramic styles. The most important ideas here are the origin and genealogy of the ceramic industry as well as the process through which Chinese elements were accepted and transformed.

As for previous Korean scholarship on the history of the ceramic industry, scholars have mainly paid attention to the beginning period of Koryŏ porcelain—the so-called "early celadon" production period. By studying the production technology and the styles of ceramic ware of Yuezhou kilns, the center of celadon production in southern China, Korean scholars have shown that a close relationship exists between early Koryŏ celadon production and Yuezhou kilns. In particular, among various kinds of early celadon ware, scholars have paid particular attention to the *haemurigup* tea bowl, the same type of ceramic ware as the Chinese bowl with *bi*-shaped foot, since it is regarded as the representative item from Yuezhou kilns. By comparing foot styles of Koryŏ celadon bowls with those of celadon bowls produced in Yuezhou kilns, many scholars have tried to explain the process of stylistic transformation of Koryŏ *haemurigup*.

---

[79] Hoam Misulgwan, *Yongin Sŏ-ri Koryŏ paekchayo*.

In early research, however, Korean scholars did not consider the possibility of Koryŏ's selective reception of various Chinese ceramic technologies and styles, simply assuming that Koryŏ must have accepted Chinese ceramic production techniques chronologically, uniformly following the stages of development that took place in China. There is no doubt that the Koryŏ celadon industry began under the absolute influence of Yuezhou kilns. Here "absolute influence" means that the Koryŏ celadon industry shared similarities with Yuezhou kilns in terms of kiln structure, kiln tools, and style and decorative patterns of ceramic ware, as well as the chemical composition of the clay forming the ceramic wares and the glaze applied to them. Hence, the suggestion that the Koryŏ porcelain industry began with the migration of a group of artisans from Yuezhou kilns is quite reasonable.

However, this focus on the relationship between the history of Koryŏ ceramics and that of Five Dynasties and Song ceramics has left unanswered many questions about ceramic style and production techniques. In other words, it has not explained the reasons why celadon and white porcelain, starting from the early celadon production period, were produced in the same kilns despite their radically different operational needs; why certain ceramic wares, including foliate-rim plates, show a stylistic tradition different from that of southern China; and why the process of production and development of the Koryŏ *haemurigup* tea bowl is radically different from that of the Chinese *haemurigup* tea bowl.

I have attempted to answer some questions that remain unsolved by previous scholarship by examining the tenth-century Koryŏ ceramic industry's relationship not only with southern Song but also with the Liao dynasty in northern China, and by considering the political and diplomatic situation surrounding Koryŏ during that time. In particular, by examining Koryŏ's relationship with northern China, rather than limiting the scope of study to southern China, I have shown that Koryŏ porcelains have a multifaceted production genealogy and stylistic tradition.

First, as for changes in production technique, this chapter focused on the introduction of the single-firing technique and the change in the shape of cup support as well as the decline of kilns in the midwestern region of the Korean peninsula, where celadon kilns in the style of Yuezhou kilns were first established. The technique of double firing had already been developed in the process of making tri-color ware during the Tang; this technique subsequently spread to Shaanxi, Henan, Hebei, and the Inner Mongolian regions. This chapter has suggested that the double-firing technique widely used for tri-color-ware production in Parhae 渤海 (698-926) and Liao as well as the double-firing technique used in Koryŏ were related to the northern Chinese ceramic industry rather than the southern Chinese. I have also argued that the beginning of this double-firing technique coincided with the production of the *haemurigup* tea bowl in Koryŏ. In addition, these Koryŏ kilns' use of small support pieces made of fire-resistant sandy soil, known as *naehwat'o* 耐火土, which were added under the foot to allow stacking of the ceramic bowls inside the kiln during the firing, was not characteristic of Yuezhou kilns. As these three phenomena occurred simultaneously without any specific external causes, I have inferred that they originated from continuous interchanges with northern China.

Together with the introduction of the new technologies, new production methods and ceramic styles also appeared in Koryŏ: transmission of Chinese white porcelains and the simultaneous production of white porcelain and celadon at the same kiln site. Since celadon and white porcelain use different materials and procedures, including firing techniques, it is fairly difficult to produce white porcelain based on celadon production facilities and technology. Nevertheless, kilns in and around Kaegyŏng, the capital of Koryŏ, first began simultaneous production of celadon and white porcelain, and kilns at Pangsan-dong in Sihŭng and at Sŏ-ri in Yongin produced a large amount of white porcelain at the same time they were producing celadon. To explain this phenomenon, I have considered the influence of northern Chinese kilns where white porcelain and related production techniques continued to be used throughout the tenth and eleventh centuries until the Jin dynasty. This chapter suggests that as the Liao began to rule over northern China and the kilns in the Liao territory produced more white porcelains to meet the increased demand, northern kilns diversified the kinds and shapes of white porcelains being produced through the introduction of techniques from Xing kilns, kilns that had a strong tradition of producing a tea bowl with a *bi*-shaped foot, as well as from Ding kilns. The fact that Koryŏ reproduced the *bi*-shaped foot, which had been prevalent during the Tang period, has intrigued many scholars. To explain this phenomenon, I have pointed out that quite a few ceramic wares with a *bi*-shaped foot, although their sizes and proportions vary, were also produced in northern China during the same period when Koryŏ produced the *haemurigup*. In particular, tea bowls with a *bi*-shaped foot were discovered at Gangwa kilns in Chifeng and at Lindong kilns located in the former Supreme Capital of Liao—kilns that reached their heights around the eleventh century. This combination of white porcelain and the *bi*-shaped foot is a common characteristic shared by northern China and Koryŏ starting from the second half of the tenth century.

The inlay technique and underglaze-iron painting technique found in kilns for the *haemurigup* tea bowl in the central region of the Korean peninsula during the late tenth century have been described here. The inlay technique of early Koryŏ was first attempted not on celadon but on white porcelains. Based on this fact, this chapter has suggested that the technique was introduced from northern China together with white porcelain production technology. In addition, this chapter also analyzed the direct and indirect transmission of the underglaze-iron painting technique from the Cizhou kiln tradition. Given the similarity in patterns used in underglaze-iron painting and considering that this technique appeared first in kilns in the central region from the late tenth century to the early eleventh century and then spread to the southern part of the peninsula, I have suggested that this technique followed the general flow of the ceramic industry in early Koryŏ.

In conclusion, although the Koryŏ porcelain industry was under the heavy influence of the southern Chinese porcelain industry in its early development, it later adopted various ceramic styles and production techniques from northern China, as Koryŏ established lively diplomatic relations and civilian interactions with northern Chinese dynasties. All these were rapid changes that occurred during the tenth century. This chapter demonstrates that Koryŏ selectively accepted elements from both northern and southern China according to its own circumstantial demands and technical capacities. The history of the Koryŏ ceramic industry followed a unique trajectory that addressed Koryŏ's own needs while reflecting many characteristics of northern and southern China.

5

The Gold Jewelry of ancient Silla: Syncretism of Northern and Southern Asian Cultures

Joo Kyeongmi

Introduction

Ancient Silla (Kr. Ko-Silla 古新羅) was a small kingdom located in the southeastern part of the Korean peninsula. It was traditionally believed to have been established in the first century B.C.E. and gradually developed into a powerful kingdom that unified the neighboring kingdoms of Koguryŏ and Paekche. By 676 Silla had developed into a much larger polity, referred to today as Unified Silla, which continued until 935.[1] Although the Unified Silla polity developed from ancient Silla, many differences can be observed in the art and culture each produced, especially in the realms of religion and artistic style. The wide spread of Buddhism and the new cultural influences from Tang China stand as the two central causes for these differences.

In this chapter I survey the special genre of art found in the tombs of ancient Silla that was made from precious metals. The people of ancient Silla believed in the immortality of the spirit and that the spirit of the deceased would live forever in the afterworld. Consequently, they constructed huge tombs for their dead ancestors; in these tombs, they buried

---

[1] For the history of ancient Silla and Unified Silla in English, see Han Young Woo, *A Review of Korean History*, vol. 1: *Ancient/Goryeo Era*, trans. Hahm Chaibong (Kyŏnggi-do: Kyŏngsaewŏn, 2010): 131-230. Here I use the term "dynasty" for Unified Silla to indicate the political difference between ancient Silla and Unified Silla. Before the unification of the Three Kingdoms, the royal line of ancient Silla was shared by three families: Kim, Pak, and Sŏk. But only the descendants of King Muyŏl (of the Kim family) maintained the royal lineage after the unification.

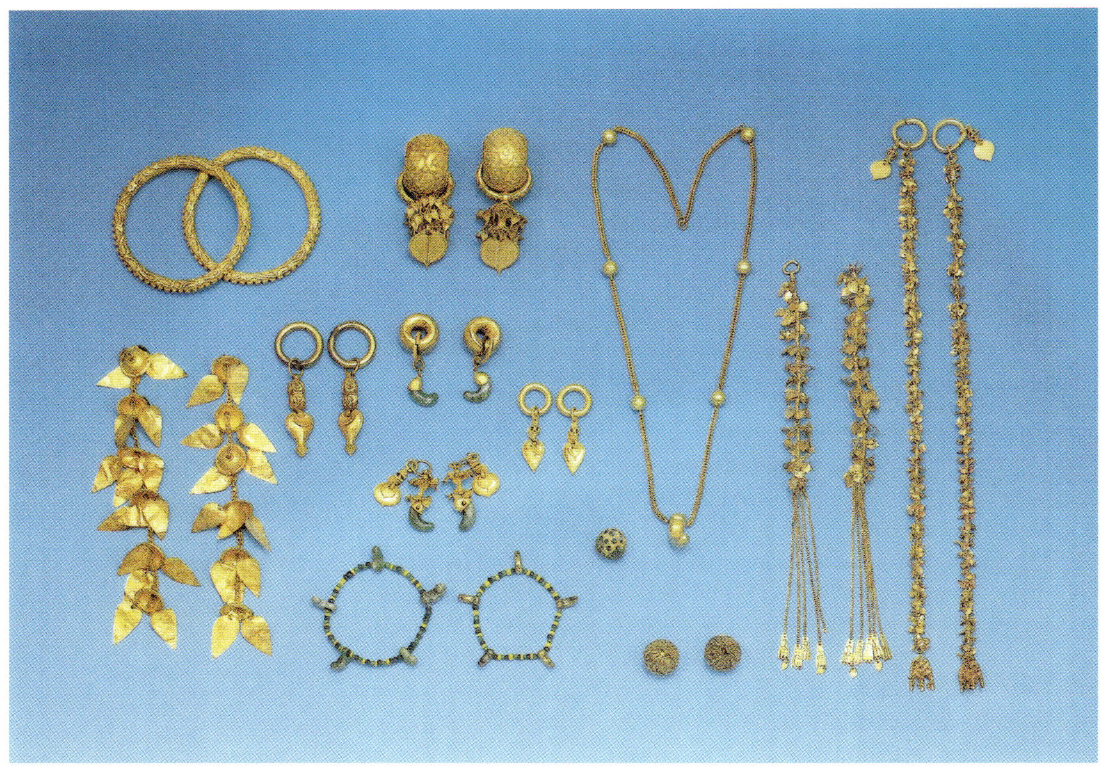

Figure 5.1 Gold earrings, bracelets, necklaces excavated from Kyŏngju. Silla, fifth-sixth century. Length of the earring on the right side: 34cm. Courtesy of the National Museum of Korea.

treasures and everyday objects for the deceased to be used in their afterlife. In the early twentieth century, Japanese archaeologists excavated ancient Silla tombs and found large quantities of gold objects, including jewelry. This archaeological revelation took the world by surprise, as no similar gold objects had been previously found in East Asia (fig. 5.1).

Since that time, Korean and Japanese scholars have investigated the origin and characteristics of ancient Silla's gold culture. Scholarly opinion held that the latter originated in the northern Asian culture that sprang from the nomadic people of the Eurasian steppes, owing to the similarity of the Silla tomb structures to those of northern Siberian kurgans.[2] From the viewpoint of material culture, it is possible that the gold jewelry and glass techniques of ancient Silla had been influenced by external elements. However, because of its distinctive style, some scholars equally maintain that the gold artistry was original to Silla culture and does not indicate outside influence.[3]

Here I suggest an alternative vision, one that posits that the gold culture of ancient Silla developed within the territory of Silla, having been influenced by the cultures of both northern Eurasia and the South Sea.[4] Early Korean historical documents indicate that people from the South Sea came to the southern part of the Korean peninsula by ship, and cultural similarities between Silla and certain South Asian maritime regions can still be identified, especially in the use of thick gold earrings and wide beaded necklaces.

---

[2] Egami Namio proposed a theory of the northern origin of ancient Silla culture in the late 1940s. He insisted that horse riders from the north advanced to the southern part of the Korean peninsula and conquered it. Egami Namio 江上波夫, *Kiba minzoku kokka: Nihon kodaishi e no apurōchi* 騎馬民族国家: 日本古代史へのアプロ ーチ [Nation of horse-rider people: Approach to Japanese ancient history] (Tokyo: Chūō Kōronsha, 1967). This "Horse-riding Theory" was later denied by many Korean and Japanese scholars because of the colonial viewpoint it presented and the relative lack of supporting material evidence. Although Egami Namio's theory has been rejected, many Korean scholars have observed and discussed a certain degree of similarities between the visual culture of ancient Silla and northern nomadic peoples. Ch'oe Pyŏnghyŏn, for example, remains open to the possibility of the migration of some nomadic tribes from northern Asia. Ch'oe Pyŏnghyŏn 崔秉鉉, *Silla kobun yŏn'gu* 新羅古墳研究 [Research on Silla tombs] (Seoul: Ilchisa, 1992). Kang Pongwŏn recently argued against these theories. Kang Pongwŏn 강봉원, "Sillasa yŏn'gu e issŏsŏ 'Kima minjok iron' ŭi chaego: tŭngja mit chaegal ŭl chungsim ŭro" 신라사 연구에 있어서 '기마민족 이론'의 재고 – 등자 및 재갈을 중심으로 [A critical reexamination of "Horse-rider Theory" in the study of Silla history: Focusing on stirrups and bits], *Chungang Asia yŏn'gu* 中央亞細亞研究 15 (December 2010): 111-135.

[3] Im Chaehae 임재해, *Silla kŭmgwan ŭi kiwŏn ŭl palk'inda* 신라금관의 기원을 밝힌다 [Illuminating the origin of Silla gold crown] (Seoul: Chisik Sanŏpsa, 2008).

[4] Kim Pyŏngmo first pointed out the cultural relationship between ancient Korea and parts of Southeast Asia based on conceptual similarities in their legends, an example being the claim that the primordial ancestor of their tribe was hatched from an egg. He also argued for the first time that these two cultures, from North Asia and from Southeast Asia, met on the territory claimed by ancient Silla and contributed to its cultural formation. Kim Pyŏngmo 金秉模, *Kŭmgwan ŭi pimil* 금관의 비밀 [Secrets of the gold crown] (Seoul: P'urŭn Yŏksa, 1998): 148-149.

The Legendary Land of Gold and Ancient Silla

In the early twentieth century, the Hungarian ethnographer Baráthosi-Balogh Benedek (1870-1945) wrote that a legendary Land of Gold thought to have been located in some unknown part of the Eurasian continent might have been in Korea.[5] He visited Korea twice, first in 1907 and then later in the early 1920s during the Japanese colonial period. He wrote about the spread of the rumor originating in the late nineteenth century that the "legendary land of gold in Asia" is located in "Korea," after which many Europeans, including a certain German Prince, came to Korea to acquire the rights to mine for gold.[6] Baráthosi-Balogh encountered more than fifty flourishing gold mines scattered around Korean rivers and mountains. According to him, many foreigners wanted to participate in the quest for gold hidden in Korea, but the Japanese colonial authorities secretly controlled the production of gold in Korea. They were eager to find new gold mines, but at that time the gold mining system in Korea was in a very bad condition and the gold of inferior grade.[7]

Early Japanese historical documents describe Silla as a country of glittering gold. In the eighth year of Chūai Tennō 仲哀天皇 (?-200), the ruler of Japan desired to conquer Silla because of its reputation as a land of gold and silver. After his death the next year, his wife Empress Jingū 神功 (ca. 169-269) invaded the territory of Silla.[8]

In addition to the Japanese record, many medieval Arab geographers wrote of Silla as a land of gold. In the ninth century, the Arab geographer Ibn Khurradādhbih (Ibn Khordadbeh, ca. 820-912) wrote that beyond China and across from Kānsū were many mountains and many kings in the land of al-Shîla where there was much gold.[9] In the early twelfth century,

---

[5] Pŏrat'osi Pŏllogŭ Penedek'ŭ (Baráthosi-Balogh Benedek) 버라토시 벌로그 베네데크, *K'oria, choyonghan ach'im ŭi nara* 코리아, 조용한 아침의 나라 [Korea, a nation of morning calm], trans. Ch'omŏ Mose (Csoma Mózes) 초머 모세 (Seoul: Chimmundang, 2005). This book was originally written in Hungarian as *Korea, a hajnalpír országa*, and published in Budapest in 1929. However, here I use the Korean translation.

[6] Baráthosi Balogh Benedek, *K'oria, choyonghan ach'im ŭi nara*, 30-31.

[7] Baráthosi Balogh Benedek, *K'oria, choyonghan ach'im ŭi nara*, 119-123.

[8] *Nihon shoki* 日本書紀 8, Chūai Tennō 仲哀天皇 8.9.5; Kojima Noriyuki 小島憲之 et al. ed., *Nihon shoki* 日本書紀 [The chronicles of Japan] (Tokyo: Shōgakkan, 1998) [hereafter Shōgakkan *Nihon shoki*], 1:410. Also see *Nihon shoki* 9, Jingū Kōgō 神功皇后 9.10.3; Shōgakkan *Nihon shoki*, 1:428-430.

[9] Ibn Khurradādhbih, *Kitab al-Masalik wa'l-mamalik* (Leiden: Brill, 1888): 70;

Al-Idrīsī (1099-1165 or 1166) wrote that many travelers from the west settled in Silla because the territory was very rich due to its abundance of gold.[10] Ibn Khurradādhbih's records of Silla's gold represent the earliest introduction of Korea to the Western world.

The credibility of these accounts by medieval Arab geographers was not verified until the autumn of 1921, when the Gold Crown Tomb (Kŭmgwanch'ong 金冠塚) in Kyŏngju was accidentally discovered.[11] After its excavation, Japanese archaeologists began to excavate the great tomb mounds in Kyŏngju. They discovered many gold artifacts, including jewelry, in the ancient tombs, finally proving that the forgotten legend of Korea as a country of gold was true.

Ancient Silla was located in the southeastern part of the Korean peninsula, and most of its gold artifacts were discovered at its capital in present-day Kyŏngju, which dated from the late fourth century to the late sixth century. Before the excavation of the Gold Crown Tomb, no one had firsthand knowledge of the splendid gold culture of ancient Silla. The gold crown found in the tomb has a unique form and style (fig. 5.2). No similar gold crown of that style or period has been found in China or Japan.

Gold crowns and earrings excavated from ancient Silla tombs are masterpieces of early Korean art, but they still await a more sophisticated understanding by Western academia.[12] In this chapter I attempt to explore these

---

M. Hartman et al., *The Encyclopaedia of Islam*, 2nd edition (Leiden: Brill, 1960): 1:842A, quoted from Muhammadŭ Kkansu 무함마드 깐수 (Mohammad Kanso), *Silla sŏyŏk kyoryusa* 신라 서역교류사 [The history of cultural exchange between Silla and the Western Regions] (Seoul: Tan'guk Taehakkyo Ch'ulp'anbu, 1992): 183.

[10] Al Idrīsī, *Nuzhat at-mushtāq fī ikhtirāq al-āfāq*, 92, quoted from Muhammadŭ Kkansu 무함마드 깐수 (Mohammad Kanso), *Silla sŏyŏk kyoryusa* 신라 서역교류사 [The history of cultural exchange between Silla and the Western Regions] (Seoul: Tan'guk Taehakkyo Ch'ulp'anbu, 1992): 193. According to Kanso, other Arabian geographers, such as al-Maqdisī and Ibn Said, wrote about Silla's gold. See *Silla sŏyŏk kyoryusa*, 133-208; Lee Hee-Soo, "Early Korea-Arabic Maritime Relations Based on Muslim Sources," *Korea Journal* 31, no. 2 (1991): 21-32.

[11] Hamada Kōsaku 濱田耕作 and Umehara Sueji 梅原末治, *Keishū Kinkanzuka to sono ihō* 慶州金冠塚と其遺寶 [The Gold Crown Tomb at Kyŏngju and its treasures], 2 vols. (Keijō [Seoul]: Chōsen Sōtokufu, 1924-1927).

[12] Recently a book on the gold crowns of Silla was published for the first time in English, with many good photos of ancient Silla's gold crafts. Lee Hansang, ed., *Gold Crowns of Silla: Treasures from a Brilliant Age*, trans. Lee Junghee (Seoul: Korea Foundation, 2010).

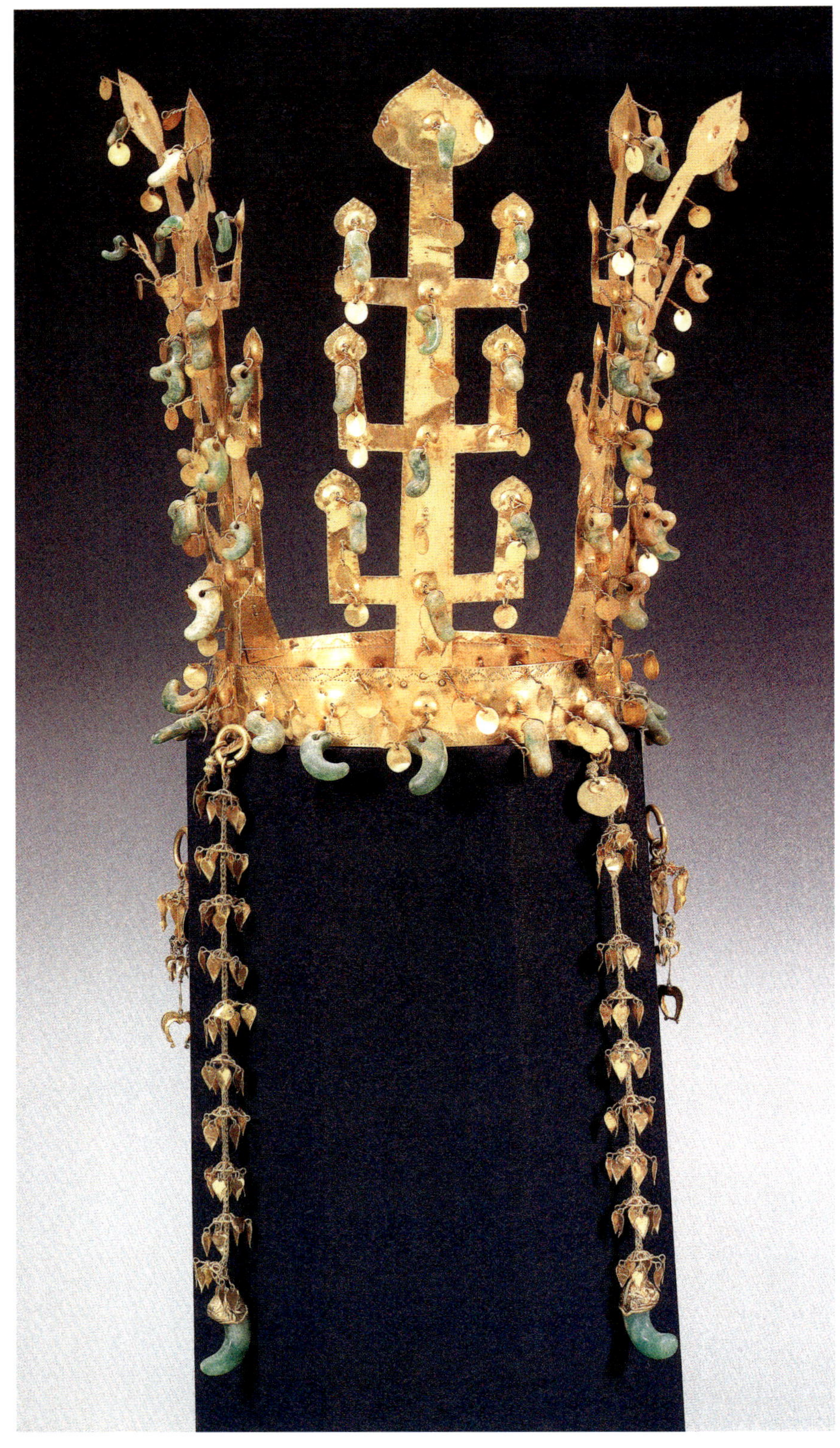

Figure 5.2 Gold crown, excavated from the Gold Crown Tomb, Kyŏngju. Silla, fifth-sixth century. H. 44.4cm. National Treasure No. 87. National Museum of Korea. Courtesy of the Gyeongju National Museum.

gold masterpieces and their implications. I argue that the creation of the idiosyncratic style of gold jewelry in ancient Silla, which has puzzled many scholars, was possible due to the syncretism of northern Asian nomadic cultures and South Asian maritime cultures. In the late fourth century, the two main trade routes of the Eurasian continent from the North and the South met in Kyŏngju, the remote southeastern corner of the Korean peninsula. The legend of the golden country started here.

Brief History of the Excavations of the Ancient Silla Tombs

Japanese scholars conducted the first excavation of tombs of ancient Silla in 1906, but all they found were earthenware and a variety of small items.[13] In 1909, they found a small amount of gold jewelry in the Kŭmch'ŏng-ni 金尺里 Tombs of the ancient Silla period,[14] but they had not yet recognized the peculiar structure of ancient Silla tombs and their hidden treasures. Before the excavation of the Gold Crown Tomb, more than six tombs of ancient Silla were excavated, but nothing was found but gold earrings.[15]

In 1921, the Gold Crown Tomb was discovered during the repair of a private house in Kyŏngju and was then excavated by Japanese archaeologists.[16]

---

[13] Imanishi Ryū 今西龍, "Shiragi kyūto Keishū fukin no kofun" 新羅舊都慶州附近の古墳 [Ancient tombs near Kyŏngju, the old capital of Silla], *Rekishi chiri* 歷史地理 11, no. 1 (1908): 130.

[14] Yatsui Seiichi 谷井濟一, "Kankoku Keishū Seigaku no ichi kofun ni tsuite" 韓國慶州西岳の一古墳に就いて [Regarding an old tomb of Sŏang-ni, in Kyŏngju, Korea], *Kōkokai* 考古界 8, no. 12 (1910): 495-501.

[15] For the historiography of the excavations of ancient Silla tombs in Kyŏngju, see Pak Yŏngbok 朴永福, "Silla kobun palgulsa: Kyŏngju chiyŏk ŭl chungsim ŭro" 新羅古墳發掘史—慶州地域을 中心으로 [Historiography of Silla tomb excavation: Focusing on the Kyŏngju region], in *Silla hwanggŭm: sinbi han hwanggŭm ŭi nara* 新羅黃金: 신비한 황금의 나라 [Silla gold: The country of marvelous gold], ed. Kungnip Kyŏngju Pangmulgwan 國立慶州博物館 [Gyeongju National Museum] (Seoul: Kungnip Kyŏngju Pangmulgwan, 2001): 294-304; Ch'a Sunch'ŏl 차순철, "Ilche kangjŏmgi ŭi Silla kobun chosa yŏn'gu e taehan kŏmt'o" 일제강점기의 신라 고분조사연구에 대한 검토 [Examination of the Japanese colonial period's investigation and research of Silla tumuli], *Munhwajae* 文化財 39 (2006): 95-130; Kungnip Kyŏngju Munhwajae Yŏn'guso 國立慶州文化財研究所 [Kyŏngju National Research Institute of Cultural Heritage], ed., *Silla kobun kich'o haksul chosa yŏn'gu I: yŏn'gu pogosŏ* 新羅古墳 基礎學術調查研究 I—研究報告書 [Basic academic investigation research on Silla tumulus I: Research report] (Kyŏngju: Kungnip Kyŏngju Munhwajae Yŏn'guso, 2007): 63-81.

[16] Hamada Kōsaku and Umehara Sueji, *Keishū Kinkanzuka to sono ihō.*

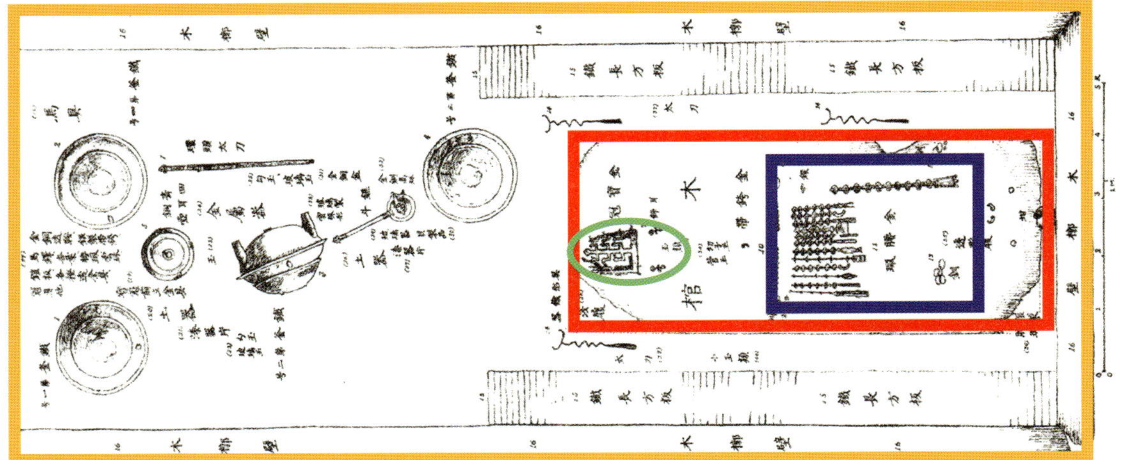

Figure 5.3 Plan of the Gold Crown Tomb. Courtesy of the author.

Yellow box: Wooden Chamber
Red box: Coffin
Green oval: Gold Crown
Blue box: Gold Belt

The tomb contained the remains of a man wearing a gold crown, gold earrings, gold bracelets, and gold rings (fig. 5.3). A large gold belt encircled his waist. More than two thousand artifacts made of gold, silver, gilt bronze, glass, and earthenware were discovered in the tomb. Although this was not an academic excavation, it revealed for the first time the structure of ancient Silla tombs, which I explain below.

After this initial excavation, Japanese archaeologists excavated more than twenty tombs and continued their search for other golden treasures.[17] Despite their ostensible academic purpose, some excavations were carried out merely as treasure hunts and even lacked subsequent excavation reports. Regardless, through those excavations archaeologists came to understand the unique tomb structure of ancient Silla, which is referred to as the "stone-piled wooden-chamber tomb" or "stone-surrounded wooden chamber tomb" (*chŏksŏk mokkwakpun* 積石木槨墳). These excavations yielded

---

[17] Kungnip Kyŏngju Munhwajae Yŏn'guso, *Silla kobun kich'o haksul chosa yŏn'gu I*, 68-69, table 15.

250

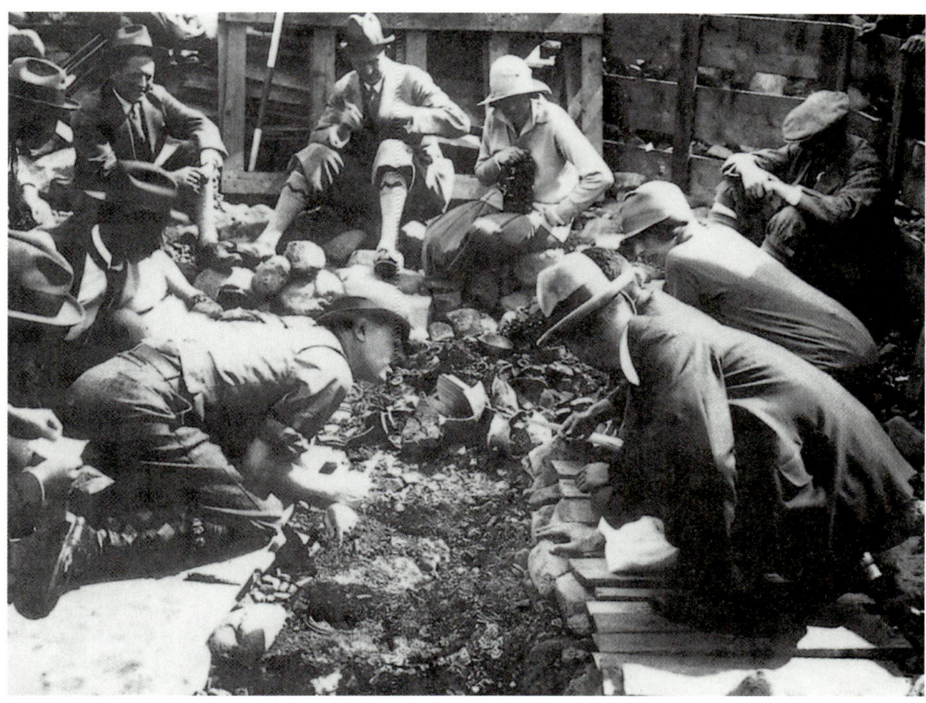

Figure 5.4 Prince Gustav and Japanese archaeologists excavating the Auspicious Phoenix Tomb, 1927. Courtesy of the Gyeongju National Museum.

many gold artifacts, including three gold crowns: one each from the Gold Crown Tomb, the Gold Bell Tomb (Kŭmnyŏngch'ong 金鈴塚), and the Auspicious Phoenix Tomb (Sŏbongch'ong 瑞鳳塚).

Among these activities, the excavation of the Auspicious Phoenix Tomb in 1926 became a well-publicized event due to the participation of Prince Gustav Adolf, later King Gustav VI of Sweden, who was an amateur archaeologist (fig. 5.4).[18] In honor of the prince's participation, the Japanese included the character *sŏ* 瑞 (or *zui* in Japanese), meaning auspicious, in the designated name of this tomb, as this character was part of the name then used for Sweden (Sŏjŏn 瑞典). This suggests that the Japanese government in Korea manipulated the archaeological excavation for

---

[18] Koizumi Akio 小泉顯夫, "Keishu Zuihōzuka no hakkutsu" 慶州瑞鳳塚の發掘 [The excavation of the Auspicious Phoenix Tomb], *Shigaku zasshi* 史學雜誌 38, no. 1 (1927): 75-83.

251

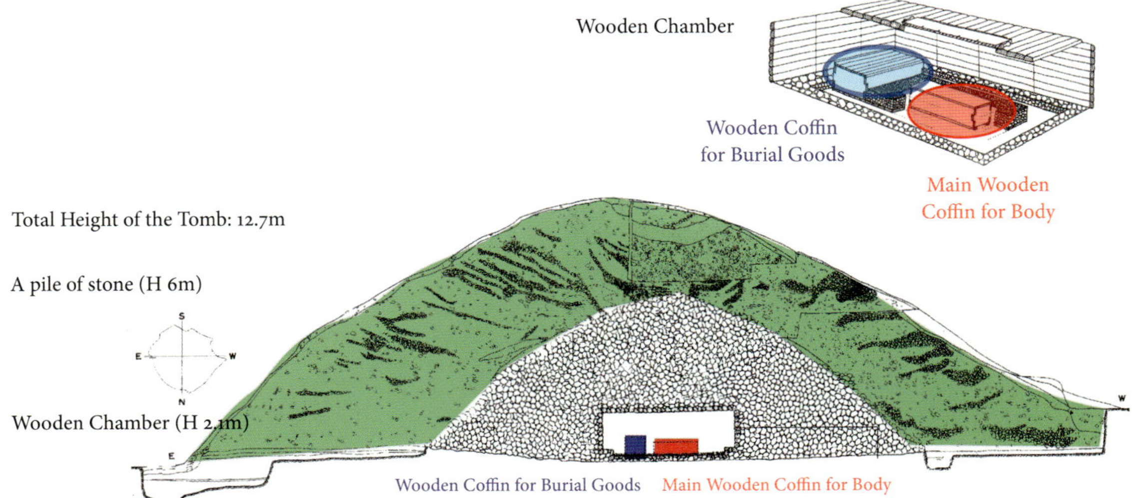

*Figure 5.5 Cross section and projection of the Heavenly
Horse Tomb, Kyŏngju. Courtesy of the author.*

propaganda purposes. Not surprisingly, the full report for this excavation
has never been published.

Although Korea gained independence in 1945, the excavation of the
tombs of ancient Silla did not fully resume until the 1970s, as part of a
government-led economic development plan. Since the founding of the
Republic of Korea, over three hundred and eighty tombs have officially
been excavated.[19] Two additional gold crowns were discovered, one at the
Heavenly Horse Tomb (Ch'ŏnmach'ong 天馬塚) and the other at the north
mound of the Great Tomb at Hwangnam (Hwangnam taech'ong pukpun
皇南大塚 北墳). The excavations of these two tombs were conducted by
Korean archaeologists, but they were also manipulated as political propaganda by President Park Chung-hee (Pak Chŏnghŭi 朴正熙, 1917-1979),
who used them to present traditional Korean culture to the world.[20] Nev-

---

[19] Kungnip Kyŏngju Munhwajae Yŏn'guso, *Silla kobun kich'o haksul chosa yŏn'gu
I*, 74-81, table 18.

[20] Han'guk Chŏngch'i Yŏn'guhoe 한국정치연구회 [Korean Politics Research
Association], ed., *Pak Chŏnghŭi rŭl nŏmŏsŏ: Pak Chŏng-hŭi wa kŭ sidae e taehan*

ertheless, these modern excavations shed new light on the study of ancient Silla culture and history.

The Heavenly Horse Tomb was excavated in 1973 by the archaeologists of the National Research Institute of Cultural Heritage (Kungnip Munhwajae Yŏn'guso 國立文化財研究所).[21] Its structure was a typical stone-piled wooden-chamber tomb (fig. 5.5). Its occupant was a man with a gold crown and a decorative iron sword. The wooden coffin holding his body was located in the center of the tomb, while another small wooden coffin with many valuables was placed at the head of the main coffin. These two wooden coffins were buried inside a larger wooden chamber with a large quantity of stones piled up around the exterior of the chamber. The height of the wooden chamber is estimated to be 2.1 meters, and the height of the stone piles at more than six meters. Earth was piled atop the stone piles, which reached a total height of approximately 12.7 meters.

More than eleven thousand artifacts were found in this tomb alone, including gold jewelry. The tomb occupant wore a gold crown, a pair of gold earrings, and a set of gold belts with hanging pendants (fig. 5.6). On his chest rested a long, broad necklace made of gold and glass beads, and on his fingers were ten gold rings. He also wore two pairs of bracelets made of gold and silver. On his left side, he had a large sword decorated with thin gold plates. Given these rich burial goods, he is presumed to have been a member of the royal family of ancient Silla who lived during the early sixth century.

The Great Tomb at Hwangnam consists of two large adjoining mounds (fig. 5.7), which had been thought, prior to the excavation, to contain a single grave. However, the National Research Institute of Cultural Heritage discovered two graves inside the tomb in 1973. The south mound held the body of an elderly man wearing a gilt-bronze crown,[22] and the north mound

---

pip'anjŏk yŏn'gu 박정희를 넘어서: 박정희와 그 시대에 대한 비판적 연구 [Beyond Park Chung-hee: Critical research on Park Chung-hee and his era] (Seoul: P'urŭn Sup, 1998): 90.

[21] Munhwajae Kwalliguk 文化財管理局 [The Office of Cultural Properties], ed., *Chŏnmach'ong* 천마총 [Heavenly Horse Tomb] (Seoul: Munhwajae Kwalliguk, 1974).

[22] Kungnip Kyŏngju Munhwajae Yŏn'guso 國立慶州文化財研究所 [Kyŏngju National Research Institute of Cultural Heritage], ed., *Hwangnam Taech'ong: Kyŏngju-si Hwangnam-dong che 98-ho kobun: nambun palgul chosa pogosŏ* 皇南大塚—慶州市皇南洞第98號古墳: 南墳發掘調查報告書 [Great Tomb at Hwangnam: Tomb No. 98 in Hwangnam-dong, Kyŏngju city: Excavation report on the south mound], 2 vols. (Seoul: Munhwajae Kwalliguk, Munhwajae Yŏn'guso, 1994).

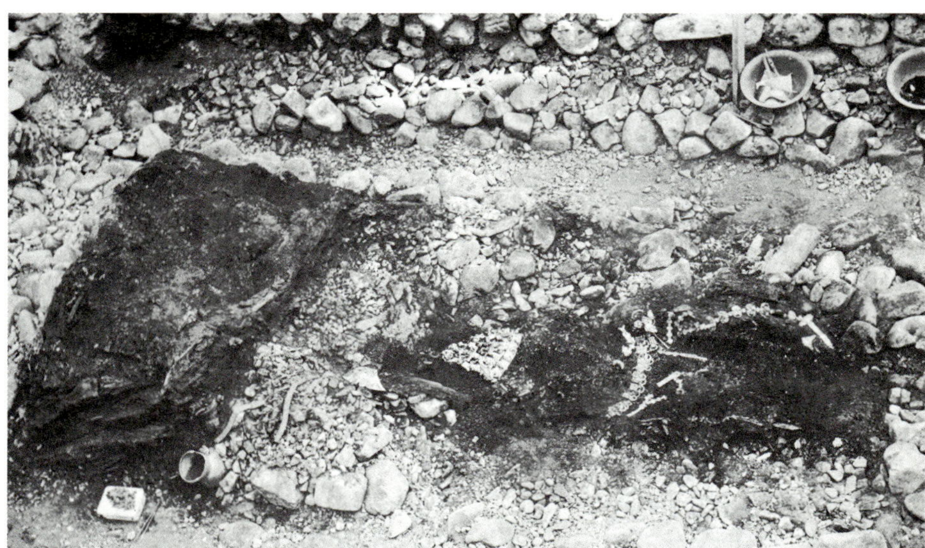

*Figure 5.6
Main coffin
burial with
gold crown and
other jewelry in
situ during ex-
cavation of the
Heavenly Horse
Tomb, Kyŏngju.
Courtesy of
the Gyeongju
Research Insti-
tute of Cultural
Heritage.*

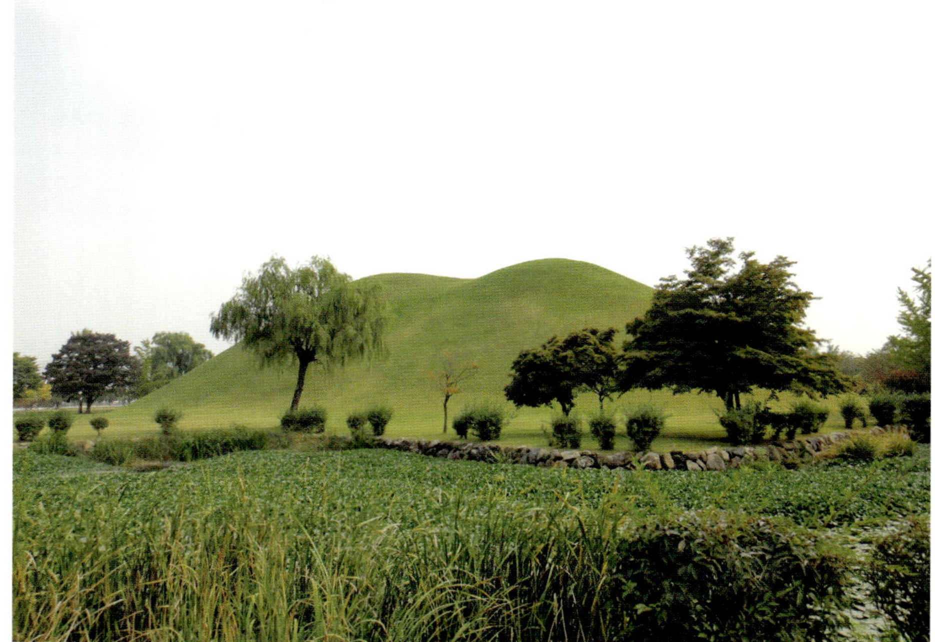

*Figure 5.7 The
Great Tomb
at Hwangnam,
Kyŏngju. Silla,
fourth-fifth cen-
tury. Courtesy of
the author.*

254

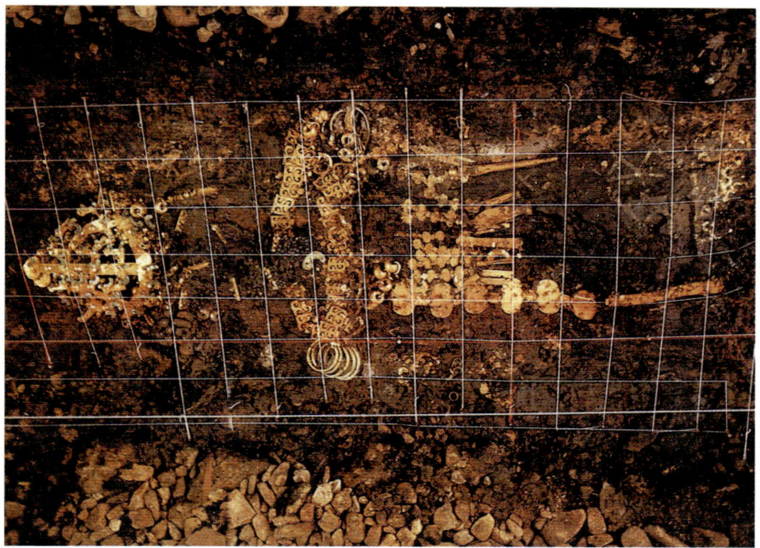

*Figure 5.8 Main coffin burial with gold crown and other jewelry in situ during
excavation of the north mound of the Great Tomb at Hwangnam, Kyŏngju.
Courtesy of the Gyeongju Research Institute of Cultural Heritage.*

held a woman with a gold crown.[23] This suggests that this Great Tomb
was built for a royal couple. Researchers believe that the man in the south
mound was a king and that his younger wife, buried in the north mound,
died after her husband. The graves are in the style of a stone-piled wooden-
chamber tomb. In the north mound, more than twenty-two thousand valuables were buried. In the south mound, more than thirty-five thousand
pieces were found.[24]

---

[23] Munhwajae Yŏn'guso 文化財研究所 [National Research Institute of Cultural
Heritage], ed., *Hwangnam Taech'ong: Kyŏngju-si Hwangnam-dong che 98-ho kobun:
Pukpun palgul chosa pogosŏ* 皇南大塚—慶州市皇南洞第98號古墳: 北墳發掘調查報
告書 [Great Tomb at Hwangnam: Tomb No. 98 in Hwangnam-dong, Kyŏngju city:
Excavation report on the north mound] (Seoul: Munhwajae Kwalliguk, Munhwa-
jae Yŏn'guso, 1985).

[24] In 2010, the National Museum of Korea held a special exhibition on the
Great Tomb at Hwangnam for the first time after its excavation. Three articles discussing controversial issues appear in the exhibition catalogue on the occupant and

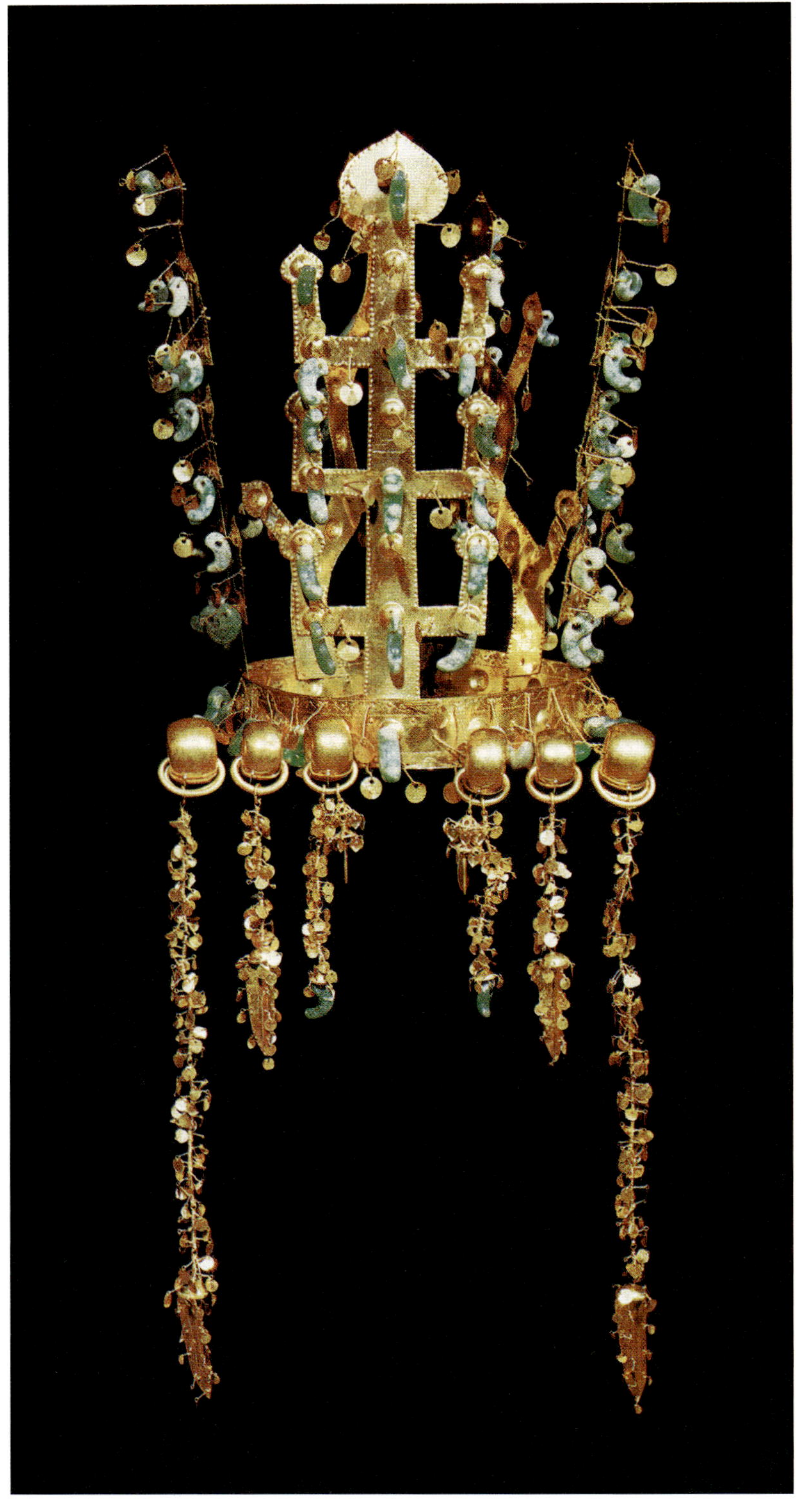

Figure 5.9 Gold crown, excavated from the north mound of the Great Tomb at Hwangnam, Kyŏngju. Silla, fourth-fifth century. H. 27.5cm. National Treasure No. 191. Courtesy of the National Museum of Korea.

The royal couple wore the same style of gold jewelry, but the woman was decorated more extravagantly, with a full set of gold jewelry (fig. 5.8), while the man wore only a set of gilt bronze and gold. The woman's most important piece of jewelry was a gold crown with six pendants (fig. 5.9). She wore a pair of gold earrings, and a long, broad necklace made of gold and glass beads lay on her chest. She wore a gold belt with many decorative pendants, eleven gold bracelets, and twelve gold rings. Her husband wore a gilt-bronze crown and other jewelry and a sword lay by his left side.

Here we encounter an enigma: Why did the queen, rather than the king, wear the gold crown and have more gold? To answer this question, we must first understand the origin of the gold crown and its meanings.

The Origin of the Gold Crown in Ancient Silla

Once the first gold crown was excavated, many scholars probed its origin and iconography.[25] Most agreed that the origin of the gold crown must be related to northern Eurasian nomadic culture. Many noted the similarity between the gold crown of Silla and the Sarmatian gold crown from southern Siberia, or the gold crown from Afghanistan,[26] because they share iconographical similarities, such as the incorporation of symbols derived from the worship of sacred trees, birds, or deer.

To date, six gold crowns have been recovered from tombs of ancient Silla (table 5.1). Five of these crowns were excavated by archaeologists, but the Kyo-dong 校洞 crown was looted by treasure hunters and then recovered by police and turned over to the Gyeongju National Museum (Kungnip Kyŏngju Pangmulgwan 國立慶州博物館).

---

chronology of the tomb, written from different viewpoints. Kungnip Chungang Pangmulgwan 國立中央博物館 [National Museum of Korea], ed., *Hwangnam Taech'ong: hwanggŭm ŭi nara Silla ŭi wangnŭng* 황남대총: 황금의 나라 신라의 왕릉 [The Great Tomb at Hwangnam: The country of gold, the royal tombs of Silla] (Seoul: Kungnip Chungang Pangmulgwan, 2010).

[25] Many publications about the Silla gold crown have been written in Korean, but few publications have appeared in English. In a recently published book, two articles addressing this topic appeared in English. See Lee Hansang, "The Gold Culture and the Gold Crowns of Silla," in *Gold Crowns of Silla*, 106-119; Sarah Milledge Nelson, "Origin, Characteristics, and Significance of Silla Gold Crowns," in *Gold Crowns of Silla*, 134-144.

[26] Lee Hansang, "The Gold Culture and the Gold Crowns of Silla," 114; Sarah Milledge Nelson, "Origin, Characteristics, and Significance of Silla Gold Crowns," 135.

Table 5.1
Gold Crowns of Ancient Silla.

	Excavation site	Excavation year	Repository	Height (cm)	Diameter (cm)	Stem	Decoration	Pendant
1	Kyŏngju Kyo-dong ruined tomb	unknown	Gyeongju National Museum	12.8	14	3 of tree shape (1 branch)	Gold leaves	uncertain
2	North mound of the Great Tomb at Hwangnam	1973	National Museum of Korea	27.3	17	3 of tree shape (each with 3 branches) + 2 of antler shape	Gold leaves + *kogok* (curved jadeite beads)	3 pairs of thick type
3	Gold Crown Tomb	1921	National Museum of Korea	27.5	19	3 of tree shape (each with 3 branches) + 2 of antler shape	Gold leaves + *kogok*	1 pair of thin type
4	Auspicious Phoenix Tomb	1926	National Museum of Korea	30.7	18.4	3 of tree shape (each with 3 branches) + 2 of antler shape	Gold leaves + *kogok* + phoenixes	1 pair of thick type
5	Gold Bell Tomb	1924	National Museum of Korea	27	15	3 of tree shape (each with 4 branches) + 2 of antler shape	Gold leaves + *kogok*	1 pair of thin type
6	Heavenly Horse Tomb	1973	Gyeongju National Museum	32.5	20	3 of tree shape (each with 4 branches) + 2 of antler shape	Gold leaves + *kogok*	1 pair of thin type

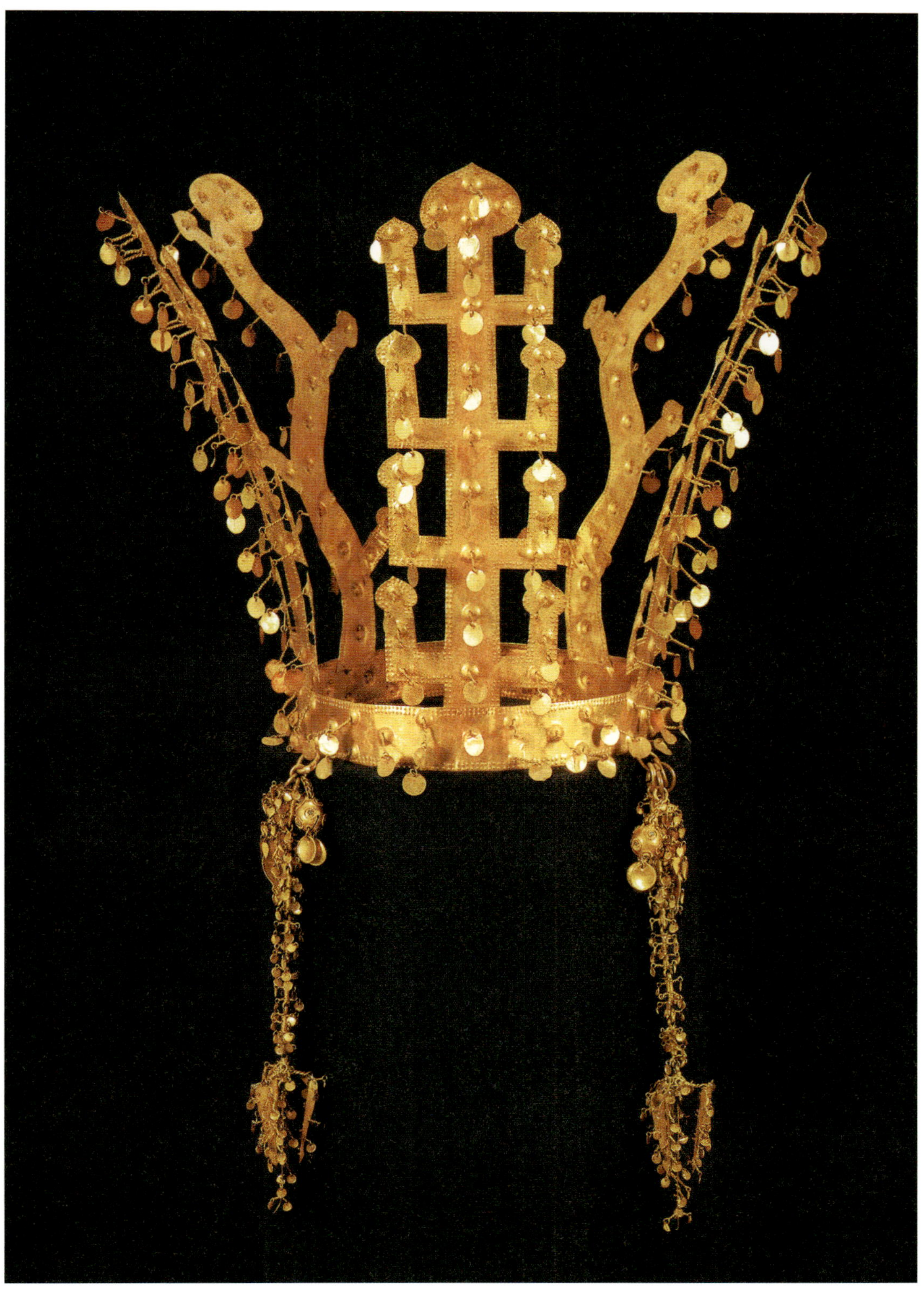

Figure 5.10 Gold crown, excavated from the Gold Bell Tomb, Kyŏngju. Silla, fifth-sixth century. H. 27cm. Treasure No. 338. National Museum of Korea. Courtesy of the Gyeongju National Museum.

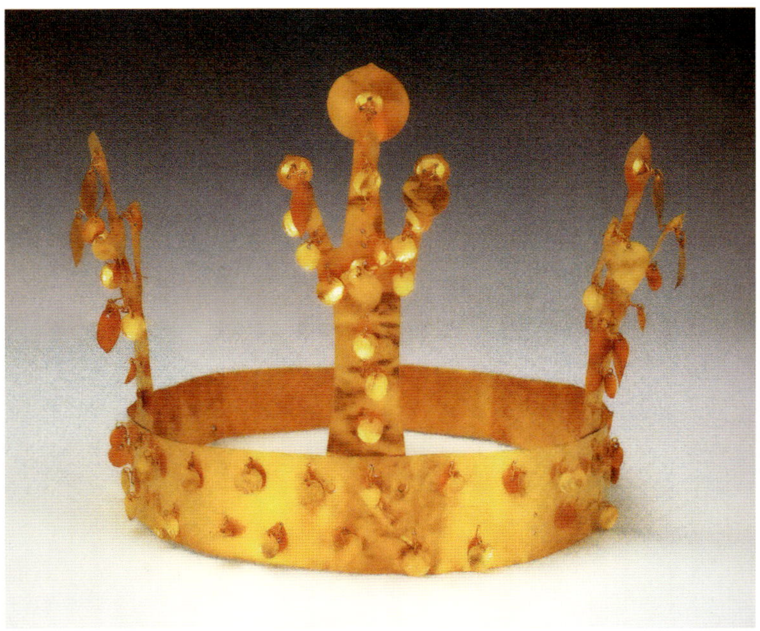

*Figure 5.11 Gold crown, excavated from a ruined tomb at Kyo-dong,
Kyŏngju. Silla, fourth-fifth century. H. 12.8cm. National Museum of
Korea. Courtesy of the Gyeongju National Museum.*

The Kyo-dong crown's shape differs slightly from those of the other five,
which share a similar shape. A round strip encircles the head, and five decorative upright stems are attached to the strip (figs. 5.2, 5.9, 5.10). Three of
the stems are shaped like a simplified and stylized tree, with three or four
pairs of angulated branches; the other two are shaped like deer antlers. All
the stems and the main strip are decorated with gold spangles in the shape
of tree leaves and green curved jadeite beads (Kr. *kogok* 曲玉), making the
crown glittery and extravagant. In addition, there is a pair of long decorative pendants hanging from the main strip, with a shape similar to that of
gold earrings recovered from the tomb.

Such a style of crown is unique to ancient Silla, and has not been found
in examples from contemporary China or other countries. Even in Koguryŏ,
another kingdom of ancient Korea, no similar crown has been found. Given

260

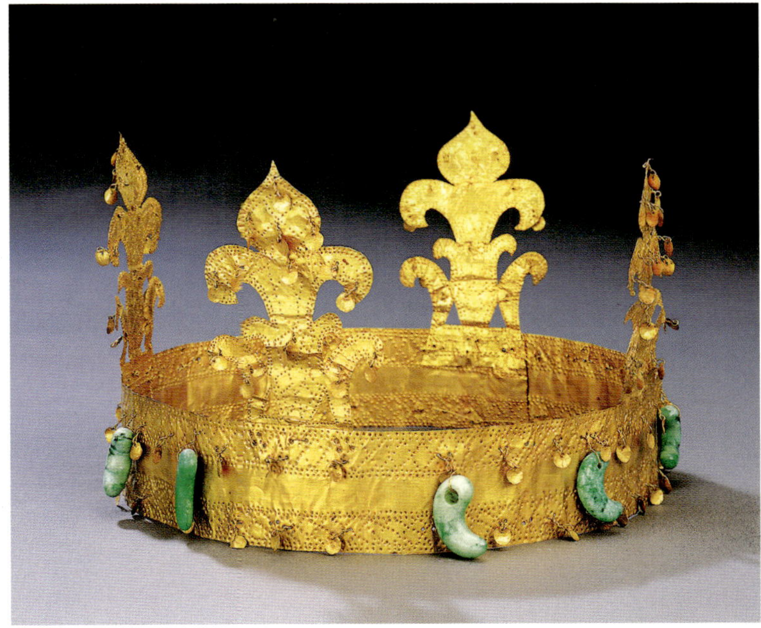

*Figure 5.12 Gold crown, excavated from an unknown tomb of Kaya. Kaya,
fifth-sixth century. H. 11.5cm. National Treasure No. 138. Courtesy of the
Leeum, Samsung Museum of Art, Korea.*

the quantity of excavated gilt-bronze crowns from all parts of its territory,
this style seems to have been prevalent in ancient Silla.

Among gold crowns of ancient Silla, the Kyo-dong crown has its
own unique style, as it is composed of one main strip and three decorative stems (fig. 5.11). Unlike other typical stems of Silla gold crowns, each
stem of the Kyo-dong crown looks like a small tree with leaves. Considering the shape of the stems, this crown more closely reflects the realistic features of Kaya crowns than the stylized features of other Silla gold
crowns. The gold crown of Kaya in the collection of the Samsung Art
Museum has one main strip and four stems resembling a tree, with decorative curved lines (fig. 5.12). A similar shape is found in the gilt-bronze
crown (fig. 5.13) excavated from Tomb 11 of the Pokch'ŏn-dong 福泉洞

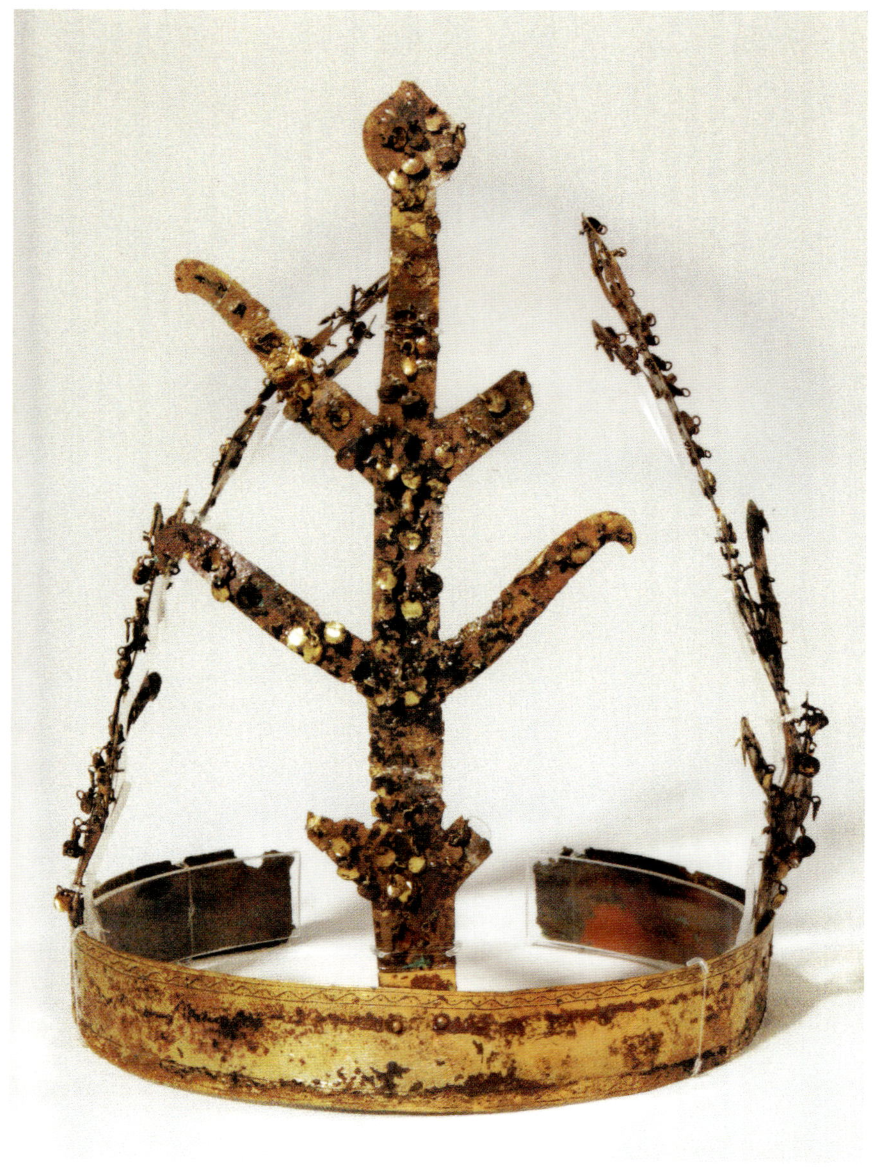

*Figure 5.13 Gilt-bronze crown, excavated from Tomb 11 at Pokch̆on-dong, Pusan.
Kaya, fifth-sixth century. H. 21.9cm. Courtesy of the Gimhae National Museum.*

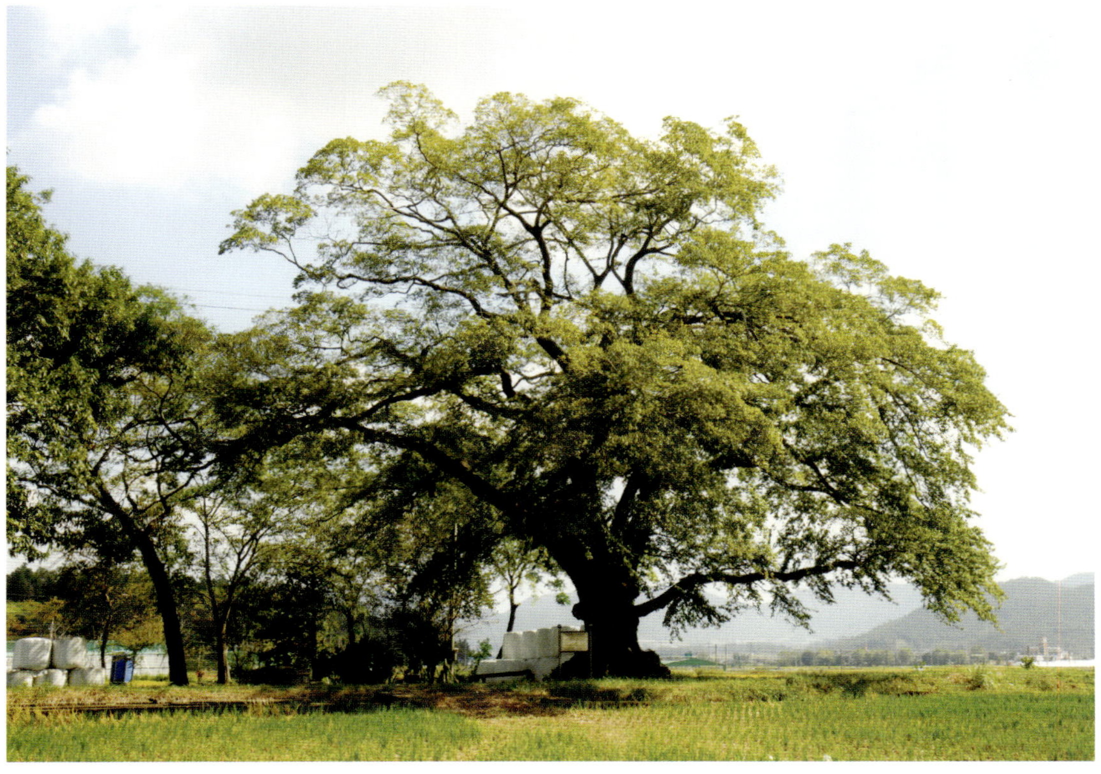

Figure 5.14 Aphananthe aspera *over 400 years old. H. 18m. Natural Monument No. 268.
Yongsan-myŏn* 蓉山面, *Changhŭng-gun* 長興郡, *Chŏlla Province, Korea. Courtesy of the author.*

cemetery in Pusan, which dates to the Kaya period.[27] This formal affinity
of the crowns of ancient Silla and Kaya may have originated from similar
religious worship of a sacred tree.

According to myth, worship of the sacred tree in early Korea began in
the time of the legendary figure Tan'gun Wanggŏm 檀君王儉. The myth

---

[27] On the excavation of this crown, see Chŏng Chingwŏn 鄭澄元 and Sin
Kyŏngch'ŏl 申敬澈, *Tongnae Pokch'ŏn-dong kobun'gun* 東萊福泉洞古墳群 [Ancient
tombs at Pokch'ŏn-dong, Tongnae], vol. 2 (Pusan: Pusan Taehakkyo Pangmulgwan,
1983): 125-127.

states that Tan'gun's father, Hwanung 桓雄, descended from heaven to the sacred tree, called the *Sindansu* 神檀樹, and ruled the human world from beneath this tree.[28] The worship of the sacred tree became widespread in northeastern Asia and throughout the Korean peninsula. In Korea, the old tradition of sacred tree worship is still practiced in many rural communities (fig. 5.14). Because an old tree near the entrance or the center of a village was believed to contain sacred power to protect the village, the people of the village held annual rituals in veneration of the tree.

In the early Three Han (Samhan 三韓, ca. 1-300 C.E.) period, each town had a sacred place called a *sodo* 蘇塗, where a tribal chief performed annual rituals. At the center of the *sodo*, there always stood a sacred tree with hanging bells and drums for worshipping a spirit.[29] This symbolic tree still exists in the form of the traditional *sottae* 솟대 in modern Korea (fig. 5.15).[30] The ancient worship of the sacred tree seems deeply connected with the tree-shaped stems on the crowns of ancient Silla and Kaya.[31] Such iconographic images are important for understanding the religious background of ancient Silla culture.

The three main upright stems of the Silla gold crown represent the image of the sacred tree, but the other two stems represent deer antlers. The worship of deer is another ancient custom from northern Asian nomadic culture. The deer hunt was an annual ritual of the kings during the Three

---

[28] This legend is recorded in the *Samguk yusa* 三國遺事. Written in the thirteenth century, the *Samguk yusa* is one of the oldest surviving historical records in Korea. For the original text, see *Samguk yusa* 1: "Kojosŏn," Han'guk Chŏngsin Munhwa Yŏn'guwŏn 韓國精神文化研究院 [Academy of Korean Studies], ed., *Yŏkchu Samguk yusa* 譯註 三國遺事 [Annotation and translation of the *Samguk yusa*] (Seoul: Ihoe Munhwasa, 2003), 1:140-141.

[29] *Hou Hanshu* 後漢書 85; *Ershisi shi* 二十四史 [The twenty-four standard histories] (Beijing: Zhonghua Shuju, 1997) [hereafter *Ershisi shi*], 3:729-730; *Sanguozhi* 三國志 30, *Ershisi shi*, 3:223-224.

[30] The *sottae* is a wooden pole with one or several wooden images of a bird on top, which stands outside a small town. The *sottae* originates in the worship of a world of trees and birds. Yi P'iryŏng 이필영, *Sottae* 솟대 [Sottae] (Seoul: Taewŏnsa, 1990): 8.

[31] Not only ancient Silla and Kaya, but also Koguryŏ and Paekche, worshipped the sacred tree. For the ancient worship of the sacred tree in Korea, see Ch'oe Chonghyŏn 최종현, "Komunhŏn e nat'anan sungmok sasang yŏn'gu" 고문헌에 나타난 숭목사상 연구 [Research on tree worship in ancient writings], *Kukt'o kyehoek* 國土計劃 37, no. 2 (February 2002): 7-23.

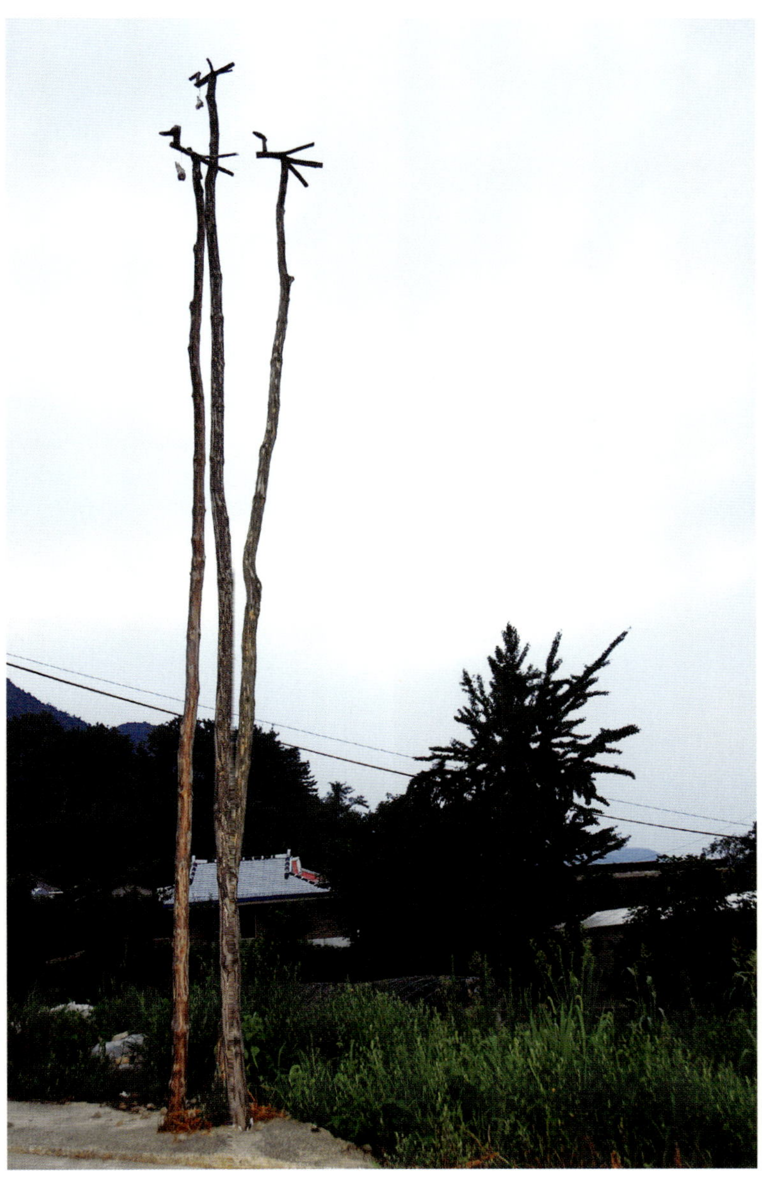

Figure 5.15 Sottæ *at Mogyok-ri* 沐浴里 *Saneo-myŏn* 山外面 *Chŏngŭp-si* 井邑市, *North Chŏlla Province. Courtesy of the author.*

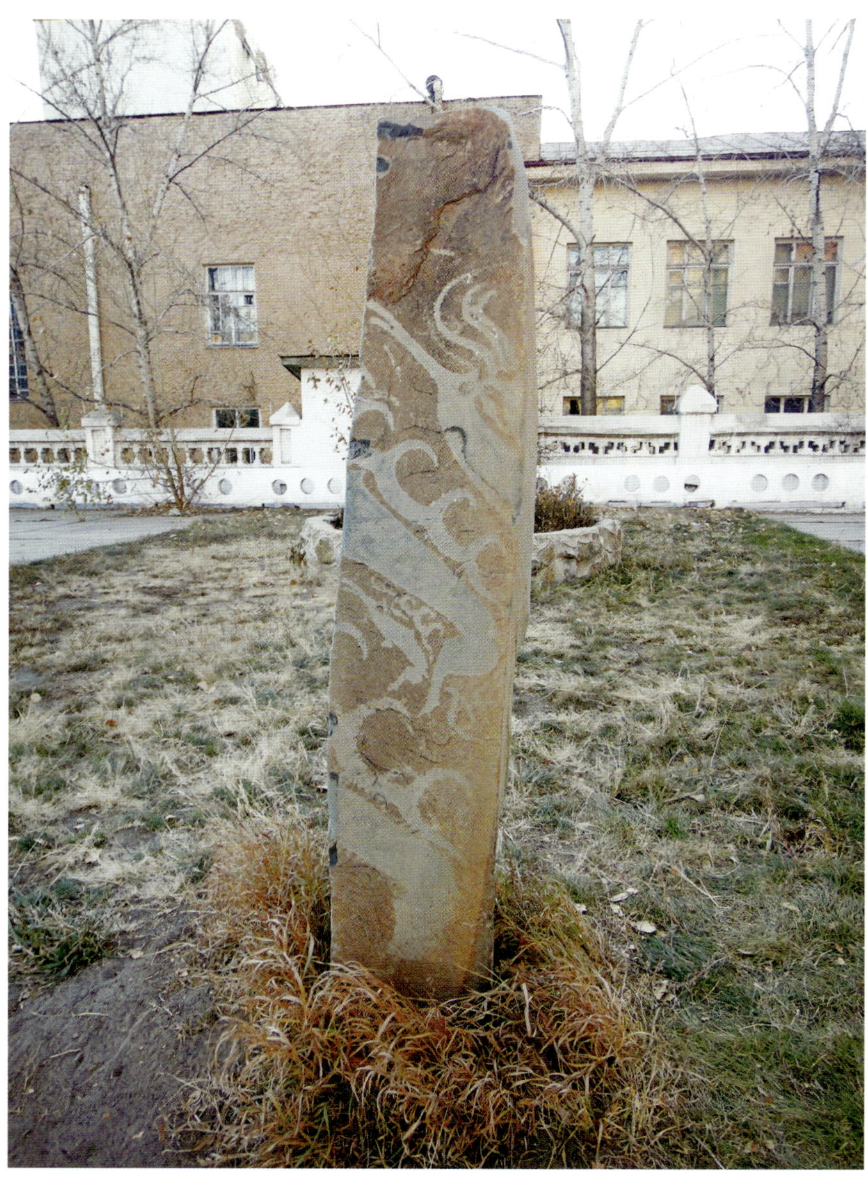

Figure 5.16 *Deer stone, Mongolia. National Museum of Mongolia,
Ulaanbaatar. Courtesy of the author.*

Kingdoms period.[32] In particular, the white deer was considered to be an auspicious symbol from heaven, promising rich harvests and peace.[33] In prehistoric times, deer worship was very popular in Mongolia and the Altai region.[34] In Mongolia, many Bronze Age deer stones can be found erected at the sites of sacred rituals (fig. 5.16).[35]

In Korea, deer images have also been found from the Bronze Age. A bronze ornament now in the collection of the Tokyo National Museum may have been used for rituals. On the surface of this bronze ornament, two deer images in the typical radiographic style appear (fig. 5.17). The figure of one deer with an arrow implies that the deer had been sacrificed to heaven. Tribal chiefs or priests of the time used either bronze ornaments with deer images or crowns with real deer antlers. Deer with antlers were also represented in the ancient rock carving at Pan'gudae 盤龜臺 in Ulsan 蔚山, and on other bronze objects in Korea.

Given these regional and historical affinities, we may assume that gold and gilt-bronze crowns with tree and antler images in ancient Silla would also represent special ornaments for ancient traditional rituals. As mentioned above, the first gold crown with antler-shaped stems was excavated from the north mound of the Great Tomb at Hwangnam (fig. 5.9). The owner of the crown could have been either a king or a tribal chief priest

---

[32] For detailed information on the ritual meaning of the deer hunt in the Three Kingdoms period, see Kim Yŏngha 金瑛河, "Samguk sidae wang ŭi t'ongch'i hyŏngt'ae yŏn'gu" 三國時代 王의 統治形態 研究 [The king's ruling system in the Three Kingdoms period] (Koryŏ Taehakkyo paksa hagwi nonmun 高麗大學校博士學位論文 [Korea University Ph.D. Dissertation], 1988): 9-60; Yi Songnan 이송란, *Silla kŭmsok kongye yŏn'gu* 신라 금속공예 연구 [Research on the metalcrafts of Silla] (Seoul: Ilchisa, 2004): 195-219.

[33] Kim Yŏngha, "Samguk sidae wang ŭi t'ongch'i hyŏngt'ae yŏn'gu," 29-40.

[34] In ancient times, deer worship was widespread throughout the northern Eurasian continent, from the Black Sea region to the Korean peninsula. It is not certain exactly which species of deer was considered to be a sacred animal in ancient Korea; however, the sacred deer of ancient northern Eurasia was the reindeer or the moose, which was larger than ordinary deer and believed to be the ancestor of a group of people as well as the animal deity of the sun. Anatoliĭ Ivanovich Martynov, *The Ancient Art of Northern Asia*, trans. and ed. Demitri B. Shimkin and Edith M. Shimkin (Urbana: University of Illinois Press, 1991): 52-73.

[35] For the Mongolian deer stones, see Pan Ling 潘玲, "Lun lushi de niandai ji xiangguan wenti" 论鹿石的年代及相关问题 [On the date of deer stones and related problems], *Kaogu Xuebao* 考古学报, no. 3 (2008): 311-336.

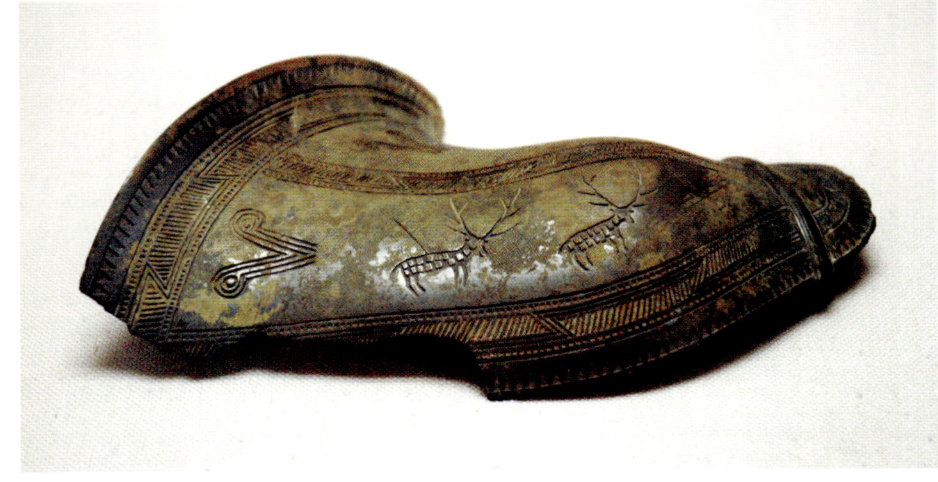

responsible for traditional ancestral rituals. In ancient Silla, important state rituals were performed by the female members of the royal family. According to the *Samguk sagi*, the second king of Silla, Namhae 南海 (r. 4-24 C.E.), built a new royal shrine for the progenitor of Silla and then ordered his sister Aro 阿老 (dates unknown) to conduct ancestral rites in it.[36] These ancestral rituals were closely related to agricultural processions and the worship of heaven, and royal women played a leading role in the rituals of the ancient Silla period.[37] The crown would have been worn as a symbolic ornament for such ritual performances.

Interestingly, all the known owners of gold crowns in southern Siberia and in Afghanistan were women as well. The typical southern Siberian gold crown of the first century shows a more natural style, with tree and deer images.[38] A crown was discovered in the Khokhlach burial mound in Novo-

---

[36] *Samguk sagi* 32: "Chesa," Han'gukhak Chungang Yŏn'guwŏn 韓國學中央研究院 [Academy of Korean Studies], ed., *Yŏkchu Samguk sagi* 譯註 三國史記 [Annotation and translation of the *Samguk sagi*] (Kyŏnggi-do Sŏngnam-si: Han'gukhak Chungang Yŏn'guwŏn Ch'ulp'anbu, 2011): 1:455.

[37] Na Hŭira 나희라, *Silla ŭi kukka chesa* 신라의 국가제사 [National rites of Silla] (Seoul: Chisik Sanŏpsa, 2003): 69-130.

[38] S.I. Kaposhina, "A Sarmatian Royal Burial at Novocherkassk," *Antiquity* 37, no. 148 (1963): 256-258; Joan Aruz et al., ed., *The Golden Deer of Eurasia: Scythian and Sarmatian Treasures from the Russian Steppes: The State Hermitage, Saint*

cherkassk, South Russia, on the head of a woman. Attached to the center of the main strip are a bust of a Greek woman, red jewels, and birdlike decorations. In this crown, we can see the iconographical origins of the tree, deer, and bird images of ancient Silla crowns. The Afghanistani gold crown excavated at Tillya-Tepe was also worn by a woman, along with gold bracelets, gold pendants, a gold necklace, and a silver ring.[39] This crown has five tree-like stems, each decorated with flowers, leaves, and birds. Although these crowns do not look exactly like the Silla crowns, the iconography of tree, deer, and bird implies the same cultural and religious traditions. In addition, several gold head ornaments with the tree shape on top were found in northeastern China in modern times. These gold ornaments are called *buyaoguan* 步搖冠 in Chinese and were used by the Xianbei 鮮卑 people, northern nomadic tribes who lived in Liaoning Province 辽宁省 and Inner Mongolia 内蒙古 in the third and fourth centuries.[40] These might have served as another direct influence on the Silla gold ornaments.[41]

Among the gold crowns of Silla, bird images were found on the upper part of the gold crown from the Auspicious Phoenix Tomb (fig. 5.18).[42] These birds look more like a chicken than a phoenix.[43] According to the

---

Petersburg, and the Archaeological Museum, Ufa (New York: Metropolitan Museum of Art; New Haven: Yale University Press, 2000): 13, fig. 13.

[39] This gold crown was discovered in the Tillya-Tepe Tomb VI, Afghanistan in 1978. Fredrik Hiebert and Pierre Cambon, eds., *Afghanistan: Hidden Treasures from the National Museum, Kabul* (Washington, DC: National Gallery of Art and National Geographic Society, 2008): 285, fig. 134.

[40] For *buyaoguan*, see Sun Ji 孙机, "Buyao, buyaoguan yu yaoye guanshi pian" 步搖, 步搖冠与搖叶饰片 [Swaying pendant pieces, swaying-pendant crowns, and swaying-leaf-crown pendants], *Wenwu* 文物, no. 11 (1991): 55-64; Liaoning sheng wenwu kaogu yanjiusuo, 辽宁省文物考古研究所 [Cultural Relic and Archaeological Institute of Liaoning Province], ed., *San Yan wenwu jingcui* 三燕文物精粹 [Cultural relics of the Three Yan] (Shenyang: Liaoning Renmin Chubanshe, 2002): Plates 29-34.

[41] Lee Hansang, "The Gold Culture and the Gold Crowns of Silla," 113-114.

[42] In the case of the gold crown from the Gold Crown Tomb, a bird's head in the shape of a chicken is chased on each side of two gold caps over each of the green curved jadeite beads that compose the hanging pendants of the crown. For illustration, see Munhwajaech'ŏng 문화재청 [The Cultural Heritage Administration of Korea], ed., *Kukpo kŭmsŏk kongye* 국보 금속공예 [National treasures, metalcraft] (Seoul: Kŭrap'ik Net'ŭ, 2009): 126.

[43] The gold headdress excavated at the Aluchaideng site in the Ordos region shows an eagle on top, which could be one origin of the birds on a gold crown in the

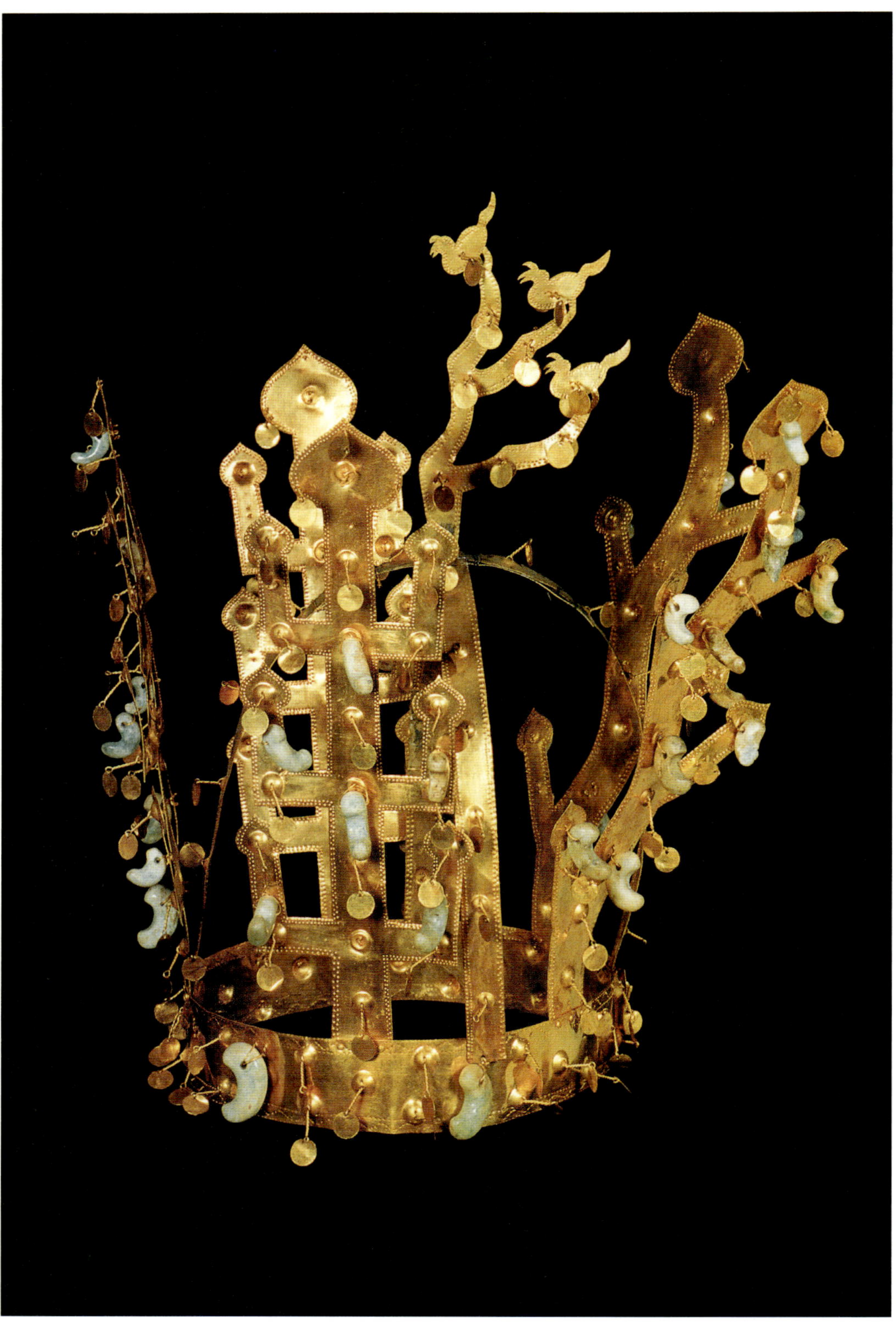

Figure 5.18 Three bird images on the top of the gold crown from the Auspicious Phoenix Tomb, Kyŏngju. H. 30.7cm. Treasure No. 339. Courtesy of the National Museum of Korea.

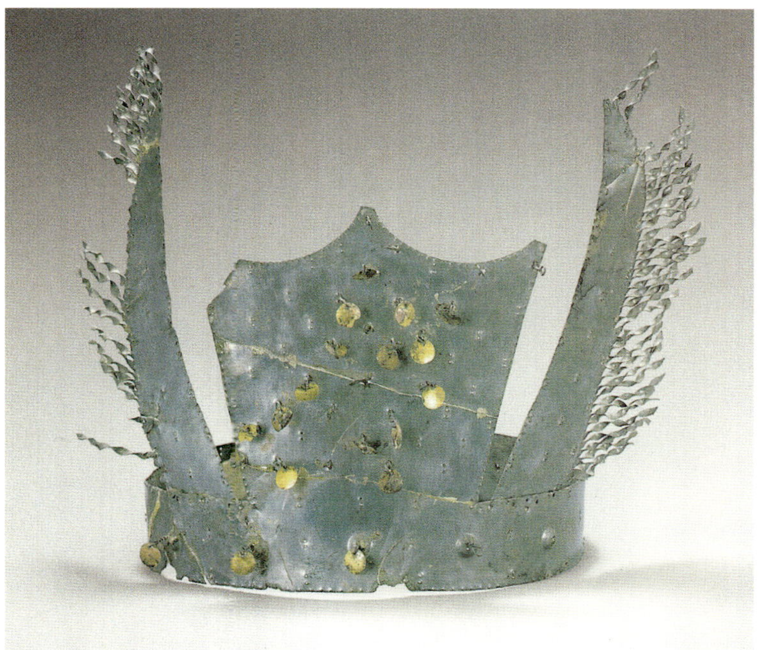

*Figure 5.19 Silver crown, excavated from the south mound of the Great Tomb at Hwangnam,
Kyŏngju. H. 20.5cm. Courtesy of the Gyeongju National Museum.*

Samguk yusa, the first Silla king's spouse was born of a chicken-like dragon.[44]
The progenitor of the Kim family, Kim Alchi 金閼智, was also said to have

Auspicious Phoenix Tomb. For illustration, see Adam T. Kessler, *Empires Beyond the
Great Wall: The Heritage of Genghis Khan* (Los Angeles: Natural History Museum
of Los Angeles County, 1994): 53, fig. 25. This bird has a shape different from that of
the Silla birds, however, and the styles of the two crowns also show slight differences.
While the worship of birds was widespread throughout northern Eurasia, there may
have been regional and temporal variations in the characters of birds.

[44] *Samguk yusa* 1: "Silla sijo Pak Hyŏkkŏse," *Yŏkchu Samguk yusa*, 3:223-225.
For an English translation, see Iryŏn, *Samguk yusa: Legends and History of the Three
Kingdoms of Ancient Korea*, trans. Tae-Hung Ha and Grafton K. Mintz (Seoul: Yonsei University Press, 1972): 50. In this English translation, the translator refers to the
mythical animal that bore the Queen as a "she-dragon." In the original text, however, it is written as *kyeryong* 鷄龍, meaning a dragon in the form of a chicken.

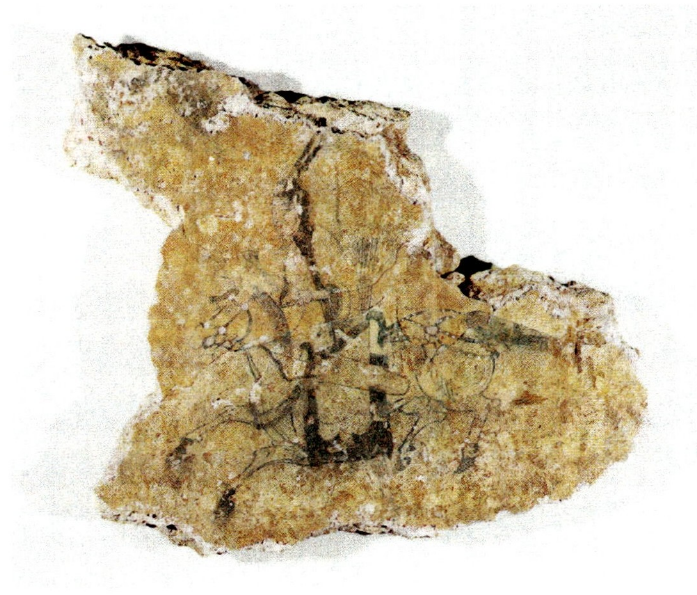

Figure 5.20 Horse rider with a hat adorned with bird feathers painted on a fragment of mural from Ssangyŏngch'ong 雙楹塚, South P'yŏngan Province. Courtesy of the National Museum of Korea.

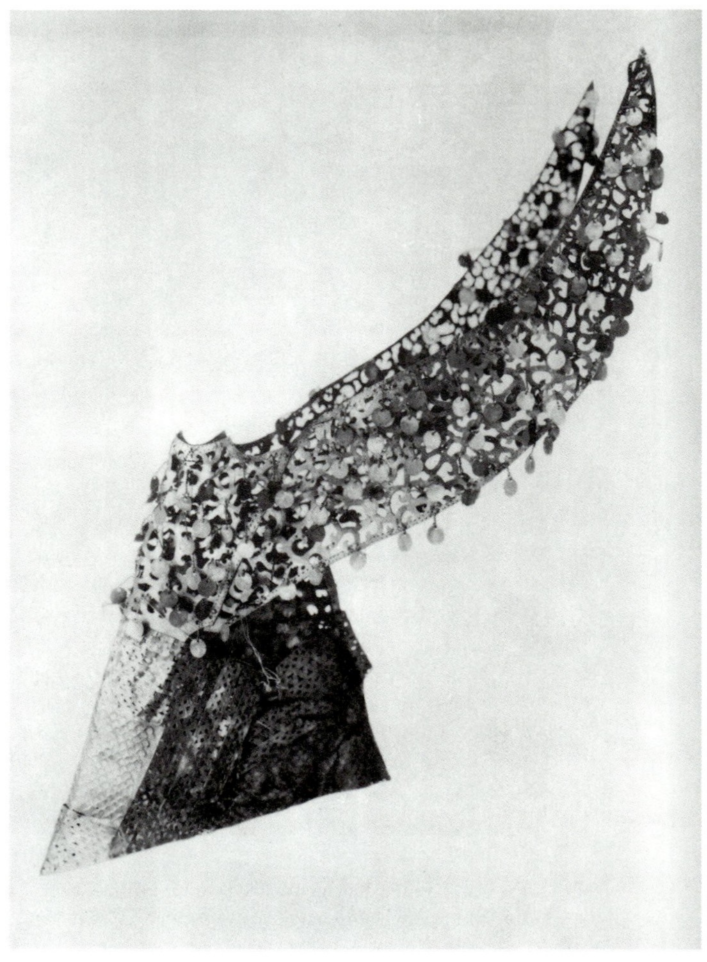

Figure 5.21 Gold crown with bird feather style decoration, from the Gold Crown Tomb, Kyŏngju. Silla, fifth-sixth century. National Museum of Korea. From Hamada Kosaku 濱田耕作 and Umehara Sueji 梅原末治, Keishū Kinkan-tsuka to sono ihō 慶州金冠塚と其遺寶 (Keijō [Seoul]: Chōsen Sōtokufu, 1924-1927): Plate 53.

been born from a golden box delivered by a heavenly white cock.[45] Such legends suggest that the worship of a heavenly chicken developed early in Silla.

Representations of birds on crowns take various forms, sometimes only appearing as feathers. In the south mound of the Great Tomb at Hwangnam, a silver crown whose stems resemble bird feathers was found (fig. 5.19). These feather-style crowns were also found in Koguryŏ and Silla. In Koguryŏ, a warrior wore a triangular silk hat with two long bird feathers (fig. 5.20). This type of crown adorned with bird feathers, or a feathered coronet, is known as *chougwan* 鳥羽冠.[46] This type of hat is transformed into metallic form in a triangular crown with feathers or horn decorations found in Silla and Paekche (fig. 5.21).[47]

These triangular crowns with decorations were misleadingly labeled "inner crowns" when they were found during the Japanese colonial period.[48] In most cases in Silla, however, these triangular crowns were buried in separate

---

[45] *Samguk yusa* 1: "Kim Alchi Haet'alwangdae," *Yŏkchu Samguk yusa*, 1:256.

[46] For the tradition of the feathered coronet in ancient Korea, see No T'aedon 노 태돈, *Yebindo e poin Koguryŏ: Tang Yi Hyŏn myo yebindo ui chougwan ul ssuŭn sajŏl e taehayŏ* 예빈도에 보인 고구려: 당 이현 묘 예빈도의 조우관을 쓴 사절 에 대하여 [Koguryŏ reflected in the painting of the envoys: About the envoy wearing *chougwan* in the tomb of Li Xian of the Tang dynasty] (Seoul: Sŏul Taehakkyo Ch'ulp'anbu, 2003). No T'aedon argued that this coronet was used only in Koguryŏ and ignored the similar crown decorations adapted to metal in ancient Silla. However, metallic decoration in the shape of bird feathers was also used on crowns in Koguryŏ. For an illustration, see Kungnip Kyŏngju Pangmulgwan, *Silla hwanggŭm*, 238-239.

[47] Although the bird-feather-style hat in Koguryŏ mural paintings and these metal crowns in Silla and Paekche share a similar style despite material differences, Korean archaeologists have distinguished between them, with the former depicting bird feathers and the latter depicting bird wings or horns. The metal crowns with feather decorations in Silla were called *choikkwan* 鳥翼冠, which means a crown with bird wings. Although these feather-shaped metal decorations have many decorations on one edge that were cut and twisted to simulate the texture of a feather, the main shape is similar to the so-called "wing-shaped" or "horn-shaped" metal decorations. Therefore, I think the "wing-shaped" or "horn-shaped" metal decorations are a simplified form of the original feather-style decoration—a change due to adoption of simpler techniques—and their meaning refers to a bird. This means that the bird-feather crown, especially that of Koguryŏ, originated in the northern bird-worshipping culture. Both the legend and worship of a heavenly bird then spread to the south in Silla and Paekche.

[48] Hamada Kōsaku and Umehara Sueji, *Keishū Kinkanzuka to sono ihō*, 2: Plates LI and LII.

sections in the graves and were not used simultaneously with the tree- and deer-style crowns. While the tree- and deer-style crown was discovered on the head of the deceased, the triangular crown with the bird feathers was buried separately, outside the coffin.[49] Therefore, these two styles of crowns were not a set, but were independently used for different purposes.

We now return to the gold crown from the north mound of the Great Tomb at Hwangnam. The female occupant, the owner of this crown, would likely be a member of a royal family who could perform the rites for her ancestors. Her husband was much older and of a lower class than she. He might have become a king by marriage. Some archaeologists argue that the south mound of the Great Tomb at Hwangnam may contain the remains of King Nulji 訥祇 (r. 417-458), who died in 458.[50] However, it is more plausible that the occupant of this tomb is King Naemul 奈勿 (r. 356-402), who died in 402, because he was not a descendant of a royal line while his wife was.[51] King Nulji was a son of King Naemul and belonged to the royal family by birth. In any case, the south mound is the earliest great mound ever excavated in ancient Silla, and would have been constructed in the early or middle fifth century.[52]

---

[49] Munhwajae Kwalliguk, *Ch'ŏnmach'ong*, plan 6; Kungnip Kyŏngju Munhwajae Yŏn'guso, *Hwangnam Taech'ong*, vol. 1: 74-77, vol. 2: plan 8.

[50] Kim Yongsŏng 金龍星 "Silla Maripkan sigi ŭi wangnŭng Hwangnam Taech'ong Nambun" 新羅 麻立干時期의 王陵 皇南大塚 南墳 [A royal tomb during the period of Maripkan in Silla: The south mound of the Great Tomb at Hwangnam], in *Hwangnam Taech'ong: hwanggŭm ŭi nara Silla ŭi wangnŭng* 황남대총: 황금의 나라 신라의 왕릉 [The Great Tomb at Hwangnam: The country of gold, the royal tombs of Silla], ed. Kungnip Chungang Pangmulgwan 國立中央博物館 [National Museum of Korea] (Seoul: Kungnip Chungang Pangmulgwan, 2010): 207-225.

[51] Yi Hŭijun 李熙濬, "Hwangnam Taech'ong nambun Naemul wangnŭngsŏl ŭi chegi paegyŏng kwa kaeyo kŭrigo ŭiŭi" 皇南大塚 南墳 奈勿王陵說의 提起 背景과 概要 그리고 意義 [The background, summary and meaning of the inference that the occupant of the south mound of the Great Tomb at Hwangnam is King Naemul], in *Hwangnam Taech'ong: hwanggŭm ŭi nara Silla ŭi wangnŭng*, 192-206.

[52] In his recent research, Ham Sunsŏp suggested that the occupant of the south mound of the Great Tomb at Hwangnam was probably King Silsŏng 實聖 (r. 402-417), a brother of King Naemul who was killed by his nephew King Nulji in 417. Ham Sunsŏp 咸舜燮, "Hwangnam Taech'ong ŭl tullŏssan nonjaeng, tto hana ŭi kanŭngsŏng" 皇南大塚을 둘러싼 論爭, 또 하나의 可能性 [Arguments regarding Hwangnam Taech'ong, and another possibility], in *Hwangnam Taech'ong: hwanggŭm ŭi nara Silla ŭi wangnŭng*, 226-245.

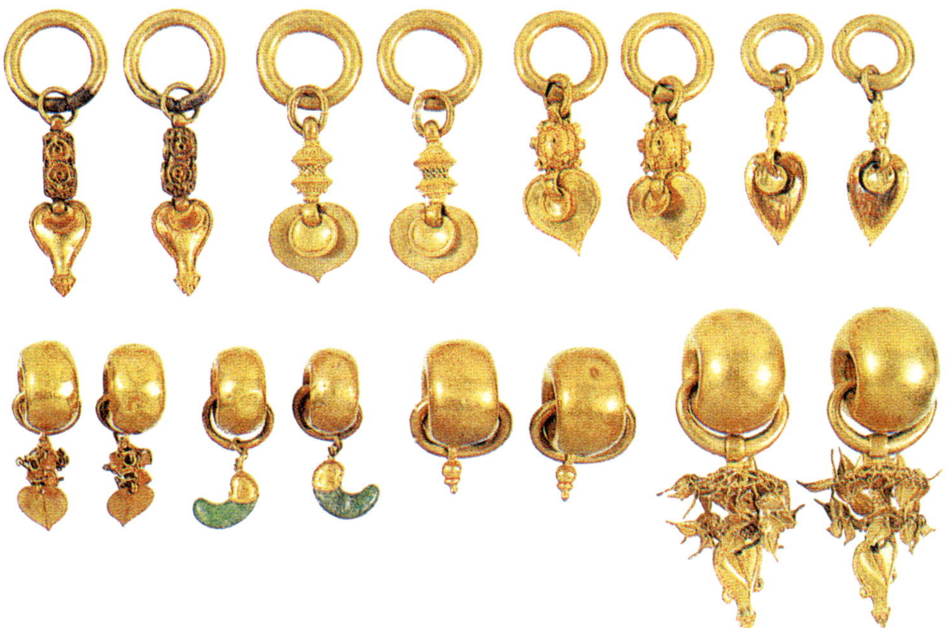

Figure 5.22
*Gold earrings.
Silla, fifth-sixth
century. Length
of the earring
in the upper
right corner:
8.1cm. Courtesy
of the Gyeongju
National
Museum.*

The gold crown is a symbol of the ancient religious authority of Silla, used during special state rituals dedicated to the ancestors. Iconographic images of trees, deer, and birds on crowns suggest a close relationship between ancient Silla and northern Eurasian cultures.

The Usage of Gold Earrings in Ancient Silla and Its Meaning

Examination of the gold earrings of Silla shows that Silla's unique earring styles had features that came not only from northern Eurasian cultures but also from South Asian maritime cultures. Gold earrings are the most common ornament found in Silla tombs (fig. 5.22). To date more than two hundred pieces of gold or gilt-bronze earrings have been found in the region once ruled by Silla.[53] The men and women wearing these

---

[53] Chu Kyŏngmi (Joo Kyeongmi) 周炅美, "Samguk sidae isik ŭi yŏn'gu: Kyŏngju chiyŏk ch'ult'o suhabu isik ŭl chungsim ŭro" 三國時代 耳飾의 研究: 慶州地域出土 垂下付耳飾을 중심으로 [Research on ear ornaments in the Three Kingdoms period

275

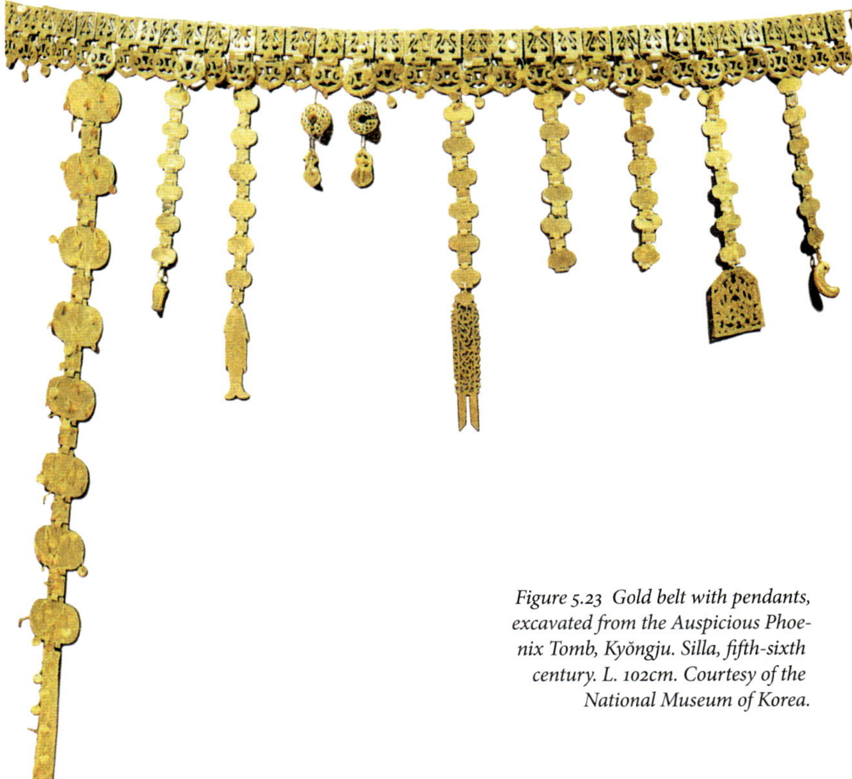

Figure 5.23 Gold belt with pendants, excavated from the Auspicious Phoenix Tomb, Kyŏngju. Silla, fifth-sixth century. L. 102cm. Courtesy of the National Museum of Korea.

gold earrings would have belonged to the high class of nobles in ancient Silla. Gold earrings have also been found in other regions, such as Paekche, Koguryŏ, and Kaya, but more gold earrings have been excavated in Silla than in any of the other regions.

Gold earrings of Silla provide a wealth of information and clues for understanding the cultural characteristics of ancient Silla. The quantity of excavated gold earrings far surpasses that of gold crowns. The former are more delicate and crafted through techniques requiring greater

of Korea: Focusing on the earrings with decorative end-pendant excavated in the Kyŏngju region], *Misul sahak yŏn'gu* 美術史學研究 211 (1996): 6-8.

276

sophistication than the latter, which were made with rather simple and easy techniques. When a craftsman made a gold crown, he first chiseled the shape of each stem and decoration from a plain, thin gold plate, and then attached the stems to a round strip with thin gold nails and wires. However, the making of gold earrings required far more advanced metalcraft techniques such as soldering, filigree, granulation, repoussé, and glass decoration.[54] Given the level of skills employed in making gold earrings, it seems likely that they would have been worn when the occupant was still alive.[55]

Some gold ornaments, such as hanging pendants for crowns or belts, had shapes resembling those of earrings. The gold crown from the north mound of the Great Tomb at Hwangnam has three pairs of pendants that resemble thick-type earrings (Kr. *t'aehwan isik* 太環耳飾) (fig. 5.9). A set of gold belts from the Auspicious Phoenix Tomb has two pendants whose shapes are also similar to those of earrings, although the main ring of the pendant has diamond-patterned perforations chiseled into it (fig. 5.23). In addition, three pairs of gold ornaments similar to thick-type earrings were excavated around the feet of the occupant of the north mound of the Great Tomb at Hwangnam.[56] In this tomb, five pairs of ornaments resembling thick-type earrings were found together with a gold belt set.[57] These ornaments are designated as "decorative pendants" (Kr. *susik* 垂飾 or *tŭrim changsik* 드림장식) used for

---

[54] Chu Kyŏngmi (Joo Kyeongmi) 周炅美, "Samguk sidae isik ŭi chejak kipŏp" 三國時代 耳飾의 製作技法 [Production techniques of ear ornaments in the Three Kingdoms period of Korea], *Kodae yŏn'gu* 古代研究 5 (May 1997): 105-140. For practical information on metalcraft techniques, see Wilhelm Braum-Felfweg, *Metal: Design & Techniques*, trans. F. Bradely (New York: Van Nostrand Reinhold Company Inc., 1975); Oppi Untracht, *Jewelry Concepts and Technology* (Garden City, NY: Doubleday & Company, Inc., 1982).

[55] There has been a long dispute on the usage of gold jewelry—whether it was made for the living or for the dead. Some scholars have claimed that the gold jewelry found in the ancient Silla tombs was made only for grave burials. Yun Seyŏng 尹世英, *Kobun ch'ult'o pujangp'um yŏn'gu* 古墳出土 副葬品 研究 [Research on the funerary objects excavated from tombs] (Seoul: Kodae Minjok Munhwa Yŏn'guso Ch'ulp'anbu, 1988): 307-309. However, others hold the opinion that some of the jewelry was used while the occupant was alive. Yi Songnan, *Silla kŭmsok kongye yŏn'gu*, 247. In my opinion, the gold crown and earrings must have been used during the lifetime of the occupant, but some kinds of metal ornaments, such as gilt-bronze shoes, would have been made only as grave goods.

[56] Munhwajae Yŏn'guso, *Hwangnam Taech'ong*, 86-87.

[57] Munhwajae Yŏn'guso, *Hwangnam Taech'ong*, 83-84.

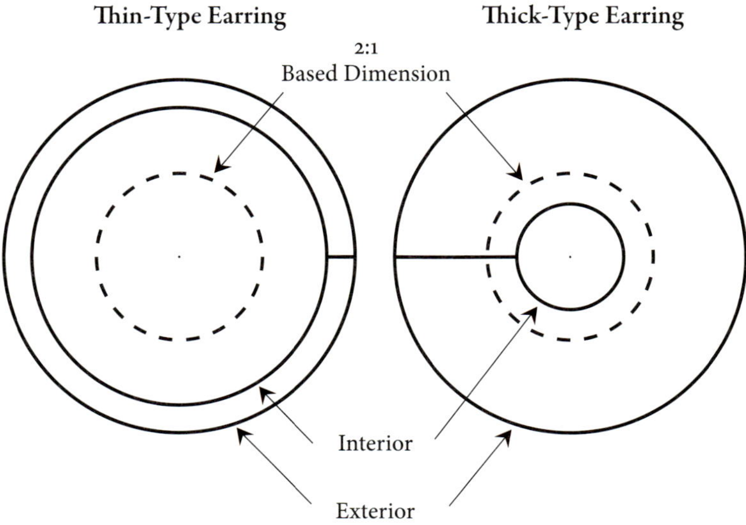

Figure 5.24 Drawing of the main ring of thick-type earring and thin-type earring, Kyŏngju. Drawing by the Korea Institute, Harvard University.

crowns, belts, or other objects, only when their location inside the tomb, verified by the archaeological excavations, has revealed their exact usage. If their original context is lost, these "decorative pendants" can be misinterpreted as earrings given their similarity with earrings in terms of style and shape. Therefore we must reconsider the real usage of many examples of gold crafts currently identified as gold earrings from Silla as well as Koguryŏ and Paekche that are currently in many different museum collections, most of which are of unknown provenance. They may be actual earrings, but at the same time they should not be automatically categorized as "earrings to be worn on the earlobe," a classification we cannot prove.

On the most basic level, the earrings can be classified into two types according to the thickness of the main ring: thick-type earrings and thin-type earrings (Kr. *sehwan isik* 細環耳飾). When laid flat, the interior and exterior diameters of the main ring can be measured. If the interior diameter of the main ring is larger than half of the external diameter of the main ring, it is categorized as a thin type. If the interior diameter is the same as or smaller than half of the external diameter, it is categorized as a thick type

278

Structure of Gold Earring

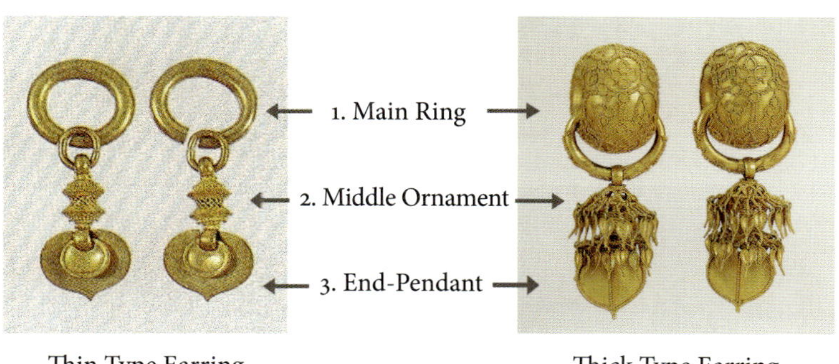

Figure 5.25 Structure of gold earrings. Courtesy of the author.

(fig. 5.24). The thin-type earrings were worn ubiquitously in early Korea by both men and women, but the thick-type earrings were worn only in Silla and Koguryŏ.[58] Moreover, the thick-type earrings were usually worn by women in Silla.[59] Thick rings are actually hollow tubes made of two or three very thin gold sheets, so they are lighter than they appear. The construction of thin rings, however, differed: some were made of gold sheets and were hollow inside, but others were made of solid gold wires. The solid rings look light, but are heavier than they appear.

The basic structure of a gold earring in the Three Kingdoms period is consistent in both types. A typical gold or gilt-bronze earring of the Three Kingdoms period consists of three parts (fig. 5.25). The first part is the main ring (Kr. *chuhwan* 主鐶) for placement in the hole of the earlobe. The second part is a middle ornament (Kr. *chunggansik* 中間飾), and the last is an

---

[58] To date, no thick-type earrings from Paekche or Kaya have been found. Chu Kyŏngmi (Joo Kyeongmi) 周炅美, "Han'guk kodae isik ŭi ch'akchang pangsik yŏn'gu" 韓國 古代 耳飾의 着裝方式 研究 [Research on the manner of wearing ear ornaments in ancient Korea], *Yŏksa minsokhak* 역사민속학 17 (December 2003): 37.

[59] Yi Hŭijun 李熙濬 "4-5 segi Silla kobun p'ijangja ŭi poksikp'um ch'akchang chŏnghyŏng" 4-5세기 신라 고분 피장자의 服飾品 着裝 定型 [Patterns of costume accessories worn by the deceased in Silla tombs from the fourth and fifth centuries], *Han'guk kogo hakpo* 韓國考古學報 47 (August 2002): 80-82.

Table 5.2
Principal Types of Middle Ornaments.

	Type name	Archetype	Variant types
1	Hollow box type		
2	Hollow sphere type		
3	Gold ball type		
4	Gold cylinder type		
5	Hollow cylinder type		
6	Gemstone type		

end-pendant (Kr. *suhasik* 垂下飾). Each part is made separately and then assembled using thin gold rings and wires. Sometimes many decorations were attached on each part. We can classify the gold earrings into many groups based on the forms and combinations of each part. The classification of earrings helps us to determine the chronology of ancient tombs of Silla.[60]

The middle ornament is the most important of the three parts in classifying earrings, because it was a small trinket made in various types that featured sophisticated techniques such as filigree, granulation, and soldering. Principal types of middle ornaments include (1) "hollow box type," (2) "hollow sphere type," (3) "gold ball type,"[61] (4) "gold cylinder type," (5) "hollow cylinder type," and (6) "gemstone type."[62] These six types are again divided into subtypes, including an archetype and many variant types with differing decorations in each (see table 5.2).

Those hollow box, hollow sphere, and hollow cylinder shapes were composed of six or more small gold rings, each of which was made of thin gold wires soldered together. Some trinkets were decorated on the surface with tiny gold granules smaller than one millimeter in size. This granulation technique, which remains quite a difficult technique even in modern times, developed in the Western world in ancient times and then spread to East Asia before the first century C.E.[63] In addition, these trinkets were dec-

---

[60] For a detailed classification of Silla gold earrings, see Itō Akio 伊藤秋男, "Mimikazari no keishikigakuteki kenkyū ni motozuku Kankoku Koshiragi jidai kofun no hennen ni kansuru ichi shian" 耳飾の型式学的研究に基づく韓国古新羅時代の古墳の編年に関する一試案 [An essay on the chronology of ancient Silla tombs based on the classification study of earrings], *Chōsen gakuhō* 朝鮮学報 64 (1972): 15-73; Chu Kyŏngmi (Joo Kyeongmi), "Samguk sidae isik ŭi yŏn'gu," 5-28; Yi Han-sang 李漢祥, "5-6 segi Silla t'aehwan isik ŭi pullyu wa p'yŏnnyŏn" 5–6世紀 新羅 太環 耳飾의 分類와 編年 [The classification and chronology of thick-type earrings during the fifth and sixth century in Silla], *Kodae yŏn'gu* 古代研究 6 (1998): 33-60.

[61] Actually, this ball is also empty inside, because it is made of two gold sheets.

[62] As in this case, there are several examples that have no gemstones but rather two gold caps for fixing the gemstone.

[63] The granulation technique was first developed in ancient Mesopotamia and Egypt, and then flourished under the ancient Etruscan and Greek gold culture. The Scythian peoples also used this technique. For the process and history of gold granulation, see Oppi Untracht, *Jewelry Concepts and Technology*, 173-184, 348-363; Jack Ogden, *Ancient Jewellery* (Berkeley: University of California Press, 1992): 51-53. This technique would be transmitted into East Asia before the first century B.C.E. by northern and central Eurasian peoples. Gold jewelry with granulation has been

Table 5.3
Principal Types of End-pendants.

	Type name	Archetype	Variant types
1	Heart leaf shape		
2	Nib shape		
3	Seed shape		
4	Curved jadeite bead		
5	Other examples		

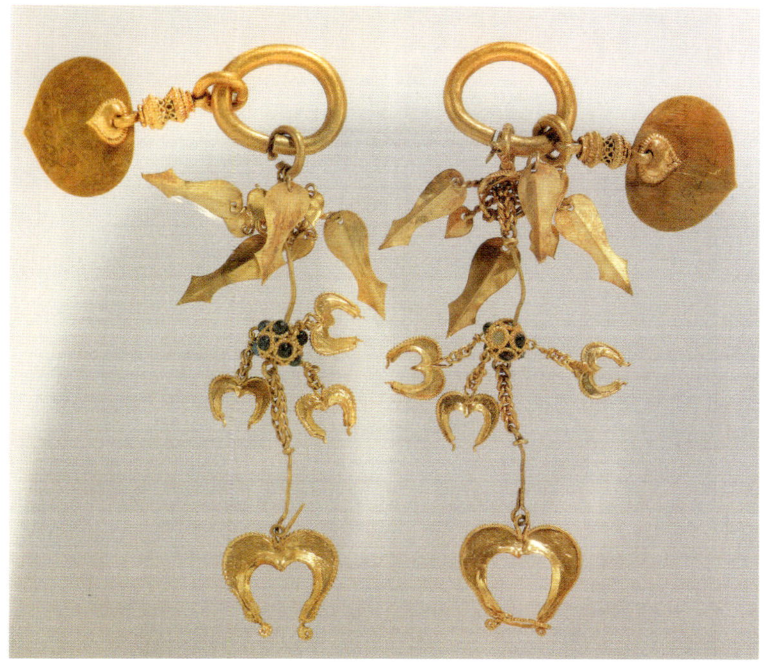

*Figure 5.26 Thin-type gold earrings, excavated from the Gold Crown Tomb,
Kyŏngju. L. 10cm. Courtesy of the Gyeongju National Museum.*

orated with many small gold leaves, beads, or glass. These gold leaves sometimes took the shape of a circle or a heart, and each leaf might be decorated
with filigree and granulation techniques. The decorations shown here are of
earrings from ancient Silla's early period. The decorations tend to become
more extravagant during the middle of the sixth century.

The forms of end-pendants are also diverse, but the most common is
(1) a heart-shaped gold leaf type. It has two or more additional small gold

---

found in ancient Xiongnu tombs in Mongolia and the ancient tombs of Tillya
Tepe in Afghanistan. In Korea, the first gold granulation work can be seen on the
gold belt buckle found in a Lelang tomb in Pyongyang dated to the first century.
Regarding the gold belt buckle of Lelang, see Munhwajaech'ŏng, *Kukpo kŭmsok
kongye*, 52-59.

leaves, or is decorated with gold granules. Other types are (2) a nib-shaped gold pendant, (3) a seed-shaped pendant,[64] (4) a green curved jadeite bead, and other extra types.[65] Like that of the middle ornament, the archetypes of end-pendants have several variant subtypes with decorations (table 5.3).

Combinations of the three earring parts are multifaceted, due to the diverse types of each part. Moreover, some earrings are composed of a set of one main ring with two middle ornaments and two end-pendants (fig. 5.26). The most common earring style in ancient Silla seems to have been a set of one main ring with a hollow-sphere-type middle ornament and heart-leaf-shaped end-pendant. The decorations of each part are added together to both parts, so the style of one whole earring is consistent.

The decoration style of Silla earrings is closely related to the chronology of the sites in which they were found.[66] The structure and decorations of the earlier earrings were simpler than those of the later ones. During the sixth century, most earrings were decorated with beaded wires and many tiny gold granules, each smaller than one millimeter (fig. 5.27). These beaded wires and granules were attached by filigree and granulation techniques, and they reveal that these high-quality gold-work techniques were highly developed

---

[64] A seed-shaped type is often discovered in the territory of Kaya, and there are a few examples in the territory of ancient Silla. This type is also closely related to Japanese earrings of the Kofun 古墳 period.

[65] End-pendants came in many variations. Here I show only three types in the shape of a bamboo leaf, a gold ball with decorations, and a tangled gold ribbon, but there are other exceptional examples besides those that appear here.

[66] There are many different opinions on the absolute chronology of the ancient tombs of Silla, but most scholars agree on the relative chronology of some stone-piled wooden-chamber tombs. One of the oldest Silla tombs ever discovered is tomb Ka-13 at Wŏlsŏngno in Kyŏngju, followed by the southern mound of the Great Tomb at Hwangnam. These are the earliest First-phase tombs. The first Second-phase tomb is the north mound of the Great Tomb at Hwangnam, and the later Second-phase tombs are the Gold Crown Tomb and the Auspicious Phoenix Tomb. The Third-phase tombs are the Gold Bell Tomb and the Heavenly Horse Tomb. The Last-phase tombs are the tomb at 215 Nosŏ-dong and the Couple's Tomb at Pomun-dong. For a comparison of diverse opinions on the chronology of ancient Silla tombs, see Ch'oe Pyŏnghyŏn 崔秉鉉, "Silla-Kaya ŭi kogohak: yŏn'gusachŏk kŏmt'o" 新羅・伽耶의 考古學—研究史的 檢討 [Historiographical review: Archaeology of Silla and Kaya], *Kuksagwan nonch'ong* 國史館論叢 33 (1992): 177-221; Kim Yongsŏng 김용성, "Silla" 신라 [Silla], in *Han'guk kogohak kangŭi* 한국 고고학 강의 [Korean archaeology lectures], ed. Han'guk Kogo Hakhoe 한국고고학회 [The Korean Archeological Society] (Seoul: Sahoe P'yŏngnon, 2007): 301-329.

284

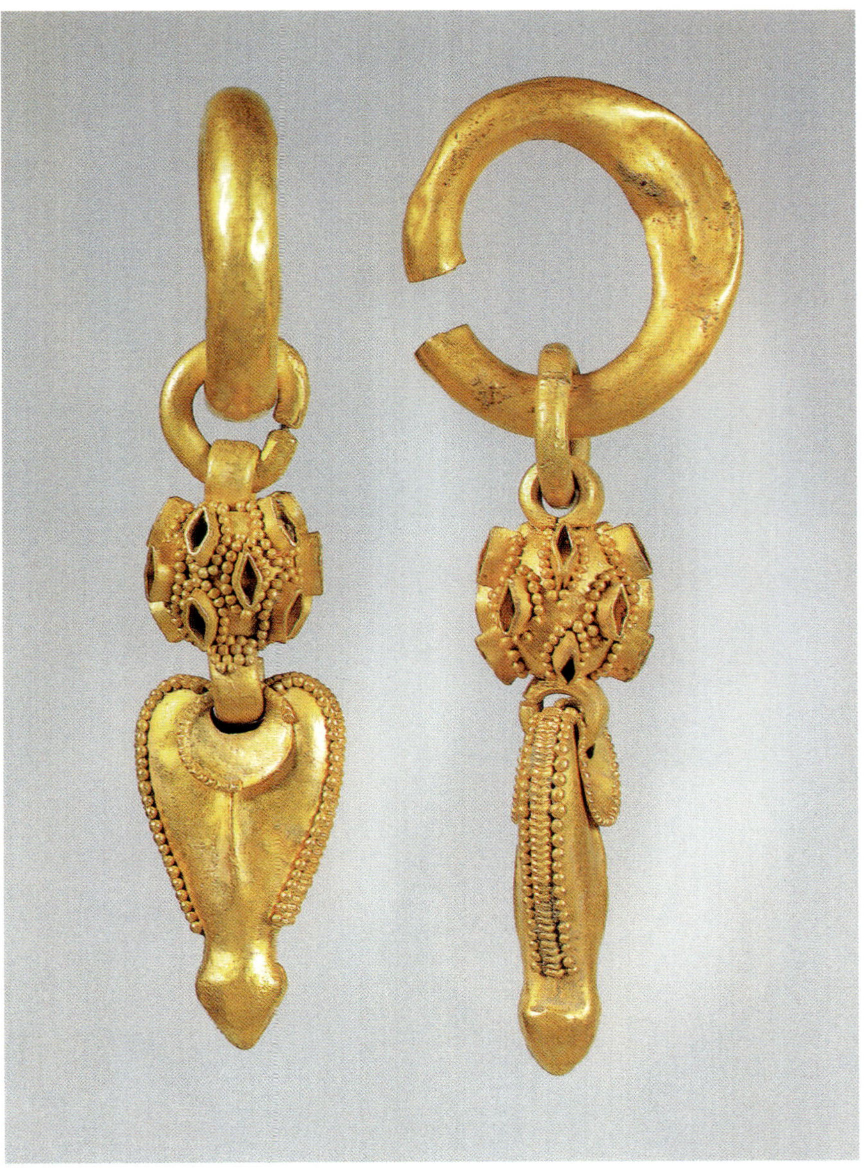

Figure 5.27 Thin-type gold earrings, excavated from Tomb 2 at 100-pŏnji 番地 *in Hwango-dong* 皇吾洞,
Kyŏngju. Silla, fifth-sixth century. L. 7.3cm. Courtesy of the Museum of Dongguk University, Gyeongju.

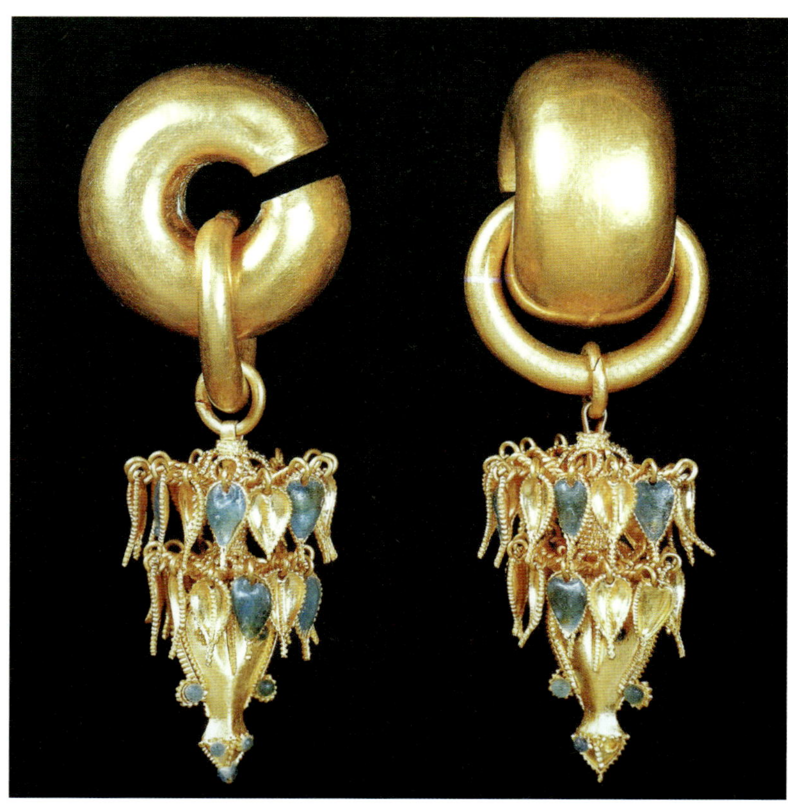

Figure 5.28 *Thick-type gold earrings, excavated from Tomb 1 at 2-chigu* 地區 *in Kyesŏng* 桂城, *Ch'angnyŏng-gun* 昌寧郡, *South Kyŏngsang Province. Silla, sixth century. Gimhae National Museum. Courtesy of the Gyeongju National Museum.*

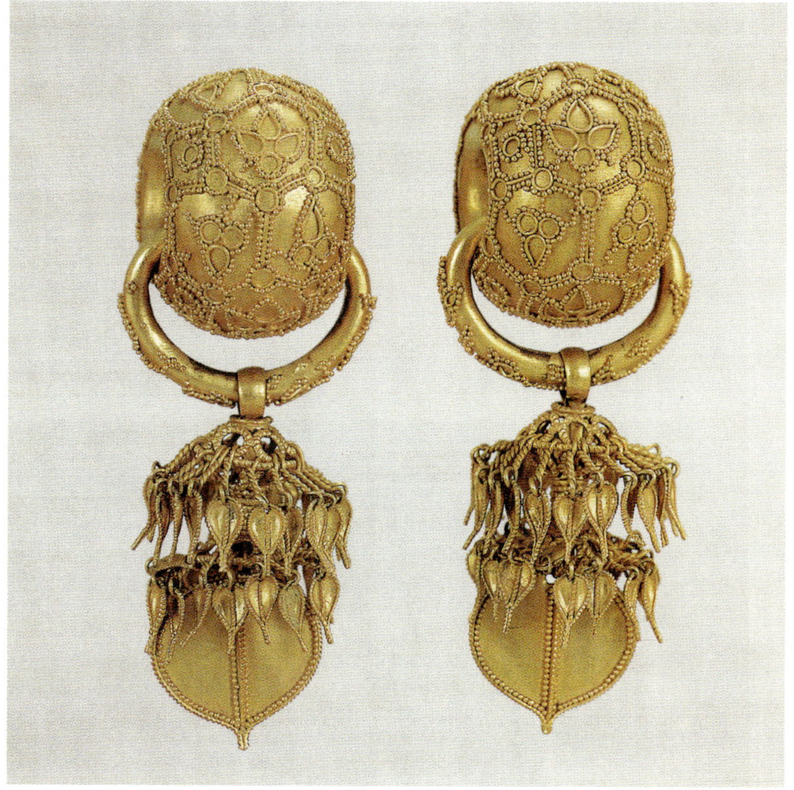

Figure 5.29 *Thick-type gold earrings, excavated from the mound of wife of the Couple's Tomb in Pomun-dong, Kyŏngju. L. 8.7cm. National Treasure No. 90. Courtesy of the National Museum of Korea.*

in ancient Silla. Sometimes blue glass or red cinnabar was attached to the surface of the gold earrings (fig. 5.28). This colorful combination of gold and blue or red gives the earrings a luxurious cast. The most extravagant gold earrings of ancient Silla are the pair excavated from the Couple's Tomb (Pubuch'ong 夫婦塚) at Pomun-dong 普門洞 in Kyŏngju (fig. 5.29).[67] These earrings are decorated with gold granulation and filigree throughout, and the middle ornament has small gold leaves attached with spire-beaded wires. The techniques employed here show the most highly advanced stage of gold metal craftsmanship. The pattern decorated with gold granules is hexagonal; I will return to the iconography of this pattern below.

The origin of these gold earrings indicates the cultural relationships enjoyed by the people of ancient Silla. The general combination of three parts of an earring would have been influenced by the nomadic peoples of northeast China from the third to the fifth centuries. Several examples of gold earrings were discovered in northeast China, where the Xianbei people flourished. Each of a pair of gold earrings excavated from the ancient Baoansi 保安寺 tomb at Yixian 义县 in Liaoning Province is composed of three parts: a thin-type main ring, a flat, semicircular middle ornament, and six long, slim end-pendants made of chains and thin gold plates (fig. 5.30).[68] An almost identical earring was excavated from tomb M198 at

---

[67] This tomb was excavated in 1915 during the Japanese colonial period, with no fully detailed excavation report released. Chōsen Sōtokufu 朝鮮總督府 [Government-General of Korea], *Chōsen koseki zufu* 朝鮮古蹟圖譜 [Illustrated book of Korean historical remains] (Seoul and Tokyo: Chōsen Sōtokufu, 1916): 344-352. Recently the Gyeongju National Museum published a new excavation report about 108 pieces of objects found inside the Couple's Tomb at Pomun-dong. Kungnip Kyŏngju Pangmulgwan 國立慶州博物館 [Gyeongju National Museum], *Kyŏngju Pomun-dong hapchangbun: Ku Kyŏngju Pomun-ri Pubuch'ong* 慶州 普門洞合葬墳—舊 慶州 普門里夫婦塚 [The double burial tomb at Pomun-dong, Kyŏngju: Previously the Couple's Tomb at Pomun-ni, Kyŏngju] (Seoul: Kungnip Kyŏngju Pangmulgwan Munhwa Chaedan, 2011). The Couple's Tomb was originally composed of two mounds for a husband and his wife, who died later. The mound for the husband is of traditional stone-piled wooden-chamber-tomb construction, but the mound for the wife is a stone-chamber tomb. So the former is the most important example of the last phase of stone-piled wooden-chamber tombs in ancient Silla. Most excavated objects from this tomb are now in the collection of the National Museum of Korea. The pair of earrings was found in the mound for the wife in the Couple's Tomb.

[68] Liu Qian 刘谦, "Liaoning Yixian Baoansi faxian de gudai muzang" 辽宁义县

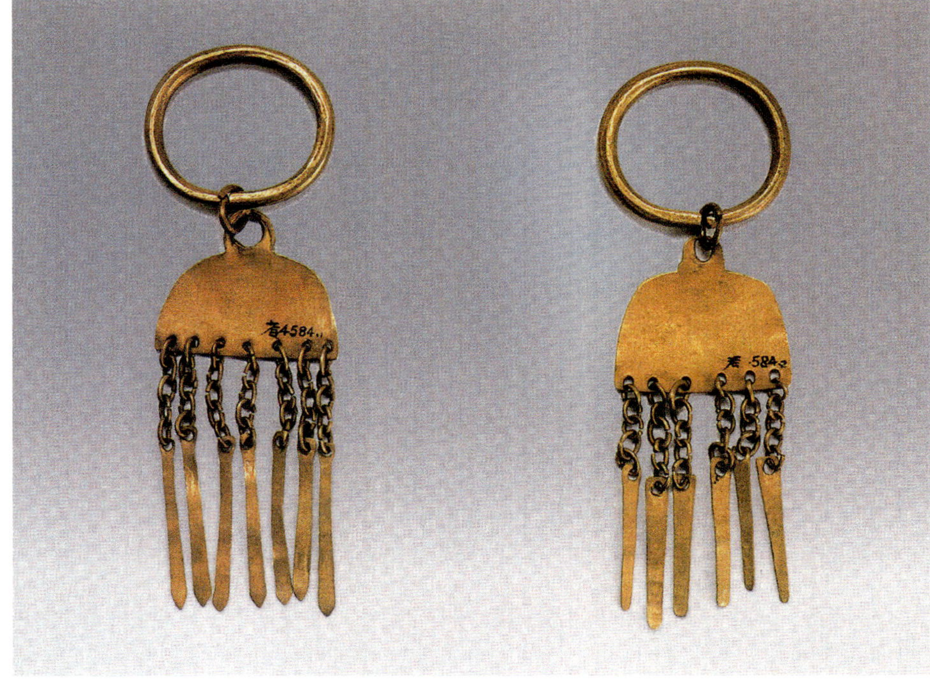

Figure 5.30 Gold earrings, excavated from the ancient Baoansi Tomb at Yixian, Liaoning Province, China. L. 5.8cm. From Liaoning Sheng Wenwu Kaoku Yanjiusuo 辽宁省文物考古研究所, *ed., San Yan wenwu jingcui* 三燕文物精粹 *(Shenyang: Liaoning Renmin Chubanshe, 2002): 42, Plate 22.*

Lamadong 喇嘛洞 also in Liaoning Province.[69] These tombs were built by the Xianbei people between the third and fourth centuries, making them one of the models for the gold earrings used in Silla. The other gold earring used by the Xianbei people is found in the Buddhist relic casket made in 481 and donated by emperor Xiaowen 孝文 (r. 471-499) of the Northern

保安寺发现的古代墓葬 [Ancient tomb excavated from Baoansi at Yixian in Liaoning], *Kaogu* 考古, no. 1 (January 1963): 53.

[69] Although an excavation report of Lamadong tombs was published in 2004, it was only a partial report and did not describe this earring. Liaoningsheng wenwu kaogu yanjiusuo 辽宁省文物考古研究所 [Liaoning Provincial Institute of Cultural Relics and Archaeology], et al., "Liaoning Beipiao Lamadong mudi 1998 nian fajue baogao" 辽宁北票喇嘛洞墓地1998年发掘报告 [Report of the excavation in 1998 of the tomb site at Lamadong, Beipiao, Liaoning], *Kaogu xuebao* 考古学报, no. 2 (2004): 209-242. The picture of this earring was published in another book. See Liaoningsheng wenwukaogu yanjiusou, ed., *San Yan wenwu jingcui*, 42, Plate 20.

288

Wei (386-534).[70] This is also a thin-type gold earring with many middle ornaments in the shape of gold balls and round leaves.[71] The end-pendants are also made of gold chains and thin gold plates and appear similar to those from the Baoansi tomb. This earring represents the later Xianbei gold ornament, and it is also composed of three parts. Significantly, these earrings of the Xianbei people may have influenced those of ancient Silla or Koguryŏ. However, the Xianbei people produced only simple and thin-type gold earrings. Neither earrings with gold granulation nor the thick-type earrings have been found in the territory of the Xianbei and other northeastern nomadic peoples.

To date, thick-type earrings with middle ornaments and end-pendants have been found only in the territory of Koguryo and Silla, and the examples from Koguryŏ are very few. The main ring of this type seems too thick to wear on ears; however, it seems that people actually had their earlobes pierced in the Three Kingdoms period.[72] According to the *Hanyuan* 翰苑, a Tang-period work, Koguryŏ people had their ears pierced with a gold ring.[73] Both thin- and thick-type rings would have been inserted into a hole in the ear. This ear-piercing custom was seen across all of the Three

---

[70] For the excavation of this Buddhist relic casket, see Liu Laicheng 刘来成 and Hebeisheng Wenhuaju Wenwu Gongzuodui 河北省文化局文物工作队 [The archaeological team, Bureau of Culture, Hebei Province], "Hebei Dingxian Beiwei shihan" 河北定县出土北魏石函 [Stone box of Northern Wei found in Dingxian, Hebei], *Kaogu* 考古, no. 5 (1966): 252-266.

[71] NHK Osaka Hōsōkyoku, NHK 大阪放送局 [NHK Osaka Broadcasting Corporation], ed., *Chūgoku no kin · gin garasu ten: Shōsōin no furusato* 中国の金·銀·ガラス展: 正倉院の故郷 [Chinese gold, silver, and glass exhibition: The hometown of Shōsōin] (Osaka: NHK Osaka Hōsōkyoku, 1992): Plate 18.

[72] Korea had a tradition of ear piercing from the Neolithic period to the Chosŏn dynasty. For the Korean ear-piercing tradition, see Chu Kyŏngmi (Joo Kyeongmi), "Han'guk kodae isik ŭi ch'akchang pangsik yŏn'gu," 31-54; Cho Hŭijin 조희진, *Sŏnbi wa p'iŏsing: Cho Hŭijin ŭi uri ot munhwa ilki* 선비와 피어싱: 조희진의 우리 옷 문화 읽기 [Confucian scholars and piercing: Cho Hŭijin's reading of our clothing culture] (Seoul: Tong Asia, 2003): 150-164.

[73] *Hanyuan* was written by the Chinese scholar Zhang Chujin 張楚金 in 660, but most of the book has been lost. Only one volume on the foreign peoples of China survives in Japan. It was reprinted in 1977. Zhang Chujin 張楚金, *Hanyuan* 翰苑 [Jp. Kan'en, Garden of literature], annotated and trans. Takeuchi Rizō 竹内理三 (Fukuoka: Dazaifu Tenmangū Bunka Kenkyūjo, 1977): 40.

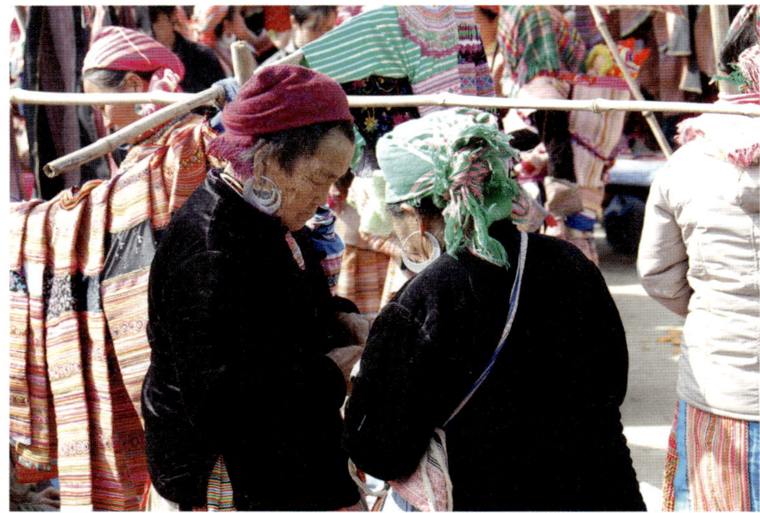

Figure 5.31 Flower Hmong people with earrings. Courtesy of the author.

Kingdoms,[74] but thick-type earrings flourished only in Silla. Since it is very hard to make a hole big enough to hold a thick-type earring in one's ear, this big hole would have been regarded as an eccentric body ornament suitable only for a special class of people in Silla or the southeastern part of the Korean peninsula.

The custom of ear piercing was common in ancient South Asia. In South and Southeast Asia, such thick gold earrings without pendants were commonly worn and have been found from Vietnam to India. The custom of wearing thick earrings in Southeast Asia persists even into modern times. In Indonesia, many thick gold earrings have been discovered on the island of Java.[75] These are simple thick rings made of gold. In 1912, a young woman with many thick earrings that had lengthened her ear lobe was found

---

[74] According to the *Suishu* 隋書 (History of the Sui dynasty) composed in 636, the costume and cultural customs of Silla were very similar to those of Koguryŏ and Paekche. *Suishu* 81, *Ershisi shi*, 7:464.

[75] John Miksic, *Old Javanese Gold* (Singapore: Ideation, 1990): 63-69, especially the pictures of Group 9 and Group 11.

among the Lerong people of northern Borneo.[76] The most important example that relates to this discussion is a stone mold for thick earrings found at
the ancient site of Óc Eo in Southern Vietnam.[77] Óc Eo is the ancient city
of the Funan (Vietnamese. Phù Nam) kingdom,[78] which flourished from
the first century to the sixth century, making it contemporary with ancient
Silla. The Flower Hmong people of northern Vietnam also still have a tradition of ear piercing (fig. 5.31), although their earrings are not the same as
the old thick earrings. However, it is in India where the tradition of thick
earrings and ear piercing has been most developed in South and Southeast
Asia from ancient to modern times.

To understand how people wore such thick earrings, we should note the
custom of ear reels (fig. 5.32). Ear reels are worn in the pierced earlobe to fix
and broaden the hole. They can be made of clay, stone, bones, or diverse metals including gold and silver. Ear reels are found everywhere people have had
the custom of pierced and elongated ears, even in ancient Greece.[79] Ear reels
have been especially popular in India, where they were used as early as Neolithic times. The clay ear reels found in ancient Kaushambi were very large,
but the shapes are similar to those found in ancient Greece.[80] Other silver ear

---

[76] Anne Richter, *Jewelry of Southeast Asia* (New York: Harry N. Abrams, Inc,
2000): 174, Fig. 103.

[77] This was excavated at the site of Óc Eo. Some earrings made by this mold
were also discovered at the same site. Louis Malleret, "L'art et la metallurgie de
l'etain dans la culture d' Oc-èo," *Artibus Asiae* 11, no. 4 (1948): 272-284, Plate I and
Plate 297. For an image of this mold, see Nancy Tingley, ed., *Arts of Ancient Viet
Nam: From River Plain to Open Sea*, (New Haven and London: Yale University
Press, 2010): 138-139, Plate 33.

[78] The culture of Óc Eo was first investigated by Louis Malleret in the early
twentieth century, and he identified this culture as the "Fu Nan" 扶南 kingdom of
ancient China. Óc Eo was an important commercial center during the first to the
sixth centuries and may be an important part of Fu Nan. For recent studies on Óc
Eo, see James C. M. Khoo, *Art & Archaeology of Fu Nan: Pre-Khmer Kingdom of the
Lower Mekong Valley* (Bangkok: Orchid Press, 2003): 1-85.

[79] Dyfri Williams and Jack Ogden, *Greek Gold: Jewelry of the Classical World*
(New York: Harry N. Abrams, 1994): 88-89, Plate 40-43. The tradition of the ear
reel originated in Egypt or India and moved to ancient Greece.

[80] M. Postel, *Ear Ornaments of Ancient India* (Bombay: Franco-Indian Pharma-
ceuticlas, 1989): 11-19, especially 15, Plate I.3. Postel calls the "ear reel" an "ear plug"
in his book, so these two terms are interchangeable.

reels made in modern Gujarat are of a conical type[81] but preserve the main design. Ancient ear reels come in flat cylinder shapes with many concentric circles on each side, with a typical diameter of more than two centimeters. Such a tradition of wearing an ear reel and thick-type earrings may have been transmitted to the southern part of the Korean peninsula through the Southern sea trade route from somewhere in India or Southeast Asia.

Ear reels were only rarely used in the southern coastal regions of Korea during the Neolithic period. At the Tongsam-dong 東三洞 shell mound in Pusan 釜山, some terracotta ear reels were excavated (fig. 5.33), the largest of which is more than nine centimeters in diameter.[82] Terracotta ear reels were also found in Tomb 65 at Taho-ri 茶戶里 in Ch'angwŏn 昌原 and in a tomb at Tohang-ni 道項里 in Haman 咸安, which date to around the first century. Despite these finds, the custom of earlobe lengthening was apparently not common in ancient Korea, because only a few rare examples of ear reels have been uncovered. It is even possible that groups of immigrants came occasionally from the sea and settled in this territory.

In the Korean peninsula, gold and silver ear reels were used only in ancient Silla in the early seventh century, just after the period of the stone-piled wooden-chamber tomb. One silver ear reel, discovered in a stone pagoda at Punhwang-sa 芬皇寺 built under the patronage of Queen Sŏndŏk 善德 (r. 632-647) in 634, has a similar shape, with concentric circles (fig. 5.34). This would have been an offering for the Buddha's relic enshrined in the pagoda, because it was discovered inside a stone reliquary that contained smaller silver and glass reliquaries.[83] Another similarly shaped pair in gold

---

[81] M. Postel, *Ear Ornaments of Ancient India*, 306, Plate A12.12.

[82] Ha Insu 河仁秀, "Tongsam-dong P'aech'ong chŏnghwa chiyŏk palgul sŏngkwa" 東三洞貝塚 淨化地域 發掘成果 [Result of the excavation on the shell mounds in Tongsam-dong purification region], in *Kogohak ŭl tonghae pon Kaya* 고고학을 통해 본 가야 [Kaya seen through archaeology], ed. Han'guk Kogo Hakhoe 한국고고학회 [The Korean Archeological Society] (Seoul: Han'guk Kogo Hakhoe, 2000): 111-133.

[83] The stone reliquary of the stone pagoda of Punhwang-sa was discovered in 1915, and there is no excavation report. For this reliquary set, see Chu Kyŏng-mi (Joo Kyeongmi), "Punhwang-sa sŏkt'ap ch'ult'o pulsari changŏmgu ŭi chaegŏmt'o" 분황사 석탑 출토 불사리장엄구의 재검토 [Reexamination of Buddhist reliquaries discovered in the stone pagoda at Punhwang-sa], *Sigak munhwa ŭi chŏnt'ong kwa haesŏk: Chŏngjae Kim Lina Kyosu chŏngnyŏn t'oeim kinyŏm misulsa nonmunjip* 시각문화의 전통과 해석: 靜齋 金理那 敎授 정년퇴임기념 미술사논문집 [Tradition and interpretation of visual culture: Festschrift of art history for the retirement of Chŏngjae, Professor Kim Lena], Chŏngjae Kim Li-na Kyosu Chŏngnyŏn T'oeim Kinyŏm Misulsa

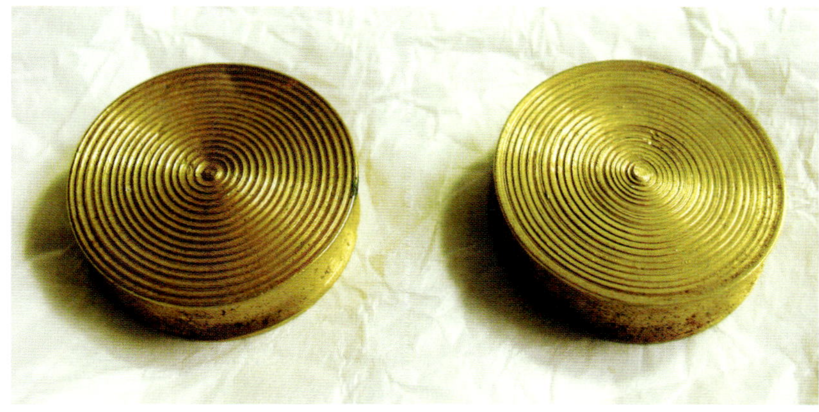

Figure 5.32 Gold ear reels, from Songnim-sa, North Kyŏngsang Province. Silla, seventh-eighth century. Diameter 2.9cm. Courtesy of the Daegu National Museum.

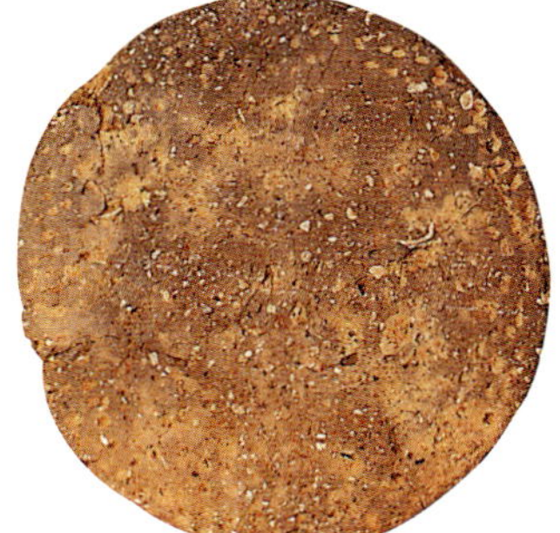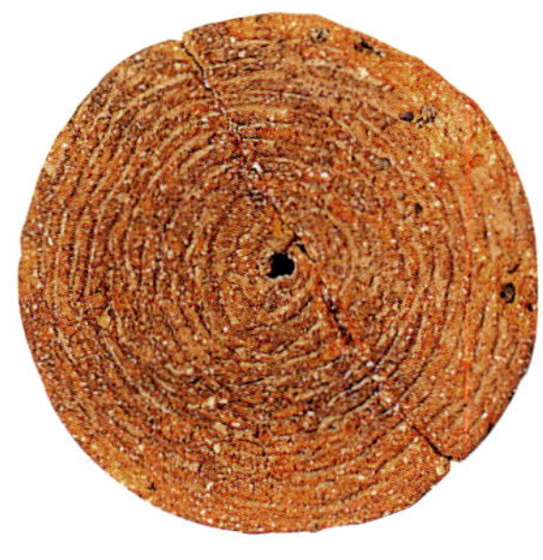

Figure 5.33 Terracotta ear reels, excavated from Tongsam-dong P'aech'ong. Neolithic period. Diameter 4.7cm. Bokcheon Museum, Pusan. Courtesy of the Busan Museum.

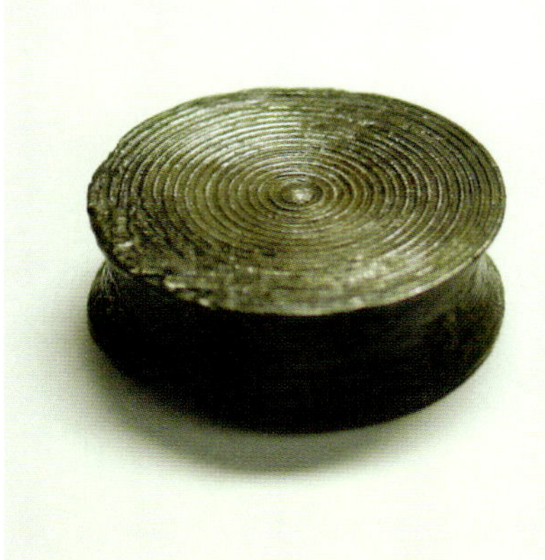

Figure 5.34 Silver ear reel, excavated from the relic crypt of Punhwang-sa Pagoda, Kyŏngju. Silla, ca. 634. Diameter 2.4cm. Courtesy of the Gyeongju National Museum.

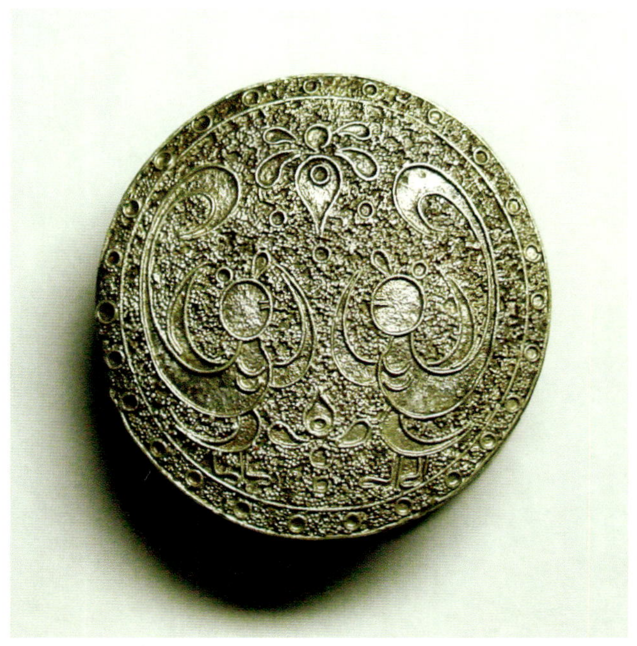

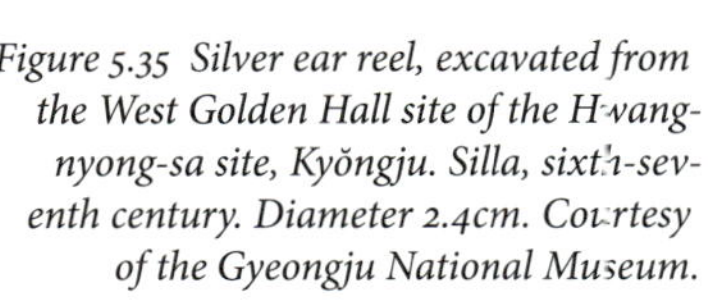

Figure 5.35 Silver ear reel, excavated from the West Golden Hall site of the Hwang-nyong-sa site, Kyŏngju. Silla, sixth-seventh century. Diameter 2.4cm. Courtesy of the Gyeongju National Museum.

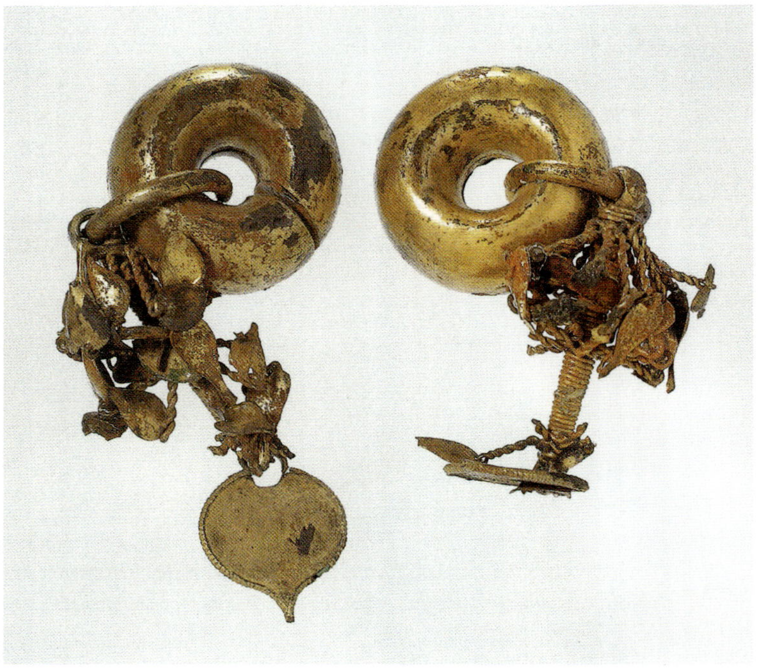

Figure 5.36 *Thick-type gilt-bronze earrings, excavated from the Hwangnyong-sa Pagoda site, Kyŏngju. Silla, seventh century. L. 10.4cm. Courtesy of the Gyeongju National Museum.*

was found in the relic crypt of a brick pagoda of Songnim-sa 松林寺 (fig. 5.32).[84] Silver ear reels were also found at the Hwangnyong-sa site, which was also built under the patronage of Queen Sŏndŏk.[85] Among these examples, a

Nonmunjip Kanhaeng Wiwŏnhoe 정재 김리나교수 정년퇴임 기념 미술사논문집 간 행위원회 [Committee for the Compilation of the Festschrift of Art History for the Retirement of Chŏngjae, Professor Kim Lena], ed. (Seoul: Yegyŏng, 2007): 277-297.

[84] Chewon Kim, "Treasures from the Songyimsa Temple in Southern Korea," *Artibus Asiae* 22, no. 1/2 (1959): 95-112. These gold ear reels were called "gilt-bronze discs" and described as "spools" in this article.

[85] At the Hwangnyong-sa site, one silver ear reel was discovered at the site of the western hall, and another two silver plates for an ear reel were discovered in the relic chamber of the wooden pagoda. Chu Kyŏngmi (Joo Kyeongmi), "Han'guk kodae isik ŭi ch'akchang pangsik yŏn'gu," 43-44; Chu Kyŏngmi (Joo Kyeongmi),

silver ear reel with a pattern of two birds in symmetrical composition, which displays delicate granulation and filigree techniques, is the most outstanding, (fig. 5.35). In addition, a pair of gilt-bronze thick-type earrings in the traditional style of ancient Silla was also found at the Hwangnyong-sa site (fig. 5.36).[86] This pair of gilt-bronze earrings is the latest example of an ancient Silla earring, and it also indicates that thick-type earrings with pendants and ear reels were used together by the nobles of ancient Silla.

The thick-type gold earrings and ear reels are impressive and significant masterpieces of gold jewelry from ancient Silla. The tradition of wearing thick earrings without pendants spread to the southern regions of early Korea by means of South Asian maritime cultures, but the thick-type earrings with pendants became popular among the nobles of ancient Silla only from the fifth to the seventh centuries. Thus the original style of these thick-type gold earrings with pendants was developed in ancient Silla under the cultural influence of both the northern nomadic peoples, who wore the thin-type earrings with pendants, and southern maritime immigrants, who wore the thick earrings without pendants.

One of the decorative patterns found on Silla earrings, known as a "turtle-shell pattern" (Kr. *kwigammun* 龜甲文), also shows the influence of South Asian maritime cultures. This pattern appears to have been related to the cult of the sea turtle, which prevailed in the southern coastal region of the Korean peninsula as well as in Southeast Asia and the Japanese archipelago. According to the *Samguk yusa*, the founder of Kŭmgwan Kaya 金官伽耶 (ca. 1-532 C.E.), King Suro 首露 (traditional dates ?-199 C.E.), descended from heaven to the highest mountain peak, called "the Turtle's Back" (Kr. Kujibong, 龜旨峯), with his brothers, in the form of eggs.[87] The turtle was believed to be a long-lived mystical creature of the sea, bestowing good luck. In the legend of King Suro, the turtle serves as a sacred animal that receives the ancestral king of Kŭmgwan Kaya as he descends from heaven to earth. Kŭmgwan Kaya was annexed by Silla in 532, and most of the people of high class in Kaya moved to Silla, especially to the Silla capital at present-day Kyŏngju.

"Hwangnyong-sa kuch'ŭng mokt'ap ŭi sari changŏm chaego" 皇龍寺九層木塔의舍利莊嚴再考 [Reexamination of the Buddhist reliquaries from the Pagoda of Hwangnyong-sa], *Yŏksa kyoyuk nonjip* 歷史敎育論集 40 (February 2008): 306-307, Plate 12.

[86] This earring was discovered with other votive objects beneath the main base stone of the pagoda.

[87] *Samguk yusa* 2: "Karak kukki," *Yŏkchu Samguk yusa*, 2:243-344.

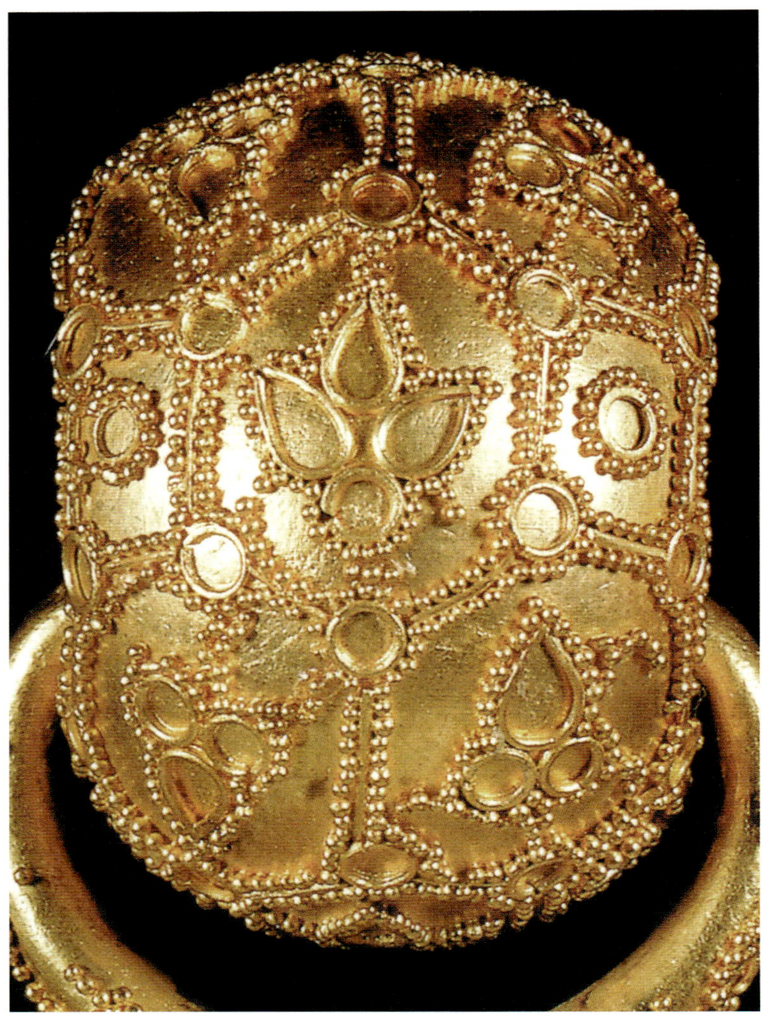

*Figure 5.37 Hexagonal pattern on the gold earring from the Couple's Tomb
(detail of figure 5.29). Courtesy of the Gyeongju National Museum.*

The most characteristic visual feature of the turtle is the hexagonal pattern on its carapace. One of the most important examples of a turtle-shell pattern found among Silla earrings is the hexagonal pattern made of tiny gold granules on the main ring of gold earrings found in the Couple's Tomb (fig. 5.37). A pair of gilt-bronze shoes found in the Decorative Shoes Tomb (Singnich'ong 飾履塚) is the most well-known example of the turtle-shell pattern and is decorated with mythical exotic animals and flowers.[88] Although there are many debates on the iconography of the turtle-shell pattern and its origin in Korea, I think the spread of the turtle-shell pattern in ancient Silla is related to the worship of the turtle in the southern part of the Korean peninsula, especially in the region near the sea.[89] Artifacts with the turtle-shell pattern are distributed broadly and including within the territories of Silla, Paekche, and Koguryŏ during the fifth and sixth centuries.[90] These artifacts were owned only by people occupying the highest class, and they are the rarest items ever found. This turtle-shell pattern must have been thought of as a representation of a sacred and precious symbol, for the local worship of the sea turtle as a sacred animal developed in the southern coastal regions, including in Kaya, which was annexed by Silla in the early

---

[88] See the pictures in Kungnip Kyŏngju Pangmulgwan, *Silla hwanggŭm*, 212-213. The Decorative Shoes Tomb was excavated in 1924, and the excavation report was published in 1932. Chōsen Sōtokufu 朝鮮總督府 [Government-General of Korea], *Taishō jūsan-nendo koseki chōsa hōkoku* 大正十三年度古蹟調査報告 [Report of investigation of ancient relics in the thirteenth year of Taishō], vol. 1: *Keishū Kinreizuka Shokurizuka hakkutsu chōsa hōkoku* 慶州金鈴塚飾履塚發掘調査報告 [Excavation reports of Gold Bell Tomb and Decorative Shoes Tomb in Kyŏngju], 2 vols. (Keijō [Seoul]: Chōsen Sōtokufu, 1932).

[89] Actually, the turtle has been viewed as a sacred animal not only in Korea but throughout Asia as well. In ancient China, the turtle was thought to be an animal related to the cosmos, as well as an animal that symbolized water, especially freshwater. Most sea turtles have hexagonal patterns on their backs; however, the back patterns of the turtles in freshwater are very diverse. Sarah Allan, *The Shape of the Turtle: Myth, Art, and Cosmos in Early China* (Albany: State University of New York Press, 1991): 103-111. According to Sarah Allan, however, the turtle was represented with circles or a grid on its back in ancient Chinese bronzes, and the shape of the turtle's plastron was important for its identification with the cosmos. Such representations of the turtle are different from the images of the turtle's back with hexagonal patterns found in ancient Silla and Paekche.

[90] Kungnip Kongju Pangmulgwan 國立公州博物館 [Gongju National Museum], *Kwigammun kwa kwimyŏnmun* 龜甲文과 鬼面文 [Turtle-shell pattern and monster-mask pattern] (Kongju: Kungnip Kongju Pangmulgwan, 1990).

sixth century. In recent studies, some scholars have maintained that this pattern was derived from a decorative art style of Sassanian Persia,[91] but the transmission route is under debate. I think this pattern may have originated outside the Korean peninsula, possibly in Sassanian Persia, but this foreign pattern could have gained popularity among the upper classes of the Three Kingdoms period in Korea due to its close connection to local worship of the sea turtle as a sacred animal. This case suggests that the meaning of a symbolic design could be decontextualized and differently received by the viewers or users from different cultures.

The gilt-bronze plates excavated from the Heavenly Horse Tomb show the relationship between the hexagonal pattern and the turtle in Silla. These metal plates are not jewelry, but decorative ornaments for harnesses, used to ensure the horseback rider's good luck (fig. 5.38). Each plate has three leaves, and each leaf has a turtle with a turtle-shell pattern on its back. We can see the transformation from the formative turtle shell design to a more elaborately designed turtle-shell pattern seen on the earrings. The Heavenly Horse Tomb was built in the early sixth century, and the Couple's Tomb in Pomun-dong was built later. This hexagonal-pattern turtle-shell design shows the influence of the southern coastal cultures in Korea, which were possibly derived from South Asian maritime cultures.

More evidence is seen in the cultural exchanges between the southern coast of Korea and South Asia. The *Samguk yusa* contains descriptions of ships coming from abroad, especially the coming of foreigners from the sea. Princess Yellow Jade (Kr. Hŏ Hwangok, 許黃玉), the spouse of King Suro and queen of Kŭmgwan Kaya, came from Ayutthaya in India by ship.[92] Sŏk T'arhae 昔脫解 (r. 57-80), the progenitor of the Sŏk family and the fourth

---

[91] Yi Songnan 李松蘭, "Silla kobun ch'ult'o kongyep'um e poinŭn oerae yoso ŭi yŏnwŏn" 新羅 古墳出土 工藝品에 보이는 外來要素의 淵源 [The origin of foreign characteristics seen in the artifacts excavated from Silla tombs], *Misul sahak yŏn'gu* 美術史學研究 203 (994): 43-75; Yi Yŏnjae 李妍宰, "Singnich'ong ch'ult'o kŭmdong singni ŭi munyang yŏn'gu" 飾履塚 출토 金銅飾履의 문양 연구 [Research on the ornamental pattern of the gilt-bronze copper shoes from Decorative Shoes Tomb], *Kangjwa misulsa* 강좌미술사 27 (2006): 129-156. Yi Songnan calls this pattern a turtle-shell pattern, but she does not discuss the iconography of the turtle in this article. By contrast, Yi Yŏnjae argues that this pattern was not regarded as a turtle-shell pattern but only a decorative hexagonal pattern. I think this is a pattern derived from abroad, but its spread in Korea is closely related to the local worship of the turtle.

[92] *Samguk yusa* 3: "Kŭmgwan-sŏng P'asa sŏkt'ap," *Yŏkchu Samguk yusa*, 3:115.

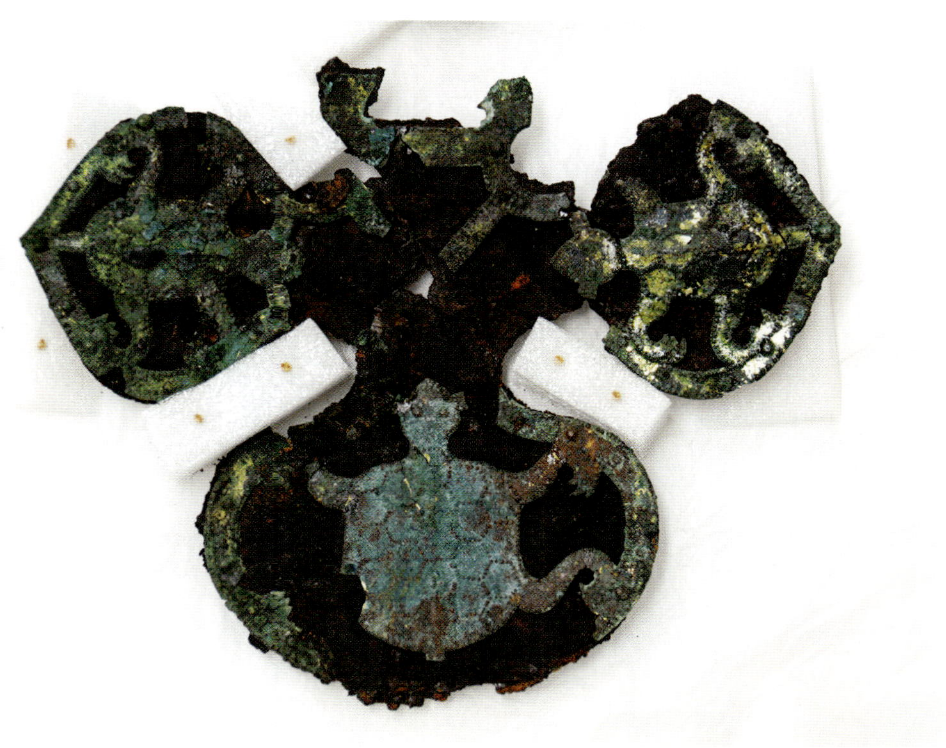

Figure 5.38 Gilt-bronze harness decorated with images of turtle, excavated from the Heavenly Horse Tomb, Kyŏngju. Silla, fifth-sixth century. 14×17cm. Courtesy of the Gyeongju National Museum.

king of ancient Silla, also sailed in from the southern sea.[93] Although the authenticity of these records has been long debated in historical studies, the material evidence, such as thick-type gold earrings, indicates the possibility of the southern Korean peninsula's cultural relationships with southern maritime cultures during this time. In addition, some scholars have suggested that special kinds of glass beads used for ornaments, such as necklaces in ancient Silla and Paekche, were imported from Southeast Asia.[94]

[93] *Samguk yusa* 1: "Chesa T'arhae Wang," *Yŏkchu Samguk yusa*, 1:245-247.

[94] Peter Francis, Jr., *Asia's Maritime Bead Trade: 300 B.C. to the Present* (Honolulu: University of Hawai'i Press, 2002): 44-48; Yi Songnan 李松蘭, "Hwangnam

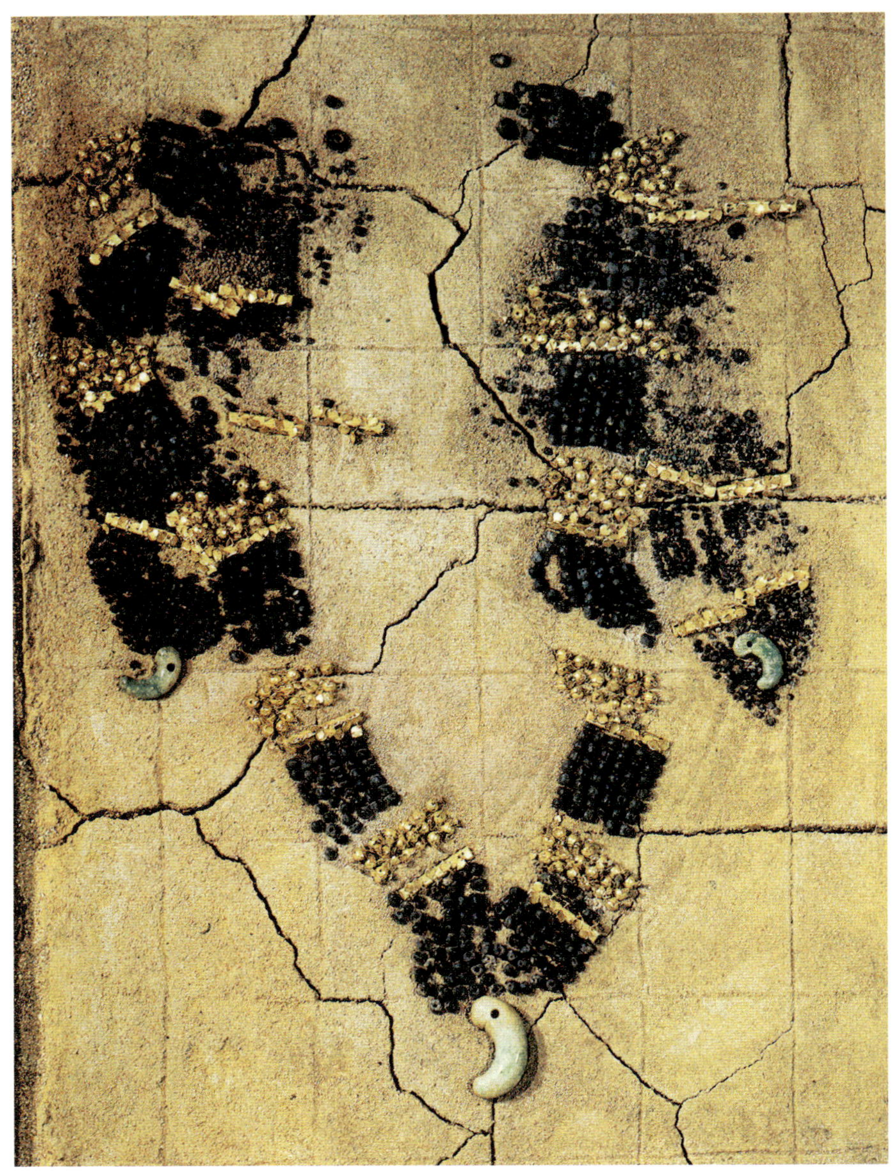

*Figure 5.39 Bead necklace, excavated from the Heavenly Horse Tomb, Kyŏngju. Silla,
sixth century. Treasure No. 619. Courtesy of the Gyeongju National Museum.*

Many kinds of beads were produced and used as jewelry in ancient Silla. The great majority of occupants of large tombs of ancient Silla, especially those of the Heavenly Horse Tomb and the Great Tomb at Hwangnam, wore a necklace made of broad and long bands of glass and gold beads (fig. 5.39). This type of necklace of ancient Silla appears to have been modeled on similar necklaces produced in India and Southeast Asia during earlier times.[95] On the other hand, the style of these necklaces is very different from that of the necklaces worn by peoples in central and northern China.[96] This long and broad bead necklace is probably another custom transmitted from the southern maritime cultures and developed in ancient Silla.

Conclusion
In this chapter, I have analyzed the gold jewelry of ancient Silla, focusing on gold crowns and earrings. But other varieties of gold jewelry, equally unique and fascinating, have been found in ancient Silla tombs. Although few historical records exist about the art and culture of ancient Silla, archaeological material provides us with a wealth of information. Today we can access many significant materials of ancient Silla that have remained intact thanks to the relatively impenetrable tomb structure used at that time. Only in the twentieth century did it become possible to verify the legend of the golden land of Silla through archaeological findings.

From the Japanese colonial period to the Republic of Korea, the major excavations of ancient Silla tombs have been conducted with the support of the government and were often manipulated for political purposes. Nevertheless, the outcomes of those quasi-political excavations have helped us to explore the cultural history of early Korea in the absence of historical documents. Initial research on the gold jewelry of ancient Silla and its relationship with the gold jewelry of other cultures was conducted by colonial Japanese scholars. Thus, the cultural identity of ancient Silla has often been

---

Taech'ong Pukpun changsik kusŭl ŭi kyebo wa padatkil muyŏk" 황남대총 북분 장식 구슬의 계보와 바닷길 무역 [The lineage of Hwangnam Taech'ong mosaic beads and sea trade route], *Kwagi kogo yŏn'gu* 科技考古研究 9 (December 2003): 51-72.

[95] The broad bead necklace in ancient India can be seen in the sculptures of Bharhut Stupa and Sanchi Stupa. Benjamin Rowland, *The Art and Architecture of India*, 3rd rev. ed. (Harmondsworth: Penguin Books, 1981): 80-111. For the modern examples in India, see Oppi Untracht, *Traditional Jewelry of India* (London: Thames and Hudson, 1997): 65-68.

[96] In addition, the people in the tomb paintings of Koguryŏ did not wear such broad, long necklaces in the style of Silla.

misinterpreted and overlooked due to the Japanese scholars' short-sightedness. The colonial scholars did not wish to acknowledge the openness and diversity of ancient Silla or its dialogues with other cultures and instead emphasized its remote geographical location as well as the idea that cultural transmission came only from northern invaders or immigrants. However, the gold culture of ancient Silla reveals more complicated cultural dialogues than those early scholars presumed. Therefore, the theory of cultural transmission only from the north has to be reconsidered and removed from consideration in future studies.

Although ancient Silla was located in a remote corner of the Korean peninsula, it enjoyed cultural exchanges with two different cultural spheres, both northern Eurasia and the South Sea, as exemplified by the many imported artifacts such as Roman glass vessels discovered in Silla tombs. The techniques of manufacturing gold artifacts in ancient Silla may have been inspired by the culture of northern nomadic people, especially the Xianbei, as well as the cultures of Lelang and Koguryŏ, which were located to the north of Silla. At the same time, the styles of Silla's gold artifacts exhibit differences from those of the northern cultures because, I argue, Silla also had cultural exchanges with South Asia. The original style of ancient Silla tombs and artifacts suddenly emerged in a complete form in the early fifth century. At that time, the maritime cultures crossing the southern sea routes would have mixed with the northern culture in the territory of ancient Silla. Ancient Silla developed into a powerful country at this time and finally achieved the unification of the Three Kingdoms in the late seventh century. Multiple cultural transmissions and the openness of ancient Silla may have contributed to its development into a powerful state.

Gold jewelry, in particular gold crowns and earrings, constitute the most attractive and representative objects from the ancient tombs of Silla. They are idiosyncratic masterpieces of early Korean art. Their original styles reflect the religious culture of ancient Silla, such as the worship of sacred trees and holy animals connecting heaven and earth. This seems to be a result of northern and southern cultural dialogues brought and initiated by immigrants and traders. We should reinterpret them with a broadened and open perspective, allowing for the syncretism of early Eurasian cultures.

CONTRIBUTORS

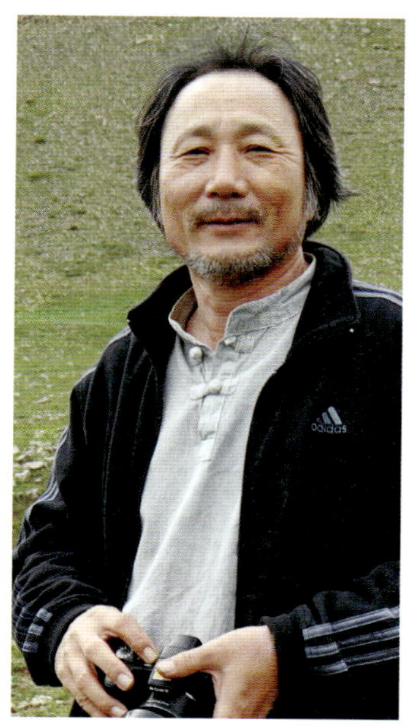

CHUNG WOOTHAK (CHŎNG U-T'AEK) 鄭于澤 is Professor of Art History in the Department of Art History at the Graduate School of Dongguk University. As a specialist in Koryŏ Buddhist painting, he has contributed to identifying and re-discovering Koryŏ Buddhist paintings scattered in museums and private collections in many countries including Japan and the United States. Until the late 1970s the existence of these Koryŏ Buddhist paintings was barely known because the great majority of them, mostly found in Japanese collections, had been misidentified as Chinese works. Chung has also studied the socio-religious contexts in which Koryŏ Buddhist paintings were commissioned, produced, and used, as well as the reception and adoption of Koryŏ Buddhist painting style in Japan. His recent research focuses on comparative studies of Buddhist paintings of Koryŏ, Song, and Xixia. His book, co-authored with Kikutake Jun'ichi 菊竹淳一, titled *Koryŏ sidae ŭi purhwa* 高麗時代의 佛畫 [Buddhist paintings of the Koryŏ period] (Seoul: Sigongsa, 1997) was published both in Korean and Japanese. Other representative publications include *Kōrai jidai Amida gazō no kenkyū* 高麗時代阿弥陀画像の研究 [A study of the painted images of Amitābha in the Koryŏ period] (Tokyo: Nagata Bunshōdō, 1990), and "Ilbon saguk chiyŏk Chosŏnjo chŏn'gi Purhwa chosa yŏn'gu" 日本 四國地域 朝鮮朝 前期 佛畫 調査 研究 [A study of the early Chosŏn Buddhist paintings surviving in the Shikoku region], *Tongak misul sahak* 동악미술사학 9 (2008).

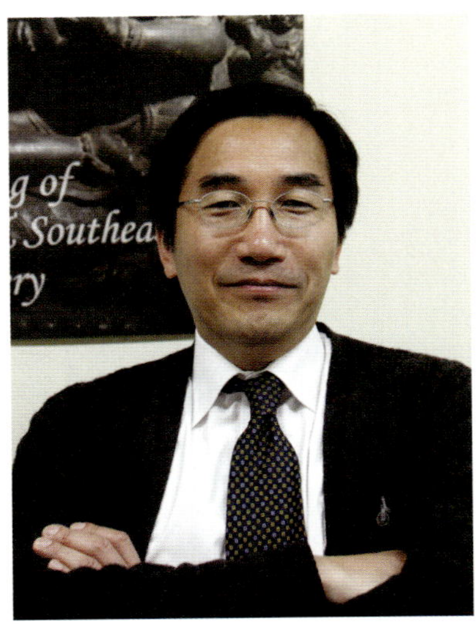

RHI JUHYUNG (YI CHU-HYŎNG) 李柱亨 is Professor of Art History at Seoul National University. He specializes in Buddhist art of South Asia, Central Asia, and Korea, and has written extensively on the traditions of these regions. Though better known for his works in English on Gandharan art, he has also published a number of works on Korean Buddhist art. Among them, "Han'guk kodae Pulgyo misul ŭi sang e taehan ŭisik kwa kyŏnghŏm" 한국 고대 불교미술의 像에 대한 意識과 경험 [The perception and experience of images in ancient Korean Buddhist art], *Misulsa wa sigak munhwa* 미술사와 시각 문화 1 (2002), which has yet to appear in English despite its initial presentation at a conference in LACMA in 2001 for the audience outside Korea, examines the way images were perceived and functioned in the Buddhist community of ancient Korea by examining literary evidence. "De Bodhgayā à Kukkuṭeśvara: la grotte-sanctuaire coréenne de Seokguram et les inspirations indiennes," in *Conférence Iéna: images et imagination—le bouddhisme en Asie* (Paris: École Française d'Etrême-Orient, 2009), traces the origin of the idiosyncratic architectural features of Sŏkkuram in a broad outlook in comparison with parallels from South and Central Asia and the Mediterranean. "The Birth of the Buddha in Korean Buddhism: Infant Buddha Images and the Ritual Bathing," in *The Birth of the Buddha*, ed. Max Deeg (Lumbini: Lumbini International Research Institute, 2011), reexamines the significance of infant Buddha images from Korea and questions their traditional association with the ritual bathing on the Buddha's birthday. Most recently, he has contributed an overview of the historical city Kyŏngju to the catalogue of the Silla art exhibition that will open at the Metropolitan Museum of Art in late 2013. In addition to his current work on books focused on Gandharan art, he plans to write comprehensive treatments of Korean Buddhist art and its scholarship by Korean scholars for the Western audience.

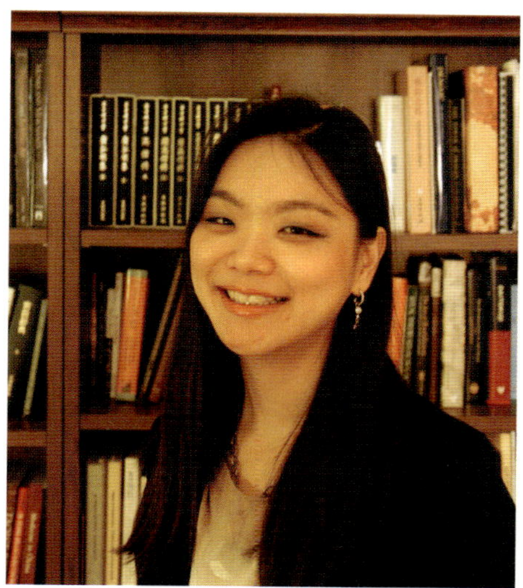

YOUN-MI KIM (KIM YŎNMI) 金延美, Assistant Professor in the Department of the History of Art at Yale University, is a specialist in Chinese Buddhist art, but her broader interest in the cross-cultural relationships between art and ritual extends to Korean and Japanese materials as well. Before joining the Yale faculty, Youn-mi Kim was an Assistant Professor in Asian art history at The Ohio State University (2011-2012) and a postdoctoral associate at the Council on East Asian Studies at Yale University (2010-2011). She is particularly interested in symbolic rituals, in which an architectural space serves as a material agent; the interplay between visibility and invisibility in Buddhist art; and the sacred spaces and religious macrocosms created by religious architecture for imaginary pilgrimages. Based on archaeological data from a medieval Chinese pagoda, she is currently working on a book manuscript titled *Art, Space, and Ritual in Medieval Buddhism: From a Liao Pagoda to Heian Japanese Esoteric Ritual*. Her article, "The Secret Link: Tracing Liao in Japanese Shingon Ritual," will appear in the *Journal of Song-Yuan Studies* 43 (2014). She is also preparing a journal article on the twin pagodas of Silla.

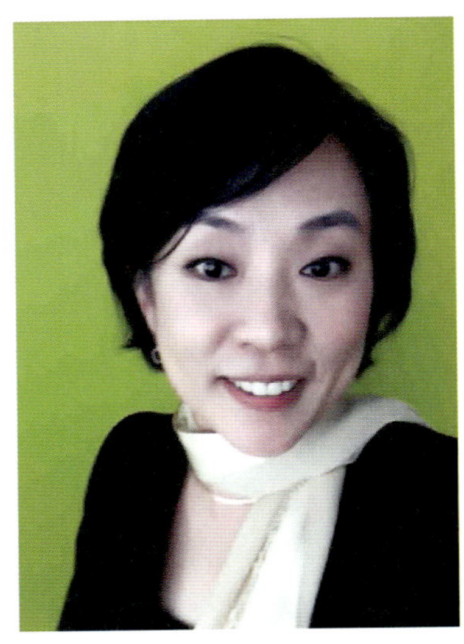

JANG NAMWON (CHANG NAM-WŎN) 張南原, Associate Professor of Art History at Ewha Womans University, specializes in the history of ceramics. She has broad research interests that include the production and the use of ceramics in premodern Korea, China, and Japan. Her research studies include not only the stylistic development of ceramics but also the social ramifications that enabled as well as caused the transmission and adoption of new ceramic technologies. In her book titled *Koryŏ chunggi chŏngja yŏn'gu* 고려중기 청자 연구 [Research on mid-Koryŏ celadon] (Seoul: Hyean, 2006), she described the social conditions and food culture that facilitated the initiation of celadon production in mid-Koryŏ, and explored Koryŏ's production, style, and consumption of celadon in the context of the larger cultural landscape of East Asia. Her representative publications also include "Koryŏ ch'o, chunggi chagi sanggam kipŏp ŭi yŏnwŏn kwa palchŏn" 고려 初·中期 瓷器 象嵌技法의 연원과 발전 [The origin and development of the early and mid-Koryŏ period porcelain inlay techniques], *Misulsa hakpo* 美術史研究 30 (June 2008); "Chosŏn sidae sangjang kongyep'um ŭi ŭimi wa kusŏng" 조선시대 喪葬 공예품의 의미와 구성 [The meaning and formation of funerary crafts in the Chosŏn period], *Misulsa yŏn'gu* 美術史研究 24 (2010); "Koryŏ chŏngja ŭi sahoejŏk kiŏk hyŏngsŏng kwajŏng ŭro pon chosŏn hugi ŭi chŏnghwang" 고려청자의 사회적 기억 형성 과정으로 본 조선후기의 정황 [Social circumstances of late Chosŏn seen from the perspective of the formation of the social memory of Koryŏ celadon], *Misulsa nondan* 美術史論壇 29 (2009); and "Ceramics Exchange between Northern China and Early Goryeo," *Journal of Korean Art and Archaeology* 5 (2011).

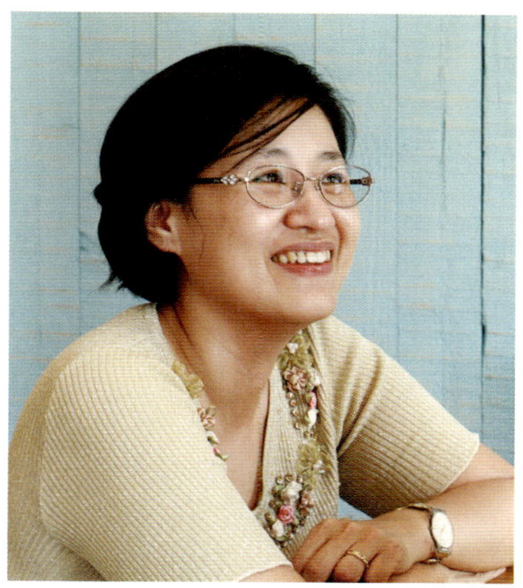

JOO KYEONGMI (CHU KYŎNGMI) 周炅美, a specialist in Korean and Chinese metal craft, is currently serving as an associate member of the Committee of Cultural Heritage at the Cultural Heritage Administration 文化財廳 in Korea; in addition, she is a lecturer at Seoul National University. She was previously a Research Professor at Pukyong National University, and a visiting scholar at Kokugakuin University, as well as a HK Research Professor at the Institute for East Asian Studies at Sogang University. Joo has conducted research on various topics related to production techniques, transmission of style, and the cultural context of metal crafts from ancient to contemporary times. Her book, *Chungguk kodae pulsari changŏm yŏn'gu* 중국 고대 불사리장엄 연구 [A Study of Buddhist reliquaries from ancient China] (Seoul: Ilchisa, 2003), examines extant reliquaries and relevant historical records from the Six Dynasties period to the Tang period, focusing on patrons and religious practices related to Buddhist reliquaries. Recently Joo has also published many journal articles on Song and Liao Buddhist reliquaries. By examining the traditional blacksmiths of Ch'ungnam Province in Korea, her recent book, *Taejangjang* 대장장 [Blacksmith] (Seoul: Minsogwŏn, 2011), explores the traditional production techniques of iron metalwork and its historical context in Korea.

Index